POEMS AND SONGS OF ROBERT BURNS

ROBERT BURNS
1759-1796

POEMS AND SONGS OF ROBERT BURNS

A COMPLETELY NEW EDITION, IN-
CLUDING OVER 60 POEMS APPEAR-
ING FOR THE FIRST TIME IN A
COLLECTED EDITION, OF WHICH
SOME HAVE NEVER BEFORE
BEEN PUBLISHED

―――――――

Edited and Introduced by
JAMES BARKE

FONTANA/Collins

This edition first published by
William Collins Sons & Co. Ltd 1960
First issued in Fontana Paperbacks 1983
Reprinted 1986

Made and printed in Great Britain by
William Collins Sons & Co. Ltd, Glasgow

INTRODUCTION

ROBERT BURNS was born on 25th January, 1759, at Alloway in Ayrshire, and died on 21st July, 1796, at Dumfries.

His father was a working gardener from south of Stonehaven, in Kincardineshire. He was a hard-working man with high ideals about human worth and conduct. By precept and example, he had much to do with Robert's education and upbringing.

By modern standards, Robert had the sketchiest of education. But at an early age he was proficient in the three Rs and well grounded in the principles of Presbyterian theology. He read what he could lay his hands on and understood what he read.

The only mystery concerning Burns, whether in boyhood or manhood, is that of the quality of his genius.

He belongs to the company of the supremely great—Beethoven, Shakespeare, Rembrandt. . .

He could read and write and remember. He was surcharged with emotion, awareness, sensibility. And despite his background and foreground of poverty and hunger and never-ceasing toil, he could laugh. He relished the gift of life as few mortals have. He paid a terrible price for this quality of enjoyment; but he paid it gladly enough. He accepted the penalties imposed by necessity.

Early, too early for his growing, undernourished body, he was at the plough and executing the orra work about a poor, under-capitalised farm. He strained his heart; he became subject to bouts of rheumatic fever or something akin to that baffling ailment.

He laboured on Mount Oliphant. He laboured on Lochlea. When his father died there, prematurely worn out and exhausted (Burns was then twenty-four years of age) he, together with his brother Gilbert, rented the farm of Mossgiel near Mauchline.

Mossgiel was doomed to failure not because Robert or Gilbert were bad farmers, but because they hadn't the necessary minimum of capital to work it economically.

But, brose-and-bannock toil apart, Robert Burns was a genius who expressed himself in poetry. As poet he could not be suppressed. As poet he triumphed. His was by no means an easy triumph—but then few triumphs of the first order are ever easy.

It was the nature of Robert Burns's experience that conditioned his poetry. He knew the nature of man and woman opposed to the bare elements of existence. His experience, if searing, was fundamental and therefore universal.

It is this supreme quality that makes Burns the first world-poet. Burns embraces all humanity. Humanity has, in turn, embraced him. So close (to give a random example) is he to Chinese thought and feeling that the Chinese have suggested that he was of their race. French, Germans, Italians, Austrians, Russians, Americans, have claimed him as their own. The unco guid, the rigidly righteous, the Holy Willies, the Hornbooks, the Cotters, the Man made to Mourn, the Mouse—none of these is exclusive to eighteenth-century Ayrshire. They are universal and timeless.

Burns wrote of them for the most part in the Scottish dialect—a dialect of the great English tongue; and yet a dialect that generations of nobly-gifted Scots have raised to the dignity of a language in its own right.

We remain baffled to know *how* he did what he did. No academic analysis of his poems and songs in relation to their metre or their antecedents tells us anything of other than purely academic interest.

An understanding of his background, his foreground and his times is not without value. But it is mainly in relation to the dominating circumstances of his time, against which Burns and his contemporaries moved, that he can best be understood.

Basically, Burns was a humanitarian. Thus he was a libertarian and equalitarian. Actually, as his *Love and Liberty* shows, he was something more—and the world has yet to catch up on that something more.

Overall, his sympathies were for the poor, the oppressed; and his sympathy extended to the animal kingdom—to the mouse, the auld mare, the wounded hare. . . . He hated all manner of cruelty, oppression and the arrogance of privilege and mere wealth.

But many other worthy poets have had similar feelings. This in itself is not enough. Burns could look and laugh at a' that. His laughter, however, is as broad as his humanity and there is no bitterness, no malice in his laughter. He laughs with life: never against it.

Burns is universal; but in his universality he is unique. There is no other poet like him. And thus, in a peculiar sense, he isn't a poet at all. He had no predecessors: he has had no disciples; and he is much too gigantic, too overflowing at too many points to be neatly, adequately or illuminatingly categorised, labelled and filed away.

Explain the mystery, the ramifications of human life, love, emotion and intellect and you can explain Robert Burns: not otherwise.

Burns's love for his fellowmen, for humanity, is all-embracing—and this despite the fact that his awareness is such that no other poet has shown such insight into the meanness, the cruelties and the follies of mankind. He is nothing of a sentimentalist.

He also loved women in the particular. He loved many women in his lifetime. Of his fifteen children, nine were born in " lawful wedlock ". But in no sense was Burns a libertine. Of no other man is it recorded that he looked upon the children he fathered in or out of wedlock as his, and not the mother's, responsibility. Burns was supremely conscious of the glory of parenthood—legitimacy or illegitimacy were meaningless words to him: he spat the morality that begot them out of his mouth.

The supreme love of his life was Jean Armour, whom he married at the age of twenty-six. It was a supremely happy and altogether fortunate marriage, even if the early years were chequered by circumstances beyond the control of either.

In 1786, while at Mossgiel, and in anticipation of emigrating to the Indies, his first volume of poems and songs was published. It was an immediate success. He was read by high and low alike.

Instead of going to the Indies, he went to Edinburgh and within a few days was acclaimed as one of the wonders of the world.

A new and enlarged edition of his poems resulted. He toured Scotland in triumph—as Caledonia's Bard.

But he endured all this without affectation or illusion. His feet remained firmly on the earth. The pattern of life in Edinburgh or elsewhere in Scotland differed in no essential from the pattern of the small Ayrshire parish. The world of men revolves on the axis of the parish pump.

After Edinburgh, there remained the problem (as ever) of earning a living. He set up as tenant-farmer in Ellisland at Dumfries. Again he was without sufficient capital to see him over the inevitable rainy day.

So he entered the Excise service as a common gauger at £50 a year. In a short space of time he rose to a foot-walk in Dumfries at £70 a year. He was an excellent farmer : he made a good Exciseman.

But he was fundamentally a poet. He could not suppress the poet in him. By having some good friends " in court " he escaped being sent to Botany Bay for treason, sedition and sympathy with the British Reform movement—a by-product of the French Revolution. *Scots Wha hae*, for example, had to be published anonymously. So savage was reaction in the saddle that William Blake observed that to defend the Bible would cost a man his life.

His public work continued, however, and he laboured (unpaid) to supply " words and music " for the collections of James Johnson and George Thomson. In a very real sense Burns was as great a musician as he was a poet.

He dedicated himself to rescuing from oblivion and neglect hundreds of songs without words—or with fragmentary or unsuitable words. He knew that a song without words dies. In supplying words to fit the melodies, he performed a feat unique in the history of art. And the fact that he produced some hundreds of songs in his Dumfries days is a noble tribute to his unflagging energy and dedicated labour.

But the flawed heart from the Mount Oliphant days, and the recurring bouts of rheumatic fever, took their toll. He died at the age of thirty-seven in the direst of poverty and haunted by the threat of a debtors' gaol. On the day of his funeral his widow, in childbed, was literally without a shilling.

He was given a grandiose military funeral with an instrumental band playing the " Dead March in Saul ". As a " turn out " it was one of the most extraordinary known to history. Had the military not been present, the " turn out " might have been even more extraordinary.

2

Burns was a genius: a many-sided genius. Despite the fact that he is the most universally-loved poet, he has yet to come into his own. There is no more flaming satire than *Holy Willie's Prayer*. There is no greater tale than *Tam o' Shanter*. If *A Man's a Man for a' that* is the Marseillaise of humanity, *Auld Lang Syne* is the world's " national " anthem. There is no more tender love song than *O, My Luve's like a red, red rose*. There is no finer epistle than *The Epistle to Davie*. There is nothing in world literature to equal the shattering, liberating cosmology of *Love and Liberty*. . . The list could be extended. The poet who laughed the Devil out of Hell (and—more difficult—banished him from Scots Presbyterian theology) and then took pity on him; the poet who asserted that the " light that led astray was light from Heaven", can be measured by no yard-stick known to letters. He is the first poet of common humanity: he is the first poet to transcend poetry.

Just as there can be no greater musician than Beethoven, there can be no greater poet than Burns. Before either can be surpassed, a new race will have to be born—a different and greater species than the *homo sapiens* hitherto known to history.

Should such a " new species " come to redeem the faults and failings of our common clay, Burns will be honoured as one of the greatest to predict such a possibility. For in a world corrupted, bedevilled and bewildered, Burns firmly believed in the perfectibility of the human race.

This may seem a dubious virtue to readers living in the middle of the twentieth century.

For all those who, whatever their faith or lack of faith, respond to the evocations of ordinary mortality, the following pages will give a lifetime of pleasure, inspiration, hope and courage—and the joy of being alive in a world shot through with terror and darkness and fear. It was in such a world that Burns wrote:

" It's coming yet, for a' that, that man to man the world o'er, shall brithers be for a' that." Who are we to say he sang in vain?

Certainly Burns is not for those who mourn, are faint-hearted, lack faith in humanity, or put their trust in legislators; who love without passion and who hate without compassion; who belittle the struggle of man against the Unknown and who blaspheme against the gift of life and put their trust in party politicians. Burns's poems and songs sing of the richness and strangeness and wonder of life. He did not write for those of little faith. Above all, he wrote for those who know that:

" The heart ay's the part ay that makes us right or wrang."

If Shakespeare (for example) be regarded as the poet who scaled the highest peaks of poetic attainment, few will dispute his unique honour and splendour and glory. But mankind cannot dwell on such peaks of rarefied experience: few indeed ever reach the plodding foothills. . .

But Burns may be likened to the broad rolling plain of mankind's triumph and travail. For here mankind weep and mourn, sing and rejoice, are born and beget their kind and die. In every stage of the journey from the cradle to the grave, Burns is triumphantly articulate.

3

This edition of Burns owes everything to the work of previous editors of Burns. It does not claim to be definitive or immaculate. What it does do is to give the reader the most complete text of Burns's poems and songs so far presented to the public. Many poems and songs are here collected for the first time. The edition is, therefore, the most complete to date.

An index to the titles and first lines is provided as the easiest method of identification. No attempt has been made here to supply a " critical apparatus " of notes. This would require a volume to itself. What cannot be understood must be skipped. But the bulk of Burns's works needs no elucidation: his general purport is always crystal clear. Nevertheless, a marginal glossary and an alphabetical glossary are included for the convenience of such readers as may care to consult them.

Where possible, the names of the tunes to which Burns wrote his words are given.

Doubtless a few more poems may yet come to light; and building on J. C. Dick, a deeper research into the songs and melodies of the eighteenth and earlier centuries may reveal some hitherto unsuspected songs " mended " by Burns.

But, for the most part, what future research or accident may reveal is not likely to detract from Burns's output: to enhance it in any way is not possible.

A number of items usually included in an edition of Burns have been deleted from this edition where research has conclusively shown that they are not from Burns's pen. Where strong doubt has persisted, it has been thought advisable, at this stage, to give Burns the benefit.

That the question of " literary taste " should have led to the exclusion of several pieces which, in the opinion of the present editor, are without offence, need cause no special heart-burning. Burns would have condoned their exclusion from a popular edition. For though he was justly proud of his bawdry, he held very definite views regarding his own productions in this line, considering them " not quite ladies' reading ".

It is regretted that the music to the songs cannot be given here. There is a physical limit to what can be encompassed in one volume. But to be unfamiliar with the music to which Burns wrote his songs is a dire handicap to an adequate awareness of his unique greatness.

4

Finally, I feel that it would be ungrateful to end this introduction without paying tribute to the help and collaboration given by my wife over many years. Indeed, without her arduous labours the accuracy of this edition would not be what it is. But for her steadfast refusal to question my final editorial judgments, I would have insisted on acknowledging her as joint-editor. Such editorial shortcomings as may exist I may fairly claim as my own.

JAMES BARKE.

CHRONOLOGY OF BURNS'S LIFE

NOTE.—By kind permission of Professor DeLancey Ferguson this Chronology is based on that compiled by him for his excellent biography of Burns entitled *Pride and Passion*, first published by the Oxford University Press in 1939. The Chronology has been re-edited by James Barke.

1759   *Jan.* 25. Robert Burns born at Alloway; eldest son of William Burnes (1721–1784) and his wife Agnes Broun (1732–1820). The other children were Gilbert (1760–1832), Agnes (1762–1834), Anabella (1764–1832), William (1767–1790), John (1769-1785), and Isabella (1771–1858).

1765   Robert and Gilbert sent to school to John Murdoch at Alloway.

1766   William Burnes rents Mount Oliphant farm.

1768   Murdoch gives up Alloway school.

1772   Robert and Gilbert attend Dalrymple parish school, week about, during summer quarter.

1773   Robert studies grammar and French with Murdoch for three weeks; writes his first song, 'Handsome Nell,' for Nellie Kilpatrick.

1774   Hard times begin at Mount Oliphant.

1775   Burns attends Hugh Rodger's school at Kirkoswald.

1777   At Whitsun, William Burnes moves from Mount Oliphant to Lochlea.

1779   Burns joins a Tarbolton dancing class 'in absolute defiance' of his father's commands.

1780   The Tarbolton Bachelors' Club organised.

1781   Burns courts Alison Begbie. His father's dispute with David MacLure, his landlord, begins. Burns joins the Freemasons. About midsummer goes to Irvine as a flax-dresser.

1782   *Jan.* 1. The Irvine shop burnt out; soon after, Burns returns to Lochlea.
       Sept. 24. William Burnes's dispute referred to arbiters.

1783   *Jan.* Burns wins a £3 prize for flax-seed.
       April. Burns begins his Commonplace Book.
       May 17. MacLure gets a writ of sequestration against William Burnes.
       Aug. 18. The 'Oversman' reports in Burnes's favour.
       Aug. 25. Burnes makes first appeal to Court of Session.
       Autumn. Robert and Gilbert secretly arrange to rent Mossgiel.

1784   *Jan.* 27. The Court of Session upholds William Burnes.
       Feb. 13. Death of William Burnes. The family moves to Mossgiel.

1785   *May* 22. Birth of Elizabeth, the poet's daughter by Elizabeth Paton.
       During the Summer Burns meets Jean Armour.
       Sept. Burns attests his marriage to Jean Armour.

Nov. 1. Burial of John Burns, the poet's youngest brother. During this year Burns began to write his satires, composed 'Love and Liberty', and in October finished his first Commonplace Book.

1786 *Jan.* (?). Burns plans emigration to Jamaica.

April 3. ' Proposals ' for the Kilmarnock *Poems* sent to press.

c. April 23. James Armour repudiates Burns as a son-in-law. Burns " repudiates " Jean Armour.

May 14. *Sunday.* Farewell and " marriage " to Highland Mary (?).

July 22. Burns transfers his share in Mossgiel to Gilbert.

July 29. Burns presides at Freemasons meeting in Mauchline.

July 30. Burns in hiding from James Armour's writ.

July 31. *Monday.* The Kilmarnock *Poems* published.

August 6. *Sunday.* Burns last penitential appearance in Mauchline Kirk.

c. Sept. 1. First postponement of Jamaica voyage.

Sept. 3. *Sunday.* Jean Armour Burns bears twins, who are christened Robert and Jean.

c. Sept. 27. Second postponement of Jamaica voyage.

Oct. Death of Highland Mary at Greenock and abandonment of Jamaica plans.

Nov. 27. Burns sets out for Edinburgh.

Nov. 29. Burns arrives in Edinburgh.

Dec. 1. Elizabeth Paton accepts Burns's settlement of her claim.

Dec. 9. Henry MacKenzie praises the Kilmarnock *Poems* in *The Lounger.*

Dec. 14. William Creech issues subscription bills for the Edinburgh edition of the *Poems.*

1787 *Jan.* 13. The Grand Lodge of Scotland toasts Burns as ' Caledonia's Bard.'

April 21. Edinburgh *Poems* published.

April 23. Burns sells his copyright to Creech for 100 guineas.

May 5–*June* 1. Burns tours the Borders with Robert Ainslie.

End of May. Vol. I of *Scots Musical Museum* published.

June 2. Burns receives Peggy Cameron's appeal.

June 8. Burns's ' *éclatant* return to Mauchline.'

End of June. Burns tours West Highlands as far as Inveraray.

Aug. 2. Burns completes his autobiographical letter to Dr. John Moore.

Aug. 8. Burns returns to Edinburgh.

Aug. 15. Burns freed of Peggy Cameron's writ.

Aug. 25–*Sept.* 16. Highland tour with William Nicol.

Oct. 4–20. Tour in Stirlingshire.

Oct. Death of poet's daughter, Jean.

Nov. Burns begins active work for the *Scots Musical Museum.*

Dec. 4. Burns meets Mrs. Agnes MacLehose. (Clarinda.)

Dec. 7. Burns dislocates his knee.

Dec. 8. The Clarinda correspondence begins.

1788 *Jan.* 4. Burns's first visit to Clarinda.

Feb. 13–14. Peak of the Clarinda correspondence: four letters in two days.

Feb. 18. Burns leaves Edinburgh.

Feb. 23. Burns returns to Mauchline; buys Jean a ' mahogany bed ' and sets up house with her, publicly testifying that they are man and wife.

Feb. 27 (?)–*Mar.* 2. Burns visits Ellisland with John Tennant.

Mar. 3. Jean bears twin girls, of whom one dies on March 10 and the other on March 22.

c. Mar. 13. Burns returns to Edinburgh.

Mar. 18. Burns signs lease of Ellisland.

Mar. 24. Burns leaves Edinburgh.

Mar. VOL. II of *Scots Musical Museum* published.

April–May. Burns receives Excise instructions at Mauchline and Tarbolton.

1788   *June* 11. Burns settles at Ellisland.

July 14. Burns's Excise commission issued.

Aug. 5. Rev. William Auld and the Mauchline Kirk Session recognise the authenticity of the marriage of Burns and Jean Armour.

Nov. 5. Centenary of the ' Glorious Revolution '.

Nov. Jenny Clow bears Burns a son.

Dec. Jean joins Burns in borrowed quarters at the Isle.

1789   *Feb.* 16. Burns goes to Edinburgh to close accounts with Creech (*Feb.* 27) and to settle Jenny Clow's suit.

Feb. 28. Burns leaves Edinburgh.

July 14. Fall of the Bastille.

c. July. Burns meets Francis Grose.

Aug. 18. Francis Wallace Burns born.

Sept. Burns begins duty as Excise officer.

Nov. Burns ill with ' malignant squinancy and low fever '.

1790   *Jan.* 27. Burns's name placed on list of those eligible for promotion as Examiners and Supervisors.

Feb. VOL. III of *Scots Musical Museum* published.

July. Burns transferred to Dumfries Third Division.

July 24. Death of William Burns in London.

Dec. 1. MS. of ' Tam o' Shanter ' sent to Grose.

1791   *Mar.* 31. Anne Park bears Burns a daughter, Elizabeth.

Apr. 9. William Nicol Burns born.

April. ' Tam o' Shanter ' published in Grose's *Antiquities of Scotland* and in the March issue of the *Edinburgh Magazine*.

June 19-22. Burns in Ayrshire to attend Gilbert's wedding.

Aug. 25. Auction of crops at Ellisland.

Sept. 10. Formal renunciation of Ellisland lease signed.

Nov. 11. Burns moves into Dumfries.

Nov. 29–*Dec.* 11. Burns in Edinburgh. Farewell to Mrs. Agnes MacLehose at Lamont's Land.

1792   *Feb.* Burns promoted to Dumfries Port Division.

Feb. 29. Capture of schooner *Rosamond*.

March. Paine's *Rights of Man* (First part) published.

April 10. Burns made honorary member of Royal Company of Archers, Edinburgh.

April 19. Sale of the *Rosamond's* carronades.

May. Paine indicted for treason ; escapes to France.

Aug. VOL. IV of *Scots Musical Museum* published.

Sept. Burns begins work for Thomson's *Select Scotish Airs*; William Smellie made freeman of Dumfries; Theatre Royal opened at Dumfries.

Nov. 13. Burns subscribes for Edinburgh *Gazetteer*.

Nov. 21. Birth of Elizabeth Riddell Burns.

Dec. First General Convention of The Friends of the People at Edinburgh.

Mid-Dec. Burns's last visit to Dunlop House.

Dec. 31. Excise inquiry into Burns's loyalty.

1793 *Jan.* 5. Burns defends himself to Graham of Fintry.

Jan. 21. French King (Louis Sixteenth) executed.

Feb. 1. France declares war against Britain.

Feb. 18. Second Edinburgh edition of *Poems* published.

March. Burns asks, and receives, burgess privileges in the Dumfries school. Mrs. MacLehose returns from the West Indies.

May 19. Burns moves to a house in Millbrae Vennel.

June. First number of Thomson's *Select Scotish Airs* published.

c. July 30–*Aug.* 2. First Galloway tour with Syme.

Aug. Thomas Muir arrested at Portpatrick. The Edinburgh " sedition " trials.

c. Aug. 30. ' Scots Wha hae ' sent to Thomson.

Dec. 9. Isabella Burns married at Mossgiel.

c. Dec. 31. Beginning of the Riddell quarrel.

1794 *Jan.* 12. Final breach with Maria Riddell.

Feb. 14. Muir, Palmer and their associates sail as convicts from Woolwich to Botany Bay.

April 21. Death of Robert Riddell.

c. May 1. Burns declines a post on the *Morning Chronicle*, London.

c. June 25–28. Second Galloway tour with Syme.

Aug. 12. Birth of James Glencairn Burns.

c. Dec. 22. Burns appointed temporary Acting Supervisor at Dumfries.

1795 *Jan.* 12. Burns posts the letter which estranged Mrs. Dunlop.

Jan. 31. Burns joins in organising the Dumfries Volunteers.

Feb. Reconciliation with Maria Riddell.

April. The Reid miniature painted. Alexander Findlater resumes his duties as Supervisor at Dumfries.

June 24. Death of William Smellie.

Sept. Death of Elizabeth Riddell Burns at Mossgiel.

Dec.–Jan. Burns ill with rheumatic fever.

1796 *Feb.* 11. Muir rescued from Botany Bay by American vessel on order of George Washington.

Mar. 12–14. Food riots in Dumfries.

July 3–16. Burns at the Brow Well.

July 18. Burns writes his last letter.

July 21. Death of Burns.

July 25. Funeral of Burns, and birth of his son Maxwell.

CONTENTS

LOVE AND LIBERTY

A Cantata

RECITATIVO

I

When lyart leaves bestrow the yird, withered;
Or, wavering like the bauckie-bird,   ground
 Bedim cauld Boreas' blast;
When hailstanes drive wi' bitter skyte, lash
And infant frosts begin to bite,
 In hoary cranreuch drest;   rime
Ae night at e'en a merry core   One; gang
 O' randie, gangrel bodies   lawless;
 In Poosie-Nansie's held the splore, vagrant
 To drink their orra duddies: carousal
  Wi' quaffing and laughing spare rags
   They ranted an' they sang, roistered
  Wi' jumping an' thumping
   The vera girdle rang.   very

2

First, niest the fire, in auld red rags next
Ane sat, weel brac'd wi' mealy bags
 And knapsack a' in order;
His doxy lay within his arm;
Wi' usquebae an' blankets warm, whisky
 She blinket on her sodger.   leered
An' ay he gies the tozie drab   flushed with
 The tither skelpin kiss,   drink
While she held up her greedy gab sounding
 Just like an aumous dish: mouth
  Ilk smack still did crack s. '' alms-dish
   Like onie cadger's whup; Each
  Then, swaggering an' staggering, hawker's
   He roar'd this ditty up:—

33

SONG

TUNE: *Soldier's Joy*

I

I am a son of Mars, who have been in many wars,
    And show my cuts and scars wherever I come:
This here was for a wench, and that other in a trench,
    When welcoming the French at the sound of the
    drum.

                  Lal de daudle, *etc.*

2

My prenticeship I past, where my leader breath'd his
    last,
    When the bloody die was cast on the heights of
    • Abram;
And I servèd out my trade when the gallant game
    was play'd,
    And the Moro low was laid at the sound of the
    drum.

3

I lastly was with Curtis among the floating batt'ries,
    And there I left for witness an arm and a limb;
Yet let my country need me, with Eliott to head me
    I'd clatter on my stumps at the sound of the drum.

4

And now, tho' I must beg with a wooden arm and
    leg ,
    And many a tatter'd rag hanging over my bum,
I'm as happy with my wallet, my bottle, and my
    callet
    As when I us'd in scarlet to follow a drum.

trull

5

What tho' with hoary locks I must stand the winter
    shocks,
    Beneath the woods and rocks oftentimes for a
    home?
When the tother bag I sell, and the tother bottle tell,
    I could meet a troop of Hell at the sound of a drum.

RECITATIVO

He ended; and the kebars sheuk   *rafters shook*
  Aboon the chorus roar;   *Over*
While frighted rattons backward leuk,   *rats*
  An' seek the benmost bore: *inmost hole*
A fairy fiddler frae the neuk,   *tiny: corner*
  He skirl'd out *Encore!*   *squeaked*
But up arose the martial chuck,   *dear*
  An' laid the loud uproar:—

SONG

TUNE: *Sodger Laddie*

I

I once was a maid, tho' I cannot tell when,
And still my delight is in proper young men.
Some one of a troop of dragoons was my daddie:
No wonder I'm fond of a sodger laddie!
              Sing, lal de dal, *etc.*

2

The first of my loves was a swaggering blade:
To rattle the thundering drum was his trade;
His leg was so tight, and his cheek was so ruddy,
Transported I was with my sodger laddie.

3

But the godly old chaplain left him in the lurch;
The sword I forsook for the sake of the church;
He riskèd the soul, and I ventur'd the body:
'Twas then I prov'd false to my sodger laddie.

4

Full soon I grew sick of my sanctified sot;
The regiment at large for a husband I got;
From the gilded spontoon to the fife I was ready
I askèd no more but a sodger laddie.

5

But the Peace it reduc'd me to beg in despair,
Till I met my old boy in a Cunningham Fair;
His rags regimental they flutter'd so gaudy:
My heart it rejoic'd at a sodger laddie.

6

And now I have liv'd—I know not how long!
But still I can join in a cup and a song;
And whilst with both hands I can hold the glass
        steady,
Here's to thee, my hero, my sodger laddie!

RECITATIVO

Poor Merry-Andrew in the neuk
        Sat guzzling wi' a tinkler-hizzie;
They mind't na wha the chorus teuk,
        Between themselves they were sae busy.
        At length, wi' drink an' courting dizzy,
He stoiter'd up an' made a face;
        Then turn'd an' laid a smack on Grizzie,
Syne tun'd his pipes wi' grave grimace:—

tinker-wench
cared not;
took

struggled

Then

SONG

TUNE: *Auld Sir Symon*

1

Sir Wisdom's a fool when he's fou;
        Sir Knave is a fool in a session:
He's there but a prentice I trow,
        But I am a fool by profession.

drunk
court

2

My grannie she bought me a beuk,
        An' I held awa to the school:
I fear I my talent misteuk,
        But what will ye hae of a fool?

book
went off

3

For drink I wad venture my neck;
        A hizzie's the half of my craft:
But what could ye other expect
        Of ane that's avowedly daft?

cracked

4

I ance was tyed up like a stirk
        For civilly swearing and quaffing;
I ance was abus'd i' the kirk
        For towsing a lass i' my daffin.

bullock;

rebuked
rumpling;
fun

5

Poor Andrew that tumbles for sport
    Let naebody name wi' a jeer:
There's even, I'm tauld, i' the Court
    A tumbler ca'd the Premier.

6

Observ'd ye yon reverend lad
    Mak faces to tickle the mob?
He rails at our mountebank squad—
    It's rivalship just i' the job!

7

And now my conclusion I'll tell,
    For faith! I'm confoundedly dry:
The chiel that's a fool for himsel,   fellow
    Guid Lord! he's far dafter than I.

RECITATIVO

Then niest outspak a raucle carlin,   sturdy
                                                    beldam
Wha kent fu' weel to cleek the sterlin,
For monie a pursie she had hookèd,
An' had in monie a well been doukèd.   ducked
Her love had been a Highland laddie,
But weary fa' the waefu' woodie!   plague upon
                                                    gallows
Wi' sighs an' sobs she thus began
To wail her braw John Highlandman:—   fine

SONG

TUNE: *O, An' Ye Were Dead, Guidman*

CHORUS

Sing hey my braw John Highlandman!
Sing ho my braw John Highlandman!
There's not a lad in a' the lan'
Was match for my John Highlandman!

I

A Highland lad my love was born,
The lalland laws he held in scorn,   lowland
But he still was faithfu' to his clan,
My gallant, braw John Highlandman.

2

kilt

With his philibeg, an' tartan plaid,
An' guid claymore down by his side,
The ladies' hearts he did trepan,
My gallant, braw John Highlandman.

3

We rangèd a' from Tweed to Spey,
An' liv'd like lords an' ladies gay,
For a lalland face he fearèd none,
My gallant, braw John Highlandman.

4

They banish'd him beyond the sea,
But ere the bud was on the tree,
Adown my cheeks the pearls ran,
Embracing my John Highlandman.

5

But Och! they catch'd him at the last,
And bound him in a dungeon fast.
My curse upon them every one—
They've hang'd my braw John Highlandman!

6

And now a widow I must mourn
The pleasures that will ne'er return;
No comfort but a hearty can
When I think on John Highlandman.

RECITATIVO

I

A pigmy scraper on a fiddle,
Wha us'd to trystes an' fairs to driddle,
buxom   Her strappin limb an' gawsie middle
                          (He reach'd nae higher)
Had hol'd his heartie like a riddle,
blown it   An' blawn't on fire.

2

Wi' hand on hainch and upward e'e,   *hip*
He croon'd his gamut, one, two, three,   *hummed*
Then in an *arioso* key
        The wee Apollo
Set off wi' *allegretto* glee
        His *giga* solo;—

SONG

TUNE: *Whistle Owre the Lave O't*   *rest*

CHORUS

I am a fiddler to my trade,
An' a' the tunes that e'er I play'a,
The sweetest still to wife or maid
   Was Whistle Owre the Lave O't.

1

Let me ryke up to dight that tear;   *reach; wipe*
An' go wi' me an' be my dear,
An' then your every care an' fear
   May whistle owre the lave o't.

2

At kirns an' weddins we'se be there,   *harvest-homes;*
An' O, sae nicely 's we will fare!   *we'll*
We'll bowse about till Daddie Care
   Sing *Whistle Owre the Lave O't.*

3

Sae merrily the banes we'll pyke,   *bones; pick*
An' sun oursels about the dyke;   *fence*
An' at our leisure, when ye like,
   We'll—whistle owre the lave o't!

4

But bless me wi' your heav'n o' charms,
An' while I kittle hair on thairms,   *tickle;*
Hunger, cauld, an' a' sic harms   *catgut*
   May whistle owre the lave o't.   *such*

RECITATIVO

1

tinker

Her charms had struck a sturdy caird
  As weel as poor gut-scraper;
He taks the fiddler by the beard,

rusty

  An' draws a roosty rapier;
He swoor by a' was swearing worth

plover

  To speet him like a pliver,
Unless he would from that time forth
  Relinquish her for ever.

2

Wi' ghastly e'e poor Tweedle-Dee

hams

  Upon his hunkers bended,
An' pray'd for grace wi' ruefu' face,

so

  An' sae the quarrel ended.
But tho' his little heart did grieve
  When round the tinkler prest her,

snigger

He feign'd to snirtle in his sleeve
  When thus the caird address'd her:—

SONG

Patch

TUNE: *Clout the Cauldron*

1

My bonie lass, I work in brass,
  A tinkler is my station;
I've travell'd round all Christian ground
  In this my occupation;
I've taen the gold, an' been enrolled
  In many a noble squadron;
But vain they search'd when off I march'd
  To go an' clout the cauldron.

2

Despise that shrimp, that wither'd imp,
  With a' his noise an' cap'rin,
An' take a share wi' those that bear
  The budget and the apron!

pot

And by that stowp, my faith an' houpe!
  And by that dear Kilbaigie!

short
commons
wet; throat

If e'er ye want, or meet wi' scant,
  May I ne'er weet my craigie!

RECITATIVO

1

The caird prevail'd: th' unblushing fair
  In his embraces sunk,
Partly wi' love o'ercome sae sair,
  An' partly she was drunk.
Sir Violino, with an air
  That show'd a man o' spunk,   spirit
Wish'd unison between the pair,
  An' made the bottle clunk
        To their health that night.

2

But hurchin Cupid shot a shaft,   urchin
  That play'd a dame a shavie: trick
The fiddler rak'd her fore and aft
  Behint the chicken cavie;   hencoop
Her lord, a wight of Homer's craft,
  Tho' limpin' wi' the spavie,   spavin
                      hobbled;
He hirpl'd up, an lap like daft,   leapt like
                      mad
  An' shor'd them ' Dainty Davie '   offered
        O' boot that night.   *Gratis*

3

He was a care-defying blade
  As ever Bacchus listed!
Tho' Fortune sair upon him laid,
  His heart, she ever miss'd it.
He had no wish but—to be glad,
  Nor want but—when he thristed,
He hated nought but—to be sad;
  An' thus the Muse suggested
        His sang that night :—

SONG

TUNE: *For A' That, An' A' That*

CHORUS

For a' that, an' a' that,
  An' twice as muckle's a' that,   much
I've lost but ane, I've twa behin',
  I've wife eneugh for a' that.

1

I am a Bard, of no regard
    Wi' gentle folks an' a' that,

staring
crowd

But Homer-like the glowrin byke,
    Frae town to town I draw that.

2

pond
brook

I never drank the Muses' stank,
    Castalia's burn, an' a' that;

foams

But there it streams, an' richly reams—
    My Helicon I ca' that.

3

Great love I bear to a' the fair,
    Their humble slave an' a' that;
But lordly will, I hold it still

thwart

    A mortal sin to thraw that.

4

In raptures sweet this hour we meet
    Wi' mutual love an' a' that;

fly; sting

But for how lang the flie may stang,
    Let inclination law that!

5

Their tricks an' craft hae put me daft,
    They've taen me in, an' a' that;
But clear your decks, an' here's the Sex!
    I like the jads for a' that.

CHORUS

For a' that, an' a' that,
    An' twice as muckle's a' that,
My dearest bluid, to do them guid,

to it

    They're welcome till't for a' that!

RECITATIVO

walls

So sung the Bard, and Nansie's wa's
Shook with a thunder of applause,
    Re-echo'd from each mouth!

emptied
their bags

They toom'd their pocks, they pawn'd their duds,

cover; tails

They scarcely left to coor their fuds,

burning

    To quench their lowin drouth.

company

Then owre again the jovial thrang
    The Poet did request

To lowse his pack, an' wale a sang,   *untie;*
   A ballad o' the best: *choose*
     He rising, rejoicing
       Between his twa Deborahs,
     Looks round him, an' found them
       Impatient for the chorus:—

SONG

TUNE: *Jolly Mortals, Fill Your Glasses*

CHORUS

A fig for those by law protected!
   Liberty's a glorious feast,
Courts for cowards were erected,
   Churches built to please the priest!

1

See the smoking bowl before us!
   Mark our jovial, ragged ring!
Round and round take up the chorus,
   And in raptures let us sing:

2

What is title, what is treasure,
   What is reputation's care?
If we lead a life of pleasure,
   'Tis no matter how or where!

3

With the ready trick and fable
   Round we wander all the day;
And at night in barn or stable
   Hug our doxies on the hay.

4

Does the train-attended carriage
   Thro' the country lighter rove?
Does the sober bed of marriage
   Witness brighter scenes of love?

5

Life is all a variorum,
   We regard not how it goes;
Let them prate about decorum,
   Who have character to lose.

6

Here's to budgets, bags and wallets!
Here's to all the wandering train!
Here's our ragged brats and callets!
One and all, cry out, Amen!

THE TWA DOGS

A Tale

'Twas in that place o' Scotland's isle
That bears the name of auld King Coil,
Upon a bonie day in June,
When wearing thro' the afternoon,
Twa dogs, that were na thrang at hame,
Forgathered ance upon a time.

busy
chance-met

The first I'll name, they ca'd him Cæsar,
Was keepit for ' his Honor's' pleasure:
His hair, his size, his mouth, his lugs,
Shew'd he was nane o' Scotland's dogs;
But whalpit some place far abroad,
Whare sailors gang to fish for cod.

ears

His lockèd, letter'd, braw brass collar
Shew'd him the gentleman an' scholar;
But tho' he was o' high degree,
The fient a pride, nae pride had he;
But wad hae spent an hour caressin,
Ev'n wi' a tinkler-gipsy's messin;
At kirk or market, mill or smiddie,
Nae tawted tyke, tho' e'er sae duddie,
But he wad stan't, as glad to see him,
An' stroan't on stanes an' hillocks wi' him.

fiend

mongrel
smithy
matted cur;
ragged
would have
stood
lanted

The tither was a ploughman's collie,
A rhyming, ranting, raving billie,
Wha for his friend an' comrade had him,
And in his freaks had Luath ca'd him,
After some dog in Highland sang,
Was made lang syne—Lord knows how lang.

rollicking;
blade

He was a gash an' faithfu' tyke,   *wise*
As ever lap a sheugh or dyke.   *ditch;*
                                            stone fence
His honest, sonsie, baws'nt face   *pleasant,*
Ay gat him friends in ilka place;   *white-*
                                            streaked
His breast was white, his tousie back   *every*
Weel clad wi' coat o' glossy black;   *shaggy*
His gawsie tail, wi' upward curl,   *joyous*
Hung owre his hurdies wi' a swirl.   *buttocks*

Nae doubt but they were fain o' ither,   *glad in*
And unco pack an' thick thegither;   *confidential*
Wi' social nose whyles snuff'd an' snowkit;   *now*
Whyles mice an' moudieworts they howkit;   *moles; dug*
Whyles scour'd awa' in lang excursion,
An' worry'd ither in diversion;
Till tir'd at last wi' monie a farce,
They sat them down upon their arse,
An' there began a lang digression
About the ' lords o' the creation.'

CÆSAR

I've aften wonder'd, honest Luath,
What sort o' life poor dogs like you have;
An' when the gentry's life I saw,
What way poor bodies liv'd ava.   *at all*

Our laird gets in his rackèd rents,
His coals, his kain, an' a' his stents: *rents in kind;*
                                            dues
He rises when he likes himsel;
His flunkies answer at the bell;
He ca's his coach; he ca's his horse;
He draws a bonie silken purse,
As lang's my tail, whare, thro' the steeks,   *stitches*
The yellow letter'd Geordie keeks.   *guinea*
                                            peeps

Frae morn to e'en it's nought but toiling,
At baking, roasting, frying, boiling;
An' tho' the gentry first are stechin,   *cramming*
Yet ev'n the ha' folk fill their pechan   *servants;*
                                            stomach
Wi' sauce, ragouts, an sic like trashtrie,
That's little short o' downright wastrie:
Our whipper-in, wee, blastit wonner,

Poor, worthless elf, it eats a dinner,
Better than onie tenant-man
His Honor has in a' the lan';
An' what poor cot-folk pit their painch in,
I own it's past my comprehension.

put; paunch — (marginal gloss)

LUATH

Trowth, Cæsar, whyles they're fash't eneugh:
A cotter howkin in a sheugh,
Wi' dirty stanes biggin a dyke,
Baring a quarry, an' sic like;
Himsel, a wife, he thus sustains,
A smytrie o' wee duddie weans,
An' nought but his han' darg to keep
Them right an' tight in thack an' rape.

sometimes; bothered · *digging* · *building* · *clearing* · *litter; brats* · *hands' labour* · *thatch and rope* — (marginal glosses)

An' when they meet wi' sair disasters,
Like loss o' health or want o' masters,
Ye maist wad think, a wee touch langer,
An' they maun starve o' cauld and hunger:
But how it comes, I never kend yet,
They're maistly wonderfu' contented;
An' buirdly chiels, an' clever hizzies,
Are bred in sic a way as this is.

small · *stout lads; young women* — (marginal glosses)

CÆSAR

But then to see how ye're negleckit,
How huff'd, an' cuff'd, an' disrespeckit!
Lord man, our gentry care as little
For delvers, ditchers, an' sic cattle;
They gang as saucy by poor folk,
As I wad by a stinking brock.

badger — (marginal gloss)

I've notic'd, on our laird's court-day,
(An' monie a time my heart's been wae),
Poor tenant bodies, scant o' cash,
How they maun thole a factor's snash:
He'll stamp an threaten, curse an' swear
He'll apprehend them, poind their gear;
While they maun staun', wi' aspect humble,
An' hear it a', an' fear an' tremble!

sad · *endure; abuse* · *seize* · *stand* — (marginal glosses)

I see how folk live that hae riches;
But surely poor-folk maun be wretches!

LUATH

They're nae sae wretched 's ane wad think:
Tho' constantly on poortith's brink,   poverty's
They're sae accustom'd wi' the sight,
The view o't gies them little fright.

Then chance an' fortune are sae guided,
They're ay in less or mair provided;
An' tho' fatigu'd wi' close employment,
A blink o' rest's a sweet enjoyment.   snatch

The dearest comfort o' their lives,
Their grushie weans an' faithfu' wives;   growing
The prattling things are just their pride,
That sweetens a' their fire-side.

An' whyles twalpennie worth o' nappy   sometimes
Can mak the bodies unco happy:
They lay aside their private cares,
To mind the Kirk and State affairs;
They'll talk o' patronage an' priests,
Wi' kindling fury i' their breasts,
Or tell what new taxation's comin,
An' ferlie at the folk in Lon'on.   marvel

As bleak-fac'd Hallowmass returns,
They get the jovial, ranting kirns,   harvest-
                                              homes
When rural life, of ev'ry station,
Unite in common recreation;
Love blinks, Wit slaps, an' social Mirth   glances
Forgets there's Care upo' the earth.

That merry day the year begins,
They bar the door on frosty win's;
The nappy reeks wi' mantling ream,   cream
An' sheds a heart-inspiring steam;
The luntin pipe, an' sneeshin mill,   smoking;
                                             snuff-box
Are handed round wi' right guid will;

conversing
cheerfully
romping

The cantie auld folks crackin crouse,
The young anes ranting thro' the house—
My heart has been sae fain to see them,
That I for joy hae barkit wi' them.

too often

well-doing

may be

indenturing

Still it's owre true that ye hae said
Sic game is now owre aften play'd;
There's monie a creditable stock
O' decent, honest, fawsont folk,
Are riven out baith root an' branch,
Some rascal's pridefu' greed to quench,
Wha thinks to knit himsel the faster
In favor wi' some gentle master,
Wha, aiblins thrang a parliamentin',
For Britain's guid his saul indentin'——

CÆSAR

going

Haith, lad, ye little ken about it:
For Britain's guid! guid faith! I doubt it.
Say rather, gaun as Premiers lead him:
An' saying aye or no 's they bid him:
At operas an' plays parading,
Mortgaging, gambling, masquerading:
Or maybe, in a frolic daft,
To Hague or Calais taks a waft,
To mak a tour an' tak a whirl,
To learn *bon ton*, an' see the worl'.

splits
road
fight; cattle
courses

muddy

venereal
sores

There, at Vienna or Versailles,
He rives his father's auld entails;
Or by Madrid he taks the rout,
To thrum guitars an' fecht wi' nowt;
Or down Italian vista startles,
Whore-hunting amang groves o' myrtles
Then bowses drumlie German-water,
To mak himsel look fair an' fatter,
An' purge the bitter ga's an' cankers
O' curst Venetian bores an' chancres.

For Britain's guid! for her destruction!
Wi' dissipation, feud an' faction.

LUATH

Hech man! dear sirs! is that the gate   *way*
They waste sae monie a braw estate!
Are we sae foughten an' harass'd   *troubled*
For gear ta gang that gate at last?   *wealth to go*

O would they stay aback frae courts,
An' please themsels wi' countra sports,
It wad for ev'ry ane be better,
The laird, the tenant, an' the cotter!
For thae frank, rantin, ramblin billies,   *those; roistering*
Fient haet o' them's ill-hearted fellows: *Not one*
Except for breakin o' their timmer,   *wasting their woods*
Or speakin lightly o' their limmer,   *mistress*
Or shootin of a hare or moor-cock,
The ne'er-a-bit they're ill to poor folk.

But will ye tell me, master Cæsar:
Sure great folk's life's a life o' pleasure?
Nae cauld nor hunger e'er can steer them,   *touch*
The vera thought o't need na fear them.

CÆSAR

Lord, man, were ye but whyles whare I am,
The gentles, ye wad ne'er envy 'em!

It's true, they need na starve or sweat,
Thro' winter's cauld, or simmer's heat;
They've nae sair wark to craze their banes,   *hard*
An' fill auld-age wi' grips an' granes: *gripes and groans*
But human bodies are sic fools,
For a' their colleges an' schools,
That when nae real ills perplex them,
They mak enow themsels to vex them;
An' ay the less they hae to sturt them,   *fret*
In like proportion, less will hurt them.

A countra fellow at the pleugh,
His acre's till'd, he's right eneugh;
A countra girl at her wheel,
Her dizzen's done, she's unco weel;   *dozen*
But gentlemen, an' ladies warst,

positive

Wi' ev'n down want o' wark are curst:
They loiter, lounging, lank an' lazy;

nothing

Tho' deil-haet ails them, yet uneasy:
Their days insipid, dull an' tasteless;
Their nights unquiet, lang an' restless.

An' ev'n their sports, their balls an' races,
Their galloping through public places,
There's sic parade, sic pomp an' art,
The joy can scarcely reach the heart.

The men cast out in party-matches,

solder

Then sowther a' in deep debauches;

One

Ae night they're mad wi' drink an' whoring,

Next

Niest day their life is past enduring.

The ladies arm-in-arm in clusters,
As great an' gracious a' as sisters;
But hear their absent thoughts o' ither,

downright

They're a' run deils an' jads thegither.
Whyles, owre the wee bit cup an' platie,
They sip the scandal-potion pretty;

live-long
books

Or lee-lang nights, wi' crabbit leuks
Pore owre the devil's pictur'd beuks;
Stake on a chance a farmer's stackyard,
An' cheat like onie unhang'd blackguard.

There's some exceptions, man an' woman;
But this is Gentry's life in common.

By this, the sun was out o' sight,

twilight

An' darker gloamin brought the night;

beetle

The bum-clock humm'd wi' lazy drone;

cattle;
lowing; field
side path

The kye stood rowtin' i' the loan;
When up they gat, an' shook their lugs,
Rejoic'd they were na *men*, but *dogs*;
An' each took aff his several way,
Resolv'd to meet some ither day.

SCOTCH DRINK

Gie him strong drink until he wink,
That's sinking in despair;
An' liquor guid to fire his bluid,
That's prest wi' grief an' care:
There let him bowse, and deep carouse,
Wi' bumpers flowing o'er,
Till he forgets his loves or debts,
An' minds his griefs no more.
SOLOMON'S PROVERBS, xxxi. 6, 7.

1

Let other poets raise a frácas
'Bout vines, an' wines, an' drucken Bacchus,
An' crabbit names an' stories wrack us,   torment
        An' grate our lug: vex; ear
I sing the juice Scotch bear can mak us,   barley
        In glass or jug.

2

O thou, my Muse! guid auld Scotch drink!
Whether thro' wimplin worms thou jink,   winding;
          frisk
Or, richly brown, ream owre the brink,   cream
        In glorious faem,   foam
Inspire me, till I lisp an' wink,
        To sing thy name!

3

Let husky wheat the haughs adorn,   hollows
An' aits set up their awnie horn,   oats; bearded
An' pease an' beans, at e'en or morn,
        Perfume the plain:
Leeze me on thee, John Barleycorn,   Blessings on
        Thou king o' grain!   thee

4

On thee aft Scotland chows her cood,   chews cud
In souple scones, the wale o' food!   pick
Or tumbling in the boiling flood
        Wi' kail an' beef;   greens
But when thou pours thy strong heart's blood,
        There thou shines chief.

5

belly

Food fills the wame, an' keeps us livin;
Tho' life 's a gift no worth receivin,
When heavy-dragg'd wi' pine an' grievin;
  But oil'd by thee,

careering

The wheels o' life gae down-hill, scrievin,
  Wi' rattlin glee.

6

muddled
Learning

Thou clears the head o' doited Lear,
Thou cheers the heart o' drooping Care;
Thou strings the nerves o' Labour sair,
  At's weary toil;
Thou ev'n brightens dark Despair
  Wi' gloomy smile.

7

dress

Aft, clad in massy siller weed,
Wi' gentles thou erects thy head;
Yet, humbly kind in time o' need,
  The poor man's wine:
His wee drap parritch, or his bread,
  Thou kitchens fine.

8

Without;
merry-
makings

Thou art the life o' public haunts:
But thee, what were our fairs and rants?
Ev'n godly meetings o' the saunts,
  By thee inspir'd,
When, gaping, they besiege the tents,
  Are doubly fir'd.

9

That merry night we get the corn in,
O sweetly, then, thou reams the horn in!

smoking
wooden
vessels
whisky
tasty sugar

Or reekin on a New-Year mornin
  In cog or bicker,
An' just a wee drap sp'ritual burn in,
  An' gusty sucker!

10

gear

When Vulcan gies his bellows breath,
An' ploughmen gather wi' their graith,

O rare! to see thee fizz an' freath *froth*
        I' th' lugget caup! *two-eared cup*
Then Burnewin comes on like death *the Blacksmith*
        At ev'ry chaup. *stroke*

11

Nae mercy, then, for airn or steel: *iron*
The brawnie, bainie, ploughman chiel, *bony; fellow*
Brings hard owrehip, wi' sturdy wheel,
        The strong forehammer,
Till block an' studdie ring an' reel, *anvil*
        Wi' dinsome clamour

12

When skirlin weanies see the light, *squalling babies*
Thou maks the gossips clatter bright, *babble*
How fumbling cuifs their dearies slight; *cheerfully dolts*
        Wae worth the name! *Woe befall*
Nae howdie gets a social night, *midwife*
        Or plack frae them. *coin*

13

When neebors anger at a plea, *law-case*
An' just as wud as wud can be, *wild*
How easy can the barley-brie *-brew*
        Cement the quarrel!
It's aye the cheapest lawyer's fee,
        To taste the barrel.

14

Alake! that e'er my Muse has reason,
To wyte her countrymen wi' treason! *charge*
But monie daily weet their weason *throat*
        Wi' liquors nice,
An' hardly, in a winter season,
        E'er spier her price. *ask*

15

Wae worth that brandy, burnin trash!
Fell source o' monie a pain an' brash! *illness*
Twins monie a poor, doylt, drucken hash, *robs; stupid, drunken oaf*
        O' half his days;
An' sends, beside, auld Scotland's cash
        To her warst faes. *foes*

16

Ye Scots, wha wish auld Scotland well!
Ye chief, to you my tale I tell,
Poor, plackless devils like mysel!
        It sets you ill,
Wi' bitter, dearthfu' wines to mell,
        Or foreign gill.

penniless
becomes
meddle

17

May gravels round his blather wrench,
An' gouts torment him, inch by inch,
Wha twists his gruntle wi' a glunch
        O' sour disdain,
Out owre a glass o' whisky-punch
        Wi' honest men!

bladder
phiz; growl

18

O Whisky! soul o' plays an' pranks!
Accept a Bardie's gratefu' thanks!
When wanting thee, what tuneless cranks
        Are my poor verses!
Thou comes—they rattle i' their ranks
        At ither's arses!

creakings

19

Thee, Ferintosh! O sadly lost!
Scotland lament frae coast to coast!
Now colic grips, an' barkin hoast
        May kill us a';
For loyal Forbés' chartered boast
        Is taen awa!

cough

20

Thae curst horse-leeches o' th' Excise,
Wha mak the whisky stells their prize!
Haud up thy han', Deil! ance, twice, thrice!
        There, seize the blinkers!
An' bake them up in brunstane pies
        For poor damn'd drinkers.

Those
stills
spies
brimstone

21

Fortune! if thou'll but gie me still
Hale breeks, a scone, an' whisky gill,

Whole
breeches

An' rowth o' rhyme to rave at will,   store
        Tak a' the rest,
An' deal't about as thy blind skill
        Directs thee best.

THE AUTHOR'S EARNEST CRY AND PRAYER

TO THE SCOTCH REPRESENTATIVES IN THE HOUSE OF COMMONS

Dearest of distillation! last and best——
——How art thou lost!——
        PARODY ON MILTON

I

Ye Irish lords, ye knights an' squires,
Wha represent our brughs an' shires,
An' doucely manage our affairs   prudently
        In Parliament,
To you a simple Bardie's prayers
        Are humbly sent.

2

Alas! my roupet Muse is haerse!   hoarse
Your Honors' hearts wi' grief 'twad pierce,
To see her sittin on her arse
        Low i' the dust,
And scriechin out prosaic verse,
        An' like to brust!

3

Tell them wha hae the chief direction,
Scotland an' me's in great affliction,
E'er sin' they laid that curst restriction
        On aqua-vitae;
An' rouse them up to strong conviction,
        An' move their pity.

4

Stand forth, an' tell yon Premier youth
The honest, open, naked truth:

thirst

Tell him o' mine an' Scotland's drouth,
   His servants humble:
The muckle deevil blaw you south,
   If ye dissemble!

5

growl
care a rap
swim

Does onie great man glunch an' gloom?
Speak out, an' never fash your thumb!
Let posts an' pensions sink or soom
   Wi' them wha grant 'em:
If honestly they canna come,
   Far better want 'em.

6

scratch;
wriggle

tale

In gath'rin votes you were na slack;
Now stand as tightly by your tack:
Ne'er claw your lug, an' fidge your back,
   An' hum an haw;
But raise your arm, an' tell your crack
   Before them a'.

7

weeping;
thistle
pint-pot;
empty

still

limpet

Paint Scotland greetin owre her thrissle;
Her mutchkin stowp as toom's a whissle;
An' damn'd excisemen in a bustle,
   Seizin a stell,
Triumphant, crushin't like a mussel,
   Or lampit shell!

8

cheek-by-
jowl; fat-
faced
pocket

Then, on the tither hand, present her—
A blackguard smuggler right behint her,
An' cheek-for-chow, a chuffie vintner
   Colleaguing join,
Pickin her pouch as bare as winter
   Of a' kind coin.

9

broken in
pieces

Is there, that bears the name o' Scot,
But feels his heart's bluid rising hot,
To see his poor auld mither's pot
   Thus dung in staves,
An' plunder'd o' her hindmost groat,
   By gallows knaves?

10

Alas! I'm but a nameless wight,
Trode i' the mire out o' sight!
But could I like Montgomeries fight,
   Or gab like Boswell,   speak
There's some sark-necks I wad draw tight, shirt-
   An' tie some hose well.

11

God bless your Honors! can ye see't,
The kind, auld, cantie carlin greet, jolly matron
             weep
An' no get warmly to your feet,
   An' gar them hear it,   make
An' tell them wi' a patriot-heat,
   Ye winna bear it?

12

Some o' you nicely ken the laws,
To round the period an' pause,
An' with rhetòric clause on clause
   To mak harangues:
Then echo thro' Saint Stephen's wa's
   Auld Scotland's wrangs.

13

Dempster, a true blue Scot I'se warran;
Thee, aith-detesting, chaste Kilkerran; oath-
An' that glib-gabbet Highland baron, smooth-
           tongued
   The Laird o' Graham;
An' ane, a chap that's damn'd auldfarran, shrewd
   Dundas his name:

14

Erskine, a spunkie Norland billie; sprightful
           fellow
True Campbells, Frederick and Ilay;
An' Livistone, the bauld Sir Willie;
   An' monie ithers,
Whom auld Demosthenes or Tully
   Might own for brithers.

15

Thee sodger Hugh, my watchman stentéd, assigned
If Bardies e'er are represented;

I ken if that your sword were wanted,
   Ye'd lend your hand;
But when there's ought to say anent it,
   Ye're at a stand.

16

Arouse, my boys! exert your mettle,
To get auld Scotland back her kettle;
bet: Or faith! I'll wad my new pleugh-pettle,
plough-staff   Ye'll see 't or lang,
smoking   She'll teach you, wi' a reekin whittle,
knife   Anither sang.

17

fretful   This while she's been in crankous mood,
Her lost Militia fir'd her bluid;
(Deil na they never mair do guid,
trick   Play'd her that pliskie!)
stark-mad   An' now she's like to rin red-wud
    About her whisky.

18

put her to 't   An' Lord! if ance they pit her till't
tuck up   Her tartan petticoat she'll kilt,
An' durk an' pistol at her belt,
    She'll tak the streets,
knife   An' rin her whittle to the hilt,
    I' the first she meets!

19

For God-sake, sirs! then speak her fair,
stroke;   An' straik her cannie wi' the hair,
gently   An' to the Muckle House repair,
the   Wi' instant speed,
Commons
learning   An' strive, wi' a' your wit an' lear,
redress   To get remead.

20

Yon ill-tongu'd tinkler, Charlie Fox,
May taunt you wi' his jeers an' mocks;
hot   But gie him't het, my hearty cocks!
scare the   E'en cowe the cadie!
varlet   An' send him to his dicing box
    An' sportin lady.

21

Tell yon guid bluid of auld Boconnock's,   *mixed-meal*
I'll be his debt twa mashlum bonnocks,   *bannocks*
An' drink his health in auld Nanse Tinnock's
        Nine times a-week.
If he some scheme, like tea an' winnocks,   *windows*
        Wad kindly seek.

22

Could he some commutation broach,
I'll pledge my aith in guid braid Scotch,
He needna fear their foul reproach
        Nor erudition,
Yon mixtie-maxtie, queer hotch-potch,   *mixed-up*
        The Coalition.

23

Auld Scotland has a raucle tongue;   *bitter*
She's just a devil wi' a rung;   *cudgel*
An' if she promise auld or young
        To tak their part,
Tho' by the neck she should be strung,
        She'll no desert.

24

And now, ye chosen Five-and-Forty,
May still your mither's heart support ye;
Then, tho' a minister grow dorty,   *pettish*
        An' kick your place,
Ye'll snap your fingers, poor an' hearty,
        Before his face.

25

God bless your Honors, a' your days,   *sups; broth;*
Wi' sowps o' kail and brats o' claes,   *scraps;*
In spite o' a' the thievish kaes,   *clothes*
        That haunt St. Jamie's!   *jack-daws*
Your humble Bardie sings an' prays,
        While Rab his name is.

POSTSCRIPT

26

Let half-starv'd slaves in warmer skies
See future wines, rich-clust'ring, rise;

Their lot auld Scotland ne'er envíes,
         But, blythe and frisky,
She eyes her freeborn, martial boys
            Tak aff their whisky.

27

sun What tho' their Phœbus kinder warms,
While fragrance blooms and Beauty charms,
When wretches range, in famish'd swarms,
          The scented groves;
Or, hounded forth, dishonor arms
          In hungry droves!

28

Their gun's a burden on their shouther;
cannot They downa bide the stink o' powther;
doubt Their bauldest thought's a hank'ring swither
         To stan' or rin,
crack;
pell-mell Till skelp—a shot—they're aff, a' throw'ther,
         To save their skin.

29

But bring a Scotsman frae his hill,
Put in his Clap in his cheek a Highland gill,
mouth Say, such is royal George's will,
         An' there's the foe!
He has nae thought but how to kill
         Twa at a blow.

30

Nae cauld, faint-hearted doubtings tease him;
Death comes, wi' fearless eye he sees him;
Wi' bluidy han' a welcome gies him;
         An' when he fa's,
His latest draught o' breathin lea'es him
         In faint huzzas.

31

eyes; shut Sages their solemn een may steek
smoke An' raise a philosophic reek,
An' physically causes seek
         In clime an' season;
But tell me whisky's name in Greek:
         I'll tell the reason.

32

Scotland, my auld, respected mither!
Tho' whiles ye moistify your leather,   *sometimes*
Till whare ye sit on craps o' heather   *heather-tops*
      Ye tine your dam,   *lose; water*
Freedom and whisky gang thegither,
      Tak aff your dram!

THE HOLY FAIR

A robe of seeming truth and trust
Hid crafty observation;
And secret hung, with poison'd crust,
The dirk of defamation:
A mask that like the gorget show'd,
Dye-varying on the pigeon;
And for a mantle large and broad,
He wrapt him in Religion.
    HYPOCRISY À-LA-MODE

I

Upon a simmer Sunday morn,
  When Nature's face is fair,
I walkèd forth to view the corn,
  An' snuff the caller air.   *cool*
The rising sun, owre Galston Muirs,
  Wi' glorious light was glintin;   *glancing*
The hares were hirplin down the furs,   *hopping*
        furrows
  The lav'rocks they were chantin   *larks*
      Fu' sweet that day.

2

As lightsomely I glowr'd abroad,   *gazed*
  To see a scene sae gay,
Three hizzies, early at the road,   *young*
        women
  Cam skelpin up the way.   *spanking*
Twa had manteeles o' dolefu' black,   *grey*
  But ane wi' lyart lining;
The third, that gaed a wee a-back,   *walked a bit*
        behind
  Was in the fashion shining
      Fu' gay that day.

3

The twa appear'd like sisters twin,
　　In feature, form, an' claes;
Their visage wither'd, lang an' thin,
　　An' sour as onie slaes:
The third cam up, hap-step-an'-lowp,
　　As light as onie lambie,
An' wi' a curchie low did stoop,
　　As soon as e'er she saw me,
　　　　Fu' kind that day.

clothes (gloss for "claes")
hop; jump (gloss for "hap-step-an'-lowp")
curtsey (gloss for "curchie")

4

Wi' bonnet aff, quoth I, 'Sweet lass,
　　I think ye seem to ken me;
I'm sure I've seen that bonie face,
　　But yet I canna name ye.'
Quo' she, an' laughin as she spak,
　　An' taks me by the han's,
'Ye, for my sake, hae gi'en the feck
　　Of a' the Ten Comman's
　　　　A screed some day.

bulk (gloss for "feck")
rip (gloss for "screed")

5

'My name is Fun—your cronie dear,
　　The nearest friend ye hae;
An' this is Superstition here,
　　An' that's Hypocrisy.
I'm gaun to Mauchline Holy Fair,
　　To spend an hour in daffin:
Gin ye 'll go there, yon runkl'd pair,
　　We will get famous laughin
　　　　At them this day.'

going (gloss for "gaun")
larking (gloss for "daffin")
wrinkled (gloss for "runkl'd")

6

Quoth I, 'Wi' a' my heart, I'll do't;
　　I'll get my Sunday's sark on,
An' meet you on the holy spot;
　　Faith, we'se hae fine remarkin!'
Then I gaed hame at crowdie-time,
　　An' soon I made me ready;
For roads were clad, frae side to side,
Wi' monie a wearie body,
　　　　In droves that day.

shirt (gloss for "sark")
we'll (gloss for "we'se")
went; porridge- (gloss for "gaed"; "crowdie-")

7

Here farmers gash, in ridin graith,
  Gaed hoddin by their cotters;
There swankies young, in braw braid-claith,
  Are springin owre the gutters.
The lasses, skelpin barefit, thrang,
  In silks an' scarlets glitter;
Wi' sweet-milk cheese, in monie a whang,
  An' farls, bak'd wi' butter,
        Fu' crump that day.

self-complacent; gear
jogging
strapping youngsters

padding; thronging

shive
small cakes
crisp

8

When by the plate we set our nose,
  Weel heapèd up wi' ha'pence,
A greedy glowr black-bonnet throws,
  An' we maun draw our tippence.
Then in we go to see the show:
  On ev'ry side they're gath'rin;
Some carryin dails, some chairs an' stools,
  An' some are busy bleth'rin
        Right loud that day.

the Elder

planks
gabbling

9

Here stands a shed to fend the show'rs,
  An' screen our countra gentry;
There Racer Jess, an' twa-three whores,
  Are blinkin at the entry.
Here sits a raw o' tittlin jads,
  Wi' heavin breasts an' bare neck;
An' there a batch o' wabster lads,
  Blackguardin frae Kilmarnock,
        For fun this day.

keep off

two or three
leering
whispering jades

weaver

10

Here some are thinkin on their sins,
  An' some upo' their claes;
Ane curses feet that fyl'd his shins,
  Anither sighs an' prays:
On this hand sits a chosen swatch,
  Wi' screw'd-up, grace-proud faces;
On that a set o' chaps, at watch,
  Thrang winkin on the lasses
        To chairs that day.

soiled

sample

Busy

11

O happy is that man an' blest!
    Nae wonder that it pride him!
Whase ain dear lass, that he likes best,
    Comes clinkin down beside him!
Wi' arm repos'd on the chair back,
    He sweetly does compose him;
Which, by degrees, slips round her neck,

And his palm   An's loof upon her bosom,
                Unkend that day.

12

Now a' the congregation o'er
    Is silent expectation;

climbs For Moodie speels the holy door,
    Wi' tidings o' damnation:

the Devil Should Hornie, as in ancient days,
    'Mang sons o' God present him;
The vera sight o' Moodie's face

hot   To's ain het hame had sent him
                Wi' fright that day.

13

Hear how he clears the points o' Faith
    Wi' rattlin and thumpin!
Now meekly calm, now wild in wrath,
    He's stampin, an' he's jumpin!
His lengthen'd chin, his turn'd-up snout,

unearthly   His eldritch squeel an' gestures,
O how they fire the heart devout—
    Like cantharidian plaisters
              On sic a day!

14

But hark! the tent has chang'd its voice;
There's peace an' rest nae langer;
For a' the real judges rise,
    They canna sit for anger:
Smith opens out his cauld harangues,
    On practice and on morals;
An' aff the godly pour in thrangs,
    To gie the jars an' barrels
              A lift that day.

15

What signifies his barren shine,
  Of moral pow'rs an' reason?
His English style, an' gesture fine
  Are a' clean out o' season.
Like Socrates or Antonine,
  Or some auld pagan heathen,
The moral man he does define,
  But ne'er a word o' faith in
      That's right that day.

16

In guid time comes an antidote
  Against sic poison'd nostrum;
For Peebles, frae the water-fit,   river's mouth
  Ascends the holy rostrum:
See, up he's got the word o' God,
  An' meek an' mim has view'd it,
While Common-sense has taen the road,
  An' aff, an' up the Cowgate
      Fast, fast that day.

17

Wee Miller niest, the guard relieves,   next
  An' orthodoxy raibles,   recites by
                                          rote
Tho' in his heart he weel believes,
  An' thinks it auld wives' fables:
But faith! the birkie wants a manse: fellow: living
  So, cannilie he hums them;   humbugs
Altho' his carnal wit an' sense
  Like hafflins-wise o'ercomes him   Nearly half
      At times that day.

18

Now butt an' ben the change-house fills, tavern
  Wi' yill-caup commentators;   ale-cup
Here's crying out for bakes an' gills,   biscuits
  An' there the pint-stowp clatters;
While thick an' thrang, an' loud an' lang,
  Wi' logic an' wi' Scripture,
They raise a din, that in the end
  Is like to breed a rupture
      O' wrath that day.

19

Blessings

    Leeze me on drink! it gies us mair
      Than either school or college;

learning
crams

It kindles wit, it waukens lear,
    It pangs us fou o' knowledge:

small beer

Be't whisky-gill or penny wheep,
    Or onie stronger potion,
It never fails, on drinkin deep,

tickle

    To kittle up our notion,
      By night or day.

20

    The lads an' lasses, blythely bent
      To mind baith saul an' body,
Sit round the table, weel content,

stir

    An' steer about the toddy:
On this ane's dress, an' that ane's leuk,
    They're makin observations;

corner

While some are cozie i' the neuk,
    An' formin assignations
      To meet some day.

21

sounds
roaring

But now the Lord's ain trumpet touts,
    Till a' the hills are rairin,
And echoes back return the shouts;
    Black Russell is na spairin:
His piercin words, like Highlan' swords,
    Divide the joints an' marrow;
His talk o' Hell, whare devils dwell,
    Our vera ' sauls does harrow '
      Wi' fright that day!

22

    A vast, unbottom'd, boundless pit,

full; flaming

    Fill'd fou o' lowin brunstane,
Whase ragin flame, an' scorchin heat,
    Wad melt the hardest whun-stane!
The half-asleep start up wi' fear,
    An' think they hear it roarin;
When presently it does appear,
    'Twas but some neebor snorin
      Asleep that day.

23

'Twad be owre lang a tale to tell,
  How monie stories past;
An' how they crouded to the yill,
  When they were a' dismist;
How drink gaed round, in cogs an' caups,
  Amang the furms an' benches;
An' cheese an' bread, frae women's laps,
  Was dealt about in lunches,   full portions
        An' dawds that day.   lumps

24

In comes a gawsie, gash guidwife,   jolly
  An' sits down by the fire,
Syne draws her kebbuck an' her knife; Then; cheese
  The lasses they are shyer:
The auld guidmen, about the grace,
  Frae side to side they bother;
Till some ane by his bonnet lays,
  An' gies them't, like a tether,   rope
        Fu' lang that day.

25

Waesucks! for him that gets nae lass, Alas!
  Or lasses that hae naething!
Sma' need has he to say a grace,
  Or melvie his braw claithing!   meal-dust
O wives, be mindfu', ance yoursel,
  How bonie lads ye wanted;
An' dinna for a kebbuck-heel
  Let lasses be affronted
        On sic a day!

26

Now Clinkumbell, wi' rattlin tow,   the bell-
  Begins to jow an' croon;   ringer; rope
                                      swing and
Some swagger hame the best they dow, toll
  Some wait the afternoon.   can
At slaps the billies halt a blink,   openings;
  Till lasses strip their shoon: fellows; bit
Wi' faith an hope, an' love an' drink, take off
  They're a' in famous tune
        For crack that day.   talk

27

How monie hearts this day converts
  O' sinners and o' lasses!
by nightfall; Their hearts o' stane, gin night, are gane
gone   As saft as onie flesh is:
There's some are fou o' love divine;
  There's some are fou o' brandy;
An' monie jobs that day begin,
fornication   May end in houghmagandie
      Some ither day.

ADDRESS TO THE DEIL

O Prince! O Chief of many thronèd pow'rs!
That led th' embattl'd seraphim to war.
                    MILTON

1

O Thou! whatever title suit thee—
Hoofie Auld Hornie, Satan, Nick, or Clootie—
Wha in yon cavern grim an' sootie,
      Clos'd under hatches,
Splashes; Spairges about the brunstane cootie,
dish
scald   To scaud poor wretches!

2

Hangman Hear me, Auld Hangie, for a wee,
An' let poor damnèd bodies be;
I'm sure sma' pleasure it can gie,
      Ev'n to a deil,
spank; scald To skelp an' scaud poor dogs like me
      An' hear us squeel.

3

Great is thy pow'r an' great thy fame;
Far kend an' noted is thy name;
flaming An' tho' yon lowin heugh's thy hame,
hollow   Thou travels far;
backward An' faith! thou's neither lag, nor lame,
bashful;
afraid   Nor blate, nor scaur.

4

Whyles, ranging like a roarin lion,   Now
For prey, a' holes an' corners trying;
Whyles, on the strong-wing'd tempest flyin,
   Tirlin the kirks;   Stripping
Whyles, in the human bosom pryin,
   Unseen thou lurks.

5

I've heard my rev'rend graunie say,
In lanely glens ye like to stray;
Or, where auld ruin'd castles grey
   Nod to the moon,
Ye fright the nightly wand'rer's way
   Wi' eldritch croon.

6

When twilight did my graunie summon,
To say her pray'rs, douce, honest woman! sedate
Aft yont the dyke she's heard you bummin, beyond
   Wi' eerie drone;
Or, rustlin, thro' the boortrees comin,   alders
   Wi' heavy groan.

7

Ae dreary, windy, winter night,
The stars shot down wi' sklentin light,   squinting
Wi' you mysel, I gat a fright:
   Ayont the lough,   pond
Ye, like a rash-buss, stood in sight,   clump of
           rushes
   Wi' waving sugh.   moan

8

The cudgel in my nieve did shake,   fist
Each bristl'd hair stood like a stake;
When wi' an eldritch, stoor ' quaick, quaick,' harsh
   Amang the springs,
Awa ye squatter'd like a drake,
   On whistling wings.

9

Let warlocks grim, an' wither'd hags,
Tell how wi' you, on ragweed nags,   ragwort

They skim the muirs an' dizzy crags,
        Wi' wicked speed;
And in kirk-yards renew their leagues,
dug-up   Owre howkit dead.

10

Thence, countra wives, wi' toil an' pain,
churn   May plunge an' plunge the kirn in vain;
For O! the yellow treasure's taen
        By witching skill;
petted,
twelve-pint   An' dawtit, twal-pint hawkie's gaen
cow; gone
dry as; bull   As yell's the bill.

11

Thence, mystic knots mak great abuse
husbands;   On young guidmen, fond, keen an' croose;
confident or
cocksure   When the best wark-lume i' the house,
tool
magic   By cantraip wit,
Is instant made no worth a louse,
nick of time   Just at the bit.

12

hoard   When thowes dissolve the snawy hoord.
surface   An' float the jinglin icy boord,
Then, water-kelpies haunt the foord,
        By your direction,
An' nighted trav'llers are allur'd
        To their destruction.

13

bog; jack-o'-   And aft your moss-traversing spunkies
lanthorus   Decoy the wight that late an' drunk is:
The bleezin, curst, mischievous monkies
        Delude his eyes,
Till in some miry slough he sunk is,
        Ne'er mair to rise.

14

When Masons' mystic word an' grip
In storms an' tempests raise you up,
must   Some cock or cat your rage maun stop,
        Or, strange to tell!
The youngest brother ye wad whip
straight   Aff straught to hell.

15

Lang syne in Eden's bonie yard,   garden
When youthfu' lovers first were pair'd,
An' all the soul of love they shar'd,
    The raptur'd hour,
Sweet on the fragrant flow'ry swaird,
    In shady bow'r.

16

Then you, ye auld, snick-drawing dog! scheming
Ye cam to Paradise incog,
An' play'd on man a cursèd brogue   trick
    (Black be your fa'!),
An' gied the infant warld a shog,   shake
    'Maist ruin'd a'.

17

D'ye mind that day when in a bizz   flurry
Wi' reekit duds, an' reestit gizz,   smoky;
             scorched wig
Ye did present your smoutie phiz   smutty
    'Mang better folk;
An' sklented on the man of Uzz   squinted
    Your spitefu' joke?

18

An' how ye gat him i' your thrall,
An' brak him out o' house an' hal',
While scabs an' botches did him gall, blotches
    Wi' bitter claw;
An' lows'd his ill-tongu'd wicked scaul— loosed; scold
    Was warst ava?   of all

19

But a' your doings to rehearse,
Your wily snares an' fechtin fierce,   fighting
Sin' that day Michael did you pierce
    Down to this time,
Wad ding a Lallan tongue, or Erse,   beat; Low-
    In prose or rhyme.   land

20

An' now, Auld Cloots, I ken ye're thinkin, Hoofs
A certain Bardie's rantin, drinkin,   roistering

hurrying

Some luckless hour will send him linkin,
              To your black Pit;

dodging

But, faith! he'll turn a corner jinkin,
              An' cheat you yet.

21

But fare-you-weel, Auld Nickie-Ben!
O' wad ye tak a thought an' men'!

perhaps

Ye aiblins might—I dinna ken—
              Still hae a stake:

sad

I'm wae to think upo' yon den,
              Ev'n for your sake!

THE DEATH AND DYING WORDS OF
Mollie   POOR MAILIE

THE AUTHOR'S ONLY PET YOWE: AN UNCO
MOURNFU' TALE

together   As Mailie, an' her lambs thegither,
one   Was ae day nibblin on the tether,
hoof; looped Upon her cloot she coost a hitch,
floundered   An' owre she warsl'd in the ditch:
               There, groanin, dying, she did lie,
doddering   When Hughoc he cam doytin by.

staring   Wi' glowrin een, an' lifted han's
               Poor Hughoc like a statue stan's;
               He saw her days were near-hand ended,
woe   But, wae's my heart! he could na mend it!
               He gapèd wide, but naething spak.
               At length poor Mailie silence brak:—

               ' O thou, whase lamentable face
               Appears to mourn my woefu' case!
               My dying words attentive hear,
               An' bear them to my Master dear.

own   ' Tell him, if e'er again he keep
much money   As muckle gear as buy a sheep—
               O, bid him never tie them mair,
               Wi' wicked strings o' hemp or hair!

But ca' them out to park or hill,   *drive*
An' let them wander at their will:
So may his flock increase, an' grow
To scores o' lambs, an' packs o' woo'!

   'Tell him, he was a Master kin',
An' ay was guid to me an' mine;
An' now my dying charge I gie him,
My helpless lambs, I trust them wi' him.

   'O, bid him save their harmless lives,
Frae dogs, an' tods, an' butchers' knives!   *foxes*
But gie them guid cow-milk their fill,   *look after*
Till they be fit to fend themsel;   *tend*
An' tent them duly, e'en an' morn,   *small quantities;*
Wi' teats o' hay an' ripps o' corn.   *handfuls*

   'An' may they never learn the gaets,   *ways*
Of ither vile, wanrestfu' pets—   *restless*
To slink thro' slaps, an' reave an' steal,   *breaches*
At stacks o' pease, or stocks o' kail!   *plants*
So may they, like their great forbears,   *ancestors*
For monie a year come thro' the sheers:
So wives will gie them bits o' bread,
An' bairns greet for them when they're dead.   *weep*

   'My poor toop-lamb, my son an' heir,   *tup*
O, bid him breed him up wi' care!
An' if he live to be a beast,
To pit some havins in his breast!   *conduct*
An' warn him—what I winna name—   *will not*
To stay content wi' yowes at hame;   *ewes*
An' no to rin an' wear his cloots,
Like other menseless, graceless brutes.   *unmannerly*

   'An' niest, my yowie, silly thing;   *ewekin;*
Gude keep thee frae a tether string!   *helpless*
O, may thou ne'er forgather up,   *make friends*
Wi' onie blastit, moorland toop;
But ay keep mind to moop an' mell,   *nibble;*
Wi' sheep o' credit like thysel!   *meddle*

   'And now, my bairns, wi' my last breath,
I lea'e my blessin wi' you baith:

.

An' when you think upo' your mither,
Mind to be kind to ane anither.

' Now, honest Hughoc, dinna fail,
To tell my master a' my tale;
An' bid him burn this cursèd tether,

bladder   An' for thy pains thou 'se get my blether.'

This said, poor Mailie turn'd her head,

eyes   An' clos'd her een amang the dead!

POOR MAILIE'S ELEGY

1

Lament in rhyme, lament in prose,
Wi' saut tears tricklin down your nose;
Our Bardie's fate is at a close,
                    Past a' remead!

remedy   The last, sad cape-stane of his woes;
                    Poor Mailie's dead!

2

worldly pelf   It's no the loss of warl's gear,
                 That could sae bitter draw the tear,
drooping   Or mak our Bardie, dowie, wear
                    The mourning weed:
                 He's lost a friend an' neebor dear
                    In Mailie dead.

3

farm   Thro' a' the toun she trotted by him;
                 A lang half-mile she could descry him;
                 Wi' kindly bleat, when she did spy him,
                    She ran wi' speed:
                 A friend mair faithfu' ne'er cam nigh him,
                    Than Mailie dead.

4

wot   I wat she was a sheep o' sense,
tact   An' could behave hersel wi' mense:

I'll say 't, she never brak a fence,
   Thro' thievish greed.
Our Bardie, lanely, keeps the spence   parlour
   Sin' Mailie's dead.

5

Or, if he wanders up the howe,   glen
Her livin image in her yowe
Comes bleatin till him, owre the knowe,   knoll
   For bits o' bread;
An' down the briny pearls rowe   roll
   For Mailie dead.

6

She was nae get o' moorlan tips,   issue; tups
           matted
Wi' tawted ket, an' hairy hips;   fleece; rumps
For her forbears were brought in ships,   ancestors
   Frae 'yont the Tweed:
A bonier fleesh ne'er cross'd the clips   fleece;shears
   Than Mailie's dead.

7

Wae worth the man wha first did shape   Woe befall
That vile, wanchancie thing—a rape!   dangerous
It maks guid fellows girn an' gape,   grin
   Wi' chokin dread;
An' Robin's bonnet wave wi' crape
   For Mailie dead.

8

O a' ye bards on bonie Doon!
An' wha on Ayr your chanters tune!   bagpipes
Come, join the melancholious croon
   O' Robin's reed!
His heart will never get aboon!   rejoice
   His Mailie's dead!

EPISTLE TO JAMES SMITH

Friendship, mysterious cement of the soul!
Sweet'ner of Life, and solder of Society!
I owe thee much——

BLAIR

1

artful   Dear Smith, the slee'st, pawkie thief,
plunder   That e'er attempted stealth or rief!
wizard-spell   Ye surely hae some warlock-breef
                Owre human hearts;
proof   For ne'er a bosom yet was prief
                Against your arts.

2

For me, I swear by sun an' moon,
above   And ev'ry star that blinks aboon,
Ye've cost me twenty pair o' shoon,
going   Just gaun to see you;
And ev'ry ither pair that's done,
taken   Mair taen I'm wi' you.

3

gossip   That auld, capricious carlin, Nature,
stunted   To mak amends for scrimpit stature,
She's turn'd you off, a human-creature
                On her first plan;
And in her freaks, on ev'ry feature
                She's wrote the Man.

4

Just now I've taen the fit o' rhyme,
seething brain   My barmie noddle 's working prime,
My fancy yerkit up sublime,
                Wi' hasty summon:
Hae ye a leisure-moment's time
                To hear what's comin?

5

Some rhyme a neebor's name to lash;
Some rhyme (vain thought!) for needfu' cash;

Some rhyme to court the countra clash,   talk
      An' raise a din;
For me, an aim I never fash;   trouble about
      I rhyme for fun.

6

The star that rules my luckless lot,
Has fated me the russet coat,
An' damn'd my fortune to the groat;
      But, in requit,
Has blest me with a random-shot
      O' countra wit.

7

This while my notion's taen a sklent,   turn
To try my fate in guid, black prent;
But still the mair I'm that way bent,
      Something cries, ' Hoolie!   Softly!
I red you, honest man, tak tent!   heed
      Ye'll shaw your folly:

8

' There's ither poets, much your betters,
Far seen in Greek, deep men o' letters,
Hae thought they had ensur'd their debtors,
      A' future ages;
Now moths deform, in shapeless tatters,
      Their unknown pages.'

9

Then farewell hopes o' laurel-boughs
To garland my poetic brows!
Henceforth I'll rove where busy ploughs
      Are whistling thrang;   at work
An' teach the lanely heights an' howes   hollows
      My rustic sang.

10

I'll wander on, wi' tentless heed   careless
How never-halting moments speed,
Till Fate shall snap the brittle thread;
      Then, all unknown,
I'll lay me with th' inglorious dead,
      Forgot and gone!

11

But why o' death begin a tale?
well   Just now we're living sound an' hale;
Then top and maintop crowd the sail,
        Heave Care o'er-side!
And large, before Enjoyment's gale,
        Let's tak the tide.

12

This life, sae far's I understand,
Is a' enchanted fairy-land,
Where Pleasure is the magic-wand,
        That, wielded right,
Maks hours like minutes, hand in hand,
        Dance by fu' light.

13

The magic-wand then let us wield;
climbed   For, ance that five-an'-forty 's speel'd,
Eld   See, crazy, weary, joyless Eild,
        Wi' wrinkl'd face,
coughing;   Comes hostin, hirplin owre the field,
limping   Wi' creepin pace.

14

twilight   When ance life's day draws near the gloamin,
Then fareweel vacant, careless roamin;
An' fareweel chearfu' tankards foamin,
        An' social noise:
An' fareweel dear, deluding Woman,
        The joy of joys!

15

O Life! how pleasant, in thy morning,
Young Fancy's rays the hills adorning!
Cold-pausing Caution's lesson scorning,
        We frisk away,
Like school-boys, at th' expected warning,
        To joy an' play.

16

We wander there, we wander here,
We eye the rose upon the brier,

Unmindful that the thorn is near,
        Among the leaves;
And tho' the puny wound appear,
        Short while it grieves.

17

Some, lucky, find a flow'ry spot,
For which they never toil'd nor swat;   *sweated*
They drink the sweet and eat the fat,
        But care or pain;   *Without*
And haply eye the barren hut
        With high disdain.

18

With steady aim, some Fortune chase;
Keen Hope does ev'ry sinew brace;
Thro' fair, thro' foul, they urge the race,
        And seize the prey:
Then cannie, in some cozie place,   *quiet; snug*
        They close the day.

19

And others like your humble servan',
Poor wights! nae rules nor roads observin,
To right or left eternal swervin,
        They zig-zag on;
Till, curst with age, obscure an' starvin,
        They aften groan.

20

Alas! what bitter toil an' straining—
But truce with peevish, poor complaining!
Is Fortune's fickle *Luna* waning?
        E'en let her gang!
Beneath what light she has remaining,
        Let's sing our sang.

21

My pen I here fling to the door,
And kneel, ye Pow'rs! and warm implore,
' Tho' I should wander *Terra* o'er,
        In all her climes,
Grant me but this, I ask no more,
        Ay rowth o' rhymes.   *plenty*

22

dripping 'Gie dreeping roasts to countra lairds,
Till icicles hing frae their beards;
clothes Gie fine braw claes to fine life-guards
And maids of honor;
ale; tinkers And yill an' whisky gie to cairds,
sicken Until they sconner.

23

'A title, Dempster merits it;
A garter gie to Willie Pitt;
Gie wealth to some be-ledger'd cit,
In cent. per cent.;
But give me real, sterling wit,
And I'm content.

24

'While ye are pleas'd to keep me hale,
meal and I'll sit down o'er my scanty meal,
water;
beeiless Be't water-brose or muslin-kail,
broth' Wi' cheerfu' face,
As lang's the Muses dinna fail
To say the grace.'

25

An anxious e'e I never throws
ear Behint my lug, or by my nose;
duck I jouk beneath Misfortune's blows
As weel's I may;
Sworn foe to sorrow, care, and prose,
I rhyme away.

26

sedate O ye douce folk that live by rule,
Grave, tideless-blooded, calm an' cool,
Compar'd wi' you—O fool! fool! fool!
How much unlike!
Your hearts are just a standing pool,
wall Your lives a dyke!

27

Nae hair-brained, sentimental traces
In your unletter'd, nameless faces!

In *arioso* trills and graces
   Ye never stray;
But *gravissímo*, solemn, basses
   Ye hum away.

28

Ye are sae grave, nae doubt ye 're wise;
Nae ferly tho' ye do despise   marvel
The hairum-scairum, ram-stam boys,   headlong
   The rattling squad:
I see ye upward cast your eyes—
   Ye ken the road!

29

Whilst I—but I shall haud me there,   hold
Wi' you I 'll scarce gang onie where—
Then, Jamie, I shall say nae mair,
   But quat my sang.   quit
Content wi' you to mak a pair,
   Whare'er I gang.

A DREAM

Thoughts, words, and deeds, the Statute blames with reason;
But surely Dreams were ne'er indicted Treason.

On reading in the public papers, the Laureate's Ode
with the other parade of June 4th, 1786, the Author was
no sooner dropt asleep, than he imagined himself trans-
ported to the Birth-day Levee: and, in his dreaming
fancy, made the following Address:

I

Guid-mornin to your Majesty!
 May Heaven augment your blisses,
On ev'ry new birth-day ye see,
 A humble Poet wishes!
My Bardship here, at your Levee,
 On sic a day as this is,
Is sure an uncouth sight to see,
 Amang thae birth-day dresses   those
   Sae fine this day.

2

busily   I see ye're complimented thrang,
                  By monie a lord an' lady;
                God Save the King 's a cuckoo sang
mighty   That's unco easy said ay:
                The poets, too, a venal gang,
                  Wi' rhymes weel-turn'd an' ready,
make; think   Wad gar you trow ye ne'er do wrang,
                  But ay unerring steady,
                              On sic a day.

3

                For me! before a Monarch's face,
                  Ev'n there I winna flatter;
                For neither pension, post, nor place,
                  Am I your humble debtor:
                So, nae reflection on your Grace,
                  Your Kingship to bespatter;
worse   There's monie waur been o' the race,
maybe   And aiblins ane been better
                              Than you this day.

4

                'Tis very true my sovereign King,
                  My skill may weel be doubted;
fellows;   But facts are chiels that winna ding,
be upset
cannot   And downa be disputed:
                Your royal nest, beneath your wing,
torn and   Is e'en right reft and clouted,
patched
                And now the third part o' the string,
                  An' less, will gang about it
                              Than did ae day.

5

                Far be't frae me that I aspire
                  To blame your legislation,
                Or say, ye wisdom want, or fire
                  To rule this mighty nation:
greatly   But faith! I muckle doubt, my sire,
                  Ye've trusted ministration
cow-shed   To chaps wha in a barn or byre
Would have   Wad better fill'd their station,
                              Than courts yon day.

6

And now ye've gien auld Britain peace,
  Her broken shins to plaister;
Your sair taxation does her fleece,
  Till she has scarce a tester: sixpence
For me, thank God, my life's a lease,
  Nae bargain wearin faster,
Or faith! I fear, that, wi' the geese,
  I shortly boost to pasture   behove
            I' the craft some day.   croft

7

I'm no mistrusting Willie Pitt,
  When taxes he enlarges,
(An' Will's a true guid tallow's get,   breed
  A name not envy spairges),   spatters
That he intends to pay your debt,
  An' lessen a' your charges;
But, God sake! let nae saving fit
  Abridge your bonie barges
            An' boats this day.

8

Adieu, my Liege! may Freedom geck   sport
  Beneath your high protection;
An' may ye rax Corruption's neck,   wring
  And gie her for dissection;
But since I'm here I'll no neglect,
  In loyal, true affection,
To pay your Queen, wi' due respect,
  My fealty an' subjection
            This great birth-day.

9

Hail, Majesty most Excellent!
  While nobles strive to please ye,
Will ye accept a compliment,
  A simple Bardie gies ye?
Thae bonie bairntime Heav'n has lent,   brood
  Still higher may they heeze ye   hoist
In bliss, till Fate some day is sent,
  For ever to release ye
            Frae care that day.

10

For you, young Potentate' o' Wales,
    I tell your Highness fairly,
Down Pleasure's stream, wi' swelling sails,
    I'm tauld ye're driving rarely;
But some day ye may gnaw your nails,
    An' curse your folly sairly,
broke   That e'er ye brak Diana's pales,
      Or rattl'd dice wi' Charlie
          By night or day.

11

colt   Yet aft a ragged cowte's been known,
old horse   To mak a noble aiver;
sedately So, ye may doucely fill a throne,
gossip   For a' their clish-ma-claver:
There, him at Agincourt wha shone,
    Few better were or braver;
And yet, wi, funny, queer Sir John,
    He was an unco shaver
          For monie a day.

12

For you, right rev'rend Osnaburg,
becomes   Nane sets the lawn-sleeve sweeter,
ear   Altho' a ribban at your lug
    Wad been a dress completer:
haughty As ye disown yon paughty dog,
    That bears the keys of Peter,
haste!   Then swith! an' get a wife to hug,
    Or trowth, ye'll stain the mitre
          Some luckless day!

13

Young, royal Tarry-breeks, I learn,
    Ye've lately come athwart her—
A glorious galley, stem an' stern
    Weel rigg'd for Venus' barter;
But first hang out that she'll discern
    Your hymeneal charter;
grappling-
iron   Then heave aboard your grapple-airn,
    An', large upon her quarter,
          Come full that day.

14

Ye, lastly, bonie blossoms a',
  Ye royal lasses dainty,
Heav'n mak you guid as weel as braw,
  An' gie you lads a-plenty!
But sneer na British boys awa!
  For kings are unco scant ay,
An' German gentles are but sma':
  They're better just than want ay
        On onie day.

15

God bless you a'! consider now,
  Ye're unco muckle dautet;   extremely;
But ere the course o' life be through,   petted
  It may be bitter sautet: salted
An' I hae seen their coggie fou,   dish
  That yet hae tarrow't at it;   tarried
But or the day was done, I trow,
  The laggen they hae clautet   bottom;
        Fu' clean that day.   scraped

THE VISION

DUAN FIRST

1

The sun had clos'd the winter day,
The curlers quat their roaring play,   ceased
And hunger'd maukin taen her way,   hare
        To kail-yards green,   kitchen-
While faithless snaws ilk step betray   gardens
        Whare she has been.   each

2

The thresher's weary flingin-tree,   flail
The lee-lang day had tired me;   live-long
And when the day had clos'd his e'e,
        Far i' the west,
Ben i' the spence, right pensivelie,   Back;
        I gaed to rest.   parlour
                                               went

3

-side
volleying
cough-; drift
structure
rats
rooftree

There, lanely by the ingle-cheek,
I sat and ey'd the spewing reek,
That fill'd, wi hoast-provoking smeek,
        The auld clay biggin;
An' heard the restless rattons squeak
        About the riggin.

4

dusty

nonsense

All in this mottie, misty clime,
I backward mus'd on wasted time:
How I had spent my youthfu' prime,
        An' done naething,
But stringing blethers up in rhyme,
        For fools to sing.

5

-shirted

Had I to guid advice but harkit,
I might, by this, hae led a market,
Or strutted in a bank and clarkit
        My cash-account:
While here, half-mad, half-fed, half-sarkit,
        Is a' th' amount.

6

weakling
horny palm

I started, mutt'ring ' Blockhead! coof! '
An' heav'd on high my waukit loof,
To swear by a' yon starry roof,
        Or some rash aith,
That I henceforth would be rhyme-proof
        Till my last breath—

7

latch

-flame

young
woman

When click! the string the snick did draw;
And jee! the door gaed to the wa';
And by my ingle-lowe I saw,
        Now bleezin bright,
A tight, outlandish hizzie, braw,
        Come full in sight.

8

peace

Ye need na doubt, I held my whisht;
The infant aith, half-form'd, was crusht;

I glowr'd as eerie's I'd been dusht,   stared;
           In some wild glen;   touched
When sweet, like modest Worth, she blusht,
           And steppèd ben.   inside

9

Green, slender, leaf-clad holly-boughs
Were twisted, gracefu', round her brows;
I took her for some Scottish Muse,
           By that same token;
And come to stop those reckless vows,
           Would soon been broken.

10

A ' hair-brain'd, sentimental trace '
Was strongly markèd in her face;
A wildly-witty, rustic grace
           Shone full upon her;
Her eye, ev'n turn'd on empty space,
           Beam'd keen with honor.

11

Down flow'd her robe, a tartan sheen,   bright
Till half a leg was scrimply seen;   barely
And such a leg! my bonie Jean
           Could only peer it;
Sae straught, sae taper, tight an' clean   straight
           Nane else came near it.

12

Her mantle large, of greenish hue,
My gazing wonder chiefly drew;
Deep lights and shades, bold-mingling, threw
           A lustre grand;
And seem'd, to my astonish'd view,
           A well-known land.

13

Here, rivers in the sea were lost;
There, mountains to the skies were toss't;
Here, tumbling billows mark'd the coast
           With surging foam;
There, distant shone Art's lofty boast,
           The lordly dome.

14

Here, Doon pour'd down his far-fetch'd floods;
There, well-fed Irwine stately thuds:
Auld hermit Ayr staw thro' his woods,
                On to the shore;
And many a lesser torrent scuds
                With seeming roar.

beats
stole

15

Low, in a sandy valley spread,
An ancient borough rear'd her head;
Still, as in Scottish story read,
                She boasts a race
To ev'ry nobler virtue bred,
                And polish'd grace.

16

By stately tow'r, or palace fair,
Or ruins pendent in the air,
Bold stems of heroes, here and there,
                I could discern;
Some seem'd to muse, some seem'd to dare
                With feature stern.

17

My heart did glowing transport feel,
To see a race heroic wheel,
And brandish round the deep-dyed steel
                In sturdy blows;
While, back-recoiling, seem'd to reel
                Their suthron foes.

18

His Country's Saviour, mark him well!
Bold Richardton's heroic swell;
The chief, on Sark who glorious fell
                In high command;
And he whom ruthless fates expel
                His native land.

19

There, where a sceptr'd Pictish shade
Stalk'd round his ashes lowly laid,

I mark'd a martial race, pourtray'd
    In colours strong:
Bold, soldier-featur'd, undismay'd,
    They strode along.

20

Thro' many a wild, romantic grove,
Near many a hermit-fancied cove
(Fit haunts for friendship or for love
    In musing mood),
An aged Judge, I saw him rove,
    Dispensing good.

21

With deep-struck, reverential awe,
The learned Sire and Son I saw:
To Nature's God, and Nature's law,
    They gave their lore;
This, all its source and end to draw,
    That, to adore.

22

Brydon's brave ward I well could spy,
Beneath old Scotia's smiling eye;
Who call'd on Fame, low standing by,
    To hand him on,
Where many a patriot-name on high,
    And hero shone.

DUAN SECOND

1

With musing-deep, astonish'd stare,
I view'd the heavenly-seeming Fair;
A whisp'ring throb did witness bear
    Of kindred sweet,
When with an elder sister's air
    She did me greet.

2

'All hail! my own inspirèd Bard!
In me thy native Muse regard!

Nor longer mourn thy fate is hard,
        Thus poorly low!
I come to give thee such reward,
        As we bestow.

3

' Know, the great Genius of this land
Has many a light aerial band,
Who, all beneath his high command,
        Harmoniously,
As arts or arms they understand,
        Their labors ply.

4

' They Scotia's race among them share:
Some fire the soldier on to dare;
Some rouse the patriot up to bare
        Corruption's heart;
Some teach the bard—a darling care—
        The tuneful art.

5

' 'Mong swelling floods of reeking gore,
They, ardent, kindling spirits pour;
Or, 'mid the venal Senate's roar,
        They, sightless, stand,
To mend the honest patriot-lore,
        And grace the hand.

6

' And when the bard, or hoary sage,
Charm or instruct the future age,
They bind the wild poetic rage
        In energy;
Or point the inconclusive page
        Full on the eye.

7

' Hence, Fullarton, the brave and young;
Hence, Dempster's zeal-inspirèd tongue;
Hence, sweet, harmonious Beattie sung
        His *Minstrel* lays,
Or tore, with noble ardour stung,
        The sceptic's bays.

8

' To lower orders are assign'd
The humbler ranks of human-kind,
The rustic bard, the laboring hind,
   The artisan;
All chuse, as various they're inclin'd,
   The various man.

9

' When yellow waves the heavy grain,
The threat'ning storm some strongly rein,
Some teach to meliorate the plain,
   With tillage-skill;
And some instruct the shepherd-train,
   Blythe o'er the hill.

10

' Some hint the lover's harmless wile;
Some grace the maiden's artless smile;
Some soothe the laborer's weary toil
   For humble gains,
And make his cottage-scenes beguile
   His cares and pains.

11

' Some, bounded to a district-space,
Explore at large man's infant race,
To mark the embryotic trace
   Of rustic bard;
And careful note each opening grace,
   A guide and guard.

12

' Of these am I—Coila my name:
And this district as mine I claim,
Where once the Campbells, chiefs of fame,
   Held ruling pow'r:
I mark'd thy embryo-tuneful flame,
   Thy natal hour.

13

' With future hope I oft would gaze,
Fond, on thy little early ways:

Thy rudely caroll'd, chiming phrase,
                In uncouth rhymes;
Fir'd at the simple, artless lays
                Of other times.

14

' I saw thee seek the sounding shore,
Delighted with the dashing roar;
Or when the North his fleecy store
                Drove thro' the sky,
I saw grim Nature's visage hoar
                Struck thy young eye.

15

' Or when the deep green-mantled earth
Warm cherish'd ev'ry flow'ret's birth,
And joy and music pouring forth
                In ev'ry grove;
,I saw thee eye the gen'ral mirth
                With boundless love.

16

' When ripen'd fields and azure skies
Call'd forth the reapers' rustling noise,
I saw thee leave their ev'ning joys,
                And lonely stalk,
To vent thy bosom's swelling rise,
                In pensive walk.

17

' When youthful Love, warm-blushing, strong,
Keen-shivering, shot thy nerves along,
Those accents grateful to thy tongue,
                Th' adorèd *Name*,
I taught thee how to pour in song
                To soothe thy flame.

18

' I saw thy pulse's maddening play,
Wild-send thee Pleasure's devious way,
Misled by Fancy's meteor-ray,
                By passion driven;
But yet the light that led astray
                Was light from Heaven.

19

' I taught thy manners-painting strains
The loves, the ways of simple swains,
Till now, o'er all my wide domains
   Thy fame extends;
And some, the pride of Coila's plains,
   Become thy friends.

20

' Thou canst not learn, nor can I show,
To paint with Thomson's landscape glow;
Or wake the bosom-melting throe
   With Shenstone's art;
Or pour, with Gray, the moving flow
   Warm on the heart.

21

' Yet, all beneath th' unrivall'd rose,
The lowly daisy sweetly blows;
Tho' large the forest's monarch throws
   His army-shade,
Yet green the juicy hawthorn grows
   Adown the glade.

22

' Then never murmur nor repine;
Strive in thy humble sphere to shine;
And trust me, not Potosi's mine,
   Nor king's regard,
Can give a bliss o'ermatching thine,
   A rustic Bard.

23

' To give my counsels all in one:
Thy tuneful flame still careful fan;
Preserve the dignity of Man,
   With soul erect;
And trust the Universal Plan
   Will all protect.

24

' And wear thou *this*.' She solemn said,
And bound the holly round my head:

The polish'd leaves and berries red
            Did rustling play;
And, like a passing thought, she fled
            In light away.

HALLOWEEN

Yes! let the rich deride. the proud disda'n,
The simple pleasures of the lowly train:
To me more dear, congenial to my heart,
One native charm, than all the gloss of art.
                          GOLDSMITH

I

Upon that night, when fairies light
    On Cassilis Downans dance,
Or owre the lays, in splendid blaze,
    On sprightly coursers prance;
Or for Colean the rout is ta'en,
    Beneath the moon's pale beams;
There, up the Cove, to stray and rove,
    Amang the rocks and streams
                To sport that night:

partures — lays
road — rout

2

Amang the bonie winding banks,
    Where Doon rins, wimplin, clear;
Where Bruce ance ruled the martial ranks,
    An' shook his Carrick spear;
Some merry, friendly, country-folks
    Together did convene,
To burn their nits, an' pou their stocks,
    An' haud their Hallowe'en
                Fu' blythe that night.

winding — wimplin
nuts; — nits
pull; plants — pou; stocks
keep — haud

3

The lasses feat an' cleanly neat,
    Mair braw than when they're fine;
Their faces blythe fu' sweetly kythe
    Hearts leal, an' warm, an' kin':
The lads sae trig, wi' wooer-babs
    Weel-knotted on their garten;

spruce — feat
fair — braw
show — kythe
loyal; kind — leal; kin'
love-knots — wooer-babs
garters — garten

Some unco blate, an' some wi' gabs   shy; talk
   Gar lasses' hearts gang startin   make; beat-
             Whyles fast at night.   ing
                                     Sometimes

4

Then, first an' foremost, thro' the kail,
   Their stocks maun a' be sought ance;   shut; eyes;
They steek their een, an' grape an' wale   grope;
   For muckle anes, an' straught anes.   choose
Poor hav'rel Will fell aff the drift,   big; straight
   An' wandered thro' the bow-kail,   foolish; lost
An' pow't, for want o' better shift,   the way
   A runt, was like a sow-tail,   cabbage
             Sae bow't that night.   pulled;
                                     choice
                                     stalk
                                     bent

5

Then, straught or crooked, yird or nane,   mould
   They roar an' cry a' throu'ther;   pell-mell
The vera wee-things, toddlin, rin   children; run
   Wi' stocks out-owre their shouther: upon
An' gif the custock 's sweet or sour,   if; pith
   Wi' joctelegs they taste them;   pocket-knives
Syne coziely, aboon the door,   Then; above
   Wi' cannie care, they 've plac'd them   prudent
            To lie that night.

6

The lasses staw frae 'mang them a',   stole
   To pou their stalks o' corn;
But Rab slips out, an' jinks about,   dodges
   Behint the muckle thorn:
He grippet Nelly hard an' fast;
   Loud skirl'd a' the lasses;   squeaked
But her tap-pickle maist was lost,
   Whan kiutlin in the fause-house   cuddling
            Wi' him that night.

7

The auld guid-wife's weel-hoordet nits   well-
   Are round an' round divided,   hoarded
An' monie lads' an' lasses' fates
   Are there that night decided:

comfortably

Some kindle couthie, side by side,
     An' burn thegither trimly;
Some start awa wi' saucy pride,

fire-place

     An' jump out-owre the chimlie
                 Fu' high that night.

8

watchful

Jean slips in twa, wi' tentie e'e;
     Wha 'twas, she wadna tell;
But this is *Jock*, an' this is *me*,

whispers

     She says in to hersel:
He bleez'd owre her, an' she owre him,
     As they wad never mair part;

chimney

Till fuff! he started up the lum,
     And Jean had e'en a sair heart
                 To see't that night.

9

Poor Willie, wi' his bow-kail runt,

precise Moll

     Was burnt wi' primsie Mallie;

huff

An' Mary, nae doubt, took the drunt,
     To be compar'd to Willie:

leaped; start

Mall's nit lap out, wi' pridefu' fling,

foot

     An' her ain fit, it burnt it;
While Willie lap, an' swoor by jing,
     'Twas just the way he wanted
                 To be that night.

10

Nell had the fause-house in her min',
     She pits hersel an' Rob in;
In loving bleeze they sweetly join,

ashes

     Till white in ase they're sobbin:
Nell's heart was dancin at the view;

by stealth,
tasted;
mouth

     She whisper'd Rob to leuk for't:
Rob, stownlins, prie'd her bonie mou,

corner

     Fu' cozie in the neuk for't,
                 Unseen that night.

11

Marian

But Merran sat behint their backs,
     Her thoughts on Andrew Bell;

gabbing

She lea'es them gashing at their cracks,
     An' slips out by hersel:

She thro' the yard the nearest taks,
  An' to the kiln she goes then,
An' darklins grapit for the bauks,   *in the dark;*
  And in the blue-clue throws then,   *cross-beams*
                Right fear't that night.

12

An' ay she win't, an' ay she swat—   *wound;*
  I wat she made nae jaukin;   *sweated*
Till something held within the pat,   *bet; trifling*
  Guid Lord! but she was quakin!   *kiln-pot*
But whether 'twas the Deil himsel,
  Or whether 'twas a bauk-en',   *beam-end*
Or whether it was Andrew Bell,
  She did na wait on talkin
             To spier that night.   *ask*

13

Wee Jenny to her graunie says,
  ' Will ye go wi' me, graunie?
I'll eat the apple at the glass,
  I gat frae uncle Johnie ':
She fuff't her pipe wi' sic a lunt,   *puffed*
  In wrath she was sae vap'rin,   *smoke*
She notic't na an aizle brunt   *cinder burnt*
  Her braw, new, worset apron   *worsted*
             Out thro' that night.

14

' Ye little skelpie-limmer's-face!
  I daur ye try sic sportin,
As seek the Foul Thief onie place,   *Devil*
  For him to spae your fortune: *tell*
Nae doubt but ye may get a sight!
  Great cause ye hae to fear it;
For monie a ane has gotten a fright,
  An' liv'd an' died deleeret,   *mad*
            On sic a night.

15

' Ae hairst afore the Sherra-moor,   *harvest;*
  I mind't as weel's yestreen—   *Sheriffmuir*
I was a gilpey then, I'm sure   *remember*
  I was na past fyfteen: *young girl*

The simmer had been cauld an' wat,
    An' stuff was unco green;
An' ay a rantin kirn we gat,
    An' just on Halloween
                It fell that night.

*grain; very
rollicking
harvest-home*

16

*chief
harvester*

son; child

off his wits

' Our stibble-rig was Rab M'Graen,
    A clever, sturdy fallow;
His sin gat Eppie Sim wi' wean,
    That lived in Achmachalla:
He gat hemp-seed, I mind it weel,
    An' he made unco light o't;
But monie a day was by himsel,
    He was sae sairly frighted
              That vera night.'

17

fighting

*sow
all merely
reached; bag*

Then up gat fechtin Jamie Fleck,
    An' he swoor by his conscience,
That he could saw hemp-seed a peck;
    For it was a' but nonsense:
The auld guidman raught down the pock,
    An' out a handfu' gied him;
Syne bad him slip frae 'mang the folk,
    Sometime when nae ane see'd him,
              An' try't that night.

18

staggered

dungfork

*trails;
crupper*

sow

He marches thro' amang the stacks,
    Tho' he was something sturtin;
The graip he for a harrow taks,
    And haurls at his curpin;
And ev'ry now and then, he says,
    ' Hemp-seed I saw thee,
An' her that is to be my lass
    Come after me, an' draw thee
            As fast this night'.

19

*scared;
awe-stricken*

He whistl'd up *Lord Lenox' March*,
    To keep his courage cheery;
Altho' his hair began to arch,
    He was sae fley'd an' eerie;

Till presently he hears a squeak,
  An' then a grane an' gruntle;   *groan*
He by his shouther gae a keek,   *round; look*
  An' tumbl'd wi' a wintle   *summersault*
              Out-owre that night.

20

He roar'd a horrid murder-shout,
  In dreadfu' desperation!
An' young an' auld come rinnin out,
  An' hear the sad narration:
He swoor 'twas hilchin Jean M'Craw,   *halting*
  Or crouchie Merran Humphie—   *hunchbacked*
Till stop! she trotted thro' them a';
  An' wha was it but grumphie   *the pig*
              Asteer that night?   *Astir*

21

Meg fain wad to the barn gaen,   *have gone*
  To winn three wechts o' naething;   *winnow;*
But for to meet the Deil her lane,   *all by herself*
  She pat but little faith in:
She gies the herd a pickle nits,   *shepherd;*
  An' twa red-cheekit apples,   *few*
To watch, while for the barn she sets,
  In hopes to see Tam Kipples
              That vera night.

22

She turns the key wi' cannie thraw,   *twist*
  An' owre the threshold ventures;
But first on Sawnie gies a ca',
  Syne bauldly in she enters:
A ratton rattl'd up the wa',   *rat*
  An' she cry'd, L—d preserve her!
An' ran thro' midden-hole an' a',
  An' pray'd wi' zeal and fervour
              Fu' fast that night.

23

They hoy't out Will, wi' sair advice;   *urged*
  They hecht him some fine braw ane;   *promised*
It chanc'd the stack he faddom't thrice,   *against*
  Was timmer-propt for thrawin: *bending*

twisted

beldam
uttered a
curse, and
made a hit
shreds
Off his fists

He taks a swirlie, auld moss-oak
    For some black gruesome carlin;
An' loot a winze, an' drew a stroke,
    Till skin in blypes cam haurlin
                Aff 's nieves that night.

24

A wanton widow Leezie was,

lively: kitten
    As cantie as a kittlin;

woods
But och! that night, amang the shaws,
    She gat a fearfu' settlin!
She thro' the whins, an' by the cairn,

careering
    An' owre the hill gaed scrievin;

brook
Whare three lairds' lands met at a burn,
    To dip her left sark-sleeve in
                Was bent that night.

25

Now; fall
Whyles owre a linn the burnie plays,
    As thro' the glen it wimpl't;

cliff
Whyles round a rocky scaur it strays,

eddy
    Whyles in a wiel it dimpl't;
Whyles glitter'd to the nightly rays,
    Wi' bickerin, dancin dazzle;

hid
Whyles cookit underneath the braes,
    Below the spreading hazel
                Unseen that night.

26

ferns;
hillside
Amang the brachens, on the brae,
    Between her an' the moon,

young cow in
the open
The Deil, or else an outler quey,
    Gat up an' gae a croon:

leaped;
sheath
Poor Leezie's heart maist lap the hool;
    Near lav'rock-height she jumpit,

lark-high
foot
But mist a fit, an' in the pool

ears
    Out-owre the lugs sne plumpit
                Wi' a plunge that night.

27

In order, on the clean hearth-stane,
    The luggies three are ranged;
And ev'ry time great care is taen
    To see them duly changed:

Auld uncle John, wha wedlock's joys
  Sin Mar's-year did desire,   *1715*
Because he gat the toom dish thrice,   *empty*
  He heav'd them on the fire
          In wrath that night.

28

Wi' merry sangs, an' friendly cracks,
  I wat they did na weary;   *wot*
An unco tales, an' funnie jokes—   *wondrous*
  Their sports were cheap an' cheery:
Till butter'd sow'ns, wi' fragrant lunt,   *steam*
  Set a' their gabs a-steerin;   *tongues*
                     wagging
Syne, wi' a social glass o' strunt,   *liquor*
  They parted aff careerin
          Fu' blythe that night.

THE AULD FARMER'S NEW-YEAR MORNING SALUTATION TO HIS AULD MARE, MAGGIE

ON GIVING HER THE ACCUSTOMED RIPP OF CORN TO HANSEL IN THE NEW-YEAR

1

A Guid New-Year I wish thee, Maggie!   *handful from*
                          the sheaf;
Hae, there's a ripp to thy auld baggie: *belly*
Tho' thou's howe-backit now, an' knaggie, *hollow-*
                          backed;
      I've seen the day   *knobby*
Thou could hae gaen like onie staggie, *gone; colt*
      Out-owre the lay.   *lea*

2

Tho' now thou's dowie, stiff, an' crazy, *drooping*
An' thy auld hide as white's a daisie,
I've seen thee dappl't, sleek an' glaizie, *shiny*
      A bonie gray:
He should been tight that daur't to raize thee, *prepared;*
      Ance in a day.   *excite*

3

Thou ance was i' the foremost rank,   *stately,*
A filly buirdly, steeve, an' swank: *compact*
                          limber

An' set weel down a shapely shank

earth

As e'er tread yird;

moat

An' could hae flown out-owre a stank

Like onie bird.

4

It's now some nine-an'-twenty year

father-in-law's
wholly as dowry

Sin' thou was my guid-father's meere;

He gied me thee, o' tocher clear,

An' fifty mark;

Tho' it was sma', 'twas weel-won gear,

strong

An' thou was stark.

5

went

When first I gaed to woo my Jenny,

mother

Ye then was trottin wi' your minnie:

sly

Tho' ye was trickie, slee, an' funnie,

mischievous

Ye ne'er was donsie;

tractable
good-tempered

But hamely, tawie, quiet, an' cannie,

An' unco sonsie.

6

That day, ye pranc'd wi' muckle pride,

bore

When ye bure hame my bonie bride:

An' sweet an' gracefu' she did ride,

Wi' maiden air!

have
challenged

Kyle-Stewart I could braggèd wide,

For sic a pair.

7

can;
stumble

Tho' now ye dow but hoyte and hobble,

stagger

An' wintle like a saumont-coble,

goer

That day, ye was a jinker noble,

wind

For heels an' win'!

wobble

An' ran them till they a' did wauble,

Far, far behin'!

8

skittish

When thou an' I were young and skiegh,

tedious

An' stable-meals at fairs were driegh,

snort;
whinny

How thou wad prance, an' snore, an' skriegh,

An' tak the road!

aloof

Town's-bodies ran, an' stood abiegh,

An' ca't thee mad.

9

When thou was corn't, an' I was mellow,
We took the road ay like a swallow:
At brooses thou had ne'er a fellow,   wedding-
               For pith an' speed;   races
But ev'ry tail thou pay't them hollow,
               Whare'er thou gaed.

10

The sma, droop-rumpl't, hunter cattle   short-rumped
Might aiblins waur't thee for a brattle;   have beat;
But sax Scotch miles thou try't their mettle,   spurt
            An' gar't them whaizle: wheeze
Nae whip nor spur, but just a wattle
             O' saugh or hazle.   willow

11

Thou was a noble fittie-lan',
As e'er in tug or tow was drawn!
Aft thee an' I, in aught hours' gaun,   going
            On guid March-weather,   to our own
Hae turn'd sax rood beside our han'   cheek
              For days thegither.

12

                           pulled rashly
Thou never braing't, an' fetch't, an' fliskit;   stopped
But thy auld tail thou wad hae whiskit,   suddenly;
An' spread abreed thy weel-fill'd brisket,   capered
             Wi' pith an' pow'r;   rooty hillocks
                           would have
Till sprittie knowes wad rair't, an' riskit,   roared;
            An' slypet owre.   cracked
                           fallen
                           smoothly
                           over

13

When frosts lay lang, an' snaws were deep,
An' threaten'd labour back to keep,
I gied thy cog a wee bit heap   dish
            Aboon the timmer: edge
I ken'd my Maggie wad na sleep
            For that, or simmer.   ere

14

In cart or car thou never reestit;
The steyest brae thou wad hae fac't it;   stiffest
                           incline

leaped;
sprang

Thou never lap, an' sten't, an' breastit,
                              Then stood to blaw;
But just thy step a wee thing hastit,

jogged along

                              Thou snoov't awa.

15

team: issue

My pleugh is now thy bairntime a',
Four gallant brutes as e'er did draw;

more

Forbye sax mae I've sell't awa,
                              That thou hast nurst;
They drew me thretteen pund an' twa.
                              The vera warst.

16

day's work

Monie a sair darg we twa hae wrought,
An' wi' the weary warl' fought!
An' monie an anxious day I thought
                              We wad be beat!
Yet here to crazy age we're brought,
                              Wi' something yet.

17

An' think na, my auld trusty servan',
That now perhaps thou's less deservin,
An' thy auld days may end in starvin;   .

bushel

                              For my last fow,

quarter-peck

A heapet stimpart, I'll reserve ane
                              Laid by for you.

18

We've worn to crazy years thegither;

totter

We'll toyte about wi' ane anither;

change

Wi' tentie care I'll flit thy tether

reserved
patch
fill your
stomach

                              To some hain'd rig,
Whare ye may nobly rax your leather
                              Wi' sma' fatigue.

THE COTTER'S SATURDAY NIGHT

INSCRIBED TO R. AIKEN, ESQ.

Let not Ambition mock their useful toil,
Their homely joys, and destiny obscure;
Nor Grandeur hear, with a disdainful smile,
The short and simple annals of the poor.
GRAY

I

My lov'd, my honor'd, much respected friend!
　No mercenary bard his homage pays;
With honest pride, I scorn each selfish end,
　My dearest meed, a friend's esteem and praise:
To you I sing, in simple Scottish lays,
The lowly train in life's sequester'd scene;
　The native feelings strong, the guileless ways;
What Aiken in a cottage would have been;
Ah! tho' his worth unknown, far happier there I
　ween!

2

November chill blaws loud wi' angry sugh;　　　wail
　The short'ning winter-day is near a close;
The miry beasts retreating frae the pleugh;
　The black'ning trains o' craws to their repose:
　The toil-worn Cotter frae his labor goes—
This night his weekly moil is at an end,
　Collects his spades, his mattocks, and his hoes,
Hoping the morn in ease and rest to spend,
And weary, o'er the moor, his course does hameward
　bend.

3

At length his lonely cot appears in view,
　Beneath the shelter of an aged tree;
Th' expectant wee-things, toddlin, stacher through　　totter
　To meet their dad, wi' flichterin' noise and glee.　　fluttering
　His wee bit ingle, blinkin bonilie,
His clean hearth-stane, his thrifty wifie's smile,
　The lisping infant, prattling on his knee,

Does a' his weary carking cares beguile,
And makes him quite forget his labor and his toil.

4

By and bye Belyve, the elder bairns come drapping in,
    At service out, amang the farmers roun';
follow;
heedful run Some ca' the pleugh, some herd, some tentie rin
quiet A cannie errand to a neebor town:
    Their eldest hope, their Jenny, woman grown,
In youthfu' bloom, love sparkling in her e'e,
    Comes hame; perhaps, to shew a braw new gown,
hard-; wages Or deposite her sair-won penny-fee,
To help her parents dear, if they in hardship be.

5

With joy unfeign'd, brothers and sisters meet,
asks And each for other's weelfare kindly spiers:
The social hours, swift-wing'd, unnotic'd fleet;
wonders Each tells the uncos that he sees or hears.
    The parents partial eye their hopeful years;
Anticipation forward points the view;
    The mother, wi' her needle and her sheers,
Makes; Gars auld claes look amaist as weel's the new;
clothes The father mixes a' wi' admonition due.

6

Their master's and their mistress's command
    The younkers a' are warned to obey;
diligent And mind their labors wi' an eydent hand,
trifle And ne'er, tho' out o' sight, to jauk or play:
    'And O! be sure to fear the Lord alway,
And mind your duty, duly, morn and night;
    Lest in temptation's path ye gang astray,
Implore His counsel and assisting might:
They never sought in vain that sought the Lord
    aright.'

But hark! a rap comes gently to the door;
    Jenny, wha kens the meaning o' the same,
Tells how a neebor lad came o'er the moor,
    To do some errands, and convoy her hame.
    The wily mother sees the conscious flame

Sparkle in Jenny's e'e, and flush her cheek;
  With heart-struck anxious care, enquires his name,
While Jenny hafflins is afraid to speak;   half
Weel-pleas'd the mother hears, it's nae wild, worth-
    less rake.

8

With kindly welcome, Jenny brings him ben;   inside
  A strappin' youth, he takes the mother's eye;
Blythe Jenny sees the visit's no ill taen;
  The father cracks of horses, pleughs, and kye.   chats; cattle
  The youngster's artless heart o'erflows wi' joy,
But blate and laithfu', scarce can weel behave;   shy:
                                        sheepish
  The mother, wi' a woman's wiles, can spy
What makes the youth sae bashfu' and sae grave;
Weel-pleas'd to think her bairn's respected like the
    lave.   rest

9

O happy love! where love like this is found:
  O heart-felt raptures! bliss beyond compare!
I've pacèd much this weary, mortal round,
  And sage experience bids me this declare:—
  ' If Heaven a draught of heavenly pleasure spare,
One cordial in this melancholy vale,
  'Tis when a youthful, loving, modest pair,
In other's arms, breathe out the tender tale
Beneath the milk-white thorn that scents the ev'ning
    gale.'

10

Is there, in human form, that bears a heart,
  A wretch! a villain! lost to love and truth!
That can, with studied, sly, ensnaring art,
  Betray sweet Jenny's unsuspecting youth?
  Curse on his perjur'd arts! dissembling, smooth!
Are honor, virtue, conscience, all exil'd?
  Is there no pity, no relenting ruth,
Points to the parents fondling o'er their child?
Then paints the ruin'd maid, and their distraction
    wild?

11

But now the supper crowns their simple board,
 The healsome parritch, chief o' Scotia's food;
The soupe their only hawkie does afford,
 That, 'yont the hallan snugly chows her cood;
 The dame brings forth, in complimental mood,
To grace the lad, her weel-hain'd kebbuck, fell;
 And aft he's prest, and aft he ca's it guid;
The frugal wifie, garrulous, will tell,
How 'twas a towmond auld, sin' lint was i' the bell.

wholesome

milk; cow

beyond; wall

-saved cheese; pungent

twelve-month; flax; flower

12

The chearfu' supper done, wi' serious face,
 They, round the ingle, form a circle wide;
The sire turns o'er, wi' patriarchal grace,
 The big ha'-Bible, ance his father's pride.
 His bonnet rev'rently is laid aside,
His lyart haffets wearing thin and bare;
 Those strains that once did sweet in Zion glide,
He wales a portion with judicious care,
And ' Let us worship God! ' he says, with solemn air.

grey side-locks

selects

13

They chant their artless notes in simple guise,
 They tune their hearts, by far the noblest aim;
Perhaps *Dundee's* wild-warbling measures rise,
 Or plaintive *Martyrs*, worthy of the name;
 Or noble *Elgin* beets the heaven-ward flame,
The sweetest far of Scotia's holy lays:
 Compar'd with these, Italian trills are tame;
The tickl'd ears no heart-felt raptures raise;
Nae unison hae they, with our Creator's praise.

fans

14

The priest-like father reads the sacred page,
 How Abram was the friend of God on high;
Or, Moses bade eternal warfare wage
 With Amalek's ungracious progeny;
 Or, how the royal Bard did groaning lie
Beneath the stroke of Heaven's avenging ire;
 Or Job's pathetic plaint, and wailing cry;
Or rapt Isaiah's wild, seraphic fire;
Or other holy Seers that tune the sacred lyre.

15

Perhaps the Christian volume is the theme:
　How guiltless blood for guilty man was shed;
How He, who bore in Heaven the second name,
　Had not on earth whereon to lay His head;
　How His first followers and servants sped;
The precepts sage they wrote to many a land:
　How he, who lone in Patmos banishèd,
Saw in the sun a mighty angel stand,
And heard great Bab'lon's doom pronounc'd by
　　Heaven's command.

16

Then kneeling down to Heaven's Eternal King,
　The saint, the father, and the husband prays:
Hope ' springs exulting on triumphant wing.'
　That thus they all shall meet in future days,
　There, ever bask in uncreated rays,
No more to sigh or shed the bitter tear,
　Together hymning their Creator's praise,
In such society, yet still more dear;
While circling Time moves round in an eternal sphere.

17

Compar'd with this, how poor Religion's pride,
　In all the pomp of method, and of art;
When men display to congregations wide
　Devotion's ev'ry grace, except the heart !
　The Power, incens'd, the pageant will desert,
The pompous strain, the sacerdotal stole:
　But haply, in some cottage far apart,
May hear, well-pleas'd, the language of the soul,
And in His Book of Life the inmates poor enroll.

18

Then homeward all take off their sev'ral way;
　The youngling cottagers retire to rest:
The parent-pair their secret homage pay,
　And proffer up to Heaven the warm request,
　That He who stills the raven's clam'rous nest,
And decks the lily fair in flow'ry pride,
　Would, in the way His wisdom sees the best,
For them and for their little ones provide;
But, chiefly, in their hearts with Grace Divine preside.

19

From scenes like these, old Scotia's grandeur springs
    That makes her lov'd at home, rever'd abroad:
Princes and lords are but the breath of kings,
    ' An honest man's the noble(st) work of God ';
    And certes, in fair Virtue's heavenly road,
The cottage leaves the palace far behind;
    What is a lordling's pomp? a cumbrous load,
Disguising oft the wretch of human kind,
Studied in arts of Hell, in wickedness refin'd!

20

O Scotia! my dear, my native soil!
    For whom my warmest wish to Heaven is sent!
Long may thy hardy sons of rustic toil
    Be blest with health, and peace, and sweet content!
    And O! may Heaven their simple lives prevent
From Luxury's contagion, weak and vile!
    Then, howe'er crowns and coronets be rent,
A virtuous populace may rise the while,
And stand a wall of fire around their much-lov'd Isle.

21

O Thou! who pour'd the patriotic tide,
    That stream'd thro' Wallace's undaunted heart,
Who dar'd to, nobly, stem tyrannic pride,
    Or nobly die, the second glorious part:
    (The patriot's God, peculiarly Thou art,
    His friend, inspirer, guardian, and reward!)
    O never, never Scotia's realm desert;
But still the patriot, and the patriot-bard
In bright succession raise, her ornament and guard!

TO A MOUSE

ON TURNING HER UP IN HER NEST WITH THE PLOUGH, NOVEMBER 1785

I

Wee, sleekit, cowrin, tim'rous beastie,   sleek
O, what a panic's in thy breastie!
Thou need na start awa sae hasty
           Wi' bickering brattle!   hurrying
                               scamper
I wad be laith to rin an' chase thee,   loth
           Wi' murdering pattle!   plough-staff

2

I'm truly sorry man's dominion
Has broken Nature's social union,
An' justifies that ill opinion
           Which makes thee startle
At me, thy poor, earth-born companion
           An' fellow mortal!

3

I doubt na, whyles, but thou may thieve;   sometimes
What then? poor beastie, thou maun live!   odd ear;
A daimen icker in a thrave   twenty-four
           'S a sma' request;   sheaves
I'll get a blessin wi' the lave,   what's left
           An' never miss't!

4

Thy wee-bit housie, too, in ruin!
Its silly wa's the win's are strewin!   feeble; winds
An' naething, now, to big a new ane,
           O' foggage green!   coarse grass
An' bleak December's win's ensuin,
           Baith snell an' keen!   bitter

5

Thou saw the fields laid bare an' waste,
An' weary winter comin fast,

An' cozie here, beneath the blast,
                Thou thought to dwell,
Till crash! the cruel coulter past
                Out thro' thy cell.

6

stubble   That wee bit heap o' leaves an' stibble,
Has cost thee monie a weary nibble!
Now thou's turned out, for a' thy trouble,
Without;
holding   But house or hald,
endure   To thole the winter's sleety dribble,
hoar-frost   An' cranreuch cauld!

7

alone   But Mousie, thou art no thy lane,
In proving foresight may be vain:
The best-laid schemes o' mice an' men
askew   Gang aft agley,
An' lea'e us nought but grief an' pain,
                For promis'd joy!

8

Still thou art blest, compared wi' me!
The present only toucheth thee:
But och! I backward cast my e'e,
                On prospects drear!
An' forward, tho' I canna see,
                I guess an' fear!

EPISTLE TO DAVIE, A BROTHER POET

1

While winds frae aff Ben-Lomond blaw,
And bar the doors wi' drivin' snaw,
fire   And hing us owre the ingle,
I set me down to pass the time,
And spin a verse or twa o' rhyme,
westland   In hamely, westlin jingle:
Right to the
chimney   While frosty winds blaw in the drift,
corner   Ben to the chimla lug,

I grudge a wee the great-folk's gift,
  That live sae bien an' snug: prosperous
    I tent less, and want less   value
      Their roomy fire-side;
  But hanker, and canker,
      To see their cursed pride.

2

It's hardly in a body's pow'r,
To keep, at times, frae being sour,
  To see how things are shar'd;
How best o' chiels are whyles in want,   chaps; sometimes
While coofs on countless thousands rant,   dolts; roister
  And ken na how to ware't;   spend
But Davie, lad, ne'er fash your head,   trouble
  Tho' we hae little gear;   wealth
We 're fit to win our daily bread,
  As lang 's we're hale and fier: whole; sound
    ' Mair spier na, nor fear na',   ask not
      Auld age ne'er mind a feg;   fig
    The last o't, the warst o't,
      Is only but to beg.

3

To lie in kilns and barns at e'en,
When banes are craz'd, and bluid is thin,
  Is, doubtless, great distress!
Yet then content could make us blest;
Ev'n then, sometimes, we'd snatch a taste
  Of truest happiness.
The honest heart that's free frae a'
  Intended fraud or guile,
However Fortune kick the ba',
  Has ay some cause to smile;
    And mind still, you'll find still,
      A comfort this nae sma';
    Nae mair then, we'll care then,
      Nae farther can we fa'.

4

What tho', like commoners of air,
We wander out, we know not where,
  But either house or hal'?   Without; holding

Yet Nature's charms, the hills and woods,
The sweeping vales, and foaming floods,
    Are free alike to all.
In days when daisies deck the ground,
    And blackbirds whistle clear,
With honest joy our hearts will bound,
    To see the coming year:
        On braes when we please then,
            We'll sit an' sowth a tune;
        Syne rhyme till't we'll time till't,
            An' sing't when we hae done.

hill-sides
hum
Then

5

It's no in titles nor in rank:
It's no in wealth like Lon'on Bank,
    To purchase peace and rest.
It's no in makin muckle, mair;
It's no in books, it's no in lear,
    To make us truly blest:
If happiness hae not her seat
    An' centre in the breast,
We may be wise, or rich, or great,
    But never can be blest!
        Nae treasures nor pleasures
            Could make us happy lang;
        The heart ay's the part ay
            That makes us right or wrang.

much, more
learning

6

Think ye, that sic as you and I,
Wha drudge and drive thro' wet and dry,
    Wi' never ceasing toil;
Think ye, are we less blest than they,
Wha scarcely tent us in their way,
    As hardly worth their while?
Alas! how oft, in haughty mood,
    God's creatures they oppress!
Or else, neglecting a' that's guid,
    They riot in excess!
        Baith careless and fearless
            Of either Heaven or Hell;
        Esteeming and deeming
            It a' an idle tale!

7

Then let us chearfu' acquiesce,
Nor make our scanty pleasures less
  By pining at our state:
And, even should misfortunes come,
I here wha sit hae met wi' some,
  An's thankfu' for them yet,   And am
They gie the wit of age to youth;
  They let us ken oursel;
They make us see the naked truth,
  The real guid and ill:
    Tho' losses and crosses
      Be lessons right severe,
      There's wit there, ye 'll get there,
        Ye'll find nae other where.

8

But tent me, Davie, ace o' hearts!   listen to
(To say aught less wad wrang the cartes,   cards
  And flatt'ry I detest)
This life has joys for you and I;
And joys that riches ne'er could buy,
  And joys the very best.
There's a' the pleasures o' the heart,
  The lover an' the frien':
Ye hae your Meg, your dearest part,
  And I my darling Jean!
    It warms me, it charms me
      To mention but her name:
    It heats me, it beets me,   kindles
      And sets me a' on flame!

9

O all ye Pow'rs who rule above!
O Thou whose very self art love!
  Thou know'st my words sincere!
The life-blood streaming thro' my heart,
Or my more dear immortal part,
  Is not more fondly dear!
When heart-corroding care and grief
  Deprive my soul of rest,
Her dear idea brings relief
  And solace to my breast.

Thou Being All-seeing,
   O, hear my fervent pray'r!
Still take her, and make her
   Thy most peculiar care!

10

All hail! ye tender feelings dear!
The smile of love, the friendly tear,
   The sympathetic glow!
Long since, this world's thorny ways
Had number'd out my weary days,
   Had it not been for you!
Fate still has blest me with a friend
   In every care and ill;
And oft a more endearing band,
   A tie more tender still.
     It lightens, it brightens
      The tenebrific scene,
     To meet with, and greet with
      My Davie or my Jean!

11

O, how that Name inspires my style!
The words come skelpin' rank an' file,
   Amaist before I ken!
The ready measure rins as fine,
As Phœbus and the famous Nine
   Were glowrin owre my pen.
My spaviet Pegasus will limp,
   Till ance he's fairly het;
And then he'll hilch, an' stilt, an' jimp,
   And rin an unco fit;
     But least then, the beast then
      Should rue this hasty ride,
     I'll light now, and dight now
      His sweaty, wizen'd hide.

Marginal glosses: spanking; overlooking; spavied; hot; hobble; limp; jump; uncommon; burst; wipe

THE LAMENT

TUNE: *Scots Queen*

OCCASIONED BY THE UNFORTUNATE ISSUE OF
A FRIEND'S AMOUR

*Alas! how oft does Goodness wound itself,
And sweet Affection prove the spring of Woe!*
HOME

1

O thou pale Orb that silent shines
   While care-untroubled mortals sleep!
Thou seest a wretch who inly pines,
   And wanders here to wail and weep!
   With Woe I nightly vigils keep,
Beneath thy wan, unwarming beam;
   And mourn, in lamentation deep,
How life and love are all a dream!

2

I joyless view thy rays adorn
   The faintly-markèd, distant hill;
I joyless view thy trembling horn
   Reflected in the gurgling rill:
   My fondly-fluttering heart, be still!
Thou busy pow'r, Remembrance, cease!
   Ah! must the agonizing thrill
For ever bar returning Peace?

3

No idly-feign'd, poetic pains
   My sad, love-lorn lamentings claim:
No shepherd's pipe—Arcadian strains;
   No fabled tortures quaint and tame.
   The plighted faith, the mutual flame,
The oft-attested Pow'rs above,
   The promis'd father's tender name,
These were the pledges of my love!

4

Encircled in her clasping arms,
   How have the raptur'd moments flown!

How have I wished for Fortune's charms,
   For her dear sake, and her's alone!
   And, must I think it! is she gone,
My secret heart's exulting boast?
   And does she heedless hear my groan?
And is she ever, ever lost?

5

O! can she bear so base a heart,
   So lost to honour, lost to truth,
As from the fondest lover part,
   The plighted husband of her youth?
   Alas! Life's path may be unsmooth!
Her way may lie thro' rough distress!
   Then, who her pangs and pains will soothe,
Her sorrows share, and make them less?

6

Ye wingèd Hours that o'er us pass'd,
   Enraptur'd more the more enjoy'd,
Your dear remembrance in my breast
   My fondly treasur'd thoughts employ'd:
   That breast, how dreary now, and void,
For her too scanty once of room!
   Ev'n ev'ry ray of Hope destroy'd,
And not a wish to gild the gloom!

7

The morn, that warns th' approaching day,
   Awakes me up to toil and woe;
I see the hours in long array,
   That I must suffer, lingering slow:
   Full many a pang, and many a throe,
Keen Recollection's direful train,
   Must wring my soul, ere Phœbus, low,
Shall kiss the distant western main.

8

And when my nightly couch I try,
   Sore-harass'd out with care and grief,
My toil-beat nerves and tear-worn eye
   Keep watchings with the nightly thief:

Or, if I slumber, Fancy, chief,
Reigns, haggard-wild, in sore affright:
    Ev'n day, all-bitter, brings relief
From such a horror-breathing night.

9

O thou bright Queen, who, o'er th' expanse
    Now highest reign'st, with boundless sway!
Oft has thy silent-marking glance
    Observ'd us, fondly-wand'ring, stray!
    The time, unheeded, sped away,
While Love's luxurious pulse beat high,
    Beneath thy silver-gleaming ray,
To mark the mutual-kindling eye.

10

O scenes in strong remembrance set!
    Scenes, never, never to return!
Scenes if in stupor I forget,
    Again I feel, again I burn!
    From ev'ry joy and pleasure torn,
Life's weary vale I wander thro';
    And hopeless, comfortless, I'll mourn
A faithless woman's broken vow!

DESPONDENCY

An Ode

I

Oppress'd with grief, oppress'd with care,
A burden more than I can bear,
    I set me down and sigh;
O Life! thou art a galling load,
Along a rough, a weary road,
    To wretches such as I!
Dim-backward, as I cast my view,
    What sick'ning scenes appear!
What sorrows yet may pierce me thro',
    Too justly I may fear!
        Still caring, despairing,
            Must be my bitter doom;
        My woes here shall close ne'er
            But with the closing tomb!

2

Happy ye sons of busy life,
Who, equal to the bustling strife,
    No other view regard!
Ev'n when the wishèd end's denied,
Yet while the busy means are plied,
    They bring their own reward:
Whilst I, a hope-abandoned wight,
    Unfitted with an aim,
Meet ev'ry sad returning night
    And joyless morn the same.
        You, bustling and justling,
            Forget each grief and pain;
        I, listless yet restless,
            Find ev'ry prospect vain.

3

How blest the Solitary's lot,
Who, all-forgetting, all-forgot,
    Within his humble cell—
The cavern, wild with tangling roots—
Sits o'er his newly-gather'd fruits,
    Beside his crystal well!
Or haply to his ev'ning thought,
    By unfrequented stream,
The ways of men are distant brought,
    A faint-collected dream;
        While praising, and raising
            His thoughts to Heav'n on high,
        As wand'ring, meand'ring,
            He views the solemn sky.

4

Than I, no lonely hermit plac'd
Where never human footsteps trac'd,
    Less fit to play the part;
The lucky moment to improve,
And just to stop, and just to move,
    With self-respecting art:
But ah! those pleasures, loves, and joys,
    Which I too keenly taste,
The Solitary can despise—
    Can want and yet be blest!

He needs not, he heeds not
   Or human love or hate;
Whilst I here must cry here
   At perfidy ingrate!

5

O enviable early days,
When dancing thoughtless pleasure's maze,
   To care, to guilt unknown!
How ill exchang'd for riper times,
To feel the follies or the crimes
   Of others, or my own!
Ye tiny elves that guiltless sport,
   Like linnets in the bush,
Ye little know the ills ye court,
   When manhood is your wish!
     The losses, the crosses
       That active man engage;
     The fears all, the tears all
       Of dim declining Age!

MAN WAS MADE TO MOURN
A Dirge

TUNE: *Peggy Bawn*

1

When chill November's surly blast
   Made fields and forests bare,
One ev'ning, as I wand'red forth
   Along the banks of Ayr,
I spied a man, whose agèd step
   Seem'd weary, worn with care,
His face was furrow'd o'er with years,
   And hoary was his hair.

2

'Young stranger, whither wand'rest thou?'
   Began the rev'rend Sage;
'Does thirst of wealth thy step constrain,
   Or youthful pleasure's rage?
Or haply, prest with cares and woes,
   Too soon thou hast began

To wander forth, with me to mourn
    The miseries of Man.

3

' The sun that overhangs yon moors,
    Out-spreading far and wide,
Where hundreds labour to support
    A haughty lordling's pride:
I've seen yon weary winter-sun
    Twice forty times return;
And ev'ry time has added proofs,
    That Man was made to mourn.

4

' O Man! while in thy early years,
    How prodigal of time!
Mis-spending all thy precious hours,
    Thy glorious, youthful prime!
Alternate follies take the sway,
    Licentious passions burn:
Which tenfold force gives Nature's law,
    That Man was made to mourn.

5

' Look not alone on youthful prime,
    Or manhood's active might;
Man then is useful to his kind,
    Supported is his right:
But see him on the edge of life,
    With cares and sorrows worn;
Then Age and Want—O ill-match'd pair!—
    Shew Man was made to mourn.

6

' A few seem favourites of Fate,
    In Pleasure's lap carest;
Yet think not all the rich and great
    Are likewise truly blest:
But oh! what crowds in ev'ry land,
    All wretched and forlorn,
Thro' weary life this lesson learn,
    That Man was made to mourn.

7

'Many and sharp the num'rous ills
  Inwoven with our frame!
More pointed still we make ourselves
  Regret, remorse, and shame!
And Man, whose heav'n-erected face
  The smiles of love adorn,—
Man's inhumanity to man
  Makes countless thousands mourn!

8

'See yonder poor, o'erlabour'd wight,
  So abject, mean, and vile,
Who begs a brother of the earth
  To give him leave to toil;
And see his lordly fellow-worm
  The poor petition spurn,
Unmindful, tho' a weeping wife
  And helpless offspring mourn.

9

'If I'm design'd yon lordling's slave—
  By Nature's law design'd—
Why was an independent wish
  E'er planted in my mind?
If not, why am I subject to
  His cruelty, or scorn?
Or why has Man the will and pow'r
  To make his fellow mourn?

10

'Yet let not this too much, my son,
  Disturb thy youthful breast:
This partial view of human-kind
  Is surely not the last!
The poor, oppressèd, honest man
  Had never, sure, been born,
Had there not been some recompense
  To comfort those that mourn!

11

'O Death! the poor man's dearest friend,
  The kindest and the best!

Welcome the hour my agèd limbs
  Are laid with thee at rest!
The great, the wealthy fear thy blow,
  From pomp and pleasure torn;
But, oh! a blest relief to those
  That weary-laden mourn!'

WINTER

A Dirge

TUNE: *MacPherson's Rant*

I

The wintry west extends his blast,
  And hail and rain does blaw;
Or the stormy north sends driving forth
  The blinding sleet and snaw:
Wild-tumbling brown, the burn comes down,
  And roars frae bank to brae:
While bird and beast in covert rest,
  And pass the heartless day.

2

' The sweeping blast, the sky o'ercast,'
  The joyless winter day
Let others fear, to me more dear
  Than all the pride of May:
The tempest's howl, it soothes my soul,
  My griefs it seems to join;
The leafless trees my fancy please,
  Their fate resembles mine!

3

Thou Pow'r Supreme, whose mighty scheme
  These woes of mine fulfil,
Here, firm I rest, they must be best,
  Because they are Thy will!
Then all I want (O, do Thou grant
  This one request of mine!):
Since to enjoy Thou dost deny,
  Assist me to resign.

A PRAYER IN THE PROSPECT
OF DEATH

1

O Thou unknown, Almighty Cause
    Of all my hope and fear!
In whose dread presence, ere an hour,
    Perhaps I must appear!

2

If I have wander'd in those paths
    Of life I ought to shun—
As something, loudly, in my breast,
    Remonstrates I have done—

3

Thou know'st that Thou hast formèd me
    With passions wild and strong;
And list'ning to their witching voice
    Has often led me wrong.

4

Where human weakness has come short,
    Or frailty stept aside,
Do Thou, All-good—for such Thou art—
    In shades of darkness hide.

5

Where with intention I have err'd,
    No other plea I have,
But, Thou art good; and Goodness still
    Delighteth to forgive.

TO A MOUNTAIN DAISY

ON TURNING ONE DOWN WITH THE PLOUGH IN APRIL 1786

1

Wee, modest, crimson-tippèd flow'r,
Thou's met me in an evil hour;
For I maun crush amang the stoure
   Thy slender stem:
To spare thee now is past my pow'r,
   Thou bonie gem.

dust

2

Alas! it's no thy neebor sweet,
The bonie lark, companion meet,
Bending thee 'mang the dewy weet,
   Wi' spreckl'd breast!
When upward-springing, blythe, to greet
   The purpling east.

wet

3

Cauld blew the bitter-biting north
Upon thy early, humble birth;
Yet cheerfully thou glinted forth
   Amid the storm,
Scarce rear'd above the parent-earth
   Thy tender form.

sparkled

4

The flaunting flow'rs our gardens yield,
High shelt'ring woods and wa's maun shield;
But thou, beneath the random bield
   O' clod or stane,
Adorns the histie stibble-field,
   Unseen, alane.

must
shelter

bare stubble

5

There, in thy scanty mantle clad,
Thy snawie bosom sun-ward spread,

Thou lifts thy unassuming head
         In humble guise;
But now the share uptears thy bed,
         And low thou lies!

6

Such is the fate of artless maid,
Sweet flow'ret of the rural shade!
By love's simplicity betray'd,
         And guileless trust;
Till she, like thee, all soil'd, is laid
         Low i' the dust.

7

Such is the fate of simple Bard,
On Life's rough ocean luckless starr'd!
Unskilful he to note the card
         Of prudent lore,
Till billows rage, and gales blow hard,
         And whelm him o'er!

8

Such fate to suffering Worth is giv'n,
Who long with wants and woes has striv'n,
By human pride or cunning driv'n
         To mis'ry's brink;
Till, wrench'd of ev'ry stay but Heav'n,
         He, ruin'd, sink!

9

Ev'n thou who mourn'st the Daisy's fate,
That fate is thine—no distant date;
Stern Ruin's plough-share drives elate,
         Full on thy bloom,
Till crush'd beneath the furrow's weight
         Shall be thy doom!

TO RUIN

1

All hail, inexorable lord!
At whose destruction-breathing word,
  The mightiest empires fall!
Thy cruel, woe-delighted train,
The ministers of grief and pain,
  A sullen welcome, all!
With stern-resolv'd, despairing eye,
  I see each aimèd dart;
For one has cut my dearest tie,
  And quivers in my heart.
    Then low'ring and pouring,
      The storm no more I dread;
    Tho' thick'ning and black'ning
      Round my devoted head.

2

And thou grim Pow'r, by Life abhorr'd,
While Life a pleasure can afford,
  O! hear a wretch's pray'r!
No more I shrink appall'd, afraid;
I court, I beg thy friendly aid,
  To close this scene of care!
When shall my soul, in silent peace,
  Resign Life's joyless day?
My weary heart its throbbings cease,
  Cold-mould'ring in the clay?
    No fear more, no tear more
      To stain my lifeless face,
    Enclaspèd and graspèd
      Within thy cold embrace!

EPISTLE TO A YOUNG FRIEND

1

I lang hae thought, my youthfu' friend,
  A something to have sent you,

Tho' it should serve nae ither end
   Than just a kind memento:
But how the subject-theme may gang,
   Let time and chance determine:
Perhaps it may turn out a sang;
   Perhaps, turn out a sermon.

2

Ye'll try the world soon, my lad;
   And, Andrew dear, believe me,
Ye'll find mankind an unco squad,   strange
   And muckle they may grieve ye:
For care and trouble set your thought,
   Ev'n when your end's attainèd;
And a' your views may come to nought,
   Where ev'ry nerve is strainèd.

3

I'll no say, men are villains a':
   The real, harden'd wicked,
Wha hae nae check but human law,
   Are to a few restricked;
But, och! mankind are unco weak   mighty
   An' little to be trusted;
If Self the wavering balance shake,
   It's rarely right adjusted!

4

Yet they wha fa' in Fortune's strife,
   Their fate we should na censure;
For still, th' important end of life
   They equally may answer:
A man may hae an honest heart,
   Tho' poortith hourly stare him;   poverty
A man may tak a neebor's part,
   Yet hae nae cash to spare him.

5

Ay free, aff han', your story tell,
   When wi' a bosom cronie;
But still keep something to yoursel
   Ye scarcely tell to onie:

Conceal yoursel as weel's ye can
   Frae critical dissection:
pry   But keek thro' ev'ry other man
   Wi' sharpen'd, sly inspection.

6

flame   The sacred lowe o' weel-plac'd love,
   Luxuriantly indulge it;
attempt But never tempt th' illicit rove,
   Tho' naething should divulge it:
I waive the quantum o' the sin,
   The hazard of concealing;
But, och! it hardens a' within,
   And petrifies the feeling!

7

To catch Dame Fortune's golden smile,
   Assiduous wait upon her;
And gather gear by ev'ry wile
   That's justify'd by honor:
Not for to hide it in a hedge,
   Nor for a train-attendant;
But for the glorious privilege
   Of being independent.

8

The fear o' Hell's a hangman's whip
   To haud the wretch in order;
But where ye feel your honour grip,
   Let that ay be your border:
Its slightest touches, instant pause—
   Debar a' side-pretences;
And resolutely keep its laws,
   Uncaring consequences.

9

The great Creator to revere
   Must sure become the creature;
But still the preaching cant forbear,
   And ev'n the rigid feature:
Yet ne'er with wits profane to range
   Be complaisance extended;
An atheist-laugh's a poor exchange
   For Deity offended!

10

When ranting round in Pleasure's ring,   frolicking
 Religion may be blinded;
Or if she gie a random sting,
 It may be little minded;
But when on Life we're tempest-driv'n—
 A conscience but a canker—
A correspondence fix'd wi' Heav'n
 Is sure a noble anchor!

11

Adieu, dear, amiable youth!
 Your heart can ne'er be wanting!
May prudence, fortitude, and truth,
 Erect your brow undaunting!
In ploughman phrase, ' God send you speed,'
 Still daily to grow wiser;
And may ye better reck the rede,   heed the
 Than ever did th' adviser!   counsel

ON A SCOTCH BARD

GONE TO THE WEST INDIES

1

A' ye wha live by sowps o' drink,   sups
A' ye wha live by crambo-clink,   rhyme
A' ye wha live and never think,
   Come, mourn wi' me!
Our billie 's gien us a' a jink,   comrade;
   An' owre the sea!   given us all
          the slip

2

Lament him a' ye rantin core,   jovial set
Wha dearly like a random-splore; frolic
Nae mair he'll join the merry roar
   In social key;
For now he's taen anither shore,
   An' owre the sea!

3

wish

The bonie lasses weel may wiss him,
And in their dear petitions place him:
The widows, wives, an' a' may bless him
        Wi' tearfu' e'e,

wot

For weel I wat they'll sairly miss him
        That's owre the sea!

4

O Fortune, they hae room to grumble!

drone

Hadst thou taen aff some drowsy bummle,

fuss

Wha can do nought but fyke an' fumble,
        'Twad been nae plea;

nimble;
wimble

But he was gleg as onie wumble,
        That's owre the sea!

5

cheerful

Auld, cantie Kyle may weepers wear,
An' stain them wi' the saut, saut tear:
'Twill mak her poor auld heart, I fear,
        In flinders flee:

splinters

He was her Laureat monie a year,
        That's owre the sea!

6

He saw Misfortune's cauld nor-west
Lang-mustering up a bitter blast;

jilt

A jillet brak his heart at last,
        Ill may she be!

berth

So, took a birth afore the mast,
        An' owre the sea.

7

rod
meal and
water

To tremble under Fortune's cummock,
On scarce a bellyfu' o' drummock,
Wi' his proud, independent stomach,
        Could ill agree;

rolled;
buttocks

So, row't his hurdies in a hammock,
        An' owre the sea.

8

He ne'er was gien to great misguiding,

pockets

Yet coin his pouches wad na bide in;

Wi' him it ne'er was under hiding,
      He dealt it free:
The Muse was a' that he took pride in,
      That's owre the sea.

9

Jamaica bodies, use him weel,
An' hap him in a cozie biel: *shelter; place*
Ye'll find him ay a dainty chiel,
      An' fou o' glee:
He wad na wrang'd the vera Deil,   *would not have*
      That's owre the sea.

10

Fareweel, my rhyme-composing billie!
Your native soil was right ill-willie;   *unkind*
But may ye flourish like a lily,
      Now bonilie!
I'll toast you in my hindmost gillie,   *last gill*
      Tho' owre the sea!

A DEDICATION

TO GAVIN HAMILTON, ESQ.

Expect na, Sir, in this narration,   *wheedling, flattering*
A fleechin, fleth'rin Dedication,
To roose you up, an' ca' you guid,   *praise*
An' sprung o' great an' noble bluid,
Because ye're surnam'd like His Grace,
Perhaps related to the race:
Then, when I'm tired—and sae are ye,
Wi' monie a fulsome, sinfu' lie—
Set up a face how I stop short,
For fear your modesty be hurt.

This may do—maun do, Sir, wi' them wha
Maun please the great-folk for a wamefou';   *bellyful*
For me! sae laigh I need na bow,   *low*
For, Lord be thankit, I can plough;
And when I downa yoke a naig,   *cannot*
Then, Lord be thankit, I can beg;
Sae I shall say, an' that's nae flatt'rin,
It's just sic poet an' sic patron.

The Poet, some guid angel help him,
Or else, I fear, some ill ane skelp him!
He may do weel for a' he's done yet,
But only he's no just begun yet.

The Patron (sir, ye maun forgie me;
I winna lie, come what will o' me),
On ev'ry hand it will allow'd be,
He's just—nae better than he should be.

I readily and freely grant,
He downa see a poor man want;
What's no his ain he winna tak it;
What ance he says, he winna break it;
Ought he can lend he'll no refus 't,
Till aft his guidness is abus'd;
And rascals whyles that do him wrang,
Ev'n that, he does na mind it lang;
As master, landlord, husband, father,
He does na fail his part in either.

But then, nae thanks to him for a' that;
Nae godly symptom ye can ca' that;
It's naething but a milder feature
Of our poor, sinfu', corrupt nature:
Ye'll get the best o' moral works,
'Mang black Gentoos, and pagan Turks,
Or hunters wild on Ponotaxi,
Wha never heard of orthodoxy.

That he's the poor man's friend in need,
The gentleman in word and deed,
It's no thro' terror of damnation:
It's just a carnal inclination,
And och! that's nae regeneration.

Morality, thou deadly bane,
Thy tens o' thousands thou hast slain!
Vain is his hope, whase stay an' trust is
In moral mercy, truth, and justice!

No—stretch a point to catch a plack;
Abuse a brother to his back;

trounce

sometimes

farthing

Steal thro' the winnock frae a whore,   window
But point the rake that taks the door;
Be to the poor like onie whunstane,
And haud their noses to the grunstane;   grindstone
Ply ev'ry art o' legal thieving;
No matter—stick to sound believing.

Learn three-mile pray'rs, an' half-mile graces,
Wi' weel-spread looves, an' lang, wry faces;   palms
Grunt up a solemn, lengthen'd groan,
And damn a' parties but your own;
I'll warrant then, ye're nae deceiver,
A steady, sturdy, staunch believer.

O ye wha leave the springs o' Calvin,
For gumlie dubs of your ain delvin!   muddy
                        puddles
Ye sons of Heresy and Error,
Ye'll some day squeel in quaking terror,
When Vengeance draws the sword in wrath,
And in the fire throws the sheath;
When Ruin, with his sweeping besom,
Just frets till Heav'n commission gies him;
While o'er the harp pale Misery moans,
And strikes the ever-deep'ning tones,
Still louder shrieks, and heavier groans!

Your pardon, sir, for this digression:
I maist forgat my Dedication;   almost
But when divinity comes 'cross me,
My readers still are sure to lose me.

So, Sir, you see 'twas nae daft vapour;   mad
But I maturely thought it proper,
When a' my works I did review,
To dedicate them, Sir, to you:
Because (ye need na tak' it ill),
I thought them something like yoursel.

Then patronize them wi' your favor
And your petitioner shall ever——
I had amaist said, ever pray,
But that's a word I need na say;
For prayin, I hae little skill o't,   extremely
                        reluctant;
I'm baith dead-sweer, an' wretched ill o't; bad at it

I'll

    But I'se repeat each poor man's pray'r,
    That kens or hears about you, Sir:——

      ' May ne'er Misfortune's gowling bark

lawyer

    Howl thro' the dwelling o' the clerk!
    May ne'er his gen'rous, honest heart,
    For that same gen'rous spirit smart!
    May Kennedy's far-honor'd name

feed

    Lang beet his hymeneal flame,
    Till Hamiltons, at least a dizzen,
    Are frae their nuptial labors risen:
    Five bonie lasses round their table,
    And sev'n braw fellows, stout an' able,
    To serve their king an' country weel,
    By word, or pen, or pointed steel!
    May Health and Peace, with mutual rays,
    Shine on the ev'ning o' his days;

great-
grandchild

    Till his wee, curlie John's ier-oe,
    When ebbing life nae mair shall flow,
    The last, sad, mournful rites bestow! '

    I will not wind a lang conclusion,
    With complimentary effusion;
    But, whilst your wishes and endeavours
    Are blest with Fortune's smiles and favours,
    I am, dear sir, with zeal most fervent,
    Your much indebted, humble servant.

    But if (which Pow'rs above prevent)
    That iron-hearted carl, Want,
    Attended, in his grim advances,
    By sad mistakes, and black mischances,
    While hopes, and joys, and pleasures fly him,
    Make you as poor a dog as I am,
    Your ' humble servant ' then no more;
    For who would humbly serve the poor?
    But, by a poor man's hopes in Heav'n!
    While recollection's pow'r is giv'n,
    If, in the vale of humble life,
    The victim sad of Fortune's strife,
    I, thro' the tender-gushing tear,
    Should recognise my master dear;
    If friendless, low, we meet together,
    Then, sir, your hand—my FRIEND and BROTHER!

TO A LOUSE

ON SEEING ONE ON A LADY'S BONNET AT CHURCH

1

Ha! whare ye gaun, ye crowlin ferlie?   crawling
Your impudence protects you sairly,   wonder
I canna say but ye strunt rarely   swagger
        Owre gauze and lace,
Tho' faith! I fear ye dine but sparely
        On sic a place.

2

Ye ugly, creepin, blastit wonner,
Detested, shunn'd by saunt an' sinner,
How daur ye set your fit upon her—   foot
        Sae fine a lady!
Gae somewhere else and seek your dinner
        On some poor body.

3

Swith! in some beggar's hauffet squattle: Off! temples
There ye may creep, and sprawl, and sprattle,   squat
Wi' ither kindred, jumping cattle,   scramble
        In shoals and nations;
Whare horn nor bane ne'er daur unsettle
        Your thick plantations.

4

Now haud you there! ye're out o' sight,   keep
Below the fatt'rils, snug an' tight;   falderals
Na, faith ye yet! ye'll no be right,
        Till ye've got on it—
The vera tapmost, tow'ring height
        O' Miss's bonnet.

5

My sooth! right bauld ye set your nose out,
As plump an' grey as onie grozet: gooseberry

rosin
deadly;
powder

O for some rank, mercurial rozet,
                    Or fell, red smeddum,
I'd gie ye sic a hearty dose o't,

breech
                    Wad dress your droddum!

6

would not
have
flannel cap
maybe;
small ragged
undervest
balloon
bonnet

I wad na been surpris'd to spy
You on an auld wife's flainen toy;
Or aiblins some bit duddie boy,
                    On's wyliecoat;
But Miss's fine Lunardi! fye!
                    How daur ye do't?

7

O Jenny, dinna toss your head,

abroad
An' set your beauties a' abroad!
Ye little ken what cursèd speed
                    The blastie's makin!

Those
Thae winks an' finger-ends, I dread,
                    Are notice takin!

8

O wad some Power the giftie gie us
To see oursels as ithers see us!
It wad frae monie a blunder free us,
                    An' foolish notion:
What airs in dress an' gait wad lea'e us,
                    An' ev'n devotion!

EPISTLE TO J. LAPRAIK

AN OLD SCOTTISH BARD, APRIL 1, 1785

1

While briers an' woodbines budding green,

partridges
calling
the hare
scudding

And paitricks scraichin loud at e'en,
An' morning poussie whiddin seen,
                    Inspire my Muse,
This freedom, in an unknown frien'
                    I pray excuse.

2

On Fasten-e'en we had a rockin,   meeting
To ca' the crack and weave our stockin;   have a chat
And there was muckle fun and jokin,
   Ye need na doubt;
At length we had a hearty yokin,   set-to
   At ' sang about.'

3

There was ae sang, amang the rest,   one
Aboon them a' it pleas'd me best,   Above
That some kind husband had addrest
   To some sweet wife:
It thirl'd the heart-strings thro' the breast,   thrilled
   A' to the life.

4

I've scarce heard ought describ'd sae weel,
What gen'rous, manly bosoms feel;
Thought I, ' Can this be Pope or Steele,
   Or Beattie's wark?'
They tald me 'twas an odd kind chiel   chap
   About Muirkirk.

5

It pat me fidgin-fain to hear't,   tingling-wild
An' sae about him there I spier't;   asked
Then a' that kent him round declar'd
   He had ingine;   genius
That nane excell'd it, few cam near't,
   It was sae fine:

6

That, set him to a pint of ale,
An' either douce or merry tale,   sober
Or rhymes an' sangs he'd made himsel,
   Or witty catches,
'Tween Inverness an' Teviotdale,
   He had few matches.

7

Then up I gat, an' swoor an aith,   swore
Tho' I should pawn my pleugh an' graith,   harness

hawker
Behind a
fence

talk

Or die a cadger pownie's death,
        At some dyke-back,
A pint an' gill I'd gie them baith,
        To hear your crack.

8

But, first an' foremost, I should tell,
Amaist as soon as I could spell,

rhyming
I to the crambo-jingle fell;
        Tho' rude an' rough—

humming
Yet crooning to a body's sel,
        Does weel eneugh.

9

I am nae poet, in a sense;
But just a rhymer like by chance,
An' hae to learning nae pretence;
        Yet, what the matter?
Whene'er my Muse does on me glance,
        I jingle at her.

10

Your critic-folk may cock their nose,
And say, ' How can you e'er propose,
You wha ken hardly verse frae prose,
        To mak a sang? '
But, by your leaves, my learned foes,
        Ye're maybe wrang.

11

What's a' your jargon o' your Schools,
Your Latin names for horns an' stools?
If honest Nature made you fools,

serves
        What sairs your grammers

stone-
breaking
Ye'd better taen up spades and shools,
        Or knappin-hammers.

12

dunderheads
A set o' dull, conceited hashes
Confuse their brains in college-classes,

young
bullocks
They gang in stirks, and come out asses,
        Plain truth to speak;

then
An' syne they think to climb Parnassus
        By dint o' Greek!

13

Gie me ae spark o' Nature's fire,
That's a' the learning I desire;
Then, tho' I drudge thro' dub an' mire   puddle
        At pleugh or cart,
My Muse, tho' hamely in attire,
        May touch the heart.

14

O for a spunk o' Allan's glee,   spark
Or Fergusson's, the bauld an' slee,   sly
Or bright Lapraik's, my friend to be,
        If I can hit it!
That would be lear eneugh for me,   learning
        If I could get it.

15

Now, sir, if ye hae friends enow,
Tho' real friends I b'lieve are few;
Yet, if your catalogue be fow,   full
        I'se no insist: I'll
But, gif ye want ae friend that's true,
        I'm on your list.

16

I winna blaw about mysel,   brag
As ill I like my fauts to tell;
But friends, an' folks that wish me well,
        They sometimes roose me;   praise
Tho', I maun own, as monie still
        As far abuse me.

17

There's ae wee faut they whyles lay to me,   one
I like the lasses—Gude forgie me!   God
For monie a plack they wheedle frae me   coin
        At dance or fair;
Maybe some ither thing they gie me,
        They weel can spare.

18

But Mauchline Race or Mauchline Fair,
I should be proud to meet you there:

We'll

We'se gie ae night's discharge to care,
   If we forgather;
And hae a swap o' rhymin-ware
   Wi' ane anither.

19

four-gill cup
we'll make
christen;
steaming
Then;
draught

The four-gill chap, we'se gar him clatter,
An' kirsen him wi' reekin water;
Syne we'll sit down an' tak our whitter,
   To cheer our heart;
An' faith, we'se be acquainted better
   Before we part.

20

worldly

manners

the hunt for
coin

Awa ye selfish, warly race,
Wha think that havins, sense, an' grace,
Ev'n love an' friendship should give place
   To Catch-the-Plack!
I dinna like to see your face,
   Nor hear your crack.

21

But ye whom social pleasure charms,
Whose hearts the tide of kindness warms,
Who hold your being on the terms,
   ' Each aid the others,'
Come to my bowl, come to my arms,
   My friends, my brothers!

22

tingle

But, to conclude my lang epistle,
As my auld pen's worn to the grissle,
Twa lines frae you wad gar me fissle,
   Who am most fervent,
While I can either sing or whistle,
   Your friend and servant.

SECOND EPISTLE TO J. LAPRAIK

APRIL 21, 1785

1

While new-ca'd kye rowte at the stake   new-driven;
An' pownies reek in pleugh or braik,   low
     smoke;
This hour on e'enin's edge I take,   harrow
          To own I'm debtor
To honest-hearted, auld Lapraik,
          For his kind letter.

2

Forjesket sair, with weary legs,   Jaded
Rattlin the corn out-owre the rigs,   ridges
Or dealing thro' amang the naigs   distributing
          Their ten-hours' bite,
My awkart Muse sair pleads and begs,
          I would na write.

3

The tapetless, ramfeezl'd hizzie,   feckless,
     exhausted
She's saft at best an' something lazy: girl
Quo' she: ' Ye ken we've been sae busy
          This month an' mair,
That trowth, my head is grown right dizzie,
          An' something sair."   aching

4

Her dowff excuses pat me mad: dull
' Conscience,' says I, ' ye thowless jad!   lazy
I'll write, an' that a hearty blaud,   screed
          This vera night;
So dinna ye affront your trade,   do not
          But rhyme it right.

5

' Shall bauld Lapraik, the king o' hearts,
Tho' mankind were a pack o' cartes,
Roose you sae weel for your deserts,   Praise
          In terms sae friendly;
Yet ye'll neglect to shaw your parts
          An' thank him kindly? '

6

twinkling

Sae I gat paper in a blink,
An' down gaed stumpie in the ink:
Quoth I: ' Before I sleep a wink,
        I vow I'll close it:

rhyme

An' if ye winna mak it clink,
        By Jove, I'll prose it!'

7

Sae I've begun to scrawl, but whether
In rhyme, or prose, or baith thegither,
Or some hotch-potch that's rightly neither,
        Let time mak proof;

nonsense
off-hand

But I shall scribble down some blether
        Just clean aff-loof.

8

My worthy friend, ne'er grudge an' carp,
Tho' Fortune use you hard an' sharp;

tickle

Come, kittle up your moorland harp
        Wi' gleesome touch!

woof

Ne'er mind how Fortune waft an' warp;
        She's but a bitch.

9

jerk;
scare
straddle

She's gien me monie a jirt an' fleg,
Sin' I could striddle owre a rig;
But, by the Lord, tho' I should beg

grey head

        Wi' lyart pow,

dance

I'll laugh an' sing, an' shake my leg,

can

        As lang's I dow!

10

Now comes the sax-an-twentieth simmer

woods

I've seen the bud upo' the timmer,

jade

Still persecuted by the limmer
        Frae year to year;

fickle gossip

But yet, despite the kittle kimmer,
        I, Rob, am here.

11

Do ye envý the city gent,

counter;
cheat

Behint a kist to lie an' sklent;

Or purse-proud, big wi' cent. per cent.
        An' muckle wame,   *stomach*
In some bit brugh to represent   *borough*
        A bailie's name?   *town magistrate's*

12

Or is't the paughty feudal thane,   *haughty*
Wi' ruffl'd sark an' glancing cane,   *shirt; shining*
Wha thinks himsel nae sheep-shank bane,
        But lordly stalks;
While caps an' bonnets aff are taen,
        As by he walks?

13

' O Thou wha gies us each guid gift!
Gie me o' wit an' sense a lift,   *load*
Then turn me, if Thou please, adrift
        Thro' Scotland wide;
Wi' cits nor lairds I wadna shift,
        In a' their pride!'

14

Were this the charter of our state,
' On pain o' hell be rich an' great,'
Damnation then would be our fate,
        Beyond remead;   *remedy*
But, thanks to heaven, that's no the gate   *way*
        We learn our creed.

15

For thus the royal mandate ran,
When first the human race began:
' The social, friendly, honest man,
        Whate'er he be,
'Tis he fulfils great Nature's plan,
        And none but he.'

16

O mandate glorious and divine!
The followers o' the ragged Nine—
Poor, thoughtless devils!—yet may shine
        In glorious light;
While sordid sons o' Mammon's line
        Are dark as night!

17

Tho' here they scrape, an' squeeze, an' growl,
Their worthless neivefu' of a soul
May in some future carcase howl,
   The forest's fright;
Or in some day-detesting owl
   May shun the light.

fistful

18

Then may Lapraik and Burns arise,
To reach their native, kindred skies,
And sing their pleasures, hopes an' joys,
   In some mild sphere;
Still closer knit in friendship's ties,
   Each passing year!

TO WILLIAM SIMPSON OF OCHILTREE

MAY, 1785

1

I gat your letter, winsome Willie;
Wi' gratefu' heart I thank you brawlie;
Tho' I maun say't, I wad be silly
   And unco vain,
Should I believe, my coaxin billie,
   Your flatterin strain.

handsomely

mighty
fellow

2

But I'se believe ye kindly meant it:
I sud be laith to think ye hinted
Ironic satire, sidelins sklented,
   On my poor Musie;
Tho' in sic phraisin terms ye've penn'd it,
   I scarce excuse ye.

I'll

sideways
squinted

wheedling

3

My senses wad be in a creel,
Should I but dare a hope to speel,

climb

Wi' Allan, or wi' Gilbertfield,
        The braes o' fame;
Or Fergusson, the writer-chiel,   *lawyer-chap*
        A deathless name.

4

(O Fergusson! thy glorious parts
Ill suited law's dry, musty arts!
My curse upon your whunstane hearts,   *whinstone*
        Ye E'nbrugh gentry!
The tythe o' what ye waste at cartes   *Would have*
        Wad stow'd his pantry!)   *stored*

5

Yet when a tale comes i' my head,
Or lasses gie my heart a screed—   *rent*
As whyles they're like to be my dead,   *sometimes;*
        (O sad disease!)   *death*
I kittle up my rustic reed;   *tickle*
        It gies me ease.

6

Auld Coila, now, may fidge fu' fain,   *tingle with*
She's gotten bardies o' her ain;   *delight*
Chiels wha their chanters winna hain,   *spare*
        But tune their lays,
Till echoes a' resound again
        Her weel-sung praise.

7

Nae Poet thought her worth his while,
To set her name in measur'd style;
She lay like some unkend-of isle
        Beside New Holland,
Or whare wild-meeting oceans boil
        Besouth Magellan.   *South of*

8

Ramsay an' famous Fergusson
Gied Forth an' Tay a lift aboon;   *a lift-up*
Yarrow an' Tweed, to monie a tune,
        Owre Scotland rings;
While Irwin, Lugar, Ayr, an' Doon
        Naebody sings.

9

Th' Illissus, Tiber, Thames, an' Seine,
Glide sweet in monie a tunefu' line:
But, Willie, set your fit to mine,
        An' cock your crest!
We'll gar our streams and burnies shine
      Up wi' the best.

foot (fit)
make; brooklets (gar; burnies)

10

We'll sing auld Coila's plains an' fells,
Her moors red-brown wi' heather bells,
Her banks an' braes, her dens an' dells,
        Whare glorious Wallace
Aft bure the gree, as story tells,
      Frae Suthron billies.

hill-sides (braes)
bore off the prize (bure the gree)

11

At Wallace' name, what Scottish blood
But boils up in a spring-tide flood?
Oft have our fearless fathers strode
        By Wallace' side,
Still pressing onward, red-wat-shod,
      Or glorious dy'd!

red-wet-shod (red-wat-shod)

12

O, sweet are Coila's haughs an' woods,
When lintwhites chant amang the buds,
And jinkin hares, in amorous whids,
        Their loves enjoy;
While thro' the braes the cushat croods
      With wailfu' cry!

hollows (haughs)
linnets (lintwhites)
sporting; (whids)
gambols (croods)
coos

13

Ev'n winter bleak has charms to me,
When winds rave thro' the naked tree;
Or frosts on hills of Ochiltree
        Are hoary gray;
Or blinding drifts wild-furious flee,
      Dark'ning the day!

14

O Nature! a' thy shews an' forms
To feeling, pensive hearts hae charms!

Whether the summer kindly warms,
            Wi' life an' light;
Or winter howls, in gusty storms,
            The lang, dark night!

15

The Muse, nae poet ever fand her,   found
Till by himsel he learn'd to wander,
Adown some trottin burn's meander,   brook's
            An' no think lang:
O, sweet to stray, an' pensive ponder
            A heart-felt sang!

16

The warly race may drudge an' drive,   worldly
Hog-shouther, jundie, stretch, an' strive;   push; ply
                                                     the elbows
Let me fair Nature's face descrive,   describe
            And I, wi' pleasure,
Shall let the busy, grumbling hive
            Bum owre their treasure.   Hum

17

Fareweel, my rhyme-composing brither!
We've been owre lang unkend to ither: too long
Now let us lay our heads thegither,
            In love fraternal:
May Envy wallop in a tether,   dangle in
            Black fiend, infernal!   a rope

18

While Highlandmen hate tolls an' taxes;
While moorlan' herds like guid, fat braxies;
While Terra Firma, on her axis,
            Diurnal turns;
Count on a friend, in faith an' practice,
            In Robert Burns.

POSTSCRIPT

19

My memory's no worth a preen: pin
I had amaist forgotten clean,

Ye bade me write you what they mean
By this New-Light,
shepherds 'Bout which our herds sae aft hae been
Maist like to fight.

20

striplings In days when mankind were but callans;
At grammar, logic, an' sic talents,
They took nae pains their speech to balance,
Or rules to gie;
vernacular But spak their thoughts in plain, braid Lallans,
Like you or me.

21

those In thae auld times, they thought the moon,
shirt Just like a sark, or pair o' shoon,
round Wore by degrees, till her last roon
Went Gaed past their viewin;
An' shortly after she was done,
They gat a new ane.

22

This past for certain, undisputed;
It ne'er cam i' their heads to doubt it,
fellows Till chiels gat up an' wad confute it,
An' ca'd it wrang;
An' muckle din there was about it,
Baith loud an' lang.

23

Some herds, weel learn'd upo' the Beuk,
maintain Wad threap auld folk the thing misteuk;
corner For 'twas the auld moon turn'd a neuk
An' out o' sight.
backwards-; An' backlins-comin to the leuk,
look She grew mair bright.

24

This was deny'd, it was affirm'd;
flocks The herds and hissels were alarm'd;
The rev'rend gray-beards rav'd an' storm'd,
That beardless laddies
Should think they better were inform'd
Than their auld daddies.

25

Frae less to mair, it gaed to sticks;
Frae words an' aiths, to clours an' nicks; *bumps; cuts*
An' monie a fallow gat his licks, *punishment*
        Wi' hearty crunt; *blow*
An some, to learn them for their tricks, *teach*
        Were hang'd an' brunt. *burned*

26

This game was play'd in monie lands,
An' Auld-Light caddies bure sic hands, *varlets; bore*
That faith, the youngsters took the sands
        Wi' nimble shanks
Till lairds forbade, by strict commands,
        Sic bluidy pranks.

27

But New-Light herds gat sic a cowe, *down-setting*
Folk thought them ruin'd stick-an-stowe; *completely*
Till now, amaist on ev'ry knowe *hillock*
        Ye'll find ane placed;
An' some, their New-Light fair avow,
        Just quite barefac'd.

28

Nae doubt the Auld-Light flocks are bleatin;
Their zealous herds are vex'd and sweatin;
Myself, I've even seen them greetin *weeping*
        Wi' girnin spite, *snarling*
To hear the moon sae sadly lie'd on
        By word an' write.

29

But shortly they will cowe the louns! *scare; rascals*
Some Auld-Light herds in neebor touns
Are mind't, in things they ca' balloons,
        To tak a flight,
An' stay ae month amang the moons
        An' see them right.

30

Guid observation they will gie them;
An' when the auld moon's gaun to lea'e them,

shard
pocket

The hindmost shaird, they'll fetch it wi' them,
    Just i' their pouch;
An' when the New-Light billies see them,
    I think they'll crouch!

31

Sae, ye observe that a' this clatter
Is naething but a ' moonshine matter ';
But tho' dull prose-folk Latin splatter
    In logic tulzie,
I hope we, Bardies, ken some better
    Than mind sic brulzie.

squabble (gloss)
such a brawl (gloss)

EPISTLE TO JOHN RANKINE

ENCLOSING SOME POEMS

1

O rough, rude, ready-witted Rankine,
The wale o' cocks for fun an' drinkin!
There's monie godly folks are thinkin'
    Your dreams and tricks
Will send you, Korah-like, a-sinkin
    Straught to Auld Nick's.

pick (gloss)

2

Ye hae sae monie cracks an' cants,
And in your wicked drucken rants,
Ye mak a devil o' the saunts,
    An' fill them fou';
And then their failings, flaws, an' wants
    Are a' seen thro'.

stories (gloss)

3

Hypocrisy, in mercy spare it!
That holy robe, O, dinna tear it!
Spare't for their sakes, wha aften wear it—
    The lads in black;
But your curst wit, when it comes near it,
    Rives't aff their back.

tears (gloss)

4

Think, wicked sinner, wha ye're skaithing: injuring
It's just the Blue-gown badge an' claithing
O' saunts; tak that, ye lea'e them naething
   To ken them by
Frae onie unregenerate heathen,
   Like you or I.

5

I've sent you here some rhyming ware
A' that I bargain'd for, an' mair;
Sae, when ye hae an hour to spare,
   I will expect,
You sang ye'll sen't, wi' cannie care,   send it
   And no neglect.

6

Tho' faith, sma' heart hae I to sing:
My Muse dow scarcely spread her wing!   can
I've play'd mysel a bonie spring,   tune
   An' danc'd my fill!
I'd better gaen an' sair't the King   have gone;
   At Bunker's Hill.   served

7

'Twas ae night lately, in my fun,
I gaed a rovin wi' the gun,   went
An' brought a paitrick to the grun'—   partridge
   A bonie hen;
And, as the twilight was begun,
   Thought nane wad ken.

8

The poor, wee thing was little hurt;
I straikit it a wee for sport,   stroked; a bit
Ne'er thinkin they wad fash me for't;   worry
   But, Deil-ma-care!
Somebody tells the Poacher-Court   the Kirk-
   The hale affair.   Session
     whole

9

Some auld, us'd hands had taen a note,
That sic a hen had got a shot;

I was suspected for the plot;
                    I scorn'd to lie;
lost my money So gat the whissle o' my groat,
                    \n' pay't the fee.

10

pick But, by my gun, o' guns the wale,
shot An' by my pouther an' my hail,
An' by my hen, an' by her tail,
                    I vow an' swear!
The game shall pay, owre moor an' dale,
next   For this, niest year!

11

clucking-chicks As soon's the clockin-time is by,
An' the wee pouts begun to cry,
I'll Lord, I'se hae sportin by an' by
                    For my gowd guinea;
Tho' I should herd the buckskin kye
                    For't, in Virginia!

12

Trowth, they had muckle for to blame!
'Twas neither broken wing nor limb,
knocks; belly But twa-three chaps about the wame,
                    Scarce thro' the feathers;
guinea An' baith a yellow George to claim
endure; nonsense   An' thole their blethers!

13

It pits me ay as mad's a hare;
So I can rhyme nor write nae mair;
tit-for-tat But pennyworths again is fair,
                    When time's expedient:
Meanwhile I am, respected Sir,
                    Your most obedient.

THE FAREWELL

TO THE BRETHREN OF ST. JAMES'S LODGE, TARBOLTON

TUNE: *Good-night, and joy be wi' you a'*

1

Adieu! a heart-warm, fond adieu;
   Dear Brothers of the *Mystic Tie*!
Ye favour'd, ye enlighten'd few,
   Companions of my social joy!
Tho' I to foreign lands must hie,
Pursuing Fortune's slidd'ry ba';   *slippery*
   With melting heart and brimful eye,
I'll mind you still, tho' far awa.

2

Oft have I met your social band,
   And spent the cheerful, festive night;
Oft, honour'd with supreme command,
   Presided o'er the *Sons of Light*;
And by that *Hieroglyphic* bright,
Which none but *Craftsmen* ever saw!
   Strong Mem'ry on my heart shall write
Those happy scenes, when far awa.

3

May Freedom, Harmony, and Love,
   Unite you in the *Grand Design*,
Beneath th' Omniscient Eye above—
   The glorious *Architect* Divine—
That you may keep th' *Unerring Line*,
Still rising by the *Plummet's Law*,
   Till *Order* bright completely shine,
Shall be my pray'r, when far awa.

4

And You farewell! whose merits claim
   Justly that *Highest Badge* to wear:
Heav'n bless your honour'd, noble Name,
   To Masonry and Scotia dear!

A last request permit me here,
When yearly ye assemble a',
health round   One round, I ask it with a tear,
To him, the Bard that's far awa.

DEATH AND DOCTOR HORNBOOK

A True Story

I

Some books are lies frae end to end,
And some great lies were never penn'd:
Ev'n ministers, they hae been kend,
         In holy rapture,
fib   A rousing whid at times to vend,
         And nail't wi' Scripture.

2

going   But this that I am gaun to tell,
Which lately on a night befel,
Is just as true's the Deil's in hell
(in effigy)   Or Dublin city:
That e'er he nearer comes oursel
         'S a muckle pity!

3

village ale;   The clachan yill had made me canty,
jolly
drunk   I was na fou, but just had plenty:
staggered   I stacher'd whyles, but yet took tent ay
now and
then; care   To free the ditches;
clear   An' hillocks, stanes, an' bushes, kend ay
         Frae ghaists an' witches.

4

stare   The rising moon began to glowr
above   The distant Cumnock Hills out-owre:
To count her horns, wi' a' my pow'r
         I set mysel;
But whether she had three or four,
         I cou'd na tell.

5

I was come round about the hill,
And todlin down on Willie's mill,
Setting my staff wi' a' my skill
                To keep me sicker;   steady
Tho' leeward whyles, against my will,   at times
                I took a bicker.   run

6

I there wi' *Something* does forgather,   put;
That pat me in an eerie swither;   ghostly
An awfu' scythe, out-owre ae shouther,   dread
                across one
                Clear-dangling, hang;   hung
A three-tae'd leister on the ither   three-pronged
                Lay, large an' lang.   fish-spear

7

Its stature seem'd lang Scotch ells twa;
The queerest shape that e'er I saw,
For fient a wame it had ava;   fiend; belly;
                And then its shanks,   at all
They were as thin, as sharp an' sma'
                As cheeks o' branks.

8

'Guid-een,' quo' I; 'Friend! hae ye been mawin,
  When ither folk are busy sawin?'
It seem'd to mak a kind o' stan',   halt
                But naething spak.
At length, says I: 'Friend! whare ye gaun? where are ye going
                Will ye go back?'   *i.e.* to the tavern

9

It spak right howe: 'My name is Death, hollow
But be na' fley'd.' Quoth I: 'Guid faith, scared
Ye're may be come to stap my breath; heed;
                But tent me, billie: comrade
I red ye weel, take care o' skaith,   advise; damage
                See, there's a gully!' large knife

10

'Gudeman,' quo' he, 'put up your whittle, blade
I'm no design'd to try its mettle;

But if I did, I wad be kittle
                    To be mislear'd:
I wad na mind it, no that spittle
                    Out-owre my beard.'

11

'Weel, weel!' says I, 'a bargain be't;

give us;
agreed

Come, gie's your hand, an' say we 're gree't;
We'll ease our shanks, an' tak a seat:
                    Come, gie's your news:

road

This while ye hae been monie a gate,
                    At monie a house.'

12

'Ay, ay!' quo' he, an' shook his head,
'It's e'en a lang, lang time indeed

cut

Sin' I began to nick the thread
                    An' choke the breath:
Folk maun do something for their bread,
                    An' sae maun Death.

13

well-nigh

'Sax thousand years are near-hand fled

butchering

Sin' I was to the butching bred,
An' monie a scheme in vain's been laid

stop; scare

                    To stap or scar me;
Till ane Hornbook's ta'en up the trade,

worst

                    And faith! he'll waur me.

14

'Ye ken Jock Hornbook i' the clachan?

scrotum;
tobacco-
pouch

Deil mak his king's-hood in a spleuchan!—
He's grown sae weel acquaint wi' *Buchan*
                    And ither chaps,

children
poke;
buttocks

The weans haud out their fingers laughin,
                    An' pouk my hips.

15

'See, here's a scythe, an' there's a dart,
They hae pierc'd monie a gallant heart;
But Doctor Hornbook wi' his art
                    An' cursèd skill,

The devil a
one

Has made them baith no worth a fart,
                    Damn'd haet they'll kill!

16

' 'Twas but yestreen, nae farther gane,   gone
I threw a noble throw at ane;
Wi' less, I'm sure, I've hundreds slain;
    But Deil-ma-care!
It just played dirl on the bane,   went tinkle
    But did nae mair.

17

' Hornbook was by wi' ready art,
An' had sae fortify'd the part,
That when I lookèd to my dart,
    It was sae blunt,
Fient haet o't wad hae pierc'd the heart cabbage-
    Of a kail-runt.   stalk

18

' I drew my scythe in sic a fury,
I near-hand cowpit wi' my hurry,   tumbled
But yet the bauld Apothecary
    Withstood the shock:
I might as weel hae try'd a quarry
    O' hard whin-rock.

19

' Ev'n them he canna get attended,
Altho' their face he ne'er had kend it,
Just shite in a kail-blade an' send it, cabbage-leaf
    As soon's he smells't,
Baith their disease and what will mend it,
    At once he tells't.

20

' And then a' doctor's saws and whittles knives
Of a' dimensions, shapes, an' mettles,
A' kinds o' boxes, mugs, and bottles,
    He's sure to hae;
Their Latin names as fast he rattles
    As A B C.

21

' Calces o' fossils, earth, and trees;
True *sal-marinum* o' the seas;

The *farina* of beans an' pease,
>> He has't in plenty;
Aqua-fontis, what you please,
>> He can content ye.

22

' Forbye some new, uncommon weapons,
Urinus spiritus of capons;
Or mite-horn shavings, filings, scrapings,
>> Distill'd *per se*;
Sal-alkali o' midge-tail-clippings,

more
>> And monie mae.'

23

' Waes me for Johnie Ged's Hole now,'

these
grazing plot;
daisies

split.

Quoth I, ' if that thae news be true!
His braw calf-ward whare gowans grew
>> Sae white and bonie,
Nae doubt they'll rive it wi' the plew:
>> They'll ruin Johnie!'

24

groaned

ditch

The creature grain'd an eldritch laugh
And says: ' Ye needna yoke the pleugh,
Kirkyards will soon be till'd eneugh,
>> Tak ye nae fear:
They'll a' be trench'd wi monie a sheugh
>> In twa-three year.

25

straw,
i.e. bed

cloth

' Whare I kill'd ane, a fair strae death
By loss o' blood or want o' breath,
This night I'm free to tak my aith,
>> That Hornbook's skill
Has clad a score i' their last claith
>> By drap an' pill.

26

weaver

fists

aching

crept quietly

' An honest wabster to his trade,
Whase wife's twa nieves were scarce weel-bred,
Gat tippence-worth to mend her head,
>> When it was sair;
The wife slade cannie to her bed,
>> But ne'er spak mair.

27

'A countra laird had taen the batts,   botts
Or some curmurring in his guts,   commotion
His only son for Hornbook sets,
            An' pays him well:
The lad, for twa guid gimmer-pets,   pet-ewes
            Was laird himsel.

28

'A bonie lass—ye kend her name—
Some ill-brewn drink had hov'd her wame;   put up;
                   belly
She trusts hersel, to hide the shame,
            In Hornbook's care;
Horn sent her aff to her lang hame
            To hide it there.

29

'That's just a swatch o' Hornbook's way;   sample
Thus goes he on from day to day,
Thus does he poison, kill, an' slay,
            An's weel paid for't;
Yet stops me o' my lawfu' prey
            Wi' his damn'd dirt:

30

'But, hark! I'll tell you of a plot,
Tho' dinna ye be speakin o't:
I'll nail the self-conceited sot,
            As dead's a herrin;
Niest time we meet, I'll wad a groat,   next; wager
            He gets his fairin!'   reward

31

But just as he began to tell,
The auld kirk-hammer strak the bell   small;
                   beyond
Some wee short hour ayont the twal,   twelve
            Which raised us baith: got us to our
                   legs
I took the way that pleas'd mysel,
            And sae did Death.

THE BRIGS OF AYR

A Poem

INSCRIBED TO JOHN BALLANTINE, ESQ., AYR

Sir, think not with a mercenary view
Some servile Sycophant approaches you.
To you my Muse would sing these simple lays,
To you my heart its grateful homage pays,
I feel the weight of all your kindness past,
But thank you not as wishing it to last;
Scorn'd be the wretch whose earth-born grov'lling
    soul
Would in his ledger-hopes his Friends enroll.
Tho' I, a lowly, nameless, rustic Bard,
Who ne'er must hope your goodness to reward,
Yet man to man, Sir, let us fairly meet,
And like masonic Level, equal greet.
How poor the balance! ev'n what Monarch's plan,
Between two noble creatures such as Man.
That to your Friendship I am strongly tied
I still shall own it, Sir, with grateful pride,
When haply roaring seas between us tumble wide.

Or if among so many cent'ries waste,
Thro the long vista of dark ages past,
Some much-lov'd honor'd name a radiance cast,
Perhaps some Patriot of distinguish'd worth,
I'll match him if My Lord will please step forth,
Or Gentleman and Citizen combine,
And I shall shew his peer in Ballantine:
Tho' honest men were parcell'd out for sale,
He might be shown a sample for the hale.

        ———————

The simple Bard, rough at the rustic plough,
Learning his tuneful trade from ev'ry bough
(The chanting linnet, or the mellow thrush,
Hailing the setting sun, sweet, in the green thorn bush;
The soaring lark, the perching red-breast shrill,
Or deep-ton'd plovers grey, wild-whistling o'er the
    hill):

.

Shall he—nurst in the peasant's lowly shed,
To hardy independence bravely bred,
By early poverty to hardship steel'd,
And train'd to arms in stern misfortune's field—
Shall he be guilty of their hireling crimes,
The servile, mercenary Swiss of rhymes?
Or labour hard the panegyric close,
With all the venal soul of dedicating prose?
No! though his artless strains he rudely sings,
And throws his hand uncouthly o'er the strings,
He glows with all the spirit of the bard,
Fame, honest fame, his great, his dear reward.
Still, if some patron's gen'rous care he trace,
Skill'd in the secret to bestow with grace;
When Ballantine befriends his humble name,
And hands the rustic stranger up to fame,
With heartfelt throes his grateful bosom swells:
The godlike bliss, to give, alone excels.

'Twas when the stacks get on their winter hap, *wrap*
And thack and rape secure the toil-won crap; *thatch; rope; crop*
Potatoe-bings are snuggèd up frae skaith *heaps;*
O' coming winter's biting, frosty breath; *damage*
The bees, rejoicing o'er their summer toils—
Unnumber'd buds' an' flowers' delicious spoils,
Seal'd up with frugal care in massive waxen piles—
Are doom'd by man, that tyrant o'er the weak,
The death o' devils smoor'd wi' brimstone reek: *smothered; smoke*
The thundering guns are heard on ev'ry side,
The wounded coveys, reeling, scatter wide;
The feather'd field-mates, bound by Nature's tie,
Sires, mothers, children, in one carnage lie:
(What warm, poetic heart but inly bleeds,
And execrates man's savage, ruthless deeds!)
Nae mair the flower in field or meadow springs;
Nae mair the grove with airy concert rings,
Except perhaps the robin's whistling glee,
Proud o' the height o' some bit half-lang tree; *small half-grown*
The hoary morns precede the sunny days;
Mild, calm, serene, widespreads the noontide blaze,
While thick the gossamour waves wanton in the rays.

'Twas in that season, when a simple Bard,
Unknown and poor—simplicity's reward!—

One
Ae night, within the ancient brugh of Ayr,
By whim inspir'd, or haply prest wi' care,
He left his bed, and took his wayward route,
And down by Simpson's wheel'd the left about
(Whether impell'd by all-directing Fate,
To witness what I after shall narrate;
Or whether, rapt in meditation high,
He wander'd forth, he knew not where nor why):
The drowsy Dungeon-Clock had number'd two,
And Wallace Tower had sworn the fact was true;
The tide-swoln Firth, with sullen-sounding roar,
Through the still night dash'd hoarse along the shore;
All else was hush'd as Nature's closèd e'e;
The silent moon shone high o'er tower and tree;
The chilly frost, beneath the silver beam,
Crept, gently-crusting, o'er the glittering stream.

When, lo! on either hand the list'ning Bard,
swish
The clanging sugh of whistling wings is heard;
Two dusky forms dart thro' the midnight air,
Swift as the gos drives on the wheeling hare;
Ane on th' Auld brig his airy shape uprears,
The ither flutters o'er the rising piers:
wizard
Our warlock rhymer instantly descried
The Sprites that owre the Brigs of Ayr preside.
(That bards are second-sighted is nae joke,
know
jack-o'-
And ken the lingo of the sp'ritual folk;
lanthorns;
Fays, spunkies, kelpies, a', they can explain them,
water-
demons
And ev'n the vera deils they brawly ken them.)
know them
well
Auld Brig appear'd of ancient Pictish race,
The vera wrinkles Gothic in his face;
wrestled
He seem'd as he wi' Time had warstl'd lang,
toughly
stubborn
Yet, teughly doure, he bade an unco bang.
New Brig was buskit in a braw new coat,
That he, at Lon'on, frae ane Adams got;
rings;
flourishes
In's hand five taper staves as smooth's a bead,
Wi' virls an' whirlygigums at the head.
The Goth was stalking round with anxious search,
Spying the time-worn flaws in ev'ry arch.
It chanc'd his new-come neebor took his e'e,
And e'en a vex'd and angry heart had he!
forbidding
Wi' thieveless sneer to see his modish mien,
river
He, down the water, gies him this guid-een:—

AULD BRIG

'I doubt na, frien', ye'll think ye're nae sheep-
   shank,
Ance ye were streekit owre frae bank to bank! *stretched across*
But gin ye be a brig as auld as me— *when*
Tho' faith, that date, I doubt, ye'll never see—
There'll be, if that day come, I'll wad a boddle, *wager a farthing*
Some fewer whigmeleeries in your noddle.' *crotchets*

NEW BRIG

'Auld Vandal! ye but show your little mense, *discretion*
Just much about it wi' your scanty sense:
Will your poor, narrow foot-path of a street,
Where twa wheel-barrows tremble when they meet,
Your ruin'd, formless bulk o' stane an' lime,
Compare wi' bonie brigs o' modern time?
There's men of taste would tak the Ducat stream,
Tho' they should cast the vera sark and swim,
E'er they would grate their feelings wi' the view
O' sic an ugly, Gothic hulk as you.'

AULD BRIG

'Conceited gowk! puff'd up wi' windy pride! *cuckoo*
This monie a year I've stood the flood an' tide;
And tho' wi' crazy eild I'm sair forfairn, *eld; worn out*
I'll be a brig when ye're a shapeless cairn! *pile of stones*
As yet ye little ken about the matter,
But twa-three winters will inform ye better. *two or three*
When heavy, dark, continued, a'-day rains *day-long*
Wi' deepening deluges o'erflow the plains;
When from the hills where springs the brawling Coil,
Or stately Lugar's mossy fountains boil,
Or where the Greenock winds his moorland course,
Or haunted Garpal draws his feeble source,
Arous'd by blustering winds an' spotting thowes, *thaws*
In monie a torrent down the snaw-broo rowes; *snow-brew rolls*
While crashing ice, borne on the roaring speat, *flood*
Sweeps dams, an' mills, an' brigs, a' to the gate; *the road*
And from Glenbuck down to the Ratton-Key *seaward*
Auld Ayr is just one lengthen'd, tumbling sea—
Then down ye'll hurl (deil nor ye never rise!), *crash*
And dash the gumlie jaups up to the pouring skies! *muddy splashes*

A lesson sadly teaching, to your cost,
That Architecture's noble art is lost! '

NEW BRIG

' Fine architecture, trowth, I needs must say't o't,

lost the trick — The Lord be thankit that we've tint the gate o't!
Gaunt, ghastly, ghaist-alluring edifices,
Hanging with threat'ning jut, like precipices;
O'er-arching, mouldy, gloom-inspiring coves,
Supporting roofs fantastic—stony groves;
Windows and doors in nameless sculptures drest,
With order, symmetry, or taste unblest;
Forms like some bedlam statuary's dream,
The craz'd creations of misguided whim;
Forms might be worshipp'd on the bended knee,
And still the second dread Command be free:
Their likeness is not found on earth, in air, or sea!
Mansions that would disgrace the building taste
Of any mason reptile, bird or beast,

muddled — Fit only for a doited monkish race,

dolts — Or frosty maids forsworn the dear embrace,
Or cuifs of later times, wha held the notion,
That sullen gloom was sterling true devotion:
Fancies that our guid brugh denies protection,
And soon may they expire, unblest with resurrection! '

AULD BRIG

coevals — ' O ye, my dear-remember'd, ancient yealings,
Were ye but here to share my wounded feelings!

provosts — Ye worthy proveses, an' monie a bailie,
Wha in the paths o' righteousness did toil ay;

sedate — Ye dainty deacons, an' ye douce conveeners,

causeway- — To whom our moderns are but causey-cleaners;
Ye godly councils, wha hae blest this town;
Ye godly brethren o' the sacred gown,

buttocks — Wha meekly gie your hurdies to the smiters;

Lawyers — And (what would now be strange), ye godly Writers;

sedate; across; water — A' ye douce folk I've borne aboon the broo,
Were ye but here, what would ye say or do!
How would your spirits groan in deep vexation
To see each melancholy alteration;
And, agonising, curse the time and place
When ye begat the base degen'rate race!

Nae langer rev'rend men, their country's glory,
In plain braid Scots hold forth a plain, braid story;
Nae langer thrifty citizens, an' douce,
Meet owre a pint or in the council-house:
But staumrel, corky-headed, graceless gentry,   half-witted
The herryment and ruin of the country;   spoliation
Men three-parts made by tailors and by barbers,
Wha waste your weel-hain'd gear on damn'd New   well-saved
    Brigs and harbours!'   wealth

NEW BRIG

' Now haud you there! for faith ye've said enough,
And muckle mair than ye can mak to through.   make good
As for your priesthood, I shall say but little,
Corbies and clergy are a shot right kittle: ravens; sort; ticklish
But, under favour o' your langer beard,
Abuse o' magistrates might weel be spar'd;
To liken them to your auld-warld squad,
I must needs say, comparisons are odd.
In Ayr, wag-wits nae mair can hae a handle
To mouth ' a Citizen,' a term o' scandal;
Nae mair the council waddles down the street,
In all the pomp of ignorant conceit;
Men wha grew wise priggin owre hops an' raisins,   haggling
Or gather'd lib'ral views in bonds and seisins;
If haply Knowledge, on a random tramp,
Had shor'd them with a glimmer of his lamp,   menaced
And would to common-sense for once betray'd them,
Plain, dull stupidity stept kindly in to aid them.'

What farther clish-ma-claver might been said,   nonsense
What bloody wars, if Sprites had blood to shed,
No man can tell; but, all before their sight,
A fairy train appear'd in order bright:
Adown the glittering stream they featly danc'd;
Bright to the moon their various dresses glanc'd;
They footed o'er the wat'ry glass so neat,
The infant ice scarce bent beneath their feet;
While arts of minstrelsy among them rung,
And soul-ennobling Bards heroic ditties sung.

O, had M'Lauchlan, thairm-inspiring sage,   (cat-) gut-
Been there to hear this heavenly band engage,

When thro' his dear strathspeys they bore with
        Highland rage;
Or when they struck old Scotia's melting airs,
The lover's raptured joys or bleeding cares;
How would his Highland lug been nobler fir'd,
And ev'n his matchless hand with finer touch inspir'd!
No guess could tell what instrument appear'd,
But all the soul of Music's self was heard;
Harmonious concert rung in every part,
While simple melody pour'd moving on the heart.

ear

The Genius of the Stream in front appears,
A venerable chief advanc'd in years;
His hoary head with water-lilies crown'd,
His manly leg with garter-tangle bound.
Next came the loveliest pair in all the ring,
Sweet Female Beauty hand in hand with Spring;
Then, crown'd with flow'ry hay, came Rural Joy,
And Summer, with his fervid-beaming eye:
All-cheering Plenty, with her flowing horn,
Led yellow Autumn wreath'd with nodding corn;
Then Winter's time-bleach'd locks did hoary show,
By Hospitality, with cloudless brow.
Next follow'd Courage, with his martial stride,
From where the Feal wild-woody coverts hide;
Benevolence, with mild, benignant air,
A female form, came from the towers of Stair;
Learning and Worth in equal measures trode
From simple Catrine, their long-lov'd abode;
Last, white-rob'd Peace, crown'd with a hazel wreath,
To rustic Agriculture did bequeath
The broken, iron instruments of death:
At sight of whom our Sprites forgat their kindling
        wrath.

THE ORDINATION

For sense, they little owe to frugal Heav'n:
To please the mob they hide the little giv'n.

1

Kilmarnock wabsters, fidge an' claw,
    An' pour your creeshie nations;
An' ye wha leather rax an' draw,
    Of a' denominations;
Swith! to the Laigh Kirk, ane an' a',
    An' there tak up your stations;
Then aff to Begbie's in a raw,
    An' pour divine libations
                For joy this day.

weavers; shrug; scratch greasy stretch

Haste!

2

Curst Common-sense, that imp o' hell,
    Cam in wi' *Maggie Lauder*:
But Oliphant aft made her yell,
    An' Russell sair misca'd her:
This day Mackinlay taks the flail,
    An' he's the boy will blaud her!
He'll clap a shangan on her tail,
    An' set the bairns to daud her
                Wi' dirt this day.

slap
cleft stick
pelt

3

Mak haste an' turn King David owre,
    An' lilt wi' holy clangor;
O' double verse come gie us four,
    An' skirl up the *Bangor*:
This day the Kirk kicks up a stoure:
    Nae mair the knaves shall wrang her,
For Heresy is in her pow'r,
    And gloriously she'll whang her
                Wi' pith this day.

shrill
dust

flog

4

Come, let a proper text be read,
    An' touch it aff wi' vigour,

laughed

How graceless Ham leugh at his dad,
 Which made Canàan a nigger;
Or Phineas drove the murdering blade
 Wi' whore-abhorring rigour;
Or Zipporah, the scauldin jad,
 Was like a bluidy tiger
      I' th' inn that day.

5

There, try his mettle on the Creed,
 And bind him down wi' caution,—
That stipend is a carnal weed
 He taks but for the fashion—
And gie him o'er the flock to feed,
 And punish each transgression;
Especial, rams that cross the breed,
 Gie them sufficient threshin:
      Spare them nae day.

6

Now auld Kilmarnock, cock thy tail,
 An' toss thy horns fu' canty;

joyful
low

Nae mair thou'lt rowte out-owre the dale,
 Because thy pasture's scanty;
For lapfu's large o' gospel kail
 Shall fill thy crib in plenty,

stalks; choice

An' runts o' grace, the pick an' wale,
 No gien by way o' dainty.

every

      But ilka day.

7

Nae mair by Babel's streams we'll weep
 To think upon our Zion;
And hing our fiddles up to sleep,

cloths

 Like baby-clouts a-dryin!
Come, screw the pegs wi' tunefu' cheep,

strings
elbows
jerk

 And o'er the thairms be tryin;
O, rare! to see our elbucks wheep,
 And a' like lamb-tails flyin
      Fu' fast this day!

8

Lang, Patronage, wi' rod o' airn,   *iron*
 Has shor'd the Kirk's undoin;   *threatened*
As lately Fenwick, sair forfairn,   *forlorn*
 Has proven to its ruin:
Our patron, honest man! Glencairn,
 He saw mischief was brewin;
An' like a godly, elect bairn,
 He's waled us out a true ane,   *chosen*
      And sound this day.

9

Now Robertson harangue nae mair,
 But steek your gab for ever;   *shut; mouth*
Or try the wicked town of Ayr,
 For there they'll think you clever;
Or, nae reflection on your lear,   *learning*
 Ye may commence a shaver;   *set up for a barber*
Or to the Netherton repair,
 An' turn a carpet-weaver
      Aff-hand this day.

10

Mu'trie and you were just a match,
 We never had sic twa drones:
Auld Hornie did the Laigh Kirk watch, *The Devil*
 Just like a winkin baudrons,   *cat*
And ay he catch'd the tither wretch,
 To fry them in his caudrons;
But now his Honor maun detach,
 Wi' a' his brimstone squadrons,
      Fast, fast this day.

11

See, see auld Orthodoxy's faes   *foes*
 She's swingein thro' the city!   *flogging*
Hark, how the nine-tail'd cat she plays!
 I vow it's unco pretty: *mighty*
There, Learning, with his Greekish face,
 Grunts out some Latin ditty;
And Common-Sense is gaun, she says,
 To mak to Jamie Beattie
      Her plaint this day.

12

But there's Morality himsel,
    Embracing all opinions;
Hear, how he gies the tither yell
    Between his twa companions!
See, how she peels the skin an' fell,
    As ane were peelin onions!
Now there, they're packèd aff to hell,
    An' banish'd our dominions,
                    Henceforth this day.

flesh under the skin

13

O happy day! rejoice, rejoice!
    Come bouse about the porter!
Morality's demure decoys
    Shall here nae mair find quarter:
Mackinlay, Russell, are the boys
    That Heresy can torture;
They'll gie her on a rape a hoyse,
    And cowe her measure shorter
                    By th' head some day.

rope; hoist

crop

14

Come, bring the tither mutchkin in,
    And here's—for a conclusion—
To ev'ry New Light mother's son,
    From this time forth, confusion!
If mair they deave us wi' their din
    Or patronage intrusion,
We'll light a spunk, and ev'ry skin
    We'll run them aff in fusion,
                    Like oil some day.

pint

deafen

match

THE CALF

To the Rev. James Steven, on his text, MALACHI iv. 2:—
'*And ye shall go forth, and grow up as calves of the stall.*'

I

Right, sir! your text I'll prove it true,
   Tho' heretics may laugh;
For instance, there's yoursel just now,
   God knows, an unco *calf*.   uncommon

2

And should some patron be so kind
   As bless you wi' a kirk,
I doubt na, sir, but then we'll find
   You're still as great a *stirk*.   yearling

3

But, if the lover's raptur'd hour
   Shall ever be your lot,
Forbid it, every heavenly Power,
   You e'er should be a *stot*!   ox

4

Tho', when some kind connubial dear
   Your but-an'-ben adorns,
The like has been that you may wear
   A noble head of *horns*.

5

And, in your lug, most reverend James,   ear
   To hear you roar and rowte,   low
Few men o' sense will doubt your claims
   To rank among the *nowte*.   cattle

6

And when ye're number'd wi' the dead
   Below a grassy hillock,
With justice they may mark your head:—
   ' Here lies a famous *bullock*! '

ADDRESS TO THE UNCO GUID

OR THE RIGIDLY RIGHTEOUS

My Son, these maxims make a rule,
An' lump them ay thegither:
The Rigid Righteous is a fool,
The Rigid Wise anither;
sifted   *The cleanest corn that e'er was dight*
chaff   *May hae some pyles o' caff in;*
So ne'er a fellow-creature slight
larking   *For random fits o' daffin.*
SOLOMON (*Eccles.* vii. 16)

I

O ye, wha are sae guid yoursel,
    Sae pious and sae holy,
Ye've nought to do but mark and tell
    Your neebours' fauts and folly;
well-going   Whase life is like a weel-gaun mill,
    Supplied wi' store o' water;
hopper   The heapet happer's ebbing still,
clapper   An' still the clap plays clatter!

2

company   Hear me, ye venerable core,
    As counsel for poor mortals
sober   That frequent pass douce Wisdom's door
giddy   For glaikit Folly's portals:
I for their thoughtless, careless sakes
put forward   Would here propone defences—
restive   Their donsie tricks, their black mistakes,
    Their failings and mischances.

3

Ye see your state wi' theirs compared,
exchange   And shudder at the niffer;
But cast a moment's fair regard,
    What makes the mighty differ?
Discount what scant occasion gave;
    That purity ye pride in;
rest   And (what's aft mair than a' the lave)
    Your better art o' hidin.

4

Think, when your castigated pulse
    Gies now and then a wallop,
What ragings must his veins convulse,
    That still eternal gallop!
Wi' wind and tide fair i' your tail,
    Right on ye scud your sea-way;
But in the teeth o' baith to sail,
    It maks an unco lee-way.   *uncommon*

5

See Social-life and Glee sit down
    All joyous and unthinking,
Till, quite transmugrify'd, they're grown
    Debauchery and Drinking:
O, would they stay to calculate,
    Th' eternal consequences,
Or—your more dreaded hell to state—
    Damnation of expenses!

6

Ye high, exalted, virtuous dames,
    Tied up in godly laces,
Before ye gie poor Frailty names,
    Suppose a change o' cases:
A dear-lov'd lad, convenience snug,
    A treach'rous inclination—
But, let me whisper i' your lug,   *ear*
    Ye're aiblins nae temptation.   *maybe*

7

Then gently scan your brother man,
    Still gentler sister woman;
Tho' they may gang a kennin wrang,
    To step aside is human:
One point must still be greatly dark,
    The moving *why* they do it;
And just as lamely can ye mark
    How far perhaps they rue it.

8

Who made the heart, 'tis He alone
    Decidedly can try us:

He knows each chord, its various tone,
   Each spring, its various bias:
Then at the balance let's be mute,
   We never can adjust it;
What's done we partly may compute,
   But know not what's resisted.

TAM SAMSON'S ELEGY

An honest man's the noblest work of God.
                                    POPE

1

Has auld Kilmarnock seen the Deil?
Or great Mackinlay thrawn his heel?
Or Robertson again grown weel
                  To preach an' read?
'Na, waur than a'!' cries ilka chiel,
                  'Tam Samson's dead!'

*worse;
everybody*

2

Kilmarnock lang may grunt an' grane,
An' sigh, an' sab, an' greet her lane,
An' cleed her bairns—man, wife an' wean—
                  In mourning weed;
To Death she's dearly pay'd the kain:
                  Tam Samson's dead!

groan
weep alone
clothe; child
rent in kind

3

The Brethren o' the mystic level
May hing their head in woefu' bevel,
While by their nose the tears will revel,
                  Like onie bead;
Death's gien the Lodge an unco devel:
                  Tam Samson's dead!

slope
*stunning
blow*

4

When Winter muffles up his cloak,
And binds the mire like a rock;
When to the loughs the curlers flock,
                  Wi' gleesome speed,
Wha will they station at the cock?—
                  Tam Samson's dead!

ponds
mark

5

He was the king of a' the core,   *company*
To guard, or draw, or wick a bore,
Or up the rink like Jehu roar
        In time o' need;
But now he lags on Death's hog-score:
        Tam Samson s dead!

6

Now safe the stately sawmont sail,   *salmon*
And trouts bedropp'd wi' crimson hail,
And eels, weel-kend for souple tail,
        And geds for greed,   *pikes*
Since, dark in Death's fish-creel, we wail,
        Tam Samson dead!

7

Rejoice, ye birring paitricks a';   *partridges*
Ye cootie moorcocks, crousely craw; *leg-plumed;*
                                      confidently
Ye maukins, cock your fud fu' braw *hares; tail*
        Withouten dread;
Your mortal fae is now awa:
        Tam Samson's dead!

8

That woefu' morn be ever mourn'd,
Saw him in shootin graith adorn'd,   *attire*
While pointers round impatient burn'd,
        Frae couples free'd; *leashes*
But och! he gaed and ne'er return'd:
        Tam Samson's dead.

9

In vain auld-age his body batters,   *ankles*
In vain the gout his ancles fetters, *brooks;*
In vain the burns cam down like waters, *lakes*
        An acre braid!
Now ev'ry auld wife, greetin, clatters: *weeping*
        'Tam Samson's dead!'

10

Owre monie a weary hag he limpit,   *moss*
An' ay the tither shot he thumpit,

feud

blast

Till coward Death behint him jumpit,
> Wi' deadly feide;
Now he proclaims wi' tout o' trumpet:
> 'Tam Samson's dead!'

11

When at his heart he felt the dagger,
He reel'd his wonted bottle-swagger,
But yet he drew the mortal trigger
> Wi' weel-aim'd heed;
'Lord, five!' he cry'd, an' owre did stagger—
> Tam Samson's dead!

Each

babble

12

Ilk hoary hunter mourn'd a brither;
Ilk sportsman-youth bemoan'd a father;
Yon auld gray stane, amang the heather,
> Marks out his head;
Whare Burns has wrote, in rhyming blether:
> 'Tam Samson's dead!'

builds

13

There low he lies in lasting rest;
Perhaps upon his mould'ring breast
Some spitefu' moorfowl bigs her nest,
> To hatch an' breed:
Alas! nae mair he'll them molest:
> Tam Samson's dead!

14

When August winds the heather wave,
And sportsmen wander by yon grave,
Three volleys let his memory crave
> O' pouther an' lead,
Till Echo answers frae her cave:
> 'Tam Samson's dead!'

more

One

15

'Heav'n rest his saul whare'er he be!'
Is th' wish o' monie mae than me:
He had twa fauts, or maybe three,
> Yet what remead?
Ae social, honest man want we:
> Tam Samson's dead!

THE EPITAPH

Tam Samson's weel-worn clay here lies:
 Ye canting zealots, spare him!
If honest worth in Heaven rise,
 Ye'll mend or ye win near him.

PER CONTRA

Go, Fame, an' canter like a filly
Thro' a' the streets an neuks o' Killie;
Tell ev'ry social honest billie   fellow
    To cease his grievin;
For, yet unskaith'd by Death's gleg gullie,   quick knife
    Tam Samson's leevin!

A WINTER NIGHT

Poor naked wretches, wheresoe'er you are,
That bide the pelting of this pityless storm!
How shall your houseless heads and unfed sides,
Your loop'd and window'd raggedness, defend you
From seasons such as these?
      SHAKESPEARE

1

When biting Boreas, fell and doure,   cruel; hard
Sharp shivers thro' the leafless bow'r;
When Phœbus gies a short-liv'd glow'r,   stare
    Far south the lift,   horizon
Dim-dark'ning thro' the flaky show'r
    Or whirling drift:

2

Ae night the storm the steeples rocked;   One
Poor Labour sweet in sleep was locked;
While burns, wi' snawy wreaths up-choked,   brooks
    Wild-eddying swirl,
Or, thro' the mining outlet bocked,   vomited
    Down headlong hurl:

3

List'ning the doors an' winnocks rattle,   windows
I thought me on the ourie cattle,   shivering

helpless

scramble
jutting rock

Or silly sheep, wha bide this brattle
          O' winter war,
And thro' the drift, deep-lairing, sprattle
          Beneath a scaur.

4

Each

Ilk happing bird—wee, helpless thing!—
That in the merry months o' spring
Delighted me to hear thee sing,
          What comes o' thee?
Whare wilt thou cow'r thy chittering wing,
          An' close thy e'e?

5

Ev'n you, on murd'ring errands toil'd,
Lone from your savage homes exil'd,
The blood-stain'd roost and sheep-cote spoil'd
          My heart forgets,
While pityless the tempest wild
          Sore on you beats!

6

Now Phœbe, in her midnight reign,
Dark-muffl'd, view'd the dreary plain;
Still crowding thoughts, a pensive train.
          Rose in my soul,
When on my ear this plaintive strain,
          Slow-solemn, stole:—

7

'Blow, blow, ye winds, with heavier gust!
And freeze, thou bitter-biting frost!
Descend, ye chilly, smothering snows!
Not all your rage, as now united, shows
  More hard unkindness unrelenting,
  Vengeful malice, unrepenting,
Than heaven-illumin'd Man on brother Man bestows!
  See stern Oppression's iron grip,
    Or mad Ambition's gory hand,
  Sending, like blood-hounds from the slip,
    Woe, Want, and Murder o'er a land!
  Ev'n in the peaceful rural vale,
  Truth, weeping, tells the mournful tale:
How pamper'd Luxury, Flatt'ry by her side,

The parasite empoisoning her ear,
  With all the servile wretches in the rear,
Looks o'er proud Property, extended wide;
  And eyes the simple, rustic hind,
  Whose toil upholds the glitt'ring show—
    A creature of another kind,
  Some coarser substance, unrefin'd—
Plac'd for her lordly use, thus far, thus vile, below!
  Where, where is Love's fond, tender throe,
  With lordly Honor's lofty brow,
    The pow'rs you proudly own?
  Is there, beneath Love's noble name,
  Can harbour, dark, the selfish aim,
    To bless himself alone?
  Mark Maiden-Innocence a prey
    To love-pretending snares:
  This boasted Honor turns away,
  Shunning soft Pity's rising sway,
Regardless of the tears and unavailing pray'rs!
  Perhaps this hour, in Misery's squalid nest,
  She strains your infant to her joyless breast,
And with a mother's fears shrinks at the rocking blast!

8

' O ye! who, sunk in beds of down,
  Feel not a want but what yourselves create,
  Think, for a moment, on his wretched fate,
Whom friends and fortune quite disown!
  Ill-satisfy'd keen nature's clam'rous call,
  Stretch'd on his straw, he lays himself to sleep;
While through the ragged roof and chinky wall,
  Chill, o'er his slumbers piles the drifty heap!
  Think on the dungeon's grim confine,
  Where Guilt and poor Misfortune pine!
  Guilt, erring man, relenting view!
  But shall thy legal rage pursue
  The wretch, already crushèd low
  By cruel Fortune's undeservèd blow?
Affliction's sons are brothers in distress;
A brother to relieve, how exquisite the bliss! '

9

I heard nae mair, for Chanticleer
  Shook off the pouthery snaw,   powdery

And hail'd the morning with a cheer,
   A cottage-rousing craw.

10

But deep this truth impress'd my mind:
   Thro' all His works abroad,
The heart benevolent and kind
   The most resembles God.

STANZAS WRITTEN IN PROSPECT OF DEATH

1

Why am I loth to leave this earthly scene?
   Have I so found it full of pleasing charms?
Some drops of joy with draughts of ill between;
   Some gleams of sunshine mid renewing storms.
Is it departing pangs my soul alarms?
   Or death's unlovely, dreary, dark abode?
For guilt, for guilt, my terrors are in arms:
   I tremble to approach an angry God,
And justly smart beneath his sin-avenging rod.

2

Fain would I say: ' Forgive my foul offence,'
   Fain promise never more to disobey.
But should my Author health again dispense,
   Again I might desert fair virtue's way;
Again in folly's path might go astray;
   Again exalt the brute and sink the man:
Then how should I for heavenly mercy pray,
   Who act so counter heavenly mercy's plan?
Who sin so oft have mourn'd, yet to temptation ran?

3

O Thou great Governor of all below!—
   If I may dare a lifted eye to Thee,—
Thy nod can make the tempest cease to blow,
   Or still the tumult of the raging sea:
With that controlling pow'r assist ev'n me
   Those headlong furious passions to confine,
For all unfit I feel my pow'rs to be
   To rule their torrent in th' allowèd line:
O, aid me with Thy help, Omnipotence Divine!

PRAYER: O THOU DREAD POWER

*Lying at a reverend friend's house one night the author
left the following verses in the room where he slept.*

1

O Thou dread Power, who reign'st above,
    I know thou wilt me hear,
When for this scene of peace and love
    I make my prayer sincere.

2

The hoary Sire—the mortal stroke,
    Long, long be pleas'd to spare:
To bless his little filial flock,
    And show what good men are.

3

She, who her lovely offspring eyes
    With tender hopes and fears—
O, bless her with a mother's joys,
    But spare a mother's tears!

4

Their hope, their stay, their darling youth,
    In manhood's dawning blush,
Bless him, Thou God of love and truth,
    Up to a parent's wish.

5

The beauteous, seraph sister-band—
    With earnest tears I pray—
Thou know'st the snares on every hand,
    Guide Thou their steps alway.

6

When, soon or late, they reach that coast,
    O'er Life's rough ocean driven,
May they rejoice, no wand'rer lost,
    A family in Heaven!

PARAPHRASE OF THE FIRST PSALM

1

The man, in life wherever plac'd,
    Hath happiness in store,
Who walks not in the wicked's way
    Nor learns their guilty lore;

2

Nor from the seat of scornful pride
    Casts forth his eyes abroad,
But with humility and awe
    Still walks before his God!

3

That man shall flourish like the trees,
    Which by the streamlets grow:
The fruitful top is spread on high,
    And firm the root below.

4

But he, whose blossom buds in guilt,
    Shall to the ground be cast,
And, like the rootless stubble, tost
    Before the sweeping blast.

5

For why? that God the good adore
    Hath giv'n them peace and rest,
But hath decreed that wicked men
    Shall ne'er be truly blest.

PRAYER UNDER THE PRESSURE OF VIOLENT ANGUISH

1

O Thou Great Being! what Thou art
    Surpasses me to know;
Yet sure I am, that known to Thee
    Are all Thy works below.

2

Thy creature here before Thee stands,
    All wretched and distrest;
Yet sure those ills that wring my soul
    Obey Thy high behest.

3

Sure Thou, Almighty, canst not act
    From cruelty or wrath!
O, free my weary eyes from tears,
    Or close them fast in death!

4

But, if I must afflicted be
    To suit some wise design,
Then man my soul with firm resolves
    To bear and not repine!

THE NINETIETH PSALM VERSIFIED

1

O Thou, the first, the greatest friend
    Of all the human race!
Whose strong right hand has ever been
    Their stay and dwelling place!

2

Before the mountains heav'd their heads
    Beneath Thy forming hand,
Before this ponderous globe itself
    Arose at Thy command;

3

That Power, which rais'd and still upholds
    This universal frame,
From countless, unbeginning time
    Was ever still the same.

4

Those mighty periods of years,
    Which seem to us so vast,

Appear no more before Thy sight
Than yesterday that's past.

5

Thou giv'st the word: Thy creature, man,
Is to existence brought;
Again Thou say'st: ' Ye sons of men,
Return ye into nought!'

6

Thou layest them, with all their cares,
In everlasting sleep;
As with a flood Thou tak'st them off
With overwhelming sweep.

7

They flourish like the morning flower
In beauty's pride array'd,
But long ere night, cut down, it lies
All wither'd and decay'd.

TO MISS LOGAN

WITH BEATTIE'S POEMS FOR A NEW-YEAR'S GIFT—JANUARY 1, 1787

1

Again the silent wheels of time
Their annual round have driv'n,
And you, tho' scarce in maiden prime,
Are so much nearer Heav'n.

2

No gifts have I from Indian coasts
The infant year to hail;
I send you more than India boasts
In Edwin's simple tale.

3

Our sex with guile, and faithless love,
Is charg'd—perhaps too true;
But may, dear maid, each lover prove
An Edwin still to you.

ADDRESS TO A HAGGIS

1

Fair fa' your honest, sonsie face,   *jolly*
Great chieftain o' the puddin-race!
Aboon them a' ye tak your place,   *Above*
        Painch, tripe, or thairm: *Paunch;*
                            small guts
Weel are ye wordy of a grace
        As lang's my arm.

2

The groaning trencher there ye fill,
Your hurdies like a distant hill,   *buttocks*
Your pin wad help to mend a mill   *skewer*
        In time o' need,
While thro' your pores the dews distil
        Like amber bead.

3

His knife see rustic Labour dight,   *wipe*
An' cut ye up wi' ready slight,   *skill*
Trenching your gushing entrails bright,
        Like onie ditch;
And then, O what a glorious sight,
        Warm-reekin, rich!

4

Then, horn for horn, they stretch an' strive: *spoon*
Deil tak the hindmost, on they drive,
Till a' their weel-swall'd kytes belyve   *bellies; by-*
        Are bent like drums;   *and-bye*
Then auld Guidman, maist like to rive,   *burst*
        ' Bethankit! ' hums.

5

Is there that owre his French *ragout*,
Or *olio* that wad staw a sow,   *sicken*
Or *fricassee* wad mak her spew
        Wi' perfect sconner,   *disgust*
Looks down wi' sneering, scornfu' view
        On sic a dinner?

6

Poor devil! see him owre his trash,
As feckless as a wither'd rash,
His spindle shank a guid whip-lash,
                    His nieve a nit;
Thro' bluidy flood or field to dash,
                    O how unfit!

weak; rush   *fist; nut*

7

But mark the Rustic, haggis-fed,
The trembling earth resounds his tread,
Clap in his walie nieve a blade,
                    He'll make it whissle;
An' legs, an' arms, an' heads will sned
                    Like taps o' thrissle.

ample   *crop*

8

Ye Pow'rs, wha mak mankind your care,
And dish them out their bill o' fare,
Auld Scotland wants nae skinking ware,
                    That jaups in luggies;
But, if ye wish her gratefu' prayer,
                    Gie her a Haggis!

watery splashes; porringers

ADDRESS TO EDINBURGH

1

Edina! Scotia's darling seat!
    All hail thy palaces and tow'rs,
Where once, beneath a Monarch's feet,
    Sat Legislation's sov'reign pow'rs:
    From marking wildly-scatt'red flow'rs,
As on the banks of Ayr I stray'd,
    And singing, lone, the ling'ring hours,
I shelter in thy honor'd shade.

2

Here Wealth still swells the golden tide,
    As busy Trade his labours plies;
There Architecture's noble pride
    Bids elegance and splendour rise:

Here Justice, from her native skies,
  High wields her balance and her rod;
    There Learning, with his eagle eyes,
Seeks Science in her coy abode.

3

Thy sons, Edina, social, kind,
  With open arms the stranger hail;
Their views enlarg'd, their lib'ral mind,
  Above the narrow, rural vale;
    Attentive still to Sorrow's wail,
Or modest Merit's silent claim:
  And never may their sources fail!
And never Envy blot their name!

4

Thy daughters bright thy walks adorn,
  Gay as the gilded summer sky,
Sweet as the dewy, milk-white thorn,
  Dear as the raptur'd thrill of joy!
    Fair Burnet strikes th' adoring eye,
Heav'n's beauties on my fancy shine:
  I see the Sire of Love on high,
And own His work indeed divine!

5

There, watching high the least alarms,
  Thy rough, rude fortress gleams afar;
Like some bold vet'ran, grey in arms,
  And mark'd with many a seamy scar:
    The pond'rous wall and massy bar,
Grim-rising o'er the rugged rock,
  Have oft withstood assailing war,
And oft repell'd th' invader's shock.

6

With awe-struck thought and pitying tears,
  I view that noble, stately dome,
Where Scotia's kings of other years,
  Fam'd heroes! had their royal home:
    Alas, how chang'd the times to come!
Their royal name low in the dust!
  Their hapless race wild-wand'ring roam!
Tho' rigid Law cries out: ' 'Twas just!'

7

Wild beats my heart to trace your steps,
    Whose ancestors, in days of yore,
Thro' hostile ranks and ruin'd gaps
    Old Scotia's bloody lion bore:
    Ev'n I, who sing in rustic lore,
Haply my sires have left their shed,
    And fac'd grim Danger's loudest roar,
Bold-following where your fathers led!

8

Edina! Scotia's darling seat!
    All hail thy palaces and tow'rs;
Where once, beneath a Monarch's feet,
    Sat Legislation's sov'reign pow'rs:
    From marking wildly-scatt'red flow'rs,
As on the banks of Ayr I stray'd,
    And singing, lone, the ling'ring hours,
I shelter in thy honour'd shade.

WRITTEN IN FRIARS CARSE HERMITAGE, ON NITHSIDE

Thou whom chance may hither lead,
Be thou clad in russet weed,
Be thou deckt in silken stole,
Grave these counsels on thy soul.

Life is but a day at most,
Sprung from night,—in darkness lost:
Hope not sunshine ev'ry hour,
Fear not clouds will always lour.

As Youth and Love with sprightly dance
Beneath thy morning star advance,
Pleasure with her siren air
May delude the thoughtless pair:
Let Prudence bless Enjoyment's cup,
Then raptur'd sip, and sip it up.

As thy day grows warm and high,
Life's meridian flaming nigh,
Dost thou spurn the humble vale?

Life's proud summits would'st thou scale?
Check thy climbing step, elate,
Evils lurk in felon wait:
Dangers, eagle-pinioned, bold,
Soar around each cliffy hold;
While cheerful Peace with linnet song
Chants the lowly dells among.

    As the shades of ev'ning close,
Beck'ning thee to long repose;
As life itself becomes disease.
Seek the chimney-nook of ease:
There ruminate with sober thought,
On all thou'st seen, and heard, and wrought;
And teach the sportive younkers round,
Saws of experience, sage and sound:
Say, man's true, genuine estimate,
The grand criterion of his fate,
Is not, Art thou high or low?
Did thy fortune ebb or flow?
Did many talents gild thy span?
Or frugal Nature grudge thee one?
Tell them, and press it on their mind,
As thou thyself must shortly find,
The smile or frown of awful Heav'n
To Virtue or to Vice is giv'n;
Say, to be just, and kind, and wise—
There solid self-enjoyment lies;
That foolish, selfish, faithless ways
Lead to be wretched, vile, and base.

    Thus resign'd and quiet, creep
To the bed of lasting sleep:
Sleep, whence thou shall ne'er awake,
Night, where dawn shall never break;
Till future life, future no more,
To light and joy the good restore,
To light and joy unknown before.

Stranger, go! Heav'n be thy guide!
Quod the beadsman of Nithside.

ODE, SACRED TO THE MEMORY OF MRS. OSWALD OF AUCHENCRUIVE

Dweller in yon dungeon dark,
Hangman of creation, mark!
Who in widow-weeds appears,
Laden with unhonoured years,
Noosing with care a bursting purse,
Baited with many a deadly curse?

STROPHE

View the wither'd beldam's face!
Can thy keen inspection trace
Aught of Humanity's sweet, melting grace?
Note that eye, 'tis rheum o'erflows—
Pity's flood there never rose.
See those hands, ne'er stretch'd to save,
Hands that took but never gave.
Keeper of Mammon's iron chest,
Lo, there she goes, unpitied and unblest,
She goes, but not to realms of everlasting rest!

ANTISTROPHE

Plunderer of Armies! lift thine eyes
(A while forbear, ye torturing fiends),
Seest thou whose step, unwilling, hither bends?
No fallen angel, hurl'd from upper skies!
'Tis thy trusty, quondam Mate,
Doom'd to share thy fiery fate:
She, tardy, hell-ward plies.

EPODE

And are they of no more avail,
Ten thousand glittering pounds a-year?
In other worlds can Mammon fail,
Omnipotent as he is here?
O bitter mockery of the pompous bier!
While down the wretched vital part is driven,
The cave-lodg'd beggar, with a conscience clear,
Expires in rags, unknown, and goes to Heaven.

ELEGY ON CAPTAIN MATTHEW HENDERSON

A GENTLEMAN WHO HELD THE PATENT FOR HIS HONOURS IMMEDIATELY FROM ALMIGHTY GOD!

> *But now his radiant course is run,*
> *For Matthew's course was bright:*
> *His soul was like the glorious sun*
> *A matchless, Heavenly light.*

1

O Death! thou tyrant fell and bloody!
The meikle Devil wi' a woodie   great; halter
Haurl thee hame to his black smiddie   Trail;smithy
         O'er hurcheon hides,   hedgehog
And like stock-fish come o'er his studdie   anvil
         Wi' thy auld sides!

2

He's gane, he's gane! he's frae us torn,   gone
The ae best fellow e'er was born!   one
Thee, Matthew, Nature's sel shall mourn,
         By wood and wild,
Where, haply, Pity strays forlorn,
         Frae man exil'd.

3

Ye hills, near neebors o' the starns,   stars
That proudly cock your cresting cairns!   mounds
Ye cliffs, the haunts of sailing yearns,   eagles
         Where Echo slumbers!
Come join ye, Nature's sturdiest bairns,
         My wailing numbers!

4

Mourn, ilka grove the cushat kens!   every
Ye hazly shaws and briery dens!   woods
Ye burnies, wimplin down your glens   brooklets, winding
         Wi' toddlin din,   purling
Or foaming, strang, wi' hasty stens,   quick leaps
         Frae lin to lin!   fall

5

Mourn, little harebells o'er the lea;
Ye stately foxgloves, fair to see;
Ye woodbines, hanging bonilie
                    In scented bowers;
Ye roses on your thorny tree,
                    The first o' flowers!

6

At dawn, when every grassy blade
Droops with a diamond at his head;
At ev'n, when beans their fragrance shed
                    I' th' rustling gale;
hares,
scudding   Ye maukins, whiddin through the glade;
                    Come join my wail!

7

Mourn, ye wee songsters o' the wood;
Ye grouse that crap the heather bud;
cloud   Ye curlews, calling thro' a clud;
                    Ye whistling plover;
partridge And mourn, ye whirring paitrick brood:
                    He's gane for ever!

8

Mourn, sooty coots, and speckled teals;
Ye fisher herons, watching eels;
Ye duck and drake, wi' airy wheels
                    Circling the lake;
Ye bitterns, till the quagmire reels,
Boom   Rair for his sake!

9

corncrakes Mourn, clam'ring craiks, at close o' day,
'Mang fields o' flow'ring clover gay!
And when you wing your annual way
                    Frae our cauld shore,
those   Tell thae far warlds wha lies in clay,
                    Wham we deplore,

10

owls   Ye houlets, frae your ivy bower
haunted   In some auld tree, or eldritch tower,

What time the moon, wi' silent glowr,   stare
        Sets up her horn,
Wail thro' the dreary midnight hour
        Till waukrife morn!   wakeful

11

O rivers, forests, hills, and plains!
Oft have ye heard my canty strains: cheerful
But now, what else for me remains
        But tales of woe?
And frae my een the drapping rains   eyes
        Maun ever flow.   Must

12

Mourn, Spring, thou darling of the year!
Ilk cowslip cup shall kep a tear: catch
Thou, Simmer, while each corny spear
        Shoots up its head,
Thy gay, green, flowery tresses shear
        For him that's dead!

13

Thou, Autumn, wi' thy yellow hair,
In grief thy sallow mantle tear!
Thou, Winter, hurling thro' the air
        The roaring blast,
Wide o'er the naked world declare
        The worth we've lost!

14

Mourn him, thou Sun, great source of light!
Mourn, Empress of the silent night!
And you, ye twinkling starnies bright,   starlets
        My Matthew mourn!
For through your orbs he's taen his flight,
        Ne'er to return.

15

O Henderson! the man! the brother!
And art thou gone, and gone for ever?
And hast thou crost that unknown river,
        Life's dreary bound?
Like thee, where shall I find another,
        The world around?

16

Go to your sculptur'd tombs, ye Great,
  In a' the tinsel trash o' state!
But by thy honest turf I'll wait,
           Thou man of worth!
And weep the ae best fellow's fate
           E'er lay in earth!

THE EPITAPH

1

Stop, passenger! my story's brief,
  And truth I shall relate, man:
I tell nae common tale o' grief,
  For Matthew was a great man.

2

If thou uncommon merit hast,
  Yet spurn'd at Fortune's door, man;
A look of pity hither cast,
  For Matthew was a poor man.

3

If thou a noble sodger art,
  That passest by this grave, man;
There moulders here a gallant heart,
  For Matthew was a brave man.

4

If thou on men, their works and ways,
  Canst throw uncommon light, man;
Here lies wha weel had won thy praise,
  For Matthew was a bright man.

5

If thou, at Friendship's sacred ca',
  Wad life itself resign, man;
Thy sympathetic tear maun fa',
  For Matthew was a kind man.

6

If thou art staunch, without a stain,
  Like the unchanging blue, man;

This was a kinsman o' thy ain,
   For Matthew was a true man.

7

If thou hast wit, and fun, and fire,
   And ne'er guid wine did fear, man;
This was thy billie, dam, and sire,   brother
   For Matthew was a queer man.

8

If onie whiggish, whingin sot,   whining
   To blame poor Matthew dare, man;
May dool and sorrow be his lot!   woe
   For Matthew was a rare man.

TO ROBERT GRAHAM OF FINTRY, ESQ.

Late crippl'd of an arm, and now a leg;
About to beg a pass for leave to beg;
Dull, listless, teas'd, dejected, and deprest
(Nature is adverse to a cripple's rest);
Will generous Graham list to his Poet's wail
(It soothes poor Misery, hearkening to her tale),
And hear him curse the light he first survey'd,
And doubly curse the luckless rhyming trade?

Thou, Nature! partial Nature! I arraign;
Of thy caprice maternal I complain:
The lion and the bull thy care have found,
One shakes the forests, and one spurns the ground;
Thou giv'st the ass his hide, the snail his shell;
Th' envenom'd wasp, victorious, guards his cell;
Thy minions kings defend, control, devour,
In all th' omnipotence of rule and power.
Foxes and statesmen subtile wiles ensure;
The cit and polecat stink, and are secure;
Toads with their poison, doctors with their drug,
The priest and hedgehog in their robes, are snug;
Ev'n silly woman has her warlike arts,
Her tongue and eyes—her dreaded spear and darts.

But O thou bitter step-mother and hard,
To thy poor, fenceless, naked child—the Bard!
A thing unteachable in world's skill,
And half an idiot too, more helpless still:
No heels to bear him from the op'ning dun,
No claws to dig, his hated sight to shun;
No horns, but those by luckless Hymen worn,
And those, alas! not, Amalthea's horn;
No nerves olfact'ry, Mammon's trusty cur,
Clad in rich Dulness' comfortable fur;
In naked feeling, and in aching pride,
He bears th' unbroken blast from ev'ry side:
Vampyre booksellers drain him to the heart,
And scorpion critics cureless venom dart.

Critics—appall'd, I venture on the name;
Those cut-throat bandits in the paths of fame;
Bloody dissectors, worse than ten Monroes:
He hacks to teach, they mangle to expose.

His heart by causeless wanton malice wrung,
By blockheads' daring into madness stung;
His well-won bays, than life itself more dear,
By miscreants torn, who ne'er one sprig must wear;
Foil'd, bleeding, tortur'd in th' unequal strife,
The hapless Poet flounders on thro' life:
Till, fled each hope that once his bosom fir'd,
And fled each Muse that glorious once inspir'd,
Low sunk in squalid, unprotected age,
Dead even resentment for his injur'd page,
He heeds or feels no more the ruthless critic's rage!
So, by some hedge, the gen'rous steed deceas'd,
For half-starv'd snarling curs a dainty feast,
By toil and famine wore to skin and bone,
Lies, senseless of each tugging bitch's son.

O Dulness! portion of the truly blest!
Calm shelter'd haven of eternal rest!
Thy sons ne'er madden in the fierce extremes
Of Fortune's polar frost, or torrid beams.
If mantling high she fills the golden cup,
With sober, selfish ease they sip it up:
Conscious the bounteous meed they well deserve,
They only wonder ' some folks ' do not starve.

The grave, sage hern thus easy picks his frog,
And thinks the mallard a sad, worthless dog.
When Disappointment snaps the clue of hope,
And thro' disastrous night they darkling grope,
With deaf endurance sluggishly they bear,
And just conclude ' that fools are fortune's care.'
So, heavy, passive to the tempest's shocks,
Strong on the sign-post stands the stupid ox.

Not so the idle Muses' mad-cap train;
Not such the workings of their moon-struck brain:
In equanimity they never dwell;
By turns in soaring heav'n, or vaulted hell.

I dread thee, Fate, relentless and severe,
With all a poet's, husband's, father's fear!
Already one strong hold of hope is lost:
Glencairn, the truly noble, lies in dust
(Fled, like the sun eclips'd as noon appears,
And left us darkling in a world of tears).
O, hear my ardent, grateful, selfish pray'r!
Fintry, my other stay, long bless and spare!
Thro' a long life his hopes and wishes crown,
And bright in cloudless skies his sun go down!
May bliss domestic smooth his private path;
Give energy to life; and soothe his latest breath,
With many a filial tear circling the bed of death!

LAMENT FOR
JAMES, EARL OF GLENCAIRN

I

The wind blew hollow frae the hills;
    By fits the sun's departing beam
Look'd on the fading yellow woods,
    That wav'd o'er Lugar's winding stream.
Beneath a craigy steep a Bard,   craggy
    Laden with years and meikle pain,   much
In loud lament bewail'd his lord,
    Whom Death had all untimely taen.

2

oak

He lean'd him to an ancient aik,
    Whose trunk was mould'ring down with years;
His locks were bleachèd white with time,
    His hoary cheek was wet wi' tears;
And as he touch'd his trembling harp,
    And as he tun'd his doleful sang,
The winds, lamenting thro' their caves,
    To echo bore the notes alang:—

3

' Ye scatter'd birds that faintly sing,
    The reliques of the vernal quire!
Ye woods that shed on a' the winds
    The honours of the agèd year!
A few short months, and, glad and gay,
    Again ye'll charm the ear and e'e;
But nocht in all revolving time
    Can gladness bring again to me.

4

' I am a bending agèd tree,
    That long has stood the wind and rain;
But now has come a cruel blast
    And my last hold of earth is gane;
Nae leaf o' mine shall greet the spring,
    Nae simmer sun exalt my bloom;
But I maun lie before the storm,
    And ithers plant them in my room.

5

' I've seen sae monie changefu' years,
    On earth I am a stranger grown:
I wander in the ways of men,
    Alike unknowing and unknown:
Unheard, unpitied, unreliev'd,

load

    I bear alane my lade o' care;
For silent, low. on beds of dust,
    Lie a' that would my sorrows share.

6

' And last (the sum of a' my griefs!)
    My noble master lies in clay;

The flow'r amang our barons bold,
  His country's pride, his country's stay:
In weary being now I pine,
  For a' the life of life is dead,
And hope has left my agèd ken,
  On forward wing for ever fled.

7

'Awake thy last sad voice, my harp!
  The voice of woe and wild despair!
Awake, resound thy latest lay,
  Then sleep in silence evermair!
And thou, my last, best, only friend,
  That fillest an untimely tomb,
Accept this tribute from the Bard
  Thou brought from Fortune's mirkest gloom.

8

'In Poverty's low barren vale,
  Thick mists obscure involv'd me round;
Though oft I turn'd the wistful eye,
  Nae ray of fame was to be found;
Thou found'st me, like the morning sun
  That melts the fogs in limpid air:
The friendless Bard and rustic song
  Became alike thy fostering care.

9

'O, why has Worth so short a date,
  While villains ripen grey with time!
Must thou, the noble, gen'rous, great,
  Fall in bold manhood's hardy prime?
Why did I live to see that day,
  A day to me so full of woe?
O, had I met the mortal shaft
  Which laid my benefactor low!

10

'The bridegroom may forget the bride
  Was made his wedded wife yestreen;
The monarch may forget the crown
  That on his head an hour has been;

The mother may forget the child
That smiles sae sweetly on her knee;
But I'll remember thee, Glencairn,
And a' that thou hast done for me! '

LINES TO SIR JOHN WHITEFOORD.
BART.

SENT WITH THE FOREGOING POEM

Thou, who thy honour as thy God rever'st,
Who, save thy mind's reproach, nought earthly fear'st.
To thee this votive off'ring I impart,
The tearful tribute of a broken heart.
The Friend thou valued'st, I the Patron lov'd;
His worth, his honour, all the world approv'd:
We'll mourn till we too go as he has gone,
And tread the shadowy path to that dark world
unknown.

TAM O' SHANTER

A Tale

Of Brownyis and of Bogillis full is this Buke.
GAWIN DOUGLAS

pedlar When chapman billies leave the street,
fellows
thirsty And drouthy neebors neebors meet;
As market-days are wearing late,
road An' folk begin to tak the gate;
ale While we sit bousing at the nappy,
full; mighty An' getting fou and unco happy,
not We think na on the lang Scots miles,
bogs; pools The mosses, waters, slaps, and styles,
breaches;
stiles That lie between us and our hame,
Whare sits our sulky, sullen dame,
Gathering her brows like gathering storm,
Nursing her wrath to keep it warm.

found This truth fand honest Tam o' Shanter,
one As he frae Ayr ae night did canter:

(Auld Ayr, wham ne'er a town surpasses.
For honest men and bonie lasses.)

O Tam, had'st thou but been sae wise,
As taen thy ain wife Kate's advice!   to have taken
                                                       good-for-
She tauld thee weel thou was a skellum,   nothing
A blethering, blustering, drunken blellum;   chattering;
                                                       babbler
That frae November till October,
Ae market-day thou was nae sober;
That ilka melder wi' the miller,   meal-
                                                       grinding
Thou sat as lang as thou had siller;   money
That ev'ry naig was ca'd a shoe on,   shod
The smith and thee gat roaring fou on;
That at the Lord's house, even on Sunday,
Thou drank wi' Kirkton Jean till Monday.
She prophesied, that, late or soon,
Thou would be found deep drown'd in Doon,
Or catch'd wi' warlocks in the mirk   wizards;
                                                       dark
By Alloway's auld, haunted kirk.

Ah! gentle dames, it gars me greet,   makes; weep
To think how monie counsels sweet,
How monie lengthen'd, sage advices
The husband frae the wife despises!

But to our tale:—Ae market-night,
Tam had got planted unco right,   uncommonly
Fast by an ingle, bleezing finely,
Wi' reaming swats, that drank divinely;   foaming
                                                       new ale
And at his elbow, Souter Johnie,   Cobbler
His ancient, trusty, drouthy cronie:
Tam lo'ed him like a very brither;
They had been fou for weeks thegither.
The night drave on wi' sangs and clatter;
And ay the ale was growing better:
The landlady and Tam grew gracious
Wi' secret favours, sweet and precious:
The Souter tauld his queerest stories;
The landlord's laugh was ready chorus:
The storm without might rair and rustle,   roar
Tam did na mind the storm a whistle.

Care, mad to see a man sae happy,
E'en drown'd himsel amang the nappy.

As bees flee hame wi' lades o' treasure,
The minutes wing'd their way wi' pleasure:
Kings may be blest but Tam was glorious,
O'er a' the ills o' life victorious!

But pleasures are like poppies spread:
You seize the flow'r, its bloom is shed;
Or like the snow falls in the river,
A moment white—then melts for ever;
Or like the Borealis race,
That flit ere you can point their place;
Or like the rainbow's lovely form
Evanishing amid the storm.
Nae man can tether time or tide;
The hour approaches Tam maun ride:
That hour, o' night's black arch the key-stane,
That dreary hour Tam mounts his beast in;
And sic a night he taks the road in,
As ne'er poor sinner was abroad in.

The wind blew as 'twad blawn its last;
The rattling showers rose on the blast;
The speedy gleams the darkness swallow'd;
Loud, deep, and lang the thunder bellow'd:
That night, a child might understand,
The Deil had business on his hand.

Weel mounted on his grey meare Meg,
A better never lifted leg,
Tam skelpit on thro' dub and mire,
Despising wind, and rain, and fire;
Whiles holding fast his guid blue bonnet,
Whiles crooning o'er some auld Scots sonnet,
Whiles glow'ring round wi' prudent cares,
Lest bogles catch him unawares:
Kirk-Alloway was drawing nigh,
Whare ghaists and houlets nightly cry.

By this time he was cross the ford,
Whare in the snaw the chapman smoor'd;
And past the birks and meikle stane,
Whare drunken Charlie brak's neck-bane;
And thro' the whins, and by the cairn,
Whare hunters fand the murder'd bairn;

(marginal glosses)
must
would have
spanked; puddle
Now
song
staring
hobgoblins
owls
across
smothered
birches; big
furze; pile of stones

And near the thorn, aboon the well,   *above*
Whare Mungo's mither hang'd hersel.
Before him Doon pours all his floods;
The doubling storm roars thro' the woods;
The lightnings flash from pole to pole;
Near and more near the thunders roll:
When, glimmering thro' the groaning trees,
Kirk-Alloway seem'd in a bleeze,
Thro' ilka bore the beams were glancing,   *every chink*
And loud resounded mirth and dancing.

    Inspiring, bold John Barleycorn!
What dangers thou canst make us scorn!
Wi' tippenny, we fear nae evil;   *ale*
Wi' usquabae, we'll face the Devil!   *whisky*
The swats sae ream'd in Tammie's noddle,
Fair play, he car'd na deils a boddle.   *not; farthing*
But Maggie stood, right sair astonish'd,
Till, by the heel and hand admonish'd,
She ventur'd forward on the light;
And, wow! Tam saw an unco sight!   *wondrous*

    Warlocks and witches in a dance:
Nae cotillion, brent new frae France,   *brand*
But hornpipes, jigs, strathspeys, and reels,
Put life and mettle in their heels.
A winnock-bunker in the east,   *window-seat*
There sat Auld Nick, in shape o' beast;
A tousie tyke, black, grim, and large,   *shaggy dog*
To gie them music was his charge:
He screw'd the pipes and gart them skirl,   *squeal*
Till roof and rafters a' did dirl.   *ring*
Coffins stood round, like open presses,   *cupboards*
That shaw'd the dead in their last dresses;
And, by some devilish cantraip sleight,   *magic device*
Each in its cauld hand held a light:
By which heroic Tam was able
To note upon the haly table,
A murderer's banes, in gibbet-airns;   *-irons*
Twa span-lang, wee, unchristen'd bairns;
A thief new-cutted frae a rape—
Wi' his last gasp his gab did gape;   *mouth*
Five tomahawks wi' bluid red-rusted;
Five scymitars wi' murder crusted;

A garter which a babe had strangled;
A knife a father's throat had mangled—
Whom his ain son o' life bereft—
The grey-hairs yet stack to the heft;
Wi' mair of horrible and awefu',
Which even to name wad be unlawfu'.
Three Lawyers' tongues, turned inside out,
Wi' lies seamed like a beggar's clout;
Three Priests' hearts, rotten, black as muck,
Lay stinking, vile, in every neuk.

stared

    As Tammie glowr'd, amaz'd, and curious,
The mirth and fun grew fast and furious;
The piper loud and louder blew,
The dancers quick and quicker flew,

took hold
beldam
sweated and
steamed
rags
tripped

They reel'd, they set, they cross'd, they cleekit,
Till ilka carlin swat and reekit,
And coost her duddies to the wark,
And linket at it in her sark!

these

    Now Tam, O Tam! had thae been queans,
A' plump and strapping in their teens!

greasy

Their sarks, instead o' creeshie flannen,
Been snaw-white seventeen hunder linen!—

These

Thir breeks o' mine, my only pair,
That ance were plush, o' guid blue hair,

buttocks
maidens

I wad hae gi'en them off my hurdies
For ae blink o' the bonie burdies!

wizened
wean
leaping;
kicking;
cudgel

    But wither'd beldams, auld and droll,
Rigwoodie hags wad spean a foal,
Louping and flinging on a crummock,
I wonder did na turn thy stomach!

well
comely;
choice
company

    But Tam kend what was what fu' brawlie:
There was ae winsome wench and wawlie,
That night enlisted in the core,
Lang after kend on Carrick shore

death

(For monie a beast to dead she shot,
An' perish'd monie a bonie boat,

much;barley

And shook baith meikle corn and bear,
And kept the country-side in fear.)

short shift;
coarse cloth

Her cutty sark, o' Paisley harn,
That while a lassie she had worn,

In longitude tho' sorely scanty,
It was her best, and she was vauntie. . . .   proud
Ah! little kend thy reverend grannie,
That sark she coft for her wee Nannie,   bought
Wi' twa pund Scots ('twas a' her riches),
Wad ever grac'd a dance of witches!   Would have

But here my Muse her wing maun cour,   stoop
Sic flights as far beyond her power:
To sing how Nannie lap and flang   leaped and
(A souple jad she was and strang);   kicked
And how Tam stood like ane bewitch'd,
And thought his very een enrich'd;
Even Satan glowr'd, and fidg'd fu' fain,   fidgeted;
And hotch'd and blew wi' might and main;   fond
Till first ae caper, syne anither,   jerked
Tam tint his reason a' thegither,   then
And roars out: ' Weel done, Cutty-sark! '   lost
And in an instant all was dark;
And scarcely had he Maggie rallied,
When out the hellish legion sallied.

As bees bizz out wi' angry fyke,   fret
When plundering herds assail their byke;   hive
As open pussie's mortal foes,   the hare's
When, pop! she starts before their nose;
As eager runs the market-crowd,
When ' Catch the thief! ' resounds aloud:
So Maggie runs, the witches follow,
Wi' monie an eldritch skriech and hollo.   unearthly

Ah, Tam! Ah, Tam! thou'll get thy fairin!
In hell they'll roast thee like a herrin!
In vain thy Kate awaits thy comin!
Kate soon will be a woefu' woman!
Now, do thy speedy utmost, Meg,
And win the key-stane of the brig;
There, at them thou thy tail may toss,
A running stream they dare na cross!
But ere the key-stane she could make,
The fient a tail she had to shake;   devil
For Nannie, far before the rest,
Hard upon noble Maggie prest,
And flew at Tam wi' furious ettle;   aim

whole

seized

But little wist she Maggie's mettle!
Ae spring brought off her master hale,
But left behind her ain grey tail:
The carlin claucht her by the rump,
And left poor Maggie scarce a stump.

Now, wha this tale o' truth shall read,
Ilk man, and mother's son, take heed:
Whene'er to drink you are inclin'd,
Or cutty sarks run in your mind,
Think! ye may buy the joys o'er dear:
Remember Tam o' Shanter's meare.

ON SEEING A WOUNDED HARE LIMP BY ME WHICH A FELLOW HAD JUST SHOT AT

1

Inhuman man! curse on thy barb'rous art,
And blasted be thy murder-aiming eye;
May never pity soothe thee with a sigh,
Nor never pleasure glad thy cruel heart!

2

Go live, poor wanderer of the wood and field,
The bitter little that of life remains!
No more the thickening brakes and verdant plains
To thee shall home, or food, or pastime yield.

3

Seek, manglèd wretch, some place of wonted rest,
No more of rest, but now thy dying bed!
The sheltering rushes whistling o'er thy head,
The cold earth with thy bloody bosom prest.

4

Oft as by winding Nith I musing, wait
The sober eve, or hail the cheerful dawn,
I'll miss thee sporting o'er the dewy lawn,
And curse the ruffian's aim, and mourn thy hapless
fate.

ADDRESS TO THE SHADE OF THOMSON

ON CROWNING HIS BUST AT EDNAM, ROXBURGHSHIRE, WITH A WREATH OF BAYS

I

While virgin Spring by Eden's flood
   Unfolds her tender mantle green,
Or pranks the sod in frolic mood,
   Or tunes Eolian strains between:

2

While Summer, with a matron grace,
   Retreats to Dryburgh's cooling shade,
Yet oft, delighted, stops to trace
   The progress of the spikey blade:

3

While Autumn, benefactor kind,
   By Tweed erects his aged head,
And sees, with self-approving mind,
   Each creature on his bounty fed:

4

While maniac Winter rages o'er
   The hills whence classic Yarrow flows,
Rousing the turbid torrent's roar,
   Or sweeping, wild, a waste of snows:

5

So long, sweet Poet of the year!
   Shall bloom that wreath thou well has won;
While Scotia, with exulting tear,
   Proclaims that Thomson was her son.

ON THE LATE CAPTAIN GROSE'S PEREGRINATIONS THRO' SCOTLAND

COLLECTING THE ANTIQUITIES OF THAT KINGDOM

1

Hear, Land o' Cakes, and brither Scots
Frae Maidenkirk to Johnie Groat's,
If there's a hole in a' your coats,
　　　　　I rede you tent it:
A chield's amang you takin notes,
　　　　　And faith he'll prent it:

look to
fellow

2

If in your bounds ye chance to light
Upon a fine, fat, fodgel wight,
O' stature short but genius bright,
　　　　　That's he, mark weel:
And wow! he has an unco sleight
　　　　　O' cauk and keel.

dumpy

skill
In chalk and
ruddle

3

By some auld, houlet-haunted biggin,
Or kirk deserted by its riggin,
It's ten to ane ye'll find him snug in
　　　　　Some eldritch part,
Wi' deils, they say, Lord safe's! colleaguin
　　　　　At some black art.

owl-
dwelling
roof

fearsome

save us

4

Ilk ghaist that haunts auld ha' or chamer,
Ye gipsy-gang that deal in glamour,
And you, deep-read in hell's black grammar,
　　　　　Warlocks and witches:
Ye'll quake at his conjúring hammer,
　　　　　Ye midnight bitches!

Each;
chamber

5

It's tauld he was a sodger bred,
And ane wad rather fa'n than fled;[1]

would have

But now he's quat the spurtle-blade
            And dog-skin wallet,
And taen the—Antiquarian trade,
            I think they call it.

quitted; pot-stick (=sword)

6

He has a fouth o' auld nick-nackets:
Rusty airn caps and jinglin jackets
Wad haud the Lothians three in tackets
            A towmont guid;
And parritch-pats and auld saut-backets
            Before the Flood.

abundance
iron
shoenails
twelvemonth
porridge-pots; salt-boxes

7

Of Eve's first fire he has a cinder;
Auld Tubalcain's fire-shool and fender;
That which distinguishèd the gender
            O' Balaam's ass;
A broomstick o' the witch of Endor,
            Weel shod wi' brass.

8

Forbye, he'll shape you aff fu' gleg
The cut of Adam's philibeg;
The knife that nicket Abel's craig
            He'll prove you fully,
It was a faulding jocteleg,
            Or lang-kail gullie.

Besides; smartly
kilt
slit; throat

Jacques de Liège (=a clasp knife)

9

But wad ye see him in his glee—
For meikle glee and fun has he—
Then set him down, and twa or three
            Guid fellows wi' him;
And port, O port! shine thou a wee,
            And then ye'll see him!

much

10

Now, by the Pow'rs o' verse and prose!
Thou art a dainty chield, O Grose!—
Whae'er o' thee shall ill suppose,
            They sair misca' thee;
I'd take the rascal by the nose,
            Wad say, 'Shame fa' thee.'

befall

ON READING IN A NEWSPAPER THE DEATH OF JOHN M'LEOD, ESQ.

BROTHER TO A YOUNG LADY, A PARTICULAR
FRIEND OF THE AUTHOR'S

1

Sad thy tale, thou idle page,
    And rueful thy alarms:
Death tears the brother of her love
    From Isabella's arms.

2

Sweetly deckt with pearly dew
    The morning rose may blow;
But cold successive noontide blasts
    May lay its beauties low.

3

Fair on Isabella's morn
    The sun propitious smil'd;
But, long ere noon, succeeding clouds
    Succeeding hopes beguil'd.

4

Fate oft tears the bosom-chords
    That Nature finest strung:
So Isabella's heart was form'd,
    And so that heart was wrung.

5

Dread Omnipotence alone
    Can heal the wound he gave—
Can point the brimful, grief-worn eyes
    To scenes beyond the grave.

6

Virtue's blossoms there shall blow,
    And fear no withering blast;
There Isabella's spotless worth
    Shall happy be at last.

THE HUMBLE PETITION OF
BRUAR WATER

TO THE NOBLE DUKE OF ATHOLE

1

My lord, I know, your noble ear
   Woe ne'er assails in vain;
Embolden'd thus, I beg you'll hear
   Your humble slave complain,
How saucy Phœbus' scorching beams,
   In flaming summer-pride,
Dry-withering, waste my foamy streams,
   And drink my crystal tide.

2

The lightly-jumping, glowrin trouts,   staring
   That thro' my waters play,
If, in their random, wanton spouts,
   They near the margin stray;
If, hapless chance! they linger lang,
   I'm scorching up so shallow,
They're left the whitening stanes amang
   In gasping death to wallow.

3

Last day I grat wi' spite and teen,   wept;
   As Poet Burns came by,   vexation
That, to a Bard, I should be seen
   Wi' half my channel dry;
A panegyric rhyme, I ween,
   Ev'n as I was, he shor'd me;   offer'd
But had I in my glory been,
   He, kneeling, wad ador'd me.   would have

4

Here, foaming down the skelvy rocks,   shelvy
   In twisting strength I rin;
There high my boiling torrent smokes,
   Wild-roaring o'er a linn: fall
Enjoying large each spring and well,
   As Nature gave them me,

I am, altho' I say't mysel,
    Worth gaun a mile to see.

going (margin)

5

Would, then, my noble master please
    To grant my highest wishes,
He'll shade my banks wi' tow'ring trees
    And bonie spreading bushes.
Delighted doubly then, my lord,
    You'll wander on my banks,
And listen monie a grateful bird
    Return you tuneful thanks.

6

The sober laverock, warbling wild,
    Shall to the skies aspire;
The gowdspink, Music's gayest child,
    Shall sweetly join the choir;
The blackbird strong, the lintwhite clear,
    The mavis mild and mellow,
The robin, pensive Autumn cheer
    In all her locks of yellow.

lark (margin)
goldfinch (margin)
linnet (margin)

7

This, too, a covert shall ensure
    To shield them from the storm;
And coward maukin sleep secure,
    Low in her grassy form:
Here shall the shepherd make his seat
    To weave his crown of flow'rs;
Or find a shelt'ring, safe retreat
    From prone-descending show'rs.

hare (margin)

8

And here, by sweet, endearing stealth,
    Shall meet the loving pair,
Despising worlds with all their wealth,
    As empty idle care:
The flow'rs shall vie, in all their charms,
    The hour of heav'n to grace;
And birks extend their fragrant arms
    To screen the dear embrace.

birches (margin)

9

Here haply too, at vernal dawn,
  Some musing Bard may stray,
And eye the smoking, dewy lawn
  And misty mountain grey;
Or, by the reaper's nightly beam,
  Mild-chequering thro' the trees,
Rave to my darkly dashing stream,
  Hoarse-swelling on the breeze.

10

Let lofty firs and ashes cool
  My lowly banks o'erspread,
And view, deep-bending in the pool,
  Their shadows' wat'ry bed:
Let fragrant birks, in woodbines drest,
  My craggy cliffs adorn,
And, for the little songster's nest,
  The close embow'ring thorn!

11

So may, old Scotia's darling hope,
  Your little angel band
Spring, like their fathers, up to prop
  Their honour'd native land!
So may, thro' Albion's farthest ken,
  To social-flowing glasses,
The grace be: 'Athole's honest men
  And Athole's bonie lasses!'

ON SCARING SOME WATER-FOWL
IN LOCH TURIT

A WILD SCENE AMONG THE HILLS OF OUGHTERTYRE

Why, ye tenants of the lake,
For me your wat'ry haunt forsake?
Tell me, fellow creatures, why
At my presence thus you fly?
Why disturb your social joys,
Parent, filial, kindred ties?—

Common friend to you and me,
Nature's gifts to all are free:
Peaceful keep your dimpling wave,
Busy feed, or wanton lave;
Or, beneath the sheltering rock,
Bide the surging billow's shock.

Conscious, blushing for our race,
Soon, too soon, your fears I trace.
Man, your proud, usurping foe,
Would be lord of all below:
Plumes himself in freedom's pride,
Tyrant stern to all beside.

The eagle, from the cliffy brow
Marking you his prey below,
In his breast no pity dwells,
Strong necessity compels:
But Man, to whom alone is giv'n
A ray direct from pitying Heav'n,
Glories in his heart humane—
And creatures for his pleasure slain!

In these savage, liquid plains,
Only known to wand'ring swains,
Where the mossy riv'let strays
Far from human haunts and ways,
All on Nature you depend,
And life's poor season peaceful spend.

Or, if Man's superior might
Dare invade your native right,
On the lofty ether borne,
Man with all his powers you scorn;
Swiftly seek, on clanging wings,
Other lakes, and other springs;
And the foe you cannot brave,
Scorn at least to be his slave.

VERSES WRITTEN WITH A PENCIL

OVER THE CHIMNEY-PIECE, IN THE PARLOUR OF THE INN AT KENMORE, TAYMOUTH

Admiring Nature in her wildest grace,
These northern scenes with weary feet I trace;
O'er many a winding dale and painful steep,
Th' abodes of covey'd grouse and timid sheep,
My savage journey, curious, I pursue,
Till fam'd Breadalbane opens to my view.
The meeting cliffs each deep-sunk glen divides:
The woods, wild-scatter'd, clothe their ample sides;
Th' outstretching lake, imbosomed 'mong the hills,
The eye with wonder and amazement fills:
The Tay meand'ring sweet in infant pride,
The palace rising on his verdant side,
The lawns wood-fring'd in Nature's native taste,
The hillocks dropt in Nature's careless haste,
The arches striding o'er the new-born stream,
The village glittering in the noontide beam—

     ·   ·   ·   ·   ·

Poetic ardors in my bosom swell,
Lone wand'ring by the hermit's mossy cell;
The sweeping theatre of hanging woods,
Th' incessant roar of headlong tumbling floods—

     ·   ·   ·   ·   ·

Here Poesy might wake her heav'n-taught lyre,
And look through Nature with creative fire;
Here, to the wrongs of Fate half reconcil'd,
Misfortune's lighten'd steps might wander wild;
And Disappointment, in these lonely bounds,
Find balm to soothe her bitter rankling wounds;
Here heart-struck Grief might heav'nward stretch
    her scan,
And injur'd Worth forget and pardon man.

     ·   ·   ·   ·   ·

LINES ON THE FALL OF FYERS
NEAR LOCH NESS

WRITTEN WITH A PENCIL ON THE SPOT

Among the heathy hills and ragged woods
The roaring Fyers pours his mossy floods;
Till full he dashes on the rocky mounds,
Where, thro' a shapeless breach, his stream resounds.
As high in air the bursting torrents flow,
As deep recoiling surges foam below,
Prone down the rock the whitening sheet descends,
And viewless Echo's ear, astonish'd, rends.
Dim-seen through rising mists and ceaseless show'rs,
The hoary cavern, wide-surrounding, lours:
Still thro' the gap the struggling river toils,
And still, below, the horrid caldron boils—

*   *   *   *   *

ON THE BIRTH OF A POSTHUMOUS
CHILD

BORN IN PECULIAR CIRCUMSTANCES OF
FAMILY DISTRESS

I

much

Sweet flow'ret, pledge o' meikle love,
  And ward o' monie a prayer,
What heart o' stane wad thou na move,
  Sae helpless, sweet, and fair!

2

hobbles

November hirples o'er the lea,
  Chill, on thy lovely form;
And gane, alas! the shelt'ring tree,
  Should shield thee frae the storm.

3

May He who gives the rain to pour,
  And wings the blast to blaw,
Protect thee frae the driving show'r,
  The bitter frost and snaw!

4

May He, the friend of Woe and Want,
  Who heals life's various stounds,   shocks
Protect and guard the mother plant,
  And heal her cruel wounds!

5

But late she flourish'd, rooted fast,
  Fair on the summer morn,
Now feebly bends she in the blast,
  Unshelter'd and forlorn.

6

Blest be thy bloom, thou lovely gem,
  Unscath'd by ruffian hand!
And from thee many a parent stem
  Arise to deck our land!

THE TWA HERDS: OR, THE HOLY TULYIE   squabble

AN UNCO MOURNFU' TALE   mighty

Blockheads with reason wicked wits abhor,
But fool with fool is barbarous civil war.
                      POPE

1

O a' ye pious godly flocks,
Weel fed on pastures orthodox,
Wha now will keep you frae the fox
      Or worrying tykes?   dogs
                    tend;
Or wha will tent the waifs an' crocks stragglers
      About the dykes?   and old ewes
                    stone fences

2

The twa best herds in a' the wast,   west
That e'er gae gospel horn a blast   gave
These five an' twenty simmers past—
      O, dool to tell!—   sad
Hae had a bitter, black out-cast   quarrel
      Atween themsel.   Between

3

O Moodie, man, an' wordy Russell,
How could you raise so vile a bustle?
Ye'll see how New-Light herds will whistle,
                An' think it fine!
such a sprain The Lord's cause gat na sic a twistle
can
remember   Sin' I hae min'.

4

O Sirs! whae'er wad hae expeckit
would have Your duty ye wad sae negleckit?
so Ye wha were no by lairds respeckit
                To wear the plaid,
But by the brutes themselves eleckit
                To be their guide!

5

What flock wi' Moodie's flock could rank,
sound; leg Sae hale an' hearty every shank?
pond Nae poison'd, soor Arminian stank
                He let them taste;
But Calvin's fountainhead they drank—
                O, sic a feast!

6

polecat, The thummart, wilcat, brock, an' tod
wildcat, Weel kend his voice thro' a' the wood;
badger and He smell'd their ilka hole an' road,
fox   Baith out and in;
An' weel he lik'd to shed their bluid
                An' sell their skin.

7

What herd like Russell tell'd his tale?
His voice was heard thro' muir and dale;
every He kend the Lord's sheep, ilka tail,
                O'er a' the height;
if An' tell'd gin they were sick or hale
                At the first sight.

8

scabbed He fine a mangy sheep could scrub;
Or nobly swing the gospel club;

Or New-Light herds could nicely drub
    And pay their skin;
Or hing them o'er the burning dub   *puddle*
    Or heave them in.

9

Sic twa—O, do I live to see't?—
Sic famous twa sud disagree't,   *should have*
An' names like villain, hypocrite,
    Ilk ither gi'en,   *Each other*
While New-Light herds wi' laughin spite
    Say neither's liein!   *lying*

10

A' ye wha tent the gospel fauld,
Thee Duncan deep, an' Peebles shaul',   *shallow*
But chiefly great apostle Auld,
    We trust in thee,
That thou wilt work them hot an' cauld
    Till they agree!

11

Consider, sirs, how we're beset:
There's scarce a new herd that we get
But comes frae 'mang that cursed set
    I winna name: *will not*
I hope frae heav'n to see them yet
    In fiery flame!

12

Dalrymple has been lang our fae,
M'Gill has wrought us meikle wae,   *much*
An' that curs'd rascal ca'd M'Quhae,
    An' baith the Shaws,
That aft hae made us black an' blae   *blue*
    Wi' vengefu' paws.

13

Auld Wodrow lang has hatch'd mischief:
We thought ay death wad bring relief,
But he has gotten to our grief
    Ane to succeed him,
A chield wha'll soundly buff our beef—   *fellow; bang*
    I meikle dread him.

14

more

Besides

An' monie mae that I could tell,
Wha fain would openly rebel,
Forby turn-coats amang oursel:
        There's Smith for ane—
I doubt he's but a greyneck still,
        An' that ye'll fin'!

15

bogs; hill-
sides

daunt

O a' ye flocks o'er a' the hills,
By mosses, meadows, moors, an' fells,
Come, join your counsel and your skills
        To cowe the lairds,
An' get the brutes the power themsels
        To chuse their herds!

16

halter

formidable

Then Orthodoxy yet may prance,
An' Learning in a woody dance,
An' that fell cur ca'd Common-sense,
        That bites sae sair,
Be banish'd o'er the sea to France—
        Let him bark there!

17

Then Shaw's an' D'rymple's eloquence,
M'Gill's close, nervous excellence,
M'Quhae's pathetic, manly sense,
        An' guid M'Math
Wha thro' the heart can brawly glance,
        May a' pack aff!

HOLY WILLIE'S PRAYER

And send the godly in a pet to pray.
POPE

1

O Thou that in the Heavens does dwell,
Wha, as it pleases best Thysel,
Sends ane to Heaven an' ten to Hell
        A' for Thy glory,
And no for onie guid or ill
        They've done before Thee!

2

I bless and praise Thy matchless might,
When thousands Thou hast left in night,
That I am here before Thy sight,
   For gifts an' grace
A burning and a shining light
   To a' this place.

3

What was I, or my generation,
That I should get sic exaltation?   such
I, wha deserv'd most just damnation
   For broken laws
Sax thousand years ere my creation,   Six
   Thro' Adam's cause!

4

When from my mither's womb I fell,
Thou might hae plung'd me deep in hell
To gnash my gooms, and weep, and wail gums
   In burning lakes,
Whare damnèd devils roar and yell,
   Chain'd to their stakes.

5

Yet I am here, a chosen sample,
To show Thy grace is great and ample:
I'm here a pillar o' Thy temple,
   Strong as a rock,
A guide, a buckler, and example
   To a' Thy flock!

6

But yet, O Lord! confess I must:
At times I'm fash'd wi' fleshly lust; irked
An' sometimes, too, in warldly trust,
   Vile self gets in;
But Thou remembers we are dust,
   Defiled wi' sin.

7

O Lord! yestreen, Thou kens, wi' Meg— last night;
             knowest
Thy pardon I sincerely beg—

O, may't ne'er be a living plague
                To my dishonour!
An' I'll ne'er lift a lawless leg
                Again upon her.

8

must   Besides, I farther maun avow—
Wi' Leezie's lass, three times, I trow—
drunk   But, Lord, that Friday I was fou,
                When I cam near her,
Or else, Thou kens, Thy servant true
would;   Wad never steer her.
meddle with

9

Maybe Thou lets this fleshly thorn
Buffet Thy servant e'en and morn,
too   Lest he owre proud and high should turn
                That he's sae gifted:
If sae, Thy han' maun e'en be borne
                Until Thou lift it.

10

Lord, bless Thy chosen in this place,
For here Thou has a chosen race!
But God confound their stubborn face
                An' blast their name,
Wha bring Thy elders to disgrace
                An' open shame!

11

Lord, mind Gau'n Hamilton's deserts!
cards   He drinks, an' swears, an' plays at cartes,
Yet has sae monie takin arts
                Wi' great and sma',
Frae God's ain Priest the people's hearts
                He steals awa.

12

And when we chasten'd him therefore,
row   Thou kens how he bred sic a splore,
And set the warld in a roar
                O' laughin at us:
Curse Thou his basket and his store,
                Kail an' potatoes!

13

Lord, hear my earnest cry and pray'r
Against that Presbyt'ry of Ayr!
Thy strong right hand, Lord, mak it bare
      Upo' their heads!
Lord, visit them, an' dinna spare,   do not
        For their misdeeds!

14

O Lord, my God! that glib-tongu'd Aiken,
My vera heart and flesh are quakin
To think how we stood sweatin, shakin,
      An' pish'd wi' dread,
While he, wi' hingin lip an' snakin,   sneering
      Held up his head.

15

Lord, in Thy day o' vengeance try him!
Lord, visit him wha did employ him!
And pass not in Thy mercy by them,
      Nor hear their pray'r,
But for Thy people's sake destroy them,
      An' dinna spare!

16

But, Lord, remember me and mine
Wi' mercies temporal and divine,
That I for grace an' gear may shine   wealth
      Excell'd by nane;
And a' the glory shall be Thine—
      Amen, Amen!

WELCOME TO A BASTART WEAN

1

Thou's welcome, wean! Mishanter fa' me,   little one;
If thoughts o' thee or yet thy mammie   Mishap be-
Shall ever daunton me or awe me,   fall
      My sweet, wee lady,
Or if I blush when thou shalt ca' me
      Tyta or daddie!

2

What tho' they ca' me fornicator,
country
gossip
An' tease my name in kintra clatter?
The mair they talk, I'm kend the better;
tattle
        E'en let them clash!
feeble
give one
annoyance
An auld wife's tongue's a feckless matter
        To gie ane fash.

3

Welcome, my bonie, sweet, wee dochter!
Tho' ye come here a wee unsought for,
And tho' your comin I hae fought for
        Baith kirk and queir;
Yet, by my faith, ye're no unwrought for—
        That I shall swear!

4

Sweet fruit o' monie a merry dint,
not all lost
My funny toil is no a' tint:
askew
Tho' thou cam to the warl' asklent,
        Which fools may scoff at,
coin
In my last plack thy part's be in't
        The better half o't.

5

worse
provided
finely;
comfortably
Tho' I should be the waur bestead,
Thou's be as braw and bienly clad,
And thy young years as nicely bred
        Wi' education,
As onie brat o' wedlock's bed
        In a' thy station.

6

Wee image o' my bonie Betty,
pet
As fatherly I kiss and daut thee,
As dear and near my heart I set thee,
        Wi' as guid will,
As a' the priests had seen me get thee
        That's out o' Hell.

7

God
Gude grant that thou may ay inherit
Thy mither's looks an' gracefu' merit,

An' thy poor, worthless daddie's spirit
        Without his failins!
'Twill please me mair to see thee heir it
        Than stocket mailins.   *farms*

8

And if thou be what I wad hae thee,
An' tak the counsel I shall gie thee,
I'll never rue my trouble wi' thee—
        The cost nor shame o't—
But be a loving father to thee,
        And brag the name o't.

THE INVENTORY

IN ANSWER TO A MANDATE BY THE SURVEYOR
OF TAXES

Sir, as your mandate did request,
I send you here a faithfu' list
O' guids an' gear an' a' my graith,   *chattels*
To which I'm clear to gie my aith.

Imprimis, then, for carriage cattle:—
I hae four brutes o' gallant mettle
As ever drew before a pettle: *plough-staff*
My lan'-afore's a guid auld ' has been,'
An' wight an' wilfu' a' his days been.   *strong*
My lan'-ahin's a weel-gaun fillie,   *well-going*
That aft has borne me hame frae Killie,   *Kilmarnock*
An' your auld borough monie a time   *Ayr*
In days when riding was nae crime.
(But ance, when in my wooing pride
I, like a blockhead, boost to ride,   *must needs*
The wilfu' creature sae I pat to—   *distress'd*
Lord, pardon a' my sins, an' that too!—
I play'd my fillie sic a shavie,   *ill turn*
She's a' bedevil'd wi' the spavie.)   *spavin*
My fur-ahin's a wordy beast   *worthy*
As e'er in tug or tow was traced.
The fourth's a Highland Donald hastie,   *stark-mad;*
A damn'd red-wud Kilburnie blastie!   *Kilbirnie*

Besides;
colt; pick

Foreby, a cowte, o' cowtes the wale,
As ever ran afore a tail:
If he be spar'd to be a beast,

fetch; £ stg.

He'll draw me fifteen pund at least.

Wheel-carriages I hae but few:

partly

Three carts, an' twa are feckly new;
An auld wheelbarrow—mair for token,

One; shafts

Ae leg an' baith the trams are broken:

axle

I made a poker o' the spin'le,

wheel

An' my auld mither brunt the trin'le.

For men, I've three mischievous boys,

Stark-devils;
fighting

Run-deils for fechtin an' for noise:
A gaudsman ane, a thrasher t' other,

David;
cattle;
fodder

Wee Davoc hauds the nowte in fother.

make them
work their
hardest

I rule them, as I ought, discreetly,
An' aften labour them completely;
An' ay on Sundays duly, nightly,
I on the *Questions* tairge them tightly:

sharp

Till, faith! wee Davoc's grown sae gleg,
Tho' scarcely langer than your leg,

rattle;

He'll screed you aff ' Effectual Calling '
As fast as onie in the dwalling.

I've nane in female servan' station
(Lord keep me ay frae a' temptation!):
I hae nae wife—and that my bliss is—

mistresses

An' ye hae laid nae tax on misses;
An' then, if kirk folks dinna clutch me,
I ken the deevils darena touch me.

brats

Wi' weans I'm mair than weel contented:
Heav'n sent me ane mair than I wanted!

good-natured

My sonsie, smirking, dear-bought Bess,
She stares the daddie in her face,
Enough of ought ye like but grace:
But her, my bonie, sweet wee lady,
I've paid enough for her already;

if
ye'll
altogether

An' gin ye tax her or her mither,
By the Lord, ye'se get them a' thegither!

But pray, remember, Mr. Aiken,
Nae kind of licence out I'm takin:

Frae this time forth, I do declare
I'se ne'er ride horse nor hizzie mair;   wench
Thro' dirt and dub for life I'll paidle,   mire and
Ere I sae dear pay for a saddle;   slush; wade
I've sturdy stumps, the Lord be thankit,
And a' my gates on foot I'll shank it.   ways
The Kirk and you may tak' you that,
It puts but little in your pat: pot
Sae dinna put me in your beuk,   do not
Nor for my ten white shillings leuk.

This list, wi' my ain hand I've wrote it,
The day and date as under notit;
Then know all ye whom it concerns,
Subscripsi huic,   ROBERT BURNS.

A MAUCHLINE WEDDING

1

When Eighty-five was seven months auld
  And wearing thro' the aught,   eight
When rolling rains and Boreas bauld
  Gied farmer-folks a faught;   Gave; fight
Ae morning quondam Mason W . . .,
  Now Merchant Master Miller,
Gaed down to meet wi' Nansie B . . .,   Went
  And her Jamaica siller   money
          To wed, that day.

2

The rising sun o'er Blacksideen
  Was just appearing fairly,
When Nell and Bess got up to dress
  Seven lang half-hours o'er early!   too
Now presses clink, and drawers jink,
  For linens and for laces:
But modest Muses only *think*
  What ladies' underdress is
          On sic a day!   such

3

But we'll suppose the stays are lac'd,
    covered — And bonie bosoms steekit,
Tho' thro' the lawn—but guess the rest!
    spy — An angel scarce durst keek it.
Then stockins fine o' silken twine
    prudent — Wi' cannie care are drawn up;
    gartered — An' garten'd tight whare mortal wight—

· · · · · · · ·

· · · · · · · ·

4

But now the gown wi' rustling sound
    Its silken pomp displays;
Sure there's nae sin in being vain
    such very — O' siccan bonie claes!
Sae jimp the waist, the tail sae vast—
    maidens — Trouth, they were bonie birdies!
O Mither Eve, ye wad been grieve
    posteriors — To see their ample hurdies
                Sae large that day!

5

    with his; — Then Sandy, wi's red jacket braw,
    Comes whip-jee-woa! about,
And in he gets the bonie twa—
    Lord, send them safely out!
And auld John Trot wi' sober phiz,
    broad;
    fine as — As braid and braw's a Bailie,
His shouthers and his Sunday's jiz
    wig
    oil — Wi' powther and wi' ulzie
                Weel smear'd that day. . .

ADAM ARMOUR'S PRAYER

I

    God — Gude pity me, because I'm little!
For though I am an elf o' mettle,
    weaver's — And can like onie wabster's shuttle
    Dodge
    cabbage-
    knife — Jink there or here,
    uncommon — Yet, scarce as lang's a guid kail-whittle,
    funny — I'm unco queer.

2

An' now Thou kens our woefu' case: knows
For Geordie's jurr we're in disgrace,   maid
Because we stang'd her through the place,
          An' hurt her spleuchan;
For whilk we daurna show our face   dare not
            Within the clachan.   hamlet

3

An' now we're dern'd in dens and hollows,   hid; glens
And hunted, as was William Wallace,
Wi' constables—thae blackguard fallows—   those
          An' sodgers baith;
But Gude preserve us frae the gallows,
            That shamefu' death!

4

Auld, grim, black-bearded Geordie's sel'—
O, shake him owre the mouth o' Hell!
There let him hing, an' roar, an' yell
          Wi' hideous din,
And if he offers to rebel,
            Then heave him in!

5

When Death comes in wi' glimmerin blink,   glance
An' tips auld drucken Nanse the wink,
May Sautan gie her doup a clink   backside
          Within his yett,   gate
An' fill her up wi' brimstone drink
           Red-reekin het.   hot

6

Though Jock an' hav'rel Jean are merry,
Some devil seize them in a hurry,
An' waft them in th' infernal wherry
          Straught through the lake,
An' gie their hides a noble curry
           Wi' oil of aik!   oak

7

As for the jurr—puir worthless body!—   creature
She's got mischief enough already;

sorely

wriggle in a
rope

Wi' stanget hips and buttocks bluidy
                    She's suffer'd sair;
But may she wintle in a woody
                    If she whore mair!

EPITHALAMIUM

1

O a' ye hymeneal powers
That rule the essence-mixing hours!
Whether in eastern monarch's bow'rs
                    Or Greenland caves,
A nuptial scene in Machlin tow'rs
                    Your presence craves.

2

Threescore-fyfteen, a blooming bride,
This night with seventy-four is ty'd;
O mak the bed baith saft an' wide
                    Wi' canie toil,
An' lay them gently side by side,
                    At least a while.

NATURE'S LAW

HUMBLY INSCRIBED TO GAVIN HAMILTON, ESQUIRE

Great Nature spoke, observant man obeyed.
                                        POPE

1

Let other heroes boast their scars,
    The marks o' sturt and strife,

struggle

But other poets sing of wars,
    The plagues o' human life!

befall

Shame fa' the fun: wi' sword and gun
    To slap mankind like lumber!
I sing his name and nobler fame
    Wha multiplies our number.

2

Great Nature spoke, with air benign:—
  ' Go on, ye human race;
This lower world I you resign;
  Be fruitful and increase.
The liquid fire of strong desire,
  I've poured it in each bosom;
Here on this hand does Mankind stand,
  And there, is Beauty's blossom! '

3

The Hero of these artless strains,
  A lowly Bard was he,
Who sung his rhymes in Coila's plains
  With meikle mirth and glee: *much*
Kind Nature's care had given his share
  Large of the flaming current;
And, all devout, he never sought
  To stem the sacred torrent.

4

He felt the powerful, high behest
  Thrill vital thro' and thro';
And sought a correspondent breast
  To give obedience due.
Propitious Powers screen'd the young flow'rs
  From mildews of abortion;
And lo! the Bard—a great reward—
  Has got a double portion!

5

Auld cantie Coil may count the day,   *jolly*
  As annual it returns,
The third of Libra's equal sway,   *September's*
  That gave another Burns,
With future rhymes an' other times
  To emulate his sire,
To sing auld Coil in nobler style
  With more poetic fire!

6

Ye Powers of peace and peaceful song,
  Look down with gracious eyes,

And bless auld Coila large and long
    With multiplying joys!
Lang may she stand to prop the land,
    The flow'r of ancient nations,
And Burnses spring her fame to sing
    To endless generations!

LINES ON MEETING WITH LORD DAER

1

know

This wot ye all whom it concerns:
I, Rhymer Rab, *alias* Burns,
                October twenty-third,
A ne'er-to-be-forgotten day,

clambered
hill

Sae far I sprachl'd up the brae
                I dinner'd wi' a Lord.

2

Lawyers'

-drunk

I've been at drucken Writers' feasts,
Nay, been bitch-fou 'mang godly Priests—
        Wi' rev'rence be it spoken!—
I've even join'd the honor'd jorum,
When mighty Squireships o' the Quorum

slake

                Their hydra drouth did sloken.

3

But wi' a Lord!—stand out my shin!
A Lord, a Peer, an Earl's son!—
            Up higher yet, my bonnet!

such

An' sic a Lord!—lang Scotch ell twa
Our Peerage he looks o'er them a',
            As I look o'er my sonnet.

4

disordered
gaze
looking
dazedly as;
an ox's bridle

But O, for Hogarth's magic pow'r
To show Sir Bardie's willyart glow'r,
            An' how he star'd an' stammer'd,
When, goavin's he'd been led wi' branks,
An' stumpin on his ploughman shanks,
            He in the parlour hammer'd!

5

To meet good Stewart little pain is,
Or Scotia's sacred Demosthénes:
        Thinks I: ' They are but men'!
But 'Burns'!—' My Lord'!—Good God! I doited,   doddered
My knees on ane anither knoited   knocked
        As faultering I gaed ben.   went to the parlour

6

I sidling shelter'd in a neuk,   corner
An' at his Lordship staw a leuk,   stole
        Like some portentous omen:
Except good sense and social glee
An' (what surpris'd me) modesty,
        I markèd nought uncommon.

7

I watch'd the symptoms o' the Great—
The gentle pride, the lordly state,
        The arrogant assuming:
The fient a pride, nae pride had he,   fiend
Nor sauce, nor state, that I could see,
        Mair than an honest ploughman!

8

Then from his Lordship I shall learn
Henceforth to meet with unconcern
        One rank as well's another;
Nae honest, worthy man need care   be perturbed
To meet with noble youthfu' Daer,
        For he but meets a brother.

ADDRESS TO THE TOOTHACHE

I

My curse upon your venom'd stang,   sting
That shoots my tortur'd gooms alang,   gums
An' thro' my lug gies monie a twang   ear
        Wi' gnawing vengeance,
Tearing my nerves wi' bitter pang,
        Like racking engines!

2

cackle
jump
heckling-
comb
backside

A' down my beard the slavers trickle,
I throw the wee stools o'er the mickle,
While round the fire the giglets keckle
    To see me loup,
An', raving mad. I wish a heckle
    Were i' their doup!

3

When fevers burn, or ague freezes,
Rheumatics gnaw, or colic squeezes,
Our neebors sympathise to ease us
    Wi' pitying moan;
But thee!—thou hell o' a' diseases,
    They mock our groan!

4

woes
Bad har-
vests; mad;
crumbling
earth

annoyance
tak'st the
prize

Of a' the num'rous human dools—
Ill-hairsts, daft bargains, cutty-stools,
Or worthy frien's laid i' the mools,
    Sad sight to see!
The tricks o' knaves, or fash o' fools—
    Thou bear'st the gree!

5

Whare'er that place be priests ca' Hell,
Whare a' the tones o' misery yell,
An' rankèd plagues their numbers tell
    In dreadfu' raw,
Thou, Toothache, surely bear'st the bell
    Amang them a'!

6

chap
makes

Give
twelve-
month's

O thou grim, mischief-making chiel,
That gars the notes o' discord squeel,
Till humankind aft dance a reel
    In gore a shoe-thick,
Gie a' the faes o' Scotland's weal
    A towmond's toothache.

LAMENT FOR THE ABSENCE OF WILLIAM CREECH, PUBLISHER

1

Auld chuckie Reekie's sair distrest,   *mother-hen*
Down droops her ance weel burnish'd crest,
Nae joy her bonie buskit nest   *trimmed*
       Can yield ava: *at all*
Her darling bird that she lo'es best,
          Willie's awa.

2

O, Willie was a witty wight,   *in: uncom-*
And had o' things an unco sleight!   *mon skill*
Auld Reekie ay he keepit tight   *in order*
       And trig an' braw;   *trim;*
But now they'll busk her like a fright—   *handsome*
          Willie's awa!   *garb*

3

The stiffest o' them a' he bow'd;
The bauldest o' them a' he cow'd;   *daunted*
They durst nae mair than he allow'd—
       That was a law:
We've lost a birkie weel worth gowd—   *blade; gold*
          Willie's awa!

4

Now gawkies, tawpies, gowks, and fools
Frae colleges and boarding schools
May sprout like simmer puddock-stools   *mushrooms*
       In glen or shaw: *wood*
He wha could brush them down to mools,   *dust*
          Willie's awa!

5

The brethren o' the Commerce-Chaumer
May mourn their loss wi' doolfu' clamour: *woeful*
He was a dictionar and grammar
       Amang them a'.
I fear they'll now mak monie a stammer:
          Willie's awa!

6

Nae mair we see his levee door
Philosophers and Poets pour,
And toothy Critics by the score
              In bloody raw:
The adjutant of a' the core,
                        Willie's awa!

7

Now worthy Greg'ry's Latin face,
Tytler's and Greenfield's modest grace,
M'Kenzie, Stewart, such a brace
              As Rome ne'er saw,

must

They a' maun meet some ither place—
                        Willie's awa!

8

Poor Burns ev'n ' Scotch Drink ' canna quicken:

cries

He cheeps like some bewilder'd chicken

mother;
brood

Scar'd frae its minnie and the cleckin

carrion-crow

              By hoodie-craw.
Grief's gien his heart an unco kickin—
                        Willie's awa!

9

ill-tongued,
snarling
railer
kill
Each;
scullion

Now ev'ry sour-mou'd, girnin blellum,
And Calvin's folk, are fit to fell him;
Ilk self-conceited critic-skellum
              His quill may draw:

finely repel
assault

He wha could brawlie ward their bellum,
                        Willie's awa!

10

meandering

Up wimpling, stately Tweed I've sped,
And Eden scenes on crystal Jed,
And Ettrick banks, now roaring red
              While tempests blaw;
But every joy and pleasure's fled:
                        Willie's awa!

11

May I be Slander's common speech,
A text for Infamy to preach,

And, lastly, streekit out to bleach   stretched
        In winter snaw,
When I forget thee, Willie Creech,
          Tho' far awa!

12

May never wicked Fortune touzle him,
May never wicked men bamboozle him,
Until a pow as auld's Methusalem   poll; old as
        He canty claw!   cheerfully
Then to the blessed new Jerusalem   scratch
        Fleet-wing awa!

VERSES IN FRIARS CARSE HERMITAGE

Thou whom chance may hither lead,
Be thou clad in russet weed,
Be thou deckt in silken stole,
Grave these maxims on thy soul:—

Life is but a day at most,
Sprung from night in darkness lost;
Hope not sunshine every hour,
Fear not clouds will always lour.
Happiness is but a name,
Make content and ease thy aim.
Ambition is a meteor-gleam;
Fame a restless airy dream;
Pleasures, insects on the wing
Round Peace, th' tend'rest flow'r of spring;
Those that sip the dew alone—
Make the butterflies thy own;
Those that would the bloom devour—
Crush the locusts, save the flower.
For the future be prepar'd:
Guard wherever thou can'st guard;
But, thy utmost duly done,
Welcome what thou can'st not shun.
Follies past give thou to air—
Make their consequence thy care.
Keep the name of Man in mind,
And dishonour not thy kind.

Reverence with lowly heart
Him, whose wondrous work thou art;
Keep His Goodness still in view—
Thy trust, and thy example too.

Stranger, go! Heaven be thy guide!
Nithside   Quod the Beadsman on Nidside.

ELEGY ON THE DEPARTED YEAR
1788

do not   For lords or kings I dinna mourn;
                 E'en let them die—for that they're born;
                 But O, prodigious to reflect,
Twelve-   A Towmont, sirs, is gane to wreck!
month   O Eighty-Eight, in thy sma' space
                 What dire events hae taken place!
                 Of what enjoyments thou hast reft us!
                 In what a pickle thou hast left us!

lost   The Spanish empire's tint a head,
dog   An' my auld teethless Bawtie's dead;
conflict;   The tulyie's teugh 'tween Pitt and Fox,
tough   An' our guidwife's wee birdie cocks:
one   The tane is game, a bluidie devil,
mighty   But to the hen-birds unco civil;
stubborn;   The tither's dour—has nae sic breedin,
manners
scratched;   But better stuff ne'er claw'd a midden.
dunghill

parsons;   Ye ministers, come mount the poupit,
pulpit   An' cry till ye be haerse an' roupet,
hoarse   For Eighty-Eight, he wished you weel,
gave;   An' gied ye a' baith gear an' meal:
money;   E'en monie a plack and monie a peck,
coin   Ye ken yoursels, for little feck!
return

wipe; eyes   Ye bonie lasses, dight your een,
                 For some o' you hae tint a frien':
                 In Eighty-Eight, ye ken, was taen
                 What ye'll ne'er hae to gie again.

cattle   Observe the vera nowte an' sheep,
dull;   How dowff an' dowilie they creep!
droopingly

Nay, even the yirth itsel does cry,   ground
For Embro' wells are grutten dry!   wept

  O Eighty-Nine, thou's but a bairn,   child
An' no owre auld, I hope, to learn!   too
Thou beardless boy, I pray tak care,
Thou now has got thy Daddie's chair:

Nae hand-cuff'd, mizzl'd, half-shackl'd Regent,   muzzled
But, like himsel, a full free agent,
Be sure ye follow out the plan
Nae waur than he did, honest man!   worse
As muckle better as ye can.   much

   January 1, 1789.

CASTLE GORDON

1

Streams that glide in Orient plains,
Never bound by Winter's chains;
  Glowing here on golden sands,
There immixed with foulest stains
  From tyranny's empurpled hands;
These, their richly gleaming waves,
I leave to tyrants and their slaves:
Give me the stream that sweetly laves
  The banks by Castle Gordon.

2

Spicy forests ever gay,
Shading from the burning ray
  Hapless wretches sold to toil;
Or, the ruthless native's way,
  Bent on slaughter, blood and spoil;
Woods that ever verdant wave,
I leave the tyrant and the slave:
Give me the groves that lofty brave
  The storms of Castle Gordon.

3

Wildly here without control
Nature reigns, and rules the whole;

In that sober pensive mood,
Dearest to the feeling soul,
    She plants the forest, pours the flood.
Life's poor day I'll, musing, rave,
And find at night a sheltering cave,
Where waters flow and wild woods wave
    By bonie Castle Gordon.

NEW YEAR'S DAY

1791

TO MRS. DUNLOP

This day Time winds th' exhausted chain,
To run the twelvemonth's length again:
I see the old, bald-pated fellow,
With ardent eyes, complexion sallow,
Adjust the unimpair'd machine
To wheel the equal, dull routine.

The absent lover, minor heir,
In vain assail him with their prayer:
Deaf as my friend, he sees them press,
Nor makes the hour one moment less.
Will you (the Major's with the hounds;
The happy tenants share his rounds;
Coila's fair Rachel's care to-day,
And blooming Keith's engaged with Gray)
From housewife cares a minute borrow
(That grandchild's cap will do to-morrow),
And join with me a-moralizing?
This day's propitious to be wise in!

First, what did yesternight deliver?
'Another year has gone for ever.'
And what is this day's strong suggestion?
'The passing moment's all we rest on!'
Rest on—for what? what do we here?
Or why regard the passing year?
Will Time, amus'd with proverb'd lore,
Add to our date one minute more?
A few days may—a few years must—
Repose us in the silent dust:

Then, is it wise to damp our bliss?
Yes: all such reasonings are amiss!
The voice of Nature loudly cries,
And many a message from the skies,
That something in us never dies;
That on this frail, uncertain state
Hang matters of eternal weight;
That future life in worlds unknown
Must take its hue from this alone,
Whether as heavenly glory bright
Or dark as Misery's woeful night.

Since, then, my honor'd first of friends,
On this poor being all depends,
Let us th' important Now employ,
And live as those who never die.
Tho' you, with days and honours crown'd,
Witness that filial circle round
(A sight life's sorrows to repulse,
A sight pale Envy to convulse),
Others now claim your chief regard:
Yourself, you wait your bright reward.

FROM ESOPUS TO MARIA

From those drear solitudes and frowsy cells,
Where Infamy with sad Repentance dwells;
Where turnkeys make the jealous portal fast,
And deal from iron hands the spare repast;
Where truant 'prentices, yet young in sin,
Blush at the curious stranger peeping in;
Where strumpets, relics of the drunken roar,
Resolve to drink, nay half—to whore—no more;
Where tiny thieves, not destin'd yet to swing,
Beat hemp for others riper for the string:
From these dire scenes my wretched lines I date,
To tell Maria her Esopus' fate.

'Alas! I feel I am no actor here!'
'Tis real hangmen real scourges bear!
Prepare, Maria, for a horrid tale
Will turn thy very rouge to deadly pale;

Will make thy hair, tho' erst from gipsy poll'd,
By barber woven and by barber sold,
Though twisted smooth with Harry's nicest care,
Like hoary bristles to erect and stare!
The hero of the mimic scene, no more
I start in Hamlet, in Othello roar;
Or, haughty Chieftain, 'mid the din of arms,
In Highland bonnet woo Malvina's charms:
While sans-culottes stoop up the mountain high,
And steal me from Maria's prying eye.
Blest Highland bonnet! once my proudest dress,
Now, prouder still, Maria's temples press!
I see her wave thy towering plumes afar,
And call each coxcomb to the wordy war!
I see her face the first of Ireland's sons,
And even out-Irish his Hibernian bronze!
The crafty Colonel leaves the tartan'd lines
For other wars, where he a hero shines;
The hopeful youth, in Scottish senate bred,
Who owns a Bushby's heart without the head,
Comes 'mid a string of coxcombs to display
That *Veni, vidi, vici,* is his way;
The shrinking Bard adown the alley skulks,
And dreads a meeting worse than Woolwich hulks,
Though there his heresies in Church and State
Might well award him Muir and Palmer's fate:
Still she, undaunted, reels and rattles on,
And dares the public like a noontide sun.
What scandal called Maria's jaunty stagger
The ricket reeling of a crooked swagger?
What slander nam'd her seeming want of art
The flimsy wrapper of a rotten heart—
Whose spleen (e'en worse than Burns's venom, when
He dips in gall unmix'd his eager pen,
And pours his vengeance in the burning line),
Who christen'd thus Maria's lyre-divine,
The idiot strum of Vanity bemus'd,
And even th' abuse of Poesy abus'd?
Who called her verse a Parish Workhouse, made
For motley foundling Fancies, stolen or strayed?

A Workhouse! Ah, that sound awakes my woes,
And pillows on the thorn my rack'd repose!

In durance vile here must I wake and weep,
And all my frowsy couch in sorrow steep:
That straw where many a rogue has lain of yore,
And vermin'd gipsies litter'd heretofore.

Why, Lonsdale, thus thy wrath on vagrants pour?
Must earth no rascal save thyself endure?
Must thou alone in guilt immortal swell,
And make a vast monopoly of Hell?
Thou know'st the Virtues cannot hate thee worse:
The Vices also, must they club their curse?
Or must no tiny sin to others fall,
Because thy guilt's supreme enough for all?

Maria, send me too thy griefs and cares,
In all of thee sure thy Esopus shares:
As thou at all mankind the flag unfurls,
Who on my fair one Satire's vengeance hurls!
Who calls thee, pert, affected, vain coquette,
A wit in folly, and a fool in wit!
Who says that fool alone is not thy due,
And quotes thy treacheries to prove it true!

Our force united on thy foes we'll turn,
And dare the war with all of woman born:
For who can write and speak as thou and I?
My periods that decyphering defy,
And thy still matchless tongue that conquers all reply!

THE HUE AND CRY OF JOHN LEWARS, A POOR MAN RUINED AND UNDONE BY ROBBERY AND MURDER

BEING AN AWEFUL WARNING TO THE YOUNG MEN OF THIS AGE, HOW THEY LOOK WELL TO THEMSELVES IN THIS DANGEROUS, TERRIBLE WORLD

I

A Thief and a Murderer! stop her who can!
  Look well to your lives and your goods!
Good people, ye know not the hazard you run,
  'Tis the far-famed and much-noted Woods.

2

While I looked at her eye, for the devil is in it,
    In a trice she whipt off my poor heart:
Her brow, cheek and lip—in another sad minute
    My peace felt her murderous dart.

3

Her features I'll tell you them over—but hold!
    She deals with your wizards and books;
And to peep in her face, if but once you're so bold,
    There's witchery kills in her looks.

4

But softly—I have it—her haunts are well known,—
    At midnight so slily I'll watch her;
And sleeping, undrest, in the dark, all alone—
    Good lord! the dear Thief how I'll catch her!

TO JOHN RANKINE

IN REPLY TO AN ANNOUNCEMENT

1

I am a keeper of the law
In some sma' points, altho' not a';
Some people tell me, gin I fa'
            Ae way or ither,
The breaking of ae point, tho sma',
            Breaks a' thegither.

if; fall
one; other

the whole

2

I hae been in for't ance or twice,
And winna say o'er far for thrice,
Yet never met wi' that surprise
            That broke my rest.
But now a rumour's like to rise—
            A whaup's i' the nest!

will not;
too surely

curlew

TO JOHN GOLDIE

AUGUST, 1785

1

O Goudie, terror o' the Whigs,
Dread o' black coats and rev'rend wigs!
Sour Bigotry on her last legs
    Girns and looks back, *snarls*
Wishing the ten Egyptian plagues
    May seize you quick.

2

Poor gapin, glowrin Superstition! *staring*
Wae's me, she's in a sad condition!
Fye! bring Black Jock, her state physician,
    To see her water!
Alas! there's ground for great suspicion
    She'll ne'er get better.

3

Enthusiasm's past redemption
Gane in a gallopin consumption:
Not a' her quacks wi' a' their gumption
    Can ever mend her;
Her feeble pulse gies strong presumption
    She'll soon surrender.

4

Auld Orthodoxy lang did grapple
For every hole to get a stapple; *stopper*
But now she fetches at the thrapple, *gurgles;*
    An' fights for breath: *windpipe*
Haste, gie her name up in the chapel,
    Near unto death!

5

'Tis you an' Taylor are the chief
To blame for a' this black mischief;
But, gin the Lord's ain folk gat leave, *if*
    A toom tar barrel *empty*
An' twa red peats wad bring relief,
    And end the quarrel.

6

For me, my skill's but very sma',
An' skill in prose I've nane ava';
But, quietlenswise between us twa,
    Weel may ye speed!
And, tho' they sud you sair misca',
    Ne'er fash your head!

at all
in confidence
should
bother

7

E'en swinge the dogs, and thresh them sicker!
The mair they squeel ay chap the thicker,
And still 'mang hands a hearty bicker
    O' something stout!
It gars an owthor's pulse beat quicker,
    An' helps his wit.

sorely
strike
between whiles; glass
makes; author's

8

There's naething like the honest nappy:
Whare'll ye e'er see men sae happy,
Or women sonsie, saft, and sappy
    'Tween morn and morn,
As them wha like to taste the drappie
    In glass or horn?

liquor
pleasant

9

I've seen me daez't upon a time,
I scarce could wink or see a styme;
Just ae hauf-mutchkin does me prime
    (Ought less is little);
Then back I rattle on the rhyme
    As gleg's a whittle.

dazed
faintest outline
one half-pint
keen; knife

TO J. LAPRAIK

(THIRD EPISTLE)

I

Guid speed and furder to you, Johnie,
Guid health, hale han's, an' weather bonie!
Now, when ye're nickin down fu' cannie
    The staff o' bread,
May ye ne'er want a stoup o' bran'y
    To clear your head!

whole hands
cutting; expertly
corn
cup

2

May Boreas never thresh your rigs, ridges
Nor kick your rickles aff their legs, ricklets
Sendin the stuff o'er muirs an' haggs broken bogs
        Like drivin wrack!
But may the tapmost grain that wags
        Come to the sack!

3

I'm bizzie, too, an' skelpin at it; busy; driving
But bitter, daudin showers hae wat it; pelting; wetted
Sae my auld stumpie-pen, I gat it, After long search
        Wi' muckle wark, clasp-knife
An' took my jocteleg, an' whatt it whittled
        Like onie clark.

4

It's now twa month that I'm your debtor
For your braw, nameless, dateless letter, fine
Abusin me for harsh ill-nature
        On holy men,
While deil a hair yoursel ye're better, devil a bit
        But mair profane!

5

But let the kirk-folk ring their bells!
Let's sing about our noble sel's:
We'll cry nae jads frae heathen hills call
        To help or roose us, inspire
But browster wives an' whisky stills—
        They are the Muses!

6

Your friendship, sir, I winna quat it; will not give it up
An' if ye mak' objections at it, to
Then hand in nieve some day we'll knot it, fist
        An' witness take;
An', when wi' usquabae we've wat it, whisky
        It winna break.

7

But if the beast and branks be spar'd horse and bridle
Till kye be gaun without the herd, kine; going; keeper

grain; rick-
yard
thatched
fire-
Some

And a' the vittel in the yard
>   An' theckit right,
I mean your ingle-side to guard
>   Ae winter night.

8

Then Muse-inspirin aqua-vitæ
Shall mak us baith sae blythe an' witty,

enervated
jolly

Till ye forget ye're auld an' gatty,
>   And be as canty
As ye were nine year less than thretty—
>   Sweet ane an' twenty!

9

shocks;
tumbled by
sun . peeps;
west
must run
leave; song

But stooks are cowpet wi' the blast,
And now the sinn keeks in the wast;
Then I maun rin amang the rest,
>   An' quat my chanter;
Sae I subscribe mysel in haste,
>   Yours, Rab the Ranter.

Sept. 13, 1785

TO THE REV. JOHN M'MATH

INCLOSING A COPY OF 'HOLY WILLIE'S PRAYER' WHICH HE HAD REQUESTED, SEPT. 17, 1785

1

shock;
reapers stoop
driving
horseplay
running,
scour

While at the stook the shearers cow'r
To shun the bitter blaudin show'r,
Or, in gulravage rinnin, scowr:
>   To pass the time,
To you I dedicate the hour
>   In idle rhyme.

2

My Musie, tir'd wi' monie a sonnet

sedate;

fearful

On gown an' ban' an' douse black-bonnet,
Is grown right eerie now she's done it,
>   Lest they should blame her,
An' rouse their holy thunder on it,
>   And anathém her.

3

I own 'twas rash, an' rather hardy,
That I, a simple, countra Bardie,
Should meddle wi' a pack sae sturdy,
   Wha, if they ken me,
Can easy wi' a single wordie   easily
    Louse Hell upon me.

4

But I gae mad at their grimaces,   furious
Their sighin, cantin, grace-proud faces,
Their three-mile prayers an' hauf-mile graces,
    Their raxin conscience,   elastic
Whase greed, revenge, an' pride disgraces
    Waur nor their nonsense. Worse than

5

There's Gau'n, misca'd waur than a beast,
Wha has mair honor in his breast
Than monie scores as guid's the priest
    Wha sae abus't him?
And may a Bard no crack his jest
    What way they've use't him?

6

See him, the poor man's friend in need,
The gentleman in word an' deed—
An' shall his fame an' honor bleed
    By worthless skellums,   railers
An' not a Muse erect her head   daunt;
    To cowe the blellums?   blusterers

7

O Pope, had I thy satire's darts
To gie the rascals their deserts,
I'd rip their rotten, hollow hearts,
    An' tell aloud
Their jugglin, hocus-pocus arts
    To cheat the crowd!

8

God knows, I'm no the thing I should be,
Nor am I even the thing I could be,

But twenty times I rather would be
           An atheist clean
Than under gospel colors hid be
           Just for a screen.

9

An honest man may like a glass,
An honest man may like a lass;
But mean revenge an' malice fause
           He'll still disdain
An' then cry zeal for gospel laws
           Like some we ken.

false

10

They take Religion in their mouth,
They talk o' Mercy, Grace, an' Truth:
For what? To gie their malice skouth
           On some puir wight;
An' hunt him down, o'er right an' ruth,
           To ruin streight.

play

straight

11

All hail, Religion! Maid divine,
Pardon a Muse sae mean as mine,
Who in her rough imperfect line
           Thus daurs to name thee;
To stigmatise false friends of thine
           Can ne'er defame thee.

12

Tho' blotch't and foul wi' monie a stain
An' far unworthy of thy train,
With trembling voice I tune my strain
           To join with those
Who boldly dare thy cause maintain
           In spite of foes:

13

In spite o' crowds, in spite o' mobs,
In spite of undermining jobs,
In spite o' dark banditti stabs
           At worth an' merit,
By scoundrels, even wi' holy robes
           But hellish spirit!

14

O Ayr! my dear, my native ground,
Within thy presbyterial bound
A candid lib'ral band is found
      Of public teachers,
As men, as Christians too, renown'd,
         An' manly preachers.

15

Sir, in that circle you are nam'd;
Sir, in that circle you are fam'd;
An' some, by whom your doctrine's blam'd
      (Which gies ye honor),
Even, Sir, by them your heart's esteem'd,
         An' winning manner.

16

Pardon this freedom I have taen,
An' if impertinent I've been,
Impute it not, good sir, in ane
      Whase heart ne'er wrang'd ye,
But to his utmost would befriend
         Ought that belang'd ye.   *was yours*

TO DAVIE

SECOND EPISTLE

1

AULD NEEBOR,
  I'm three times doubly o'er your debtor
For your auld-farrant, frien'ly letter;   *old-*
Tho' I maun say't, I doubt ye flatter,   *fashioned*
      Ye speak sae fair: *must*
For my puir, silly, rhymin clatter   *babble*
         Some less maun sair.   *serve*

2

Hale be your heart, hale be your fiddle!   *Whole*
Lang may your elbuck jink an' diddle   *elbow; dance*
To cheer you thro' the weary widdle   *and shake*
      O' war'ly cares,   *wriggle*
Till bairns' bairns kindly cuddle   *worldly*
         Your auld grey hairs!   *grand-*
                                         children;
                                         fondle

3

afraid;
foolish

But Davie, lad, I'm red ye're glaikit:

should;
whipped
fidget
Such hands;
let off
spared

I'm tauld the Muse ye hae negleckit;
An' gif it's sae, ye sud be lickit
Until ye fyke;
Sic han's as you sud ne'er be faiket,
Be hain't wha like.

4

Tearing,
make; rhyme
Now dazed
Freemasons
too
Fine

For me, I'm on Parnassus' brink,
Rivin the words to gar them clink;
Whyles daez't wi' love, whyles daez't wi' drink
Wi' jads or Masons,
An' whyles, but ay owre late I think,
Braw sober lessons.

5

-have it

Of a' the thoughtless sons o' man
Commen' me to the Bardie clan:
Except it be some idle plan
O' rhymin clink—
The devil-haet that I sud ban!—
They never think.

6

pocket; fist
careering
worry

Nae thought, nae view, nae scheme o' livin,
Nae cares to gie us joy or grievin,
But just the pouchie put the nieve in,
An' while ought's there,
Then, hiltie-skiltie, we gae scrievin,
An' fash nae mair.

7

Blessings
almost
a-field
girl
homespun

Leeze me on rhyme! It's ay a treasure,
My chief, amaist my only pleasure;
At hame, a-fiel', at wark or leisure,
The Muse, poor hizzie!
Tho' rough an' raploch be her measure,
She's seldom lazy.

8

Stick
world; ill-
turn

Haud to the Muse, my dainty Davie:
The warl' may play you monie a shavie,

But for the Muse, she'll never leave ye,
        Tho' e'er sae puir;
Na, even tho' limpin wi' the spavie   spavin
        Frae door to door!

LOOK UP AND SEE!

1

Noo, Davie Sillar, that's the plan,
Quo I, last night, when in my han
I gaed your latest screed a scan
        Rebukin me
About your model name-sake man—
        Look up and see!

2

Altho it may be unexpectit,
An' few the facts hae yet detectit,
My Bible hasna been negleckit
        Sin I was wee,
And nae sma lore I hae colleckit,—
        Look up and see!

3

Bad as I am, or hae been ca'd
By jauds that lang hae at me jaw'd
And priests that fain my pash had claw'd,
        I winna lee,
King David's life ye less can laud,—
        Look up and see!

4

Gin I had but a Gowdie's airt
At treating him to his desert,
This saintship after God's ain he'rt,
        As said to be,
I'd prove a villain maist expert—
        Look up and see!

5

Ay, though that Jesus styled Divine
Is shown to be o' David's line

Thro mair than ae poor concubine,
          The pedigree

plagued

Has plaguit ither heids than mine,—
          Look up and see!

6

I'm sure, my frien, ye never heard
That I, although like him a Bard,
Wi' daft, unseemly dancin garr'd
          My shanks to flee,
Till a' the decencies were jarr'd—
          Look up and see!

7

His wife, at least ane o' the lot,
Since by the score he had them got,
For thinkin him a filthy snot—
          Saul's dochter she—
A cruel curse at her he shot—
          Look up and see!

8

And neist his tricks wi' Abigail:

began

Her man or lang begood to ail
And was as ye may read the tale
          Alloo'd to dee;
Syne David did the widow nail—
          Look up and see!

9

And wha his conduct could defen
When like a coward, as we ken,
He sacrificed sae mony men
          Upon the plea
God bann'd the Census Takkers pen?—
          Look up and see!

10

He was a cruel Man o' War
And for his plunder traivell'd far
Defenceless fowk to mash and mar

blood

          And spill their bree
In bluidy streams among the glaur—
          Look up and see!

11

And some for unco little cause
He cut wi' harrows and wi' saws:
Wha likes for that may shout huzzahs,
        I'll never gie
Sic fiendish deeins my applause—   doings
        Look up and see!

12

None spared he in his anger wild;
Not age itself, nor yet the child,
Although upon the sword it smiled
        Or crow'd in glee—
How *can* the texts be reconciled?—
        Look up and see!

13

For David, as the Scriptures say,
As black a rascal in his day
As ony Tyrant noo we hae
        Or e'er may dree
Was God's especial protegé—
        Look up and see!

14

Can parsons, think ye, close the lid
And keep the awfu' story hid
On hoo the rascal—God forbid   how
        We e're sud pree
What he to puir Uriah did—
        Look up and see!

15

And since the Psalmist, as we learn,
Gat stown Bath-Sheba twice wi' bairn   stolen
He must hae had a hert o' airn   iron
        To shut his e'e
To Nathan's reprimandin stern—
        Look up and see!

16

Fine stock they were we maun alloo!   allow
Himsel—we ken wha he cam through—

And Solomon they'd gar us true
    Bore Wisdom's Key,
But here's my best advice to you—
    Look up and see!

17

Foul-mouth'd auld Davie also was
And mony proofs your Bible has
O' his inspired profaneness as
    Ye maun agree
If 'tis as in my copy 'twas—
    Look up and see!

18

E'en lyin on the bed o' Death
The scoundrel, bent on spreadin scaith,
Kept up his cursin tongue, in faith
    Ne'er stoppit he
Till Cloutie chokit aff his breath—
    Look up and see!

19

And yet in face o' a' his record,
His lang career sae vilely checker'd,
And hoo his licht sae aften flicker'd,
    In Heaven hie
Nae angel's seat is better siccar'd—
    Look up and see!

20

I've read my Bible, Davie man,
And that's the reason hoo I stan
Opposed to a' the pious ban
    That bow the knee
To saints o' royal David's clan—
    Look up and see!

21

Should a' be true the prophets tell,
If I the lines am fit to spell,
King David mair o' dirt should smell
    Than Deity,
And gin there's sic a place as Hell—
    Look up and see!

TO JOHN KENNEDY, DUMFRIES HOUSE

1

Now, Kennedy, if foot or horse
E'er bring you in by Mauchlin Corss   Cross
(Lord, man, there's lasses there wad force   would
         A hermit's fancy;
And down the gate in faith! they're worse   way
         An' mair unchancy):   dangerous

2

But as I'm sayin, please step to Dow's,
An' taste sic gear as Johnie brews,   stuff
Till some bit callan bring me news   small boy
         That ye are there;
An' if we dinna hae a bowse,
         I'se ne'er drink mair.   I'll

3

It's no I like to sit an' swallow,   not that
Then like a swine to puke an' wallow;
But gie me just a true guid fallow
         Wi' right ingíne,   wit
And spunkie ance to mak us mellow,   liquor
         An' then we'll shine!   enough

4

Now if ye're ane o' warl's folk,   the world's
Wha rate the wearer by the cloak,
An' sklent on poverty their joke   squint
         Wi' bitter sneer,
Wi' you nae friendship I will troke,   barter
         Nor cheap nor dear.

5

But if, as I'm informèd weel,
Ye hate as ill's the vera Deil
The flinty heart that canna feel—
         Come, sir, here's tac you!   to
Hae, there's my han', I wiss you weel,   take; wish
         An' Gude be wi' you!

TO GAVIN HAMILTON, ESQ., MAUCHLINE

RECOMMENDING A BOY

I hold it, Sir, my bounden duty
To warn you how that Master Tootie,
   Alias Laird M'Gaun,
Was here to hire yon lad away
'Bout whom ye spak the tither day,
     An' wad hae done't aff han';
But lest he learn the callan tricks—
     As faith! I muckle doubt him—
Like scrapin out auld Crummie's nicks,
     An' tellin lies about them,
       As lieve then, I'd have then
        Your clerkship he should sair,
      If sae be ye may be
        Not fitted otherwhere.

Altho' I say't, he's gleg enough,
An' bout a house that's rude an' rough
     The boy might learn to swear;
But then wi' *you* he'll be sae taught,
An' get sic fair example straught,
     I hae na onie fear:
Ye'll catechise him every quirk,
     An' shore him weel wi' ' Hell ';
An' gar him follow to the kirk—
     Ay when ye gang yoursel!
      If ye, then, maun be then
        Frae hame this comin Friday,
      Then please, Sir, to lea'e, Sir,
        The orders wi' your lady.

My word of honour I hae gien,
In Paisley John's that night at e'en
     To meet the ' warld's worm,'
To try to get the twa to gree,
An' name the airles an' the fee
     In legal mode an' form:
I ken he weel a snick can draw,
     When simple bodies let him;

An' if a Devil be at a',
 In faith he's sure to get him.
  To phrase you an' praise you,
   Ye ken, your Laureat scorns:
  The pray'r still you share still
   Of grateful MINSTREL BURNS.

TO MR. M'ADAM OF CRAIGEN-GILLAN

IN ANSWER TO AN OBLIGING LETTER HE SENT
IN THE COMMENCEMENT OF MY POETIC CAREER

1

Sir, o'er a gill I gat your card,   *drink*
 I trow it made me proud.
'See wha taks notice o' the Bard!'
 I lap, and cry'd fu' loud.   *danced*

2

Now deil-ma-care about their jaw,
 The senseless, gawky million! *cuckooing*
I'll cock my nose aboon them a': *above*
 I'm roos'd by Craigen-Gillan! *praised*

3

'Twas noble, sir; 'twas like yoursel,
 To grant your high protection:
A great man's smile, ye ken fu' well,
 Is ay a blest infection.

4

Tho', by his banes wha in a tub *Diogenes*
 Match'd Macedonian Sandy!   *Alexander*
               Magnus
On my ain legs thro' dirt and dub *puddle*
 I independent stand ay;

5

And when those legs to guid warm kail *broth*
 Wi' welcome canna bear me,
A lee dyke-side, a sybow-tail,   *stone fence;*
 An' barley-scone shall cheer me. *onion-*

6

Heaven spare you lang to kiss the breath
   O' monie flow'ry simmers,
An' bless your bonie lasses baith

lovable girls

   (I'm tauld they're loosome kimmers)!

7

An' God bless young Dunaskin's laird,
   The blossom of our gentry,
An' may he wear an auld man's beard,
   A credit to his country!

REPLY TO AN INVITATION

Sir,
   Yours this moment I unseal,
     And faith! I'm gay and hearty.
   To tell the truth and shame the Deil,

drunk;
the Devil

     I am as fou as Bartie.

Thursday;
true

But Foorsday, Sir, my promise leal,
     Expect me o' your partie,

climb

If on a beastie I can speel

trundle

     Or hurl in a cartie.
         Yours,—Robert Burns.

TO DR. MACKENZIE

An Invitation to a Masonic Gathering

Friday first's the day appointed
By our Right Worshipful Anointed
   To hold our grand procession,

screed

To get a blaud o' Johnie's morals,

sample

An' taste a swatch o' Manson's barrels
   I' th' way of our profession.
Our Master and the Brotherhood

would

   Wad a' be glad to see you.
For me, I wad be mair than proud
   To share the mercies wi' you.

danger

   If Death, then, wi' skaith then

menacing

     Some mortal heart is hechtin,

bully

   Inform him, an' storm him,

fight

     That Saturday ye'll fecht him.

EPISTLE TO DR. JOHN MACKENZIE

1

DEAR THINKER JOHN,
    Your creed I like it past expression,
    I'm sure, o' truth, it's nae transgression
    To say the great Westminster Session,
        Wi a' their clatter,
    In Carraches or large Confession
      Ne'er made a better.

2

For me, I ken a weel ploughed rigg,
I ken a handsome hizzie's leg
When, springing taper straught and trig,   straight
    It fires my fancy;
But *system-Sandy* mills to bigg
    Is nae that chancy.

3

Sma skill in *holy war* I boast,
My wee bit spunk o' *Latin's* lost,
An *Logic* gies me ay the hoast
    An' cuts my win,   wind
So I maun tak the rear-guard post
    Far, far behind.

4

I see the poopet ance a week,   pulpit
An' carefu' every sentence cleek;
Or if frae —— a smirking keek   (Jean?)
    Spoil my devotion,
My carnal een I instant steek   eyes
    Wi' double caution.

5

Still, tho' nae staunch polemic head
O lang-win'd Athanasian breed,
I hae a wee-bit cantie *creed*
    Just ae my ain,
An tho' uncouthly it may read,
    It's unco plain.

6

Tho' human-kind be sae at odds,
Poor Waspish, animated clods,
There's just twa patent turnpike roads
     They a maun gang
To dark futurity's abodes—
     The *right* an' *wrang*.

7

If, spite of a' its crooks an' thraws,
The heav'nward road your fancy draws,
If ye *resemble* ought their laws
     An' ways that's there,
Then march awa and never pause:
     Your conduct's fair.

8

But if ye think, within yoursel,
You'll fairly tak your chance o' hell,
An' honestly your notion tell,
     Free, unashamed,
Then faith, I see nae how that well
     Ye can be blam'd.

9

But here the conduct I call evil:
Some at their heart wad sair the devil,
Yet groan, and drone, an' sigh, and snivel,
     An' pray and cant,
An' be to heaven as fair an' civil
     As ony saunt.

serve

saint

10

Thae rotten-hearted twa-fac'd wretches,
Wi a' their hypocritic fetches,
I would rejoice in well-splic'd stitches
     O' hempen string
Out owre a tree, the sons o' bitches,
     To see them swing.

11

Ye see my skill's but very sma,
Some folk may think I've nane ava,

But we sall gie our pens a claw
  Some ither time,
An' hae a bout between us twa
  At prose an' rhyme.

12

Farewell, dear death-defying John!
Aft hunt-the-gowke for you he's gone,
But some day he'll come down the loan
  Wi spurtlin shanks,   *stick-like*
An' grip ye till he gar you groan,   *make*
  By way of Thanks.

13

But first, before that come to pass:
May ye toom many a social glass,   *empty*
An' bless a dear warm-hearted lass
  That likes you some;
Then after fifty simmers grass
  E'en let him come!

TO JOHN KENNEDY

A Farewell

Farewell, dear friend! may guid luck hit you,
And 'mong her favourites admit you!
If e'er Detraction shore to smit you,   *threaten;*
          May nane believe him!   *smite*
And onie deil that thinks to get you,
          Good Lord, deceive him!

TO WILLIE CHALMERS' SWEETHEART

1

Wi' braw new branks in mickle pride,   *fine; bridle*
  And eke a braw new brechan,   *collar*
My Pegasus I'm got astride,
  And up Parnassus pechin: *blowing*
Whyles owre a bush wi' downward crush
  The doited beastie stammers;   *stupid*
Then up he gets, and off he sets
  For sake o' Willie Chalmers.

2

I doubt na, lass, that weel kend name
    May cost a pair o' blushes:
I am nae stranger to your fame,
    Nor his warm-urgèd wishes:
Your bonie face, sae mild and sweet,
    His honest heart enamours;
And faith! ye'll no be lost a whit,
bestowed   Tho' wair'd on Willie Chalmers.

3

Auld Truth hersel might swear ye're fair,
    And Honor safely back her;
And Modesty assume your air,
    And ne'er a ane mistak her;
eyes   And sic twa love-inspiring een
    Might fire even holy palmers:
Nae wonder then they've fatal been
    To honest Willie Chalmers!

4

offer   I doubt na Fortune may you shore
prim-lipped,   Some mim-mou'd, pouther'd priestie,
powdered
Much   Fu' lifted up wi' Hebrew lore
    And band upon his breastie;
But O, what signifies to you
    His lexicons and grammars?
The feeling heart's the royal blue,
    And that's wi' Willie Chalmers.

5

staring   Some gapin, glowrin countra laird
struggle   May warsle for your favour:
scratch; ear;   May claw his lug, and straik his beard,
stroke
cough   And hoast up some palaver.
My bonie maid, before ye wed
Such; dunces   Sic clumsy-witted hammers,
spank   Seek Heaven for help, and barefit skelp
    Awa wi' Willie Chalmers.

6

Forgive the Bard! My fond regard
    For ane that shares my bosom
Inspires my Muse to gie'm his dues,
devil a bit;   For deil a hair I roose him.
flatter

May Powers aboon unite you soon,   *above*
  And fructify your ámours,
And every year come in mair dear
  To you and Willie Chalmers!

TO AN OLD SWEETHEART

WRITTEN ON A COPY OF HIS POEMS

I

Once fondly lov'd and still remember'd dear,
  Sweet early object of my youthful vows,
Accept this mark of friendship, warm, sincere—
  (Friendship! 'tis all cold duty now allows);

2

And when you read the simple artless rhymes,
  One friendly sigh for him—he asks no more—
Who, distant, burns in flaming torrid climes,
  Or haply lies beneath th' Atlantic roar.

EXTEMPORE TO GAVIN HAMILTON

STANZAS ON NAETHING

I

To you, Sir, this summons I've sent
  (Pray, whip till the pownie is fraething!);   *foaming*
But if you demand what I want,
  I honestly answer you—naething.

2

Ne'er scorn a poor Poet like me
  For idly just living and breathing,
While people of every degree
  Are busy employed about—naething.

3

Poor Centum-per-Centum may fast,
  And grumble his hurdies their claithing;   *grudge;*
He'll find, when the balance is cast,   *buttocks;*
  He's gane to the Devil for—naething.   *clothing*

4

The courtier cringes and bows;
    Ambition has likewise its plaything—
A coronet beams on his brows;
    And what is a coronet?—Naething.

5

Some quarrel the Presbyter gown,
    Some quarrel Episcopal graithing;
But every good fellow will own
    The quarrel is a' about—naething.

rail at
vestments

6

The lover may sparkle and glow,
    Approaching his bonie bit gay thing;
But marriage will soon let him know
    He's gotten—a buskit-up naething.

little

tricked-out

7

The Poet may jingle and rhyme
    In hopes of a laureate wreathing,
And when he has wasted his time,
    He's kindly rewarded with—naething.

8

The thundering bully may rage,
    And swagger and swear like a heathen;
But collar him fast, I'll engage,
    You'll find that his courage is—naething.

9

Last night with a feminine Whig—
    A poet she couldna put faith in!
But soon we grew lovingly big,
    I taught her, her terrors were—naething.

10

Her Whigship was wonderful pleased,
    But charmingly tickled wi' ae thing;
Her fingers I lovingly squeezed,
    And kissed her, and promised her—naething.

one

11

The priest anathèmas may threat—
  Predicament, sir, that we're baith in;
But when Honor's reveillé is beat,
  The holy artillery's—naething.

12

And now I must mount on the wave:
  My voyage perhaps there is death in;
But what is a watery grave?
  The drowning a Poet is—naething.

13

And now, as grim Death's in my thought,
  To you, Sir, I make this bequeathing:
My service as long as ye've ought,
  And my friendship, by God, when ye've—
    naething.

REPLY TO A TRIMMING EPISTLE
RECEIVED FROM A TAILOR

1

What ails ye now, ye lousie bitch,
To thresh my back at sic a pitch?   *punish; such*
Losh, man, hae mercy wi' your natch!   *Lord; notch-*
      Your bodkin's bauld: *ing weapon*
I didna suffer half sae much   *needle*
      Frae Daddie Auld.

2

What tho' at times, when I grow crouse,   *merry*
I gie their wames a random pouse,
Is that enough for you to souse
      Your servant sae?
Gae mind your seam, ye prick-the-louse
      An' jag-the-flae!   *flea*

3

King David o' poetic brief   *writ*
Wrocht 'mang the lassies sic mischief

As fill'd his after-life with grief
rows   An' bloody rants;
         An' yet he's rank'd amang the chief
old-time   O' lang-syne saunts.
saints

4

canters   And maybe, Tam, for a' my cants,
sprees   My wicked rhymes an' drucken rants,
-Hoofie's I'll gie auld Cloven-Clootie's haunts
wondrous   An unco slip yet,
          An' snugly sit amang the saunts
                                    At Davie's hip yet!

5

faith; Kirk-   But, fegs! the Session says I maun
Session;
must   Gae fa' upo' anither plan
making;   Than garrin lasses coup the cran,
capsize the
pot   Clean heels owre body,
suffer   An' sairly thole their mither's ban
midwife   Afore the howdy.

6

          This leads me on to tell for sport
          How I did wi' the Session sort:
The Bellman Auld Clinkum at the inner port
                                   Cried three times:—'Robin!
          Come hither lad, and answer for't,
                                   Ye're blam'd for jobbin!'

7

          Wi' pinch I put a Sunday's face on,
toddled off An' snoov'd awa' before the Session:
          I made an open, fair confession—
                                   I scorn'd to lie—
then;   An' syne Mess John, beyond expression,
                                   Fell foul o' me.

8

          A fornicator-loun he call'd me,
fault   An' said my faut frae bliss expell'd me.
          I own'd the tale was true he tell'd me,
                                   'But, what the matter?'
          (Quo' I) 'I fear unless ye geld me,
                                   I'll ne'er be better!'

9

'Geld you!' (quo' he) 'an' what for no?   why not
If that your right hand, leg, or toe
Should ever prove your sp'ritual foe,
    You should remember
To cut it aff; an' what for no
    Your dearest member?'

10

'Na, na' (quo' I), 'I'm no for that,
Gelding's nae better than 'tis ca't;
I'd rather suffer for my faut
    A hearty flewit,   stripe
As sair owre hip as ye can draw't,
    Tho' I should rue it.

11

'Or, gin ye like to end the bother,
To please us a'—I've just ae ither: one other
When next wi' yon lass I forgather,   meet
    Whate'er betide it,
I'll frankly gie her't a' thegither,
    An' let her guide it.'

12

But, Sir, this pleas'd them warst of a',
An' therefore, Tam, when that I saw,
I said 'Guid-night,' an' cam awa,
    An' left the Session:
I saw they were resolvèd a'
    On my oppression.

TO ROBERT AIKEN

I

Assist me, Coila, while I sing
 The virtues o' a crony
That in the blessings friendships bring
 Has ne'er been match'd by mony.
And wha's the man sic land to gain?
 There can be nae mistakin',
As if there could be mair than ane—
 Step forrat Robert Aiken!   forward

2

When I had neither poun' nor plack
   To rub on ane anither;
When hope's horizon seemed as black
   As midnicht a'-the-gither:
When chased and challenged by the law
   My he'rt was after quakin',

stood; friend   Wha stude my steady fiere for a'?—
   O, wha but Robert Aiken!

3

When he and she baith young and auld
   Were bent on my undoin',

lies; bold   And tried by lees and scandals bauld
   To drive me clean to ruin:
Wha never aince withdrew his smile,

gossip   Or listened to the claikin'?—
Ah, he's a frien' that's worth the while,
   A man like Robert Aiken!

4

When first I tried my rustic pen
   In little bits o' rhymin'
Wha introduced me but and ben
   And helped me in my climbin'?
Wha advertised abroad my name,
   'A minstrel in the makin','
Wha fairly read me into fame,
   But Lawyer Robert Aiken!

5

And when wi' muckle qualms I socht
   To get my poems printed,
While mony 'frien's' nae copies bocht
   And some, their orders stinted:
Wha by the dizzen and the score
   The names to me was rakin'?—
The king o' a' the buyin' corps
   Was surely Robert Aiken!

6

The time will come when I'll be deemed
   A poet grander, greater,
Than ever prophesied or dreamed

The loodest, proodest prater.
Then let this fact be published too
    That at the bard's awakin'
The truest, kindest friend he knew
    Was honest Robert Aiken!

TO MAJOR LOGAN

1

Hail, thairm-inspirin, rattlin Willie!   string-
Tho' Fortune's road be rough an' hilly
To every fiddling, rhyming billie,   brother
          We never heed,
But take it like the unbrack'd filly   unbroken
          Proud o' her speed.

2

When, idly goavin, whyles we saunter,   mooning;
Yirr! Fancy barks, awa we canter,   sometimes
Up hill, down brae, till some mishanter,   mishap
          Some black bog-hole,
Arrests us; then the scathe an' banter
          We're forced to thole.   endure

3

Hale be your heart! hale be your fiddle!   Whole
Lang may your elbuck jink an' diddle,   elbow dance
To cheer you through the weary widdle   and shake
          O' this vile warl',   wriggle
Until you on a cummock driddle,
          A grey-hair'd carl.   old man

4

Come wealth, come poortith, late or soon,   poverty
Heaven send your heart-strings ay in tune,
And screw your temper-pins aboon   fiddle-pegs
          (A fifth or mair)   above
The melancholious, sairie croon   sorrowful
          O' cankrie Care.   note
                                        crabbed

5

May still your life from day to day,
Nae *lente largo* in the play
But *allegretto forte* gay,
            Harmonious flow,
A sweeping, kindling, bauld strathspey—
            Encore! Bravo!

bold

6

A' blessings on the cheery gang,
Wha dearly like a jig or sang,
An' never think o' right an' wrang
            By square an' rule,
But as the clegs o' feeling stang
            Are wise or fool.

gadflies;
sting

7

My hand-wal'd curse keep hard in chase
The harpy, hoodock, purse-proud race,
Wha count on poortith as disgrace!
            Their tuneless hearts,
May fireside discords jar a bass
            To a' their parts!

hand-picked
(*i.e.* choicest)
grasping

8

But come, your hand, my careless brither!
I' th' ither warl', if there's anither—
An' that there is, I've little swither
            About the matter—
We, cheek for chow, shall jog thegither—
            I'se ne'er bid better!

world
doubt

cheek by
jowl;
together
I'll; ask

9

We've faults and failins—granted clearly!
We're frail, backsliding mortals merely;
Eve's bonie squad, priests wyte them sheerly
            For our grand fa';
But still, but still—I like them dearly . . .
            God bless them a'!

blame;
wholly

10

Ochon for poor Castalian drinkers,
When they fa' foul o' earthly jinkers!

gamesters

The witching, curs'd, delicious blinkers   *oglers*
    Hae put me hyte,   *furious*
An' gart me weet my waukrife winkers   *made; wet;*
    Wi' girnin spite.   *wakeful eyes*
                                                            snarling

11

But by yon moon—and that's high swearin!—
An' every star within my hearin,
An' by her een wha was a dear ane   *eyes*
    I'll ne'er forget,
I hope to gie the jads a clearin   *jades*
    In fair play yet!

12

My loss I mourn, but not repent it;
I'll seek my pursie whare I tint it;   *lost*
Ance to the Indies I were wonted,   *escaped*
    Some cantraip hour   *witching*
By some sweet elf I'll yet be dinted:
    Then *vive l'amour!*

13

Faites mes baissemains respectueusè
To sentimental sister Susie
And honest Lucky: no to roose you,   *flatter*
    Ye may be proud,
That sic a couple Fate allows ye   *such*
    To grace your blood.

14

Nae mair at present can I measure,
An' trowth! my rhymin ware's nae treasure;
But when in Ayr, some half-hour's leisure,
    Be't light, be't dark,
Sir Bard will do himself the pleasure
    To call at Park.

TO THE GUIDWIFE OF
WAUCHOPE HOUSE

(MRS. SCOTT)

I

GUID WIFE,

remember   I mind it weel, in early date,
bashful   When I was beardless, young, and blate,
   An' first could thresh the barn,
hold; a day's work   Or haud a yokin at the pleugh,
exhausted   An', tho' forfoughten sair eneugh,
mighty   Yet unco proud to learn;
   When first amang the yellow corn
   A man I reckon'd was,
others each   An' wi the lave ilk merry morn
ridge   Could rank my rig and lass:
reaping   Still shearing, and clearing
row of shocks   The tither stookèd raw,
gossip; nonsense   'Wi' clavers an' havers
away   Wearing the day awa.

2

E'en then, a wish (I mind its pow'r),
A wish that to my latest hour
   Shall strongly heave my breast,
That I for poor auld Scotland's sake
Some usefu' plan or book could make,
   Or sing a sang at least.
The rough burr-thistle spreading wide
barley   Amang the bearded bear,
-shears   I turn'd the weeder-clips aside,
   An' spar'd the symbol dear.
   No nation, no station
   My envy e'er could raise;
without   A Scot still, but blot still,
   I knew nae higher praise.

3

But still the elements o' sang
In formless jumble, right an' wrang,
   Wild floated in my brain;

Till on that hairst I said before,   harvest;
My partner in the merry core,   mentioned
   She rous'd the forming strain.   band
I see her yet, the sonsie quean   pleasant lass
   That lighted up my jingle,
Her witching smile, her pauky een   artful eyes
   That gart my heart-strings tingle!   made
    I firèd, inspirèd,
      At ev'ry kindling keek, glance
    But, bashing and dashing,   abashing;
      I fearèd ay to speak.   peacocking

4

Hale to the sex! (ilk guid chiel says):   Health;
Wi' merry dance on winter days,   each; fellow
   An' we to share in common!
The gust o' joy, the balm of woe,
The saul o' life, the heav'n below   soul
   Is rapture-giving Woman.
Ye surly sumphs, who hate the name,   churls
   Be mindfu' o' your mither:
She, honest woman, may think shame
   That ye're connected with her!
    Ye're wae men, ye're nae men   sad
      'That slight the lovely dears;
    To shame ye, disclaim ye,
      Ilk honest birkie swears.   fellow

5

For you, no bred to barn and byre,   not;
Wha sweetly tune the Scottish lyre,   cowhouse
   Thanks to you for your line!
The marl'd plaid ye kindly spare,
By me should gratefully be ware;   worn
   'Twad please me to the nine.   perfection
I'd be mair vauntie o' my hap,   proud; wrap
   Douce hingin owre my curple,   sedately
                                hanging;
Than onie ermine ever lap,   crupper
   Or proud imperial purple.   folded
    Farewell, then! lang hale, then,   long health
      An' plenty be your fa'! lot
    May losses and crosses
      Ne'er at your hallan ca'! porch

TO WM. TYTLER, ESQ., OF WOODHOUSELEE

WITH AN IMPRESSION OF THE AUTHOR'S PORTRAIT

1

Reverèd defender of beauteous Stuart,
    Of Stuart!—a name once respected,
A name which to love was once mark of a true heart,
    But now 'tis despis'd and neglected!

2

Tho' something like moisture conglobes in my eye—
    Let no one misdeem me disloyal!
A poor friendless wand'rer may well claim a sigh—
    Still more, if that wand'rer were royal.

3

My Fathers that name have rever'd on a throne;
    My Fathers have fallen to right it:
Those Fathers would spurn their degenerate son,
    That name, should he scoffingly slight it.

4

Still in prayers for King George I most heartily join,
    The Queen, and the rest of the gentry;
Be they wise, be they foolish, is nothing of mine:
    Their title's avow'd by my country.

5

But why of that epocha make such a fuss
    That gave us the Hanover stem?
If bringing them over was lucky for us,
    I'm sure 'twas as lucky for them.

6

But loyalty—truce! we're on dangerous ground:
    Who knows how the fashions may alter?
The doctrine, to-day that is loyalty sound,
    To-morrow may bring us a halter!

7

I send you a trifle, a head of a Bard,
  A trifle scarce worthy your care;
But accept it, good Sir, as a mark of regard,
  Sincere as a saint's dying prayer.

8

Now Life's chilly evening dim-shades on your eye,
  And ushers the long dreary night;
But you, like the star that athwart gilds the sky,
  Your course to the latest is bright.

TO MR. RENTON OF LAMERTON

Your billet, Sir, I grant receipt;
anywhere Wi' you I'll canter onie gate,
world Tho' 'twere a trip to yon blue warl'
fellows Where birkies march on burning marl:
Then, Sir, God willing, I'll attend ye,
And to His goodness I commend ye.

TO MISS ISABELLA MACLEOD

1

The crimson blossom charms the bee,
  The summer sun the swallow:
So dear this tuneful gift to me
  From lovely Isabella.

2

Her portrait fair upon my mind
  Revolving time shall mellow,
And mem'ry's latest effort find
  The lovely Isabella.

3

No Bard nor lover's rapture this
  In fancies vain and shallow!
She is, so come my soul to bliss,
  The Lovely Isabella!

TO MISS FERRIER

1

Nae heathen name shall I prefix
    Frae Pindus or Parnassus;
Auld Reekie dings them a' to sticks
    For rhyme-inspiring lasses.

Edinburgh knocks

2

Jove's tunefu' dochters three times three
    Made Homer deep their debtor;
But gien the body half an e'e,
    Nine Ferriers wad done better!

daughters
given; fellow
would have

3

Last day my mind was in a bog;
    Down George's Street I stoited;
A creeping, cauld, prosaic fog
    My very senses doited;

Yesterday
stumbled
muddled

4

Do what I dought to set her free,
    My saul lay in the mire:
Ye turned a neuk, I saw your e'e,
    She took the wing like fire!

could
soul
corner

5

The mournfu' sang I here enclose,
    In gratitude I send you,
And pray, in rhyme as weel as prose,
    A' guid things may attend you!

SYLVANDER TO CLARINDA

1

When dear Clarinda, matchless fair,
    First struck Sylvander's raptur'd view,
He gaz'd, he listened to despair—
    Alas! 'twas all he dared to do.

2

Love from Clarinda's heavenly eyes
   Transfix'd his bosom thro' and thro',
But still in Friendship's guarded guise—
   For more the demon fear'd to do.

3

That heart, already more than lost,
   The imp beleaguer'd all *perdu*;
For frowning Honor kept his post—
   To meet that frown he shrunk to do.

4

His pangs the Bard refus'd to own,
   Tho' half he wish'd Clarinda knew;
But Anguish wrung the unweeting groan—
   Who blames what frantic Pain must do?

5

That heart, where motley follies blend,
   Was sternly still to Honor true:
To prove Clarinda's fondest friend
   Was what a lover, sure, might do!

6

The Muse his ready quill employ'd;
   No nearer bliss he could pursue;
That bliss Clarinda cold deny'd—
   ' Send word by Charles how you do!'

7

The chill behest disarm'd his Muse,
   Till Passion all impatient grew:
He wrote, and hinted for excuse,
   ' 'Twas 'cause he'd nothing else to do.'

8

But by those hopes I have above!
   And by those faults I dearly rue!
The deed, the boldest mark of love,
   For thee that deed I dare to do!

9

O, could the Fates but name the price
  Would bless me with your charms and you,
With frantic joy I'd pay it thrice,
  If human art or power could do!

10

Then take, Clarinda, friendship's hand
  (Friendship, at least, I may avow),
And lay no more your chill command—
  I'll write, whatever I've to do.

TO CLARINDA

(WITH A PRESENT OF A PAIR OF DRINKING GLASSES)

1

Fair Empress of the Poet's soul
  And Queen of poetesses;
Clarinda, take this little boon,
  This humble pair of glasses;

2

And fill them high with generous juice,
  As generous as your mind;
And pledge me in the generous toast:
  ' The whole of human kind! '

3

' To those who love us! ' second fill;
  But not to those whom *we* love,
Lest we love those who love not us!
  A third:—' To thee and me, love! '

4

' Long may we live! Long may we love!
  And long may we be happy!
And may we never want a glass
  Well charg'd with generous nappy! '

TO MISS CRUIKSHANK

A VERY YOUNG LADY

WRITTEN ON THE BLANK LEAF OF A BOOK,
PRESENTED TO HER BY THE AUTHOR

I

Beauteous Rosebud, young and gay,
Blooming on thy early May,
Never may'st thou, lovely flower,
Chilly shrink in sleety shower!
Never Boreas' hoary path,
Never Eurus' pois'nous breath,
Never baleful stellar lights,
Taint thee with untimely blights!
Never, never reptile thief
Riot on thy virgin leaf!
Nor even Sol too fiercely view
Thy bosom blushing still with dew!

2

May'st thou long, sweet crimson gem,
Richly deck thy native stem;
Till some ev'ning, sober, calm,
Dropping dews and breathing balm,
While all around the woodland rings,
And ev'ry bird thy requiem sings,
Thou, amid the dirgeful sound,
Shed thy dying honours round,
And resign to parent Earth
The loveliest form she e'er gave birth.

TO HUGH PARKER

In this strange land, this uncouth clime,
A land unknown to prose or rhyme;
Where words ne'er cros't the Muse's heckles,   hackles
Nor limpit in poetic shackles:
A land that Prose did never view it,
Except when drunk he stacher't thro' it: staggered
Here, ambush'd by the chimla cheek,   chimney corner
Hid in an atmosphere of reek,   smoke

I hear a wheel thrum i' the neuk,
I hear it—for in vain I leuk:
The red peat gleams, a fiery kernel
Enhuskèd by a fog infernal.
Here, for my wonted rhyming raptures,
I sit and count my sins by chapters;
For life and spunk like ither Christians,
I'm dwindled down to mere existence;
Wi' nae converse but Gallowa' bodies,
Wi' nae kend face but Jenny Geddes.
Jenny, my Pegasean pride,
Dowie she saunters down Nithside,
And ay a westlin leuk she throws,
While tears hap o'er her auld brown nose!
Was it for this wi' cannie care
Thou bure the Bard through many a shire?
At howes or hillocks never stumbled,
And late or early never grumbled?
O, had I power like inclination,
I'd heeze thee up a constellation!
To canter with the Sagitarre,
Or loup the Ecliptic like a bar,
Or turn the Pole like any arrow;
Or, when auld Phœbus bids good-morrow,
Down the Zodíac urge the race,
And cast dirt on his godship's face:
For I could lay my bread and kail
He'd ne'er cast saut upo' thy tail!
Wi' a' this care and a' this grief,
And sma', sma' prospect of relief,
And nought but peat reek i' my head,
How can I write what ye can read?—
Tarbolton, twenty-fourth o' June,
Ye'll find me in a better tune;
But till we meet and weet our whistle,
Tak this excuse for nae epistle.

TO ALEX. CUNNINGHAM

1

My godlike friend—nay, do not stare:
  You think the praise is odd-like?
But ' God is Love,' the saints declare:
  Then surely thou art god-like!

2

And is thy ardour still the same,
  And kindled still in Anna?
Others may boast a partial flame,
  But thou art a volcano!

3

Even Wedlock asks not love beyond
  Death's tie-dissolving portal;
But thou, omnipotently fond,
  May'st promise love immortal!

4

Thy wounds such healing powers defy,
  Such symptoms dire attend them,
That last great antihectic try—
  Marriage perhaps may mend them.

5

Sweet Anna has an air—a grace,
  Divine, magnetic, touching!
She takes, she charms—but who can trace
  The process of bewitching?

TO ROBERT GRAHAM, ESQ.,
OF FINTRY

REQUESTING A FAVOUR

When Nature her great master-piece design'd,
And fram'd her last, best work, the human mind,
Her eye intent on all the wondrous plan,
She form'd of various stuff the various Man.

The useful many first, she calls them forth—
Plain plodding Industry and sober Worth:
Thence peasants, farmers, native sons of earth,
And merchandise' whole genus take their birth;
Each prudent cit a warm existence finds,
And all mechanics' many-apron'd kinds.
Some other rarer sorts are wanted yet—
The lead and buoy are needful to the net:
The *caput mortuum* of gross desires
Makes a material for mere knights and squires;
The martial phosphorus is taught to flow;
She kneads the lumpish philosophic dough,
Then marks th' unyielding mass with grave designs—
Law, physic, politics, and deep divines;
Last, she sublimes th' Aurora of the poles,
The flashing elements of female souls.

The order'd system fair before her stood;
Nature, well pleas'd, pronounc'd it very good;
Yet ere she gave creating labour o'er,
Half-jest, she tried one curious labour more.
Some spumy, fiery, *ignis fatuus* matter,
Such as the slightest breath of air might scatter;
With arch-alacrity and conscious glee
(Nature may have her whim as well as we:
Her Hogarth-art, perhaps she meant to show it),
She forms the thing, and christens it—a Poet:
Creature, tho' oft the prey of care and sorrow,
When blest to-day, unmindful of to-morrow;
A being form'd t'amuse his graver friends;
Admir'd and prais'd—and there the wages ends;
A mortal quite unfit for Fortune's strife,
Yet oft the sport of all the ills of life;
Prone to enjoy each pleasure riches give,
Yet haply wanting wherewithal to live;
Longing to wipe each tear, to heal each groan,
Yet frequent all unheeded in his own.

But honest Nature is not quite a Turk:
She laugh'd at first, then felt for her poor work.
Viewing the propless climber of mankind,
She cast about a standard tree to find;
In pity for his helpless woodbine state,
She clasp'd his tendrils round the truly great:

A title, and the only one I claim,
To lay strong hold for help on bounteous Graham.

Pity the hapless Muses' tuneful train!
Weak, timid landsmen on life's stormy main,
Their hearts no selfish, stern, absorbent stuff,
That never gives—tho' humbly takes—enough:
The little Fate allows, they share as soon,
Unlike sage, proverb'd Wisdom's hard-wrung boon.
The world were blest did bliss on them depend—
Ah, that ' the friendly e'er should want a friend! '
Let Prudence number o'er each sturdy son
Who life and wisdom at one race begun,
Who feel by reason, and who give by rule
(Instinct's a brute, and Sentiment a fool!),
Who make poor ' will do ' wait upon ' I should '—
We own they're prudent, but who owns they're good?
Ye wise ones, hence! ye hurt the social eye,
God's image rudely etch'd on base alloy!
But come ye who the godlike pleasure know,
Heaven's attribute distinguish'd—to bestow!
Whose arms of love would grasp all human race:
Come thou who giv'st with all a courtier's grace—
Friend of my life, true patron of my rhymes,
Prop of my dearest hopes for future times!

Why shrinks my soul, half blushing, half afraid,
Backward, abash'd to ask thy friendly aid?
I know my need, I know thy giving hand,
I tax thy friendship at thy kind command.
But there are such who court the tuneful Nine
(Heavens! should the branded character be mine!),
Whose verse in manhood's pride sublimely flows,
Yet vilest reptiles in their begging prose.
Mark, how their lofty independent spirit
Soars on the spurning wing of injur'd merit!
Seek you the proofs in private life to find?
Pity the best of words should be but wind!
So to Heaven's gates the lark's shrill song ascends,
But grovelling on the earth the carol ends.
In all the clam'rous cry of starving want,
They dun Benevolence with shameless front;
Oblige them, patronise their tinsel lays—
They persecute you all your future days!

Ere my poor soul such deep damnation stain,
My horny fist assume the plough again!
The pie-bald jacket let me patch once more!
On eighteenpence a week I've liv'd before.
Tho', thanks to Heaven, I dare even that last shift,
I trust, meantime, my boon is in thy gift:
That, plac'd by thee upon the wish'd-for height,
With man and nature fairer in her sight,
My Muse may imp her wing for some sublimer flight.

IMPROMPTU TO CAPTAIN RIDDELL

ON RETURNING A NEWSPAPER

1

Your News and Review, Sir,
I've read through and through, Sir,
With little admiring or blaming:
The Papers are barren
Of home-news or foreign—
No murders or rapes worth the naming.

2

Our friends, the Reviewers,
Those chippers and hewers,
Are judges of mortar and stone, Sir;
But of meet or unmeet
In a fabric complete
I'll boldly pronounce they are none, Sir.

3

My goose-quill too rude is
To tell all your goodness
Bestow'd on your servant, the Poet;
Would to God I had one
Like a beam of the sun,
And then all the world, Sir, should know it!

REPLY TO A NOTE FROM CAPTAIN RIDDELL

Dear Sir, at onie time or tide
I'd rather sit wi' you than ride,
  Tho' 'twere wi' royal Geordie:
And trowth! your kindness soon and late
Aft gars me to mysel look blate—   *makes; sheepish*
  The Lord in Heaven reward ye!

TO JAMES TENNANT OF GLENCONNER

Auld comrade dear and brither sinner,
How's a' the folk about Glenconner?
How do you this blae eastlin wind,   *livid; easterly*
That's like to blaw a body blind?
For me, my faculties are frozen,
My dearest member nearly dozen'd.   *torpid*
I've sent you here, by Johnie Simson,
Twa sage philosophers to glimpse on:
Smith wi' his sympathetic feeling,
An' Reid to common sense appealing.
Philosophers have fought and wrangled,
An' meikle Greek an' Latin mangled,   *much*
Till, wi' their logic-jargon tir'd
And in the depth of science mir'd,
To common sense they now appeal—
What wives and wabsters see and feel!   *women; weavers*
But, hark ye, friend! I charge you strictly,
Peruse them, an' return them quickly:
For now I'm grown sae cursed douse   *serious*
I pray and ponder butt the house;   *in the kitchen*
My shins my lane I there sit roastin,   *alone*
Perusing Bunyan, Brown, an' Boston;
Till by an' by, if I haud on,   *hold*
I'll grunt a reàl gospel groan.
Already I begin to try it,
To cast me een up like a pyet,   *eyes; magpie*
When by the gun she tumbles o'er,
Flutt'ring an' gasping in her gore:
Sae shortly you shall see me bright,   *So*
A burning an' a shining light.

My heart-warm love to guid auld Glen,
pick   The ace an' wale of honest men:
When bending down wi'' auld grey hairs
Beneath the load of years and cares,
May He who made him still support him,
An' views beyond the grave comfórt him!
His worthy fam'ly far and near,
wealth   God bless them a' wi' grace and gear!

My auld schoolfellow, preacher Willie,
-brother   The manly tar, my Mason-billie,
And Auchenbay, I wish him joy;
If he's a parent, lass or boy,
May he be dad and Meg the mither
Just five-and-forty years thegither!
And no forgetting wabster Charlie,
promises I'm tauld he offers very fairly.
Sandie   An', Lord, remember singing Sannock
whole   Wi' hale breeks, saxpence, an' a bannock!
And next, my auld acquaintance, Nancy,
Since she is fitted to her fancy,
directed to An' her kind stars hae airted till her
chap; little A guid chiel wi' a pickle siller!
My kindest, best respects, I sen' it,
To cousin Kate, an' sister Janet:
Tell them, frae me, wi' chiels be cautious,
may be; For, faith! they'll aiblins fin' them fashious;
troublesome To grant a heart is fairly civil,
But to grant a maidenhead's the devil!
An' lastly, Jamie, for yoursel,
May guardian angels tak a spell,
An' steer you seven miles south o' Hell!
But first, before you see Heaven's glory,
May ye get monie a merry story,
Monie a laugh and monie a drink,
coin   And ay eneugh o' needfu' clink!

Now fare ye weel, an' joy be wi' you!
For my sake, this I beg it o' you:
Assist poor Simson a' ye can;
Ye'll fin' him just an honest man.
leave; song Sae I conclude, and quat my chanter,
Yours, saint or sinner,

                    RAB THE RANTER

TO JOHN M'MURDO

WITH SOME OF THE AUTHOR'S POEMS

I

O, could I give thee India's wealth,
  As I this trifle send!
Because thy Joy in both would be
  To share them with a friend!

2

But golden sands did never grace
  The Heliconian stream;
Then take what gold could never buy—
  An honest Bard's esteem.

SONNET TO ROBERT GRAHAM, ESQ., OF FINTRY

ON RECEIVING A FAVOUR, 19TH AUGUST, 1789

I call no Goddess to inspire my strains:
A fabled Muse may suit a Bard that feigns.
Friend of my life! my ardent spirit burns,
And all the tribute of my heart returns,
For boons accorded, goodness ever new,
The gift still dearer, as the giver you.

Thou orb of day! thou other paler light!
And all ye many sparkling stars of night!
If aught that giver from my mind efface,
If I that giver's bounty e'er disgrace,
Then roll to me along your wand'ring spheres
Only to number out a villain's years!

I lay my hand upon my swelling breast,
And grateful would, but cannot, speak the rest.

EPISTLE TO DR. BLACKLOCK

1

proud
in health;
jolly
little
excursion
set you up

Wow, but your letter made me vauntie!
And are ye hale, and weel, and cantie?
I kend it still, your wee bit jauntie
      Wad bring ye to:
Lord send you ay as weel's I want ye,
      And then ye'll do!

2

Devil

The Ill-Thief blaw the Heron south,
And never drink be near his drouth!
He tauld mysel by word o' mouth,
      He'd tak my letter:

trusted; chap
asked

I lippen'd to the chiel in trowth,
      And bade nae better.

3

may be

But aiblins honest Master Heron
Had at the time some dainty fair one

spend

To ware his theologic care on
      And holy study,

souls;
learning

And, tired o' sauls to waste his lear on,
      E'en tried the body.

4

companion

But what d'ye think, my trusty fier?
I'm turned a gauger—Peace be here!
Parnassian queens, I fear, I fear,
      Ye'll now disdain me,
And then my fifty pounds a year
      Will little gain me!

5

giddy
winding
Dance

Ye glaikit, gleesome, dainty damies,
Wha by Castalia's wimplin streamies
Lowp, sing, and lave your pretty limbies,
      Ye ken, ye ken,
That strang necessity supreme is
      'Mang sons o' men.

6

I hae a wife and twa wee laddies;
They maun hae brose and brats o' duddies:
Ye ken yoursels my heart right proud is—
        I need na vaunt—
But I'll sned besoms, thraw saugh woodies,
        Before they want.

must;
scraps of clothes

prune; weave willow twigs

7

Lord help me thro' this warld o' care!
I'm weary—sick o't late and air!
Not but I hae a richer share
        Than monie ithers;
But why should ae man better fare,
        And a' men brithers?

early

one

8

Come, firm Resolve, take thou the van,
Thou stalk o' carl-hemp in man!
And let us mind, faint heart ne'er wan
        A lady fair:
Wha does the utmost that he can
        Will whyles do mair.

male-hemp
remember

sometimes

9

But to conclude my silly rhyme
(I'm scant o' verse and scant o' time):
To make a happy fireside clime
        To weans and wife,
That's the true pathos and sublime
        Of human life.

children

10

My compliments to sister Beckie,
And eke the same to honest Lucky;
I wat she is a daintie chuckie
        As e'er tread clay:
And gratefully, my guid auld cockie,
        I'm yours for ay.

hen
trod

TO A GENTLEMAN

WHO HAD SENT A NEWSPAPER, AND OFFERED
TO CONTINUE IT FREE OF EXPENSE

Kind Sir, I've read your paper through,
And faith, to me 'twas really new!
How guessed ye, Sir, what maist I wanted?
This monie a day I've grain'd and gaunted,
To ken what French mischief was brewin;
Or what the drumlie Dutch were doin;
That vile doup-skelper, Emperor Joseph,
If Venus yet had got his nose off;
Or how the collieshangie works
Atween the Russians and the Turks;
Or if the Swede, before he halt,
Would play anither Charles the Twalt;
If Denmark, any body spak o't;
Or Poland, wha had now the tack o't;
How cut-throat Prussian blades were hingin;
How libbet Italy was singin;
If Spaniard, Portuguese, or Swiss
Were sayin or takin aught amiss;
Or how our merry lads at hame
In Britain's court kept up the game:
How royal George—the Lord leuk o'er him!—
Was managing St. Stephen's quorum;
If sleekit Chatham Will was livin,
Or glaikit Charlie got his nieve in;
How Daddie Burke the plea was cookin;
If Warren Hastings' neck was yeukin;
How cesses, stents, and fees were rax'd,
Or if bare arses yet were tax'd;
The news o' princes, dukes, and earls,
Pimps, sharpers, bawds, and opera-girls;
If that daft buckie, Geordie Wales,
Was threshin still at hizzies' tails;
Or if he was grown oughtlins douser,
And no a perfect kintra cooser:
A' this and mair I never heard of,
And, but for you, I might despair'd of.
So, gratefu', back your news I send you,
And pray a' guid things may attend you!

Glosses (left margin):
groaned;
gaped
muddy
bottom-
smacker
squabble
Between
Twelfth
spoke of it
lease
hanging
castrated
assembly
crafty
giddy; fist
itching
assessments;
dues in kind;
extended
mad younker
wenches'
aught
sedater
country
stallion

TO PETER STUART

Dear Peter, dear Peter,
We poor sons of metre
Are often negleckit, ye ken;
    For instance your sheet, man
    (Tho' glad I'm to see't, man),
I get it no ae day in ten.   not one

TO JOHN MAXWELL, ESQ.
OF TERRAUGHTIE

ON HIS BIRTH-DAY

1

Health to the Maxwells' vet'ran Chief!
Health ay unsour'd by care or grief!
Inspir'd, I turn'd Fate's sibyl leaf
                This natal morn:
I see thy life is stuff o' prief,   stuff of proof
                Scarce quite half-worn.

2

This day thou metes threescore eleven,
And I can tell that bounteous Heaven
(The second-sight, ye ken, is given
                To ilka Poet)   every
On thee a tack o' seven times seven,   lease
                Will yet bestow it.

3

If envious buckies view wi' sorrow   younkers
Thy lengthen'd days on thy blest morrow,
May Desolation's lang-teeth'd harrow,
                Nine miles an' hour,
Rake them, like Sodom and Gomorrah,
                In brunstane stoure!   dust

4

But for thy friends, and they are monie,
Baith honest men and lasses bonie,

loving;
quiet

May couthie Fortune, kind and cannie
　　　　In social glee,
Wi' mornings blythe and e'enings funny
　　　　Bless them and thee!

5

fellow

touch

Fareweel, auld birkie! Lord be near ye,
And then the Deil, he daurna steer ye!
Your friends ay love, your foes ay fear ye!
　　　　For me, shame fa' me,

befall

next; do not

If neist my heart I dinna wear ye,
　　　　While Burns they ca' me!

TO WILLIAM STEWART

1

chimney-
corner
must

In honest Bacon's ingle-neuk
　　Here maun I sit and think,
Sick o' the warld and warld's folk,
　　An' sick, damn'd sick, o' drink!

2

I see, I see there is nae help,
　　But still doun I maun sink,

low

Alas

Till some day *laigh enough* I yelp:—
　　'Wae worth that cursed drink!'

3

Last night;
drunk
hiccup

Yestreen, alas! I was sae fu'
　　I could but yisk and wink;
And now, this day, sair, sair I rue

sorely

　　The weary, weary drink.

4

Satan, I fear thy sooty claws,
　　I hate thy brunstane stink,
And ay I curse the luckless cause,

sup

　　The wicked soup o' drink.

5

In vain I would forget my woes
　　In idle rhyming clink,
For, past redemption damn'd in Prose,
　　I can do nought but drink.

6

To you my trusty, well try'd friend,
     May heaven still on you blink,   smile
And may your life flow to the end,
     Sweet as a dry man's drink!

INSCRIPTION TO MISS GRAHAM
OF FINTRY

1

Here, where the Scottish Muse immortal lives
     In sacred strains and tuneful numbers join'd,
Accept the gift! Though humble he who gives,
     Rich is the tribute of the grateful mind.

2

So may no ruffian feeling in thy breast,
     Discordant, jar thy bosom-chords among!
But Peace attune thy gentle soul to rest,
     Or Love ecstatic wake his seraph song!

3

Or Pity's notes in luxury of tears,
     As modest Want the tale of woe reveals;
While conscious Virtue all the strain endears,
     And heaven-born Piety her sanction seals!

REMORSEFUL APOLOGY

1

The friend whom, wild from Wisdom's way,
     The fumes of wine infuriate send
(Not moony madness more astray),
     Who but deplores that hapless friend?

2

Mine was th' insensate, frenzied part—
     Ah! why should I such scenes outlive?
Scenes so abhorrent to my heart!
     'Tis thine to pity and forgive.

TO COLLECTOR MITCHELL

1

true   Friend of the Poet tried and leal,
        Wha wanting thee might beg or steal;
big   Alake, alake, the meikle Deil
               Wi' a' his witches
dancing   Are at it, skelpin jig an' reel
pockets   In my poor pouches!

2

would   I modestly fu' fain wad hint it,
        That One-pound-one, I sairly want it;
maid   If wi' the hizzie down ye sent it,
               It would be kind;
throbbed   And while my heart wi' life-blood dunted,
               I'd bear't in mind!

3

go   So may the Auld Year gang out moanin
        To see the New come laden, groanin
down the
road   Wi' double plenty o'er the loanin
               To thee and thine:
        Domestic peace and comforts crownin
whole   The hale design!

POSTSCRIPT

4

beaten   Ye've heard this while how I've been licket,
nailed   And by fell Death was nearly nicket:
sleeve-waist-
coat   Grim loon! He got me by the fecket,
               And sair me sheuk;
leapt   But by guid luck I lap a wicket,
corner   And turn'd a neuk.

5

        But by that health, I've got a share o't,
        And by that life, I'm promis'd mair o't,
health;
welfare   My hale and weel, I'll tak a care o't
more watch-
ful   A tentier way;
        Then farewell Folly, hide and hair o't,
              For ance and ay!

TO COLONEL DE PEYSTER

1

My honor'd Colonel, deep I feel
Your interest in the Poet's weal:
Ah! now sma' heart hae I to speel   climb
     The steep Parnassus,
Surrounded thus by bolus pill
     And potion glasses.

2

O, what a canty warld were it,   jolly
Would pain and care and sickness spare it,
And Fortune favor worth and merit
     As they deserve,
And ay a rowth—roast-beef and claret!—   plenty
     Syne, wha wad starve?   Then; would

3

Dame Life, tho' fiction out may trick her,
And in paste gems and frippery deck her,
Oh! flickering, feeble, and unsicker   uncertain
     I've found her still:
Ay wavering, like the willow-wicker,
     'Tween good and ill!

4

Then that curst carmagnole, Auld Satan,
Watches, like baudrons by a ratton,   the cat: rat
Our sinfu' saul to get a claut on   soul; clutch
     Wi' felon ire;
Syne, whip! his tail ye'll ne'er cast saut on—   salt
     He's aff like fire.

5

Ah Nick! Ah Nick! it is na fair,
First showing us the tempting ware,
Bright wines and bonie lasses rare,
     To put us daft;   send us wild
Syne weave, unseen, thy spider snare   Then
     O' Hell's damned waft!   weft

6

Poor Man, the flie, aft bizzes by,
And aft, as chance he comes thee nigh,
itches   Thy damn'd auld elbow yeuks wi' joy
       And hellish pleasure,
Already in thy fancy's eye
certain   Thy sicker treasure!

7

topsy-turvy   Soon, heels o'er gowdie, in he gangs,
tongs [for
singeing]   And, like a sheep-head on a tangs,
grinning   Thy girnin laugh enjoys his pangs
       And murdering wrestle,
As, dangling in the wind, he hangs
       A gibbet's tassle.

8

But lest you think I am uncivil
tedious   To plague you with this draunting drivel,
Abjuring a' intentions evil,
quit   I quat my pen:
The Lord preserve us frae the Devil!
       Amen! Amen!

TO MISS JESSIE LEWARS

Thine be the volumes, Jessie fair,
And with them take the Poet's prayer:
That Fate may in her fairest page,
With ev'ry kindliest, best presage
Of future bliss enrol thy name;
With native worth, and spotless fame,
And wakeful caution, still aware
Of ill—but chief Man's felon snare!
All blameless joys on earth we find,
And all the treasures of the mind—
These be thy guardian and reward!
So prays thy faithful friend, the Bard.

INSCRIPTION

WRITTEN ON THE BLANK LEAF OF A COPY OF
THE LAST EDITION OF MY POEMS, PRESENTED
TO THE LADY WHOM, IN SO MANY FICTITIOUS
REVERIES OF PASSION, BUT WITH THE MOST AR-
DENT SENTIMENTS OF REAL FRIENDSHIP, I HAVE
SO OFTEN SUNG UNDER THE NAME OF CHLORIS

I

'Tis Friendship's pledge, my young, fair Friend,
   Nor thou the gift refuse;
Nor with unwilling ear attend
   The moralising Muse.

2

Since thou in all thy youth and charms
   Must bid the world adieu
(A world 'gainst peace in constant arms),
   To join the friendly few;

3

Since, thy gay morn of life o'ercast,
   Chill came the tempest's lour
(And ne'er Misfortune's eastern blast
   Did nip a fairer flower);

4

Since life's gay scenes must charm no more:
   Still much is left behind,
Still nobler wealth hast thou in store—
   The comforts of the mind!

5

Thine is the self-approving glow
   Of conscious honor's part;
And (dearest gift of Heaven below)
   Thine Friendship's truest heart;

6

The joys refin'd of sense and taste,
   With every Muse to rove:
And doubly were the Poet blest,
   These joys could he improve.

PROLOGUE

SPOKEN BY MR. WOODS ON HIS BENEFIT
NIGHT, MONDAY, 16TH APRIL, 1787

When by a generous Public's kind acclaim
That dearest need is granted—honest fame;
When here your favour is the actor's lot,
Nor even the man in private life forgot;
What breast so dead to heavenly Virtue's glow
But heaves impassion'd with the grateful throe?

Poor is the task to please a barb'rous throng:
It needs no Siddons's powers in Southern's song.
But here an ancient nation, fam'd afar
For genius, learning high, as great in war.
Hail, Caledonia, name for ever dear!
Before whose sons I'm honor'd to appear!
Where every science, every nobler art,
That can inform the mind or mend the heart,
Is known (as grateful nations oft have found),
Far as the rude barbarian marks the bound!
Philosophy, no idle pedant dream,
Here holds her search by heaven-taught Reason's
    beam;
Here History paints with elegance and force
The tide of Empire's fluctuating course;
Here *Douglas* forms wild Shakespeare into plan,
And Harley rouses all the God in man.
When well-form'd taste and sparkling wit unite
With manly lore, or female beauty bright
(Beauty, where faultless symmetry and grace
Can only charm us in the second place),
Witness my heart, how oft with panting fear,
As on this night, I've met these judges here!
But still the hope Experience taught to live:
Equal to judge, you're candid to forgive.
No hundred-headed Riot here we meet,
With Decency and Law beneath his feet;
Nor Insolence assumes fair Freedom's name:
Like Caledonians you applaud or blame!

O Thou, dread Power, Whose empire-giving hand
Has oft been stretch'd to shield the honor'd land!

Strong may she glow with all her ancient fire;
May every son be worthy of his sire;
Firm may she rise, with generous disdain
At Tyranny's, or direr Pleasure's chain;
Still self-dependent in her native shore,
Bold may she brave grim Danger's loudest roar,
Till Fate the curtain drop on worlds to be no more!

PROLOGUE SPOKEN AT THE THEATRE OF DUMFRIES

ON NEW YEAR'S DAY EVENING, 1790

No song nor dance I bring from yon great city
That queens it o'er our taste—the more's the pity!
Tho', by the bye, abroad why will you roam?
Good sense and taste are natives here at home.
But not for panegýric I appear:
I come to wish you all a good New Year!
Old Father Time deputes me here before ye,
Not for to preach, but tell his simple story.
The sage, grave Ancient cough'd, and bade me say:
' You're one year older this important day.'
If wiser too—he hinted some suggestion,
But 'twould be rude, you know, to ask the question;
And with a would-be-roguish leer and wink
He bade me on you press this one word—Think!

Ye sprightly youths, quite flush with hope and
        spirit,
Who think to storm the world by dint of merit,
To you the dotard has a deal to say,
In his sly, dry, sententious, proverb way!
He bids you mind, amid your thoughtless rattle,
That the first blow is ever half the battle;
That, tho' some by the skirt may try to snatch him,
Yet by the forelock is the hold to catch him;
That, whether doing, suffering, or forbearing,
You may do miracles by persevering.

Last, tho' not least in love, ye youthful fair,
Angelic forms, high Heaven's peculiar care!
To you old Bald-Pate smoothes his wrinkled brow,

And humbly begs you'll mind the important—Now!
To crown your happiness he asks your leave,
And offers bliss to give and to receive.

For our sincere, tho' haply weak endeavours,
With grateful pride we own your many favours;
And howsoe'er our tongues may ill reveal it,
Believe our glowing bosoms truly feel it.

SCOTS PROLOGUE FOR
MRS. SUTHERLAND

ON HER BENEFIT-NIGHT AT THE THEATRE,
DUMFRIES, MARCH 3RD, 1790

What needs this din about the town o' Lon'on,
How this new play an' that new song is comin?
Why is outlandish stuff sae meikle courted?
Does Nonsense mend like brandy—when imported?
Is there nae poet, burning keen for fame,
Will bauldly try to gie us plays at hame?
For Comedy abroad he need na toil:
A knave and fool are plants of every soil.
Nor need he stray as far as Rome or Greece
To gather matter for a serious piece:
There's themes enow in Caledonian story
Would show the tragic Muse in a' her glory.

Is there no daring Bard will rise and tell
How glorious Wallace stood, how hapless fell?
Where are the Muses fled that could produce
A drama worthy o' the name o' Bruce?
How here, even here, he first unsheath'd the sword
'Gainst mighty England and her guilty lord,
And after monie a bloody, deathless doing,
Wrench'd his dear country from the jaws of Ruin!
O, for a Shakespeare, or an Otway scene
To paint the lovely, hapless Scottish Queen!
Vain all th' omnipotence of female charms
'Gainst headlong, ruthless, mad Rebellion's arms!
She fell, but fell with spirit truly Roman,
To glut the vengeance of a rival woman:

much

A woman (tho' the phrase may seem uncivil)
As able—and as cruel—as the Devil!
One Douglas lives in Home's immortal page,
But Douglasses were heroes every age;
And tho' your fathers, prodigal of life,
A Douglas followed to the martial strife,
Perhaps, if bowls row right, and Right succeeds,   roll
Ye yet may follow where a Douglas leads!

  As ye hae generous done, if a' the land
Would take the Muses' servants by the hand;
Not only hear, but patronize, befriend them,
And where ye justly can commend, commend them;
And aiblins, when they winna stand the test,   perhaps; will
                                                        not
Wink hard, and say: 'The folks hae done their
      best!'
Would a' the land do this, then I'll be caition   go bail
Ye'll soon hae Poets o' the Scottish nation
Will gar Fame blaw until her trumpet crack,   make
And warsle Time, an' lay him on his back!   grapple

For us and for our stage, should onie spier:—   ask
'Whase aught thae chiels maks a' this bustle here?'   Who owns
                                                        those fellows
My best leg foremost, I'll set up my brow:—
'We have the honor to belong to you!'
We're your ain bairns, e'en guide us as ye like,
But like good mithers, shore before ye strike;   warn
And gratefu' still, I trust ye'll ever find us
For gen'rous patronage and meikle kindness
We've got frae a' professions, setts an' ranks:
God help us! we're but poor—ye'se get but thanks!   ye'll

THE RIGHTS OF WOMAN

An Occasional Address

SPOKEN BY MISS FONTENELLE ON HER
BENEFIT NIGHT, DUMFRIES, NOVEMBER 26, 1792

While Europe's eye is fix'd on mighty things,
The fate of empires and the fall of kings;
While quacks of State must each produce his plan,
And even children lisp the Rights of Man;

Amid this mighty fuss just let me mention,
The Rights of Woman merit some attention.

First, in the sexes' intermix'd connexion
One sacred Right of Woman is Protection:
The tender flower, that lifts its head elate,
Helpless must fall before the blasts of fate,
Sunk on the earth, defac'd its lovely form,
Unless your shelter ward th' impending storm.

Our second Right—but needless here is caution—
To keep that right inviolate's the fashion:
Each man of sense has it so full before him,
He'd die before he'd wrong it—'tis Decorum!
There was, indeed, in far less polish'd days,
A time, when rough rude Man had naughty ways:
Would swagger, swear, get drunk, kick up a riot,
Nay, even thus invade a lady's quiet!
Now, thank our stars! these Gothic times are fled;
Now, well-bred men—and you are all well-bred—
Most justly think (and we are much the gainers)
Such conduct neither spirit, wit, nor manners.

For Right the third, our last, our best, our dearest:
That right to fluttering female hearts the nearest,
Which even the Rights of Kings, in low prostration,
Most humbly own—'tis dear, dear Admiration!
In that blest sphere alone we live and move;
There taste that life of life—Immortal Love.
Smiles, glances, sighs, tears, fits, flirtations, airs—
'Gainst such an host what flinty savage dares?
When awful Beauty joins with all her charms,
Who is so rash as rise in rebel arms?

But truce with kings, and truce with constitutions,
With bloody armaments and revolutions;
Let Majesty your first attention summon:
Ah! ça ira! the Majesty of Woman!

ADDRESS

SPOKEN BY MISS FONTENELLE ON HER BENEFIT NIGHT, DECEMBER 4TH, 1793, AT THE THEATRE, DUMFRIES

Still anxious to secure your partial favor,
And not less anxious, sure, this night than ever,
A Prologue, Epilogue, or some such matter,
'Twould vamp my bill, said I, if nothing better:
So sought a Poet roosted near the skies;
Told him I came to feast my curious eyes;
Said, nothing like his works was ever printed;
And last, my prologue-business slily hinted.
' Ma'am, let me tell you,' quoth my man of rhymes,
' I know your bent—these are no laughing times:
Can you—but, Miss, I own I have my fears—
Dissolve in pause, and sentimental tears?
With laden sighs, and solemn-rounded sentence,
Rouse from his sluggish slumbers, fell Repentance?
Paint Vengeance, as he takes his horrid stand,
Waving on high the desolating brand,
Calling the storms to bear him o'er a guilty land?'

I could no more! Askance the creature eyeing:—
' D'ye think,' said I, ' this face was made for crying?
I'll laugh, that's poz—nay more, the world shall
    know it;
And so, your servant! gloomy Master Poet!'

  Firm as my creed, Sirs, 'tis my fix'd belief
That Misery's another word for Grief.
I also think (so may I be a bride!)
That so much laughter, so much life enjoy'd.

Thou man of crazy care and ceaseless sigh,
Still under bleak Misfortune's blasting eye;
Doom'd to that sorest task of man alive—
To make three guineas do the work of five;
Laugh in Misfortune's face—the beldam witch—
Say, you'll be merry, tho' you can't be rich!

Thou other man of care, the wretch in love!
Who long with jiltish arts and airs hast strove;

Who, as the boughs all temptingly project,
Measur'st in desperate thought—a rope—thy neck—
Or, where the beetling cliff o'erhangs the deep,
Peerest to meditate the healing leap:
Would'st thou be cur'd, thou silly, moping elf?
Laugh at her follies, laugh e'en at thyself;
Learn to despise those frowns now so terrific,
And love a kinder: that's your grand specific.

To sum up all: be merry, I advise;
And as we're merry, may we still be wise!

ADDRESS OF BEELZEBUB

To the Right Honorable the Earl of Breadalbane,
President of the Right Honorable the Highland Society,
which met on the 23rd of May last, at the *Shakespeare*,
Covent Garden, to concert ways and means to frustrate
the designs of five hundred Highlanders who, as the
Society were informed by Mr. M'Kenzie of Applecross,
were so audacious as to attempt an escape from their law-
ful lords and masters whose property they were, by
emigrating from the lands of Mr. Macdonald of Glen-
gary to the wilds of Canada, in search of that fantastic
thing—Liberty.

Long life, my lord, an' health be yours,
Unharmed   Unskaith'd by hunger'd Highland boors!
ragged   Lord grant nae duddie, desperate beggar,
Wi' dirk, claymore, or rusty trigger,
rob   May twin auld Scotland o' a life
She likes—as lambkins like a knife!

Faith! you and Applecross were right
To keep the Highland hounds in sight!
offer   I doubt na! they wad bid nae better
Than let them ance out owre the water!
those   Then up amang thae lakes and seas,
They'll mak what rules and laws they please:
Some daring Hancock, or a Franklin,
May set their Highland bluid a-ranklin;
Some Washington again may head them,
Or some Montgomerie, fearless, lead them;

Till (God knows what may be effected
When by such heads and hearts directed)
Poor dunghill sons of dirt an' mire
May to Patrician rights aspire!
Nae sage North now, nor sager Sackville,
To watch and premier owre the pack vile!
An' whare will ye get Howes and Clintons
To bring them to a right repentance?
To cowe the rebel generation,   scare
An' save the honor o' the nation?
They, an' be damn'd! what right hae they
To meat or sleep or light o' day,
Far less to riches, pow'r, or freedom,
But what your lordship likes to gie them?

But hear, my lord! Glengary, hear!
Your hand's owre light on them, I fear: too
Your factors, grieves, trustees, and bailies,
I canna say but they do gaylies: gaily
They lay aside a' tender mercies,   strip;
An' tirl the hullions to the birses.   slovens;
                                                        bristles;
Yet while they're only poind and herriet,   distrained;
They'll keep their stubborn Highland spirit.   robbed
But smash them! crush them a' to spails,
An' rot the dyvors i' the jails!   bankrupts
The young dogs, swinge them to the labour:
Let wark an' hunger mak them sober!   girls; at
The hizzies, if they're aughtlins fawsont,   all good-
Let them in Drury Lane be lesson'd!   looking
An' if the wives an' dirty brats   begging;
Come thiggin at your doors an' yetts,   gates
Flaffin wi' duds an' grey wi' beas',   flapping with
                                                        rags; vermin
Frightin awa your deuks an' geese,   ducks
Get out a horsewhip or a jowler,   bull dog
The langest thong, the fiercest growler,
An' gar the tatter'd gypsies pack   make
Wi' a' their bastards on their back!

Go on, my Lord! I lang to meet you,   long
An' in my ' house at hame ' to greet you.
Wi' common lords ye shanna mingle: shall not
The benmost neuk beside the ingle,   inmost
At my right han' assigned your seat   corner;
'Tween Herod's hip an' Polycrate,   fireside

weary

Or (if you on your station tarrow)
Between Almagro and Pizarro,
A seat, I'm sure ye're weel deservin't;
An' till ye come—your humble servant,
                                    BEELZEBUB.

Hell,
1st *June, Anno Mundi* 5790

BIRTHDAY ODE FOR
31ST DECEMBER 1787

Afar the illustrious Exile roams,
    Whom kingdoms on this day should hail,
An inmate in the casual shed,
On transient pity's bounty fed,
    Haunted by busy Memory's bitter tale!
Beasts of the forest have their savage homes,
    But He, who should imperial purple wear,
Owns not the lap of earth where rests his royal head:
    His wretched refuge dark despair,
While ravening wrongs and woes pursue,
And distant far the faithful few
    Who would his sorrows share!

False flatterer, Hope, away,
    Nor think to lure us as in days of yore!
We solemnize this sorrowing natal day,
    To prove our loyal truth—we can no more—
And, owning Heaven's mysterious sway,
    Submissive, low, adore.
Ye honor'd, mighty Dead,
    Who nobly perish'd in the glorious cause,
    Your King, your Country, and her laws:
From great Dundee, who smiling Victory led
    And fell a Martyr in her arms
    (What breast of northern ice but warms!),
To bold Balmerino's undying name,
Whose soul of fire, lighted at Heaven's high flame,
Deserves the proudest wreath departed heroes claim!

Not unrevenged your fate shall lie,
    It only lags, the fatal hour:

Your blood shall with incessant cry
    Awake at last th' unsparing Power.
As from the cliff, with thundering course,
    The snowy ruin smokes along
With doubling speed and gathering force,
Till deep it, crushing, whelms the cottage in the vale,
    So Vengeance' arm, ensanguin'd, strong,
    Shall with resistless might assail,
    Usurping Brunswick's pride shall lay,
And Stewart's wrongs and yours with tenfold weight
    repay.

Perdition, baleful child of night,
Rise and revenge the injured right
    Of Stewart's royal race!
Lead on the unmuzzled hounds of Hell,
Till all the frighted echoes tell
    The blood-notes of the chase!
Full on the quarry point their view,
Full on the base usurping crew,
The tools of faction and the nation's curse!
    Hark how the cry grows on the wind;
    They leave the lagging gale behind;
    Their savage fury, pityless, they pour;
    With murdering eyes already they devour!
    See Brunswick spent, a wretched prey,
    His life one poor despairing day,
Where each avenging hour still ushers in a worse!
    Such Havoc, howling all abroad,
        Their utter ruin bring,
    The base apostates to their God
        Or rebels to their King!

ODE TO THE DEPARTED
REGENCY BILL

Daughter of Chaos' doting years,
Nurse of ten thousand hopes and fears!
Whether thy airy, unsubstantial shade
(The rights of sepulture now duly paid)
Spread abroad its hideous form
On the roaring civil storm,

Deafening din and warring rage
Factions wild with factions wage;
  Or Underground
  Deep-sunk, profound
Among the demons of the earth,
  With groans that make
  The mountains shake
Thou mourn thy ill-starr'd blighted birth;
Or in the uncreated Void,
  Where seeds of future being fight,
With lighten'd step thou wander wide
  To greet thy mother—Ancient Night—
And as each jarring monster-mass is past,
Fond recollect what once thou wast:
In manner due, beneath this sacred oak,
Hear, Spirit, hear! thy presence I invoke!

  By a Monarch's heaven-struck fate;
  By a disunited State;
  By a generous Prince's wrongs;
  By a Senate's war of tongues;
  By a Premier's sullen pride
  Louring on the changing tide;
  By dread Thurlow's powers to awe—
  Rhetoric, blasphemy and law;
  By the turbulent ocean,
  A Nation's commotion;
  By the harlot-caresses
  Of Borough addresses;
  By days few and evil;
  (Thy portion, poor devil!),
  By Power, Wealth, and Show—the Gods by
    men adored;
  By nameless Poverty their Hell abhorred;
    By all they hope, by all they fear,
    Hear! and Appear!

Stare not on me, thou ghostly Power,
Nor, grim with chain'd defiance, lour!
No Babel-structure would I build
  Where, Order exil'd from his native sway,
Confusion might the Regent-sceptre wield,
  While all would rule and none obey,

Go, to the world of Man relate
The story of thy sad, eventful fate;
And call presumptuous Hope to hear
And bid him check his blind career;
And tell the sore-prest sons of Care
  Never, never to despair!

Paint Charles's speed on wings of fire,
The object of his fond desire,
Beyond his boldest hopes, at hand.
Paint all the triumph of the Portland Band
(Hark! how they lift the joy-exulting voice,
And how their num'rous creditors rejoice!);
But just as hopes to warm enjoyment rise,
Cry ' Convalescence! ' and the vision flies.
Then next pourtray a dark'ning twilight gloom
  Eclipsing sad a gay, rejoicing morn,
While proud Ambition to th' untimely tomb
  By gnashing, grim, despairing fiends is borne!
Paint Ruin, in the shape of high Dundas
  Gaping with giddy terror o'er the brow:
In vain he struggles, the Fates behind him press,
  And clamorous Hell yawns for her prey below!
How fallen That, whose pride late scaled the skies!
And This, like Lucifer, no more to rise!
  Again pronounce the powerful word:
See Day, triumphant from the night, restored!

Then know this truth, ye Sons of Men
  (Thus ends thy moral tale:)
Your darkest terrors may be vain,
  Your brightest hopes may fail!

A NEW PSALM FOR THE CHAPEL
OF KILMARNOCK

ON THE THANKSGIVING-DAY FOR HIS MAJESTY'S RECOVERY

I

O, sing a new song to the Lord!
  Make, all and every one,
A joyful noise, ev'n for the King
  His restoration!

2

The sons of Belial in the land
   Did set their heads together.
' Come, let us sweep them off,' said they,
   ' Like an o'erflowing river! '

3

They set their heads together, I say,
   They set their heads together:
On right, and left, and every hand,
   We saw none to deliver.

4

Thou madest strong two chosen ones,
   To quell the Wicked's pride:
That Young Man, great in Issachar,
   The burden-bearing tribe;

5

And him, among the Princes, chief
   In our Jerusalem,
The Judge that's mighty in Thy law,
   The man that fears Thy name.

6

Yet they, even they with all their strength,
   Began to faint and fail;
Even as two howling, rav'ning wolves
   To dogs do turn their tail.

7

Th' ungodly o'er the just prevail'd;
   For so Thou hadst appointed,
That Thou might'st greater glory give
   Unto Thine own anointed!

8

And now Thou hast restored our State,
   Pity our Kirk also;
For she by tribulations
   Is now brought very low!

9

Consume that high-place, Patronage,
  From off Thy holy hill;
And in Thy fury burn the book
  Even of that man M'Gill!

10

Now hear our prayer, accept our song,
  And fight Thy chosen's battle!
We seek but little, Lord, from Thee:
  Thou kens we get as little!

INSCRIBED TO
THE RIGHT HON. C. J. FOX

How Wisdom and Folly meet, mix, and unite,
How Virtue and Vice blend their black and their
    white,
How Genius, th' illustrious father of fiction,
Confounds rule and law, reconciles contradiction,
I sing. If these mortals, the critics, should bustle,
I care not, not I: let the critics go whistle!

But now for a Patron, whose name and whose glory
At once may illústrate and honor my story:—

Thou first of our orators, first of our wits,
Yet whose parts and acquirements seem mere lucky
    hits;
With knowledge so vast and with judgment so strong,
No man with the half of 'em e'er could go wrong;
With passions so potent and fancies so bright,
No man with the half of 'em e'er could go right;
A sorry, poor, misbegot son of the Muses,
For using thy name, offers fifty excuses.

Good Lord, what is Man! For as simple he looks,
Do but try to develop his hooks and his crooks!
With his depths and his shallows, his good and his
    evil,
All in all he's a problem must puzzle the Devil.

On his one ruling passion Sir Pope hugely labors,
That, like th' old Hebrew walking-switch, eats up its
　　neighbours.
Human Nature's his show-box—your friend, would
　　you know him?
Pull the string, Ruling Passion—the picture will show
　　him.
What pity, in rearing so beauteous a system,
One trifling particular—Truth—should have miss'd
　　him!
For, spite of his fine theoretic positions,
Mankind is a science defies definitions.

Some sort all our qualities each to its tribe,
And think Human Nature they truly describe:
Have you found this, or t'other? There's more in
　　the wind,
As by one drunken fellow his comrades you'll find.
But such is the flaw, or the depth of the plan
In the make of that wonderful creature called Man,
No two virtues, whatever relation they claim,
Nor even two different shades of the same,
Though like as was ever twin brother to brother,
Possessing the one shall imply you 've the other.

But truce with abstraction, and truce with a Muse
Whose rhymes you'll perhaps, Sir, ne'er deign to
　　peruse!
Will you leave your justings, your jars, and your
　　quarrels,
Contending with Billy for proud-nodding laurels?
My much-honour'd Patron, believe your poor Poet,
Your courage much more than your prudence, you
　　show it.
In vain with Squire Billy for laurels you struggle:
He'll have them by fair trade—if not, he will smuggle;
Nor cabinets even of kings would conceal 'em,
He'd up the back-stairs, and by God he would steal
　　'em!
Then feats like Squire Billy's, you ne'er can achieve
　　'em;
It is not, out-do him—the task is, out-thieve him!

ON GLENRIDDELL'S FOX BREAKING
HIS CHAIN

A FRAGMENT, 1791

Thou, Liberty, thou art my theme:
Not such as idle poets dream,
Who trick thee up a heathen goddess
That a fantastic cap and rod has!
Such stale conceits are poor and silly:
I paint thee out a Highland filly,
A sturdy, stubborn, handsome dapple,
As sleek's a mouse, as round's an apple,
That, when thou pleasest, can do wonders,
But when thy luckless rider blunders,
Or if thy fancy should demur there,
Wilt break thy neck ere thou go further.

These things premis'd, I sing a Fox—
Was caught among his native rocks,
And to a dirty kennel chained—
How he his liberty regained.

Glenriddell! a Whig without a stain,
A Whig in principle and grain,
Could'st thou enslave a free-born creature,
A native denizen of Nature?
How could'st thou, with a heart so good
(A better ne'er was sluiced with blood),
Nail a poor devil to a tree,
That ne'er did harm to thine or thee?

The staunchest Whig Glenriddell was,
Quite frantic in his country's cause;
And oft was Reynard's prison passing,
And with his brother-Whigs canvássing
The rights of men, the powers of women,
With all the dignity of Freemen.

Sir Reynard daily heard debates
Of princes', kings', and nations' fates,
With many rueful, bloody stories
Of tyrants, Jacobites, and Tories:

From liberty how angels fell,
That now are galley-slaves in Hell;
How Nimrod first the trade began
Of binding Slavery's chains on man;
How fell Semiramis—God damn her!—
Did first, with sacrilegious hammer
(All ills till then were trivial matters)
For Man dethron'd forge hen-peck fetters;
How Xerxes, that abandoned Tory,
Thought cutting throats was reaping glory,
Until the stubborn Whigs of Sparta
Taught him great Nature's Magna Charta;
How mighty Rome her fiat hurl'd
Resistless o'er a bowing world,
And, kinder than they did desire,
Polish'd mankind with sword and fire:
With much too tedious to relate
Of ancient and of modern date,
But ending still how Billy Pitt
(Unlucky boy!) with wicked wit
Has gagg'd old Britain, drained her coffer,
As butchers bind and bleed a heifer.

Thus wily Reynard, by degrees
In kennel listening at his ease,
Suck'd in a mighty stock of knowledge,
As much as some folks at a college;
Knew Britain's rights and constitution,
Her aggrandisement, diminution;
How Fortune wrought us good from evil:
Let no man, then, despise the Devil,
As who should say: ' I ne'er can need him,'
Since we to scoundrels owe our Freedom.

ON THE COMMEMORATION OF
RODNEY'S VICTORY

KING'S ARMS, DUMFRIES, 12TH APRIL, 1793

Instead of a song, boys, I'll give you a toast:
Here's the Mem'ry of those on the Twelfth that we
    lost!—

We lost, did I say?—No, by Heav'n, that we found!
For their fame it shall live while the world goes
  round.
The next in succession I'll give you: the King!
And who would betray him, on high may he swing!
And here's the grand fabric, our Free Constitution
As built on the base of the great Revolution!
And, longer with Politics not to be cramm'd,
Be Anarchy curs'd, and be Tyranny damn'd!
And who would to Liberty e'er prove disloyal,
May his son be a hangman—and he his first trial!

ODE FOR GENERAL WASHINGTON'S BIRTHDAY

No Spartan tube, no Attic shell,
  No lyre Æolian I awake.
'Tis Liberty's bold note I swell:
  Thy harp, Columbia, let me take!
See gathering thousands, while I sing,
A broken chain, exulting, bring
    And dash it in a tyrant's face,
  And dare him to his very beard,
  And tell him he no more is fear'd,
    No more the despot of Columbia's race!
  A tyrant's proudest insults brav'd,
They shout a People freed! They hail an Empire
  sav'd!
  Where is man's godlike form?
    Where is that brow erect and bold,
    That eye that can unmov'd behold
  The wildest rage, the loudest storm
  That e'er created Fury dared to raise?
  Avaunt! thou caitiff, servile, base,
  That tremblest at a despot's nod,
  Yet, crouching under the iron rod,
    Canst laud the arm that struck th' insulting blow!
Art thou of man's Imperial line?
Dost boast that countenance divine?
  Each skulking feature answers: No!
But come, ye sons of Liberty,
Columbia's offspring, brave as free,

In danger's hour still flaming in the van,
Ye know, and dare maintain, The Royalty of Man!

Alfred, on thy starry throne
    Surrounded by the tuneful choir,
    The Bards that erst have struck the patriot lyre,
    And rous'd the freeborn Briton's soul of fire,
No more thy England own!
Dare injured nations form the great design
    To make detested tyrants bleed?
    Thy England execrates the glorious deed!
    Beneath her hostile banners waving,
    Every pang of honour braving,
England in thunder calls: ' The Tyrant's cause is
    mine! '
That hour accurst how did the fiends rejoice,
And Hell thro' all her confines raise th' exulting
    voice!
That hour which saw the generous English name
Link't with such damnèd deeds of everlasting shame!

Thee, Caledonia, thy wild heaths among,
Fam'd for the martial deed, the heaven-taught song,
    To thee I turn with swimming eyes!
Where is that soul of Freedom fled?
Immingled with the mighty dead
    Beneath that hallow'd turf where Wallace lies!
Hear it not, Wallace, in thy bed of death!
    Ye babbling winds, in silence sweep!
    Disturb not ye the hero's sleep,
Nor give the coward secret breath!
Is this the ancient Caledonian form,
Firm as her rock, resistless as her storm?
Show me that eye which shot immortal hate,
    Blasting the Despot's proudest bearing!
Show me that arm which, nerv'd with thundering
    fate,
    Braved Usurpation's boldest daring!
Dark-quench'd as yonder sinking star,
No more that glance lightens afar,
That palsied arm no more whirls on the waste of
    war.

ELECTION BALLAD

AT CLOSE OF THE CONTEST FOR REPRESENTING
THE DUMFRIES BURGHS, 1790

Addressed to Robert Graham of Fintry

1

Fintry, my stay in worldly strife,
Friend o' my Muse, friend o' my life,
    Are ye as idle's I am?
Come, then! Wi' uncouth kintra fleg   *country action*
O'er Pegasus I'll fling my leg,
    And ye shall see me try him!

2

But where shall I gae rin or ride,   *go run*
That I may splatter nane beside?   *splash*
    I wad na be uncivil: *would not*
In mankind's various paths and ways
There's ay some doytin body strays,   *doddering creature*
    And I ride like a devil.

3

Thus I break aff wi' a' my birr,   *force*
An' down yon dark, deep alley spur,
    Where Theologics dander: *saunter*
Alas! curst wi' eternal fogs,
And damn'd in everlasting bogs,
    As sure's the Creed I'll blunder!

4

I'll stain a band, or jaup a gown,   *splash*
Or rin my reckless, guilty crown
    Against the haly door!
Sair do I rue my luckless fate,   *Sore*
When, as the Muse an' Deil wad hae't,
    I rade that road before!

5

Suppose I take a spurt, and mix
Amang the wilds o' Politics—
    Electors and elected—

Where dogs at Court (sad sons o' bitches!)
Septennially a madness touches,
      Till all the land's infected?

6

All hail, Drumlanrig's haughty Grace,
Discarded remnant of a race
      Once godlike—great in story!
Thy fathers' virtues all contrasted,
The very name of Douglas blasted,
      Thine that inverted glory!

7

Hate, envy, oft the Douglas bore;
But thou hast superadded more,
      And sunk them in contempt!
Follies and crimes have stain'd the name;
But, Queensberry, thine the virgin claim,
      From aught that's good exempt!

8

I'll sing the zeal Drumlanrig bears,
Who left the all-important cares
      Of fiddlers, whores, and hunters,
And, bent on buying Borough Towns,
Came shaking hands wi' wabster-loons,
      And kissing barefit bunters.

weaver
rascals
harlots

9

Combustion thro' our boroughs rode,
Whistling his roaring pack abroad
      Of mad unmuzzled lions,
As Queensberry buff-and-blue unfurl'd,
And Westerha' and Hopeton hurl'd
      To every Whig defiance.

10

But cautious Queensberry left the war
(Th' unmanner'd dust might soil his star;
      Besides, he hated bleeding),
But left behind him heroes bright,
Heroes in Cæsarean fight
      Or Ciceronian pleading.

11

O, for a throat like huge Mons-Meg,
To muster o'er each ardent Whig,
   Beneath Drumlanrig's banner!
Heroes and heroines commix,
All in the field of politics,
   To win immortal honor!

12

M'Murdo and his lovely spouse
(Th' enamour'd laurels kiss her brows!)
   Led on the Loves and Graces:
She won each gaping burgess' heart,
While he, *sub rosa*, played his part
   Among their wives and lasses.

13

Craigdarroch led a light-arm'd core: company
Tropes, metaphors, and figures pour,
   Like Hecla streaming thunder.
Glenriddell, skill'd in rusty coins,
Blew up each Tory's dark designs
   And bared the treason under.

14

In either wing two champions fought:
Redoubted Staig, who set at nought
   The wildest savage Tory;
And Welsh, who ne'er yet flinch'd his ground,
High-wav'd his magnum-bonum round   double-
   With Cyclopeian fury.   quart

15

Miller brought up th' artillery ranks,
The many-pounders of the Banks,
   Resistless desolation!
While Maxwelton, that baron bold,
'Mid Lawson's port entrench'd his hold
   And threaten'd worse damnation.

16

To these what Tory hosts oppos'd,
With these what Tory warriors clos'd,
   Surpasses my descriving:

Squadrons, extended long and large,
With furious speed rush to the charge,
   Like furious devils driving.

17

What verse can sing, what prose narrate
The butcher deeds of bloody Fate
   Amid this mighty tulyie?
Grim Horror girn'd, pale Terror roar'd,
As Murther at his thrapple shor'd,
   And Hell mix'd in the brulyie.

tussle
snarled
weasand
threatened
brangle

18

As Highland craigs by thunder cleft,
When lightnings fire the stormy lift,
   Hurl down with crashing rattle,
As flames among a hundred woods,
As headlong foam a hundred floods—
   Such is the rage of Battle!

crags
sky

19

The stubborn Tories dare to die:
As soon the rooted oaks would fly
   Before th' approaching fellers!
The Whigs come on like Ocean's roar,
When all his wintry billows pour
   Against the Buchan Bullers.

20

Lo, from the shades of Death's deep night
Departed Whigs enjoy the fight,
   And think on former daring!
The muffled murtherer of Charles
The Magna Charter flag unfurls,
   All deadly gules its bearing.

21

Nor wanting ghosts of Tory fame:
Bold Scrimgeour follows gallant Graham,
   Auld Covenanters shiver . . .
Forgive! forgive! much-wrong'd Montrose!
Now Death and Hell engulph thy foes,
   Thou liv'st on high for ever!

22

Still o'er the field the combat burns;
The Tories, Whigs, give way by turns;
  But Fate the word has spoken;
For woman's wit and strength o' man,
Alas! can do but what they can:
  The Tory ranks are broken.

23

O, that my een were flowing burns!   *eyes; brooks*
My voice a lioness that mourns
  Her darling cubs' undoing
That I might greet, that I might cry,   *weep*
While Tories fall, while Tories fly
  From furious Whigs pursuing!

24

What Whig but melts for good Sir James,
Dear to his country by the names,
  Friend, Patron, Benefactor?
Not Pulteney's wealth can Pulteney save;
And Hopeton falls—the generous, brave!—
  And Stewart bold as Hector.

25

Thou, Pitt, shalt rue this overthrow,
And Thurlow growl this curse of woe,
  And Melville melt in wailing!
Now Fox and Sheridan rejoice,
And Burke shall sing:—' O Prince, arise!
  Thy power is all prevailing! '

26

For your poor friend, the Bard, afar
He sees and hears the distant war,
  A cool spectator purely:
So, when the storm the forest rends,
The robin in the hedge descends,
  And, patient, chirps securely.

27

Now, for my friends' and brethren's sakes,
And for my dear-lov'd Land o' Cakes,
  I pray with holy fire:—

would

Lord, send a rough-shod troop o' Hell
O'er a' wad Scotland buy or sell,
        To grind them in the mire!

WHY SHOULD WE IDLY WASTE OUR PRIME

1

Why should we idly waste our prime
  Repeating our oppressions?
Come rouse to arms! 'Tis now the time
  To punish past transgressions.
'Tis said that Kings can do no wrong—
  Their murderous deeds deny it,
And, since from us their power is sprung,
  We have a right to try it.
Now each true patriot's song shall be:—
' Welcome Death or Libertie! '

2

Proud Priests and Bishops we'll translate
  And canonize as Martyrs;
The guillotine on Peers shall wait;
  And Knights shall hang in garters.
Those Despots long have trode us down,
  And Judges are their engines:
Such wretched minions of a Crown
  Demand the people's vengeance!
To-day 'tis *theirs*. To-morrow we
Shall don the Cap of Libertie!

3

The Golden Age we'll then revive:
  Each man will be a brother;
In harmony we all shall live,
  And share the earth together;
In Virtue train'd, enlighten'd Youth
  Will love each fellow-creature;
And future years shall prove the truth
  That Man is good by nature:
Then let us toast with three times three
The reign of Peace and Libertie!

THE TREE OF LIBERTY

1

Heard ye o' the Tree o' France,
    And wat ye what's the name o't?   wot
Around it a' the patriots dance—
    Weel Europe kens the fame o't!
It stands where ance the Bastile stood—
    A prison built by kings, man,
When Superstition's hellish brood
    Kept France in leading-strings, man.

2

Upo' this tree there grows sic fruit,   such
    Its virtues a' can tell, man:
It raises man aboon the brute,   above
    It mak's him ken himsel', man!
Gif ance the peasant taste a bit,   If
    He's greater than a lord, man,
And wi' the beggar shares a mite
    O' a' he can afford, man.

3

This fruit is worth a' Afric's wealth:
    To comfort us 'twas sent, man,
To gie the sweetest blush o' health,
    And mak' us a' content, man!
It clears the een, it cheers the heart,   eyes
    Mak's high and low guid friends, man,
And he wha acts the traitor's part,
    It to perdition sends, man.

4

My blessings ay attend the chiel,   fellow
    Wha pitied Gallia's slaves, man,
And staw a branch, spite o' the Deil,   stole
    Frae 'yont the western waves, man!   beyond
Fair Virtue water'd it wi' care,
    And now she sees wi' pride, man,
How weel it buds and blossoms there,
    Its branches spreading wide, man.

5

But vicious folk ay hate to see
    The works o' Virtue thrive, man.
The courtly vermin's bann'd the tree,
wept   And grat to see it thrive, man!
King Louis thought to cut it down,
very   When it was unco sma', man;
For this the watchman crack'd his crown,
    Cut aff his head and a', man.

6

then   A wicked crew syne, on a time,
oath   Did tak' a solemn aith, man,
It ne'er should flourish to its prime—
wot   I wat they pledg'd their faith, man!
went Awa they gaed wi' mock parade,
    Like beagles hunting game, man,
But soon grew weary o' the trade,
    And wish'd they'd been at hame, man.

7

Fair Freedom, standing by the tree,
    Her sons did loudly ca', man.
She sang a sang o' Liberty,
    Which pleas'd them ane and a', man.
By her inspir'd, the new-born race
    Soon drew the avenging steel, man.
gave The hirelings ran—her foes gied chase,
    And bang'd the despot weel, man.

8

Let Britain boast her hardy oak,
    Her poplar, and her pine, man!
Auld Britain ance could crack her joke,
    And o'er her neighbours shine, man!
But seek the forest round and round,
    And soon 'twill be agreed, man,
That sic a tree can not be found
    'Twixt London and the Tweed, man.

9

Without this tree alake this life
    Is but a vale o' woe, man,

A scene o' sorrow mix'd wi' strife,
　　Nae real joys we know, man;
We labour soon, we labour late,
　　To feed the titled knave, man,
And a' the comfort we're to get,
　　Is that ayont the grave, man.　　　　　　　　beyond

10

Wi' plenty o' sic trees, I trow,
　　The warld would live in peace, man.
The sword would help to mak' a plough,
　　The din o' war wad cease, man.
Like brethren in a common cause,
　　We'd on each other smile, man;
And equal rights and equal laws
　　Wad gladden every isle, man.

11

Wae worth the loon wha wadna eat　　　　woe befall
　　Sic halesome, dainty cheer, man!　　　the fellow
I'd gie the shoon frae aff my feet,
　　To taste the fruit o't here, man!
Syne let us pray, Auld England may　　　　Then
　　Sure plant this far-famed tree, man;
And blythe we'll sing, and herald the day
　　That gives us liberty, man.

I'LL GO AND BE A SODGER

1

O, why the deuce should I repine,
　　And be an ill foreboder?
I'm twenty-three and five feet nine,
　　I'll go and be a sodger.

2

I gat some gear wi' meikle care,　　　　　wealth;
　　I held it weel thegither;　　　　　　　much
But now it's gane—and something mair:　　together
　　I'll go and be a sodger.

APOSTROPHE TO FERGUSSON

INSCRIBED ABOVE AND BELOW HIS PORTRAIT

Curse on ungrateful man, that can be pleas'd
And yet can starve the author of the pleasure!

O thou, my elder brother in misfortune,
By far my elder brother in the Muse,
With tears I pity thy unhappy fate!
Why is the Bard unfitted for the world,
Yet has so keen a relish of its pleasures?

AH, WOE IS ME, MY MOTHER DEAR

Jeremiah, chap. xv. verse 10

I

Ah, woe is me, my Mother dear!
    A man of strife ye've born me:
For sair contention I maun bear;   *must*
    They hate, revile, and scorn me.

2

I ne'er could lend on bill or band,
    That five per cent. might blest me;   *might have blest*
And borrowing, on the tither hand,   *other*
    The deil a ane wad trust me.   *would*

3

Yet I, a coin-denyèd wight,
    By Fortune quite discarded,
Ye see how I am day and night
    By lad and lass blackguarded!

INSCRIBED ON A WORK OF HANNAH MORE'S

PRESENTED TO THE AUTHOR BY A LADY

Thou flatt'ring mark of friendship kind,
Still may thy pages call to mind
  The dear, the beauteous donor!
Tho' sweetly female ev'ry part,
Yet such a head and—more—the heart
  Does both the sexes honor:
She show'd her taste refin'd and just,
  When she selected thee,
Yet deviating, own I must,
  For so approving me:
    But, kind still, I mind still   *remember*
      The giver in the gift;
    I'll bless her, and wiss her   *wish*
      A Friend aboon the lift.   *in the heavens*

LINES WRITTEN ON A BANK NOTE

Wae worth thy power, thou cursed leaf!   *Woe befall*
Fell source of a' my woe and grief,   *Deadly*
For lack o' thee I've lost my lass,
For lack o' thee I scrimp my glass!
I see the children of affliction
Unaided, through thy curs'd restriction.
I've seen the oppressor's cruel smile
Amid his hapless victims' spoil;
And for thy potence vainly wish'd
To crush the villain in the dust.
For lack o' thee I leave this much-lov'd shore,
Never, perhaps, to greet old Scotland more.

THE FAREWELL

The valiant, in himself, what can he suffer?
Or what does he regard his single woes?
But when, alas! he multiplies himself,
To dearer selves, to the lov'd tender fair,
To those whose bliss, whose beings hang upon him,
To helpless children,—then, Oh then he feels
The point of misery festering in his heart,
And weakly weeps his fortunes like a coward:
Such, such am I!—undone!

THOMSON's *Edward and Eleanora*

I

Farewell, old Scotia's bleak domains,
Far dearer than the torrid plains,
    Where rich ananas blow!
Farewell, a mother's blessing dear,
A brother's sigh, a sister's tear,
    My Jean's heart-rending throe!
Farewell, my Bess! Tho' thou'rt bereft
    Of my paternal care,
A faithful brother I have left,
    My part in him thou'lt share!
        Adieu too, to you too,
            My Smith, my bosom frien';
        When kindly you mind me,
            O, then befriend my Jean!

remember

2

What bursting anguish tears my heart?
From thee, my Jeany, must I part?
    Thou, weeping, answ'rest: 'No!'
Alas! misfortune stares my face,
And points to ruin and disgrace—
    I for thy sake must go!
Thee, Hamilton, and Aiken dear,
    A grateful, warm adieu:
I with a much-indebted tear
    Shall still remember you!
        All-hail, then, the gale then
            Wafts me from thee, dear shore!
        It rustles, and whistles—
            I'll never see thee more!

ELEGY ON THE DEATH OF ROBERT RUISSEAUX

1

Now Robin lies in his last lair,
He'll gabble rhyme, nor sing nae mair;
Cauld Poverty wi' hungry stare
   Nae mair shall fear him; *terrify*
Nor anxious Fear, nor cankert Care, *crabbed*
   E'er mair come near him.

2

To tell the truth, they seldom fash'd him, *bothered*
Except the moment that they crush'd him;
For sune as Chance or Fate had hush'd 'em, *soon*
   Tho' e'er sae short,
Then wi' a rhyme or sang he lash'd 'em,
   And thought it sport.

3

Tho' he was bred to kintra-wark, *country-*
And counted was baith wight and stark, *both stout;*
Yet that was never Robin's mark *strong*
   To mak a man;
But tell him, he was learned and clark, *scholarly*
   Ye roos'd him then! *flattered*

VERSES INTENDED TO BE WRITTEN BELOW A NOBLE EARL'S PICTURE

1

Whose is ... .ble, dauntless brow?
Whose whose that eye of fire?
And whose that generous princely mien,
 Ev'n rooted foes admire?

2

Stranger! to justly show that brow
 And mark that eye of fire,
Would take His hand, whose vernal tints
 His other works admire!

3

Bright as a cloudless summer sun,
　　With stately port he moves;
His guardian Seraph eyes with awe
　　The noble Ward he loves.

4

Among the illustrious Scottish sons
　　That Chief thou may'st discern:
Mark Scotia's fond-returning eye—
　　It dwells upon Glencairn.

ELEGY ON THE DEATH OF SIR JAMES HUNTER BLAIR

1

The lamp of day with ill-presaging glare,
　　Dim, cloudy, sank beneath the western wave;
Th' inconstant blast howl'd thro' the darkening air,
　　And hollow whistled in the rocky cave.

2

Lone as I wander'd by each cliff and dell,
　　Once the lov'd haunts of Scotia's royal train;
Or mus'd where limpid streams, once hallow'd, well,
　　Or mould'ring ruins mark the sacred Fane.

bubble up

3

Th' increasing blast roared round the beetling rocks,
　　The clouds, swift-wing'd, flew o'er the starry sky,
The groaning trees untimely shed their locks,
　　And shooting meteors caught the startled eye.

4

The paly moon rose in the livid east,
　　And 'mong the cliffs disclos'd a stately form
In weeds of woe, that frantic beat her breast,
　　And mix'd her wailings with the raving storm.

5

Wild to my heart the filial pulses glow:
　　'Twas Caledonia's trophied shield I view'd,

Her form majestic droop'd in pensive woe,
   The lightning of her eye in tears imbued;

6

Revers'd that spear redoubtable in war,
   Reclined that banner, erst in fields unfurl'd,
That like a deathful meteor gleam'd afar,
   And brav'd the mighty monarchs of the world.

7

' My patriot son fills an untimely grave! '
   With accents wild and lifted arms, she cried;
' Low lies the hand that oft was stretch'd to save,
   Low lies the heart that swell'd with honor's pride.

8

' A weeping country joins a widow's tear;
   The helpless poor mix with the orphan's cry;
The drooping Arts surround their patron's bier;
   And grateful Science heaves the heart-felt sigh.

9

' I saw my sons resume their ancient fire;
   I saw fair Freedom's blossoms richly blow.
But ah! how hope is born but to expire!
   Relentless fate has laid their guardian low.

10

' My patriot falls, but shall he lie unsung,
   While empty greatness saves a worthless name?
No: every Muse shall join her tuneful tongue,
   And future ages hear his growing fame.

11

' And I will join a mother's tender cares
   Thro' future times to make his virtues last,
That distant years may boast of other Blairs! '—
   She said, and vanish'd with the sweeping blast.

ON THE DEATH OF LORD PRESIDENT DUNDAS

Lone on the bleaky hills, the straying flocks
Shun the fierce storms among the sheltering rocks;
Down foam the rivulets, red with dashing rains;
The gathering floods burst o'er the distant plains;
Beneath the blast the leafless forests groan;
The hollow caves return a hollow moan.
Ye hills, ye plains, ye forests, and ye caves,
Ye howling winds, and wintry swelling waves,
Unheard, unseen, by human ear or eye,
Sad to your sympathetic glooms I fly,
Where to the whistling blast and water's roar
Pale Scotia's recent wound I may deplore!
O heavy loss, thy country ill could bear!
A loss these evil days can ne'er repair!
Justice, the high vicegerent of her God,
Her doubtful balance eyed, and sway'd her rod;
Hearing the tidings of the fatal blow,
She sank, abandon'd to the wildest woe.
Wrongs, injuries, from many a darksome den,
Now gay in hope explore the paths of men.
See from his cavern grim Oppression rise,
And throw on Poverty his cruel eyes!
Keen on the helpless victim let him fly,
And stifle, dark, the feebly-bursting cry!
Mark Ruffian Violence, distained with crimes,
Rousing elate in these degenerate times!
View unsuspecting Innocence a prey,
As guileful Fraud points out the erring way;
While subtile Litigation's pliant tongue
The life-blood equal sucks of Right and Wrong!
Hark, injur'd Want recounts th' unlisten'd tale,
And much-wrong'd Mis'ry pours th' unpitied wail!

Ye dark, waste hills, ye brown, unsightly plains,
Congenial scenes, ye soothe my mournful strains.
Ye tempests, rage! ye turbid torrents, roll!
Ye suit the joyless tenor of my soul.
Life's social haunts and pleasures I resign;
Be nameless wilds and lonely wanderings mine,
To mourn the woes my country must endure:
That wound degenerate ages cannot cure.

ELEGY ON WILLIE NICOL'S MARE

TUNE: *Chevy Chase*

I

Peg Nicholson was a good bay mare
  As ever trod on airn;   iron
But now she's floating down the Nith,
  And past the mouth o' Cairn.

2

Peg Nicholson was a good bay mare,
  An' rode thro' thick an' thin;
But now she's floating down the Nith,
  And wanting even the skin.

3

Peg Nicholson was a good bay mare,
  And ance she bore a priest;
But now she's floating down the Nith,
  For Solway fish a feast.

4

Peg Nicholson was a good bay mare,
  An' the priest he rode her sair;   hard
And much oppress'd, and bruis'd she was,
  As priest-rid cattle are.

LINES ON FERGUSSON

I

Ill-fated genius! Heaven-taught Fergusson!
  What heart that feels, and will not yield a tear
To think Life's sun did set, e'er well begun
  To shed its influence on thy bright career!

2

O, why should truest Worth and Genius pine
  Beneath the iron grasp of Want and Woe,
While titled knaves and idiot-greatness shine
  In all the splendour Fortune can bestow?

ELEGY ON THE LATE MISS BURNET OF MONBODDO

1

Life ne'er exulted in so rich a prize
   As Burnet, lovely from her native skies;
Nor envious Death so triumph'd in a blow
   As that which laid th' accomplish'd Burnet low.

2

Thy form and mind, sweet maid, can I forget?
   In richest ore the brightest jewel set!
In thee high Heaven above was truest shown,
   For by His noblest work the Godhead best is known.

3

In vain ye flaunt in summer's pride, ye groves!
   Thou crystal streamlet with thy flowery shore,
Ye woodland choir that chaunt your idle loves,
   Ye cease to charm: Eliza is no more.

4

Ye heathy wastes immix'd with reedy fens,
   Ye mossy streams with sedge and rushes stor'd,
Ye rugged cliffs o'erhanging dreary glens,
   To you I fly: ye with my soul accord.

5

Princes whose cumb'rous pride was all their worth,
   Shall venal lays their pompous exit hail,
And thou, sweet Excellence! forsake our earth,
   And not a Muse with honest grief bewail?

6

We saw thee shine in youth and beauty's pride
   And Virtue's light, that beams beyond the spheres;
But, like the sun eclips'd at morning tide,
   Thou left us darkling in a world of tears.

7

The parent's heart that nestled fond in thee,
   That heart how sunk, a prey to grief and care!
So deckt the woodbine sweet yon aged tree,
   So, rudely ravish'd, left it bleak and bare.

PEGASUS AT WANLOCKHEAD

I

With Pegasus upon a day
    Apollo, weary flying
(Through frosty hills the journey lay),
    On foot the way was plying.

2

Poor slip-shod, giddy Pegasus
    Was but a sorry walker;
To Vulcan then Apollo goes
    To get a frosty caulker.

3

Obliging Vulcan fell to work,
    Threw by his coat and bonnet,
And did Sol's business in a crack—
    Sol paid him in a sonnet.

4

Ye Vulcan's sons of Wanlockhead,
    Pity my sad disaster!
My Pegasus is poorly shod—
    I'll pay you like my master!

ON SOME COMMEMORATIONS
OF THOMSON

I

Dost thou not rise, indignant Shade,
    And smile wi' spurning scorn,
When they wha wad hae starved thy life
    Thy senseless turf adorn?

2

They wha about thee mak sic fuss	such
Now thou art but a name,	
Wad seen thee damn'd ere they had spar'd	would have
Ae plack to fill thy wame.	One farthing

3

climbed; hill

Helpless, alane, thou clamb the brae
 Wi' meikle honest toil,

clutched
hard-

And claucht th' unfading garland there,
 Thy sair-won, rightful spoil.

4

And wear it there! and call aloud
 This axiom undoubted:—
Would thou hae Nobles' patronage?
 First learn to live without it!

5

those that
have

' To whom hae much, more shall be given '
 Is every great man's faith;
But he, the helpless, needful wretch,
 Shall lose the mite he hath.

ON JOHN M'MURDO

Blest be M'Murdo to his latest day!
No envious cloud o'ercast his evening ray!
No wrinkle furrow'd by the hand of care,
Nor ever sorrow, add one silver hair!
O may no son the father's honor stain,
Nor ever daughter give the mother pain!

ON HEARING A THRUSH SING IN A MORNING WALK IN JANUARY

Sing on, sweet thrush, upon the leafless bough,
Sing on, sweet bird, I listen to thy strain:
See aged Winter, 'mid his surly reign,
At thy blythe carol clears his furrowed brow.
So in lone Poverty's dominion drear
Sits meek Content with light, unanxious heart,
Welcomes the rapid moments, bids them part,
Nor asks if they bring ought to hope or fear.
I thank Thee, Author of this opening day,
Thou whose bright sun now gilds yon orient skies!

Riches denied, Thy boon was purer joys:
What wealth could never give nor take away!
Yet come, thou child of Poverty and Care,
The mite high Heav'n bestowed, that mite with
    thee I'll share.

IMPROMPTU ON MRS. RIDDEL'S BIRTHDAY

4TH NOVEMBER, 1793

I

Old Winter, with his frosty beard,
Thus once to Jove his prayer preferred:—
' What have I done of all the year,
To bear this hated doom severe?
My cheerless suns no pleasure know;
Night's horrid car drags dreary slow;
My dismal months no joys are crowning,
But spleeny, English hanging, drowning.

2

Now Jove, for once be mighty civil:
To counterbalance all this evil
Give me, and I've no more to say,
Give me Maria's natal day!
That brilliant gift shall so enrich me,
Spring, Summer, Autumn, cannot match me.'
' 'Tis done! ' says Jove; so ends my story,
And Winter once rejoiced in glory.

SONNET ON THE DEATH OF ROBERT RIDDELL OF GLENRIDDELL

No more, ye warblers of the wood, no more,
Nor pour your descant grating on my soul!
Thou young-eyed Spring, gay in thy verdant stole,
More welcome were to me grim Winter's wildest roar!
How can ye charm, ye flowers, with all your dyes?
Ye blow upon the sod that wraps my friend.
How can I to the tuneful strain attend?
That strain flows round the untimely tomb where
    Riddell lies.

Yes, pour, ye warblers, pour the notes of woe,
And soothe the Virtues weeping o'er his bier!
The man of worth—and ' hath not left his peer '!—
Is in his ' narrow house ' for ever darkly low.
Thee, Spring, again with joy shall others greet;
Me, memory of my loss will only meet.

A SONNET UPON SONNETS

Fourteen, a sonneteer thy praises sings;
What magic myst'ries in that number lie!
Your hen hath fourteen eggs beneath her wings
That fourteen chickens to the roost may fly.
Fourteen full pounds the jockey's stone must be;
His age fourteen—a horse's prime is past.
Fourteen long hours too oft the Bard must fast;
Fourteen bright bumpers—bliss he ne'er must see!
Before fourteen, a dozen yields the strife;
Before fourteen—e'en thirteen's strength is vain.
Fourteen good years—a woman gives us life;
Fourteen good men—we lose that life again.
What lucubrations can be more upon it?
Fourteen good measur'd verses make a sonnet.

TRAGIC FRAGMENT

All villain as I am—a damnèd wretch,
A hardened, stubborn, unrepenting sinner—
Still my heart melts at human wretchedness,
And with sincere, tho' unavailing, sighs
I view the helpless children of distress.
With tears indignant I behold the oppressor
Rejoicing in the honest man's destruction,
Whose unsubmitting heart was all his crime.
Ev'n you, ye hapless crew! I pity you;
Ye, whom the seeming good think sin to pity:
Ye poor, despised, abandoned vagabonds,
Whom Vice, as usual, has turn'd o'er to ruin.
Oh! but for friends and interposing Heaven,
I had been driven forth, like you forlorn,
The most detested, worthless wretch among you!

O injured God! Thy goodness has endow'd me
With talents passing most of my compeers,
Which I in just proportion have abused,
As far surpassing other common villains
As Thou in natural parts has given me more.

REMORSE

Of all the numerous ills that hurt our peace,
That press the soul, or wring the mind with anguish,
Beyond comparison the worst are those
By our own folly, or our guilt brought on:
In ev'ry other circumstance, the mind
Has this to say:—' It was no deed of mine.'
But, when to all the evil of misfortune
This sting is added:—' Blame thy foolish self! '
Or, worser far, the pangs of keen remorse,
The torturing, gnawing consciousness of guilt,
Of guilt, perhaps, where we've involvèd others,
The young, the innocent, who fondly lov'd us;
Nay, more, that very love their cause of ruin!
O burning Hell! in all thy store of torments
There's not a keener lash!
Lives there a man so firm, who, while his heart
Feels all the bitter horrors of his crime,
Can reason down its agonizing throbs,
And, after proper purpose of amendment,
Can firmly force his jarring thoughts to peace?
O happy, happy, enviable man!
O glorious magnanimity of soul!

RUSTICITY'S UNGAINLY FORM

1

Rusticity's ungainly form
  May cloud the highest mind;
But when the heart is nobly warm,
  The good excuse will find.

2

Propriety's cold, cautious rules
  Warm Fervour may o'erlook;

But spare poor Sensibility
    Th' ungentle, harsh rebuke.

ON WILLIAM CREECH

A little upright, pert, tart, tripping wight,
And still his precious self his dear delight;
Who loves his own smart shadow in the streets
Better than e'er the fairest She he meets.
Much specious lore, but little understood
(Veneering oft outshines the solid wood),
His solid sense by inches you must tell,
But mete his subtle cunning by the ell!
A man of fashion, too, he made his tour,
Learn'd ' Vive la bagatelle et vive l'amour':
So travell'd monkies their grimace improve,
Polish their grin—nay, sigh for ladies' love!
His meddling vanity, a busy fiend,
Still making work his selfish craft must mend.

ON WILLIAM SMELLIE

. . . . . Crochallan came:
The old cock'd hat, the brown surtout the same;
His grisly beard just bristling in its might
('Twas four long nights and days to shaving-night);
His uncomb'd, hoary locks, wild-staring, thatch'd
A head for thought profound and clear unmatch'd;
Yet, tho' his caustic wit was biting rude,
His heart was warm, benevolent, and good.

SKETCH FOR AN ELEGY

I

Craigdarroch, fam'd for speaking art
And every virtue of the heart,
Stops short, nor can a word impart
        To end his sentence,
When mem'ry strikes him like a dart
        With auld acquaintance.

2

Black James—whase wit was never laith,   loth
But, like a sword had tint the sheath,   which had
                                             lost
Ay ready for the work o' death—
          He turns aside,
And strains wi' suffocating breath
          His grief to hide.

3

Even Philosophic Smellie tries
To choak the stream that floods his eyes!   choke
So Moses wi' a hazel-rice   -rod
          Came o'er the stane;
But, tho' it cost him speaking twice,
          It gush'd amain.

4

Go to your marble graffs, ye great,   vaults
In a' the tinkler-trash of state!
But by thy honest turf I'll wait,
          Thou man of worth,
And weep the ae best fallow's fate   one
          E'er lay in earth!

PASSION'S CRY

Mild zephyrs waft thee to life's farthest shore,
Nor think of me and my distresses more!
Falsehood accurst! No! Still I beg a place,
Still near thy heart some little, little trace!
For that dear trace the world I would resign:
O, let me live, and die, and think it mine!

By all I lov'd, neglected, and forgot,
No friendly face e'er lights my squalid cot.
Shunn'd, hated, wrong'd, unpitied, unredrest
The mock'd quotation of the scorner's jest;
Ev'n the poor support of my wretched life,
Snatched by the violence of legal strife;
Oft grateful for my very daily bread.
To those my family's once large bounty fed;

A welcome inmate at their homely fare,
My griefs, my woes, my sighs, my tears they share:
Their vulgar souls unlike the souls refined,
The fashion'd marble of the polish'd mind.

' I burn, I burn, as when thro' ripen'd corn
By driving winds the crackling flames are borne.'
Now, maddening-wild, I curse that fatal night,
Now bless the hour that charm'd my guilty sight.
In vain the Laws their feeble force oppose:
Chain'd at his feet, they groan Love's vanquish'd foes.
In vain Religion meets my shrinking eye:
I dare not combat, but I turn and fly.
Conscience in vain upbraids th' unhallow'd fire.
Love grasps his scorpions—stifled they expire.
Reason drops headlong from his sacred throne,
Your dear idea reigns, and reigns alone;
Each thought intoxicated homage yields,
And riots wanton in forbidden fields.

By all on high adoring mortals know;
By all the conscious villain fears below;
By what, alas! much more my soul alarms—
My doubtful hopes once more to fill thy arms—
Ev'n shouldst thou, false, forswear the guilty tie,
Thine and thine only I must live and die!

TO CLARINDA

In vain would Prudence with decorous sneer
Point out a cens'ring world, and bid me fear:
Above that world on wings of love I rise.
I know its worst, and can that worst despise.
Wronged, injured, shunned, unpitied, unredrest,
' The mocked quotation of the scorner's jest,'
Let Prudence' direst bodements on me fall,
Clarinda, rich reward! o'erpays them all.
As low-borne mists before the sun remove,
So shines, so reigns unrivalled mighty LOVE.
In vain the laws their feeble force oppose;
Chained at his feet, they groan Love's vanquished
    foes;
In vain Religion meets my shrinking eye;
I dare not combat, but I turn and fly:

Conscience in vain upbraids th' unhallowed fire;
Love grasps his scorpions, stifled they expire:
Reason drops headlong from his sacred throne,
Thy dear idea reigns, and reigns alone;
Each thought intoxicated homage yields,
And riots wanton in forbidden fields.

By all on High, adoring mortals know!
By all the conscious villain fears below,
By what, Alas! much more my soul alarms,
My doubtful hopes once more to fill thy arms!
E'en shouldst thou, false, forswear each guilty tie,
Thine, and thine only, I must live and die!

THE CARES O' LOVE

HE

The cares o' Love are sweeter far
    Than onie other pleasure;
And if sae dear its sorrows are,
    Enjoyment, what a treasure!

SHE

I fear to try, I dare na try
    A passion sae ensnaring;
For light's her heart and blythe's her song
    That for nae man is caring.

EPIGRAM ON SAID OCCASION

1

O Death, had'st thou but spar'd his life,
    Whom we this day lament!
We freely wad exchanged the wife,
    An' a' been weel content.

2

Ev'n as he is, cauld in his graff,   grave
    The swap we yet will do't;   exchange
Tak thou the carlin's carcase aff,
    Thou'se get the saul o' boot.   into the
                                             bargain

ANOTHER

One Queen Artemisa, as old stories tell,
When depriv'd of her husband she lovèd so well,
In respect for the love and affection he'd show'd her,
She reduc'd him to dust and she drank up the powder.
But Queen Netherplace, of a diff'rent complexion,
When call'd on to order the fun'ral direction,
Would have eat her dead lord, on a slender pretence,
Not to show her respect, but—to save the expense!

AT ROSLIN INN

My blessings on ye, honest wife!
    I ne'er was here before;
stuff   Ye've wealth o' gear for spoon and knife:
    Heart could not wish for more.
worry   Heav'n keep you clear o' sturt and strife,
beyond   Till far ayont fourscore,
    And by the Lord o' death and life,
go   I'll ne'er gae by your door!

TO AN ARTIST

Dear ——, I 'll gie ye some advice,
    You'll tak it no uncivil:
You shouldna paint at angels, man,
    But try and paint the Devil.
delicate   To paint an angel's kittle wark,
Satan   Wi' Nick there's little danger:
long-known   You'll easy draw a lang-kent face,
    But no sae weel a stranger.

ON ELPHINSTONE'S TRANSLATION OF MARTIAL

O thou whom Poesy abhors,
Whom Prose has turnèd out of doors,
that   Heard'st thou yon groan?—Proceed no further!
'Twas laurel'd Martial calling ' Murther! '

ON JOHNSON'S OPINION
OF HAMPDEN

For shame!
Let Folly and Knavery
Freedom oppose:
'Tis suicide, Genius,
To mix with her foes.

UNDER THE PORTRAIT
OF MISS BURNS

Cease, ye prudes, your envious railing!
Lovely Burns has charms: confess!
True it is she had ae failing: one
Had ae woman ever less?

ON MISS AINSLIE IN CHURCH

Fair maid, you need not take the hint,
Nor idle texts pursue;
'Twas guilty sinners that he meant,
Not angels such as you.

AT INVERARAY

1

Whoe'er he be that sojourns here,
I pity much his case,
Unless he come to wait upon
The Lord their God, ' His Grace.'

2

There's naething here but Highland pride
And Highland scab and hunger:
If Providence has sent me here,
'Twas surely in an anger.

AT CARRON IRONWORKS

not; works   We cam na here to view your warks
        In hopes to be mair wise,
go   But only, lest we gang to Hell,
        It may be nae surprise.
knocked   But when we tirl'd at your door
could not   Your porter dought na bear us:
permit
gates   Sae may, should we to Hell's yetts come,
fellow; serve   Your billie Satan sair us.

ON SEEING THE ROYAL PALACE AT STIRLING IN RUINS

Here Stewarts once in glory reign'd,
And laws for Scotland's weal ordain'd;
But now unroof'd their palace stands,
Their sceptre fallen to other hands:
Fallen indeed, and to the earth,
Whence grovelling reptiles take their birth!
The injured Stewart line is gone,
A race outlandish fills their throne:
An idiot race, to honour lost—
Who know them best despise them most.

REPLY TO THE THREAT OF A CENSORIOUS CRITIC

With Æsop's lion, Burns says:—' Sore I feel
Each other blow: but damn that ass's heel! '

A HIGHLAND WELCOME

When Death's dark stream I ferry o'er
    (A time that surely shall come),
In Heaven itself I'll ask no more
    Than just a Highland welcome.

AT WHIGHAM'S INN, SANQUHAR

Envy, if thy jaundiced eye
Through this window chance to spy,
To thy sorrow thou shalt find,
All that's generous, all that's kind.
Friendship, virtue, every grace,
Dwelling in this happy place.

VERSICLES ON SIGN-POSTS

1

He looked
Just as your sign-post Lions do,
With aspect fierce and quite as harmless too.

2

(PATIENT STUPIDITY)

So heavy, passive to the tempest's shocks,
Dull on the sign-post stands the stupid ox.

3

His face with smile eternal drest
Just like the landlord to his guest,
High as they hang with creaking din
To index out the Country Inn.

4

A head, pure, sinless quite of brain and soul,
The very image of a barber's poll:
Just shews a human face, and wears a wig,
And looks, when well friseur'd, amazing big.

ON MISS JEAN SCOTT

O, had each Scot of ancient times
Been, Jeanie Scott, as thou art,
The bravest heart on English ground
Had yielded like a coward.

ON CAPTAIN FRANCIS GROSE

The Devil got notice that Grose was a-dying,
So whip! at the summons, old Satan came flying;
But when he approach'd where poor Francis lay
    moaning,
And saw each bed-post with its burthen a-groaning,
Astonish'd, confounded, cries Satan:—' By God,
I'd want him ere take such a damnable load! '

AN EXTEMPORANEOUS EFFUSION ON BEING APPOINTED TO THE EXCISE

Searching auld wives' barrels,
    Ochon, the day
That clarty barm should stain my laurels;
    But—what'll ye say?
These movin' things ca'd wives an' weans
Wad move the very hearts o' stanes.

dirty (gloss for "clarty")
children (gloss for "weans")

ON MISS DAVIES

Ask why God made the gem so small,
    And why so huge the granite?
Because God meant mankind should set
    That higher value on it.

ON A BEAUTIFUL COUNTRY SEAT

We grant they're thine, those beauties all,
    So lovely in our eye:
Keep them, thou eunuch, Cardoness,
    For others to enjoy.

THE TYRANT WIFE

Curs'd be the man, the poorest wretch in life,
The crouching vassal to the tyrant wife!
Who has no will but by her high permission;
Who has not sixpence but in her possession;
Who must to her his dear friend's secret tell;
Who dreads a curtain lecture worse than hell!
Were such the wife had fallen to my part,
I'd break her spirit, or I'd break her heart:
I'd charm her with the magic of a switch,
I'd kiss her maids, and kick the perverse bitch.

AT JOHN BACON'S BROWNHILL INN

At Brownhill we always get dainty good cheer
And plenty of bacon each day in the year;
We've a' thing that's nice, and mostly in season: every
But why always bacon?—come, tell me the reason?

THE TOADEATER

Of Lordly acquaintance you boast,
   And the Dukes that you dined with yestreen;
Yet an insect's an insect at most,
   Tho' it crawl on the curl of a Queen!

IN LAMINGTON KIRK

As cauld a wind as ever blew,
A cauld kirk, and in't but few,
As cauld a minister's ever spak—
Ye'se a' be het or I come back!   hot

THE KEEKIN GLASS

How daur ye ca' me ' Howlet-face,'   Owl-
   Ye blear-e'ed, wither'd spectre?
Ye only spied the keekin-glass,   looking-
   An' there ye saw your picture.

AT THE GLOBE TAVERN, DUMFRIES

I

The greybeard, old Wisdom, may boast of his
  treasures,
 Give me with gay Folly to live!
I grant him his calm-blooded, time-settled pleasures,
 But Folly has raptures to give.

2

  My bottle is a holy pool,
sorrow That heals the wounds o' care an' dool,
  And pleasure is a wanton trout—
  An ye drink it, ye'll find him out.

3

  In politics if thou would'st mix,
   And mean thy fortunes be;
  Bear this in mind: Be deaf and blind,
   Let great folks hear and see.

YE TRUE LOYAL NATIVES

Ye true ' Loyal Natives ' attend to my song:
In uproar and riot rejoice the night long!
corps From Envy and Hatred your core is exempt,
But where is your shield from the darts of Contempt?

ON COMMISSARY GOLDIE'S BRAINS

  Lord, to account who does Thee call,
   Or e'er dispute Thy pleasure?
  Else why within so thick a wall
   Enclose so poor a treasure?

EXTEMPORE:

ON BEING TOLD BY W—— L—— OF THE CUSTOMS,
DUMBLIN, THAT COMMISSARY GOLDIE DID NOT
SEEM DISPOSED TO PUSH THE BOTTLE

Friend Commissar, since we are met and happy,
Pray why should we part without having more nappy?
Bring in t'other bottle, for faith I am dry—
Thy drink thou can'st part with and neither can I.

IN A LADY'S POCKET BOOK

Grant me, indulgent Heaven, that I may live
To see the miscreants feel the pains they give!
Deal Freedom's sacred treasures free as air,
Till Slave and Despot be but things that were!

EPIGRAMS ON THE EARL OF GALLOWAY

I

What dost thou in that mansion fair?
   Flit, Galloway, and find
Some narrow, dirty, dungeon cave,
   The picture of thy mind.

2

No Stewart art thou, Galloway:
   The Stewarts all were brave.
Besides, the Stewarts were but fools,
   Not one of them a knave.

3

Bright ran thy line, O Galloway,
   Thro' many a far-famed sire!
So ran the far-famed Roman way,
   And ended in a mire.

4

Spare me thy vengeance, Galloway!
   In quiet let me live:
I ask no kindness at thy hand,
   For thou hast none to give.

ON AN OLD ACQUAINTANCE WHO SEEMED TO PASS THE BARD WITHOUT NOTICE

I

Dost hang thy head, Billy, asham'd that thou
   knowest me?
'Tis paying in kind a just debt that thou owest me.

2

Dost blush, my dear Billy, asham'd of thyself,
　A Fool and a Cuckold together?
The fault is not thine, insignificant elf,
　Thou wast not consulted in either.

EXTEMPORE

ON BEING REQUESTED TO WRITE ON THE BLANK LEAF OF AN ELEGANTLY BOUND BIBLE

Free thro' the leaves ye maggots make your windings;
But for the Owner's sake oh spare the bindings!

EPIGRAM ON JAMES SWAN

(ON HIS BEING ELECTED COUNCILLOR AND BAILLIE, 22ND SEPTEMBER, 1794)

Baillie Swan, Baillie Swan,
Let you do what you can—
God hae mercy on honest Dumfries;
But e'er the year's done,
Good Lord! Provost John
Will find that his *Swans* are but *Geese*.

EPITAPH FOR J—— H——

WRITER IN AYR

Here lies a Scots mile of a chiel,
If he's in heaven, Lord, fill him weel!

ON ALEXANDER FINDLATER, SUPERVISOR, DUMFRIES EXCISE

The Exciseman and the gentleman in one
I point thee Findlater, for thou'st the man

ON EDMUND BURKE BY AN OPPONENT AND A FRIEND TO WARREN HASTINGS

Oft have I wonder'd that on Irish ground
No poisonous Reptile has ever been found:
Revealed stands the secret of great Nature's work:
She preservèd her poison to create a Burke!

ON WEDDING RINGS

She asked why wedding rings are made of gold;
I ventured this to instruct her;
Why, madam, love and lightning are the same,
On earth they glance, from Heaven they came.
Love is the soul's electric flame,
And gold its best conductor.

TO A VIOLET

Go, little flower: go bid thy name impart
Each hope, each wish, each beating of my heart;
Go, soothe her sorrows, bid all anguish cease,
Go, be the bearer of thyself—heart's ease.

EPIGRAM

TO —— OF C——DER, ON SOME GENTLEMEN
BEING REFUSED PERMISSION TO TAKE A VIEW
OF THE ARCHITECTURE, ETC., OF C——DER-
HOUSE

Why shut your doors and windows thus,
   With such a jealous dread?
We are no children come to eat
   Your works of gingerbread.

EXCHANGE OF EPIGRAMS

BOYD:

Dear Burns, your wit how can you flash
  On such a wretch as this is?

BURNS:

Dear Boyd, how can I let him pass,
  The hangman so remiss is?

ON MR. PITT'S HAIR-POWDER TAX

Pray, Billy Pitt, explain thy rigs,
  This new poll-tax of thine!
' I mean to mark the GUINEA pigs
  From other common SWINE.'

ON THE LAIRD OF LAGGAN

When Morine, deceas'd, to the Devil went down,
'Twas nothing would serve him but Satan's own
    crown.
' Thy fool's head,' quoth Satan, ' that crown shall
    wear never:
I grant thou'rt as wicked, but not quite so clever.'

ON MARIA RIDDELL

' Praise Woman still,' his lordship roars,
  ' Deserv'd or not, no matter! '
But thee whom all my soul adores,
  There Flattery cannot flatter!
Maria, all my thought and dream,
  Inspires my vocal shell:
The more I praise my lovely theme,
  The more the truth I tell.

ON MISS FONTENELLE

Sweet naïveté of feature,
  Simple, wild, enchanting elf,
Not to thee, but thanks to Nature
  Thou art acting but thyself.
Wert thou awkward, stiff, affected,
  Spurning Nature, torturing art,
Loves and Graces all rejected,
  Then indeed thou'dst act a part.

KIRK AND STATE EXCISEMEN

Ye men of wit and wealth, why all this sneering
'Gainst poor Excisemen? Give the cause a hearing.
What are your Landlord's rent-rolls? Taxing ledgers!
What Premiers? What ev'n Monarchs? Mighty
  Gaugers!
Nay, what are Priests (those seeming godly wisemen)?
What are they, pray, but Spiritual Excisemen!

ON THANKSGIVING FOR A NATIONAL VICTORY

Ye hypocrites! are these your pranks?
To murder men, and give God thanks?
Desist for shame! Proceed no further:
God won't accept your thanks for Murther.

PINNED TO MRS. WALTER RIDDELL'S CARRIAGE

If you rattle along like your mistress's tongue,
  Your speed will out-rival the dart;
But, a fly for your load, you'll break down on the road,
  If your stuff be as rotten's her heart.

TO DR. MAXWELL

ON MISS JESSY STAIG'S RECOVERY

Maxwell, if merit here you crave,
   That merit I deny:
You save fair Jessie from the grave!—
   An Angel could not die!

TO THE BEAUTIFUL
MISS ELIZA J——N

ON HER PRINCIPLES OF LIBERTY AND EQUALITY

How, ' Liberty! ' Girl, can it be by thee nam'd?
' Equality,' too! Hussey, art not asham'd?
Free and Equal indeed, while mankind thou en-
   chainest,
And over their hearts a proud Despot so reignest.

TO THE HON. WM. R. MAULE
OF PANMURE

EXTEMPORE:

ON SEEING THE HON. WM. R. MAULE OF PANMURE DRIVING AWAY IN HIS FINE AND ELEGANT PHAETON ON THE RACE GROUND AT TINWALD DOWNS, OCTOBER, 1794

Thou Fool, in thy phaeton towering.
   Art proud when that phaeton's prais'd?
'Tis the pride of a Thief's exhibition
   When higher his pillory's rais'd.

ON SEEING MRS. KEMBLE IN YARICO

Kemble, thou cur'st my unbelief
   Of Moses and his rod:
At Yarico's sweet notes of grief
   The rock with tears had flow'd.

ON DR. BABINGTON'S LOOKS

That there is a falsehood in his looks
    I must and will deny:
They say their Master is a knave,
    And sure they do not lie.

ON ANDREW TURNER

In Se'enteen Hunder'n Forty-Nine
The Deil gat stuff to mak a swine,
    An' coost it in a corner;
But wilily he chang'd his plan,
An' shap'd it something like a man,
    An' ca'd it Andrew Turner.

chucked

THE SOLEMN LEAGUE
AND COVENANT

The Solemn League and Covenant
    Now brings a smile, now brings a tear.
But sacred Freedom, too, was theirs:
    If thou'rt a slave, indulge thy sneer.

TO JOHN SYME OF RYEDALE

WITH A PRESENT OF A DOZEN OF PORTER

O had the malt thy strength of mind,
    Or hops the flavour of thy wit,
'Twere drink for first of human kind—
    A gift that e'en for Syme were fit.

ON A GOBLET

There's Death in the cup, so beware!
    Nay, more—there is danger in touching!
But who can avoid the fell snare?
    The man and his wine's so bewitching!

APOLOGY TO JOHN SYME

No more of your guests, be they titled or not,
    And cookery the first in the nation:
Who is proof to thy personal converse and wit
    Is proof to all other temptation.

TO CAPTAIN GORDON

ON BEING ASKED WHY I WAS NOT TO BE OF THE PARTY WITH HIM AND HIS BROTHER KENMURE AT SYME'S

1

Dost ask, dear Captain, why from Syme
    I have no invitation,
When well he knows he has with him
    My first friends in the nation?

2

Is it because I love to toast,
    And round the bottle hurl?
No! there conjecture wild is lost,
    For Syme, by God, 's no churl!

3

Is't lest with bawdy jests I bore,
    As oft the matter of fact is?
No! Syme the theory can't abhor—
    Who loves so well the practice.

4

Is it a fear I should avow
    Some heresy seditious?
No! Syme (but this is *entre nous*)
    Is quite an old Tiresias.

5

In vain Conjecture thus would flit
    Thro' mental clime and season:
In short, dear Captain, Syme's a Wit—
    Who asks of Wits a reason?

6

Yet must I still the *sort* deplore
  That to my griefs adds one more,
In balking me the social hour
  With you and noble Kenmure.

ON MR. JAMES GRACIE

Gracie, thou art a man of worth,
  O, be thou Dean for ever!
May he be damn'd to Hell henceforth,
  Who fauts thy weight or measure!   challenges

AT FRIARS CARSE HERMITAGE

To Riddell, much-lamented man,
  This ivied cot was dear:
Wand'rer, dost value matchless worth?
  This ivied cot revere.

FOR AN ALTAR OF INDEPENDENCE

AT KERROUGHTRIE, THE SEAT OF MR. HERON

Thou of an independent mind,
With soul resolv'd, with soul resign'd,
Prepar'd Power's proudest frown to brave,
Who wilt not be, nor have a slave,
Virtue alone who dost revere,
Thy own reproach alone dost fear:
Approach this shrine, and worship here.

VERSICLES TO JESSIE LEWARS

THE TOAST

Fill me with the rosy wine;
Call a toast, a toast divine;
Give the Poet's darling flame;
Lovely Jessie be her name:
Then thou mayest freely boast
Thou hast given a peerless toast.

THE MENAGERIE

1

Talk not to me of savages
　From Afric's burning sun!
No savage e'er can rend my heart
　As, Jessie, thou hast done.

2

But Jessie's lovely hand in mine
　A mutual faith to plight—
Not even to view the heavenly choir
　Would be so blest a sight.

JESSIE'S ILLNESS

Say, sages, what's the charm on earth
　Can turn Death's dart aside?
It is not purity and worth,
　Else Jessie had not died!

HER RECOVERY

But rarely seen since Nature's birth
　The natives of the sky!
Yet still one seraph's left on earth,
　For Jessie did not die.

ON MARRIAGE

That hackney'd judge of human life,
　The Preacher and the King,
Observes:—' The man that gets a wife
　He gets a noble thing.'
But how capricious are mankind,
　Now loathing, now desirous!
We married men, how oft we find
　The best of things will tire us!

A POET'S GRACE

BEFORE MEAT

O Thou, who kindly dost provide
  For ev'ry creature's want!
We bless the God of Nature wide
  For all Thy goodness lent.
And if it please Thee, heavenly Guide,
  May never worse be sent;
But, whether granted or denied,
  Lord, bless us with content.

AFTER MEAT

O Thou, in whom we live and move,
  Who made the sea and shore,
Thy goodness constantly we prove,
  And, grateful, would adore;
And, if it please Thee, Power above!
  Still grant us with such store
The friend we trust, the fair we love,
  And we desire no more.

AT THE GLOBE TAVERN

BEFORE MEAT

1

O Lord, when hunger pinches sore,
  Do Thou stand us in stead,
And send us from Thy bounteous store
  A tup- or wether-head.   sheep's-head

AFTER MEAT

1

Lord Thee we thank, and Thee alone,
  For temporal gifts we little merit!
At present we will ask no more:
  Let William Hislop bring the spirit.

2

O Lord, since we have feasted thus,
  Which we so little merit,

meat   Let Meg now take the flesh away,
                And Jock bring in the spirit.

3

O Lord, we do Thee humbly thank
   For that we little merit:
Now Jean may tak the flesh away,
   And Will bring in the spirit.

EPITAPH ON A HENPECKED SQUIRE

As father Adam first was fool'd,
   A case that's still too common,
Here lies a man a woman rul'd:
   The Devil ruled the woman.

ON A CELEBRATED RULING ELDER

Cobbler   Here Souter Hood in death does sleep:
                In hell, if he's gane thither,
money
take good
care of it   Satan, gie him thy gear to keep;
                He'll haud it weel thegither.

ON A NOISY POLEMIC

those   Below thir stanes lie Jamie's banes:
                O Death, it's my opinion,
gabbling   Thou ne'er took such a bleth'rin bitch
                Into thy dark dominion.

ON WEE JOHNIE

Hic jacet WEE *Johnie*

Whoe'er thou art, O reader, know,
   That Death has murder'd Johnie,
An' here his *body* lies fu' low—
   For *saul* he ne'er had onie.

FOR ROBERT AIKEN, Esq.

Know thou, O stranger to the fame
  Of this much lov'd, much honour'd name!
(For none that knew him need be told),
  A warmer heart Death ne'er made cold.

FOR GAVIN HAMILTON, Esq.

The poor man weeps—here Gavin sleeps,
  Whom canting wretches blam'd;
But with such as he, where'er he be,
  May I be sav'd or damn'd.

ON JAMES GRIEVE, LAIRD OF BOGHEAD, TARBOLTON

Here lies Boghead amang the dead
  In hopes to get salvation;
But if such as he in Heav'n may be,
  Then welcome—hail! damnation.

ON WM. MUIR IN TARBOLTON MILL

An honest man here lies at rest,
As e'er God with His image blest:
The friend of man, the friend of truth,
The friend of age, and guide of youth:
Few hearts like his—with virtue warm'd,
Few heads with knowledge so inform'd:
If there's another world, he lives in bliss;
If there is none, he made the best of this.

ON JOHN RANKINE

Ae day, as Death, that gruesome carl,   One; fellow
Was driving to the tither warl'   other world
A mixtie-maxtie, motley squad
And monie a guilt-bespotted lad:

preachers
and lawyers

Black gowns of each denomination,
And thieves of every rank and station,
From him that wears the star and garter

swings

To him that wintles in a halter:
Asham'd himself to see the wretches,
He mutters, glow'ring at the bitches:—
' By God I'll not be seen behint them,
Nor 'mang the sp'ritual core present them,
Without at least ae honest man
To grace this damn'd infernal clan! '
By Adamhill a glance he threw,
' Lord God! ' quoth he, ' I have it now,
There's just the man I want, i' faith! '
And quickly stoppit Rankine's breath.

ON TAM THE CHAPMAN

As Tam the chapman on a day
Wi' Death forgather'd by the way,
Weel pleas'd he greets a wight so famous.
And Death was nae less pleas'd wi' Thomas,
Wha cheerfully lays down his pack,

chat

And there blaws up a hearty crack:
His social, friendly, honest heart
Sae tickled Death, they could na part;
Sae, after viewing knives and garters.
Death taks him hame to gie him quarters.

ON HOLY WILLIE

I

sore

Here Holy Willie's sair worn clay
        Taks up its last abode;

soul

His saul has taen some other way—
        I fear, the left-hand road.

2

Stop! there he is as sure's a gun!

creature

        Poor, silly body, see him!

ground

Nae wonder he's as black's the grun—
        Observe wha's standing wi' him!

3

Your brunstane Devilship, I see,   brimstone
  Has got him there before ye!
But haud your nine-tail-cat a wee,   withhold;
  Till ance you've heard my story.   for a little

4

Your pity I will not implore,
  For pity ye have nane.
Justice, alas! has gi'en him o'er,
  And mercy's day is gane.

5

But hear me, Sir, Deil as ye are,
  Look something to your credit:
A cuif like him wad stain your name,   dastard
  If it were kent ye did it!   known

ON JOHN DOVE, INNKEEPER

1

Here lies Johnie Pigeon:
What was his religion
  Whae'er desires to ken
To some other warl'   world
Maun follow the carl,   old fellow
  For here Johnie Pigeon had nane!

2

Strong ale was ablution;
Small beer, persecution;
  A dram was *memento mori*;
But a full flowing bowl
Was the saving his soul,
  And port was celestial glory!

ON A WAG IN MAUCHLINE

1

Lament him, Mauchline husbands a',
  He aften did assist ye;
For had ye staid hale weeks awa',   whole
  Your wives they ne'er had missed ye!

2

[together

    Ye Mauchline bairns, as on ye pass
        To school in bands thegither,
    O, tread ye lightly on his grass—
        Perhaps he was your father!

ON ROBERT FERGUSSON

ON THE TOMBSTONE IN THE CANONGATE CHURCHYARD

**HERE LIES ROBERT FERGUSSON
BORN SEPT. 5TH, 1751
DIED OCT. 16TH, 1774**

No sculptur'd Marble here, nor pompous lay,
    No storied Urn nor animated Bust;
This simple stone directs pale Scotia's way
    To pour her sorrow o'er the Poet's dust.

ADDITIONAL STANZAS

NOT INSCRIBED

1

She mourns, sweet tuneful youth, thy hapless fate:
    Tho' all the powers of song thy fancy fir'd,
Yet Luxury and Wealth lay by in State,
    And, thankless, starv'd what they so much admir'd.

2

This humble tribute with a tear he gives,
    A brother Bard—he can no more bestow:
But dear to fame thy Song immortal lives,
    A nobler monument than Art can show.

FOR WILLIAM NICOL

such

    Ye maggots, feed on Nicol's brain,
        For few sic feasts you've gotten;
    And fix your claws in Nicol's heart,
        For deil a bit o't's rotten.

FOR WILLIAM CRUIKSHANK, A.M.

Now honest William's gaen to Heaven,
   I wat na gin't can mend him:
The fauts he had in Latin lay,
   For nane in English kent them.

*I know not
if it
faults
knew*

ON ROBERT MUIR

What man could esteem, or what woman could love,
   Was he who lies under this sod:
If such Thou refusest admission above,
   Then whom wilt Thou favour, Good God?

ON A LAP-DOG

1

In wood and wild, ye warbling throng,
   Your heavy loss deplore:
Now half extinct your powers of song—
   Sweet Echo is no more.

2

Ye jarring, screeching things around,
   Scream your discordant joys:
Now half your din of tuneless sound
   With Echo silent lies.

MONODY

ON A LADY (MARIA RIDDELL) FAMED FOR HER CAPRICE

1

How cold is that bosom which Folly once fired!
   How pale is that cheek where the rouge lately
     glisten'd!
How silent that tongue which the echoes oft tired!
   How dull is that ear which to flatt'ry so listen'd!

2

If sorrow and anguish their exit await,
　　From friendship and dearest affection remov'd,
How doubly severer, Maria, thy fate!
　　Thou diedst unwept, as thou livedst unlov'd.

3

Loves, Graces, and Virtues, I call not on you:
　　So shy, grave, and distant, ye shed not a tear.
But come, all ye offspring of Folly so true,
　　And flowers let us cull for Maria's cold bier!

4

We'll search through the garden for each silly flower,
　　We'll roam thro' the forest for each idle weed,
But chiefly the nettle, so typical, shower,
　　For none e'er approach'd her but rued the rash
　　　deed.—

5

We'll sculpture the marble, we'll measure the lay:
　　Here Vanity strums on her idiot lyre!
There keen Indignation shall dart on his prey,
　　Which spurning Contempt shall redeem from his
　　　ire!

THE EPITAPH

Here lies, now a prey to insulting neglect,
　　What once was a butterfly, gay in life's beam:
Want only of wisdom denied her respect,
　　Want only of goodness denied her esteem.

FOR MR. WALTER RIDDELL

So vile was poor Wat, such a miscreant slave,
That the worms ev'n damn'd him when laid in his
　　grave.
' In his scull there's a famine,' a starved reptile cries;
' And his heart, it is poison,' another replies.

ON A NOTED COXCOMB

(CAPT. WM. RODDICK, OF CORBISTON)

Light lay the earth on Billie's breast,
  His chicken heart's so tender;
But build a castle on his head—
  His scull will prop it under.

ON CAPT. LASCELLES

When Lascelles thought fit from this world to depart,
Some friends warmly spoke of embalming his heart.
A bystander whispers:—'Pray don't make so much
    o't—
The subject is poison, no reptile will touch it.'

ON A GALLOWAY LAIRD

(DAVID MAXWELL OF CARDONESS)

NOT QUITE SO WISE AS SOLOMON

Bless Jesus Christ, O Cardoness,
  With grateful lifted eyes,
Who taught that not the soul alone
  But body too shall rise!
For had He said:—' The soul alone
  From death I will deliver,'
Alas! alas! O Cardoness,
  Then hadst thou lain for ever!

ON WM. GRAHAM OF MOSSKNOWE

' Stop thief! ' Dame Nature call'd to Death,
As Willie drew his latest breath:
' How shall I make a fool again?
My choicest model thou hast taen.'

ON JOHN BUSHBY OF TINWALD DOWNS

Here lies John Bushby—honest man!
Cheat him, Devil—if you can!

ON A SUICIDE

Here lies in earth a root of Hell
  Set by the Deil's ain dibble:
This worthless body damn'd himsel
  To save the Lord the trouble.

ON A SWEARING COXCOMB

Here cursing, swearing Burton lies,
A buck, a beau, or ' Dem my eyes! '
Who in his life did little good,
And his last words were:—' Dem my blood! '

ON JEAN ARMOUR

O Jeany, thou hast stolen away my soul !
In vain I strive against the lov'd idea:
Thy tender image sallies on my thoughts,
My firm resolves become an easy prey !

IN SOME FUTURE ECCENTRIC PLANET

Where Wit may sparkle all its rays,
  Uncurst with Caution's fears ;
And Pleasure, basking in the blaze,
  Rejoice for endless years !

FOR GABRIEL RICHARDSON

Here brewer Gabriel's fire's extinct,
  And empty all his barrels:
He's blest—if as he brew'd, he drink—
  In upright, virtuous morals.

REEKIE'S TOWN

Now, God in heaven bless Reekie's town
  With plenty, joy and peace !
And may her wealth and fair renown
  To latest times increase ! ! !

ON AN INNKEEPER NICKNAMED 'THE MARQUIS'

Here lies a mock Marquis, whose titles were shamm'd.
If ever he rise, it will be to be damn'd.

CORN RIGS ARE BONIE

TUNE: *Corn Rigs*

CHORUS

Corn rigs, an' barley rigs,
  An' corn rigs are bonie:
I'll ne'er forget that happy night,
  Amang the rigs wi' Annie.

1

It was upon a Lammas night,
  When corn rigs are bonie,   ridges
Beneath the moon's unclouded light,
  I held awa to Annie;
The time flew by, wi' tentless heed;   careless
  Till, 'tween the late and early,   dark and
Wi' sma' persuasion she agreed   dawn
  To see me thro' the barley.

2

The sky was blue, the wind was still,
  The moon was shining clearly;
I set her down, wi' right good will,
  Amang the rigs o' barley:

knew

I ken't her heart was a' my ain;
 I lov'd her most sincerely;
I kiss'd her owre and owre again,
 Amang the rigs o' barley.

3

I lock'd her in my fond embrace;
 Her heart was beating rarely:
My blessings on that happy place,
 Amang the rigs o' barley!
But by the moon and stars so bright,
 That shone that hour so clearly!
She ay shall bless that happy night
 Amang the rigs o' barley.

4

I hae been blythe wi' comrades dear;
 I hae been merry drinking;

money-
making

I hae been joyfu' gath'rin gear;
 I hae been happy thinking:
But a' the pleasures e'er I saw,
 Tho' three times doubl'd fairly—
That happy night was worth them a',
 Amang the rigs o' barley.

SONG: COMPOSED IN AUGUST

TUNE: *Port Gordon*

1

western

Now westlin winds and slaught'ring guns
 Bring Autumn's pleasant weather;

moorcock

The gorcock springs on whirring wings
 Amang the blooming heather:
Now waving grain, wide o'er the plain,
 Delights the weary farmer;
The moon shines bright, as I rove by night
 To muse upon my charmer.

2

The paitrick lo'es the fruitfu' fells,
 The plover lo'es the mountains;
The woodcock haunts the lonely dells,

heron

 The soaring hern the fountains;

Thro' lofty groves the cushat roves,
   The path o' man to shun it;
The hazel bush o'erhangs the thrush,
   The spreading thorn the linnet.

3

Thus ev'ry kind their pleasure find,
   The savage and the tender;
Some social join, and leagues combine,
   Some solitary wander:
Avaunt, away, the cruel sway!
   Tyrannic man's dominion!
The sportsman's joy, the murd'ring cry,
   The flutt'ring, gory pinion!

4

But, Peggy dear, the evening's clear,
   Thick flies the skimming swallow,
The sky is blue, the fields in view
   All fading-green and yellow:
Come let us stray our gladsome way,
   And view the charms of Nature;
The rustling corn, the fruited thorn,
   And ilka happy creature.   *every*

5

We'll gently walk, and sweetly talk,
   While the silent moon shines clearly;
I'll clasp thy waist, and, fondly prest,
   Swear how I lo'e thee dearly:
Not vernal show'rs to budding flow'rs,
   Not Autumn to the farmer,
So dear can be as thou to me,
   My fair, my lovely charmer!

FROM THEE ELIZA

TUNE: *Gilderoy*

I

From thee Eliza, I must go,
   And from my native shore:
The cruel fates between us throw
   A boundless ocean's roar;

But boundless oceans, roaring wide
   Between my Love and me,
They never, never can divide
   My heart and soul from thee.

2

Farewell, farewell, Eliza dear,
   The maid that I adore!
A boding voice is in mine ear,
   We part to meet no more!
But the latest throb that leaves my heart,
   While Death stands victor by,
That throb, Eliza, is thy part,
   And thine that latest sigh!

JOHN BARLEYCORN

A Ballad

TUNE: *Lull Me Beyond Thee*

1

There was three kings into the east,
   Three kings both great and high,
And they hae sworn a solemn oath
   John Barleycorn should die.

2

They took a plough and plough'd him down,
   Put clods upon his head,
And they hae sworn a solemn oath
   John Barleycorn was dead.

3

But the cheerful Spring came kindly on,
   And show'rs began to fall;
John Barleycorn got up again,
   And sore surpris'd them all.

4

The sultry suns of Summer came,
   And he grew thick and strong:
His head weel arm'd wi' pointed spears,
   That no one should him wrong.

5

The sober Autumn enter'd mild,
  When he grew wan and pale;
His bending joints and drooping head
  Show'd he began to fail.

6

His colour sicken'd more and more,
  He faded into age;
And then his enemies began
  To show their deadly rage.

7

They've taen a weapon long and sharp,
  And cut him by the knee;
Then ty'd him fast upon a cart,
  Like a rogue for forgerie.

8

They laid him down upon his back,
  And cudgell'd him full sore.
They hung him up before the storm,
  And turn'd him o'er and o'er.

9

They fillèd up a darksome pit
  With water to the brim,
They heavèd in John Barleycorn—
  There, let him sink or swim!

10

They laid him out upon the floor,
  To work him farther woe;
And still, as signs of life appear'd,
  They toss'd him to and fro.

11

They wasted o'er a scorching flame
  The marrow of his bones;
But a miller us'd him worst of all,
  For he crush'd him between two stones.

12

And they hae taen his very heart's blood,
  And drank it round and round;
And still the more and more they drank,
  Their joy did more abound.

13

John Barleycorn was a hero bold,
  Of noble enterprise;
For if you do but taste his blood,
  'Twill make your courage rise.

14

'Twill make a man forget his woe;
  'Twill heighten all his joy:
'Twill make the widow's heart to sing,
  Tho' the tear were in her eye.

15

Then let us toast John Barleycorn,
  Each man a glass in hand;
And may his great posterity
  Ne'er fail in old Scotlànd!

A FRAGMENT: WHEN GUILFORD GOOD

TUNE: *The Black Watch*

1

When Guilford good our pilot stood,
  An' did our hellim thraw, man;
Ae night, at tea, began a plea,
  Within Americà, man:
Then up they gat the maskin-pat,
  And in the sea did jaw, man;
An' did nae less, in full Congress,
  Than quite refuse our law, man.

2

Then thro' the lakes Montgomery takes,
  I wat he was na slaw, man;
Down Lowrie's Burn he took a turn,
  And Carleton did ca', man:

helm turn

tea-pot
dash

But yet, whatreck, he at Quebec   *what matter*
  Montgomery-like did fa', man,
Wi' sword in hand, before his band,
  Amang his en'mies a', man.

3

Poor Tammy Gage within a cage
  Was kept at Boston-ha', man;
Till Willie Howe took o'er the knowe   *hill*
  For Philadelphià, man;
Wi' sword an' gun he thought a sin
  Guid Christian bluid to draw, man;
But at New-York wi' knife an' fork
  Sir-Loin he hackèd sma', man.

4

Burgoyne gaed up, like spur an' whip,
  Till Fraser brave did fa', man;
Then lost his way, ae misty day,
  In Saratoga shaw, man.   *wood*
Cornwallis fought as lang's he dought,   *could*
  An' did the buckskins claw, man;
But Clinton's glaive frae rust to save,
  He hung it to the wa', man.

5

Then Montague, an' Guilford too,
  Began to fear a fa', man;
And Sackville doure, wha stood the stoure   *obstinate;*
  The German chief to thraw, man: *fight*
For Paddy Burke, like onie Turk,   *thwart*
  Nae mercy had at a', man;
An' Charlie Fox threw by the box,
  An' lows'd his tinkler jaw, man.   *let loose*

6

Then Rockingham took up the game,
  Till death did on him ca', man;
When Shelburne meek held up his cheek,
  Conform to gospel law, man:
Saint Stephen's boys, wi' jarring noise,
  They did his measures thraw, man;
For North an' Fox united stocks,
  An' bore him to the wa', man.

7

Then clubs an' hearts were Charlie's cartes:
    He swept the stakes awa', man,
Till the diamond's ace, of Indian race,
    Led him a sair *faux pas*, man:

cheers   The Saxon lads, wi' loud placads,
    On Chatham's boy did ca', man;
An' Scotland drew her pipe an' blew:

worst   ' Up, Willie, waur them a', man!'

8

Behind the throne then Granville's gone,
    A secret word or twa, man;

sly   While slee Dundas arous'd the class
North of   Be-north the Roman wa', man:
garb   An' Chatham's wraith, in heav'nly graith,
    (Inspirèd bardies saw, man),
Wi' kindling eyes, cry'd: ' Willie, rise!
    Would I hae fear'd them a', man?'

9

But, word an' blow, North, Fox, and Co.
golfed   Gowff'd Willie like a ba' man,
rose; cast; Till Suthron raise an' coost their claise
clothes   Behind him in a raw, man:
bagpipes An' Caledon threw by the drone,
blade   An' did her whittle draw, man;
An' swoor fu' rude, thro' dirt an' bluid,
    To mak it guid in law, man.

MY NANIE, O

TUNE: (*As Title*)

I

Behind yon hills where Stinchar flows
    'Mang moors an' mosses many, O,
The wintry sun the day has clos'd,
    AndI 'll awa to Nanie, O.

2

western The westlin wind blaws loud an' shill,
dark   The night's baith mirk and rainy, O;

But I'll get my plaid, an' out I'll steal,
  An' owre the hill to Nanie, O.

3

My Nanie's charming, sweet, an' young;
  Nae artfu' wiles to win ye, O:
May ill befa' the flattering tongue
  That wad beguile my Nanie, O!

4

Her face is fair, her heart is true;
  As spotless as she's bonie, O,
The op'ning gowan, wat wi' dew,   daisy
  Nae purer is than Nanie, O.

5

A country lad is my degree,
  An' few there be that ken me, O;
But what care I how few they be?
  I'm welcome ay to Nanie, O.

6

My riches a's my penny-fee,
  An' I maun guide it cannie, O;   manage; carefully
But warl's gear ne'er troubles me,
  My thoughts are a'—my Nanie, O.

7

Our auld guidman delights to view
  His sheep an' kye thrive bonie, O;   kine
But I'm as blythe that hauds his pleugh,
  An' has nae care but Nanie, O.

8

Come weel, come woe, I care na by;   do not care
  I'll tak what Heav'n will send me, O:
Nae ither care in life have I,
  But live, an' love my Nanie, O.

GREEN GROW THE RASHES, O

TUNE: *(As Title)*

CHORUS
Green grow the rashes, O;
Green grow the rashes, O;
The sweetest hours that e'er I spend,
Are spent among the lasses, O.

I

There's nought but care on ev'ry han',
    In every hour that passes, O:
What signifies the life o' man,
    An' 'twere na for the lasses, O.

2

worldly   The war'ly race may riches chase,
    An' riches still may fly them, O;
An' tho' at last they catch them fast,
    Their hearts can ne'er enjoy them, O.

3

quiet   But gie me a cannie hour at e'en,
    My arms about my dearie, O,
worldly   An' war'ly cares an' war'ly men
topsy-turvy   May a' gae tapsalteerie, O!

4

grave   For you sae douce, ye sneer at this;
    Ye're nought but senseless asses, O;
world   The wisest man the warl' e'er saw,
    He dearly lov'd the lasses, O.

5

Auld Nature swears, the lovely dears
    Her noblest work she classes, O:
Her prentice han' she try'd on man,
    An' then she made the lasses, O.

AGAIN REJOICING NATURE

TUNE: *Jockey's Grey Breeks*

CHORUS

And maun I still on Menie doat,
  And bear the scorn that's in her e'e?
For it's jet, jet-black, an' it's like a hawk,
  An' it winna let a body be.

I

Again rejoicing Nature sees
  Her robe assume its vernal hues:
Her leafy locks wave in the breeze,
  All freshly steep'd in morning dews.

2

In vain to me the cowslips blaw,
  In vain to me the vi'lets spring;
In vain to me in glen or shaw,
  The mavis and the lintwhite sing.   linnet

3

The merry ploughboy cheers his team,
  Wi' joy the tentie seedsman stalks;   careful
But life to me's a weary dream,
  A dream of ane that never wauks.   wakes

4

The wanton coot the water skims,
  Amang the reeds the ducklings cry,
The stately swan majestic swims,
  And ev'ry thing is blest but I.

5

The sheep-herd steeks his faulding slap,   shuts;
  And o'er the moorlands whistles shill;   fold-gate
Wi' wild, unequal, wand'ring step,
  I meet him on the dewy hill.

6

And when the lark, 'tween light and dark,
  Blythe waukens by the daisy's side,
And mounts and sings on flittering wings,
  A woe-worn ghaist I hameward glide.

7

Come winter, with thine angry howl,
  And raging, bend the naked tree;
Thy gloom will soothe my cheerless soul,
  When nature all is sad like me!

THE GLOOMY NIGHT IS GATHERING FAST

TUNE: *Roslin Castle*

1

The gloomy night is gath'ring fast,
Loud roars the wild inconstant blast;
Yon murky cloud is filled with rain,
I see it driving o'er the plain;
The hunter now has left the moor,
The scatt'red coveys meet secure;
While here I wander, prest with care,
Along the lonely banks of Ayr.

2

The Autumn mourns her rip'ning corn
By early Winter's ravage torn;
Across her placid, azure sky,
She sees the scowling tempest fly;
Chill runs my blood to hear it rave:
I think upon the stormy wave,
Where many a danger I must dare,
Far from the bonie banks of Ayr.

3

'Tis not the surging billows' roar,
'Tis not that fatal, deadly shore;
Tho' death in ev'ry shape appear,
The wretched have no more to fear:

But round my heart the ties are bound,
That heart transpierc'd with many a wound;
These bleed afresh, those ties I tear,
To leave the bonie banks of Ayr.

4

Farewell, old Coila's hills and dales,
Her heathy moors and winding vales;
The scenes where wretched Fancy roves,
Pursuing past unhappy loves!
Farewell my friends! farewell my foes!
My peace with these, my love with those—
The bursting tears my heart declare,
Farewell, my bonie banks of Ayr.

NO CHURCHMAN AM I

TUNE: *Prepare, my dear Brethren*

I

No churchman am I for to rail and to write,
No statesman nor soldier to plot or to fight,
No sly man of business contriving a snare,
For a big-belly'd bottle's the whole of my care.

2

The peer I don't envy, I give him his bow;
I scorn not the peasant, tho' ever so low;
But a club of good fellows, like those that are here,
And a bottle like this, are my glory and care.

3

Here passes the squire on his brother—his horse,
There centum per centum, the cit with his purse,
But see you *The Crown*, how it waves in the air?
There a big-belly'd bottle still eases my care.

4

The wife of my bosom, alas! she did die;
For sweet consolation to church I did fly;
I found that old Solomon provèd it fair,
That a big-belly'd bottle's a cure for all care.

5

I once was persuaded a venture to make;
A letter inform'd me that all was to wreck;
But the pursy old landlord just waddlèd up stairs,
With a glorious bottle that ended my cares.

6

' Life's cares they are comforts '—a maxim laid down
By the Bard, what d'ye call him? that wore the
    black gown;
And faith I agree with th' old prig to a hair:
For a big-belly'd bottle's a heav'n of a care.

A STANZA ADDED IN A MASON LODGE

Then fill up a bumper and make it o'erflow,
And honours Masonic prepare for to throw:
May ev'ry true Brother of the Compass and Square
Have a big-belly'd bottle, when harass'd with care!

LAMENT OF MARY QUEEN OF SCOTS

ON THE APPROACH OF SPRING

TUNE: *Mary Queen of Scots' Lament*

1

Now Nature hangs her mantle green
    On every blooming tree,
And spreads her sheets o' daisies white
    Out o'er the grassy lea;
Now Phœbus cheers the crystal streams,
    And glads the azure skies:
But nought can glad the weary wight
    That fast in durance lies.

2

larks

Now laverocks wake the merry morn,
    Aloft on dewy wing;
The merle, in his noontide bow'r,
    Makes woodland echoes ring;
The mavis wild wi' monie a note
    Sings drowsy day to rest:
In love and freedom they rejoice,
    Wi' care nor thrall opprest.

3

Now blooms the lily by the bank,
    The primrose down the brae;   hill-side
The hawthorn's budding in the glen,
    And milk-white is the slae: sloe
The meanest hind in fair Scotland
    May rove their sweets amang;
But I, the Queen of a' Scotland,
    Maun lie in prison strang.   must

4

I was the Queen o' bonie France,
    Where happy I hae been;
Fu' lightly rase I in the morn,
    As blythe lay down at e'en:
And I'm the sov'reign of Scotland,
    And monie a traitor there;
Yet here I lie in foreign bands
    And never-ending care.

5

But as for thee, thou false woman,
    My sister and my fae,   foe
Grim vengeance yet shall whet a sword
    That thro' thy soul shall gae!   go
The weeping blood in woman's breast
    Was never known to thee;
Nor th' balm that draps on wounds of woe
    Frae woman's pitying e'e.

6

My son! my son! may kinder stars
    Upon thy fortune shine;
And may those pleasures gild thy reign,
    That ne'er wad blink on mine!   glance
God keep thee frae thy mother's faes,
    Or turn their hearts to thee;
And where thou meet'st thy mother's friend,
    Remember him for me!

7

O! soon, to me, may summer suns
    Nae mair light up the morn!

Nae mair to me the autumn winds
   Wave o'er the yellow corn!
And, in the narrow house of death,
   Let winter round me rave;
And the next flow'rs that deck the spring
   Bloom on my peaceful grave.

THE WHISTLE

A Ballad

TUNE: (*As Title*)

1

I sing of a Whistle, a Whistle of worth,
I sing of a Whistle, the pride of the North,
Was brought to the court of our good Scottish King,
And long with this Whistle all Scotland shall ring.

2

Old Loda, still rueing the arm of Fingal,
The God of the Bottle sends down from his hall:
' This Whistle's your challenge, to Scotland get o'er,
And drink them to Hell, Sir! or ne'er see me more! '

3

Old poets have sung, and old chronicles tell,
What champions ventur'd, what champions fell:
The son of great Loda was conqueror still,
And blew on the Whistle their requiem shrill.

4

Till Robert, the lord of the Cairn and the Scaur,
Unmatch'd at the bottle, unconquer'd in war,
He drank his poor god-ship as deep as the sea;
No tide of the Baltic e'er drunker than he.

5

Thus Robert, victorious, the trophy has gain'd;
Which now in his house has for ages remain'd;
Till three noble chieftains, and all of his blood,
The jovial contest again have renew'd.

6

Three joyous good fellows, with hearts clear of flaw;
Craigdarroch, so famous for wit, worth, and law;
And trusty Glenriddel, so skilled in old coins;
And gallant Sir Robert, deep-read in old wines.

7

Craigdarroch began, with a tongue smooth as oil,
Desiring Glenriddel to yield up the spoil;
Or else he would muster the heads of the clan,
And once more, in claret, try which was the man.

8

' By the gods of the ancients! ' Glenriddel replies,
' Before I surrender so glorious a prize,
I'll conjure the ghost of the great Rorie More,
And bumper his horn with him twenty times o'er.'

9

Sir Robert, a soldier, no speech would pretend,
But he ne'er turn'd his back on his foe, or his friend;
Said:—' Toss down the Whistle, the prize of the
    field,'
And, knee-deep in claret, he'd die ere he'd yield.

10

To the board of Glenriddel our heroes repair,
So noted for drowning of sorrow and care;
But for wine and for welcome not more known to
    fame
Than the sense, wit, and taste, of a sweet lovely dame.

11

A Bard was selected to witness the fray,
And tell future ages the feats of the day;
A Bard who detested all sadness and spleen,
And wish'd that Parnassus a vineyard had been.

12

The dinner being over, the claret they ply,
And ev'ry new cork is a new spring of joy;
In the bands of old friendship and kindred so set,
And the bands grew the tighter the more they were
    wet.

13

Gay Pleasure ran riot as bumpers ran o'er;
company   Bright Phœbus ne'er witness'd so joyous a core,
And vow'd that to leave them he was quite forlorn,
Till Cynthia hinted he'd see them next morn.

14

Six bottles a-piece had well wore out the night,
When gallant Sir Robert, to finish the fight,
Turn'd o'er in one bumper a bottle of red,
And swore 'twas the way that their ancestor did.

15

Then worthy Glenriddel, so cautious and sage,
No longer the warfare ungodly would wage:
A high Ruling Elder to wallow in wine!
He left the foul business to folks less divine.

16

The gallant Sir Robert fought hard to the end;
But who can with Fate and quart bumpers contend?
Though Fate said, a hero should perish in light;
So uprose bright Phœbus—and down fell the knight.

17

Next uprose our Bard, like a prophet in drink:—
' Craigdarroch thou'lt soar when creation shall sink!
But if thou would flourish immortal in rhyme,
Come—one bottle more—and have at the sublime!

18

' Thy line, that have struggled for freedom with
          Bruce,
Shall heroes and patriots ever produce:
So thine be the laurel, and mine be the bay;
The field thou hast won, by yon bright God of Day!'

THE KIRK'S ALARM

TUNE: *Come let us prepare*

1

Orthodox! orthodox!—
Wha believe in John Knox—
Let me sound an alarm to your conscience:
    A heretic blast
    Has been blawn i' the Wast,   West
That what is not sense must be nonsense—
        Orthodox!
That what is not sense must be nonsense.

2

Dr. Mac! Dr. Mac!
You should stretch on a rack,
To strike wicked Writers wi' terror:
    To join faith and sense,
    Upon onie pretence,
Was heretic, damnable error—
        Dr. Mac!
'Twas heretic, damnable error.

3

Town of Ayr! Town of Ayr!
It was rash, I declare,
To meddle wi' mischief a-brewing:
    Provost John is still deaf
    To the church's relief,
And Orator Bob is its ruin—
        Town of Ayr!
And Orator Bob is its ruin.

4

D'rymple mild! D'rymple mild!
Tho' your heart's like a child,
An' your life like the new-driven snaw,
    Yet that winna save ye: will not
    Auld Satan must have ye,
For preaching that three's ane and twa—
        D'rymple mild!
For preaching that three's ane and twa.

5

Calvin's sons! Calvin's sons!
Seize your sp'ritual guns,
Ammunition you never can need:
Your hearts are the stuff
Will be powther enough,
And your skulls are store-houses o' lead—
Calvin's sons!
Your skulls are store-houses o' lead.

6

Rumble John! Rumble John!
Mount the steps with a groan,
Cry:—' The book is wi' heresy cramm'd';
Then lug out your ladle,
Deal brimstone like adle,
And roar every note o' the damn'd—
Rumble John!
And roar every note o' the damn'd.

cow-lant

7

Simper James! Simper James!
Leave the fair Killie dames—
There's a holier chase in your view:
I'll lay on your head
That the pack ye'll soon lead,
For puppies like you there's but few—
Simper James!
For puppies like you there's but few.

Kilmarnoc

8

Singet Sawnie! Singet Sawnie!
Are ye herding the penny,
Unconscious what evils await?
Wi' a jump, yell, and howl
Alarm every soul,
For the Foul Thief is just at your gate—
Singet Sawnie!
The Foul Thief is just at your gate.

Shrivelled
guarding

the Devil

9

Daddie Auld! Daddie Auld!
There's a tod in the fauld,
A tod meikle waur than the clerk:

fox
much worse;
lawyer

Tho' ye can do little skaith,   damage
    Ye'll be in at the death,
And gif ye canna bite, ye may bark—   if
        Daddie Auld!
For gif ye canna bite ye may bark.

10

Davie Rant! Davie Rant!
    In a face like a saunt
And a heart that would poison a hog,
    Raise an impudent roar,
    Like a breaker lee-shore,
Or the Kirk will be tint in a bog—   lost
        Davie Rant!
Or the Kirk will be tint in a bog.

11

Jamie Goose! Jamie Goose!
    Ye hae made but toom roose   empty
In hunting the wicked lieutenant;   reputation
    But the Doctor's your mark,
    For the Lord's haly ark,
He has cooper'd, and ca'd a wrang pin in't—   knocked
        Jamie Goose!
He has cooper'd and ca'd a wrang pin in't.

12

Poet Willie! Poet Willie!
    Gie the Doctor a volley,
Wi' your ' Liberty's chain ' and your wit:
    O'er Pegasus' side
    Ye ne'er laid a stride,
Ye but smelt, man, the place where he shit—
        Poet Willie!
Ye smelt but the place where he shit.

13

Andro Gowk! Andro Gowk!   Cuckoo
    Ye may slander the Book,
And the Book not the waur, let me tell ye: worse
    Ye are rich, and look big,
    But lay by hat and wig,
And ye'll hae a calf's head o' sma' value—
        Andro Gowk!
Ye'll hae a calf's head o' sma' value.

14

Barr Steenie! Barr Steenie!
What mean ye? what mean ye?
If ye 'll meddle nae mair wi' the matter,
Ye may hae some pretence
conduct   To havins and sense
Wi' people wha ken ye nae better—
Barr Steenie!
Wi' people wha ken ye nae better.

15

Irvine-side! Irvine-side!
Wi' your turkey-cock pride,
Of manhood but sma' is your share:
Ye've the figure, 'tis true,
foes   Even your faes will allow,
dare not   And your friends daurna say ye hae mair—
Irvine-side!
Your friends daurna say ye hae mair.

16

Muirland Jock! Muirland Jock!
Whom the Lord gave a stock
Wad set up a tinkler in brass,
If ill manners were wit,
There's no mortal so fit
To prove the poor Doctor an ass—
Muirland Jock!
To prove the poor Doctor an ass.

17

Holy Will! Holy Will!
There was wit i' your skull,
When ye pilfer'd the alms o' the poor:
material   The timmer is scant,
When ye're taen for a saunt
rope   Wha should swing in a rape for an hour—
Holy Will!
Ye should swing in a rape for an hour.

18

Poet Burns! Poet Burns!
-spanking   Wi' your priest-skelping turns,
Why desert ye your auld native shire?

Your Muse is a gipsy,
Yet were she ev'n tipsy,
She could ca' us nae waur than we are—   worse
    Poet Burns!
Ye could ca' us nae waur than we are.

POSTSCRIPTS

I

Afton's Laird! Afton's Laird!
When your pen can be spared,
A copy of this I bequeath,
    On the same sicker score   strict
    As I mention'd before,   conditions
To that trusty auld worthy, Clackleith—
    Afton's Laird!
To that trusty auld worthy, Clackleith.

2

Factor John! Factor John!
Whom the Lord made alone,
And ne'er made another thy peer,
    Thy poor servant, the Bard,
    In respectful regard
He presents thee this token sincere—
    Factor John!
He presents thee this token sincere.

ON CAPTAIN GROSE

WRITTEN ON AN ENVELOPE, ENCLOSING A LETTER TO HIM

TUNE: *Sir John Malcolm*

I

Ken ye ought o' Captain Grose?
            Igo and ago
If he's among his friends or foes?
            Iram, coram, dago
Is he south, or is he north?
            Igo and ago
Or drownèd in the River Forth?
            Iram, coram, dago

2

creatures

Is he slain by Hielan' bodies?
      Igo and ago
And eaten like a wether haggis?
      Iram, coram, dago
Is he to Abra'm's bosom gane?
      Igo and ago

holding;
belly

Or haudin Sarah by the wame?
      Iram, coram, dago

3

Where'er he be, the Lord be near him!
      Igo and ago
As for the Deil, he daur na steer him.
      Iram, coram, dago
But please transmit th' enclosèd letter
      Igo and ago
Which will oblige your humble debtor
      Iram, coram, dago

4

So may ye hae auld stanes in store,
      Igo and ago
The very stanes that Adam bore!
      Iram, coram, dago
So may ye get in glad possession,
      Igo and ago
The coins o' Satan's coronation!
      Iram, coram, dago

THE FÊTE CHAMPETRE

TUNE: *Killiecrankie*

I

O, wha will to Saint Stephen's House,
  To do our errands there, man?
O, wha will to Saint Stephen's House
  O' th' merry lads of Ayr, man?
Or will ye send a man o' law?
  Or will ye send a sodger?
Or him wha led o'er Scotland a'

big

  The meikle Ursa-Major?

2

Come, will ye court a noble lord,
  Or buy a score o' lairds, man?
For Worth and Honour pawn their word,
  Their vote shall be Glencaird's, man.
Ane gies them coin, ane gies them wine,
  Anither gies them clatter;   talk
Annbank, wha guess'd the ladies' taste,
  He gies a Fête Champetre.

3

When Love and Beauty heard the news
  The gay green-woods amang, man,
Where, gathering flowers and busking bowers,   dressing
  They heard the blackbird's sang, man;
A vow, they seal'd it with a kiss,
  Sir Politics to fetter:
As theirs alone the patent bliss
  To hold a Fête Champetre.

4

Then mounted Mirth on gleesome wing,
  O'er hill and dale she flew, man;
Ilk wimpling burn, ilk crystal spring,   Each
  Ilk glen and shaw she knew, man.   winding
She summon'd every social sprite,   wood
  That sports by wood or water,
On th' bonie banks of Ayr to meet
  And keep this Fête Champetre.

5

Cauld Boreas wi' his boisterous crew
  Were bound to stakes like kye, man;   cows
And Cynthia's car, o' silver fu',   full
  Clamb up the starry sky, man: Climbed
Reflected beams dwell in the streams,
  Or down the current shatter;
The western breeze steals through the trees
  To view this Fête Champetre.

6

How many a robe sae gaily floats,
  What sparkling jewels glance, man,

To Harmony's enchanting notes,
   As moves the mazy dance, man!
The echoing wood, the winding flood
   Like Paradise did glitter,
gate   When angels met at Adam's yett
   To hold their Fête Champetre.

7

When Politics came there to mix
adder-   And make his ether-stane, man,
He circled round the magic ground,
   But entrance found he nane, man:
left   He blush'd for shame, he quat his name,
   Forswore it every letter,
Wi' humble prayer to join and share
   This festive Fête Champetre.

THE FIVE CARLINS

TUNE: *Chevy Chase*

I

matrons   There was five carlins in the South:
   They fell upon a scheme
To send a lad to London Town
   To bring them tidings hame:

2

Nor only bring them tidings hame,
   But do their errands there:
maybe gold;   And aiblins gowd and honor baith
both   Might be that laddie's share.

3

There was Maggie by the banks o' Nith,
   A dame wi' pride eneugh;
And Marjorie o' the Monie Lochs,
   A carlin auld and teugh;

4

smirking   And Blinkin Bess of Annandale,
   That dwelt near Solway-side;
And Brandy Jean, that took her gill
   In Galloway sae wide;

5

And Black Joán, frae Crichton Peel,
  O' gipsy kith an' kin:
Five wighter carlins were na found   more
  The South countrie within.   influential

6

To send a lad to London Town
  They met upon a day;
And monie a knight and monie a laird
  This errand fain wad gae.   would go

7

O, monie a knight and monie a laird
  This errand fain wad gae;
But nae ane could their fancy please,
  O, ne'er a ane but tway!   two]

8

The first ane was a belted Knight,
  Bred of a Border band;
And he wad gae to London Town,
  Might nae man him withstand;

9

And he wad do their errands weel,
  And meikle he wad say;   much
And ilka ane at London court   every
  Wad bid to him guid-day.

10

The neist cam in, a Soger boy,   next
  And spak wi' modest grace;
And he wad gae to London Town,
  If sae their pleasure was.

11

He wad na hecht them courtly gifts,   promise
  Nor meikle speech pretend;
But he wad hecht an honest heart
  Wad ne'er desert his friend.

12

Now wham to chuse and wham refuse
    At strife thae carlins fell;
For some had gentle folk to please,
    And some wad please themsel.

those

themselves

13

Then out spak mim-mou'd Meg o' Nith,
    And she spak up wi' pride,
And she wad send the Soger lad,
    Whatever might betide.

-mouthed

14

For the auld Guidman o' London court
    She didna care a pin;
But she wad send the Soger lad
    To greet his eldest son.

the King

15

Then up sprang Bess o' Annandale,
    And swore a deadly aith,
Says:—' I will send the belted Knight,
    Spite of you carlins baith!

oath

16

' For far-aff fowls hae feathers fair,
    And fools o' change are fain;
But I hae tried this Border Knight:
    I'll try him yet again.'

fond

17

Then Brandy Jean spak owre her drink:—
    ' Ye weel ken, kimmers a',
The auld Guidman o' London court,
    His back's been at the wa';

gossips

18

' And monie a friend that kiss'd his caup
    Is now a fremit wight;
But it's ne'er be sae wi' Brandy Jean—
    I'll send the Border Knight.'

cup
hostile

19

Says Black Joán frae Crichton Peel,
  A carlin stoor and grim:—   *stern*
' The auld Guidman or the young Guidman   *the Prince*
  For me may sink or swim!

20

' For fools will prate o' right or wrang,
  While knaves laugh in their slieve;
But wha blaws best the horn shall win—
  I'll spier nae courtier's leave! '   *ask*

21

Then slow raise Marjorie o' the Lochs,
  And wrinkled was her brow,
Her ancient weed was russet gray,
  Her auld Scots heart was true:—

22

' There's some great folk set light by me,
  I set as light by them;
But I will send to London Town
  Wham I lo'e best at hame.'

23

Sae how this sturt and strife may end,   *turmoil*
  There's naebody can tell.
God grant the King and ilka man
  May look weel to themsel!

ELECTION BALLAD FOR WESTERHA'

TUNE: *Up an' waur them a' Willie*

CHORUS

Up and waur them a', Jamie,
  Up and waur them a'!
The Johnstones hae the guidin o't:
  Ye turncoat Whigs, awa!

I

The Laddies by the banks o' Nith
  Wad trust his Grace wi' a', Jamie;   *Would*

serve   But he'll sair them as he sair'd the King—
run   Turn tail and rin awa, Jamie.

2

stood   The day he stude his country's friend,
scratch   Or gied her faes a claw, Jamie,
won   Or frae puir man a blessin wan—
                 That day the Duke ne'er saw, Jamie.

3

                 But wha is he, his country's boast?
                 Like him there is na twa, Jamie!
youngster   There s no a callant tents the kye
herds; cow   But kens o' Westerha', Jamie.

4

                 To end the wark, here's Whistlebirk—
                 Lang may his whistle blaw, Jamie!—
                 And Maxwell true, o' sterling blue,
                 And we'll be Johnstones a', Jamie.

BALLADS ON MR. HERON'S ELECTION,

1795

BALLAD FIRST

TUNE: *For a' that*

1

                 Wham will we send to London town,
                 To Parliament and a' that?
                 Or wha in a' the country round
have   The best deserves to fa' that?
                   For a' that, and a' that,
                   Thro' Galloway and a' that,
                   Where is the Laird or belted Knight
                   That best deserves to fa' that?

2

gate   Wha sees Kerroughtree's open yett—
                 And wha is't never saw that?—
                 Wha ever wi' Kerroughtree met,
                 And has a doubt of a' that?

For a' that, and a' that,
  Here's Heron yet for a' that!
The independent patriot,
  The honest man, and a' that!

3

Tho' wit and worth, in either sex,
  Saint Mary's Isle can shaw that,
Wi' Lords and Dukes let Selkirk mix,
  And weel does Selkirk fa' that.   *well; suit*
    For a' that, and a' that,
    Here's Heron yet for a' that!
An independent commoner
  Shall be the man for a' that.

4

But why should we to Nobles jeuk,   *bend*
  And it against the law, that,
And even a Lord may be a gowk,   *cuckoo (i.e.*
  Wi' ribban, star, and a' that?   *dolt)*
    For a' that, and a' that,
    Here's Heron yet for a' that!
A Lord may be a lousy loon,
  Wi' ribban, star, and a' that.

5

A beardless boy comes o'er the hills
  Wi's uncle's purse and a' that;   *With his*
But we'll hae ane frae 'mang oursels,   *from among*
  A man we ken, and a' that.
    For a' that, and a' that,
    Here's Heron yet for a' that!
We are na to be bought and sold,
  Like nowte, and naigs, and a' that.   *cattle; nags*

6

Then let us drink:—' The Stewartry,
  Kerroughtree's laird, and a' that,
Our representative to be':
  For weel he's worthy a' that!
    For a' that, and a' that,
    Here's Heron yet for a' that!
A House of Commons such as he,
  They wad be blest that saw that.

BALLAD SECOND: THE ELECTION

TUNE: *Fy, Let Us A' to The Bridal*

I

Fy, let us a' to Kirkcudbright,
    For there will be bickerin there;
For Murray's light horse are to muster,
    An' O, how the heroes will swear!
And there will be Murray commander,
    An' Gordon the battle to win:
Like brothers, they'll stan' by each other,
    Sae knit in alliance and kin.

2

An' there'll be black-nebbit Johnie,
    The tongue o' the trump to them a':
Gin he get na Hell for his haddin,
    The Deil gets nae justice ava!
And there'll be Kempleton's birkie,
    A boy no sae black at the bane;
But as to his fine nabob fortune—
    We'll e'en let the subject alane!

-beaked
Jew's-harp
inheritance
at all
younker
bone

3

An' there'll be Wigton's new sheriff—
    Dame Justice fu' brawly has sped:
She's gotten the heart of a Bushby,
    But Lord! what's become o' the head?
An' there'll be Cardoness, Esquire,
    Sae mighty in Cardoness' eyes:
A wight that will weather damnation,
    For the Devil the prey would despise.

finely

4

An' there'll be Douglasses doughty,
    New christening towns far and near:
Abjuring their democrat doings
    An' kissing the arse of a peer!
An' there'll be Kenmure sae generous,
    Wha's honor is proof to the storm:
To save them from stark reprobation
    He lent them his name to the firm!

5

But we winna mention Redcastle,   *will not*
   The body—e'en let him escape!   *creature*
He'd venture the gallows for siller,   *money*
   An' 'twere na the cost o' the rape!   *rope*
An' whare is our King's Lord Lieutenant,
   Sae famed for his gratefu' return?
The billie is getting his Questions   *fellow;*
   To say at St. Stephen's the morn!   *Catechism*
    to-morrow

6

An' there'll be lads o' the gospel:
   Muirhead, wha's as guid as he's true;
An' there'll be Buittle's Apostle,
   Wha's mair o' the black than the blue;
An' there'll be folk frae St. Mary's,
   A house o' great merit and note: *The Devil a*
The Deil ane but honors them highly,   *one*
   The Deil ane will gie them his vote!

7

An' there'll be wealthy young Richard,
   Dame Fortune should hang by the neck:
But for prodigal thriftless bestowing,
   His merit had won him respect.
An' there'll be rich brither nabobs;
   Tho' nabobs, yet men o' the first!
An' there'll be Collieston's whiskers,
   An' Quinton—o' lads no the warst!

8

An' there'll be Stamp-Office Johnie:
   Tak tent how ye purchase a dram!   *Take heed*
An' there'll be gay Cassencarry,
   An' there'll be Colonel Tam;
An' there'll be trusty Kerroughtree,
   Wha's honour was ever his law:
If the virtues were pack't in a parcel,
   His worth might be sample for a'!

9

An' can we forget the auld Major,
   Wha'll ne'er be forgot in the Greys?   *Scots Greys*

Our flatt'ry we'll keep for some other:
    Him only it's justice to praise!
An' there'll be maiden Kilkerran,
    An' also Barskimming's guid Knight.
An' there'll be roaring Birtwhistle—
    Yet luckily roars in the right!

10

An' there frae the Niddlesdale border
    Will mingle the Maxwells in droves:

Tough
gapes

Teuch Johnie, Staunch Geordie, and Wattie
    That girns for the fishes an' loaves!

Bawdry

An' there'll be Logan's M'Doual—
    Sculdudd'ry an' he will be there!
An' also the wild Scot o' Galloway,
    Sogering, gunpowther Blair!

11

Then hey the chaste interest of Broughton.
    An' hey for the blessings 'twill bring!
It may send Balmaghie to the Commons—
    In Sodom 'twould mak him a King!
An' hey for the sanctified Murray
    Our land wha wi' chapels has stor'd;
He founder'd his horse among harlots,
    But gie'd the auld naig to the Lord!

BALLAD THIRD:
JOHN BUSHBY'S LAMENTATION

TUNE: *The Children in the Wood*

1

'Twas in the Seventeen Hunder year
    O' grace, and Ninety-Five,

saddest

That year I was the wae'est man
    Of onie man alive.

2

In March the three-an'-twentieth morn,
    The sun raise clear an' bright;
But O, I was a waefu' man,

the fall

    Ere to-fa' o' the night!

3

Yerl Galloway lang did rule this land   Earl
   Wi' equal right and fame,
Fast knit in chaste and holy bands
   With Broughton's noble name.

4

Yerl Galloway's man o' men was I,
   And chief o' Broughton's host:
So twa blind beggars, on a string,
   The faithfu' tyke will trust!   dog

5

But now Yerl Galloway's sceptre's broke,
   And Broughton's wi' the slain,
And I my ancient craft may try,
   Sin' honesty is gane.

6

'Twas by the banks o' bonie Dee,
   Beside Kirkcudbright's towers,
The Stewart and the Murray there
   Did muster a' their powers.

7

Then Murray on the auld grey yaud
   Wi' wingèd spurs did ride:
That auld grey yaud a' Nidsdale rade,
   He staw upon Nidside.   stole

8

An' there had na been the Yerl himsel,
   O, there had been nae play!
But Garlies was to London gane,
   And sae the kye might stray.   cattle

9

And there was Balmaghie, I ween—
   In front rank he wad shine;
But Balmaghie had better been
   Drinkin' Madeira wine.

10

And frae Glenkens cam to our aid
   A chief o' doughty deed:
In case that worth should wanted be,
   O' Kenmure we had need.

11

And by our banners march'd Muirhead,
   And Buittle was na slack,
Whase haly priesthood nane could stain,
   For wha could dye the black?

12

And there was grave Squire Cardoness,
   Look'd on till a' was done:
Sae in the tower o' Cardoness
owl   A howlet sits at noon.

13

And there led I the Bushby clan:
   My gamesome billie, Will,
And my son Maitland, wise as brave,
   My footsteps follow'd still.

14

The Douglas and the Heron's name,
   We set nought to their score;
The Douglas and the Heron's name
   Had felt our weight before.

15

But Douglasses o' weight had we:
   The pair o' lusty lairds,
For building cot-houses sae fam'd,
kitchen-   And christenin kail-yards.
gardens

16

And then Redcastle drew his sword
   That ne'er was stain'd wi' gore
Save on a wand'rer lame and blind,
   To drive him frae his door.

17

And last cam creepin Collieston,
  Was mair in fear than wrath;
Ae knave was constant in his mind—   One
  To keep that knave frae scaith.   harm

BALLAD FOURTH: THE TROGGER   packman

TUNE: *Buy broom besoms*

CHORUS

> *Buy braw troggin*   fine wares
>   *Frae the banks o' Dee!*
> *Wha wants troggin*
>   *Let him come to me!*

1

Wha will buy my troggin,
  Fine election ware,
Broken trade o' Broughton,
  A' in high repair?

2

There's a noble Earl's
  Fame and high renown,
For an auld sang—it's thought
  The guids were stown.   goods; stolen

3

Here's the worth o' Broughton
  In a needle's e'e.   eye
Here's a reputation
  Tint by Balmaghie.   lost

4

Here's its stuff and lining,
  Cardoness's head—
Fine for a soger,
  A' the wale o' lead.   pick

5

mortgage

Here's a little wadset—
    Buittle's scrap o' truth,
Pawn'd in a gin-shop,
    Quenching holy drouth.

6

Here's an honest conscience
    Might a prince adorn,
Bushby's
residence
Frae the downs o' Tinwald—
    So was never worn!

7

Here's armorial bearings
    Frae the manse o' Urr:
The crest, a sour crab-apple
    Rotten at the core.

8

buzzard
hawk
Here is Satan's picture,
    Like a bizzard gled
Pouncing poor Redcastle,
toad
    Sprawlin like a taed.

9

Here's the font where Douglas
    Stane and mortar names,
Lately used at Caily
    Christening Murray's crimes.

10

Here's the worth and wisdom
    Collieston can boast:
By a thievish midge
    They had been nearly lost.

11

Here is Murray's fragments
    O' the Ten Commands,
Bushby
Gifted by Black Jock
    To get them aff his hands.

12
Saw ye e'er sic troggin?—   such
    If to buy ye're slack,
Hornie's turnin chapman: The Devil
    He'll buy a' the pack!

THE DEAN OF THE FACULTY

A New Ballad

TUNE: *The Dragon of Wantley*

1

Dire was the hate at Old Harlaw
    That Scot to Scot did carry;
And dire the discord Langside saw
    For beauteous, hapless Mary.
But Scot to Scot ne'er met so hot,
    Or were more in fury seen, Sir,
Than 'twixt Hal and Bob for the famous job,
    Who should be the Faculty's Dean, Sir.

2

This Hal for genius, wit, and lore
    Among the first was number'd;
But pious Bob, 'mid learning's store
    Commandment the Tenth remember'd.
Yet simple Bob the victory got,
    And won his heart's desire:
Which shows that Heaven can boil the pot,
    Tho' the Deil piss in the fire.

3

Squire Hal, besides, had in this case
    Pretensions rather brassy;
For talents, to deserve a place,
    Are qualifications saucy.
So their worships of the Faculty,
    Quite sick of Merit's rudeness,
Chose one who should owe it all, d'ye see,
    To their gratis grace and goodness.

4

As once on Pisgah purg'd was the sight
    Of a son of Circumcision,
So, may be, on this Pisgah height
    Bob's purblind mental vision.
Nay, Bobby's mouth may be open'd yet,
    Till for eloquence you hail him,
And swear that he has the Angel met
    That met the Ass of Balaam.

5

In your heretic sins may ye live and die,
    Ye heretic Eight-and-Thirty!
But accept, ye sublime majority,
    My congratulations hearty!
With your honors, as with a certain King,
    In your servants this is striking,
The more incapacity they bring
    The more they're to your liking.

THE TARBOLTON LASSES

TUNE: (*Unknown*)

1

If ye gae up to yon hill-tap,
    Ye'll there see bonie Peggy:
She kens her father is a laird,
    And she forsooth's a leddy.

pretty

lady

2

There's Sophy tight, a lassie bright,
    Besides a handsome fortune:
Wha canna win her in a night
    Has little art in courtin.

3

Gae down by Faile, and taste the ale,
    And tak a look o' Mysie:
She's dour and din, a deil within,
    But aiblins she may please ye.

*stubborn;
muddy of
complexion
perhaps*

4

If she be shy, her sister try,
   Ye'll maybe fancy Jenny:
If ye'll dispense wi' want o' sense,
   She kens hersel she's bonie.

5

As ye gae up by yon hillside,   *that*
   Spier in for bonie Bessy: *Call*
She'll give ye a beck, and bid ye light,
   And handsomely address ye.

6

There's few sae bonie, nane sae guid
   In a' King George' dominion:
If ye should doubt the truth of this,
   It's Bessy's ain opinion.

THE RONALDS OF THE BENNALS

TUNE: (*Unknown*)

1

In Tarbolton, ye ken, there are proper young men,
   And proper young lasses and a', man:
But ken ye the Ronalds that live in the Bennals?
   They carry the gree frae them a', man.   *bear the*
                                               bell

2

Their father's a laird, and weel he can spare't: *Broad:*
   Braid money to tocher them a', man;   *to dower*
To proper young men, he'll clink in the hand   *chink*
   Gowd guineas a hunder or twa, man.   *Gold*

3

There's ane they ca' Jean, I'll warrant ye've seen
   As bonie a lass or as braw, man;   *well-dressed*
But for sense and guid taste she'll vie wi' the best,
   And a conduct that beautifies a', man.

4

The charms o' the min', the langer they shine
   The mair admiration they draw, man;
While peaches and cherries, and roses and lilies,
   They fade and they wither awa, man.

5

If ye be for Miss Jean, tak this frae a frien',
   A hint o' a rival or twa, man:
would go   The Laird o' Blackbyre wad gang through the fire,
   If that wad entice her awa, man.

6

The Laird o' Braehead has been on his speed
twelvemonth   For mair than a towmond or twa, man:
stretch   The Laird o' the Ford will straught on a board,
   If he canna get her at a', man.

7

Then Anna comes in, the pride o' her kin,
   The boast of our bachelors a', man:
pleasant   Sae sonsy and sweet, sae fully complete,
   She steals our affections awa, man.

8

choice   If I should detail the pick and the wale
about   O' lasses that live here awa, man,
fault   The faut wad be mine, if they didna shine
   The sweetest and best o' them a', man.

9

I lo'e her mysel, but darena weel tell,
   My poverty keeps me in awe, man;
For making o' rhymes, and working at times,
   Does little or naething at a', man.

10

would not   Yet I wadna choose to let her refuse
   Nor hae't in her power to say na, man:
For though I be poor, unnoticed, obscure,
   My stomach's as proud as them a', man.

11

Though I canna ride in well-booted pride,
    And flee o'er the hills like a craw, man,
I can haud up my head wi' the best o' the breed,   *hold*
    Though fluttering ever so braw, man.   *fine*

12

My coat and my vest, they are Scotch o' the
    best;
    O' pairs o' guid breeks I hae twa, man,   *trousers*
And stockings and pumps to put on my stumps,
    And ne'er a wrang steek in them a', man.   *stitch*

13

My sarks they are few, but five o' them new—   *shirts*
    Twal' hundred, as white as the snaw, man!
A ten-shillings hat, a Holland cravat—
    There are no monie Poets sae braw, man!   *well-dressed*

14

I never had frien's weel stockit in means,
    To leave me a hundred or twa, man;
Nae weel-tocher'd aunts, to wait on their drants   *dowered;*
    And wish them in hell for it a', man.   *prosings*

15

I never was cannie for hoarding o' money,   *careful*
    Or claughtin't together at a', man;   *grasping it*
I've little to spend and naething to lend,
    But devil a shilling I awe, man.   *owe*

THE BELLES OF MAUCHLINE

TUNE: *Bonie Dundee*

1

In Mauchline there dwells six proper young belles,
The pride of the place and its neighbourhood a',
Their carriage and dress, a stranger would guess,
In Lon'on or Paris they'd gotten it a'.

2

handsomely
dressed

Miss Millar is fine, Miss Markland's divine,
Miss Smith she has wit, and Miss Betty is braw,
There's beauty and fortune to get wi' Miss Morton;
But Armour's the jewel for me o' them a'.

ON GENERAL DUMOURIER'S DESERTION

FROM THE FRENCH REPUBLICAN ARMY

TUNE: *Robin Adair*

1

You're welcome to Despots,
                    Dumourier!
You're welcome to Despots,
                    Dumourier!
How does Dampiere do?
Ay, and Bournonville too?
Why did they not come along with you,
                    Dumourier?

2

I will fight France with you,
                    Dumourier,
I will fight France with you,
                    Dumourier;
I will fight France with you,
I will take my chance with you,
By my soul, I'll dance with you,
                    Dumourier!

3

Then let us fight about,
                    Dumourier!
Then let us fight about,
                    Dumourier!
Then let us fight about
Till Freedom's spark be out,
Then we'll be damn'd, no doubt,
                    Dumourier.

EXTEMPORE IN THE COURT OF SESSION

TUNE: *Killiecrankie*

LORD ADVOCATE

He clench'd his pamphlets in his fist,
  He quoted and he hinted,
Till in a declamation-mist
  His argument, he tint it: lost
He gapèd for't, he grapèd for't,   groped
  He fand it was awa, man;   found
But what his common sense came short,
  He ekèd out wi' law, man.

MR. ERSKINE

Collected, Harry stood awee,   a moment
  Then open'd out his arm, man;
His lordship sat wi' ruefu' e'e,   eye
  And ey'd the gathering storm, man;
Like wind-driv'n hail it did assail,
  Or torrents owre a linn, man;   cascade
The Bench sae wise lift up their eyes,
  Hauf-wauken'd wi' the din, man.

I MURDER HATE BY FIELD OR FLOOD

TUNE: *(Unknown)*

I

I murder hate by field or flood,
  Tho' Glory's name may screen us.
In wars at hame I'll spend my blood—
  Life-giving wars of Venus.
The deities that I adore
  Are Social Peace and Plenty:
I'm better pleas'd to make one more
  Than be the death of twenty.

2

I would not die like Socrates,
    For all the fuss of Plato;
Nor would I with Leonidas,
    Nor yet would I with Cato;
The zealots of the Church and State
    Shall ne'er my mortal foes be;
But let me have bold Zimri's fate
    Within the arms of Cozbi.

ON CHLORIS

REQUESTING ME TO GIVE HER A SPRIG OF BLOSSOMED THORN

TUNE: (*Unknown*)

From the white-blossom'd sloe my dear Chloris
    requested
A sprig, her fair breast to adorn:
' No, by Heaven! ' I exclaim'd, ' let me perish for
    ever,
    Ere I plant in that bosom a thorn! '

MY AUNTIE JEAN

TUNE: *John Anderson, my jo*

My auntie Jean held to the shore,
    As Ailsa boats cam' back;
And she has coft a feather bed
    For twenty and a plack;
And in it she wan fifty mark,
    Before a towmond sped;
O! what a noble bargain
    Was auntie Jeanie's bed.

MY GIRL SHE'S AIRY

TUNE: *Black Joke*

My girl she's airy, she's buxom and gay;
Her breath is as sweet as the blossoms in May;
  A touch of her lips it ravishes quite.
She's always good natur'd, good humor'd and
    free;
She dances, she glances, she smiles upon me;
  I never am happy when out of her sight.
Her slender neck her handsome waist
Her hair well curl'd her stays well lac'd

  .   .   .   .
    .   .   .   .

And O for the joys of a long winter night.

YOUNG PEGGY

TUNE: *Loch Errochside*

1

Young Peggy blooms our boniest lass:
  Her blush is like the morning,
The rosy dawn the springing grass
  With early gems adorning;
Her eyes outshine the radiant beams
  That gild the passing shower,
And glitter o'er the crystal streams,
  And cheer each fresh'ning flower.

2

Her lips, more than the cherries bright—
  A richer dye has graced them—
They charm the admiring gazer's sight,
  And sweetly tempt to taste them.
Her smile is as the evening mild,
  When feather'd pairs are courting,
And little lambkins wanton wild,
  In playful bands disporting.

3

Were Fortune lovely Peggy's foe,
  Such sweetness would relent her:
As blooming Spring unbends the brow
  Of surly, savage Winter.
Detraction's eye no aim can gain
  Her winning powers to lessen,
And fretful Envy grins in vain
  The poison'd tooth to fasten.

4

Ye Pow'rs of Honour, Love, and Truth,
  From ev'ry ill defend her!
Inspire the highly-favour'd youth
  The destinies intend her!
Still fan the sweet connubial flame
  Responsive in each bosom,
And bless the dear parental name
  With many a filial blossom!

BONIE DUNDEE

TUNE: *Adew Dundee*

1

' O, whar gat ye that hauver-meal bannock? '
  ' O silly blind body, O, dinna ye see?
I gat it frae a young, brisk sodger laddie
  Between Saint Johnston and bonie Dundee.
O, gin I saw the laddie that gae me't!
  Aft has he doudl'd me up on his knee:
May Heaven protect my bonie Scots laddie,
  And send him hame to his babie and me!

2

' My blessin's upon thy sweet, wee lippie!
  My blessin's upon thy bonie e'e brie!
Thy smiles are sae like my blythe sodger laddie,
  Thou's ay the dearer and dearer to me!
But I'll big a bow'r on yon bonie banks,
  Whare Tay rins wimplin by sae clear;
And I'll cleed thee in the tartan sae fine,
  And mak thee a man like thy daddie dear.'

Marginal glosses:
do not
Perth
would that
dandled
eyebrow
Thou art
build
meandering
clothe

TO THE WEAVER'S GIN YE GO

TUNE: (*As Title*)

should

CHORUS

To the weaver's gin ye go, fair maids,
To the weaver's gin ye go,
I rede you right, gang ne'er at night,
To the weaver's gin ye go.

warn you
true; go

1

My heart was ance as blythe and free
  As simmer days were lang;
But a bonie, westlin weaver lad
  Has gart me change my sang.

once

western
made

2

My mither sent me to the town,
  To warp a plaiden wab;
But the weary, weary warpin o't
  Has gart me sigh and sab.

sob

3

A bonie, westlin weaver lad
  Sat working at his loom;
He took my heart, as wi' a net,
  In every knot and thrum.

4

I sat beside my warpin-wheel,
  And ay I ca'd it roun';
And every shot and every knock,
  My heart it gae a stoun.

drove

ache

5

The moon was sinking in the west
  Wi' visage pale and wan,
As my bonie, westlin weaver lad
  Convoy'd me thro' the glen.

6

But what was said, or what was done,
  Shame fa' me gin I tell;
But O! I fear the kintra soon
  Will ken as weel's mysel!

befall; if
country

O, WHISTLE AN' I'LL COME TO YE, MY LAD

TUNE: (*As Title*)

CHORUS

O, whistle an' I'll come to ye, my lad!
O, whistle an' I'll come to ye, my lad!
Tho' father an' mother an' a' should gae mad,
O, whistle an' I'll come to ye, my lad!

go

1

spy
not; -gate;
ajar
Then
not

But warily tent when ye come to court me,
And come nae unless the back-yett be a-jee;
Syne up the back-style, and let naebody see,
And come as ye were na comin to me,
And come as ye were na comin to me!

2

Go; fly

glance

At kirk, or at market, whene'er ye meet me,
Gang by me as tho' that ye car'd na a flie;
But steal me a blink o' your bonie black e'e,
Yet look as ye were na lookin to me,
Yet look as ye were na lookin to me!

3

sometimes;
disparage;
little

entice

Ay vow and protest that ye care na for me,
And whyles ye may lightly my beauty a wee;
But court na anither tho' jokin ye be,
For fear that she wyle your fancy frae me,
For fear that she wyle your fancy frae me!

I'M O'ER YOUNG TO MARRY YET

TUNE: (*As Title*)

CHORUS

I'm o'er young, I'm o'er young,
I'm o'er young to marry yet!
I'm o'er young, 'twad be a sin
To tak me frae my mammie yet.

1

I am my mammie's ae bairn,   only child
    Wi' unco folk I weary, Sir,   strange
And lying in a man's bed,
    I'm fley'd it make me eerie, Sir.   I fear

2

Hallowmass is come and gane,
    The nights are lang in winter, Sir,
And you an' I in ae bed—   one
    In trowth, I dare na venture, Sir!

3

Fu' loud and shrill the frosty wind
    Blaws thro' the leafless timmer, Sir,   woods
But if ye come this gate again,   way
    I'll aulder be gin simmer, Sir.   older be by

THE BIRKS OF ABERFELDIE   birches

TUNE: *The Birks of Abergeldie*

CHORUS

Bonie lassie, will ye go,
Will ye go, will ye go?
Bonie lassie, will ye go
    To the birks of Aberfeldie?

1

Now simmer blinks on flow'ry braes,   shines;
And o'er the crystal streamlets plays,   slopes
Come, let us spend the lightsome days
    In the birks of Aberfeldie!

2

The little birdies blythely sing,
While o'er their heads the hazels hing,   hang
Or lightly flit on wanton wing
    In the birks of Aberfeldie.

3

The braes ascend like lofty wa's,
The foaming stream, deep-roaring, fa's
O'er hung with fragrant-spreading shaws,   woods
    The birks of Aberfeldie.

4

falls;
brooklet
wets

The hoary cliffs are crown'd wi' flowers,
White o'er the linns the burnie pours,
And, rising, weets wi' misty showers
    The birks of Aberfeldie.

5

Let Fortune's gifts at random flee,
They ne'er shall draw a wish frae me,
Supremely blest wi' love and thee
    In the birks of Aberfeldie.

MACPHERSON'S FAREWELL

TUNE: *MacPherson's Rant*

CHORUS

jovially
went

Sae rantingly, sae wantonly,
   Sae dauntingly gaed he,
He play'd a spring, and danc'd it round
   Below the gallows-tree.

1

Farewell, ye dungeons dark and strong,
   The wretch's destinie!
MacPherson's time will not be long
   On yonder gallows-tree.

2

O, what is death but parting breath?
   On many a bloody plain
I've dar'd his face, and in this place
   I scorn him yet again!

3

Untie these bands from off my hands,
   And bring to me my sword,
And there's no a man in all Scotland
   But I'll brave him at a word.

4

trouble

I've liv'd a life of sturt and strife;
   I die by treacherie:
It burns my heart I must depart,
   And not avengèd be.

5

Now farewell light, thou sunshine bright,
     And all beneath the sky!
May coward shame distain his name,
     The wretch that dare not die!

MY HIGHLAND LASSIE. O

TUNE: *MacLauchlin's Scots-Measure*

CHORUS

Within the glen sae bushy, O,
Aboon the plain sae rashy, O,   Above;
I set me down wi' right guid will   rushy
To sing my Highland lassie, O!

1

Nae gentle dames, tho' ne'er sae fair,   No highborn
Shall ever be my Muse's care:
Their titles a' are empty show—
Gie me my Highland lassie, O!   Give

2

O, were yon hills and vallies mine,
Yon palace and yon gardens fine,
The world then the love should know
I bear my Highland lassie, O!

3

But fickle Fortune frowns on me,
And I maun cross the raging sea;   must
But while my crimson currents flow
I'll love my Highland lassie, O.

4

Altho' thro' foreign climes I range,
I know her heart will never change;
For her bosom burns with honour's glow,
My faithful Highland lassie, O.

5

For her I'll dare the billows' roar,
For her I'll trace a distant shore,
That Indian wealth may lustre throw
Around my Highland lassie, O.

6

She has my heart, she has my hand,
My secret troth and honour's band!
'Till the mortal stroke shall lay me low,
I'm thine, my Highland lassie, O!

CHORUS

Farewell the glen sae bushy, O!
Farewell the plain sae rashy, O!
To other lands I now must go
To sing my Highland lassie, O.

THO' CRUEL FATE

TUNE: *She Rose and Let Me In*

Tho' cruel fate should bid us part
    Far as the pole and line,
Her dear idea round my heart
    Should tenderly entwine.
Tho' mountains rise, and deserts howl,
    And oceans roar between,
Yet dearer than my deathless soul
    I still would love my Jean.

STAY, MY CHARMER

TUNES: *An gille dubh ciar dubh*—Urbani's *Pit-a-Patty*

I

Feel, oh feel my bosom beating
As the busy moments fleeting,
Pit-a-patty still repeating
    Like the little mallet's blow
    Like the little mallet's blow.

2

Stay, my charmer, can you leave me?
Cruel. cruel to deceive me!
Well you know how much you grieve me:
    Cruel charmer, can you go?
    Cruel charmer, can you go?

3

By my love so ill-requited,
By the faith you fondly plighted,
By the pangs of lovers slighted,
    Do not, do not leave me so!
    Do not, do not leave me so!

STRATHALLAN'S LAMENT

TUNE: (*As Title*)

1

Thickest night, surround my dwelling!
    Howling tempests, o'er me rave!
Turbid torrents wintry-swelling,
    Roaring by my lonely cave!
Crystal streamlets gently flowing,
    Busy haunts of base mankind,
Western breezes softly blowing,
    Suit not my distracted mind.

2

In the cause of Right engagèd,
    Wrongs injurious to redress,
Honour's war we strongly wagèd,
    But the heavens deny'd success.
Ruin's wheel has driven o'er us:
    Not a hope that dare attend,
The wide world is all before us,
    But a world without a friend.

MY HOGGIE
lamb

TUNE: (*As Title*)

1

What will I do gin my hoggie die?   should
    My joy, my pride, my hoggie!
My only beast, I had nae mae,   no more
    And vow but I was vogie!   vain
The lee-lang night we watched the fauld,   live-long; fold
    Me and my faithfu' doggie;
We heard nocht but the roaring linn   waterfall
    Amang the braes sae scroggie.   hill-sides; scrubby

2

owl
snipe
fox

dawn

strange dog;
leaped;
stone fence
almost

But the houlet cry'd frae the castle wa',
    The blitter frae the boggie,
The tod reply'd upon the hill:
    I trembled for my hoggie.
When day did daw, and cocks did craw,
    The morning it was foggie,
An unco tyke lap o'er the dyke,
    And maist has kill'd my hoggie!

JUMPIN JOHN

TUNE: (*As Title*)

CHORUS

The lang lad they ca' Jumpin John
    Beguil'd the bonie lassie!
The lang lad they ca' Jumpin John
    Beguil'd the bonie lassie!

1

would not
believe it;
liquor

Her daddie forbad, her minnie forbad;
    Forbidden she wadna be:
She wadna trow't, the browst she brew'd
    Wad taste sae bitterlie!

2

ewe; half
thirty
dowry;
daughter

A cow and a cauf, a yowe and a hauf,
    And thretty guid shillins and three:
A vera guid tocher! a cotter-man's dochter,
    The lass with the bonie black e'e!

UP IN THE MORNING EARLY

TUNE: (*As Title*)

CHORUS

Up in the morning's no for me,
    Up in the morning early!
When a' the hills are covered wi' snaw,
    I'm sure it's winter fairly!

1

Cauld blaws the wind frae east to west,
  The drift is driving sairly,   sorely
Sae loud and shrill's I hear the blast—
  I'm sure it's winter fairly!

2

The birds sit chittering in the thorn,
  A' day they fare but sparely;   All
And lang's the night frae e'en to morn—
  I'm sure it's winter fairly.

THE YOUNG HIGHLAND ROVER

TUNE: *Morag*

1

Loud blaw the frosty breezes,
  The snaws the mountains cover.
Like winter on me seizes,
  Since my young Highland rover
  Far wanders nations over.
Where'er he go, where'er he stray,
  May Heaven be his warden!
Return him safe to fair Strathspey
  And bonie Castle Gordon!

2

The trees, now naked groaning,
  Shall soon wi' leaves be hinging, hanging
The birdies, dowie moaning,   droopingly
  Shall a' be blythely singing,
  And every flower be springing:
Sae I'll rejoice the lee-lang day, live-long
  When (by his mighty Warden)
My youth's return'd to fair Strathspey
  And bonie Castle Gordon.

THE DUSTY MILLER

TUNE: (*As Title*)

1

Hey the dusty miller
And his dusty coat!
He will spend a shilling
Ere   Or he win a groat.
Dusty was the coat,
Dusty was the colour,
Dusty was the kiss
That I gat frae the miller!

2

Hey the dusty miller
And his dusty sack!
Leeze me on the calling
Fills the dusty peck!
Fills the dusty peck,
Brings the dusty siller!
I wad gie my coatie
For the dusty miller!

I DREAM'D I LAY

TUNE: (*As Title*)

1

I dream'd I lay where flowers were springing
Gaily in the sunny beam,
List'ning to the wild birds singing,
By a falling crystal stream;
Straight the sky grew black and daring,
Thro' the woods the whirlwinds rave,
Trees with agèd arms were warring
turbid   O'er the swelling, drumlie wave.

2

Such was my life's deceitful morning,
Such the pleasures I enjoy'd!

But lang or noon loud tempests, storming,   ere
    A' my flowery bliss destroy'd.   All
Tho' fickle Fortune has deceiv'd me
    (She promis'd fair, and perform'd but ill),
Of monie a joy and hope bereav'd me,
    I bear a heart shall support me still.

DUNCAN DAVISON

TUNE: *Ye'll ay be welcome back again*

1

There was a lass, they ca'd her Meg,
    And she held o'er the moors to spin;
There was a lad that follow'd her,
    They ca'd him Duncan Davison.
The moor was dreigh, and Meg was skeigh,   dull; skittish
    Her favour Duncan could na win;
For wi' the rock she wad him knock,   distaff
    And ay she shook the temper-pin.

2

As o'er the moor they lightly foor,   fared
    A burn was clear, a glen was green;
Upon the banks they eas'd their shanks,
    And ay she set the wheel between:
But Duncan swoor a haly aith,   holy oath
    That Meg should be a bride the morn;   to-morrow
Then Meg took up her spinnin-graith,   -instruments
    And flang them a' out o'er the burn.   across the
                                        brook

3

We will big a wee, wee house,   build
    And we will live like king and queen,
Sae blythe and merry's we will be,
    When ye set by the wheel at e'en!   aside
A man may drink, and no be drunk;
    A man may fight, and no be slain;
A man may kiss a bonie lass,
    And ay be welcome back again!

THENIEL MENZIES' BONIE MARY

TUNE: *Ruffian's Rant*

CHORUS

Theniel Menzies' bonie Mary,
Theniel Menzies' bonie Mary,
lost   *Charlie Grigor tint his plaidie,*
Kissin Theniel's bonie Mary!

I

In comin by the brig o' Dye,
while   At Darlet we a blink did tarry;
dawning   As day was dawin in the sky,
We drank a health to bonie Mary.

2

eyes   Her een sae bright, her brow sae white,
side   Her haffet locks as brown's a berry,
And ay they dimpl't wi' a smile,
The rosy cheeks o' bonie Mary.

3

leaped; live- We lap an' danc'd the lee-lang day,
long
sad   Till piper-lads were wae and weary;
tune   But Charlie gat the spring to pay,
For kissin Theniel's bonie Mary.

LADY ONLIE, HONEST LUCKY

TUNE: *Ruffian's Rant*

CHORUS

Lady Onlie, honest lucky,
Buchan   *Brews guid ale at shore o' Bucky:*
I wish her sale for her guid ale,
The best on a' the shore o' Bucky!

I

A' the lads o' Thorniebank,
go   When they gae to the shore o' Bucky,
They'll step in an' tak a pint
Wi' Lady Onlie, honest lucky.

2

Her house sae bien, her curch sae clean—   snug;
   I wat she is a dainty chuckie,   kerchief
And cheery blinks the ingle-gleede   old dear
   O' Lady Onlie, honest lucky!   glances;
                                               -blaze

THE BANKS OF THE DEVON

TUNE: *Bhannerach 'dhon na chrie*

I

How pleasant the banks of the clear winding Devon,
   With green spreading bushes and flow'rs blooming
     fair!
But the boniest flow'r on the banks of the Devon
   Was once a sweet bud on the braes of the Ayr.   slopes
Mild be the sun on this sweet blushing flower,
   In the gay rosy morn, as it bathes in the dew!
And gentle the fall of the soft vernal shower,
   That steals on the evening each leaf to renew!

2

O, spare the dear blossom, ye orient breezes,
   With chill, hoary wing as ye usher the dawn!
And far be thou distant, thou reptile that seizes
   The verdure and pride of the garden or lawn!
Let Bourbon exult in his gay gilded lilies,
   And England triumphant display her proud rose!
A fairer than either adorns the green vallies,
   Where Devon, sweet Devon, meandering flows.

DUNCAN GRAY

TUNE: (*As Title*)

I

Weary fa' you, Duncan Gray!   Woe befall
   (Ha, ha, the girdin o't!),   girthing
Wae gae by you, Duncan Gray!   Woe go with
   (Ha, ha, the girdin o't!).
When a' the lave gae to their play,   rest
Then I maun sit the lee-lang day,   must;
                                          live-long
And jeeg the cradle wi' my tae,   jog; toe
   And a' for the girdin o't!

2

Bonie was the Lammas moon
   (Ha, ha, the girdin o't!)
Glowrin a' the hills aboon
   (Ha, ha, the girdin o't!)
The girdin brak, the beast cam down,
I tint my curch and baith my shoon,
And Duncan, ye're an unco loun—
   Wae on the bad girdin o't!

above

kerchief;
shoes
terrible
rogue

3

But Duncan, gin ye'll keep your aith
   (Ha, ha, the girdin o't!)
I'se bless you wi' my hindmost breath
   (Ha, ha, the girdin o't!)
Duncan, gin ye'll keep your aith,
The beast again can bear us baith,
And auld Mess John will mend the skaith
   And clout the bad girdin o't.

if; oath

I'll

damage
patch

THE PLOUGHMAN

TUNE: *(As Title)*

CHORUS

Then up wi't a', my ploughman lad,
   And hey, my merry ploughman!
Of a' the trades that I do ken,
   Commend me to the ploughman!

1

The ploughman, he's a bonie lad,
   His mind is ever true, jo!
His garters knit below his knee,
   His bonnet it is blue, jo.

2

I hae been east, I hae been west,
   I hae been at St. Johnston;
The boniest sight that e'er I saw
   Was the ploughman laddie dancin.

Perth

3

Snaw-white stockings on his legs
    And siller buckles glancin,   silver
A guid blue bonnet on his head,
    And O, but he was handsome!

4

Commend me to the barn-yard   stack-
    And the corn mou, man!   heap
I never got my coggie fou   little
    Till I met wi' the ploughman.   dish full

LANDLADY, COUNT THE LAWIN   reckoning

TUNE: *Hey Tutti, Taiti*

CHORUS

Hey tutti, taiti,
How tutti, taiti,
Hey tutti, taiti,
Wha's fou now?   drunk

1

Landlady, count the lawin,
The day is near the dawin;   dawning
Ye're a' blind drunk, boys,
    And I'm but jolly fou.

2

Cog, an ye were ay fou,   Stoup; full
Cog, an ye were ay fou,
I wad sit and sing to you,
    If ye were ay fou!

3

Weel may ye a' be!   all
Ill may ye never see!
God bless the king
    And the companie!

RAVING WINDS AROUND HER BLOWING

TUNE: *MacGrigor of Rora's Lament*

1

Raving winds around her blowing,
Yellow leaves the woodlands strowing,
By a river hoarsely roaring,
Isabella stray'd deploring:—
' Farewell hours that late did measure
Sunshine days of joy and pleasure!
Hail, thou gloomy night of sorrow—
Cheerless night that knows no morrow!

2

' O'er the Past too fondly wandering,
On the hopeless Future pondering,
Chilly Grief my life-blood freezes,
Fell Despair my fancy seizes.
Life, thou soul of every blessing,
Load to Misery most distressing,
Gladly how would I resign thee,
And to dark Oblivion join thee!'

HOW LANG AND DREARY IS THE NIGHT

TUNE: *A Gaelic Air*

CHORUS

For O, her lanely nights are lang,
And O, her dreams are eerie,
full of fear *And O, her widow'd heart is sair,*
That's absent frae her dearie!

1

How lang and dreary is the night,
When I am frae my dearie!
I restless lie frae e'en to morn,
Tho' I were ne'er sae weary.

2

When I think on the lightsome days
  I spent wi' thee, my dearie,
And now what seas between us roar,
  How can I be but eerie?

3

How slow ye move, ye heavy hours!
  The joyless day how dreary!
It was na sae ye glinted by,   *sparkled*
  When I was wi' my dearie!

MUSING ON THE ROARING OCEAN

TUNE: *Druimionn Dubh*

1

Musing on the roaring ocean,
  Which divides my love and me,
Wearying heav'n in warm devotion
  For his weal where'er he be: *welfare*

2

Hope and Fear's alternate billow
  Yielding late to Nature's law,
Whispering spirits round my pillow,
  Talk of him that's far awa.

3

Ye whom sorrow never wounded,
  Ye who never shed a tear,
Care-untroubled, joy-surrounded,
  Gaudy day to you is dear!

4

Gentle night, do thou befriend me!
  Downy sleep, the curtain draw!
Spirits kind, again attend me,
  Talk of him that's far awa!

BLYTHE WAS SHE

TUNE: *Andro and his Cutty Gun*

CHORUS

in kitchen
and parlour

Blythe, blythe and merry was she,
Blythe was she butt and ben,
Blythe by the banks of Earn,
And blythe in Glenturit glen!

I

oak
birch wood

By Oughtertyre grows the aik,
On Yarrow banks the birken shaw;
But Phemie was a bonier lass

heights

Than braes o' Yarrow ever saw.

2

Her looks were like a flow'r in May,
Her smile was like a simmer morn.
She trippèd by the banks o' Earn

light as

As light's a bird upon a thorn.

3

Her bonie face it was as meek
As onie lamb upon a lea.
The evening sun was ne'er sae sweet

glance

As was the blink o' Phemie's e'e.

4

The Highland hills I've wander'd wide,
As o'er the Lawlands I hae been,
But Phemie was the blythest lass
That ever trod the dewy green.

conquer

TO DAUNTON ME

TUNE: (*As Title*)

CHORUS

To daunton me, to daunton me,
An auld man shall never daunton me! } *Bis.*

1

The blude-red rose at Yule may blaw,
The simmer lilies bloom in snaw,
The frost may freeze the deepest sea,
But an auld man shall never daunton me.

2

To daunton me, and me sae young,
Wi' his fause heart and flatt'ring tongue:
That is the thing you ne'er shall see,
For an auld man shall never daunton me.

3

For a' his meal and a' his maut,   malt
For a' his fresh beef and his saut,
For a' his gold and white monie,
An auld man shall never daunton me.

4

His gear may buy him kye and yowes,   money; kine;
His gear may buy him glens and knowes;   sheep
                                          knolls
But me he shall not buy nor fee,   hire
For an auld man shall never daunton me.

5

He hirples twa-fauld as he dow,   hobbles two-
                                          fold; can
Wi' his teethless gab and his auld beld pow, mouth; bald
And the rain rains down frae his red blear'd e'e— pate
That auld man shall never daunton me!

O'ER THE WATER TO CHARLIE

TUNE: *Over the Water to Charlie*

CHORUS

We'll o'er the water, we'll o'er the sea,
We'll o'er the water to Charlie!
Come weal, come woe, we'll gather and go,
And live and die wi' Charlie!

1

Come boat me o'er, come row me o'er,
Come boat me o'er to Charlie!

I'll gie John Ross another bawbee
To boat me o'er to Charlie.

2

I lo'e weel my Charlie's name,
  Tho' some there be abhor him;
going But O, to see Auld Nick gaun hame,
  And Charlie's faes before him!

3

I swear and vow by moon and stars
  And sun that shines so early,
If I had twenty thousand lives,
  I'd die as aft for Charlie!

A ROSE-BUD, BY MY EARLY WALK

TUNE: *A Rose-bud*

1

A rose-bud, by my early walk
field-path Adown a corn-inclosèd bawk,
Sae gently bent its thorny stalk,
  All on a dewy morning.
Ere twice the shades o' dawn are fled,
In a' its crimson glory spread
And drooping rich the dewy head,
  It scents the early morning.

2

Within the bush her covert nest
A little linnet fondly prest,
The dew sat chilly on her breast,
  Sae early in the morning.
She soon shall see her tender brood,
The pride, the pleasure o' the wood,
Amang the fresh green leaves bedew'd,
  Awake the early morning.

3

So thou, dear bird, young Jeany fair,
On trembling string or vocal air
Shall sweetly pay the tender care
guards   That tents thy early morning!

So thou, sweet rose-bud, young and gay,
Shalt beauteous blaze upon the day,
And bless the parent's evening ray
    That watch'd thy early morning!

AND I'LL KISS THEE YET

TUNE: *Braes o' Balquhidder*

CHORUS

And I'll kiss thee yet, yet,
    And I'll kiss thee o'er again,
And I'll kiss thee yet, yet,
    My bonie Peggy Alison.

1

When in my arms, wi' a' thy charms,
    I clasp my countless treasure, O,
I seek nae mair o' Heav'n to share
    Than sic a moment's pleasure, O!   such

2

And by thy een sae bonie blue   eyes
    I swear I'm thine for ever, O!
And on thy lips I seal my vow,
    And break it shall I never, O!

RATTLIN, ROARIN WILLIE

TUNE: (*As Title*)

1

O, rattlin, roarin Willie,
    O, he held to the fair,
An' for to sell his fiddle
    And buy some other ware;
But parting wi' his fiddle,
    The saut tear blin't his e'e—
And, rattlin, roarin Willie,
    Ye're welcome hame to me!

2

'O Willie, come sell your fiddle,
　O, sell your fiddle sae fine!
O Willie come sell your fiddle
　And buy a pint o' wine!'
'If I should sell my fiddle,
　The warld would think I was mad;

merry

For monie a rantin day
　My fiddle and I hae had.'

3

quietly
looked in

As I cam by Crochallan,
　I cannily keekit ben,
Rattlin, roarin Willie
　Was sitting at yon boord-en':
Sitting at yon boord-en',
　And amang guid companie!
Rattlin, roarin Willie,
　Ye're welcome hame to me.

WHERE, BRAVING ANGRY WINTER'S STORMS

TUNE: *Lament for Abercairney*

1

Where, braving angry winter's storms,
　The lofty Ochils rise,
Far in their shade my Peggy's charms
　First blest my wondering eyes:
As one who by some savage stream
　A lonely gem surveys,
Astonish'd doubly, marks it beam
　With art's most polish'd blaze.

2

Blest be the wild, sequester'd glade,
　And blest the day and hour,
Where Peggy's charms I first survey'd,
　When first I felt their pow'r!
The tyrant Death with grim control
　May seize my fleeting breath,
But tearing Peggy from my soul
　Must be a stronger death.

O TIBBIE, I HAE SEEN THE DAY

TUNE: *Invercauld's Reel*

CHORUS

O Tibbie, I hae seen the day,
Ye wadna been sae shy!
For laik o' gear ye lightly me,
But, trowth, I care na by.

would not
have
lack of
wealth;
scorn
I care not
although
you do

1

Yestreen I met you on the moor,
Ye spak na, but gaed by like stoure!
Ye geck at me because I'm poor—
    But fient a hair care I!

Last night
spoke not;
went;
blowing dust
toss your
head
fiend

2

When comin hame on Sunday last,
Upon the road as I cam past,
Ye snufft an' gae your head a cast—
    But, trowth, I care't na by!

gave
cared

3

I doubt na, lass, but ye may think,
Because ye hae the name o' clink,
That ye can please me at a wink,
    Whene'er ye like to try.

wealth

4

But sorrow tak him that's sae mean,
Altho' his pouch o' coin were clean,
Wha follows onie saucy quean,
    That looks sae proud and high!

5

Altho' a lad were e'er sae smart,
If that he want the yellow dirt,
Ye'll cast your head anither airt,
    And answer him fu' dry.

direction

6

But if he hae the name o' gear,
Ye'll fasten to him like a brier,
Tho' hardly he for sense or lear
    Be better than the kye.

learning
kine

7

But, Tibbie, lass, tak my advice:
Your daddie's gear maks you sae nice,
ask   The Deil a ane wad spier your price,
    Were ye as poor as I.

8

There lives a lass beside yon park,
shift   I'd rather hae her in her sark
Than you wi' a' your thousand mark,
makes   That gars you look sae high.

CLARINDA, MISTRESS OF MY SOUL

TUNE: *Clarinda*

1

Clarinda, mistress of my soul,
   The measur'd time is run!
The wretch beneath the dreary pole
   So marks his latest sun.

2

To what dark cave of frozen night
   Shall poor Sylvander hie,
Depriv'd of thee, his life and light,
   The sun of all his joy?

3

We part—but, by these precious drops
   That fill thy lovely eyes,
No other light shall guide my steps
   Till thy bright beams arise!

4

She, the fair sun of all her sex,
   Has blest my glorious day;
And shall a glimmering planet fix
   My worship to its ray?

THE WINTER IT IS PAST

TUNE: (*As Title*)

I

The winter it is past, and the simmer comes at last,
    And the small birds sing on ev'ry tree:
The hearts of these are glad, but mine is very sad,
    For my love is parted from me.

2

The rose upon the brier by the waters running clear
    May have charms for the linnet or the bee:
Their little loves are blest, and their little hearts at
        rest,
    But my lover is parted from me.

3

My love is like the sun in the firmament does run—
    Forever is constant and true;
But his is like the moon, that wanders up and down,
    And every month it is new.

4

All you that are in love, and cannot it remove,
    I pity the pains you endure,
For experience makes me know that your hearts are
        full of woe,
    A woe that no mortal can cure.

I LOVE MY LOVE IN SECRET

TUNE: (*As Title*)

CHORUS

My Sandy O, my Sandy O,
My bonie, bonie Sandy O!
Tho' the love that I owe
To thee I dare na show,
Yet I love my love in secret,
    My Sandy O!

1

gave

My Sandy gied to me a ring
Was a' beset wi' diamonds fine;
But I gied him a far better thing,
I gied my heart in pledge o' his ring.

2

gold
salt; rolled
half

My Sandy brak a piece o' gowd,
While down his cheeks the saut tears row'd;
He took a hauf, and gied it to me,
And I'll keep it till the hour I die.

SWEET TIBBIE DUNBAR

TUNE: *Johnny MacGill*

1

O, wilt thou go wi' me, sweet Tibbie Dunbar?
O, wilt thou go wi' me, sweet Tibbie Dunbar?
Wilt thou ride on a horse, or be drawn in a car,
Or walk by my side, O sweet Tibbie Dunbar?

2

I care na thy daddie, his lands and his money;
I care na thy kin, sae high and sae lordly;
But say that thou'lt hae me for better or waur,
And come in thy coatie, sweet Tibbie Dunbar.

FINE FLOWERS IN THE VALLEY

TUNE: *(As Title)*

1

She sat down below a thorn,
    Fine flowers in the valley,
And there she has her sweet babe born
    And the green leaves they grow rarely.

2

Smile na sae sweet, my bonie babe
    Fine flowers in the valley,
And ye smile sae sweet, ye'll smile me dead,
    And the green leaves they grow rarely.

3

She's taen out her little penknife
    Fine flowers in the valley,
And twinn'd the sweet babe o' its life,
    And the green leaves they grow rarely.

4

She's howket a grave by the light o' the moon,   *dug*
    Fine flowers in the valley,
And there she's buried her sweet babe in,
    And the green leaves they grow rarely.

5

As she was going to the church,
    Fine flowers in the valley,
She saw a sweet babe in the porch,
    And the green leaves they grow rarely.

6

O sweet babe and thou were mine,
    Fine flowers in the valley,
I wad cleed thee in the silk so fine   *clothe*
    And the green leaves they grow rarely.

7

O mother dear, when I was thine,
    Fine flowers in the valley,
You did na prove to me sae kind,
    And the green leaves they grow rarely.

SONG: ANNA THY CHARMS

TUNE: *Bonny Mary*

I

Anna thy charms my bosom fire,
    And waste my soul with care;
But ah! how bootless to admire
    When fated to despair!

2

Yet in thy presence, lovely Fair,
    To hope may be forgiven:
For sure 'twere impious to despair
    So much in sight of Heaven.

MY SOGER LADDIE

TUNE: (*As Title*)

CHORUS

My soger laddie, I lang hae lo'ed weel,
Now nearer my heart I tender thee still:
To Country thou'rt loyal, to friendship thou'rt steady,
My blessin gae wi' thee, my soger laddie.

I

My soger laddie gaed over the sea,
won And there he wan fame and laurels to me;
And now her embraces thy country has ready
To welcome thee hame, my soger laddie.

AS I WAS A WAND'RING

TUNE: *Rinn m'eudial mo mhealladh*

CHORUS

Weel, since he has left me, may pleasure gae wi' him;
I may be distress'd but I winna complain:
I'll flatter my fancy I may get anither
My heart it shall never be broken for ane.

I

As I was a wand'ring ae midsummer e'enin
  The pipers and youngsters were makin their game,
Amang them I spyed my faithless fause luver,
  Which bled a' the wounds o' my dolour again.

2

I could na get sleepin till dawin, for greetin;
  The tears trickl'd down like the hail and the rain:
Had I na got greetin, my heart wad a broken,
  For oh, luve forsaken's a tormenting pain!

3

Although he has left me for greed o' the siller,
  I dinna envý him the gains he can win:
I rather wad bear a' the lade o' my sorrow,
  Than ever hae acted sae faithless to him.

HEY HOW JOHNIE LAD

TUNE: *The Lasses of the Ferry*

1

Hey, how, my Johnie lad, ye're no sae kind's ye sud   *should*
   hae been;
Gin your voice I had na kent, I cou'd na eithly trow
   my een.
Sae weel's ye might hae touzled me, and sweetly
   prie'd my mou bedeen;   *mouth*
Hey, how, my Johnie lad, ye're no sae kind's ye sud   *forthwith*
   hae been.

2

My Father he was at the pleugh, my Mither she was
   at the mill,
My Billie he was at the moss, and no ane near our
   sport to spill,   *spoil*
The feint a Body was therein there was nae fear of
   being seen,
Hey, how, my Johnie lad, ye're no sae kind's ye sud
   hae been.

3

Wad ony lad wha lo'ed her weel, hae left his bonny
   lass her lane,
To sigh and greet ilk langsome hour, and think her
   sweetest minutes gane,
O, had ye been a wooer leal, we shu'd hae met wi'
   hearts mair keen,
Hey, how, my Johnie lad, ye're no sae kind's ye sud
   hae been.

4

But I maun hae anither joe, whase love gangs never
   out o' mind,
And winna let the moment pass, when to a lass he
   can be kind,
Then gang your wa's to blinken Bess, nae mair for   *ways*
   Johnie shall she green,   *long for*
Hey, how, my Johnie lad, ye're no sae kind's ye sud
   hae been.

O FARE YE WEEL MY AULD WIFE

TUNE: (*As Title*)

I

O, fare ye weel, my auld wife!
  Sing bum bibery bum,
O fare ye weel my auld wife!
  Sing bum.
O fare ye weel my auld wife!

trouble The steerer up o' sturt and strife,
malt The maut's aboon the meal the night
    Wi' some.

2

An fare ye weel, my pyke-staff,
  Sing bum bibery bum,
An fare ye weel, my pyke-staff,
  Sing bum.
An fare ye weel, my pyke-staff,

strike Nae mair wi' you my wife I'll baff,
  The maut's aboon the meal the night
    Wi' some.

THE SHEPHERD'S WIFE

TUNE: (*Title not traced*)

I

hill The shepherd's wife cries o'er the knowe,
  'Will ye come hame, will ye come hame?'
The shepherd's wife cries o'er the knowe,

by even 'Will ye come hame again e'en jo?'
'O what will ye gie me to my supper,
  Gin I come hame, gin I come hame,
O what will ye gie me to my supper,
  Gin I come hame again e'en jo?'

2

'Ye'se get a panfu' o' plumpin parridge,
  And butter in them, and butter in them,
Ye'se get a panfu' o' plumpin parridge,
  Gin ye'll come hame again e'en, jo?'

'Ha, ha, how! that's naething that dow,
   I winna come hame, I canna come hame;
Ha, ha, how! that's naething that dow,
   I winna come hame gin e'en jo.'

3

The shepherd's wife cries o'er the knowe,
   'Will ye come hame, will ye come hame?'
The shepherd's wife cries o'er the knowe,
   'Will he come hame again e'en jo?'
'O what will ye gie me to my supper,
   Gin I come hame, gin I come hame,
O what will ye gie me to my supper,
   Gin I come hame again e'en jo?'

4

'A reekin fat hen, weel fryth'd i' the pan,
   Gin ye'll come hame, gin ye'll come hame,
A reekin fat hen weel fryth'd i' the pan,
   Gin ye'll come hame again e'en jo.'
'Ha, ha, how! that's naething that dow,
   I winna come hame, I canna come hame;
Ha, ha, how! that's naething that dow,
   I winna come hame gin e'en, jo.'

5

The shepherd's wife cries o'er the knowe,
   'Will ye come hame, will ye come hame?'
The shepherd's wife cries o'er the knowe,
   'Will ye come hame again e'en jo?'
'O what will ye gie me to my supper,
   Gin I come hame, gin I come hame,
O what will ye gie me to my supper,
   Gin I come hame again e'en jo?'

6

'A weel made bed and a pair o' clean sheets,
   Gin ye'll come hame, gin ye'll come hame,
A weel made bed and a pair o' clean sheets,
   Gin ye'll come hame again e'en, jo.'
'Ha, ha, how! that's naething that dow,
   I winna come hame, I canna come hame;
Ha, ha, how! that's naething that dow,
   I winna come hame gin e'en, jo.'

7

The shepherd's wife cries o'er the knowe,
  ' Will ye come hame, will ye come hame? '
The shepherd's wife cries o'er the knowe,
  ' Will ye come hame again e'en jo? '
' O what will ye gie me to my supper,
  Gin I come hame, gin I come hame,
O what will ye gie me to my supper,
  Gin I come hame again e'en jo? '

8

' A luving wife in lily white linens,
  Gin ye 'll come hame, gin ye 'll come hame,
A luving wife in lily white linens,
  Gin ye 'll come hame again e'en, jo.'
' Ha, ha, how! that's something that dow,
  I will come hame, I will come hame;
Ha, ha, how! that's something that dow,
  I will come hame again e'en, jo.'

MY FIDDLE AND I

TUNE: *Green Sleeves*

1

Green sleeves and tartan ties
  Mark my true love where she lies:
I'll be at her or she rise,
  My fiddle and I thegither.

2

Be it by the crystal burn,
  Be it by the milk-white thorn;
I shall rouse her in the morn,
  My fiddle and I thegither.

I COURTED A LASSIE

TUNE: (*Unknown*)

CHORUS

And e'en let her gang—and e'en let her gang,
And e'en let her gang, say I.

I

I courted a lassie, I courted her lang,
   The lassie she did comply;
But she has proved fickle and broken her vow,
   And e'en let her gang, say I.

NAE BIRDIES SANG THE MIRKY HOUR

TUNE: *Sweet Willy*

I

Nae birdies sang the mirky hour
   Amang the braes o' Yarrow,
But slumber'd on the dewy boughs,
   To wait the wauk'ning morrow.

2

' Where shall I gang, my ain true love,
   Where shall I gang to hide me;
For weel ye ken, i' ye're father's bow'r,
   It wad be death to find me.'

3

' O, go you to yon tavern house,
   An' there count o'er your lawin,
An' if I be a woman true,
   I'll meet you in the dawin.'

4

O, he's gone to yon tavern house,
   An' ay he counted his lawin,
An' ay he drank to her gude health—
   Was to meet him in the dawin.

5

O, he's gone to yon tavern house,
   An' counted owre his lawin,
When in there cam three arméd men
   To meet him in the dawin.

6

' O, woe be unto woman's wit,
   It has beguiléd many!

She promiséd to come hersel,
    But she sent three men to slay me.'

          •   •   •   •   •

7

' Get up, get up, now Sister Ann,
    I fear we've wrought you sorrow;
Get up, ye'll find your true love slain
    Among the banks of Yarrow.

8

She sought him east, she sought him west,
    She sought him braid and narrow,
cleft, rock   Till in the clintin of a craig,
    She found him drown'd in Yarrow.

9

She's ta'en three links of her yellow hair
    That hung down long and yellow;
And she's tied it about sweet Willie's waist,
    An' drawn him out of Yarrow.

          •   •   •   •   •

10

I made my love a suit of clothes,
    I clad him all in tartan;
But ere the morning sun arose
garter   He was a' bluid to the gartan.

          •   •   •   •   •

AS LATE BY A SODGER I CHANCED TO PASS

TUNE: *I'll mak you be fain to follow me*

1

As late by a sodger I chancèd to pass,
I heard him a courtin a bonie young lass,
' My hinny, my life, my dearest,' quo he,
' I'll mak you be fain to follow me.'
' Gin I should follow you a poor sodger lad
Ilk ane o' my cummers wad think I was mad.
For battles I never shall lang to see,
I'll never be fain to follow thee.'

2

'To follow me, I think ye may be glad,
A part o' my supper, a part o' my bed,
A part o' my bed, wherever it be,
I'll mak ye be fain to follow me.
Come try my knapsack on your back,
Alang the king's highgate we'll pack,
Between Saint Johnston and bonie Dundee,
I'll mak you be fain to follow me.'

O DEAR MINNY, WHAT SHALL I DO?

TUNE: *O dear minny*

CHORUS

O dear minny, what shall I do?
O dear minny, what shall I do?
O dear minny, what shall I do?
'*Daft thing, doylt thing, do as I do.*'

1

If I be black, I canna be lo'ed;
If I be fair I canna be gude;
If I be lordly, the lads will look by me:
O dear minny, what shall I do?

LASSIE, LEND ME YOUR BRAW HEMP HECKLE

TUNE: *The Bob o' Dumblane*

1

Lassie, lend me your braw hemp heckle,
  And I'll lend you my thrippling-kame;   comb
My heckle is broken, it canna be gotten,
  And we'll gae dance the Bob o' Dumblane.

2

Twa gaed to the wood, to the wood, to the wood,
  Twa gaed to the wood—three cam hame;
An it be na weel bobbit, weel bobbit, weel bobbit,
  An it be na weel bobbit, we'll bob it again.

O, GALLOWAY TAM CAM HERE TO WOO

TUNE: *Galloway Tam*

1

red-brown

O, Galloway Tam cam here to woo;
I'd rather we'd gien him the brawnit cow;
For our lass Bess may curse and ban
The wanton wit o' Galloway Tam.

2

O, Galloway Tam cam here to shear;
I'd rather we'd gien him the gude gray mare;
He kist the gudewife and strack the gudeman;
And that's the tricks o' Galloway Tam.

THE COLLIER HAS A DOCHTER

TUNE: *The collier's bonie lassie*

The Collier has a dochter,
    And O, she's wonder bonie!
A laird he was that sought her,
    Rich baith in lands and money:
She wadna hae a laird,
    Nor wad she be a lady,
But she wad hae a collier
    The color o' her daddie.

SHE PLAY'D THE LOON OR SHE WAS MARRIED

TUNE: *My wife's a wanton wee thing*

CHORUS

My wife's a wanton wee thing,
My wife's a wanton wee thing,
My wife's a wanton wee thing,
    She winna be guided by me.

I

She play'd the loon or she was married,   strumpet
She play'd the loon or she was married,
She play'd the loon or she was married,
    She'll do it again or she die.

2

She sell'd her coat and she drank it,
She sell'd her coat and she drank it,
She row'd hersel in a blanket,—
    She winna be guided by me.

3

She mind't na when I forbade her,
She mind't na when I forbade her,
I took a rung and I claw'd her,
    And a braw gude bairn was she.

THERE'S CAULD KAIL IN ABERDEEN

TUNE: *Cauld Kail*

CHORUS

My coggie, Sirs, my coggie, Sirs,   dish
* I cannot want my coggie:*
I wadna gie my three-girr'd cap,   -hooped dish
* For e'er a quean on Bogie.*

I

There's cauld kail in Aberdeen,
  And castocks in Strathbogie,   cabbage
When ilka lad maun hae his lass,   stalks
  Then fye, gie me my coggie.

2

There's Johnie Smith has got a wife
  That scrimps him o' his coggie,
If she were mine, upon my life
  I wad douk her in a bogie.   duck; bog

WHEN WE GAED TO THE BRAES O' MAR

TUNE: *Up, and warn a', Willie*

CHORUS

Up, and warn a', Willie,
Warn, warn a';
To hear my canty Highland sang
Relate the thing I saw, Willie.

1

When we gaed to the braes o' Mar,
-show   And to the weapon-shaw, Willie;
Wi' true design to serve the king
    And banish Whigs awa, Willie.
Up, and warn a', Willie,
    Warn, warn a';
For lords and lairds came there bedeen,
    And wow! but they were braw, Willie.

2

But when the standard was set up,
    Right fierce the wind did blaw Willie,
nut   The royal nit upon the tap
    Down to the ground did fa', Willie.
Up, and warn a', Willie,
    Warn, warn a';
Then second-sighted Sandie said
    We'd do nae gude at a', Willie.

3

But when the army join'd at Perth,
    The bravest e'er ye saw, Willie,
We didna doubt the rogues to rout,
    Restore our king an a', Willie.
Up, and warn a', Willie,
    Warn, warn a';
The pipers play'd frae right to left
    O whirry Whigs awa, Willie.

4

But when we march'd to Sherramuir
  And there the rebels saw, Willie;
Brave Argyle attack'd our right,
  Our flank, and front and a', Willie;
  Up, and warn a', Willie,
      Warn, warn a';
  ¡Traitor Huntly soon gave way,
      Seaforth, St. Clair and a', Willie.

5

But brave Glengary on our right
  The rebels' left did claw, Willie;
He there the greatest slaughter made
  That ever Donald saw, Willie;
  Up, and warn a', Willie,
      Warn, warn a';
  And Whittam fyled his breeks for fear,   soiled
      And fast did rin awa, Willie.

6

For he ca'd us a Highland mob,
  And soon he'd slay us a', Willie;
But we chas'd him back to Stirling brig—
  Dragoons, and foot, and a', Willie.
  Up, and warn a', Willie,
      Warn, warn a';
  At length we rallied on a hill,
      And briskly up did draw, Willie.

7

But when Argyle did view our line
  And them in order saw, Willie,
He straight gaed to Dumblane again,
  And back his left did draw, Willie.
  Up, and warn a', Willie,
      Warn, warn a';
  Then we to Auchterairder march'd
      To wait a better fa', Willie.

8

Now if ye spier wha wan the day,
  I've tell'd you what I saw, Willie,

We baith did fight, and baith did beat,
   And baith did rin awa, Willie.
Up, and warn a', Willie,
     Warn, warn a';
For second-sighted Sandie said
    We'd do nae gude at a', Willie.

SIR JOHN COPE TRODE THE NORTH RIGHT FAR

TUNE: *Johnie Cope*

CHORUS

Hey! Johnie Cope, are ye wauking yet?
Or are ye sleeping I would wit;
O, haste ye get up, for the drums do beat;
O fye! Cope, rise in the morning.

1

Sir John Cope trode the north right far,
Yet ne'er a rebel he cam naur,
Until he landed at Dunbar
   Right early in a morning.

near

2

He wrote a challenge from Dunbar,
' Come fight me, Charlie, an ye daur,
If it be not by the chance of war
   I'll give you a merry morning.'

dare

3

When Charlie look'd the letter upon,
He drew his sword the scabbard from—
' So Heaven restore to me my own,
   I'll meet you, Cope, in the morning.'

4

Cope swore, with many a bloody word,
That he would fight them gun and sword,
But he fled frae his nest like an ill-scar'd bird,
   And Johnie took wing in the morning.

5

It was upon an afternoon,
Sir Johnie march'd to Preston town,
He says, ' My lads come lean you down,
    And we'll fight the boys in the morning.'

6

But when he saw the Highland lads,
Wi' tartan trews and white cockauds,
Wi' swords, and guns, and rungs, and gauds—
    O Johnie, he took wing in the morning.

7

On the morrow when he did rise,
He looked between him and the skies ;
He saw them wi' their naked thighs,
    Which fear'd him in the morning.

8

O, then he flew into Dunbar,
Crying for a man of war ;
He thought to have passed for a rustic tar,
    And gotten awa in the morning.

9

Sir Johnie into Berwick rade,
Just as the devil had been his guide ;
Gien him the warld he would na stay'd
    To foughten the boys in the morning.   *fight*

10

Says the Berwickers unto Sir John :
' O what's become of all your men ? '
' In faith,' says he, ' I dinna ken—
    I left them a' this morning.'

11

Says Lord Mark Car—' Ye are na blate   *shy*
To bring us the news o' your ain defeat,
I think you deserve the back o' the gate !
    Get out o' my sight this morning.'

THERE LIV'D A MAN IN YONDER GLEN

TUNE: *Johnie Blunt*

1

There liv'd a man in yonder glen,
    And john Blunt was his name, O;
malt   He maks gude maut, and he brews gude ale,
    And he bears a wondrous fame, O.

2

porch   The wind blew in the hallan ae night,
    Fu' snell out o'er the moor, O;
' Rise up, rise up, auld Luckie.' he says,
    ' Rise up and bar the door, O;'

3

pact   They made a paction 'tween them twa,
    They made it firm and sure, O,
Whae'er sud speak the foremost word,
    Should rise and bar the door, O.

4

lost; road   Three travellers that had tint their gate,
    As thro' the hills they foor, O;
They airted by the line o' light
    Fu' straught to Johnie Blunt's door, O.

5

dragged   They haurl'd auld Luckie out o' her bed,
    And laid her on the floor, O;
But never a word auld Luckie wad say,
    For barrin o' the door, O.

6

' Ye've eaten my bread, ye hae druken my ale,
    And ye'll mak my auld wife a whore, O.'—
' Aha! Johnie Blunt! ye hae spoke the first
      word,—
    Get up and bar the door, O.'

UPON THE LOMONDS I LAY, I LAY

TUNE: *The Campbells are comin*

CHORUS

The Campbells are comin, Oho! Oho!
The Campbells are comin, Oho! Oho!
The Campbells are comin to bonie Lochleven,
The Campbells are comin, Oho! Oho!

I

Upon the Lomonds I lay, I lay,
 Upon the Lomonds I lay, I lay,
I lookèd down to bonie Lochleven
 And saw three bonie perches play.

2

Great Argyle he goes before;
 He maks his cannons and guns to roar,
Wi' sound o' trumpet, pipe and drum;
 The Campbells are comin, Oho! Oho!

3

The Campbells they are a' in arms,
 Their loyal faith and truth to show,
Wi' banners rattling in the wind,
 The Campbells are comin, Oho! Oho!

TWA BONIE LADS WERE SANDY AND JOCKIE

TUNE: *Jenny's Lamentation*

Twa bonie lads were Sandy and Jockie,
Jockie was lo'ed but Sandy unlucky,
Jockie was laird baith of hills and of vallies,
But Sandy was nought but the king o' gude fellows.
Jockie lo'ed Madgie, for Madgie had money,
And Sandy lo'ed Mary for Mary was bonie,
Ane wedded for love, ane wedded for treasure,
So Jockie had siller and Sandy had pleasure.

IT'S UP WI' THE SOUTERS O' SELKIRK

TUNE: *The Souters o' Selkirk*

Cobblers

It's up wi' the Souters o' Selkirk,
    And down wi' the Earl of Hume,
And here is to a' the braw laddies
    That wear the single-sol'd shoon.
It's up wi' the Souters o' Selkirk,
    For they are baith trusty and leal,
And up wi' the lads o' the Forest,
    And down wi' the Merse to the deil!

shoes — appears beside "That wear the single-sol'd shoon."

OUR LORDS ARE TO THE MOUNTAINS GANE

TUNE: *Druimionn dubh*

1

Our lords are to the mountains gane,
    A hunting o' the fallow deer;
And they hae gripit Hughie Graham,
    For stealing o' the bishop's mare.

gripped — appears beside "And they hae gripit Hughie Graham,"

2

And they hae tied him hand and foot,
    And led him up thro' Stirling town;
The lads and lassies met him there,
    Cried 'Hughie Graham thou art a loun'.

3

'O lowse my right hand free,' he says,
    'And put my braid sword in the same,
He's no in Stirling town this day,
    Daur tell the tale to Hughie Graham.'

loosen — appears beside "'O lowse my right hand free,' he says,"
Dare — appears beside "Daur tell the tale to Hughie Graham.'"

4

Up then bespake the brave Whitefoord,
    As he sat by the bishop's knee;
'Five hundred white stots I'll gie you,
    If ye'll let Hughie Graham gae free.'

cattle — appears beside "'Five hundred white stots I'll gie you,"

5

' O haud your tongue,' the bishop says,
  ' And wi' your pleading let me be;
For tho' ten Grahams were in his coat,
  Hughie Graham this day shall die.'

6

Up then bespake the fair Whiteford,
  As she sat by the bishop's knee,
' Five hundred white pence I'll gie you,
  If ye'll gie Hughie Graham to me.'

7

' O haud your tongue now lady fair,
  And wi' your pleading let it be;
Altho' ten Grahams were in his coat,
  It's for my honor he maun die.'

8

They've taen him to the gallows knowe,
  He lookèd to the gallows tree,
Yet never color left his cheek,
  Nor ever did he blin' his e'e.

9

At length he lookèd round about,
  To see whatever he could spy,
And there he saw his auld fathèr,
  And he was weeping bitterly.

10

' O haud your tongue, my father dear
  And wi' your weeping let it be;
For tho' they rob me o' my life,
  They cannot o' the Heaven hie.   high

11

' And ye may gie my brother John
  My sword that's bent in the middle clear,
And let him come at twelve o'clock,
  And see me pay the bishop's mare.

12

'And ye may gie my brother James
    My sword that's bent in the middle brown,
And bid him come at four o'clock,
    And see his brother Hugh cut down.

13

'Remember me to Maggy, my wife,
    The niest time ye gang o'er the moor,
Tell her she staw the bishop's mare,
    Tell her she was the bishop's whore.

next

stole

14

'And ye may tell my kith and kin
    I never did disgrace their blood;
And when they meet the bishop's cloak,
    To make it shorter by the hood.'

AS I CAM DOWN BY YON CASTLE WA'

TUNE: *(As Title)*

1

As I cam down by yon castle wa',
    And in by yon garden green,
O, there I spied a bonie, bonie lass,
    But the flower-borders were us between.

2

A bonie, bonie lassie she was,
    As ever mine eyes did see:
'O, five hundred pounds would I give,
    For to have such a pretty bride as thee.'

3

'To have such a pretty bride as me,
    Young man ye are sairly mistaen;
Tho' ye were king o' fair Scotland,
    I wad disdain to be your queen.'

sorely
mistaken

4

'Talk not so very high, bonie lass,
    O talk not so very, very high:
The man at the fair that wad sell,
    He maun learn at the man that wad buy.

would
must

5

'I trust to climb a far higher tree,
  And herry a far richer nest: rob
Tak this advice o' me bonie lass,
  Humility wad set thee best.'

O, WHERE HAE YE BEEN LORD
RONALD, MY SON?

TUNE: (*As Title*)

1

'O, where hae ye been Lord Ronald, my son?
O, where hae ye been Lord Ronald, my son?'
'I hae been wi' my sweetheart, mother, make my
    bed soon,
For I'm weary wi' the hunting, and fain wad lie
    down.'

2

'What got ye frae your sweetheart, Lord Ronald,
    my son?
What got ye frae your sweetheart, Lord Ronald,
    my son?'
'I hae got deadly poison, mother, make my bed soon,
For life is a burden that soon I'll lay down.'

AS I WENT OUT AE MAY MORNING

TUNE: (*As Title*)

1

As I went out ae May morning,
  A May morning it chanc'd to be;
There I was aware of a weel-far'd maid,
  Cam linkin o'er the lea to me.

2

O, but she was a weel-far'd maid,
  The boniest lass that's under the sun;
I spier'd gin she could fancy me,   asked
  But her answer was, 'I am too young.

3

'To be your bride I am too young,
    To be your loun wad shame my kin,
So therefore pray young man begone,
    For you never, never shall my favour win.'

4

But amang yon birks and hawthorns green,
    Where roses blaw and woodbines hing,
O, there I learn'd my bonie lass,
    That she was not a single hour too young.

5

The lassie blush'd, the lassie sigh'd,
    And the tear stood twinklin in her e'e;
'O kind Sir, since ye hae done me this wrang,
    It's pray when will ye marry me,'

6

'It's of that day tak ye nae heed,
    For that's a day ye ne'er shall see;
For ought that passed between us twa,
    Ye had your share as weel as me.'

7

She wrang her hands, she tore her hair,
    She crièd out most bitterlie,
'O, what will I say to my mammie

false
    When I gae hame wi' a *fause storie*.'

8

malt 'O, as ye maut, so maun ye brew,
cask   And as ye brew, so maun ye tun:
But come to my arms, my ae bonie lass,
    For ye never shall rue what ye now hae done.'

THERE WAS A BATTLE IN THE NORTH

TUNE: *A Country Lass*

1

There was a battle in the north,
    And nobles there was many,
And they hae kill'd Sir Charlie Hay,
    And they laid the wyte on Geordie.   blame

2

O, he has written a lang letter—
    He sent it to his lady:—
' Ye maun cum up to Enbrugh town
    To see what words o' Geordie.'

3

When first she look'd the letter on,
    She was baith red and rosy;
But she had na read a word but twa,
    Till she wallow't like a lily.

4

' Gar get to me my gude grey steed,
    My menzie a' gae wi' me;   servants
For I shall neither eat nor drink
    Till Enbrugh town shall see me.'

5

And she has mountit her gude grey steed,
    Her menzie a' gaed wi' her;   servants
And she did neither eat nor drink
    Till Enbrugh town did see her.

6

And first appear'd the fatal block,
    And syne the aix to head him,   axe
And Geordie cam down the stair
    And bands o' airn upon him.   iron

7

But tho' he was chain'd in fetters strang,
 O' airn and steel sae heavy,
There was na ane in a' the court
 Sae bra' a man as Geordie.

8

O, she's down on her bended knee,
 I wat she's pale and weary;
' O pardon, pardon, noble king
 And gie me back my Dearie!

9

' I hae born seven sons to my Geordie dear
 The seventh ne'er saw his daddie:
O, pardon, pardon, noble king,
 Pity a waefu' lady! '

10

' Gar bid the headin'-man mak haste! '
 Our king reply'd fu' lordly:
' O noble king, tak a' that's mine
 But gie me back my Geordie.'

11

The Gordons cam and the Gordons ran
 And they were stark and steady;
And ay the word amang them a',
 Was, ' Gordons keep you ready.'

12

An aged lord at the king's right hand
 Says: ' Noble king, but hear me:—
Gar her tell down five thousand pound,
 And gie her back her Dearie.'

13

Some gae her marks, some gae her crowns,
 Some gae her dollars many;
And she's tell'd down five thousand pound,
 And she's gotten again her Dearie.

14

She blinkit blythe in her Geordie's face,
    Says: ' Dear I've bought thee, Geordie,
But there sud been bluidy bouks on the green   bodies
    Or I had tint my laddie.'   lost

15

He claspit her by the middle sma',
    And he kist her lips sae rosy,
' The fairest flower o' woman-kind
    Is my sweet bonie Lady.'

O, I FORBID YOU MAIDENS A'

TUNE: *Tam Lin*

1

O, I forbid you maidens a',
    That wear gowd on your hair,   gold
To come or gae by Carterhaugh,
    For young Tam Lin is there.

2

There's nane that gaes by Carterhaugh   goes
    But they leave him a wad;
Either their rings, or green mantles,
    Or else their maidenhead.

3

Janet has belted her green kirtle
    A little aboon her knee;
And she has broded her yellow hair
    A little aboon her bree;   brow
And she's awa to Carterhaugh
    As fast as she can hie!

4

But when she cam to Carterhaugh,
    Tam Lin was at the well,
And there she fand his steed standing,
    But away was himsel.

5

two

She hadna pu'd a double rose,
 A rose but only twae,
Till up then started young Tam Lin
 Says, ' Lady thou's pu' nae mae.

6

' Why pu's thou the rose, Janet,
 And why breaks thou the wand!
Or, why comes thou to Carterhaugh
 Withoutten my command?'

7

' Carterhaugh it is my ain;
 My daddie gave it me,
I'll come and gang by Carterhaugh,
 And ask nae leave at thee.'

8

Janet has kilted her green kirtle
 A little aboon her knee,
And she has snooded her yellow hair
 A little aboon her bree,
And she is to her father's ha'
 As fast as she can hie.

9

Four and twenty ladies fair
 Were playing at the ba',
And out then cam the fair Janet
 Ance the flower amang them a',

10

Four and twenty ladies fair
 Were playing at the chess,
And out then cam the fair Janet
 As green as ony glass.

11

Out then spak an auld grey knight
 Lay o'er the castle wa';
And says: ' Alas! fair Janet for thee
 But we'll be blamèd a'.'

12

'Haud your tongue, ye auld fac'd knight,
    Some ill death may ye die,
Father my bairn on whom I will,
    I'll father nane on thee.'

13

Out then spak her father dear,
    And he spak meek and mild,
'And ever alas! Sweet Janet,' he says—
    'I think thou gaes wi' child.'

14

'If that I gae wi' child, father,
    Mysel maun bear the blame,
There's ne'er a laird about your ha',
    Shall get the bairn's name.

15

'If my love were an earthly knight,
    As he's an elfin gray,
I wadna gie my ain true-love
    For nae lord that ye hae.

16

'The steed that my true-love rides on
    Is lighter than the wind;
Wi' siller he is shod before,   silver
    Wi' burning gowd behind.'   gold

17

Janet has kilted her green kirtle
    A little aboon her knee;
And she has snooded her yellow hair
    A little aboon her bree;
And she's awa to Carterhaugh
    As fast as she can hie.

18

When she cam to Carterhaugh,
    Tam Lin was at the well;
And there she fand his steed standing,
    But away was himsel.

19

She hadna pu'd a double rose,
 A rose but only twae;
Till up then started young Tam Lin
 Says, ' Lady thou's pu' nae mae.

20

' Why pu's thou the rose, Janet,
 Amang the groves sae green,
And a' to kill the bonie babe
 That we gat us between? '

21

' O, tell me tell me, Tam Lin,' she says,
 ' For's sake that died on tree,
If e'er ye was in holy chapel,
 Or Christendom did see.'

22

' Roxbrugh he was my grandfather
 Took me with him to bide,
And ance it fell upon a day,
 That wae did me betide.

23

' And ance it fell upon a day,
 A cauld day and a snell,
When we were frae the hunting come
 That frae my horse I fell.

24

' The Queen o' Fairies she caught me
 In yon green hill to dwell,
And pleasant is the fairy-land:—
 But, an eerie tale to tell!

25

' Ay, at the end o' seven years
 We pay a tiend to hell!
I am sae fair and fu' o' flesh
 I'm fear'd it be mysel.

26

'But the night is Hallowe'en, lady,
　The morn is Hallowday;
Then win me, win me, an ye will,
　For weel I wat ye may.

27

'Just at the mirk and midnight hour
　The fairy folk will ride;
And they that wad their true-love win
　At Milecross they maun bide.'

28

'But how shall I thee ken, Tam Lin,
　Or how my true-love know,
Amang sae mony unco knights
　The like I never saw.'

29

'O first let pass the black, lady,
　And syne let pass the brown;
But quickly run to the milk-white steed,
　Pu' ye his rider down.

30

'For I'll ride on the milk-white steed,
　And ay nearest the town,
Because I was an earthly knight
　They gie me that renown.

31

'My right hand will be glov'd, lady,
　My left hand will be bare,
Cockt up shall my bonnet be
　And kaim'd down shall my hair;
And thae's the tokens I gie thee—
　Nae doubt I will be there:

32

'They'll turn me in your arms, lady,
　Into an esk and adder,
But hold me fast and fear me not—
　I am your bairn's father.

33

'They'll turn me to a bear sae grim,
　And then a lion bold;
But hold me fast and fear me not,
　As ye shall love your child.

34

'Again they'll turn me in your arms
　To a red het gaud of airn;
But hold me fast and fear me not,
　I'll do to you nae harm.

35

'And last they'll turn me in your arms
　Into the burning lead:
Then throw me into well water:
　O! throw me in wi' speed.

36

'And then I'll be your ain true love,
　I'll turn a naked knight;
Then cover me wi' your green mantle,
　And cover me out o' sight.'

37

Gloomy, gloomy was the night,
　And eerie was the way,
As fair Jenny in her green mantle,
　To Milecross she did gae.

38

About the middle o' the night,
　She heard the bridles ring;
This lady was as glad at that
　As any earthly thing.

39

First she let the black pass by,
　And syne she let the brown;
But quickly she ran to the milk-white steed,
　And pu'd the rider down.

40

Sae weel she minded what he did say
  And young Tam Lin did win;
Syne cover'd him wi' her green mantle,
  As blythe's a bird in Spring.

41

Out then spak the queen o' fairies,
  Out of a bush o' broom;
' Them that has gotten young Tam Lin
  Has gotten a stately groom.'

42

Out then spak the queen o' fairies,
  And an angry queen was she:
' Shame betide her ill-far'd face,
  And an ill death may she die,
For she's taen awa the boniest knight
  In a' my companie.

43

' But had I kend, Tam Lin,' she says,
  ' What now this night I see,
I wad hae taen out thy twa grey een,
  And put in twa een o' tree.'

AFTEN HAE I PLAY'D AT THE CARDS AND THE DICE

TUNE: *The rantin laddie*

1

Aften hae I play'd at the cards and the dice,
  For the love of a bonie rantin laddie;
But now I maun sit in my father's kitchen neuk,   nook
  And balou a bastard babie.

2

For my father he will not me own,
  And my mother she neglects me,
And a' my friends hae lightlied me,
  And their servants they do slight me.

3

But had I a servant at my command—
    As aft times I've had many,
That wad rin wi' a letter to bonie Glenswood—
    Wi' a letter to my rantin laddie.

run

4

'Oh, is he either a laird or a lord,
    Or is he but a cadie,
That ye do him ca' sae aften by name,
    Your bonie, bonie rantin laddie.'

5

'Indeed he is baith a laird and a lord,
    And he never was a cadie,
For he is the Earl o' bonie Aboyne,
    And he is my rantin laddie.'

6

'O ye'se get a servant at your command,
    As aft times ye've had many,
That sall rin wi' a letter to bonie Glenswood—
    A letter to your rantin laddie.'

7

When Lord Aboyne did the letter get,
    O, but he blinket bonie;
But or he had read three lines of it,
    I think his heart was sorry.

8

'O, wha is he daur be sae bauld,
    Sae cruelly to use my lassie?'
(But I'll tak her to bonie Aboyne
    Where oft she did caress me.)

dare; bold

9

'For her father he will not her know,
    And her mother she does slight her;
And a' her friends hae lightlied her,
    And their servants they neglect her.'

10

'Go raise to me my five hundred men,
  Make haste and make them ready;
With a milkwhite steed under every ane
  For to bring hame my lady.'

11

As they came in through Buchan-shire,
  They were a company bonie,
With a gude claymore in every hand
  And O, but they shin'd bonie.

OUR YOUNG LADY'S A-HUNTIN GANE

TUNE: *The rowin't in her apron*

1

Our young lady's a-huntin gane,
Sheets nor blankets has she taen,
But she's born her auld son or she cam hame,
  And she's row'd him in her apron.   wrapped

2

Her apron was o' the hollan fine,
Laid about wi' laces nine;
She thought it a pity her babie should tyne,
  And she's row'd him in her apron.

3

Her apron was o' the hollan sma',
Laid about wi' laces a',
She thought it a pity her babe to let fa';
  And she row'd him in her apron.

4

Her father says within the ha',
Among the knights and nobles a':—
'I think I hear a babie ca'   call
  In the chamber among our young ladies.'

5

'O father dear! it is a bairn,
I hope it will do you nae harm,
For the laddie I lo'ed, and he'll lo'e me again,
    For the rowin't in my apron.'

6

'O, is he a gentleman, or is a clown,
That has brought thy fair body down?
I would not for a' this town
    The rowin't in thy apron.'

7

'Young Terreagles is nae clown,
He is the toss of Edinborrow town,
And he'll buy me a braw new gown
    For the rowin't in my apron.'

8

'It's I hae castles, I hae towers,
I hae barns, and I hae bowers;
An' that is mine it shall be thine
    For the rowin't in thy apron.'

'O, FOR MY AIN KING,' QUO' GUDE WALLACE

TUNE: *Gude Wallace*

1

'O, for my ain king,' quo' gude Wallace,
    'The rightfu' king of fair Scotland,
blood   Between me and my sovereign blude,
sown   I think I see some ill seed sawn.'

2

leaped   Wallace out over yon river he lap,
    And he has lighted low down on yon plain,
And he was aware of a gay ladie,
    As she was at the well washing.

3

'What tydins, what tydins, fair lady,' he says,
  'What tydins hast thou to tell unto me—
What tydins, what tydins, fair lady,' he says,
  'What tydins hae ye in the south countrie?'

4

'Low down in yon wee Ostler-house
  There is fyfteen Englishmen,
And they are seekin for gude Wallace;
  It's him to take, and him to hang.'

5

'There's nocht in my purse,' quo' gude Wallace,
  'There's nocht, not even a bare pennie;
But I will down to yon wee Ostler-house
  Thir fyfteen Englishmen to see.'   These

6

And when he cam in to yon wee Ostler-house
  He bad *benedicite* be there;   bade
(The Englishmen at the table sat
  The wine-fac'd captain at him did stare.)

7

'Where was ye born, auld crookit carl,   crooked
  Where was ye born—in what countrie?'
'I am a true Scot born and bred,
  And an auld crookit carl just sic as ye see.'   such

8

'I wad gie fyfteen shillings to onie crookit carl—
  To onie crookit carl just sic as ye,
If ye will get me gude Wallace,
  For he is the man I wad very fain see.'

9

He hit the proud captain alang the chaft blade.
  That never a bit o' meal he ate mair;
And he sticket the rest at the table where they sat,
  And he left them a' lyin sprawlin there.

10

'Get up, get up, gudewife,' he says,
    'And get to me some dinner in haste;
For it will soon be three lang days
    since   Sin I a bit o' meat did taste.'

11

The dinner was na weel readie,
    Nor was it on the table set,
Till other fyfteen Englishmen
    gate   Were a' lighted about the yett.

12

'Come out, come out, now gude Wallace,
    This is the day that thou maun die;'
depend   'I lippen nae sae little to God,' he says,
    'Altho' I be but ill wordie.'

13

The gudewife had an auld gudeman,
    By gude Wallace he stiffly stood;
Till ten o' the fyfteen Englishmen
    Before the door lay in their blude.

14

The other five to the greenwood ran,
    branch   And he hang'd these five upon a grain;
And on the morn wi' his merry men a'
    He sat at dine in Lochmaben town.

NEAR EDINBURGH WAS A YOUNG SON BORN

TUNE: *Hynde Horn*

1

Near Edinburgh was a young son born,—
    Hey lilelu an' a how low lan',
An' his name it was callèd young Hynhorn,
    An' it's hey down down, deedle airo.

2

Seven long years he served the king,—
  Hey lilelu, &c.
And it's a' for the sake of his daughter Jean,—
  An' it's hey down, &c.

3

The king an angry man was he,—
He sent young Hynhorn to the sea.

   *   *   *   *   *

4

An' on his finger she put a ring,
(Wi' three shining diamonds set therein.)
When your ring turns pale and wan,
Then I'm in love wi' another man.

   *   -   *   *   *

5

Upon a day he look'd at his ring,
It was as pale as any thing.

6

He's left the sea, and he's come to the lan'.
And there he met an auld beggar man.
' What news, what news, my auld beggar man,
What news, what news by sea or by lan'? '

7

' Nae news, nae news,' the auld beggar said,
' But the king's daughter Jean is going to be wed.'
' Cast off, cast off, thy auld beggar weed,
An' I'll gie thee my gude grey steed.'

   *   *   *   *

8

When he cam to our gude king's yett,
He sought a glass o' wine for young Hynhorn's
    sake.
He drank out the wine and he put in the ring,
And he bade them carry't to the king's dochter
    Jean.

   *   *   *   *   *

9

'O gat ye't by sea, or gat ye't by lan',
O gat ye't aff a dead man's han'?'
'I gat na't by sea, I gat na't by lan',
But I gat it out of your own fair han'.'

*   *   *   *   *

10

'Go, take away my bridal gown,
And I'll follow him frae town to town.'
'Ye need na leave your bridal gown,
For I'll make ye ladie o' mony a town.'

WHAT MERRIMENT HAS TAEN THE WHIGS

TUNE: *The German lairdie*

CHORUS

Sing heedle liltie, teedle liltie,
Andum, tandum, tandie,
Sing fal de dal, de dal lal lal,
Sing howdle liltie dandie.

1

What merriment has taen the Whigs
I think they be gaen mad, Sir,
Wi' playing up their Whiggish jigs,
Their dancin may be sad, Sir.

2

The Revolution principles
Has put their heads in bees, Sir;
They 're a' fa'en out amang themsels—
Deil tak the first that grees, Sir.

O, THAT I WERE WHERE HELEN LIES

TUNE: *Where Helen lies*

1

O, that I were where Helen lies!
Night and day on me she cries;
O, that I were where Helen lies
　　In fair Kirkconnel lee.

2

O Helen fair! beyond compare,
A ringlet of thy flowing hair,
I'll wear it still for evermair
　　Until the day I die.

3

Curs'd be the hand that shot the shot,
And curs'd the gun that gave the crack,
Into my arms bird Helen lap,　　　　　　leaped
　　And died for sake o' me.

4

O think na ye but my heart was sair,
My love fell down and spake nae mair,
There did she swoon wi' meikle care
　　On fair Kirkconnel lee.

5

I lighted down, my sword did draw,
I cutted him in pieces sma';
I cutted him in pieces sma'
　　On fair Kirkconnel lee.

6

O Helen chaste, thou wert modest
If I were with thee I were blest,
Where thou lies low, and takes thy rest
　　On fair Kirkconnel lee.

7

I wish my grave was growing green,
A winding sheet put o'er my een,　　　　eyes
And I in Helen's arms lying
　　In fair Kirkconnel lee!

8

I wish I were where Helen lies!
Night and day on me she cries;
O, that I were where Helen lies
    On fair Kirkconnel lee.

O HEARD YE OF A SILLY HARPER?

TUNE: *The Lochmaben harper*

1

O, heard ye of a silly harper
    Liv'd long in Lochmaben town?
How he did gang to fair England   } *bis*
    To steal King Henry's wanton brown.

2

But first he gaed to his gude-wife
    Wi' a' the speed that he could thole:—
' This wark,' quo' he, ' will never work   } *bis*
    Without a mare that has a foal.'

3

Quo' she, ' thou has a gude grey mare
high   That'll rin o'er hills baith low and hie;
Gae tak the grey mare in thy hand,   } *bis*
    And leave the foal at hame wi' me.'

4

' And tak a halter in thy hose,
    And o' thy purpose dinna fail,
wrap   But wap it o'er the wanton's nose,   } *bis*
    And tie her to the grey mare's tail.

5

' Syne ca' her out at yon back yeate,
    O'er moss and muir and ilka dale,
For she'll ne'er let the wanton bite,   } *bis*
    Till she come hame to her ain foal.'

6

So he is up to England gane,
    Even as fast as he can hie,
gate   Till he came to King Henry's yeate—   } *bis*
    And wha was there but King Henry?

7

'Come in,' quo' he, 'thou silly blind harper,
    And of thy harping let me hear ':
'O! by my sooth,' quo' the silly blind harper, } *bis*
    'I'd rather hae stabling for my mare.'

8

The king looks o'er his left shoulder,
    And says unto his stable groom:—
'Gae tak the silly poor harper's mare,
    And tie her 'side my wanton brown.' } *bis*

9

And ay he harpèd, and ay he carpit,
    Till a' the lords gaed through the floor;
They thought the music was sae sweet
    That they forgot the stable door. } *bis*

10

And ay he harpit, and ay he carpit,
    Till a' the nobles were sound asleep;
Then quietly he took aff his shoon
    And saftly down the stair did creep. } *bis*

11

Syne to the stable door he hies
    Wi' tread as light as light could be,
And when he open'd and gaed in,
    There he fand thirty good steeds and three. } *bis*   found

12

He took the halter frae his hose,
    And of his purpose did na fail;
He slipt it o'er the wanton's nose,
    And tied it to his grey mare's tail. } *bis*

13

He ca'd her out at yon back yeate
    O'er moss and muir and ilka dale;
And she loot ne'er the wanton bite,
    But held her still gaun at her tail. } *bis*   let

14

The grey mare was right swift o' fit,
　　And did na fail to find the way,
For she was at Lochmaben yeate　　⎫bis
　　Fu' lang three hours ere it was day.⎭

15

When she came to the harper's door,
neigh　　There she gae many a nicher and snear;
'Rise,' quo' the wife, 'thou lazy lass,　⎫bis
　　Let in thy master and his mare.'　　⎭

16

put; clothes   Then up she raise, pat on her claes,
　　And lookit out through the lock-hole:
'O! by my sooth, then,' quo' the lass,　⎫bis
　　'Our mare has gotten a braw big foal.'⎭

17

'Come haud thy peace thou foolish lass,
　　The moon's but glancing in thy e'e;
whole   I'd wad my haill fee 'gainst a groat　⎫bis
　　It's bigger than e'er our foal will be.'⎭

18

The neighbours too that heard the noise
　　Cried to the wife to put her in;
'By my sooth, then,' quoth the wife　⎫bis
　　'She's better than ever he rade on.'⎭

19

But on the morn at fair daylight,
　　When they had ended a' their cheer:
stolen   King Henry's wanton brown was stawn,　⎫bis
　　And eke the poor auld harper's mare.⎭

20

'Alace! alace!' says the silly blind harper;
　　'Alace! alace! that I came here,
lost   In Scotland I've tint a braw cowte foal,　⎫
　　In England they've stawn my gude grey ⎬bis
　　mare.'　　　　　　　　　　　　　　⎭

21

'Come haud thy tongue, thou silly blind harper,
    And of thy *alacing* let me be,
For thou shall get a better mare,
    And weel paid shall thy cowte foal be.
For thou shall get a better mare,
    And weel paid shall thy cowte foal be.'

'TWAS PAST ONE O'CLOCK

TUNE: *Cold frosty morning*

1

'Twas past one o'clock in a cauld frosty morning
    When cankert November blaws over the plain,
I heard the kirk-bell repeat the loud warning
    As restless I sought for sweet slumber in vain:
Then up I arose, the silver moon shining bright,
Mountains and vallies appearing all hoary white;
Forth I would go amid the pale, silent night,
    To visit the fair one, the cause of my pain.

2

Sae gently I staw to my lovely maid's chamber,   stole
    And rapp'd at her window, low down on my knee,
Begging that she would awauk from sweet slumber,
    Awauk from sweet slumber and pity me:
For, that a stranger to a' pleasure, peace and rest,
Love into madness had fir èd my tortur'd breast,
And that I should be of a' men the maist unblest,
    Unless she would pity my sad miserie!

3

My true love arose and whisper èd to me—
    (The moon look èd in and envy'd my love's
        charms;—)
'An innocent maiden, ah, would you undo me!'
    I made no reply, but leapt into her arms:
Bright Phoebus peep'd over the hills and found me
        there;
As he has done, now, seven lang years and mair,
A faithfuller, constanter, kinder, more loving pair,
    His sweet chearing beam nor enlightens nor warms.

THE QUEEN O' THE LOTHIANS CAM CRUISIN TO FIFE

TUNE: (*As Title*)

1

The Queen o' the Lothians cam cruisin to Fife,
  Fal de ral, lal de ral, lario,
To see gin a wooer wad tak her for life.
  Sing hey, fal lal de ral, lal de ral, lal de ral,
  Hey, fal lal de ral, lairo.

2

She had na been lang at the brow o' the hill,
Till Jockie cam down to visit Lochnell.

3

nook   He took the aunt to the neuk o' the ha',
Whare naebody heard, and whare naebody saw.

4

'Madam,' he says, ' I've thought on your advice,
afraid   I wad marry your niece, but I'm fley'd she'll be nice.'

5

'Jockie,' she says, ' the wark's done to your hand,
I've spoke to my niece, and she's at your command.'

6

'But troth, Madam, I canna woo,
For aft I hae tried it, and ay I fa' thro'.

7

'But, O dear Madam, and I'se wad begin,
For I 'm as fley'd to do it, as it were a sin.'

8

Jenny cam in, and Jockie ran out.
'Madam,' she says, ' what hae ye been about? '

9

'Jenny,' she says, ' I've been workin for you,
For what do you think, Jockie's came here to woo.

10

'Now, Jenny, tak care, and dash na the lad,
For offers like him are na ay to be had.'   *not always*

11

'Madam, I'll tak the advice o' the wise.
I ken the lad's worth, and I own he's a prize.'

12

Then she cries but the house, 'Jockie, come here,
Ye've naething to do but the question to spier.'

13

The question was spier'd, and the bargain was struck,
The neebors cam in, and wish'd them gude luck.

BROOM BESOMS

TUNE: *Buy broom besoms*

CHORUS

Buy broom besoms! Wha will buy them now?
Fine heather ringers, better never grew.

1

I maun hae a wife, whatsoe'er she be;
An she be a woman, that's eneugh for me.

2

If that she be bony, I shall think her right:
If that she be ugly, where's the odds at night?

3

O, an she be young, how happy shall I be?
If that she be auld, the sooner she will die.

4

If that she be fruitfu', O! what joy is there!
If she should be barren, less will be my care.

5

Be she green or gray; be she black or fair;
Let her be a woman, I shall seek nae mair.

6

If she like a drappie, she and I'll agree;
If she dinna like it, there's the mair for me.

BROOM BESOMS

Second Set

TUNE: *Buy broom besoms*

CHORUS

Buy broom besoms! Wha will buy them now?
Fine heather ringers, better never grew.

1

Young and souple was I, when I lap the dyke;

ditch   Now I'm auld and frail, I douna step a syke.

2

Young and souple was I, when at Lautherslack,
Now I'm auld and frail, and lie at Nansie's back.

3

Had she gien me butter, when she gae me bread,

bolder; bald   I wad looked baulder, wi' my beld head.

EVER TO BE NEAR YE!

TUNE: *The Sutor's Dochter*

1

Ever to be near ye!
Whaur ye bide or whaur ye stray,
To comfort and to cheer ye!
Be your fortune what it may,
Hearken noo and hear ye:
I'd be happy nicht and day
Ever to be near ye;
Happy I'd be nicht and day
Ever to be near ye!

2

Ever to be near ye!
Neither rocks nor currents rife
  Ever need to fear ye
Frae the stress and frae the strife
  Couthiely I'll steer ye,—
Thro' the stormy sea o' life,
  Ever to be near ye!
Thro' the stormy sea o' life,
  Ever to be near ye!

3

Ever to be near ye!
Good and bonny as ye are,
  Wha could nae revere ye?
In your circle or afar
  Nane there is to peer ye:
O, for better or for waur,
  Ever to be near ye!
O, for better or for waur,
  Ever to be near ye!

TO MR. GOW, VISITING DUMFRIES

TUNE: *Tullochgorum*

1

Thrice welcome, king o' rant and reel!
Whaur is the bard to Scotia leal
Wha wadna sing o' sic a chiel   such
  And sic a glorious fiddle!

2

It's but a weary warl' at best,
Wauf an' weary—aften dreary—
It's but a weary warl' at best,
  A wauf and weary widdle!

3

It's but a weary warl' at best
Gang north, or sooth, or east, or west,
But we will never mak' protest
  When near you and your fiddle.

4

Let prosy parsons pray and preach,
And wise professors try to teach
The secrets far beyond their reach
    As Stradivari's fiddle!

5

We'll leave them to themsel's to read
Things sae vexin'—and perplexin'—
We'll leave them to themsel's to read
    Life's cabalistic riddle!—

6

We'll leave them to themsel's to read
To spin their scheme and mak' their creed;
Come, screw your pins and gie's a screed
    Frae your unrivall'd fiddle!

7

Nae fabled wizard's wand, I trow,
Had e'er the magic airt o' Gow,
When wi' a wave he draws his bow
    Across his wondrous fiddle!

art

8

Sic fays and fairies come and dance—
Lightly tripping—hopping, skipping—
Sic fays and fairies come and dance,
    Their maister in the middle!

9

Sic fays and fairies come and dance,
So gently glide and spryly prance,
And noo retreat and noo advance
    When he strikes up his fiddle!

10

In brisk strathspey or plaintive air
What rival can wi' you compare?
O' wha could think a hank o' hair
    Could thus transform a fiddle?

11

What are the notes o' lyre or lute—
Wizzent, wheezy—slim and sleezy—
What are the notes o' lyre or lute?—
    Inconsequential diddle!

12

What are the notes o' lyre or lute?—
O' pipes, piano, fife, or flute,
Wi' a' that ye can execute,
    On your enchanting fiddle!

13

Wha doesna joy to hear the ring
O' ilka bonny lilt and spring
That ye frae recollection bring
    And wheedle through your fiddle!

14

The sumph that wadna praises gie   churl
A soulless clod maun surely be;
A chiel should never hae to dee
    That half like you can fiddle!

ELIBANKS AND ELIBRAES

TUNE: *Killiecrankie*

1

O, Elibanks and Elibraes
    It was but aince I saw ye
But a' my days I'll sing your praise
    Whaever may misca' ye.
Your trees were in their freshest bloom,
    Your birds were singin' cheery
When thro' your wavin' yellow broom
    I wander'd wi' my dearie!

2

How sweet the siller mornin' sped   silver
    In cheerful contemplation!
How fast the gowden gloamin' fled   golden
    In loving conversation!

Noo doon the bank and up the brae
How could I ever weary
such   In sic a place on sic a day
Wi' sic a bonnie dearie!

3

O, Elibanks and Elibraes,
Aye pleasant be your waters!
May a' your sons hae winning ways,
And lovely be your daughters!
My life to me maun surely be
Existence dull and dreary
If I forget the day we met
When I was wi' my dearie!

HIGHLAND HARRY

TUNE: *Highlander's Lament*

CHORUS

O, for him back again!
O, for him back again!
I wad gie a' Knockhaspie's land
For Highland Harry back again.

1

My Harry was a gallant gay,
strode   Fu' stately strade he on the plain,
But now he's banish'd far away:
I'll never see him back again.

2

rest; go   When a' the lave gae to their bed,
drooping   I wander dowie up the glen,
weep   I set me down, and greet my fill,
And ay I wish him back again.

3

O, were some villains hangit high,
every; own   And ilka body had their ain,
Then I might see the joyfu' sight,
My Highland Harry back again!

THE TAILOR FELL THRO' THE BED

TUNE: *I rede ye beware o the ripells you man,*

I

The tailor fell thro' the bed, thimble an' a',
The tailor fell thro' the bed, thimble an' a';
The blankets were thin, and the sheets they were
  sma'—
The tailor fell thro' the bed, thimble an' a'!

2

The sleepy bit lassie, she dreaded nae ill,   small
The sleepy bit lassie, she dreaded nae ill;
The weather was cauld, and the lassie lay still:
She thought that a tailor could do her nae ill!

3

Gie me the groat again, cannie young man!   gentle
Gie me the groat again, cannie young man!
The day it is short, and the night it is lang—
The dearest siller that ever I wan!

4

There's somebody weary wi' lying her lane,   alone
There's somebody weary wi' lying her lane!
There's some that are dowie, I trow wad be fain   drooping;
To see the bit tailor come skippin again.   glad

AY WAUKIN, O   awake

TUNE: (*As Title*)

CHORUS

Ay waukin, O,
  Waukin still and weary:
Sleep I can get nane
  For thinking on my dearie.

1

Simmer's a pleasant time:
    Flowers of every colour,
crag   The water rins owre the heugh,
    And I long for my true lover.

2

When I sleep I dream,
apprehensive   When I wauk I'm eerie,
Sleep I can get nane
    For thinkin on my dearie.

3

Lanely night comes on,
rest   A' the lave are sleepin,
I think on my bonie lad,
eyes;
weeping   And I bleer my een wi' greetin.

BEWARE O' BONIE ANN

TUNE: *Bonie Ann*

1

warn you   Ye gallants bright, I rede you right,
true   Beware o' bonie Ann!
Her comely face sae fu' o' grace,
    Your heart she will trepan.

2

eyes   Her een sae bright like stars by night,
    Her skin is like the swan.
trim   Sae jimply lac'd her genty waist
    That sweetly ye might span.

3

Youth, Grace, and Love attendant move,
    And Pleasure leads the van:
In a' their charms, and conquering arms,
    They wait on bonie Ann.

4

The captive bands may chain the hands,
    But Love enslaves the man:
fine   Ye gallants braw, I rede you a',
    Beware o' bonie Ann!

LANG HAE WE PARTED BEEN

TUNE: *Laddie, Lie Near Me*

CHORUS

Near me, near me,
Lassie, lie near me!
Lang hast thou lien thy lane,   alone
Lassie, lie near me!

1

Lang hae we parted been,
   Lassie, my dearie;
Now we are met again—
   Lassie, lie near me!

2

A' that I hae endur'd,
   Lassie, my dearie,
Here in thy arms is cur'd—
   Lassie, lie near me!

THE GARD'NER WI' HIS PAIDLE   spade

TUNE: *The Gardener's March*

1

When rosy May comes in wi' flowers
To deck her gay, green-spreading bowers,
Then busy, busy are his hours,
     The gard'ner wi' his paidle.

2

The crystal waters gently fa',
The merry birds are lovers a',
The scented breezes round him blaw—
     The gard'ner wi' his paidle.

3

When purple morning starts the hare
To steal upon her early fare,
Then thro' the dew he maun repair—   must
     The gard'ner wi' his paidle.

4

When Day, expiring in the west,
The curtain draws o' Nature's rest,
He flies to her arms he lo'es best,
   The gard'ner wi' his paidle.

ON A BANK OF FLOWERS

TUNE: *The Bashful Lover*

1

On a bank of flowers in a summer day,
 For summer lightly drest,
The youthful, blooming Nelly lay
 With love and sleep opprest;
When Willie, wand'ring thro' the wood,
Who for her favour oft had sued—
  He gaz'd, he wish'd,
  He fear'd, he blush'd,
And trembled where he stood.

2

Her closèd eyes, like weapons sheath'd,
 Were seal'd in soft repose;
Her lips, still as she fragrant breath'd,
 It richer dyed the rose;
The springing lilies, sweetly prest,
Wild-wanton kiss'd her rival breast:
  He gaz'd, he wish'd,
  He fear'd, he blush'd,
His bosom ill at rest.

3

Her robes, light-waving in the breeze,
 Her tender limbs embrace;
Her lovely form, her native ease,
 All harmony and grace.
Tumultuous tides his pulses roll,
A faltering, ardent kiss he stole:
  He gaz'd, he wish'd,
  He fear'd, he blush'd,
And sigh'd his very soul.

4

As flies the partridge from the brake
  On fear-inspirèd wings,
So Nelly starting, half-awake,
  Away affrighted springs.
But Willie follow'd—as he should;
He overtook her in the wood;
    He vow'd, he pray'd,
    He found the maid
Forgiving all, and good.

THE DAY RETURNS

TUNE: *Seventh of November*

1

The day returns, my bosom burns,
  The blissful day we twa did meet!
Tho' winter wild in tempest toil'd,
  Ne'er summer sun was half sae sweet.
Than a' the pride that loads the tide,
  And crosses o'er the sultry line,
Than kingly robes, than crowns and globes,
  Heav'n gave me more—it made thee mine!

2

While day and night can bring delight,
  Or Nature aught of pleasure give,
While joys above my mind can move,
  For thee, and thee alone, I live!
When that grim foe of Life below
  Comes in between to make us part,
The iron hand that breaks our band,
  It breaks my bliss, it breaks my heart!

MY LOVE SHE'S BUT A LASSIE YET

TUNE: (*As Title*)

CHORUS

My love, she's but a lassie yet,
My love, she's but a lassie yet!
We'll let her stand a year or twa,
She'll no be half sae saucy yet!

I

I rue the day I sought her, O!
I rue the day I sought her, O!
Wha gets her need na say he's woo'd,
But he may say he has bought her, O.

2

Come draw a drap o' the best o't yet,
Come draw a drap o' the best o't yet!
Gae seek for pleasure whare ye will,
But here I never missed it yet.

3

We're a' dry wi' drinkin o't,
We're a' dry wi' drinkin o't!
The minister kiss't the fiddler's wife—
He could na preach for thinkin o't!

JAMIE, COME TRY ME

TUNE: (*As Title*)

CHORUS

Jamie, come try me,
Jamie, come try me!
If thou would win my love,
Jamie, come try me!

I

If thou should ask my love,
Could I deny thee?
If thou would win my love,
Jamie, come try me!

2

If thou should kiss me, love,
    Wha could espy thee?
If thou wad be my love,
    Jamie, come try me!

THE SILVER TASSIE

TUNE: *The Secret Kiss*

1

Go, fetch to me a pint o' wine,
    And fill it in a silver tassie,
That I may drink before I go
    A service to my bonie lassie!
The boat rocks at the pier o' Leith,
    Fu' loud the wind blaws frae the Ferry,
The ship rides by the Berwick-Law,
    And I maun leave my bonie Mary.   must

2

The trumpets sound, the banners fly,
    The glittering spears are rankèd ready,
The shouts o' war are heard afar,
    The battle closes deep and bloody.
It's not the roar o' sea or shore
    Wad mak me langer wish to tarry,
Nor shouts o' war that's heard afar:
    It 's leaving thee, my bonie Mary!

THE LAZY MIST

TUNE: *(As Title)*

1

The lazy mist hangs from the brow of the hill,
Concealing the course of the dark winding rill.
How languid the scenes, late so sprightly, appear,
As Autumn to Winter resigns the pale year!

2

The forests are leafless, the meadows are brown,
And all the gay foppery of summer is flown.
Apart let me wander, apart let me muse,
How quick Time is flying, how keen Fate pursues!

3

How long I have liv'd, but how much liv'd in vain!
How little of life's scanty span may remain!
What aspects old Time in his progress has worn!
What ties cruel Fate in my bosom has torn!

4

How foolish, or worse, till our summit is gain'd!
And downward, how weaken'd, how darken'd, how
    pain'd!
Life is not worth having with all it can give:
For something beyond it poor man, sure, must live.

THE CAPTAIN'S LADY

TUNE: (*As Title*)

CHORUS

O, mount and go,
    Mount and make you ready!
O, mount and go,
    And be the Captain's Lady!

1

When the drums do beat,
    And the cannons rattle,
Thou shalt sit in state,
    And see thy love in battle:

2

When the vanquish'd foe
    Sues for peace and quiet,
To the shades we'll go,
    And in love enjoy it.

directions

OF A' THE AIRTS

TUNE: *Miss Admiral Gordon's Strathspey*

1

Of a' the airts the wind can blaw
    I dearly like the west,
For there the bonie lassie lives,
    The lassie I lo'e best.

There wild woods grow, and rivers row,   roll
  And monie a hill between,
But day and night my fancy's flight
  Is ever wi' my Jean.

2

I see her in the dewy flowers—
  I see her sweet and fair.
I hear her in the tunefu' birds—
  I hear her charm the air.
There's not a bonie flower that springs
  By fountain, shaw, or green,   wood
There's not a bonie bird that sings,
  But minds me o' my Jean.   reminds

CARL, AN THE KING COME   if

TUNE: (*As Title*)

CHORUS

Carl, an the King come,
Carl, an the King come,
Thou shalt dance, and I will sing,
Carl, an the King come!

1

An somebodie were come again,
Then somebodie maun cross the main,   must
And every man shall hae his ain,   own
  Carl, an the King come!

2

I trow we swappèd for the worse: swopped
We gae the boot and better horse,   gave
And that we'll tell them at the Cross,
  Carl, an the King come!

3

Coggie, an the King come,   Stoup
Coggie, an the King come,   I'll be full;
I'll be fou, and thou'se be toom,   (*i.e.* drunk);
  Coggie, an the King come!   thou'lt;
                           empty

WHISTLE O'ER THE LAVE O'T

TUNE: (*As Title*)

rest of it

I

First when Maggie was my care,
Heav'n, I thought, was in her air;

ask no
more

Now we're married, spier nae mair,
    But—whistle o'er the lave o't!
Meg was meek, and Meg was mild,
Sweet and harmless as a child:
Wiser men than me's beguiled—
    Whistle o'er the lave o't!

2

How we live, my Meg and me,
How we love, and how we gree,

care nothing

I care na by how few may see—
    Whistle o'er the lave o't!
Wha I wish were maggots' meat,
Dish'd up in her winding-sheet,
I could write (but Meg wad see't)—
    Whistle o'er the lave o't!

O, WERE I ON PARNASSUS HILL

TUNE: *My Love is lost to me*

I

O, were I on Parnassus hill,
Or had o' Helicon my fill,
That I might catch poetic skill
    To sing how dear I love thee!

must

But Nith maun be my Muses' well,
My Muse maun be thy bonie sel',

gaze

On Corsincon I'll glowr and spell,
    And write how dear I love thee.

2

Then come, sweet Muse, inspire my lay!

live-long

For a' the lee-lang simmer's day
I couldna sing, I couldna say
    How much, how dear I love thee.

I see thee dancing o'er the green,
Thy waist sae jimp, thy limbs sae clean,
Thy tempting lips, thy roguish een—   eyes
    By Heaven and Earth I love thee!

3

By night, by day, a-field, at hame,
The thoughts o' thee my breast inflame,
And ay I muse and sing thy name—
    I only live to love thee.
Tho' I were doom'd to wander on,
Beyond the sea, beyond the sun,
Till my last weary sand was run,
    Till then—and then—I 'd love thee!

THERE'S A YOUTH IN THIS CITY

TUNE: *Niel Gow's Lament*

I

There's a youth in this city, it were a great pity
  That he from our lasses should wander awa';
For he's bonie an braw, weel-favor'd witha',   smart
  An' his hair has a natural buckle an' a'.   curl

2

His coat is the hue o' his bonnet sae blue,
  His fecket is white as the new-driven snaw,   waistcoat
His hose they are blae, and his shoon like the slae,   blue; sloe
  And his clear siller buckles, they dazzle us a'.

3

For beauty and fortune the laddie's been courtin;
  Weel-featur'd, weel-tocher'd, weel-mounted, an'   -dowered
    braw,
But chiefly the siller that gars him gang till her—   money;
  The penny's the jewel that beautifies a'!   makes; go to

4

There's Meg wi' the mailen, that fain wad a haen him.   farm; gladly
  And Susie, wha's daddie was laird of the Ha',   would have
                                                      had
There's lang-tocher'd Nancy maist fetters his fancy;   almost
  But the laddie's dear sel he loes dearest of a'.   self

MY HEART'S IN THE HIGHLANDS

TUNE: *The Musket Salute*

CHORUS

My heart's in the Highlands, my heart is not here,
My heart's in the Highlands a-chasing the deer,
A-chasing the wild deer and following the roe—
My heart's in the Highlands, wherever I go!

1

Farewell to the Highlands, farewell to the North,
The birthplace of valour, the country of worth!
Wherever I wander, wherever I rove,
The hills of the Highlands for ever I love.

2

Farewell to the mountains high cover'd with snow,
Farewell to the straths and green valleys below,
Farewell to the forests and wild-hanging woods,
Farewell to the torrents and loud-pouring floods!

JOHN ANDERSON MY JO

TUNE: (*As Title*)

1

John Anderson my jo, John,
    When we were first acquent,
acquainted
Your locks were like the raven,
straight
    Your bonie brow was brent;
bald
But now your brow is beld, John,
    Your locks are like the snaw,
pate
But blessings on your frosty pow,
    John Anderson my jo!

2

John Anderson my jo, John,
    We clamb the hill thegither,
climbed;
together
And monie a cantie day, John,
jolly
    We've had wi' ane anither;

Now we maun totter down, John,   *must*
  And hand in hand we'll go,
And sleep thegither at the foot,
  John Anderson my jo!

AWA', WHIGS, AWA'

TUNE: (*As Title*)

CHORUS

Awa', Whigs, awa'!
  Awa', Whigs, awa'!
Ye're but a pack o' traitor louns,
  Ye'll do nae guid at a'.

1

Our thrissles flourish'd fresh and fair,   *thistles*
  And bonie bloom'd our roses;
But Whigs cam like a frost in June,
  An' wither'd a' our posies.

2

Our ancient crown's fa'n in the dust—
  Deil blin' them wi' the stoure o't,   *dust-whirl*
An' write their names in his black beuk,   *book*
  Wha gae the Whigs the power o't!

3

Our sad decay in church and state
  Surpasses my descriving.   *describing*
The Whigs cam o'er us for a curse,
  And we hae done wi' thriving.

4

Grim Vengeance lang has taen a nap,
  But we may see him waukin—   *awake*
Gude help the day when Royal heads
  Are hunted like a maukin!   *hare*

Drive; ewes
knolls

CA' THE YOWES TO THE KNOWES

TUNE: *Ca' the Yowes*

CHORUS

Ca' the yowes to the knowes,
Ca' them whare the heather grows,
brooklet;
rolls
Ca' them whare the burnie rowes,
My bonie dearie!

I

went
As I gaed down the water-side,
There I met my shepherd lad:
wrapped
He row'd me sweetly in his plaid,
called
And he ca'd me his dearie.

2

go
'Will ye gang down the water-side,
And see the waves sae sweetly glide
Beneath the hazels spreading wide,
The moon it shines fu' clearly?'

3

such
'I was bred up in nae sic school,
My shepherd lad, to play the fool,
sorrow
An' a' the day to sit in dool,
An' naebody to see me.'

4

'Ye sall get gowns and ribbons meet,
Calf-
Cauf-leather shoon upon your feet,
And in my arms ye'se lie and sleep,
An' ye sall be my dearie.'

5

'If ye'll but stand to what ye've said,
I'll go
I'se gang wi' you, my shepherd lad,
And ye may row me in your plaid,
And I sall be your dearie.'

6

wind
'While waters wimple to the sea,
shines;
sky; high
While day blinks in the lift sae hie,
Till clay-cauld death sall blin' my e'e,
Ye sall be my dearie.'

O, MERRY HAE I BEEN

TUNE: *Lord Breadalbane's March*

1

O, merry hae I been teethin a heckle,   heckling-
  An' merry hae I been shapin a spoon!   comb
O, merry hae I been cloutin a kettle,   patching
  An' kissin my Katie when a' was done!
O, a' the lang day I ca' at my hammer,   knock
  An' a' the lang day I whistle an' sing!
O, a' the lang night I cuddle my kimmer,   mistress
  An' a' the lang night as happy's a king!

2

Bitter in dool, I lickit my winnins   sorrow;
  O' marrying Bess, to gie her a slave.   supped;
Blest be the hour she cool'd in her linens,   earnings
  And blythe be the bird that sings on her grave!   winding-
Come to my arms, my Katie, my Katie,   sheet
  An' come to my arms, and kiss me again!
Drucken or sober, here's to thee, Katie,
  And blest be the day I did it again!

A MOTHER'S LAMENT

TUNE: *Finlayston House*

1

Fate gave the word—the arrow sped,
  And pierc'd my darling's heart,
And with him all the joys are fled
  Life can to me impart.
By cruel hands the sapling drops,
  In dust dishonor'd laid:
So fell the pride of all my hopes,
  My age's future shade.

2

The mother linnet in the brake
  Bewails her ravish'd young:
So I for my lost darling's sake
  Lament the live-day long.

Death, oft I've fear'd thy fatal blow!
Now fond I bare my breast!
O, do thou kindly lay me low,
With him I love at rest!

THE WHITE COCKADE

TUNE: *(As Title)*

CHORUS

rollicking

O, he's a ranting, roving lad!
He is a brisk an' a bonie lad!
Betide what may, I will be wed,
And follow the boy wi' the White Cockade!

1

My love was born in Aberdeen,
The boniest lad that e'er was seen;
But now he makes our hearts fu' sad—
He takes the field wi' his White Cockade.

2

distaff; flax
white-faced

I'll sell my rock, my reel, my tow,
My guid gray mare and hawkit cow,
To buy mysel a tartan plaid,
To follow the boy wi' the White Cockade.

hills

THE BRAES O' BALLOCHMYLE

TUNE: *(As Title)*

1

The Catrine woods were yellow seen,
   The flowers decay'd on Catrine lea;
lark
Nae lav'rock sang on hillock green,
eye
   But nature sicken'd on the e'e;
Thro' faded groves Maria sang,
   Hersel in beauty's bloom the while,
And aye the wild-wood echoes rang:—
   ' Farèweel the braes o' Ballochmyle!

2

' Low in your wintry beds, ye flowers,
　　Again ye'll flourish fresh and fair;
Ye birdies, dumb in with'ring bowers,
　　Again ye'll charm the vocal air;
　　But here, alas! for me nae mair
Shall birdie charm, or floweret smile:
　　Fareweel the bonie banks of Ayr!
Fareweel! fareweel sweet Ballochmyle! '

THE RANTIN DOG, THE DADDIE O'T   rollicking

TUNE: *Whare wad bonie Annie lie ?*

1

O, wha my babie-clouts will buy?   -clothes
O, wha will tent me when I cry?   attend to
Wha will kiss me where I lie?—
　　The rantin dog, the daddie o't!

2

O, wha will own he did the faut?   fault
O, what will buy the groanin maut?   midwife's ale
O, wha will tell me how to ca't?—   name it
　　The rantin dog, the daddie o't!

3

When I mount the creepie-chair,
Wha will sit beside me there?
Gie me Rob, I'll seek nae mair—
　　The rantin dog, the daddie o't!

4

Wha will crack to me my lane?   talk; alone
Wha will mak me fidgin fain?   desirous
Wha will kiss me o'er again?—
　　The rantin dog, the daddie o't!

THOU LINGERING STAR

TUNE: *Captain Cook's Death*

I

Thou ling'ring star with less'ning ray,
  That lov'st to greet the early morn,
Again thou usher'st in the day
  My Mary from my soul was torn.
O Mary, dear departed shade!
  Where is thy place of blissful rest?
See'st thou thy lover lowly laid?
  Hear'st thou the groans that rend his breast?

2

That sacred hour can I forget,
  Can I forget the hallow'd grove,
Where, by the winding Ayr, we met
  To live one day of parting love?
Eternity cannot efface
  Those records dear of transports past,
Thy image at our last embrace—
  Ah! little thought we 'twas our last!

3

Ayr, gurgling, kiss'd his pebbled shore,
  O'erhung with wild woods thickening green;
The fragrant birch and hawthorn hoar
  'Twin'd amorous round the raptur'd scene;
The flowers sprang wanton to be prest,
  The birds sang love on every spray,
Till too, too soon, the glowing west
  Proclaim'd the speed of wingèd day.

4

Still o'er these scenes my mem'ry wakes,
  And fondly broods with miser-care.
Time but th' impression stronger makes,
  As streams their channels deeper wear.
O Mary, dear departed shade!
  Where is thy place of blissful rest?
See'st thou thy lover lowly laid?
  Hear'st thou the groans that rend his breast?

EPPIE ADAIR

TUNE: (*As Title*)

CHORUS

An' O my Eppie,
My jewel, my Eppie!
Wha wadna be happy   wouldn't
Wi' Eppie Adair?

1

By love and by beauty
By law and by duty,
I swear to be true to
My Eppie Adair!

2

A' pleasure exile me,   All
Dishonour defile me,
If e'er I beguile thee,
My Eppie Adair!

THE BATTLE OF SHERRAMUIR

TUNE: *Cameronian Rant*

1

' O, cam ye here the fight to shun,
    Or herd the sheep wi' me, man?
Or were ye at the Sherra-moor,
    Or did the battle see, man? '
' I saw the battle, sair and teugh,   sore and tough
And reekin-red ran monie a sheugh;   furrow
My heart for fear gae sough for sough,   gave; sigh
To hear the thuds, and see the cluds   clouds
O' clans frae woods in tartan duds,   clothes
    Wha glaum'd at kingdoms three, man.   grasped

2

' The red-coat lads wi' black cockauds
    To meet them were na slaw, man: not slow
They rush'd and push'd and bluid outgush'd,
    And monie a bouk did fa', man!   trunk

The great Argyle led on his files,
I wat they glanc'd for twenty miles;
They hough'd the clans like nine-pin kyles,
They hack'd and hash'd, while braid-swords clash'd,
And thro' they dash'd, and hew'd and smash'd,
    Till fey men died awa, man.

wot; shone
hocked;
skittles

fated

3

' But had ye seen the philibegs
    And skyrin tartan trews, man,
When in the teeth they daur'd our Whigs
    And Covenant trueblues, man!
In lines extended lang and large,
When baig'nets o'erpower'd the targe,
And thousands hasten'd to the charge,
Wi' Highland wrath they frae the sheath
Drew blades o' death, till out o' breath
    They fled like frighted dows, man! '

kilts
flaring;
trousers
dared

bayonets

pigeons

4

' O, how Deil! Tam, can that be true?
    The chase gaed frae the north, man!
I saw mysel, they did pursue
    The horsemen back to Forth, man;
And at Dunblane, in my ain sight,
They took the brig wi' a' their might,
And straught to Stirling wing'd their flight;
But, cursed lot! the gates were shut,
And monie a huntit poor red-coat,
    For fear amaist did swarf, man! '

how the
Devil
went

bridge

almost;
swoon

5

' My sister Kate cam up the gate
    Wi' crowdie unto me, man:
She swoor she saw some rebels run
    To Perth and to Dundee, man!
Their left-hand general had nae skill;
The Angus lads had nae good will
That day their neebors' bluid to spill;
For fear by foes that they should lose
Their cogs o' brose, they scar'd at blows,
    And hameward fast did flee, man.

road
meal and
water

mugs of
porridge

6

'They've lost some gallant gentlemen,
  Amang the Highland clans, man!
I fear my Lord Panmure is slain,
  Or in his en'mies' hands, man.
Now wad ye sing this double flight,
Some fell for wrang, and some for right,
But monie bade the world guid-night:
Say, pell and mell, wi' muskets' knell
How Tories fell, and Whigs to Hell
  Flew off in frighted bands, man!'

JOCKIE WAS THE BLYTHEST LAD

TUNE: (*As Title*)

1

Young Jockie was the blythest lad,
  In a' our town or here awa: round about
Fu' blythe he whistled at the gaud,   goad
  Fu' lightly danc'd he in the ha'.

2

He roos'd my een sae bonie blue,   praised; eyes
  He roos'd my waist sae genty sma';   trimly
An' ay my heart cam to my mou',   mouth
  When ne'er a body heard or saw.

3

My Jockie toils upon the plain
  Thro' wind and weet, thro' frost and snaw;
And o'er the lea I leuk fu' fain,   longingly
  When Jockie's owsen hameward ca'.   oxen; drive

4

An' ay the night comes round again,
  When in his arms he taks me a',
An' ay he vows he'll be my ain
  As lang's he has a breath to draw.

A WAUKRIFE MINNIE

TUNE: (*As Title*)

wakeful
mother

1

going

honey

'Whare are you gaun, my bonie lass?
    Whare are you gaun, my hinnie?'
She answer'd me right saucilie:—
    'An errand for my minnie!'

2

brookside;
if; must

'O, whare live ye, my bonie lass?
    O, whare live ye, my hinnie?'
'By yon burnside, gin ye maun ken,
    In a wee house wi' my minnie!'

3

went

half

But I foor up the glen at e'en
    To see my bonie lassie,
And lang before the grey morn cam
    She was na hauf sae saucy.

4

woe befall;
polecat;
stop;
crowing
woman
bit ere the
dawn

O, weary fa' the waukrife cock,
    And the foumart lay his crawin!
He wauken'd the auld wife frae her sleep
    A wee blink or the dawin.

5

wot; rose

big; -cudgel
well-thrashed

An angry wife I wat she raise,
    And o'er the bed she brought her,
And wi' a meikle hazel-rung
    She made her a weel-pay'd dochter.

6

'O, fare-thee-weel, my bonie lass!
    O, fare-thee-weel, my hinnie!
Thou art a gay and a bonie lass,
    But thou has a waukrife minnie!'

THO' WOMEN'S MINDS

TUNE: *For a' that*

CHORUS

For a' that, an' a' that,
  And twice as meikle's a' that,   much as
The bonie lass that I loe best,
  She'll be my ain for a' that!

1

Tho' women's minds like winter winds
  May shift, and turn, an' a' that,
The noblest breast adores them maist—   most
  A consequence, I draw that.

2

Great love I bear to a' the fair,
  Their humble slave, an' a' that;
But lordly will, I hold it still
  A mortal sin to thraw that.   contradict

3

But there is ane aboon the lave,
  Has wit, and sense, and a' that;
A bonie lass, I like her best,
  And wha a crime dare ca' that?

4

In rapture sweet this hour we meet,
  Wi' mutual love an' a' that,
But for how lang the flie may stang,   fly; sting
  Let inclination law that!

5

Their tricks an' craft hae put me daft,
  They've taen me in an' a' that,
But clear your decks, and here's:—'The Sex?'
  I like the jads for a' that!   jades

malt

WILLIE BREW'D A PECK O' MAUT

TUNE: (*As Title*)

CHORUS

full (*i.e.*
drunk)
droplet
crow; dawn
-brew

We are na fou, we're nae that fou,
But just a drappie in our e'e!
The cock may craw, the day may daw,
And ay we'll taste the barley-bree!

I

O. Willie brewed a peck o' maut,
    And Rob and Allan cam to prie.
Three blyther hearts that lee-lang night
    Ye wad na found in Christendie.

live-long
would not
have;
Christendom

2

Here are we met three merry boys,
    Three merry boys I trow are we;
And monie a night we've merry been,
    And monie mae we hope to be!

more

3

It is the moon, I ken her horn,
    That's blinkin in the lift sae hie?
She shines sae bright to wyle us hame,
    But, by my sooth, she'll wait a wee!

shining;
sky; high
entice

4

Wha first shall rise to gang awa,
    A cuckold, coward loun is he!
Wha first beside his chair shall fa',
    He is the King amang us three!

go
rogue

KILLIECRANKIE

TUNE: *An' ye had been where I hae been*

CHORUS

If
would not
have; jolly

heights

An ye had been whare I hae been,
Ye wad na been sae cantie, O!
An ye had seen what I hae seen
On the braes o' Killiecrankie, O!

1

'Whare hae ye been sae braw, lad?   fine
 Whare hae ye been sae brankie, O? spruce
Whare hae ye been sae braw, lad?
 Cam ye by Killiecrankie, O?'

2

'I faught at land, I faught at sea,
 At hame I faught my auntie, O;
But I met the Devil and Dundee
 On the braes o' Killiecrankie, O.

3

'The bauld Pitcur fell in a furr,   furrow
 An' Clavers gat a clankie, O,   knock
Or I had fed an Athole gled   Else; hawk
 On the braes o' Killiecrankie, O!'

THE BLUE-EYED LASSIE

TUNE: (*As Title*)

1

I gaed a waefu' gate yestreen,   I went a
 A gate I fear I'll dearly rue: woeful way
I gat my death frae twa sweet een, last night
 Twa lovely een o' bonie blue!   eyes
'Twas not her golden ringlets bright,
 Her lips like roses wat wi' dew, wet
Her heaving bosom lily-white:
 It was her een sae bonie blue.

2

She talk'd, she smil'd, my heart she wyl'd, snared
 She charm'd my soul I wist na how;
And ay the stound, the deadly wound, ache
 Cam frae her een sae bonie blue.
But 'spare to speak, and spare to speed'—
 She'll aiblins listen to my vow: may be
Should she refuse, I'll lay my dead death
 To her twa een sae bonie blue.

THE BANKS OF NITH

TUNE: *Robie donna gorach*

1

The Thames flows proudly to the sea,
  Where royal cities stately stand;
But sweeter flows the Nith to me,
  Where Cummins ance had high command.
  When shall I see that honor'd land,
That winding stream I love so dear?
  Must wayward Fortune's adverse hand
For ever—ever keep me here?

2

How lovely, Nith, thy fruitful vales,
  Where bounding hawthorns gaily bloom,
And sweetly spread thy sloping dales,
  Where lambkins wanton thro' the broom!
  Tho' wandering now must be my doom
Far from thy bonie banks and braes,
  May there my latest hours consume
Amang my friends of early days!

TAM GLEN

TUNE: *Mall Roe in the Morning*

1

sister

My heart is a-breaking, dear tittie,
  Some counsel unto me come len',
To anger them a' is a pity,
  But what will I do wi' Tam Glen?

2

such; fine
poverty;
shift

I'm thinking, wi' sic a braw fellow
  In poortith I might mak a fen'.
What care I in riches to wallow,

must not

  If I mauna marry Tam Glen?

3

There's Lowrie the laird o' Dumeller:
  ' Guid day to you,' brute! he comes ben.   in
He brags and he blaws o' his siller,   money
  But when will he dance like Tam Glen?

4

My minnie does constantly deave me,   mother;
  And bids me beware o' young men.   deafen
They flatter, she says, to deceive me—
  But wha can think sae o' Tam Glen?

5

My daddie says, gin I'll forsake him,   if
  He'd gie me guid hunder marks ten.
But if it's ordain'd I maun take him,
  O, wha will I get but Tam Glen?

6

Yestreen at the valentines' dealing,   Last night
  My heart to my mou gied a sten,   mouth;
For thrice I drew ane without failing,   spring
  And thrice it was written ' Tam Glen'!

7

The last Halloween I was waukin
  My droukit sark-sleeve, as ye ken—   wetted shift
His likeness came up the house staukin,   stalking
  And the very grey breeks o' Tam Glen!   breeches

8

Come, counsel, dear tittie, don't tarry!
  I'll gie ye my bonie black hen,
Gif ye will advise me to marry   If
  The lad I lo'e dearly, Tam Glen.

CRAIGIEBURN WOOD

TUNE: (*As Title*)

CHORUS

Beyond thee, dearie, beyond thee, dearie,
And O, to be lying beyond thee!
O, sweetly, soundly, weel may he sleep
That's laid in the bed beyond thee!

I

Sweet closes the ev'ning on Craigieburn Wood
 And blythely awaukens the morrow;
But the pride o' the spring in the Craigieburn Wood
 Can yield me naught but sorrow.

2

I see the spreading leaves and flowers,
 I hear the wild birds singing;
But pleasure they hae nane for me,
 While care my heart is wringing.

3

must   I can na tell, I maun na tell,
 I daur na for your anger;
But secret love will break my heart,
 If I conceal it langer.

4

I see thee gracefu', straight, and tall,
 I see thee sweet and bonie;
But O, what will my torment be,
 If thou refuse thy Johnie!

5

To see thee in another's arms
 In love to lie and languish,
death   'Twad be my dead, that will be seen—
 My heart wad burst wi' anguish!

6

But, Jeanie, say thou wilt be mine,
 Say thou lo'es nane before me,
And a' my days o' life to come
 I'll gratefully adore thee.

FRAE THE FRIENDS AND LAND I LOVE

TUNE: *Carronside*

I

Frae the friends and land I love
  Driv'n by Fortune's felly spite,   relentless
Frae my best belov'd I rove,
  Never mair to taste delight!
Never mair maun hope to find   must
  Ease frae toil, relief frae care.
When remembrance wracks the mind,
  Pleasures but unveil despair.

2

Brightest climes shall mirk appear,   gloomy
  Desert ilka blooming shore,   every
Till the Fates, nae mair severe,
  Friendship, love, and peace restore;
Till Revenge wi' laurell'd head
  Bring our banish'd hame again,
And ilk loyal, bonie lad   each
  Cross the seas, and win his ain!

JOHN, COME KISS ME NOW

TUNE: *(As Title)*

CHORUS

O John, come kiss me now, now, now!
O John, my love, come kiss me now!
* O John, come kiss me by and by,*
For weel ye ken the way to woo!

I

O, some will court and compliment,
  And ither some will kiss and daut; others; pet
But I will mak o' my guidman,   husband
  My ain guidman—it is nae faut!   fault

2

O, some will court and compliment,
    And ither some will prie their mou',
And some will hause in ither's arms,
    And that's the way I like to do!

taste
cuddle

COCK UP YOUR BEAVER

TUNE: (*As Title*)

1

When first my brave Johnie lad came to this town,
He had a blue bonnet that wanted the crown,
But now he has gotten a hat and a feather—
Hey, brave Johnie lad, cock up your beaver!

2

spruce

Cock up your beaver, and cock it fu' sprush!
We'll over the border and gie them a brush:
There's somebody there we'll teach better be-
    haviour—
Hey, brave Johnie lad, cock up your beaver!

MY TOCHER'S THE JEWEL

dowry's

TUNE: *The Highway to Edinburgh*

1

much

O, meikle thinks my luve o' my beauty,
    And meikle thinks my luve o' my kin;
finely
But little thinks my luve I ken brawlie
    My tocher's the jewel has charms for him.
honey
It's a' for the apple he'll nourish the tree,
It's a' for the hiney he'll cherish the bee!
much;
money
    My laddie's sae meikle in luve wi' the siller,
He canna hae luve to spare for me!

2

hansel-

Your proffer o' luve's an airle-penny,
    My tocher's the bargain ye wad buy;
if
But an ye be crafty, I am cunnin,
    Sae ye wi' anither your fortune may try.

Ye're like to the timmer o' yon rotten wood,   timber
  Ye're like to the bark o' yon rotten tree:
Ye'll slip frae me like a knotless thread,
  An' ye'll crack ye're credit wi' mair nor me!

GUIDWIFE, COUNT THE LAWIN

Hostess;
reckoning

TUNE: *(As Title)*

CHORUS

Then, guidwife, count the lawin,
  The lawin, the lawin!
Then, guidwife, count the lawin,
  And bring a coggie mair!

1

Gane is the day, and mirk's the night,   Gone; dark's
But we'll ne'er stray for faut o' light,   want
For ale and brandy's stars and moon,
And blude-red wine's the risin sun.

2

There's wealth and ease for gentlemen,   simple; fight
And semple folk maun fecht and fen';   and defend
                                         (*i.e.* shift for
But here we're a' in ae accord   themselves)
For ilka man that's drunk's a lord.   one
                                       every

3

My coggie is a haly pool,   stoup; holy
That heals the wounds o' care and dool,   sorrow
And Pleasure is a wanton trout:
An ye drink it a', ye'll find him out!   If

THERE'LL NEVER BE PEACE TILL JAMIE COMES HAME

TUNE: *There are few good fellows when Jamie's awa?*

1

By yon castle wa' at the close of the day,
I heard a man sing, tho' his head it was grey,
And as he was singing, the tears doon came:—
' There'll never be peace till Jamie comes hame!

2

' The Church is in ruins, the State is in jars,
Delusions, oppressions, and murderous wars,
We dare na weel say't, but we ken wha's to blame—
There 'll never be peace till Jamie comes hame!

3

fine   ' My seven braw sons for Jamie drew sword,
weep; earth   But now I greet round their green beds in the yerd;
It brak the sweet heart o' my faithfu' auld dame—
There 'll never be peace till Jamie comes hame!

4

' Now life is a burden that bows me down,
since; lost;   Sin I tint my bairns, and he tint his crown;
children   But till my last moments my words are the same—
There 'll never be peace till Jamie comes hame! '

WHAT CAN A YOUNG LASSIE

TUNE: *What shall I do with an auld man?*

1

What can a young lassie,
What shall a young lassie,
What can a young lassie
   Do wi' an auld man?
Bad luck on the penny
mother   That tempted my minnie
To sell her puir Jenny
money   For siller an' lan'!

2

He 's always compleenin
Frae mornin to eenin;
coughs;   He hoasts and he hirples
hobbles   The weary day lang;
He 's doylt and he 's dozin;
stupid;   His blude it is frozen—
torpid   O, dreary's the night
               Wi' a crazy auld man!

3

He hums and he hankers,
He frets and he cankers,
I never can please him
   Do a' that I can.
He's peevish an' jealous
Of a' the young fellows—
O, dool on the day   woe
   I met wi' an auld man!

4

My auld auntie Katie
Upon me taks pity,
I'll do my endeavour
   To follow her plan:
I'll cross him an' wrack him
Until I heartbreak him,
And then his auld brass
   Will buy me a new pan.

THE BONIE LAD THAT'S FAR AWA

TUNE: (*As Title*)

1

O, how can I be blythe and glad,
   Or how can I gang brisk and braw,   go: fine
When the bonie lad that I lo'e best
   Is o'er the hills and far awa?

2

It's no the frosty winter wind,
   It's no the driving drift and snaw;
But ay the tear comes in my e'e
   To think on him that's far awa.

3

My father pat me frae his door,   put
   My friends they hae disown'd me a';
But I hae ane will tak my part—
   The bonie lad that's far awa.

4

A pair o' glooves he bought to me,
fillets; gave   And silken snoods he gae me twa,
And I will wear them for his sake,
   The bonie lad that's far awa.

5

O, weary Winter soon will pass,
clothe;
birchwoods   And Spring will cleed the birken shaw,
And my sweet babie will be born,
   And he'll be hame that's far awa!

I DO CONFESS THOU ART SAE FAIR

TUNE: *The Cuckoo*

1

I do confess thou art sae fair,
would have;
ears   I wad been o'er the lugs in luve,
not Had I na found the slightest prayer
   That lips could speak thy heart could muve.
I do confess thee sweet, but find
   Thou art so thriftless o' thy sweets,
Thy favours are the silly wind
every   That kisses ilka thing it meets.

2

See yonder rosebud rich in dew,
   Amang its native briers sae coy,
soon; loses How sune it tines its scent and hue,
pulled   When pu'd and worn a common toy!
Such Sic fate ere lang shall thee betide,
   Tho' thou may gaily bloom awhile,
And sune thou shalt be thrown aside,
   Like onie common weed, an' vile.

SENSIBILITY HOW CHARMING

TUNE: *Cornwallis's Lament*

1

Sensibility how charming,
   Thou, my friend, can'st truly tell!
But Distress with horrors arming
   Thou alas! hast known too well!

2

Fairest flower, behold the lily
    Blooming in the sunny ray:
Let the blast sweep o'er the valley,
    See it prostrate in the clay.

3

Hear the woodlark charm the forest,
    Telling o'er his little joys;
But alas! a prey the surest
    To each pirate of the skies!

4

Dearly bought the hidden treasure
    Finer feelings can bestow:
Chords that vibrate sweetest pleasure
    Thrill the deepest notes of woe.

YON WILD MOSSY MOUNTAINS

TUNE: *Phoebe*

1

Yon wild mossy mountains sae lofty and wide,
That nurse in their bosom the youth o' the Clyde,
Where the grouse lead their coveys thro' the heather
    to feed,
And the shepherd tents his flock as he pipes on his   tends
    reed.

2

Not Gowrie's rich valley nor Forth's sunny shores
To me hae the charms o' yon wild, mossy moors;
For there, by a lanely, sequesterèd stream,
Resides a sweet lassie, my thought and my dream.

3

Amang thae wild mountains shall still be my path,   those
Ilk stream foaming down its ain green, narrow   Each
    strath;
For there wi' my lassie the lang day I rove,
While o'er us unheeded flie the swift hours o' love.

4

She is not the fairest, altho' she is fair;
O' nice education but sma' is her share;
Her parentage humble as humble can be;
But I lo'e the dear lassie because she lo'es me.

5

must

To Beauty what man but maun yield him a prize,
In her armour of glances, and blushes, and sighs?
And when Wit and Refinement hae polish'd her
    darts,

eyes

They dazzle our een, as they flie to our hearts.

6

But kindness, sweet kindness, in the fond-sparkling e'e
Has lustre outshining the diamond to me,
And the heart beating love as I 'm clasp'd in her arms,
O, these are my lassie's all-conquering charms!

Hell

I HAE BEEN AT CROOKIEDEN

TUNE: *The Old Highland Laddie*

I

I hae been at Crookieden—
    My bonie laddie, Highland laddie!

William of Cumberland

Viewing Willie and his men—
    My bonie laddie, Highland laddie!
There our foes that burnt and slew—
    My bonie laddie, Highland laddie!
There at last they gat their due—
    My bonie laddie, Highland laddie!

2

corner

Satan sits in his black neuk—
    My bonie laddie, Highland laddie!
Breaking sticks to roast the Duke—
    My bonie laddie, Highland laddie!
The bloody monster gae a yell—
    My bonie laddie, Highland laddie!
And loud the laugh gaed round a' Hell—
    My bonie laddie, Highland laddie!

IT IS NA, JEAN, THY BONIE FACE

TUNE: *The Maid's Complaint*

1

It is na, Jean, thy bonie face   *not*
  Nor shape that I admire,
Altho' thy beauty and thy grace
  Might weel awauk desire.
Something in ilka part o' thee   *every*
  To praise, to love, I find;
But, dear as is thy form to me,
  Still dearer is thy mind.

2

Nae mair ungen'rous wish I hae,
  Nor stronger in my breast,
Than, if I canna mak thee sae,   *so*
  At least to see thee blest:
Content am I, if Heaven shall give
  But happiness to thee,
And, as wi' thee I wish to live,
  For thee I'd bear to dee.

EPPIE MACNAB

TUNE: (*As Title*)

1

O, saw ye my dearie, my Eppie Macnab?
O, saw ye my dearie, my Eppie Macnab?
 ' She's down in the yard, she's kissin the laird,
She winna come hame to her ain Jock Rab!'   *will not*

2

O, come thy ways to me, my Eppie Macnab!
O, come thy ways to me, my Eppie Macnab!
  Whate'er thou has done, be it late, be it soon,
Thou's welcome again to thy ain Jock Rab.   *art*

3

What says she, my dearie, my Eppie Macnab?
What says she, my dearie, my Eppie Macnab?

know

   ' She lets thee to wit that she has thee forgot,
And for ever disowns thee, her ain Jock Rab.'

4

O, had I ne'er seen thee, my Eppie Macnab!
O, had I ne'er seen thee, my Eppie Macnab!
   As light as the air and as fause as thou's fair,
Thou's broken the heart o' thy ain Jock Rab!

WHA IS THAT AT MY BOWER DOOR?

TUNE: *Lass an' I come near thee*

1

   ' Wha is that at my bower door?'
     ' O, wha is it but Findlay!'

go your way,
ye shall not
must

   ' Then gae your gate, ye'se nae be here.'
     ' Indeed maun I!' quo' Findlay.

do

   ' What mak ye, sae like a thief?'
     ' O, come and see!' quo' Findlay.
   ' Before the morn ye'll work mischief?'
     ' Indeed will I!' quo' Findlay.

2

If

   ' Gif I rise and let you in '—
     ' Let me in!' quo' Findlay—

awake

   ' Ye'll keep me wauken wi' your din?'
     ' Indeed will I!' quo' Findlay.
   ' In my bower if ye should stay '—
     ' Let me stay!' quo' Findlay—
   ' I fear ye'll bide till break o' day?'
     ' Indeed will I!' quo' Findlay.

3

   ' Here this night if ye remain '—
     ' I'll remain!' quo' Findlay—
   ' I dread ye'll learn the gate again?'
     ' Indeed will I!' quo' Findlay.

'What may pass within this bower?
  ('Let it pass!' quo' Findlay!)
'Ye maun conceal till your last hour'—
  'Indeed will I!' quo' Findlay.

BONIE WEE THING

TUNE: (*As Title*)

CHORUS

Bonie wee thing, cannie wee thing,   gentle
  Lovely wee thing, wert thou mine,
I wad wear thee in my bosom
  Lest my jewel it should tine.   lose

I

Wishfully I look and languish
  In that bonie face o' thine,
And my heart it stounds wi' anguish,   aches
  Lest my wee thing be na mine.

2

Wit and Grace and Love and Beauty
  In ae constellation shine!   one
To adore thee is my duty,
  Goddess o' this soul o' mine!

AE FOND KISS

TUNE: *Rory Dall's Port*

I

Ae fond kiss, and then we sever!
Ae farewell, and then forever!
Deep in heart-wrung tears I'll pledge thee,
Warring sighs and groans I'll wage thee.

2

Who shall say that Fortune grieves him,
While the star of hope she leaves him?
Me, nae cheerfu' twinkle lights me,
Dark despair around benights me.

3

I'll ne'er blame my partial fancy:
Naething could resist my Nancy!
But to see her was to love her,
Love but her, and love for ever.

4

Had we never lov'd sae kindly,
Had we never lov'd sae blindly,
Never met—or never parted—
We had ne'er been broken-hearted.

5

Fare-thee-weel, thou first and fairest!
Fare-thee-weel, thou best and dearest!
every   Thine be ilka joy and treasure,
Peace, Enjoyment, Love and Pleasure!

6

Ae fond kiss, and then we sever!
Ae farewell, alas, for ever!
Deep in heart-wrung tears I'll pledge thee,
Warring sighs and groans I'll wage thee.

LOVELY DAVIES

TUNE: *Miss Muir*

1

O, how shall I, unskilfu', try
    The Poet's occupation?
The tunefu' Powers, in happy hours
    That whisper inspiration,
must   Even they maun dare an effort mair
    Than aught they ever gave us,
Ere they rehearse in equal verse
    The charms o' lovely Davies.

2

Each eye, it cheers, when she appears,
    Like Phœbus in the morning,
When past the shower, and every flower
    The garden is adorning!

As the wretch looks o'er Siberia's shore,
 When winter-bound the wave is,
Sae droops our heart, when we maun part
 Frae charming, lovely Davies.

3

Her smile's a gift frae 'boon the lift,   above;
 That maks us mair than princes.   sky
A sceptred hand, a king's command,
 Is in her darting glances.
The man in arms 'gainst female charms,
 Even he her willing slave is:
He hugs his chain, and owns the reign
 Of conquering lovely Davies.

4

My Muse to dream of such a theme
 Her feeble powers surrenders;
The eagle's gaze alone surveys
 The sun's meridian splendours.
I wad in vain essay the strain—
 The deed too daring brave is!
I'll drap the lyre, and, mute, admire   drop
 The charms o' lovely Davies.

THE WEARY PUND O' TOW   pound; yarn

TUNE: (*As Title*)

CHORUS

The weary pund, the weary pund,
 The weary pund o' tow!
I think my wife will end her life
 Before she spin her tow.

1

I bought my wife a stane o' lint   stone: flax
 As guid as e'er did grow,
And a' that she has made o' that
 Is ae puir pund o' tow.   one poor

2

           hole in the
           wall
There sat a bottle in a bole   At the back
 Beyont the ingle low;   of the fire-
           place

other suck
wet the dusty

And ay she took the tither souk
   To drouk the stourie tow.

3

Quoth I:—' For shame, ye dirty dame,
   Gae spin your tap o' tow! '
She took the rock, and wi' a knock
   She brake it o'er my pow.

bunch
distaff
pate

4

At last her feet—I sang to see't!—
   Gaed foremost o'er the knowe,
And or I wad anither jad,
   I'll wallop in a tow.

went; hill
wed
kick heels;
rope

have

I HAE A WIFE O' MY AIN

TUNE: (*As Title*)

1

I hae a wife o' my ain,
   I'll partake wi' naebody:
I'll take cuckold frae nane,
   I'll gie cuckold to naebody.

2

I hae a penny to spend,
   There—thanks to naebody!
I hae naething to lend,
   I'll borrow frae naebody.

3

I am naebody's lord,
   I'll be slave to naebody.
I hae a guid braid sword,
   I'll tak dunts frae naebody.

blows

4

I'll be merry and free,
   I'll be sad for naebody,
Naebody cares for me,
   I care for naebody.

WHEN SHE CAM BEN, SHE BOBBED

into the
parlour;
curtseyed

TUNE: *When she cam ben she bobbit*

1

O, when she cam ben, she bobbéd fu' law!   low
O, when she cam ben, she bobbéd fu' law!
And when she cam' ben, she kiss'd Cockpen,
And syne she deny'd she did it at a'!   then; at all

2

And was na Cockpen right saucy witha'?
And was na Cockpen right saucy witha',
In leaving the dochter o' a lord,
And kissin a collier lassie an' a'?

3

' O, never look down, my lassie, at a'!
O, never look down, my lassie, at a'!
Thy lips are as sweet, and thy figure complete,
As the finest dame in castle or ha'.

4

' Tho' thou hast nae silk, and holland sae sma',   fine
Tho' thou hast nae silk, and holland sae sma',
Thy coat and thy sark are thy ain handywark,   shift
And Lady Jean was never sae braw. '

O, FOR ANE-AND-TWENTY, TAM   One-

TUNE: *The Moudiewart*

CHORUS

An' O, for ane-and-twenty, Tam!
And hey, sweet ane-and-twenty, Tam!
I'll learn my kin a rattlin sang
An I saw ane-and-twenty, Tam.   If

1

They snool me sair, and haud me down,   snub; sore;
    And gar me look like bluntie, Tam;   keep
But three short years will soon wheel roun'—   make; a
    And then comes ane-and-twenty, Tam!   stupid

2

handful of
money

A gleib o' lan', a claut o' gear
  Was left me by my auntie, Tam.

Of; ask

At kith or kin I needna spier,
  An I saw ane-and-twenty, Tam.

3

dolt

They'll hae me wed a wealthy coof,
  Tho' I mysel hae plenty, Tam;

palm

But hear'st thou, laddie—there's my loof:
  I'm thine at ane-and-twenty, Tam!

O, KENMURE'S ON AND AWA, WILLIE

TUNE: (*As Title*)

I

O, Kenmure's on and awa, Willie,
  O, Kenmure's on and awa!
An' Kenmure's lord's the bravest lord
  That ever Galloway saw!

2

Success to Kenmure's band, Willie,
  Success to Kenmure's band!
There's no a heart that fears a Whig
  That rides by Kenmure's hand.

3

Here's Kenmure's health in wine, Willie,
  Here's Kenmure's health in wine!
There ne'er was a coward o' Kenmure's blude,
  Nor yet o' Gordon's line.

4

O, Kenmure's lads are men, Willie,
  O, Kenmure's lads are men!
Their hearts and swords are metal true,

foes

  And that their faes shall ken.

5

They'll live or die wi' fame, Willie,
  They'll live or die wi' fame!
But soon wi' sounding Victorie
  May Kenmure's lord come hame!

6

Here's him that's far awa, Willie,
  Here's him that's far awa!
And here's the flower that I lo'e best—
  The rose that's like the snaw!

O, LEEZE ME ON MY SPINNIN-WHEEL

TUNE: *Sweet's the lass that loves me*

1

O, leeze me on my spinnin-wheel!
And leeze me on my rock and reel,   *distaff*
Frae tap to tae that cleeds me bien,   *top to toe; clothes;*
And haps me fiel and warm at e'en!   *comfortably wraps; well*
I'll set me down, and sing and spin,   *place*
While laigh descends the summer sun,   *low*
Blest wi' content, and milk and meal—
O, leeze me on my spinnin-wheel!

2

On ilka hand the burnies trot,   *either; brooklets*
And meet below my theekit cot.   *thatched*
The scented birk and hawthorn white   *birch*
Across the pool their arms unite,
Alike to screen the birdie's nest
And little fishes' caller rest.   *cool*
The sun blinks kindly in the biel,   *glances; shelter*
Where blythe I turn my spinnin-wheel.

3

On lofty aiks the cushats wail,   *oaks*
And Echo cons the doolfu' tale.   *doleful*
The lintwhites in the hazel braes,   *linnets; slopes*
Delighted, rival ither's lays.   *each other's*
The craik amang the claver hay,   *corncrake; clover*
The paitrick whirrin o'er the ley,   *partridge; meadow*
The swallow jinkin round my shiel,   *darting; cottage*
Amuse me at my spinnin-wheel.

4

Wi' sma to sell and less to buy,   *little*
Aboon distress, below envý,   *Above*

O, wha wad leave this humble state
For a' the pride of a' the great?
Amid their flaring, idle toys,
noisy   Amid their cumbrous, dinsome joys,
Can they the peace and pleasure feel
Of Bessy at her spinnin-wheel?

MY COLLIER LADDIE

TUNE: (*As Title*)

1

' O, whare live ye, my bonie lass,
call   And tell me how they ca' ye?'
' My name,' she says, ' is Mistress Jean,
And I follow the collier laddie.'

2

' O, see you not yon hills and dales
finely   The sun shines on sae brawlie?
They a' are mine, and they shall be thine,
if   Gin ye'll leave your collier laddie!

3

go   ' An' ye shall gang in gay attire,
adorned   Weel buskit up sae gaudy,
And ane to wait on every hand,
Gin ye'll leave your collier laddie!'

4

' Tho' ye had a' the sun shines on,
And the earth conceals sae lowly,
I wad turn my back on you and it a',
And embrace my collier laddie.

5

' I can win my five pennies in a day,
An' spend it at night fu' brawlie,
corner   And make my bed in the collier's neuk
And lie down wi' my collier laddie.

6

' Loove for loove is the bargain for me,
   Tho' the wee cot-house should haud me,   hold
And the warld before me to win my bread—
   And fair fa' my collier laddie! '   good befall

NITHSDALE'S WELCOME HAME

TUNE: (*As Title*)

I

The noble Maxwells and their powers
   Are coming o'er the border;
And they'll gae big Terreagles' towers,   go build
   And set them a' in order;
And they declare Terreagles fair,
   For their abode they choose it:
There's no a heart in a' the land
   But's lighter at the news o't!

2

Tho' stars in skies may disappear,
   And angry tempests gather,
The happy hour may soon be near
   That brings us pleasant weather;
The weary night o' care and grief
   May hae a joyfu' morrow;
So dawning day has brought relief—
   Fareweel our night o' sorrow!

IN SIMMER, WHEN THE HAY WAS MAWN

TUNE: *The Country Lass*

I

In simmer, when the hay was mawn
   And corn wav'd green in ilka field,   every
While claver blooms white o'er the ley,   clover;
   And roses blaw in ilka bield,   pasture / sheltered
   Blythe Bessie in the milking shiel   spot / shed
Says:—' I'll be wed, come o't what will! '
   Out spake a dame in wrinkled eild:—   eld
' O' guid advisement comes nae ill.

2

many a one

> 'It's ye hae wooers monie ane,
>   And lassie, ye're but young, ye ken!

sensibly
choose
well-stocked
kitchen;
parlour
Full; cow-
shed

> Then wait a wee, and cannie wale
>   A routhie butt, a routhie ben.
>   There Johnie o' the Buskie-Glen,
>   Fu' is his barn, fu' is his byre.
>   Tak this frae me, my bonie hen:

fans

>   It's plenty beets the luver's fire!'

3

> 'For Johnie o' the Buskie-Glen

fly

>   I dinna care a single flie:

crops; kine

> He lo'es sae weel his craps and kye,
>   He has nae love to spare for me.

glance; eye

>   But blythe's the blink o' Robie's e'e,

wot
One; give

> And weel I wat he lo'es me dear:
>   Ae blink o' him I wad na gie

wealth

> For Buskie-Glen and a' his gear.'

4

fight

> 'O thoughtless lassie, life's a faught!

quietest way

>   The canniest gate, the strife is sair.

full-handed;
fighting
terrible

> But ay fu'-han't is fechtin best:
>   A hungry care's an unco care.
>   But some will spend, and some will spare,

must

> An' wilfu' folk maun hae their will.

Then

>   Syne as ye brew, my maiden fair,

ale

> Keep mind that ye maun drink the yill!'

5

ridges

> 'O, gear will buy me rigs o' land,
>   And gear will buy me sheep and kye!

lawful

> But the tender heart o' leesome loove

gold and
silver

>   The gowd and siller canna buy!
>   We may be poor, Robie and I;
>   Light is the burden luve lays on;
>   Content and loove brings peace and joy:
> What mair hae Queens upon a throne?'

FAIR ELIZA

TUNE: *A Gaelic air*

1

Turn again, thou fair Eliza!
  Ae kind blink before we part!   One: glance
Rew on thy despairing lover—   Take pity
  Canst thou break his faithfu' heart?
Turn again, thou fair Eliza!
  If to love thy heart denies,
For pity hide the cruel sentence
  Under friendship's kind disguise!

2

Thee, dear maid, hae I offended?
  The offence is loving thee.
Canst thou wreck his peace for ever,
  Wha for thine wad gladly die?
While the life beats in my bosom,
  Thou shalt mix in ilka throe.   every
Turn again, thou lovely maiden,
  Ae sweet smile on me bestow!   One

3

Not the bee upon the blossom
  In the pride o' sinny noon,   sunny
Not the little sporting fairy
  All beneath the simmer moon,
Not the Poet in the moment
  Fancy lightens in his e'e,
Kens the pleasure, feels the rapture,
  That thy presence gies to me.

YE JACOBITES BY NAME

TUNE: (*As Title*)

1

Ye Jacobites by name,
  Give an ear, give an ear!
Ye Jacobites by name,
  Give an ear!

faults

must

Ye Jacobites by name,
Your fautes I will proclaim,
Your doctrines I maun blame—
    You shall hear!

2

What is Right, and what is Wrang.
    By the law, by the law?
What is Right, and what is Wrang
    By the law?
What is Right, and what is Wrang?
A short sword and a lang,
A weak arm and a strang
    For to draw!

3

What makes heroic strife
    Famed afar, famed afar?
What makes heroic strife
    Famed afar?
What makes heroic strife?
To whet th'assassin's knife,
Or hunt a Parent's life
    Wi' bluidy war!

4

Then let your schemes alone,
    In the State, in the State!
Then let your schemes alone.
    In the State!
Then let your schemes alone,
Adore the rising sun,
And leave a man undone
    To his fate!

THE POSIE

TUNE: (As Title)

1

O, luve will venture in where it daur na weel be seen!
O, luve will venture in, where wisdom ance hath been!
But I will doun yon river rove amang the wood sae
    green,

pluck

    And a' to pu' a posie to my ain dear May!

2

The primrose I will pu', the firstling o' the year,
And I will pu' the pink, the emblem o' my dear,
For she's the pink o' womankind, and blooms without
    a peer—
    And a' to be a posie to my ain dear May!

3

I'll pu' the budding rose when Phœbus peeps in view,
For it's like a baumy kiss o' her sweet, bonie mou.   balmy
The hyacinth's for constancy wi' its unchanging blue—
    And a' to be a posie to my ain dear May!

4

The lily it is pure, and the lily it is fair,
And in her lovely bosom I'll place the lily there.
The daisy's for simplicity and unaffected air—
    And a' to be a posie to my ain dear May!

5

The hawthorn I will pu', wi' its locks o' siller gray,
Where, like an agèd man, it stands at break o' day;
But the songster's nest within the bush I winna tak   will not
    away—
    And a' to be a posie to my ain dear May!

6

The woodbine I will pu' when the e'ening star is
    near,
And the diamond draps o' dew shall be her een sae   eyes
    clear!
The violet's for modesty, which weel she fa's to   claims
    wear—
    And a' to be a posie to my ain dear May!

7

I'll tie the posie round wi' the silken band o' luve.
And I'll place it in her breast, and I'll swear by a'
    above,
That to my latest draught o' life the band shall ne'er
    remove,
    And this will be a posie to my ain dear May!

THE BANKS O' DOON

TUNE: *Caledonian Hunt's Delight*

I

slopes

Ye banks and braes o' bonie Doon,
  How can ye bloom sae fresh and fair?
How can ye chant, ye little birds,
  And I sae weary fu' o' care!
Thou'll break my heart, thou warbling bird,
  That wantons thro' the flowering thorn!
Thou minds me o' departed joys,
  Departed never to return.

2

Aft hae I rov'd by bonie Doon
  To see the rose and woodbine twine,
every

And ilka bird sang o' its luve,
  And fondly sae did I o' mine.
plucked

Wi' lightsome heart I pu'd a rose,
  Fu' sweet upon its thorny tree!
stole

And my fause luver staw my rose—
  But ah! he left the thorn wi' me.

WILLIE WASTLE

TUNE: *Sic a Wife as Willie had*

I

Willie Wastle dwalt on Tweed,
  The spot they ca'd it Linkumdoddie.
weaver

Willie was a wabster guid
have stolen
  Could stown a clue wi' onie bodie.
stubborn;
dun

He had a wife was dour and din,
Tinker
  O, Tinkler Maidgie was her mither!
Such

Sic a wife as Willie had,
  I wad na gie a button for her.

2

She has an e'e (she has but ane),
  The cat has twa the very colour,
besides

Five rusty teeth, forbye a stump,
deaven
  A clapper-tongue wad deave a miller;

A whiskin beard about her mou,
  Her nose and chin they threaten ither;   *each other*
Sic a wife as Willie had,
  I wad na gie a button for her.

3

She's bow-hough'd, she's hem-shin'd,   *bandy*
  Ae limpin leg a hand-breed shorter;   *one;*
                                       -breadth
She's twisted right, she's twisted left,
  To balance fair in ilka quarter;   *either*
She has a hump upon her breast,
  The twin o' that upon her shouther: *shoulder*
Sic a wife as Willie had,
  I wad na gie a button for her.

4

Auld baudrans by the ingle sits,   *Old pussie*
  An' wi' her loof her face a-washin;   *palm*
But Willie's wife is nae sae trig,   *trim*
  She dights her grunzie wi' a hushion; *wipes; snout*
Her walie nieves like midden-creels,   *ample fists*
  Her face wad fyle the Logan Water: *foul*
Sic a wife as Willie had,
  I wad na gie a button for her.

LADY MARY ANN

TUNE: (*As Title*)

I

O, Lady Mary Ann looks o'er the Castle wa',
She saw three bonie boys playing at the ba',
The youngest he was the flower amang them a'—
  My bonie laddie's young, but he's growin yet!

2

' O father, O father, an ye think it fit,
We'll send him a year to the college yet;
We'll sew a green ribbon round about his hat,
  And that will let them ken he's to marry yet! '

3

Lady Mary Ann was a flower in the dew,
Sweet was its smell and bonie was its hue,
And the longer it blossom'd the sweeter it grew,
  For the lily in the bud will be bonier yet.

4

oak
straight

Young Charlie Cochran was the sprout of an aik;
Bonie and bloomin and straucht was its make;
The sun took delight to shine for its sake,
　　And it will be the brag o' the forest yet.

5

The simmer is gane when the leaves they were green,
And the days are awa that we hae seen;
But far better days I trust will come again,
　　For my bonie laddie's young, but he's growin yet.

A PARCEL OF ROGUES IN A NATION

TUNE: (*As Title*)

1

Fareweel to a' our Scottish fame,
　　Fareweel our ancient glory!
Fareweel ev'n to the Scottish name,
　　Sae famed in martial story!
Now Sark rins over Solway sands,
　　An' Tweed rins to the ocean,
To mark where England's province stands—
　　Such a parcel of rogues in a nation!

2

What force or guile could not subdue
　　Thro' many warlike ages
Is wrought now by a coward few
　　For hireling traitor's wages.
The English steel we could disdain,
　　Secure in valour's station;
But English gold has been our bane—
　　Such a parcel of rogues in a nation!

3

O, would, or I had seen the day
　　That Treason thus could sell us,
My auld grey head had lien in clay
　　Wi' Bruce and loyal Wallace!
Even when
without

But pith and power, till my last hour
　　I'll mak this declaration:—
'We're bought and sold for English gold'—
　　Such a parcel of rogues in a nation!

KELLYBURN BRAES

TUNE: (*As Title*)

1

There livèd a carl in Kellyburn Braes   old man
   (Hey and the rue grows bonie wi' thyme),
And he had a wife was the plague o' his days
   (And the thyme it is wither'd, and rue is in prime).

2

Ae day as the carl gaed up the lang glen   One
   (Hey and the rue grows bonie wi' thyme),
He met wi' the Devil, says:—' How do you fen?'   are you getting on
   (And the thyme it is wither'd, and rue is in prime).

3

' I've got a bad wife, sir, that's a' my complaint
   (Hey and the rue grows bonie wi' thyme),
For, saving your presence, to her ye're a saint,
   (And the thyme it is wither'd, and rue is in prime).

4

' It's neither your stot nor your staig I shall crave   steer; young horse
   (Hey and the rue grows bonie wi' thyme),
' But gie me your wife, man, for her I must have'
   (And the thyme it is wither'd, and rue is in prime).

5

' O welcome most kindly!' the blythe carl said
   (Hey and the rue grows bonie wi' thyme),
' But if ye can match her ye're waur than ye're ca'd '   worse
   (And the thyme it is wither'd, and rue is in prime).

6

The Devil has got the auld wife on his back
   (Hey and the rue grows bonie wi' thyme),
And like a poor pedlar he's carried his pack
   (And the thyme it is wither'd, and rue is in prime).

7

He's carried her hame to his ain hallan-door   porch-
   (Hey and the rue grows bonie wi' thyme),
Syne bade her gae in for a bitch and a whore   Then; go
   (And the thyme it is wither'd, and rue is in prime).

8

Then straight he makes fifty, the pick o' his band
    (Hey and the rue grows bonie wi' thyme),
Turn out on her guard in the clap o' a hand
    (And the thyme it is wither'd, and rue is in prime).

9

beldam; mad

The carlin gaed thro' them like onie wud bear
    (Hey and the rue grows bonie wi' thyme):
Whae'er she gat hands on cam near her nae mair
    (And the thyme it is wither'd, and rue is in prime).

10

smoky small

A reekit wee deevil looks over the wa
    (Hey and the rue grows bonie wi' thyme):—
' O help, maister, help, or she'll ruin us a'! '
    (And the thyme it is wither'd, and rue is in prime).

11

The Devil he swore by the edge o' his knife
    (Hey and the rue grows bonie wi' thyme),
He pitied the man that was tied to a wife
    (And the thyme it is wither'd, and rue is in prime).

12

The Devil he swore by the kirk and the bell
    (Hey and the rue grows bonie wi' thyme),
He was not in wedlock, thank Heav'n, but in Hell
    (And the thyme it is wither'd, and rue is in prime).

13

Then Satan has travell'd again wi' his pack
    (Hey and the rue grows bonie wi' thyme),
And to her auld husband he's carried her back
    (And the thyme it is wither'd, and rue is in prime).

14

most

' I hae been a Devil the feck o' my life
    (Hey and the rue grows bonie wi' thyme),
But ne'er was in Hell till I met wi' a wife.'
    (And the thyme it is wither'd, and rue is in prime).

THE SLAVE'S LAMENT

TUNE: (*As Title*)

I

It was in sweet Senegal
That my foes did me enthral
  For the lands of Virginia, -ginia, O!
Torn from that lovely shore,
And must never see it more,
  And alas! I am weary, weary, O!

2

All on that charming coast
Is no bitter snow and frost,
  Like the lands of Virginia, -ginia O!
There streams for ever flow,
And the flowers for ever blow,
  And alas! I am weary, weary, O!

3

The burden I must bear,
While the cruel scourge I fear,
  In the lands of Virginia, -ginia, O!
And I think on friends most dear
With the bitter, bitter tear,
  And alas! I am weary, weary, O!

THE SONG OF DEATH

TUNE: *Oran an aoig*

I

Farewell, thou fair day, thou green earth, and ye skies,
  Now gay with the broad setting sun!
Farewell, loves and friendships, ye dear tender ties—
  Our race of existence is run!
Thou grim King of Terrors! thou Life's gloomy foe,
  Go, frighten the coward and slave!
Go, teach them to tremble, fell tyrant, but know,
  No terrors has thou to the brave!

2

Thou strik'st the dull peasant—he sinks in the dark,
    Nor saves e'en the wreck of a name!
Thou strik'st the young hero—a glorious mark,
    He falls in the blaze of his fame!
In the field of proud honour, our swords in our hands,
    Our king and our country to save,
While victory shines on Life's last ebbing sands,
    O, who would not die with the brave?

SWEET AFTON

TUNE: *Afton Water*

1

slopes

Flow gently, sweet Afton, among thy green braes!
Flow gently, I'll sing thee a song in thy praise!
My Mary's asleep by thy murmuring stream—
Flow gently, sweet Afton, disturb not her dream!

2

Thou stock dove whose echo resounds thro' the glen,
Ye wild whistling blackbirds in yon thorny den.
Thou green-crested lapwing, thy screaming forbear—
I charge you, disturb not my slumbering fair!

3

How lofty, sweet Afton, thy neighbouring hills,
Far mark'd with the courses of clear, winding rills!
There daily I wander, as noon rises high,
My flocks and my Mary's sweet cot in my eye.

4

How pleasant thy banks and green vallies below,
Where wild in the woodlands the primroses blow;
There oft, as mild ev'ning weeps over the lea.

birch

The sweet-scented birk shades my Mary and me.

5

Thy crystal stream, Afton, how lovely it glides,
And winds by the cot where my Mary resides!
How wanton thy waters her snowy feet lave,
As, gathering sweet flowerets, she stems thy clear
    wave!

6

Flow gently, sweet Afton, among thy green braes!
Flow gently, sweet river, the theme of my lays!
My Mary's asleep by thy murmuring stream—
Flow gently, sweet Afton, disturb not her dream!

BONIE BELL

TUNE: (*As Title*)

1

The smiling Spring comes in rejoicing,
  And surly Winter grimly flies.
Now crystal clear are the falling waters,
  And bonie blue are the sunny skies.
Fresh o'er the mountains breaks forth the morning,
  The ev'ning gilds the ocean's swell:
All creatures joy in the sun's returning,
  And I rejoice in my bonie Bell.

2

The flowery Spring leads sunny Summer,
  The yellow Autumn presses near;
Then in his turn comes gloomy Winter,
  Till smiling Spring again appear.
Thus seasons dancing, life advancing,
  Old Time and Nature their changes tell;
But never ranging, still unchanging,
  I adore my bonie Bell.

THE GALLANT WEAVER

TUNE: (*As Title*)

1

Where Cart rins rowin to the sea   rolling
By monie a flower and spreading tree,
There lives a lad. the lad for me—
  He is a gallant weaver!
O, I had wooers aught or nine,
They gied me rings and ribbons fine,   gave
And I was fear'd my heart wad tine,   afraid;
  And I gied it to the weaver.   be lost

2

deed of
settlement

My daddie sign'd my tocher-band
To gie the lad that has the land;
But to my heart I'll add my hand,
    And give it to the weaver.
While birds rejoice in leafy bowers,
While bees delight in opening flowers
While corn grows green in summer showers,
    I love my gallant weaver.

work away

HEY, CA' THRO'

TUNE: (*As Title*)

CHORUS

Hey, ca' thro', ca' thro',
much to do
For we hae mickle ado!
Hey, ca' thro', ca' thro',
For we hae mickle ado!

1

old men
Up wi' the carls of Dysart
    And the lads o' Buckhaven,
gossips
And the kimmers o' Largo
    And the lasses o' Leven!

2

We hae tales to tell,
    And we hae sangs to sing;
We hae pennies to spend,
    And we hae pints to bring.

3

We 'll live a' our days,
    And them that comes behin',
Let them do the like
weal h
    And spend the gear they win!

O, CAN YE LABOUR LEA

TUNE: (*As Title*)

CHORUS

O, can ye labour lea, young man,
O, can ye labour lea?
Gae back the gate ye came again—   Go; way
Ye'se never scorn me!   Ye shall;
despise

I

I fee'd a man at Martinmas   hired
Wi' airle-pennies three;   hansel-
But a' the faut I had to him
He couldna labour lea.

2

O, clappin's guid in Febarwar,   stroking
An' kissin's sweet in May;
But what signifies a young man's love,
An't dinna last for ay?   If it do not

3

O, kissin is the key o' love
An' clappin is the lock;
An' makin of's the best thing
That e'er a young thing got!

THE DEUK'S DANG O'ER MY DADDIE   duck has
knocked

TUNE: (*As Title*)

I

The bairns gat out wi' an unco shout:—   children;
' The deuk's dang o'er my daddie, O! '   surprising
' The fien-ma-care,' quo' the feirrie auld wife,   fiend-may-;
' He was but a paidlin body, O!   lusty
creature
He paidles out, and he paidles in,
An' he paidles late and early, O!
This seven lang years I hae lien by his side,
An' he is but a fusionless carlie, O! '   sapless old
mannikin

2

hold
> ' O, haud your tongue, my feirrie auld wife,
>   O, haud your tongue, now Nansie, O!

so have
testy
> I've seen the day, and sae hae ye,
>   Ye wad na been sae donsie, O.
> I've seen the day ye butter'd my brose,
>   And cuddl'd me late and early, O;

cannot-do is
feel it sorely
> But downa-do's come o'er me now,
>   And och, I find it sairly, O! '

false

SHE'S FAIR AND FAUSE

TUNE: *The Lads of Leith*

I

> She's fair and fause that causes my smart;

much; long
>   I lo'ed her meikle and lang;
> She's broken her vow, she's broken my heart;

go
ninny;
plenty;
money
lo; t
>   And I may e'en gae hang.
> A coof cam in wi' routh o' gear,
> And I hae tint my dearest dear;
> But Woman is but warld's gear,

go
>   Sae let the bonie lass gang!

2

> Whae'er ye be that Woman love,
>   To this be never blind:

No wonder
is it
> Nae ferlie 'tis, tho' fickle she prove,

nature
>   A woman has't by kind.
> O Woman lovely, Woman fair,

fallen
> An angel form's faun to thy share,

have given
> 'Twad been o'er meikle to gien thee mair!
>   I mean an angel mind.

THE DEIL'S AWA WI' TH' EXCISEMAN

TUNE: *The Hemp-dresser*

CHORUS

> *The Deil's awa, the Deil's awa,*
> *The Deil's awa wi' th' Exciseman!*
> *He's danc'd awa, he's danc'd awa,*
> *He's danc'd awa wi' th' Exciseman!*

1

The Deil cam fiddlin thro' the town,
  And danc'd awa wi' th' Exciseman,
And ilka wife cries:—' Auld Mahoun,   *every*
  I wish you luck o' the prize, man!

2

' We'll mak our maut, and we'll brew our drink,   *malt*
  We'll laugh, sing, and rejoice, man,
And monie braw thanks to the meikle black Deil,   *handsome; big*
  That danc'd awa wi' th' Exciseman.

3

' There's threesome reels, there's foursome reels,
  There's hornpipes and strathspeys, man,
But the ae best dance ere cam to the land   *one*
  Was *The Deil's Awa wi' th' Exciseman!* '

THE LOVELY LASS OF INVERNESS

TUNE: (*As Title*)

1

The lovely lass of Inverness,
  Nae joy nor pleasure can she see;
For e'en to morn she cries ' Alas! '
  And ay the saut tear blin's her e'e:—   *salt*

2

' Drumossie moor, Drumossie day—
  A waefu' day it was to me!   *woeful*
For there I lost my father dear,
  My father dear and brethren three.

3

Their winding-sheet the bluidy clay,
  Their graves are growin green to see,
And by them lies the dearest lad
  That ever blest a woman's e'e.

4

Now wae to thee, thou cruel lord,   *William of Cumberland*
  A bluidy man I trow thou be,
For monie a heart thou hast made sair   *sore*
  That ne'er did wrang to thine or thee! '

A RED, RED ROSE

TUNE: *Major Graham*

1

O, my luve's like a red, red rose,
  That's newly sprung in June.
O, my luve's like the melodie,
  That's sweetly play'd in tune.

2

As fair art thou, my bonie lass,
  So deep in luve am I,
And I will luve thee still, my Dear,
go Till a' the seas gang dry.

3

Till a' the seas gang dry, my Dear,
  And the rocks melt wi' the sun!
O I will luve thee still, my Dear,
  While the sands o' life shall run.

4

And fare thee weel, my only Luve,
  And fare thee weel a while!
And I will come again, my Luve,
  Tho' it were ten thousand mile!

AS I STOOD BY YON ROOFLESS TOWER

TUNE: *Cumnock Psalms*

CHORUS

A lassie all alone was making her moan,
  Lamenting our lads beyond the sea :—
' *In the bluidy wars they fa', and our honor's gane an' a',*
must *And broken-hearted we maun die.'*

1

As I stood by yon roofless tower,
  Where the wa'flow'r scents the dewy air,
owl Where the houlet mourns in her ivy bower,
  And tells the midnight moon her care:

2

The winds were laid, the air was still,
  The stars they shot along the sky,
The tod was howling on the hill,   fox
  And the distant-echoing glens reply.

3

The burn, adown its hazelly path,   brook
  Was rushing by the ruin'd wa',
Hasting to join the sweeping Nith,
  Whase roarings seem'd to rise and fa'.

4

The cauld blae North was streaming forth   livid
  Her lights, wi' hissing, eerie din:
Athort the lift they start and shift,   athwart
  Like Fortune's favours, tint as win.   lost as soon
                                          as won

5

Now, looking over firth and fauld,   fold
  Her horn the pale-faced Cynthia rear'd,
When lo! in form of minstrel auld
  A stern and stalwart ghaist appear'd.   ghost

6

And frae his harp sic strains did flow,   such
  Might rous'd the slumbering Dead to hear,   as might
But O, it was a tale of woe   have
  As ever met a Briton's ear!

7

He sang wi' joy his former day,
  He, weeping, wail'd his latter times:
But what he said—it was nae play!—
  I winna ventur't in my rhymes.   will not

O, AN YE WERE DEAD, GUIDMAN

if; husband

TUNE: *(As Title)*

CHORUS

cudgel

stall

> *Sing, round about the fire wi' a rung she ran,*
> *An' round about the fire wi' a rung she ran:—*
> *'Your horns shall tie you to the staw,*
> *An' I shall bang your hide, guidman!'*

1

O. an ye were dead, guidman,
A green turf on your head, guidman!
I wad bestow my widowhood
roistering   Upon a rantin Highlandman!

2

six

There's sax eggs in the pan, guidman,
There's sax eggs in the pan, guidman:
There's ane to you, and twa to me,
And three to our John Highlandman!

3

A sheep-head's in the pot. guidman,
A sheep-head's in the pot, guidman:
broth   The flesh to him, the broo to me,
An' the horns become your brow, guidman!

old long ago

AULD LANG SYNE

TUNE: *(As Title)*

CHORUS

> *And for auld lang syne, my jo,*
> *For auld lang syne,*
> *We'll tak a cup o' kindness yet,*
> *For auld lang syne.*

1

Should auld acquaintance be forgot,
    And never brought to mind?
Should auld acquaintance be forgot,
    And days o' lang syne?

2

And surely ye'll be your pint-stowp!   pay for
    And surely I'll be mine!
And we'll tak a cup o' kindness yet,
    For auld lang syne.

3

We twa hae run about the braes   hillsides
    And pu'd the gowans fine;   pulled;
                                            wild daisies
But we've wander'd mony a weary foot
    Sin auld lang syne.   since

4

We twa hae paidl'd i' the burn,   waded
                                            brook
    Frae mornin' sun till dine;   noon
But seas between us braid hae roar'd   broad
    Sin auld lang syne.

5

And there's a hand, my trusty fiere!   chum
    And gie's a hand o' thine!   give me
And we'll tak a right gude-willy waught,   good-will
                                            drink
    For auld lang syne.

LOUIS, WHAT RECK I BY THEE

TUNE: (*As Title*)

I

Louis, what reck I by thee,
    Or Geordie on his ocean?
Dyvor beggar louns to me!   bankrupt;
                                            fellows
    I reign in Jeanie's bosom.

2

Let her crown my love her law
    And in her breast enthrone me,
Kings and nations—swith awa!   off away
    Reif randies, I disown ye.   Thieving
                                            rascals

HAD I THE WYTE?

TUNE: *Come kiss with me*

Was I to blame?

1

Had I the wyte? had I the wyte?
　　Had I the wyte? she bade me!
high　She watch'd me by the hie-gate side,
lane;　　And up the loan she shaw'd me;
showed
would not　And when I wadna venture in,
lad　　A coward loon she ca'd me!
way　Had Kirk and State been in the gate,
　　I'd lighted when she bade me.

2

led me in　Sae craftilie she took me ben
noise　　And bade me mak nae clatter:—
surly;　' For our ramgunshoch, glum guidman
husband
beyond　Is o'er ayont the water.'
　Whae'er shall say I wanted grace
fondle　　When I did kiss and dawte her,
Then;　Let him be planted in my place,
transgressor　　Syne say I was the fautor!

3

　Could I for shame, could I for shame,
have refused　　Could I for shame refus'd her?
would not;　And wadna manhood been to blame
have been　　Had I unkindly used her?
wool-comb　He claw'd her wi' the ripplin-kame,
blue　　And blae and bluidy bruis'd her—
such　When sic a husband was frae hame,
would have　　What wife but wad excus'd her!

4

wiped; eyes　I dighted ay her een sae blue,
cursed;　　An' bann'd the cruel randy,
scoundrel
wot; mouth　And, weel I wat, her willin mou'
　　Was sweet as sugarcandie.
sunset　At gloamin-shot, it was, I wot,
　　I lighted—on the Monday,
Tuesday's　But I cam thro' the Tyseday's dew
　　To wanton Willie's brandy.

COMIN THRO' THE RYE

TUNE: *Miller's Wedding*

CHORUS

O Jenny's a' weet, poor body,   wet;
   Jenny's seldom dry: creature
She draigl't a' her petticoatie,   draggled
   Comin thro' the rye!

1

Comin thro' the rye, poor body,
   Comin thro' the rye,
She draigl't a' her petticoatie,
   Comin thro' the rye!

2

Gin a body meet a body   Should
   Comin thro' the rye,
Gin a body kiss a body,
   Need a body cry?

3

Gin a body meet a body
   Comin thro' the glen,
Gin a body kiss a body,
   Need the warld ken?

4

Gin a body meet a body
   Comin thro' the grain;
Gin a body kiss a body,
   The thing's a body's ain.

YOUNG JAMIE

TUNE: *The carlin o' the glen*

1

Young Jamie, pride of a' the plain,
Sae gallant and sae gay a swain,
Thro' a' our lasses he did rove,
And reign'd resistless King of Love.

2

briars

mournfully

But now, wi' sighs and starting tears,
He strays amang the woods and breers;
Or in the glens and rocky caves
His sad complaining dowie raves:—

3

' I. wha sae late did range and rove,
And chang'd with every moon my love—
I little thought the time was near,
Repentance I should buy sae dear.

4

suffer

' The slighted maids my torments see,
And laugh at a' the pangs I dree;
While she, my cruel. scornful Fair,
Forbids me e'er to see her mair.'

OUT OVER THE FORTH

TUNE: *Charles Graham's welcome hame*

1

Out over the Forth, I look to the north—
But what is the north, and its Highlands to me?
The south nor the east gie ease to my breast,
The far foreign land or the wide rolling sea!

2

go

love

But I look to the west, when I gae to rest,
That happy my dreams and my slumbers may be;
For far in the west lives he I loe best,
The man that is dear to my babie and me.

WANTONNESS FOR EVERMAIR

TUNE: *Wantonness*

Wantonness for evermair,
   Wantonness has been my ruin.
Yet for a' my dool and care
It's wantonness for evermair.
   I hae lo'ed the Black, the Brown;
I hae lo'ed the Fair, the Gowden!   Golden
   A' the colours in the town—
I hae won their wanton favour.

CHARLIE HE'S MY DARLING

TUNE: *(As Title)*

CHORUS

An' Charlie he's my darling,
My darling, my darling,
Charlie he's my darling—
*   The Young Chevalier!*

I

'Twas on a Monday morning
   Right early in the year,
That Charlie came to our town—
   The Young Chevalier!

2

As he was walking up the street
   The city for to view,
O, there he spied a bonie lass
   The window looking thro'!

3

Sae light's he jimpèd up the stair,
   And tirl'd at the pin;   rasped
And wha sae ready as hersel'
   To let the laddie in!

4

He set his Jenny on his knee,
   All in his Highland dress;

finely well

For brawlie weel he kend the way
        To please a bonie lass.

5

It's up yon heathery mountain
scrubby   And down yon scroggy glen,
daren't go   We daurna gang a-milking
        For Charlie and his men!

THE LASS O' ECCLEFECHAN

TUNE: *Jack Latin*

1

' Gat ye me, O, gat ye me,
        Gat ye me wi' naething?
Rock an' reel, an' spinning wheel,
big   A mickle quarter basin:
Moreover;   Bye attour, my gutcher has
goodsire
high; low   A heich house and a laich ane,
All besides   A' forbye my bonie sel,
to 1st   The toss o' Ecclefechan! '

2

hold   ' O, haud your tongue now, Lucky Lang,
jabber   O, haud your tongue and jauner!
kept to the I held the gate till you I met,
strait path
Then   Syne I began to wander:
        I tint my whistle and my sang,
lost   I tint my peace and pleasure;
grave   But your green graff, now Lucky Lang,
direct   Wad airt me to my treasure.'

THE COOPER O' CUDDY

TUNE: *Bab at the bowster*

CHORUS

We'll hide the cooper behint the door,
Behint the door, behint the door,
We'll hide the cooper behint the door
basket   *And cover him under a mawn, O.*

1

The Cooper o' Cuddy came here awa,   here about
He ca'd the girrs out o'er us a',   knocked;
                        hoops
An' our guidwife has gotten a ca',   knock
  That's anger'd the silly guidman, O.

2

He sought them out, he sought them in,
Wi ' Deil hae her! ' an' ' Deil hae him! '
But the body he was sae doited and blin',   creature;
                        stupid
  He wist na where he was gaun, O.   going

3

They cooper'd at e'en, they cooper'd at morn,
Till our guidman has gotten the scorn:
On ilka brow she's planted a horn,   each
  And swears that there they sall stan', O!   shall

FOR THE SAKE O' SOMEBODY

TUNE: (*As Title*)

1

My heart is sair—I dare na tell—   sore
  My heart is sair for Somebody:
I could wake a winter night
  For the sake o' Somebody.
    O-hon! for Somebody!
    O-hey! for Somebody!
I could range the world around
  For the sake o' Somebody.

2

Ye Powers that smile on virtuous love,
  O, sweetly smile on Somebody!
Frae ilka danger keep him free,   each
  And send me safe my Somebody!
    O-hon! for Somebody!
    O-hey! for Somebody!
I wad do—what wad I not?—
  For the sake o' Somebody!

THE CARDIN O'T

TUNE: *(As Title)*

CHORUS

The cardin o't, the spinnin o't,
The warpin o't, the winnin o't!
each   *When ilka ell cost me a groat,*
stole   *The tailor staw the lynin o't.*

I

bought   I coft a stane o' haslock woo,
web   To mak a wab to Johnie o't,
For Johnie is my only jo—
I lo'e him best of onie yet!

2

For tho' his locks be lyart gray.
bald above   And tho' his brow be beld aboon,
Yet I hae seen him on a day
the whole
parish   The pride of a' the parishen.

THERE'S THREE TRUE
GUID FELLOWS

TUNE: *Three guid fellows ayont the glen*

CHORUS

There's three true guid fellows,
There's three true guid fellows,
There's three true guid fellows,
beyond   *Down ayont yon glen!*

I

dawning   It's now the day is dawin,
before
nightfall   But or night do fa' in,
Whase cock's best at crawin,
shall   Willie, thou sall ken!

SAE FLAXEN WERE HER RINGLETS

TUNE: *Oonagh's Waterfall*

1

Sae flaxen were her ringlets,
  Her eyebrows of a darker hue,
Bewitchingly o'er-arching
  Twa laughing een o' bonie blue.   eyes
Her smiling, sae wyling,   coaxing
  Wad make a wretch forget his woe!
What pleasure, what treasure,
  Unto those rosy lips to grow!
Such was my Chloris' bonie face,
  When first that bonie face I saw,
And ay my Chloris' dearest charm—
  She says she lo'es me best of a'!

2

Like harmony her motion,
  Her pretty ankle is a spy
Betraying fair proportion
  Wad make a saint forget the sky!   Would
Sae warming, sae charming,
  Her faultless form and gracefu' air,
Ilk feature—auld Nature   Each
  Declar'd that she could dae nae mair!   do no more
Hers are the willing chains o' love
  By conquering beauty's sovereign law,
And ay my Chloris' dearest charm—
  She says she lo'es me best of a'.

3

Let others love the city,
  And gaudy show at sunny noon!
Gie me the lonely valley,
  The dewy eve, and rising moon,
Fair beaming, and streaming
  Her silver light the boughs amang,
While falling, recalling,
  The amorous thrush concludes his sang!
There, dearest Chloris, wilt thou rove
  By wimpling burn and leafy shaw,   winding
  brook; wood
And hear my vows o' truth and love,
  And say thou lo'es me best of a'?

THE LASS THAT MADE
THE BED TO ME

TUNE: (*As Title*)

1

When Januar' wind was blawin cauld,
    As to the North I took my way,

darksome   The mirksome night did me enfauld,
    I knew na where to lodge till day.
By my guid luck a maid I met
    Just in the middle o' my care,
And kindly she did me invite
    To walk into a chamber fair.

2

I bow'd fu' low unto this maid,
    And thank'd her for her courtesie;
I bow'd fu' low unto this maid,
    An' bade her mak a bed to me.
She made the bed baith large and wide,
    Wi' twa white hands she spread it down,
She put the cup to her rosy lips,
    And drank:—' Young man, now sleep ye
     soun'.'

3

She snatch'd the candle in her hand,
    And frae my chamber went wi' speed,
But I call'd her quickly back again

more   To lay some mair below my head:
pillow A cod she laid below my head,
    And servèd me with due respeck,
And, to salute her wi' a kiss,
    I put my arms about her neck.

4

Hold   ' Haud aff your hands, young man,' she said,
do not   ' And dinna sae uncivil be;
Gif ye hae onie luve for me,
    O, wrang na my virginitie! '

gold Her hair was like the links o' gowd,
    Her teeth were like the ivorie,
Her cheeks like lilies dipt in wine,
    The lass that made the bed to me!

5

Her bosom was the driven snaw,
    Twa drifted heaps sae fair to see;
Her limbs the polish'd marble stane,
    The lass that made the bed to me!
I kiss'd her o'er and o'er again,
    And ay she wist na what to say.
I laid her 'tween me an' the wa'—
    The lassie thocht na lang till day.   *deemed it not long*

6

Upon the morrow, when we raise,   *rose*
    I thank'd her for her courtesie,
But ay she blush'd, and ay she sigh'd,
    And said:—'Alas, ye've ruin'd me!'
I clasp'd her waist, and kiss'd her syne,   *then*
    While the tear stood twinklin in her e'e.   *eye*
I said:—'My lassie, dinna cry,
    For ye ay shall mak the bed to me.'

7

She took her mither's holland sheets,
    An' made them a' in sarks to me.   *shirts*
Blythe and merry may she be,
    The lass that made the bed to me!
The bonie lass made the bed to me,
    The braw lass made the bed to me!   *handsome*
I'll ne'er forget till the day I die,
    The lass that made the bed to me.

SAE FAR AWA

TUNE: *Dalkeith Maiden Bridge*

1

O, sad and heavy should I part
    But for her sake sae far awa,
Unknowing what my way may thwart—
    My native land sae far awa.

2

Thou that of a' things Maker art,
    That formed this Fair sae far awa,
Gie body strength, then I'll ne'er start   *Give*
    At this my way sae far awa!

3

How true is love to pure desert!
So mine in her sae far awa,
And nocht can heal my bosom's smart,
While, O, she is sae far awa!

4

Nane other love, nane other dart
I feel, but hers sae far awa;
But fairer never touched a heart,
Than hers, the Fair sae far awa.

THE REEL O' STUMPIE

TUNE: (*As Title*)

1

wrap; roll   Wap and rowe, wap and rowe,
little feet   Wap and rowe the feetie o't,
             I thought I was a maiden fair,
its little cry   Till I heard the greetie o't!

2

             My daddie was a fiddler fine,
mother   My minnie she made mantie, O,
quean (*i.e.*   And I myself a thumpin quine,
lass)   And danc'd the Reel o' Stumpie, O.

I'LL AY CA' IN BY YON TOWN

TUNE: *I'll gae nae mair to your town*

CHORUS

call   *I'll ay ca' in by yon town*
          An by yon garden green again!
          I'll ay ca' in by yon town,
          And see my bonie Jean again.

1

     There's nane shall ken, there's nane can guess
same way   What brings me back the gate again,
     But she, my fairest faithfu' lass,
by stealth   And stow'nlins we sall meet again.

2

She'll wander by the aiken tree,   oaken
  When trystin time draws near again;   meeting
And when her lovely form I see,
  O haith! she's doubly dear again.   faith

O, WAT YE WHA'S IN YON TOWN   wot

TUNE: *I'll gae nae mair to your town*

CHORUS

O, wat ye wha's in yon town
  Ye see the e'enin sun upon?   evening
The dearest maid's in yon town
  That e'enin sun is shining on!

I

Now haply down yon gay green shaw   wood
  She wanders by yon spreading tree.
How blest ye flowers that round her blaw!
  Ye catch the glances o' her e'e.

2

How blest ye birds that round her sing,
  And welcome in the blooming year!
And doubly welcome be the Spring,
  The season to my Jeanie dear!

3

The sun blinks blythe in yon town,   glances
  Among the broomy braes sae green;   heights
But my delight in yon town,
  And dearest pleasure, is my Jean.

4

Without my Love, not a' the charms
  O' Paradise could yield me joy;
But gie me Jeanie in my arms,
  And welcome Lapland's dreary sky!

5

My cave wad be a lover's bower,
  Tho' raging Winter rent the air,
And she a lovely little flower,
  That I wad tent and shelter there.   tend

6

O, sweet is she in yon town
   The sinkin sun's gane down upon!
A fairer than's in yon town
   His setting beam ne'er shone upon.

7

If angry Fate be sworn my foe,
   And suff'ring I am doom'd to bear,
I'd careless quit aught else below,
   But spare, O, spare me Jeanie dear!

8

For, while life's dearest blood is warm,
One   Ae thought frae her shall ne'er depart,
And she, as fairest is her form,
   She has the truest, kindest heart.

O MAY, THY MORN

TUNE: *The Rashes*

1

O May, thy morn was ne'er sae sweet
dark   As the mirk night o' December!
For sparkling was the rosy wine,
   And private was the chamber,
And dear was she I dare na name,
   But I will ay remember.

2

And here's to them that, like oursel,
   Can push about the jorum!
And here's to them that wish us weel—
   May a' that's guid watch o'er 'em!
And here's to them we dare na tell,
   The dearest o' the quorum!

AS I CAME O'ER THE CAIRNEY MOUNT

TUNE: *The Highland Lassie*

CHORUS

O, my bonie Highland lad!
My winsome, weel-faur'd Highland laddie!   well-favoured
Wha wad mind the wind and rain
Sae weel row'd in his tartan plaidie!   wrapped

1

As I came o'er the Cairney mount
  And down among the blooming heather,
Kindly stood the milking-shiel   -shed
  To shelter frae the stormy weather.

2

Now Phœbus blinkit on the bent,   shone;
  And o'er the knowes the lambs were bleating;   meadow knolls
But he wan my heart's consent
  To be his ain at the neist meeting.   next

HIGHLAND LADDIE

TUNE: *The Highland Laddie*

1

The bonniest lad that e'er I saw—
  Bonie laddie, Highland laddie!
Wore a plaid and was fu' braw—   fine
  Bonie Highland laddie!
On his head a bonnet blue—
  Bonie laddie, Highland laddie!
His royal heart was firm and true—
  Bonie Highland laddie!

2

'Trumpets sound and cannons roar,
  Bonie lassie, Lawland lassie!—   Lowland
And a' the hills wi' echoes roar,
  Bonie Lawland lassie!

Glory, Honour, now invite—
   Bonie lassie, Lawland lassie!—
For freedom and my King to fight,
   Bonie Lawland lassie! '

3

' The sun a backward course shall take,
   Bonie laddie, Highland laddie!
Ere aught thy manly courage shake,
   Bonie Highland laddie!
Go, for yoursel' procure renown,
   Bonie laddie, Highland laddie,
And for your lawful King his crown,
   Bonie Highland laddie! '

WILT THOU BE MY DEARIE?

TUNE: *The Sutor's Dochter*

1

Wilt thou be my dearie?
When Sorrow wrings thy gentle heart,
   O, wilt thou let me cheer thee?
By the treasure of my soul—
   That's the love I bear thee—
I swear and vow that only thou
   Shall ever be my dearie!
Only thou, I swear and vow,
   Shall ever be my dearie!

2

Lassie, say thou lo'es me,
Or, if thou wilt na be my ain,   *own*
   Say na thou'lt refuse me!
If it winna, canna be,   *will not*
   Thou for thine may choose me,
Let me, lassie, quickly die,
   Trusting that thou lo'es me!
Lassie, let me quickly die,
   Trusting that thou lo'es me!

LOVELY POLLY STEWART

TUNE: *Ye're welcome Charlie Stewart*

CHORUS

O lovely Polly Stewart,
O charming Polly Stewart,
There's ne'er a flower that blooms in May,
That's half so fair as thou art!

I

The flower it blaws, it fades, it fa's,
    And art can ne'er renew it;
But Worth and Truth eternal youth
    Will gie to Polly Stewart!

2

May he whase arms shall fauld thy charms   enfold
    Possess a leal and true heart!   loyal
To him be given to ken the heaven
    He grasps in Polly Stewart!

THE HIGHLAND BALOU

TUNE: *(As Title)*

I

Hee balou, my sweet wee Donald,
Picture o' the great Clanronald!
Brawlie kens our wanton Chief   Finely
Wha gat my young Highland thief.

2

Leeze me on thy bonie craigie!   Blessings;
An thou live, thou'll steal a naigie,   throat
Travel the country thro' and thro',   horse
And bring hame a Carlisle cow!

3

Thro' the Lawlands, o'er the Border,
Weel, my babie, may thou furder,   advance
Herry the louns o' the laigh Countrie,   rogues;
Syne to the Highlands hame to me!   lowlands
    Then

soft cakes;
barley

BANNOCKS O' BEAR MEAL

TUNE: *The Killogie*

CHORUS

Bannocks o' bear meal,
Bannocks o' barley,
Here's to the Highlandman's
Bannocks o' barley!

1

brangle

Wha in a brulyie
    Will first cry ' a parley '?
Never the lads
    Wi' the bannocks o' barley!

2

woeful

Wha, in his wae days,
    Were loyal to Charlie?
Wha but the lads
    Wi' the bannocks o' barley!

WAE IS MY HEART

TUNE: *(As Title)*

1

Wae is my heart, and the tear's in my e'e;
Lang, lang joy's been a stranger to me:
Forsaken and friendless my burden I bear,
And the sweet voice o' pity ne'er sounds in my ear.

2

Love, thou hast pleasures—and deep hae I lov'd!

sorely

Love thou has sorrows—and sair hae I prov'd!
But this bruisèd heart that now bleeds in my breast,
I can feel by its throbbings, will soon be at rest.

3

O, if I were where happy I hae been,
Down by yon stream and yon bonie castle green!
For there he is wand'ring and musing on me,
Wha wad soon dry the tear frae his Phillis' e'e!

HERE'S HIS HEALTH IN WATER

TUNE: *The job of journey work*

I

Altho' my back be at the wa',   wall
  And tho' he be the fautor,   transgressor
Altho' my back be at the wa',
  Yet here's his health in water!
O, wae gae by his wanton sides,   woe go
  Sae brawly's he could flatter!   finely as
Till for his sake I'm slighted sair
  And dree the kintra clatter!   endure the talk of the countryside
But, tho' my back be at the wa',
  Yet here's his health in water!

THE WINTER OF LIFE

TUNE: *East Indian Air*

I

But lately seen in gladsome green,
  The woods rejoiced the day;
Thro' gentle showers the laughing flowers
  In double pride were gay;
But now our joys are fled
  On winter blasts awa,
Yet maiden May in rich array
  Again shall bring them a'.

2

But my white pow—nae kindly thowe   poll: thaw
  Shall melt the snaws of Age!
My trunk of eild, but buss and bield,   eild; without bush and shelter
  Sinks in Time's wintry rage.
O, Age has weary days
  And nights o' sleepless pain!
Thou golden time o' youthfu' prime,
  Why comes thou not again?

THE TAILOR

TUNE: *The Drummer*

I

The tailor he cam here to sew,
And weel he kend the way to woo,
For ay he pree'd the lassie's mou',
    As he gaed but and ben, O.
    For weel he kend the way, O,
    The way, O, the way, O!
    For weel he kend the way, O,
    The lassie's heart to win, O!

tasted
went from
kitchen to
parlour

2

The tailor rase and shook his duds,
The flaes they flew awa in cluds!
And them that stay'd gat fearfu' thuds—
    The tailor prov'd a man, O!
    For now it was the gloamin,
    The gloamin, the gloamin!
    For now it was the gloamin,
    When a' the rest are gaun, O!

rose: clothes
fleas; clouds

dusk

going

THERE GROWS A BONIE BRIER-BUSH

TUNE: *The Bonie Brier-Bush*

I

There grows a bonie brier-bush in our kail-yard,
There grows a bonie brier-bush in our kail-yard;
And below the bonie brier-bush there's a lassie and
    a lad,
And they're busy, busy courting in our kail-yard.

kitchen-
garden

2

We'll court nae mair below the buss in our kail-yard,
We'll court nae mair below the buss in our kail-yard:
We'll awa to Athole's green, and there we'll no be
    seen,
Where the trees and the branches will be our safe-
    guard.

bush

not

3

Will ye go to the dancin in Carlyle's ha'?   hall
Will ye go to the dancin in Carlyle's ha',
Where Sandy and Nancy I'm sure will ding them a'?   beat
I winna gang to the dance in Carlyle-ha'!   will not go

4

What will I do for a lad when Sandie gangs awa!
What will I do for a lad when Sandie gangs awa!
I will awa to Edinburgh, and win a pennie fee,   earn; hire
And see an onie lad will fancy me.   if

5

He's comin frae the north that's to marry me,
He's comin frae the north that's to marry me,
A feather in his bonnet and a ribbon at his knee—
He's a bonie, bonie laddie, an yon be he!   that one

HERE'S TO THY HEALTH

TUNE: *Laggan Burn*

1

Here's to thy health, my bonie lass!
    Guid night and joy be wi' thee!
I'll come nae mair to thy bower-door
    To tell thee that I lo'e thee.
O, dinna think, my pretty pink,
    But I can live without thee: But that
I vow and swear I dinna care   do not
    How lang ye look about ye!

2

Thou'rt ay sae free informing me
    Thou hast nae mind to marry,   desire
I'll be as free informing thee
    Nae time hae I to tarry.
I ken thy freens try ilka means   friends;
    Frae wedlock to delay thee   every
(Depending on some higher chance),
    But fortune may betray thee.

3

I ken they scorn my low estate,
    But that does never grieve me,

For I'm as free as any he—
    Sma' siller will relieve me!

a little money

I'll count my health my greatest wealth
    Sae lang as I'll enjoy it.
I'll fear nae scant, I'll bode nae want
    As lang's I get employment.

4

But far off fowls hae feather's fair,
    And, ay until ye try them,
Tho' they seem fair, still have a care—
    They may prove as bad as I am!

twelve

But at twel at night, when the moon shines
    bright,
    My dear, I'll come and see thee,
For the man that loves his mistress weel,
    Nae travel makes him weary.

IT WAS A' FOR OUR RIGHTFU' KING

TUNE: *Mally Stuart*

1

It was a' for our rightfu' king
    We left fair Scotland's strand;
It was a' for our rightfu' king,
    We e'er saw Irish land,
        My dear—
    We e'er saw Irish land.

2

Now a' is done that men can do,
    And a' is done in vain,
My Love and Native Land fareweel,

must

    For I maun cross the main,
        My dear—
    For I maun cross the main.

3

He turn'd him right and round about
    Upon the Irish shore,

gave

And gae his bridle reins a shake,
    With adieu for evermore,
        My dear—
    And adieu for evermore!

4

The soger frae the wars returns,
   The sailor frae the main,
But I hae parted frae my love
   Never to meet again,
         My dear—
   Never to meet again.

5

When day is gane, and night is come,
   And a' folk bound to sleep,
I think on him that's far awa
   The lee-lang night, and weep,   live-long
         My dear—
   The lee-lang night and weep.

THE HIGHLAND WIDOW'S LAMENT

TUNE: (*As Title*)

1

O. I am come to the low countrie—
   Ochon, ochon, ochrie!—
Without a penny in my purse
   To buy a meal to me.

2

It was na sae in the Highland hills—   not so
   Ochon, ochon, ochrie!—
Nae woman in the country wide
   Sae happy was as me.

3

For then I had a score o' kye—   kine
   Ochon, ochon, ochrie!—
Feeding on yon hill sae high
   And giving milk to me.

4

And there I had three score o' yowes—   ewes
   Ochon, ochon, ochrie!—
Skipping on yon bonie knowes   knolls
   And casting woo' to me.   wool

5

I was the happiest of a' the clan—
  sorely Sair, sair may I repine!—
pick of the clan For Donald was the brawest man,
  And Donald he was mine.

6

Till Charlie Stewart cam at last
  Sae far to set us free:
My Donald's arm was wanted then
  For Scotland and for me.

7

woeful Their waefu' fate what need I tell?
  Right to the wrang did yield:
My Donald and his country fell
  Upon Culloden field.

8

Ochon! O Donald, O!
  Ochon, ochon, ochrie!
Nae woman in the warld wide
  Sae wretched now as me!

THOU GLOOMY DECEMBER

TUNE: *Thro' the lang moor*

1

Once more Ance mair I hail thee, thou gloomy December!
  Ance mair I hail thee wi' sorrow and care!
Sad was the parting thou makes me remember:
  Parting wi' Nancy, O, ne'er to meet mair!

2

Fond lovers' parting is sweet, painful pleasure,
  Hope beaming mild on the soft parting hour;
But the dire feeling, O farewell for ever!
  Anguish unmingled and agony pure!

3

Wild as the winter now tearing the forest,
  Till the last leaf o' the summer is flown—
Such is the tempest has shaken my bosom,
  Till my last hope and last comfort is gone!

4

Still as I hail thee, thou gloomy December,
  Still shall I hail thee wi' sorrow and care;
For sad was the parting thou makes me remember:
  Parting wi' Nancy, O, ne'er to meet mair!

MY PEGGY'S FACE

TUNE: (*As Title*)

1

My Peggy's face, my Peggy's form
The frost of hermit Age might warm.
My Peggy's worth, my Peggy's mind
Might charm the first of human kind.

2

I love my Peggy's angel air,
Her face so truly heavenly fair,
Her native grace so void of art;
But I adore my Peggy's heart.

3

The lily's hue, the rose's dye,
The kindling lustre of an eye—
Who but owns their magic sway?
Who but knows they all decay?

4

The tender thrill, the pitying tear,
The generous purpose nobly dear,
The gentle look that rage disarms—
These are all immortal charms.

STEER HER UP

rouse

TUNE: (*As Title*)

1

O, steer her up, an' haud her gaun—
  Her mither's at the mill, jo,
An' gin she winna tak a man,   ff: will not
  E'en let her tak her will, jo.

threaten
call for
should she
scold

First shore her wi' a gentle kiss,
　　And ca' anither gill, jo,
An' gin she tak the thing amiss,
　　E'en let her flyte her fill, jo.

2

not bashful

to
waste
one rebuff

find

O steer her up, an' be na blate,
　　An' gin she tak it ill, jo,
Then leave the lassie till her fate,
　　And time nae langer spill, jo!
Ne'er break your heart for ae rebute,
　　But think upon it still, jo,
That gin the lassie winna do't,
　　Ye'll fin' anither will, jo.

WEE WILLIE GRAY

TUNE: *Totum Fogg*

I

Wee Willie Gray an' his leather wallet,
Peel a willow-wand to be him boots and jacket!
The rose upon the brier will be him trouse and
　　doublet—
The rose upon the brier will be him trouse and
　　doublet!

shirt: crava:
fly

Wee Willie Gray and his leather wallet,
Twice a lily-flower will be him sark and gravat!
Feathers of a flie wad feather up his bonnet—
Feathers of a flie wad feather up his bonnet!

WE'RE A' NODDIN

TUNE: *(As Title)*

CHORUS

We're a' noddin,
Nid nid noddin,
We're a' noddin
At our house at hame!

1

'Guid e'en to you, kimmer,   gossip
    And how do ye do?'
'Hiccup!' quo' kimmer,
    'The better that I'm fou!,   drunk

2

Kate sits i' the neuk,   corner
    Suppin hen-broo.   chicken-
Deil tak Kate   broth
    An she be na noddin too!

3

'How's a' wi' you, kimmer?   How are all
    And how do you fare?'
'A pint o' the best o't,
    And twa pints mair!'

4

'How's a' wi you, kimmer?
    And how do ye thrive?
How monie bairns hae ye?'
    Quo' kimmer, 'I hae five.'

5

'Are they a' Johnie's?'
    'Eh! atweel na: in truth
Twa o' them were gotten
    When Johnie was awa!'

6

Cats like milk,
    And dogs like broo;   broth
Lads like lasses weel,
    And lasses lads too.

MY WIFE SHE DANG ME   beat
TUNE: (*As Title*)
CHORUS

O, ay my wife she dang me,
An' aft my wife she bang'd me!
If ye gie a woman a' her will,
Guid faith! she'll soon o'er-gang ye.   go beyond
    control

1

On peace an' rest my mind was bent,
 And, fool I was! I married;
But never honest man's intent
 Sae cursedly miscarried.

2

sorry   Some sairie comfort at the last,
these   When a' thir days are done, man:
      My ' pains o' hell ' on earth is past,
above   I'm sure o' bliss aboon, man.

SCROGGAM

TUNE: (*As Title*)

1

dwelt   There was a wife wonn'd in Cockpen,
            Scroggam!
    She brew'd guid ale for gentlemen:
    Sing Auld Cowl, lay you down by me—
    Scroggam, my dearie, ruffum!

2

daughter   The guidwife's dochter fell in a fever,
            Scroggam!
    The priest o' the parish fell in anither:
    Sing Auld Cowl, lay you down by me—
    Scroggam, my dearie, ruffum!

3

together   They laid the twa i' the bed thegither,
            Scroggam!
one; other That the heat o' the tane might cool the tither;
    Sing Auld Cowl, lay you down by me—
    Scroggam, my dearie, ruffum!

O, GUID ALE COMES

TUNE: *The Bottom of the Punch Bowl*

CHORUS

O, guid ale comes, and guid ale goes,
Guid ale gars me sell my hose,   makes
Sell my hose, and pawn my shoon—
Guid ale keeps my heart aboon!   my heart up.

1

I had sax owsen in a pleugh,   six oxen
And they drew a' weel eneugh:
I sell'd them a' just ane by ane—
Guid ale keeps the heart aboon!

2

Guid ale hauds me bare and busy,   keeps
Gars me moop wi' the servant hizzie,   meddle; girl
Stand i' the stool when I hae dune—   censure
Guid ale keeps the heart aboon!

ROBIN SHURE IN HAIRST   reaped; harvest

TUNE: *Rob shear'd in hairst*

CHORUS

Robin shure in hairst,
I shure wi' him:
Fient a heuk had I,   Fiend; sickle
Yet I stack by him.   stuck

1

I gaed up to Dunse   went
    To warp a wab o' plaiden,   web of coarse woollen
At his daddie's yett   gate
    Wha met me but Robin!

2

Was na Robin bauld,   Wasn't; bold
    Tho' I was a cottar?
Play'd me sic a trick,   such
    An' me the Eller's dochter!   Elder's daughter

3

Robin promis'd me
   A' my winter vittle:
Fient haet he had but three
   Guse feathers and a whittle!

food
Fiend have it
(i.e. Nothing)
Goose-quills;
knife

DOES HAUGHTY GAUL INVASION THREAT?

TUNE: *Push about the jorum*

1

Does haughty Gaul invasion threat?
   Then let the loons beware, Sir!
There's wooden walls upon our seas
   And volunteers on shore, Sir!
The Nith shall run to Corsincon,
   And Criffel sink in Solway,
Ere we permit a foreign foe
   On British ground to rally!

rascals

2

O, let us not, like snarling tykes,
   In wrangling be divided,
Till, slap! come in an unco loun,
   And wi' a rung decide it!
Be Britain still to Britain true,
   Amang oursels united!
For never but by British hands
   Maun British wrangs be righted!

dogs

foreign
cudgel

must;
wrongs

3

The kettle o' the Kirk and State,
   Perhaps a clout may fail in't;
But Deil a foreign tinkler loon
   Shall ever ca' a nail in't!
Our fathers' blude the kettle bought,[1]
   And wha wad dare to spoil it,
By Heav'ns! the sacrilegious dog
   Shall fuel be to boil it!

patch
tinker
drive

4

The wretch that would a tyrant own,
　　And the wretch, his true-sworn brother,
Who would set the mob above the throne,
　　May they be damn'd together!
Who will not sing *God save the King*
　　Shall hang as high's the steeple;
But while we sing *God save the King*,
　　We'll ne'er forget the People!

O, ONCE I LOV'D A BONIE LASS

TUNE: *I am a man unmarried*

1

O. once I lov'd a bonie lass,
　　Ay, and I love her still!
And whilst that virtue warms m, breast,
　　I'll love my handsome Nell.

2

As bonie lasses I hae seen,
　　And monie full as braw,　　　　　　fine
But for a modest gracefu' mien
　　The like I never saw.

3

A bonie lass, I will confess,
　　Is pleasant to the e'e;
But without some better qualities
　　She's no a lass for me.

4

But Nelly's looks are blythe and sweet,
　　And, what is best of a',
Her reputation is complete
　　And fair without a flaw.

5

She dresses ay sae clean and neat,
　　Both decent and genteel;
And then there's something in her gait
　　Gars onie dress look weel.　　　　　makes

6

A gaudy dress and gentle air
　　May slightly touch the heart;
But it's innocence and modesty
　　That polishes the dart.

7

'Tis this in Nelly pleases me,
　　'Tis this enchants my soul;
For absolutely in my breast
　　She reigns without controul.

MY LORD A-HUNTING

TUNE: *My Lady's Gown*

CHORUS

gores　　　　　*My lady's gown, there's gairs upon't,*
golden　　　　*And gowden flowers sae rare upon't;*
stays; bodice　*But Jenny's jimps and jirkinet,*
much more　　*My lord thinks meikle mair upon't!*

1

My lord a-hunting he is gane,
But hounds or hawks wi' him are nane;
By Colin's cottage lies his game,
If Colin's Jenny be at hame.

2

My lady's white, my lady's red,
And kith and kin o' Cassillis' blude;
dowry　　　　But her ten-pund lands o' tocher guid
Were a' the charms his lordship lo'ed.

3

bog　　　　Out o'er yon muir, out o'er yon moss,
moor-　　　Whare gor-cocks thro' the heather pass,
dwells　　　There wons auld Colin's bonie lass,
A lily in a wilderness.

4

Sae sweetly move her genty limbs,
Like music notes o' lovers' hymns!
eyes　　　　The diamond-dew in her een sae blue,
Where laughing love sae wanton swims!

5

My lady's dink, my lady's drest,   trim
The flower and fancy o' the west;
But the lassie that a man lo'es best,
O, that's the lass to mak him blest!

MEG O' THE MILL

TUNE: *O ken ye what Meg, etc.*

1

O, ken ye what Meg o' the Mill has gotten?   got
An' ken ye what Meg o' the Mill has gotten?
A braw new naig wi' the tail o' a rottan,   horse; rat
And that's what Meg o' the Mill has gotten!

2

O. ken ye what Meg o' the Mill lo'es dearly?
An, ken ye what Meg o' the Mill lo'es dearly?
A dram o' guid strunt in a morning early,   liquor
And that's what Meg o' the Mill lo'es dearly!

3

O, ken ye how Meg o' the Mill was married?
An' ken ye how Meg o' the Mill was married?
The priest he was oxter'd, the clark he was carried, held up
And that's how Meg o' the Mill was married!   under the
                                                    arms

4

O, ken ye how Meg o' the Mill was bedded?
An' ken ye how Meg o' the Mill was bedded?
The groom gat sae fu' he fell awald beside it,   bridegroom;
And that's how Meg o' the Mill was bedded!   drunk;
                                                    backways

JOCKIE'S TA'EN THE PARTING KISS

TUNE: *Bonie lass tak a man*

I

Jockie's ta'en the parting kiss,
  O'er the mountains he is gane,
And with him is a' my bliss—
  Nought but griefs with me remain.

2

Spare my luve, ye winds that blaw,
  Plashy sleets and beating rain!
Spare my luve, thou feathery snaw,
  Drifting o'er the frozen plain!

3

When the shades of evening creep
  O'er the day's fair gladsome e'e,
Sound and safely may he sleep,
awakening   Sweetly blythe his waukening be!

4

He will think on her he loves,
  Fondly he'll repeat her name;
For where'er he distant roves,
  Jockie's heart is still at hame.

palm ## O, LAY THY LOOF IN MINE, LASS

TUNE: *The Cordwarner's March*

CHORUS

O, lay thy loof in mine, lass,
In mine, lass, in mine, lass,
And swear on thy white hand, lass,
own   *That thou wilt be my ain!*

I

A slave to Love's unbounded sway,
He aft has wrought me meikle wae;
foe But now he is my deadly fae,
  Unless thou be my ain.

2

There's monie a lass has broke my rest,
That for a blink I hae lo'ed best;
But thou art queen within my breast,
    For ever to remain.

CAULD IS THE E'ENIN BLAST

TUNE: *Peggy Ramsay*

1

Cauld is the e'enin blast
    O' Boreas o'er the pool,
An' dawin, it is dreary,   dawning
    When birks are bare at Yule.   birches;
                                   Chrismas-
                                   tide

2

O, cauld blaws the e'enin blast,
    When bitter bites the frost,
And in the mirk and dreary drift   dark
    The hills and glens are lost!

3

Ne'er sae murky blew the night
    That drifted o'er the hill,
But bonie Peg-a-Ramsay
    Gat grist to her mill.

THERE WAS A BONIE LASS

TUNE: *A Bonie Lass*

1

There was a bonie lass, and a bonie, bonie lass,
    And she loed her bonie laddie dear,
Till War's loud alarms tore her laddie frae her arms
    Wi' monie a sigh and a tear.

2

Over sea, over shore, where the cannons loudly roar,
    He still was a stranger to fear,
And nocht could him quail, or his bosom assail,   nought
    But the bonie lass he loed sae dear.

THERE'S NEWS, LASSES, NEWS

TUNE: (*As Title*)

CHORUS

child
pillow
not go

The wean wants a cradle,
   And the cradle wants a cod,
An' I'll no gang to my bed
   Until I get a nod. ·

I

There's news, lasses, news,
   Guid news I've to tell!
There's a boatfu' o' lads
   Come to our town to sell!

2

'Father,' quo' she, 'Mither,' quo' she,
   'Do what you can:
I'll no gang to my bed
   Until I get a man!'

3

croft-ridge
earth
woe befall;
pasture-
must
plough it

I hae as guid a craft rig
   As made o' yird and stane;
And waly fa' the ley-crap
   For I maun till'd again.

O, THAT I HAD NE'ER BEEN MARRIED

TUNE: *Crowdie*

CHORUS

meal and
water

Ance crowdie, twice crowdie,
   Three times crowdie in a day!
Gin ye crowdie onie mair,
   Ye'll crowdie a' my meal away.

1

O, that I had ne'er been married,
  I wad never had nae care!
Now I've gotten wife an bairns,   children
  An' they cry ' Crowdie ' evermair.

2

Waefu' Want and Hunger fley me,   scare
  Glowrin by the hallan en';   the end of
                                                    the porch
Sair I fecht them at the door,   Hard; fight
  But ay I'm eerie they come ben.   frightened;
                                                    in

MALLY'S MEEK, MALLY'S SWEET   Mollie's

TUNE: (*As Title*)

CHORUS

Mally's meek, Mally's sweet,
Mally's modest and discreet,
Mally's rare, Mally's fair,
Mally's ev'ry way complete.

1

As I was walking up the street,
A barefit maid I chanc'd to meet;
But O, the road was very hard
For that fair maiden's tender feet!

2

It were mair meet that those fine feet
  Were weel laced up in silken shoon!
An' 'twere more fit that she should sit
  Within yon chariot gilt aboon!   above

3

Her yellow hair, beyond compare,
  Comes tumbling down her swan-white neck,
And her twa eyes, like stars in skies,
  Would keep a sinking ship frae wreck!

WANDERING WILLIE

TUNE: *Here awa, there awa*

I

Here awa, there awa, wandering Willie,
hold   Here awa, there awa, haud awa hame!
oneCome to my bosom, my ae only dearie,
    And tell me thou bring'st me my Willie the same.

2

Loud tho' the Winter blew cauld at our parting,
    'Twas na the blast brought the tear in my e'e:
SummerWelcome now Simmer, and welcome my Willie,
    The Simmer to Nature, my Willie to me!

3

Rest, ye wild storms in the cave o' your slumbers—
    How your wild howling a lover alarms!
Awake; rollWauken, ye breezes, row gently, ye billows,
    And waft my dear laddie ance mair to my arms.

4

remembers notBut O, if he's faithless, and minds na his Nannie,
    Flow still between us, thou wide-roaring main!
May I never see it, may I never trow it,
    But, dying, believe that my Willie's my ain!

BRAW LADS O' GALLA WATER

Handsome

TUNE: *The Brave Lads of Galla Water*

I

heightsBraw, braw lads on Yarrow braes,
    They rove amang the blooming heather;
woodsBut Yarrow braes nor Ettrick shaws
    Can match the lads o' Galla Water.

2

But there is ane, a secret ane,
Above   Aboon them a' I loe him better;
And I'll be his, and he'll be mine,
    The bonie lad o' Galla Water.

3

Altho' his daddie was nae laird,   much dowry
   And tho' I hae nae meikle tocher,
Yet, rich in kindest, truest love,
   We'll tent our flocks by Galla Water.   watch

4

It ne'er was wealth, it ne'er was wealth,
   That coft contentment, peace, and pleasure: bought
The bands and bliss o' mutual love,
   O, that's the chiefest warld's treasure!

AULD ROB MORRIS

TUNE: (As Title)

1

There's Auld Rob Morris that wons in yon glen,   dwells
He's the king o' guid fellows and wale of auld men: pick
He has gowd in his coffers, he has owsen and kine,   gold
And ae bonie lassie, his dautie and mine.   one; pet

2

She's fresh as the morning the fairest in May,
She's sweet as the ev'ning amang the new hay,
As blythe and as artless as the lambs on the lea,
And dear to my heart as the light to my e'e.

3

But O, she's an heiress, auld Robin's a laird,
And my daddie has nocht but a cot-house and yard!   garden
A wooer like me maunna hope to come speed: mustn't
The wounds I must hide that will soon be my dead.   death

4

The day comes to me, but delight brings me nane;   brings me
The night comes to me, but my rest it is gane;   no delight
I wander my lane like a night-troubled ghaist,   alone; ghost
And I sigh as my heart it wad burst in my breast.

5

O, had she but been of a lower degree,
I then might hae hop'd she wad smil'd upon me!   would have
O, how past descriving had then been my bliss,   describing
As now my distraction no words can express!

OPEN THE DOOR TO ME, O

TUNE: *Open the door softly*

I

O, open the door some pity to shew,
    If love it may na be, O!
Tho' thou hast been false, I'll ever prove true—
    O, open the door to me, O!

2

Cauld is the blast upon my pale cheek,
    But caulder thy love for me, O:
The frost, that freezes the life at my heart,
    Is nought to my pains frae thee, O!

3

The wan moon sets behind the white wave,
    And Time is setting with me, O:
False friends, false love, farewell! for mair
    I'll ne'er trouble them nor thee, O!

4

She has open'd the door, she has open'd it wide,
    She sees the pale corse on the plain, O,
' My true love! ' she cried, and sank down by his
        side—
    Never to rise again, O!

WHEN WILD WAR'S DEADLY BLAST

TUNE: *The Mill, Mill O*

I

When wild War's deadly blast was blawn,
    And gentle Peace returning,
Wi' monie a sweet babe fatherless
    And monie a widow mourning,
I left the lines and tented field,
    Where lang I'd been a lodger,
My humble knapsack a' my wealth,
    A poor and honest sodger.

2

A leal, light heart was in my breast,   loyal
    My hand unstain'd wi' plunder,
And for fair Scotia, hame again,
    I cheery on did wander:
I thought upon the banks o' Coil,
    I thought upon my Nancy,
And ay I mind't the witching smile   remembered
    That caught my youthful fancy.

3

At length I reach'd the bonie glen,
    Where early life I sported.
I pass'd the mill and trysting thorn,
    Where Nancy aft I courted.
Wha spied I but my ain dear maid,
    Down by her mother's dwelling,
And turn'd me round to hide the flood
    That in my een was swelling!   eyes

4

Wi' alter'd voice, quoth I:—'Sweet lass,
    Sweet as yon hawthorn's blossom,
O, happy, happy may he be,
    That's dearest to thy bosom!
My purse is light, I've far to gang,   go
    And fain wad be thy lodger;
I've serv'd my king and country lang—
    Take pity on a sodger.'

5

Sae wistfully she gaz'd on me,
    And lovelier was than ever.
Quo' she:—'A sodger ance I lo'ed,
    Forget him shall I never.
Our humble cot, and hamely fare,
    Ye freely shall partake it;
That gallant badge—the dear cockade—
    Ye're welcome for the sake o't!'

6

She gaz'd, she redden'd like a rose,
    Syne, pale like onie lily,   Then
She sank within my arms, and cried:—
    'Art thou my ain dear Willie?'

'By Him who made yon sun and sky,
By whom true love's regarded,
I am the man! And thus may still
    True lovers be rewarded!

7

'The wars are o'er and I'm come hame,
    And find thee still true-hearted.
wealth   Tho' poor in gear, we're rich in love,
we'll   And mair, we'se ne'er be parted.'
gold   Quo' she:—'My grandsire left me gowd,
farm   A mailen plenish'd fairly!
And come, my faithfu' sodger lad,
    Thou'rt welcome to it dearly!'

8

For gold the merchant ploughs the main,
    The farmer ploughs the manor;
But glory is the sodger's prize,
    The sodger's wealth is honor!
The brave poor sodger ne'er despise,
    Nor count him as a stranger:
Remember he's his country's stay
    In day and hour of danger.

DUNCAN GRAY

TUNE: (*As Title*)

I

Duncan Gray cam here to woo
    (Ha, ha, the wooing o't!)
Christmas On blythe Yule-Night when we were fou
Eve; drunk   (Ha, ha, the wooing o't!).
cast Maggie coost her head fu' high,
askance; Look'd asklent and unco skeigh,
very skittish
Made; off Gart poor Duncan stand abeigh—
    Ha, ha, the wooing o't!

2

wheedled Duncan fleech'd, and Duncan pray'd
    (Ha, ha, the wooing o't!),
Meg was deaf as Ailsa Craig
    (Ha, ha, the wooing o't!).

Duncan sigh'd baith out and in,   both
Grat his een baith bleer't an' blin',   Wept; eyes
Spak o' lowpin o'er a linn—   leaping;
    Ha, ha, the wooing o't!   waterfall

3

Time and Chance are but a tide
    (Ha, ha, the wooing o't!):
Slighted love is sair to bide   hard to
    (Ha, ha, the wooing o't!).   endure
' Shall I like a fool,' quoth he,
' For a haughty hizzie die?   jade
She may gae to—France for me! '—   go
    Ha, ha, the wooing o't!

4

How it comes, let doctors tell
    (Ha, ha, the wooing o't!):
Meg grew sick, as he grew hale
    (Ha, ha, the wooing o't!).
Something in her bosom wrings,
For relief a sigh she brings,
And O! her een they spak sic things!—   eyes; such
    Ha, ha, the wooing o't!

5

Duncan was a lad o' grace
    (Ha, ha, the wooing o't!),
Maggie's was a piteous case
    (Ha, ha, the wooing o't!):
Duncan could na be her death,
Swelling pity smoor'd his wrath;   smothered
Now they're crouse and canty baith—   proud; jolly
    Ha, ha, the wooing o't!

DELUDED SWAIN, THE PLEASURE

TUNE: *The collier's bonie lassie*

I

Deluded swain, the pleasure
    The fickle Fair can give thee
Is but a fairy treasure—
    Thy hopes will soon deceive thee:

The billows on the ocean,
  The breezes idly roaming,
The cloud's uncertain motion,
  They are but types of Woman!

2

O, art thou not ashamèd
  To doat upon a feature?
If Man thou would'st be namèd,
  Despise the silly creature!
Go, find an honest fellow,
  Good claret set before thee,
Hold on till thou art mellow,
  And then to bed in glory!

HERE IS THE GLEN

TUNE: *Banks of Cree*

1

Here is the glen, and here the bower
  All underneath the birchen shade,
The village-bell has toll'd the hour—
  O, what can stay my lovely maid?
'Tis not Maria's whispering call—
  'Tis but the balmy-breathing gale,
Mixed with some warbler's dying fall
  The dewy star of eve to hail!

2

It is Maria's voice I hear!—
  So calls the woodlark in the grove
His little faithful mate to cheer:
  At once 'tis music and 'tis love!
And art thou come? And art thou true?
  O, welcome, dear, to love and me,
And let us all our vows renew
  Along the flowery banks of Cree!

LET NOT WOMEN E'ER COMPLAIN

TUNE: *Duncan Gray*

1

Let not women e'er complain
  Of inconstancy in love!
Let not women e'er complain
  Fickle man is apt to rove!
Look abroad thro' Nature's range,
Nature's mighty law is change:
Ladies, would it not be strange
  Man should then a monster prove?

2

Mark the winds, and mark the skies,
  Ocean's ebb and ocean's flow.
Sun and moon but set to rise.
  Round and round the seasons go.
Why then, ask of silly man
To oppose great Nature's plan?
We'll be constant, while we can—
  You can be no more, you know!

LORD GREGORY

TUNE: *(As Title)*

1

O, mirk, mirk is this midnight hour,   dark
  And loud the tempest's roar!
A waefu' wanderer seeks thy tower—
  Lord Gregory, ope thy door.

2

An exile frae her father's ha',   hall
  And a' for sake o' thee,
At least some pity on me shaw,   show
  If love it may na be.

3

Lord Gregory mind'st thou not the grove   rememb'rest
  By bonie Irwine side,
Where first I own'd that virgin love
  I lang, lang had denied?

4

How aften didst thou pledge and vow,
    Thou wad for ay be mine!
And my fond heart, itsel' sae true,
    It ne'er mistrusted thine.

5

Hard is thy heart, Lord Gregory,
    And flinty is thy breast:
Thou bolt of Heaven that flashest by,
    O, wilt thou bring me rest!

6

Ye mustering thunders from above,
    Your willing victim see,
But spare and pardon my fause love
    His wrangs to Heaven and me!

O POORTITH CAULD

cold poverty

TUNE: *Cauld Kail*

CHORUS

such

O. why should Fate sic pleasure have
Life's dearest bands untwining?
Or why sae sweet a flower as love
Depend on Fortune's shining?

I

O Poortith cauld and restless Love,
    Ye wrack my peace between ye!

wreck

Yet poortith a' I could forgive,
    An 'twere na for my Jeanie.

If

2

The warld's wealth when I think on,
    Its pride and a' the lave o't—

rest

My curse on silly coward man,
    That he should be the slave o't!

3

Her een sae bonie blue betray
    How she repays my passion;

eyes

But prudence is her o'erword ay:
    She talks o' rank and fashion.

4

O, wha can prudence think upon,
  And sic a lassie by him?
O, wha can prudence think upon,
  And sae in love as I am?

5

How blest the wild-wood Indian's fate!
  He woos his artless dearie—
The silly bogles, Wealth and State,   hobgoblins
  Can never make him eerie.   fearful

O, STAY, SWEET WARBLING WOOD-LARK

TUNE: *Whare shall our guidman lie*

1

O, stay, sweet warbling wood-lark, stay,
Nor quit for me the trembling spray!
A hapless lover courts thy lay,
  Thy soothing, fond complaining.
Again, again that tender part,
That I may catch thy melting art!
For surely that wad touch her heart,
  Wha kills me wi' disdaining.

2

Say, was thy little mate unkind,
And heard thee as the careless wind?
O, nocht but love and sorrow join'd   nothing
  Sic notes o' woe could wauken!   Such;
Thou tells o' never-ending care,   awake
O' speechless grief and dark despair—
For pity's sake, sweet bird, nae mair,
  Or my poor heart is broken!

SAW YE BONIE LESLEY

TUNE: *The collier's bonie lassie*

1

O, saw ye bonie Lesley,
   As she gaed o'er the Border?
She's gane, like Alexander,
   To spread her conquests farther!

went

2

To see her is to love her,
   And love but her for ever;
For Nature made her what she is,
   And never made anither!

3

Thou art a queen, fair Lesley—
   Thy subjects, we before thee!
Thou art divine, fair Lesley—
   The hearts o' men adore thee.

4

The Deil he could na skaith thee,
   Or aught that wad belang thee:
He'd look into thy bonie face,
   And say:—' I canna wrang thee! '

harm
belong to

5

The Powers aboon will tent thee,
   Misfortune sha'na steer thee:
Thou'rt like themsel' sae lovely,
   That ill they'll ne'er let near thee.

above;
guard
meddle with

6

Return again, fair Lesley,
   Return to Caledonie!
That we may brag we hae a lass
   There's nane again sae bonie.

SWEET FA'S THE EVE

TUNE: *Craigieburn Wood*

1

Sweet fa's the eve on Craigieburn,
    And blythe awakes the morrow,
But a' the pride o' Spring's return
    Can yield me nocht but sorrow.   nothing

2

I see the flowers and spreading trees,
    I hear the wild birds singing;
But what a weary wight can please,
    And Care his bosom is wringing?

3

Fain, fain would I my griefs impart,
    Yet dare na for your anger;
But secret love will break my heart,
    If I conceal it langer.

4

If thou refuse to pity me,
    If thou shalt love another,
When yon green leaves fade frae the tree,
    Around my grave they'll wither.

YOUNG JESSIE

TUNE: *Bonie Dundee*

1

True hearted was he, the sad swain o' the Yarrow,
    And fair are the maids on the banks of the Ayr;
But by the sweet side o' the Nith's winding river
    Are lovers as faithful and maidens as fair:
To equal young Jessie seek Scotia all over—
    To equal young Jessie you seek it in vain!
Grace, beauty, and elegance fetter her lover,
    And maidenly modesty fixes the chain.

2

Fresh is the rose in the gay, dewy morning,
    And sweet is the lily at evening close;
But in the fair presence o' lovely young Jessie
    Unseen is the lily, unheeded the rose.
Love sits in her smile, a wizard ensnaring;
eyes   Enthron'd in her een he delivers his law:
And still to her charms she alone is a stranger:
    Her modest demeanour's the jewel of a'.

ADOWN WINDING NITH

TUNE: *The muckin o' Geordy's byre*

CHORUS

Awa wi' your belles and your beauties—
They never wi' her can compare!
Whaever hae met wi' my Phillis
Has met wi' the Queen o' the Fair!

1

Adown winding Nith I did wander
    To mark the sweet flowers as they spring.
Adown winding Nith I did wander
    Of Phillis to muse and to sing.

2

The Daisy amus'd my fond fancy,
    So artless, so simple, so wild:
' Thou emblem,' said i, ' o' my Phillis '—
    For she is Simplicity's child.

3

The rose-bud's the blush o' my charmer,
    Her sweet balmy lip when 'tis prest.
How fair and how pure is the lily!
    But fairer and purer her breast.

4

Yon knot of gay flowers in the arbour,
    They ne'er wi' my Phillis can vie:
Her breath is the breath of the woodbine,
    Its dew-drop o' diamond her eye.

5

Her voice is the song o' the morning,
    That wakes thro' the green-spreading grove,
When Phebus peeps over the mountains
    On music, and pleasure, and love.

6

But Beauty, how frail and how fleeting!
    The bloom of a fine summer's day!
While Worth in the mind o' my Phillis
    Will flourish without a decay.

A LASS WI' A TOCHER   dowry

TUNE: *Balin a mone*

CHORUS

Then hey for a lass wi' a tocher,
Then hey for a lass wi' a tocher,
Then hey for a lass wi' a tocher,
    The nice yellow guineas for me!

1

Awa wi' your witchcraft o' Beauty's alarms,
The slender bit beauty you grasp in your arms!
O, gie me the lass that has acres o' charms!
O, gie me the lass wi' the weel-stockit farms!

2

Your Beauty's a flower in the morning that blows,
And withers the faster the faster it grows;
But the rapturous charm o' the bonie green knowes,   knolls
Ilk spring they're new deckit wi' bonie white yowes!   ewes

3

And e'en when this Beauty your bosom has blest,
The brightest o' Beauty may cloy when possess'd;
But the sweet, yellow darlings wi' Geordie impress'd,
The langer ye hae them, the mair they're carest!

BLYTHE HAE I BEEN ON YON HILL

TUNE: *The Quaker's Wife*

I

Blythe hae I been on yon hill
  As the lambs before me,
Careless ilka thought, and free
  As the breeze flew o'er me.
Now nae langer sport and play
  Mirth or sang can please me:
Lesley is sae fair and coy,
  Care and anguish seize me.

every

2

Heavy, heavy is the task,
  Hopeless love declaring!
Trembling, I dow nocht but glow'r
  Sighing, dumb despairing!
If she winna ease the thraws
  In my bosom swelling,
Underneath the grass-green sod
  Soon maun be my dwelling.

can do nothing but stare

will not; throes

must

BY ALLAN STREAM

TUNE: *Allan Water*

I

By Allan stream I chanc'd to rove,
  While Phebus sank beyond Benledi;
The winds were whispering thro' the grove,
  The yellow corn was waving ready;
I listen'd to a lover's sang,
  An' thought on youthfu' pleasures monie,
And ay the wild-wood echoes rang:—
  ' O, my love Annie's very bonie!

2

' O, happy be the woodbine bower,
  Nae nightly bogle make it eerie!
Nor ever sorrow stain the hour,
  The place and time I met my dearie!

hobgoblin; fearful

Her head upon my throbbing breast,
　　She, sinking, said:—" I'm thine for ever! "
While monie a kiss the seal imprest—
　　The sacred vow we ne'er should sever.'

3

The haunt o' Spring's the primrose-brae.   -bank
　　The Summer joys the flocks to follow.
How cheery thro' her short'ning day
　　Is Autumn in her weeds o' yellow!
But can they melt the glowing heart,
　　Or chain the soul in speechless pleasure,
Or thro' each nerve the rapture dart,
　　Like meeting her, our bosom's treasure?

CANST THOU LEAVE ME

TUNE: *Ruffian's Rant*

CHORUS

Canst thou leave me thus, my Katie!
　　Canst thou leave me thus, my Katie!
Well thou know'st my aching heart,
　　And canst thou leave me thus for pity?

I

Is this thy plighted, fond regard:
　　Thus cruelly to part, my Katie?
Is this thy faithful swain's reward:
　　An aching broken heart, my Katie?

2

Farewell! And ne'er such sorrows tear
　　That fickle heart of thine, my Katie!
Thou may'st find those will love thee dear,
　　But not a love like mine, my Katie.

COME, LET ME TAKE THEE

TUNE: *Cauld Kail*

1

Come, let me take thee to my breast,
  And pledge we ne'er shall sunder,
And I shall spurn as vilest dust
  The world's wealth and grandeur!
And do I hear my Jeanie own
  That equal transports move her?
I ask for dearest life alone,
  That I may live to love her.

2

Thus in my arms, wi' a' her charms,
  I clasp my countless treasure,
I'll seek nae mair o' Heav'n to share
  Than sic a moment's pleasure!
And by thy een sae bonie blue
  I swear I'm thine for ever,
And on thy lips I seal my vow,
  And break it shall I never!

such

eyes

CONTENTED WI' LITTLE

TUNE: *Lumps of Pudding*

1

Contented wi' little and cantie wi' mair,
Whene'er I forgather wi' Sorrow and Care,
I gie them a skelp, as they're creepin alang,
Wi' a cog o' guid swats and an auld Scottish sang.

jolly

smack

new ale

2

I whyles claw the elbow o' troublesome Thought;
But Man is a soger, and Life is a faught.
My mirth and guid humour are coin in my pouch,
And my Freedom's my lairdship nae monarch daur touch.

sometimes

scratch

fight

3

A towmond o' trouble, should that be my fa',
A night o' guid fellowship sowthers it a':

twelve-month; lot

solders

When at the blythe end o' our journey at last,
Wha the Deil ever thinks o' the road he has past?

4

Blind Chance, let her snapper and stoyte on her way,   stumble;
    stagger
Be't to me, be't frae me, e'en let the jade gae!   go
Come Ease or come Travail, come Pleasure or Pain,
My warst word is:—' Welcome, and welcome again! '   worst

FAREWELL, THOU STREAM

TUNE: *Alace yat I came owr the moor*

I

Farewell, thou stream that winding flows
    Around Eliza's dwelling!
O Mem'ry, spare the cruel throes
    Within my bosom swelling:
Condemn'd to drag a hopeless chain
    And yet in secret languish,
To feel a fire in every vein
    Nor dare disclose my anguish!

2

Love's veriest wretch, unseen, unknown,
    I fain my griefs would cover:
The bursting sigh, th' unweeting groan   unconscious.
    Betray the hapless lover.
I know thou doom'st me to despair,
    Nor wilt, nor canst relieve me;
But, O Eliza, hear one prayer—
    For pity's sake forgive me!

3

The music of thy voice I heard,
    Nor wist while it enslav'd me!
I saw thine eyes, yet nothing fear'd,
    Till fears no more had sav'd me!
Th' unwary sailor thus, aghast
    The wheeling torrent viewing,
'Mid circling horrors sinks at last
    In overwhelming ruin.

HAD I A CAVE

TUNE: *Robin Adair*

1

Had I a cave
  On some wild distant shore,
Where the winds howl
  To the wave's dashing roar,
      There would I weep my woes,
      There seek my lost repose,
      Till grief my eyes should close,
Ne'er to wake more!

2

Falsest of womankind,
  Can'st thou declare
All thy fond, plighted vows
  Fleeting as air?
      To thy new lover hie,
      Laugh o'er thy perjury,
      Then in thy bosom try
What peace is there!

HERE'S A HEALTH

TUNE: *Here's a health to them that's awa*

CHORUS

Here's a health to ane I loe dear!
Here's a health to ane I loe dear!
Thou art sweet as the smile when fond lovers meet,
And soft as their parting tear,
        Jessy—
And soft as their parting tear!

1

must

Altho' thou maun never be mine,
  Altho' even hope is denied,
'Tis sweeter for thee despairing
  Than ought in the world beside,
        Jessy—
  Than ought in the world beside!

2

I mourn thro' the gay, gaudy day,
  As hopeless I muse on thy charms;
But welcome the dream o' sweet slumber!
  For then I am lockt in thine arms,
          Jessy—
  For then I am lockt in thine arms!

3

I guess by the dear angel smile
  I guess by the love-rolling e'e;
But why urge the tender confession,
  'Gainst Fortune's fell, cruel decree,
          Jessy—
  'Gainst Fortune's fell, cruel decree.

HOW CRUEL ARE THE PARENTS

TUNE: *John Anderson my jo*

1

How cruel are the parents
  Who riches only prize,
And to the wealthy booby
  Poor Woman sacrifice!
Meanwhile the hapless daughter
  Has but a choice of strife:
To shun a tyrant father's hate
  Become a wretched wife!

2

The ravening hawk pursuing,
  The trembling dove thus flies:
To shun impending ruin
  Awhile her pinion tries,
Till, of escape despairing,
  No shelter or retreat,
She trusts the ruthless falconer,
  And drops beneath his feet.

HUSBAND, HUSBAND, CEASE YOUR STRIFE

TUNE: *My jo, Janet*

I

'Husband, husband, cease your strife,
  Nor longer idly rave, sir!
Tho' I am your wedded wife,
  Yet I am not your slave, sir.'
' One of two must still obey,
  Nancy, Nancy!
Is it Man or Woman, say,
  My spouse Nancy?'

2

' If 'tis still the lordly word,
  Service and obedience,
I'll desert my sov'reign lord,
  And so goodbye, allegiance!'
' Sad will I be so bereft,
  Nancy, Nancy!
Yet I'll try to make a shift,
  My spouse Nancy!'

3

' My poor heart, then break it must,
  My last hour I am near it:
When you lay me in the dust,
  Think, how will you bear it?'
' I will hope and trust in Heaven,
  Nancy, Nancy!
Strength to bear it will be given,
  My spouse Nancy.'

4

' Well, sir, from the silent dead,
  Still I'll try to daunt you:
Ever round your midnight bed
  Horrid sprites shall haunt you!'
' I'll wed another like my dear,
  Nancy, Nancy!
Then all Hell will fly for fear,
  My spouse Nancy!'

IT WAS THE CHARMING MONTH

TUNE: *Dainty Davie*

CHORUS

Lovely was she by the dawn,
  Youthful Chloe, charming Chloe,
Tripping o'er the pearly lawn,
  The youthful, charming Chloe!

1

It was the charming month of May,
When all the flow'rs were fresh and gay,
One morning, by the break of day,
  The youthful, charming Chloe
From peaceful slumber she arose,
Girt on her mantle and her hose,
And o'er the flow'ry mead she goes—
  The youthful, charming Chloe!

2

The feather'd people you might see
Perch'd all around on every tree!
With notes of sweetest melody
  They hail the charming Chloe,
Till, painting gay the eastern skies,
The glorious sun began to rise,
Outrival'd by the radiant eyes
  Of youthful, charming Chloe.

LAST MAY A BRAW WOOER   fine

TUNE: *The Lothian Lassie*

1

Last May a braw wooer cam down the lang glen,
  And sair wi' his love he did deave me.   deafen
I said there was naething I hated like men:
  The deuce gae wi' him to believe me, believe me—   go
  The deuce gae wi' him to believe me!

2

He spak o' the darts in my bonie black een,   eyes
  And vow'd for my love he was diein.
I said, he might die when he liket for Jean:

The Lord forgie me for liein, for liein—
The Lord forgie me for liein!

3

farm;
landlord

A weel-stockèt mailen, himsel for the laird,
And marriage aff-hand were his proffers:

let

I never loot on that I kenn'd it, or car'd,

worse

But thought I might hae waur offers, waur offers—
But thought I might hae waur offers.

4

But what wad ye think? In a fortnight or less
(The Deil tak his taste to gae near her!)
He up the Gate-Slack to my black cousin, Bess!
Guess ye how, the jad! I could bear her, could
bear her—
Guess ye how, the jad! I could bear her.

5

next
cattle-fair

But a' the niest week, as I petted wi' care,
I gaed to the tryste o' Dalgarnock,
And wha but my fine fickle lover was there?

stared

I glowr'd as I'd seen a warlock, a warlock—
I glowr'd as I'd seen a warlock.

6

shoulder;
glance

But owre my left shouther I gae him a blink,
Lest neebours might say I was saucy.
My wooer he caper'd as he'd been in drink,
And vow'd I was his dear lassie, dear lassie—
And vow'd I was his dear lassie!

7

asked;
affable
If
shoes;
shapeless

I spier'd for my cousin fu' couthy and sweet:
Gin she had recover'd her hearin?
And how her new shoon fit her auld, shachl'd feet?
But heavens! how he fell a swearin, a swearin—
But heavens! how he fell a swearin!

8

He beggèd, for gudesake, I wad be his wife,
Or else I wad kill him wi' sorrow;
So e'en to preserve the poor body in life,

must

I think I maun wed him to-morrow, to-morrow—
I think I maun wed him to-morrow!

MY NANIE'S AWA

TUNE: *There are few good fellows when Jamie's awa*

1

Now in her green mantle blythe Nature arrays,
And listens the lambkins that bleat o'er the braes, *heights*
While birds warble welcomes in ilka green shaw, *every; wood*
But to me it's delightless—my Nanie's awa.

2

The snawdrap and primrose our woodlands adorn,
And violets bathe in the weet o' the morn. *wet [i.e.dew]*
They pain my sad bosom, sae sweetly they blaw:
They mind me o' Nanie—and Nanie's awa!

3

Thou lav'rock, that springs frae the dews of the lawn
The shepherd to warn o' the grey-breaking dawn,
And thou mellow mavis, that hails the night-fa,
Give over for pity—my Nanie's awa.

4

Come Autumn, sae pensive in yellow and grey,
And soothe me wi' tidings o' Nature's decay!
The dark, dreary Winter and wild-driving snaw
Alane can delight me—now Nanie's awa.

NOW ROSY MAY

TUNE: *Dainty Davie*

CHORUS

Meet me on the Warlock Knowe, *knoll*
Dainty Davie, Dainty Davie!
There I'll spend the day wi' you,
My ain dear Dainty Davie. *own*

1

Now rosy May comes in wi' flowers
To deck her gay, green-spreading bowers;
And now comes in the happy hours
    To wander wi' my Davie.

2

The crystal waters round us fa',
The merry birds are lovers a',
The scented breezes round us blaw,
    A wandering wi' my Davie.

3

When purple morning starts the hare
To steal upon her early fare,
Then thro' the dews I will repair
    To meet my faithfu' Davie.

4

When day, expiring in the west,
The curtain draws o' Nature's rest,
I flee to his arms I loe the best:
    And that's my ain dear Davie!

NOW SPRING HAS CLAD

TUNE: (*Unknown*)

1

Now spring has clad the grove in green,
    And strew'd the lea wi' flowers;
The furrow'd, waving corn is seen
    Rejoice in fostering showers;
While ilka thing in nature join
    Their sorrows to forego,
O, why thus all alone are mine
    The weary steps o' woe!

every

2

The trout within yon wimpling burn
    Glides swift, a silver dart,
And, safe beneath the shady thorn,
    Defies the angler's art:
My life was ance that careless stream,
    That wanton trout was I,
But Love wi' unrelenting beam
    Has scorch'd my fountains dry.

winding

3

The little floweret's peaceful lot,
    In yonder cliff that grows,

Which, save the linnet's flight, I wot,   guess
  Nae ruder visit knows,
Was mine, till Love has o'er me past,
  And blighted a' my bloom;
And now beneath the withering blast
  My youth and joy consume.

4

The waken'd lav'rock warbling springs,
  And climbs the early sky,
Winnowing blythe his dewy wings
  In Morning's rosy eye:
As little reck't I Sorrow's power,
  Until the flowery snare
O' witching Love in luckless hour
  Made me the thrall o' care!

5

O, had my fate been Greenland snows
  Or Afric's burning zone,
Wi' Man and Nature leagu'd my foes,
  So Peggy ne'er I'd known!
The wretch, whose doom is ' hope nae mair,'
  What tongue his woes can tell,
Within whose bosom, save Despair,
  Nae kinder spirits dwell!

O, THIS IS NO MY AIN LASSIE

TUNE: *This is no mine ain house*

CHORUS

O, this is no my ain lassie,
  Fair tho' the lassie be:
Weel ken I my ain lassie—
  Kind love is in her e'e.

1

I see a form, I see a face,
Ye weel may wi' the fairest place:
It wants to me the witching grace,
  The kind love that's in her e'e.

2

She's bonie, blooming, straight, and tall,
And lang has had my heart in thrall;
And ay it charms my very saul,
  The kind love that's in her e'e.

3

artful
glance
sharp; eyes

A thief sae pawkie is my Jean,
To steal a blink by a' unseen!
But gleg as light are lover's een,
  When kind love is in the e'e.

4

It may escape the courtly sparks,
It may escape the learned clerks;
But well the watching lover marks
  The kind love that's in her e'e.

wot;
who

O, WAT YE WHA THAT LO'ES ME

TUNE: *Morag*

CHORUS

O, that's the lassie o' my heart,
  My lassie ever dearer!
O, that's the queen o' womankind,
  And ne'er a ane to peer her!

1

O, wat ye wha that lo'es me,
  And has my heart a keeping?
O, sweet is she that lo'es me
  As dews o' summer weeping,
  In tears the rosebuds steeping!

2

If thou shalt meet a lassie
  In grace and beauty charming,
That e'en thy chosen lassie,
  Erewhile thy breast sae warming,
such
  Had ne'er sic powers alarming:—

3

If thou hadst heard her talking
  (And thy attention's plighted),
That ilka body talking   every
  But her by thee is slighted,   Except
  And thou art all-delighted:—

4

If thou hast met this fair one,
  When frae her thou hast parted,
If every other fair one
  But her thou hast deserted,
  And thou art broken-hearted:—

SCOTS, WHA HAE

TUNE: *Hey, tutti taitie*

1

Scots, wha hae wi' Wallace bled,
Scots, wham Bruce has aften led,
Welcome to your gory bed
        Or to victorie!

2

Now's the day, and now's the hour:
See the front o' battle lour,
See approach proud Edward's power—
        Chains and slaverie!

3

Wha will be a traitor knave?
Wha can fill a coward's grave?
Wha sae base as be a slave?—
        Let him turn, and flee!

4

Wha for Scotland's King and Law
Freedom's sword will strongly draw,
Freeman stand or freeman fa',
        Let him follow me!

5

By Oppression's woes and pains,
By your sons in servile chains,
We will drain our dearest veins
        But they shall be free!

6

Lay the proud usurpers low!
Tyrants fall in every foe!
Liberty's in every blow!
        Let us do, or die!

THEIR GROVES O' SWEET MYRTLE

TUNE: *Humours of Glen*

1

Their groves o' sweet myrtle let foreign lands reckon,
    Where bright-beaming summers exalt the perfume!
ferns   Far dearer to me yon lone glen o' green breckan,
brook   Wi' the burn stealing under the lang, yellow broom;
Far dearer to me are yon humble broom bowers,
wild daisy   Where the blue-bell and gowan lurk lowly, unseen;
For there, lightly tripping among the wild flowers,
    A-list'ning the linnet, aft wanders my Jean.

2

Tho' rich is the breeze in their gay, sunny vallies,
    And cauld Caledonia's blast on the wave,
Their sweet-scented woodlands that skirt the proud
    palace,
    What are they?—The haunt of the tyrant and
    slave!
The slave's spicy forests and gold-bubbling fountains
    The brave Caledonian views wi' disdain:
He wanders as free as the winds of his mountains,
    Save Love's willing fetters—the chains o' his Jean.

THINE AM I

TUNE: *The Quaker's Wife*

1

Thine am I, my faithful Fair,
  Thine my lovely Nancy!
Ev'ry pulse along my veins,
  Ev'ry roving fancy!
To thy bosom lay my heart
  There to throb and languish.
Tho' despair had wrung its core,
  That would heal its anguish.

2

Take away those rosy lips
  Rich with balmy treasure!
Turn away thine eyes of love,
  Lest I die with pleasure!
What is life when wanting love?
  Night without a morning!
Love the cloudless summer's sun,
  Nature gay adorning.

THOU HAST LEFT ME EVER, JAMIE

TUNE: *Fee him, father, fee him*

1

Thou hast left me ever, Jamie,
  Thou hast left me ever!
Thou hast left me ever, Jamie,
  Thou hast left me ever!
Aften hast thou vow'd that Death
  Only should us sever;
Now thou'st left thy lass for ay—
  I maun see thee never, Jamie,   must
  I'll see thee never!

2

Thou hast me forsaken, Jamie,
  Thou hast me forsaken!

Thou hast me forsaken, Jamie,
    Thou hast me forsaken!
Thou canst love another jo,
    While my heart is breaking;
eyes   Soon my weary een I'll close,
more   Never mair to waken, Jamie,
        Never mair to waken!

HIGHLAND MARY

TUNE: *Lady Catherine Ogle*

I

Ye banks and braes and streams around
    The castle o' Montgomery,
Green be your woods, and fair your flowers,
turbid   Your waters never drumlie!
unfold   There Summer first unfald her robes,
    And there the langest tarry!
For there I took the last fareweel
    O' my sweet Highland Mary!

2

birch   How sweetly bloom'd the gay, green birk,
    How rich the hawthorn's blossom,
As underneath their fragrant shade
    I clasp'd her to my bosom!
The golden hours on angel wings
    Flew o'er me and my dearie:
For dear to me as light and life
    Was my sweet Highland Mary.

3

Wi' monie a vow and lock'd embrace
    Our parting was fu' tender;
And, pledging aft to meet again,
    We tore oursels asunder.
But O, fell Death's untimely frost,
    That nipt my flower sae early!
Now green's the sod, and cauld's the clay,
    That wraps my Highland Mary!

4

O, pale, pale now, those rosy lips
    I aft hae kiss'd sae fondly;
And clos'd for ay, the sparkling glance
    That dwalt on me sae kindly;
And mouldering now in silent dust
    That heart that lo'ed me dearly!
But still within my bosom's core
    Shall live my Highland Mary.

MY CHLORIS, MARK

TUNE: *On the Cold Ground*

1

My Chloris, mark how green the groves,
    The primrose banks how fair!
The balmy gales awake the flowers,
    And wave thy flaxen hair

2

The lav'rock shuns the palace gay,   lark
    And o'er the cottage sings:
For Nature smiles as sweet, I ween,
    To shepherds as to kings.

3

Let minstrels sweep the skilfu' string
    In lordly, lighted ha':   hall
The shepherd stops his simple reed,
    Blythe in the birken shaw.   birch wood

4

The princely revel may survey
    Our rustic dance wi' scorn;
But are their hearts as light as ours
    Beneath the milk-white thorn?

5

The shepherd in the flowery glen
    In shepherd's phrase will woo:
The courtier tells a finer tale—
    But is his heart as true?

6

Here wild-wood flowers I've pu'd, to deck
That spotless breast o' thine:
The courtier's gems may witness love—
But 'tis na love like mine!

FAIREST MAID ON DEVON BANKS

TUNE: *Rothiemurchie's Rant*

CHORUS

Fairest maid on Devon banks,
Crystal Devon, winding Devon,
Wilt thou lay that frown aside,
And smile as thou wert wont to do?

1

Full well thou know'st I love thee dear—
Couldst thou to malice lend an ear!
O, did not Love exclaim:—' Forbear,
Nor use a faithful lover so!'

2

Then come, thou fairest of the fair,
Those wonted smiles, O, let me share,
And by thy beauteous self I swear
No love but thine my heart shall know!

LASSIE WI' THE LINT-WHITE LOCKS

TUNE: *Rothiemurchie's Rant*

CHORUS

Lassie wi' the lint-white locks,
Bonie lassie, artless lassie,
Wilt thou wi' me tent the flocks—
Wilt thou be my dearie, O?

tend

1

clothes

Now Nature cleeds the flowery lea,
And a' is young and sweet like thee,
O, wilt thou share its joys wi' me,
And say thou'lt be my dearie, O?

2

The primrose bank, the wimpling burn,   *meandering*
The cuckoo on the milk-white thorn,
The wanton lambs at early morn
   Shall welcome thee, my dearie, O.

3

And when the welcome simmer shower
Has cheer'd ilk drooping little flower,   *each*
We'll to the breathing woodbine-bower
   At sultry noon, my dearie, O.

4

When Cynthia lights wi' silver ray
The weary shearer's hameward way,   *reaper's*
Thro' yellow waving fields we'll stray,
   And talk o' love, my dearie, O.

5

And when the howling wintry blast
Disturbs my lassie's midnight rest,
Enclaspèd to my faithfu' breast,
   I'll comfort thee, my dearie, O.

LONG, LONG THE NIGHT

TUNE: *Ay, waukin, O*

CHORUS

Long, long the night,
   Heavy comes the morrow,
While my soul's delight
   Is on her bed of sorrow.

1

Can I cease to care,
   Can I cease to languish,
While my darling fair
   Is on the couch of anguish!

2

Ev'ry hope is fled,
   Ev'ry fear is terror:
Slumber ev'n I dread,
   Ev'ry dream is horror.

3

Hear me, Powers Divine:
O, in pity, hear me!
Take aught else of mine,
But my Chloris spare me!

LOGAN WATER

TUNE: (*As Title*)

1

O Logan, sweetly didst thou glide
That day I was my Willie's bride,
And years sin syne hae o'er us run
Like Logan to the simmer sun.
But now thy flowery banks appear
Like drumlie winter, dark and drear,
While my dear lad maun face his faes
Far, far frae me and Logan braes.

since then
have

dull
must
slopes

2

Again the merry month of May
Has made our hills and vallies gay;
The birds rejoice in leafy bowers,
The bees hum round the breathing flowers;
Blythe Morning lifts his rosy eye,
And Evening's tears are tears o' joy:
My soul delightless a' surveys,
While Willie's far frae Logan braes.

3

Within yon milk-white hawthorn bush,
Amang her nestlings sits the thrush:
Her faithfu' mate will share her toil,
Or wi' his song her cares beguile.
But I wi' my sweet nurslings here,
Nae mate to help, nae mate to cheer,
Pass widow'd nights and joyless days,
While Willie's far frae Logan braes.

4

O, wae upon you, Men o' State,
That brethren rouse in deadly hate!

As ye make monie a fond heart mourn,
Sae may it on your heads return!
Ye mindna 'mid your cruel joys   remember
The widow's tears, the orphan's cries;   not
But soon may peace bring happy days,
And Willie hame to Logan braes!

YON ROSY BRIER

TUNE: *I wish my love were in a mire*

I

O, bonie was yon rosy brier   yonder
   That blooms sae far frae haunt o' man,
And bonie she—and ah, how dear!—
   It shaded frae the e'enin sun!

2

Yon rosebuds in the morning dew,
   How pure among the leaves sae green!
But purer was the lover's vow
   They witnessed in their shade yestreen.   last night

3

All in its rude and prickly bower,
   That crimson rose how sweet and fair!
But love is far a sweeter flower
   Amid life's thorny path o' care.

4

The pathless wild and wimpling burn,   winding
   Wi' Chloris in my arms, be mine,
And I the warld nor wish nor scorn—
   Its joys and griefs alike resign!

WHERE ARE THE JOYS

TUNE: *Saw ye my father?*

I

Where are the joys I hae met in the morning,
   That danc'd to the lark's early sang?
Where is the peace that awaited my wand'ring
   At e'ening the wild-woods amang?

2

Nae mair a-winding the course o' yon river
　　And marking sweet flowerets sae fair,
Nae mair I trace the light footsteps o' Pleasure,
　　But Sorrow and sad-sighing Care.

3

Is it that Summer's forsaken our vallies,
　　And grim, surly Winter is near?
No, no, the bees humming round the gay roses
　　Proclaim it the pride o' the year.

4

Fain wad I hide what I fear to discover,
　　Yet lang, lang, too well hae I known:
A' that has causèd the wreck in my bosom
　　Is Jenny, fair Jenny alone!

5

Time cannot aid me, my griefs are immortal,
　　Not Hope dare a comfort bestow.
Come then, enamor'd and fond of my anguish,
　　Enjoyment I'll seek in my woe!

BEHOLD THE HOUR

TUNE: *Oran gaoil*

1

Behold the hour, the boat arrive!
　　Thou goest, the darling of my heart!
Sever'd from thee, can I survive?
　　But Fate has will'd and we must part.
I'll often greet the surging swell,
　　Yon distant isle will often hail:—
' E'en here I took the last farewell;
　　There, latest mark'd her vanish'd sail.'

2

Along the solitary shore,
　　While flitting sea-fowl round me cry,
Across the rolling, dashing roar,
　　I'll westward turn my wistful eye:—

'Happy, thou Indian grove,' I'll say,
  'Where now my Nancy's path may be!
While thro' thy sweets she loves to stray,
  O, tell me, does she muse on me?'

FORLORN MY LOVE

TUNE: *Let me in this ae night*

CHORUS

O, wert thou, love, but near me,
But near, near, near me,
How kindly thou would cheer me,
  And mingle sighs with mine, love!

1

Forlorn my love, no comfort near,
Far, far from thee I wander here;
Far, far from thee, the fate severe,
  At which I most repine, love.

2

Around me scowls a wintry sky,
Blasting each bud of hope and joy,
And shelter, shade, nor home have I
  Save in these arms of thine, love.

3

Cold, alter'd friendship's cruel part,
To poison Fortune's ruthless dart!
Let me not break thy faithful heart,
  And say that fate is mine, love!

4

But, dreary tho' the moments fleet,
O, let me think we yet shall meet!
That only ray of solace sweet
  Can on thy Chloris shine, love!

Drive; ewes;
knolls

CA' THE YOWES TO THE KNOWES

TUNE: *Ca' the Yowes*

Second Set

CHORUS

Ca' the yowes to the knowes,
Ca' them where the heather grows,
brooklet
runs
Ca' them where the burnie rowes,
My bonie dearie.

1

Hark, the mavis' e'ening sang
Sounding Clouden's woods amang,
go
Then a-faulding let us gang,
My bonie dearie.

2

We'll gae down by Clouden side,
Thro' the hazels, spreading wide
O'er the waves that sweetly glide
To the moon sae clearly.

3

Yonder Clouden's silent towers,
Where, at moonshine's midnight hours,
O'er the dewy bending flowers
Fairies dance sae cheery.

4

hobgoblin
Ghaist nor bogle shalt thou fear—
Thou'rt to Love and Heav'n sae dear
Nocht of ill may come thee near,
My bonie dearie.

5

Fair and lovely as thou art,
stolen
Thou hast stown my very heart;
I can die—but canna part,
My bonie dearie.

HOW CAN MY POOR HEART

TUNE: *O'er the hills and far away*

1

How can my poor heart be glad
When absent from my sailor lad?
How can I the thought forego—
He's on the seas to meet the foe?
Let me wander, let me rove,
Still my heart is with my love.
Nightly dreams and thoughts by day
Are with him that's far away.
  On the seas and far away,
   On stormy seas and far away—
   Nightly dreams and thoughts by day,
   Are ay with him that's far away.

2

When in summer noon I faint,
As weary flocks around me pant,
Haply in this scorching sun
My sailor's thund'ring at his gun.
Bullets, spare my only joy!
Bullets, spare my darling boy!
Fate, do with me what you may,
Spare but him that's far away!
  On the seas and far away,
   On stormy seas and far away—
   Fate, do with me what you may,
   Spare but him that's far away!

3

At the starless, midnight hour
When Winter rules with boundless power,
As the storms the forests tear,
And thunders rend the howling air,
Listening to the doubling roar
Surging on the rocky shore,
All I can—I weep and pray
For his weal that's far away.

On the seas and far away,
On stormy seas and far away,
All I can—I weep and pray
For his weal that's far away.

4

Peace, thy olive wand extend
And bid wild War his ravage end;
Man with brother man to meet,
And as brother kindly greet!
Then may Heaven with prosperous gales
Fill my sailor's welcome sails,
To my arms their charge convey,
My dear lad that's far away!
   On the seas and far away,
   On stormy seas and far away,
   To my arms their charge convey,
   My dear lad that's far away!

IS THERE FOR HONEST POVERTY

TUNE: *For a' that*

1

Is there for honest poverty
   That hings his head, an' a' that?   *hings* — hangs
The coward slave, we pass him by—
   We dare be poor for a' that!
For a' that, an' a' that,
   Our toils obscure, an' a' that,
The rank is but the guinea's stamp,
   The man's the gowd for a' that.   *gowd* — gold

2

What though on hamely fare we dine,
   Wear hoddin grey, an' a' that?   *hoddin* — coarse grey woollen
Gie fools their silks, and knaves their wine—
   A man's a man for a' that.
For a' that, an' a' that,
   Their tinsel show, an' a' that,
The honest man, tho' e'er sae poor,
   Is king o' men for a' that.

3

Ye see yon birkie ca'd ' a lord,'   fellow;
  Wha struts, an' stares, an' a' that?   called
Tho' hundreds worship at his word,
  He's but a cuif for a' that.   dolt
For a' that, an' a' that,
  His ribband, star, an' a' that,
The man o' independent mind,
  He looks an' laughs at a' that.

4

A prince can mak a belted knight,
  A marquis, duke, an' a' that!
But an honest man's aboon his might—   above
  Guid faith, he mauna fa' that!   must not
For a' that, an' a' that,
  Their dignities, an' a' that,
The pith o' sense an' pride o' worth
  Are higher rank than a' that.

5

Then let us pray that come it may
  (As come it will for a' that)
That Sense and Worth o'er a' the earth
  Shall bear the gree an' a' that!   have the
For a' that, an' a' that,   first place
  It's comin yet for a' that,
That man to man the world o'er
  Shall brithers be for a' that.

MARK YONDER POMP

TUNE: *Deil tak the wars*

1

Mark yonder pomp of costly fashion
  Round the wealthy, titled bride!
But, when compar'd with real passion,
  Poor is all that princely pride.

2

What are the showy treasures?
What are the noisy pleasures?
The gay, gaudy glare of vanity and art!

The polish'd jewel's blaze
May draw the wond'ring gaze,
And courtly grandeur bright
The fancy may delight,
But never, never can come near the heart!

3

But did you see my dearest Chloris
In simplicity's array,
Lovely as yonder sweet opening flower is,
Shrinking from the gaze of day:

4

O, then, the heart alarming
And all resistless charming,
In love's delightful fetters she chains the willing
soul!
Ambition would disown
The world's imperial crown!
Ev'n Avarice would deny
His worshipp'd deity,
And feel thro' every vein love's raptures roll!

O, LET ME IN THIS AE NIGHT

one

TUNE: *Will ye lend me your loom, lass?*

CHORUS

O, let me in this ae night,
This ae, ae, ae night!
O, let me in this ae night,
And rise, and let me in!

1

awake;
know

foot

O lassie, are ye sleepin yet,
Or are ye waukin, I wad wit?
For Love has bound me hand an' fit,
And I would fain be in, jo.

2

wet

shines

Thou hear'st the winter wind an' weet:
Nae star blinks thro' the driving sleet!
Tak pity on my weary feet,
And shield me frae the rain, jo.

3

The bitter blast that round me blaws,
Unheeded howls, unheeded fa's:
The cauldness o' thy heart's the cause
   Of a' my care and pine, jo.

HER ANSWER

CHORUS

I tell you now this ae night,
This ae, ae, ae night,
And ance for a' this ae night,
I winna let ye in, jo.   will not

I

O, tell me na o' wind an' rain,   not
Upbraid na me wi' cauld disdain,
Gae back the gate ye cam again,   way
   I winna let ye in, jo!

2

The snellest blast at mirkest hours,   keenest;
                             darkest
That round the pathless wand'rer pours
Is nocht to what poor she endures,   nothing
   That's trusted faithless man, jo.

3

The sweetest flower that deck'd the mead,
Now trodden like the vilest weed—
Let simple maid the lesson read!
   The weird may be her ain, jo.   fate: own

4

The bird that charm'd his summer day,
And now the cruel fowler's prey,
Let that to witless woman say:—
   'The gratefu' heart of man,' jo.

O PHILLY, HAPPY BE THAT DAY

TUNE: *The Sow's Tail to Geordie*

CHORUS

gold
do not

HE AND SHE. *For a' the joys that gowd can gie,*
I dinna care a single flie!
The $\left\{ \begin{matrix} lad \\ lass \end{matrix} \right\}$ *I love's the* $\left\{ \begin{matrix} lad \\ lass \end{matrix} \right\}$ *for me,*
And that's my ain dear $\left\{ \begin{matrix} Willy \\ Philly \end{matrix} \right\}$

I

HE. O Philly, happy be that day
When, roving thro' the gather'd hay,
My youthfu' heart was stown away,
And by thy charms, my Philly!

stolen

SHE. O Willy, ay I bless the grove
Where first I own'd my maiden love,
Whilst thou did pledge the Powers above
To be my ain dear Willy.

2

HE. As songsters of the early year
Are ilka day mair sweet to hear,
So ilka day to me mair dear
And charming is my Philly.

each
succeeding

SHE. As on the brier the budding rose
Still richer breathes, and fairer blows,
So in my tender bosom grows
The love I bear my Willy.

3

HE. The milder sun and bluer sky,
That crown my harvest cares wi' joy,
Were ne'er sae welcome to my eye
As is a sight o' Philly.

SHE. The little swallow's wanton wing,
Tho' wafting o'er the flowery spring,
Did ne'er to me sic tidings bring
As meeting o' my Willy.

such

4

HE. The bee, that thro' the sunny hour
    Sips nectar in the op'ning flower,
    Compar'd wi' my delight is poor
      Upon the lips o' Philly.
SHE. The woodbine in the dewy weet,   *wet*
    When ev'ning shades in silence meet,
    Is nocht sae fragrant or sae sweet   *nothing*
      As is a kiss o' Willy.

5

HE. Let Fortune's wheel at random rin,
    And fools may tyne, and knaves may win!   *lose*
    My thoughts are a' bound up on ane,
      And that's my ain dear Philly.
SHE. What's a' the joys that gowd can gie?
    I dinna care a single flie!
    The lad I love's the lad for me,
      And that's my ain dear Willy.

O, WERE MY LOVE

TUNE: *Gin my love were yon red rose*

1

O, were my love yon lilac fair
    Wi' purple blossoms to the spring,
And I a bird to shelter there,
    When wearied on my little wing,
How I wad mourn when it was torn
    By Autumn wild and Winter rude!
But I wad sing on wanton wing,
    When youthfu' May its bloom renew'd.

2

O, gin my love were yon red rose,   *if*
    That grows upon the castle wa',
And I myself a drap o' dew
    Into her bonie breast to fa',
O, there, beyond expression blest,
    I'd feast on beauty a' the night,
Seal'd on her silk-saft faulds to rest,   *-soft; folds*
    Till fley'd awa by Phœbus' light!   *scared*

SLEEP'ST THOU

TUNE: *Deil tak the wars*

1

Sleep'st thou, or wauk'st thou, fairest creature?
  Rosy Morn now lifts his eye,
Numbering ilka bud, which Nature
  Waters wi' the tears o' joy.
  Now to the streaming fountain
  Or up the heathy mountain
The hart, hind, and roe, freely, wildly-wanton stray;
  In twining hazel bowers
  His lay the linnet pours;
  The laverock to the sky
  Ascends wi' sangs o' joy,
While the sun and thou arise to bless the day!

each

2

Phœbus, gilding the brow of morning,
  Banishes ilka darksome shade,
Nature gladdening and adorning:
  Such to me my lovely maid!
  When frae my Chloris parted,
  Sad, cheerless, broken-hearted,
The night's gloomy shades, cloudy, dark, o'ercast my
    sky;
  But when she charms my sight
  In pride of Beauty's light,
  When thro' my very heart
  Her beaming glories dart,
'Tis then—'tis then I wake to life and joy!

THERE WAS A LASS

TUNE: (*Unknown*)

1

There was a lass, and she was fair!
  At kirk and market to be seen
When a' our fairest maids were met,
  The fairest maid was bonie Jean.

2

And ay she wrought her country wark,
   And ay she sang sae merrilie:
The blythest bird upon the bush
   Had ne'er a lighter heart than she!

3

But hawks will rob the tender joys,
   That bless the little lintwhite's nest,   linnet's
And frost will blight the fairest flowers,
   And love will break the soundest rest.

4

Young Robie was the brawest lad,   handsomest
   The flower and pride of a' the glen,
And he had owsen, sheep, and kye,   oxen: kine
   And wanton naigies nine or ten.   horses

5

He gaed wi' Jeanie to the tryste,   went
   He danc'd wi' Jeanie on the down,
And, lang ere witless Jeanie wist,
   Her heart was tint, her peace was stown!   lost; stolen

6

As in the bosom of the stream
   The moon-beam dwells at dewy e'en,
So, trembling pure, was tender love
   Within the breast of bonie Jean.

7

And now she works her country's wark,
   And ay she sighs wi' care and pain,
Yet wist na what her ail might be,   knew not;
   Or what wad make her weel again.   complaint
      well

8

But did na Jeanie's heart loup light,   not: leap
   And did na joy blink in her e'e,   glance
As Robie tauld a tale o' love
   Ae e'enin on the lily lea?   One

9

While monie a bird sang sweet o' love,
   And monie a flower blooms o'er the dale,

His cheek to hers he aft did lay,
   And whisper'd thus his tender tale:—

10

' O Jeanie fair, I lo'e thee dear.
   O, canst thou think to fancy me?
Or wilt thou leave thy mammie's cot,
tend   And learn to tent the farms wi' me?

11

cowhouse ' At barn or byre thou shalt na drudge,
   Or naething else to trouble thee,
But stray amang the heather-bells,
   And tent the waving corn wi' me.'

12

Now what could artless Jeanie do?
   She had nae will to say him na!
At length she blush'd a sweet consent,
   And love was ay between them twa.

meadow-
ridge

THE LEA-RIG

TUNE: *My ain kind dearie, O*

1

When o'er the hill the eastern star
folding   Tells bughtin time is near, my jo,
And owsen frae the furrow'd field
dull   Return sae dowf and weary, O,
Down by the burn, where scented birks
   Wi' dew are hangin clear, my jo,
I'll meet thee on the lea-rig,
   My ain kind dearie, O.

2

At midnight hour in mirkest glen
frightened I'd rove, and ne'er be eerie, O,
went   If thro' that glen I gaed to thee,
   My ain kind dearie, O!
Altho' the night were ne'er sae wild,
   And I were ne'er sae weary, O,
I'll meet thee on the lea-rig,
   My ain kind dearie, O.

3

The hunter lo'es the morning sun
  To rouse the mountain deer, my jo;
At noon the fisher takes the glen
  Adown the burn to steer, my jo:
Gie me the hour o' gloamin grey—   twilight
  It maks my heart sae cheery, O,
To meet thee on the lea-rig,
  My ain kind dearie, O!

MY WIFE'S A WINSOME WEE THING

TUNE: *My wife's a wanton wee thing*

CHORUS

She is a winsome wee thing,
She is a handsome wee thing,
She is a lo'esome wee thing,
  This sweet wee wife o' mine!

1

I never saw a fairer,
I never lo'ed a dearer,
And neist my heart I'll wear her,   next
  For fear my jewel tine.   be lost

2

The warld's wrack, we share o't;
The warstle and the care o't,
Wi' her I'll blythely bear it,
  And think my lot divine.

MARY MORISON

TUNE: *Duncan Davison*

1

O Mary, at thy window be!
  It is the wish'd, the trysted hour.
Those smiles and glances let me see,
  That make the miser's treasure poor.

bear the
struggle

How blythely wad I bide the stoure,
A weary slave frae sun to sun,
  Could I the rich reward secure—
The lovely Mary Morison!

2

Last night

went

fine
the other

Yestreen, when to the trembling string
  The dance gaed thro' the lighted ha',
To thee my fancy took its wing,
  I sat, but neither heard or saw:
  Tho' this was fair, and that was braw,
And yon the toast of a' the town,
  I sigh'd and said amang them a':—
  'Ye are na Mary Morison!'

3

fault
give

cannot

O Mary, canst thou wreck his peace
  Wha for thy sake wad gladly die?
Or canst thou break that heart of his
  Whase only faut is loving thee?
  If love for love thou wilt na gie,
At least be pity to me shown:
  A thought ungentle canna be
The thought o' Mary Morison.

A RUINED FARMER

TUNE: *Go from my window, love, do*

1

The sun he is sunk in the west,
All creatures retirèd to rest,
While here I sit, all sore beset
      With sorrow, grief, and woe:
And it's O fickle Fortune, O!

2

The prosperous man is asleep,
Nor hears how the whirlwinds sweep;
But Misery and I must watch
      The surly tempests blow:
And it's O fickle Fortune, O!

3

There lies the dear Partner of my breast,
Her cares for a moment at rest!
Must I see thee, my youthful pride,
   Thus brought so very low?—
And it's O fickle Fortune, O!

4

There lie my sweet babies in her arms:
No anxious fear their little hearts alarms;
But for their sake my heart does ache,
   With many a bitter throe:
And it's O fickle Fortune, O!

5

I once was by Fortune carest,
I once could relieve the distress;
Now life's poor support, hardly earn'd,
   My fate will scarce bestow:
And it's O fickle Fortune, O!

6

No comfort, no comfort I have!
How welcome to me were the grave!
But then my wife and children dear—
   O, whither would they go?
And it's O fickle Fortune, O!

7

O, whither, O, whither shall I turn,
All friendless, forsaken, forlorn?
For in this world Rest or Peace
   I never more shall know:
And it's O fickle Fortune, O!

MONTGOMERIE'S PEGGY

TUNE: *Galla Water*

1

Altho' my bed were in yon muir,   yonder
 Amang the heather, in my plaidie,
Yet happy, happy would I be,
 Had I my dear Montgomerie's Peggy.

2

When o'er the hill beat surly storms,
  And winter nights were dark and rainy,
I'd seek some dell, and in my arms
  I'd shelter dear Montgomerie's Peggy.

3

Were I a Baron proud and high,
  And horse and servants waiting ready,
'twould give   Then a' 'twad gie o' joy to me—
sharing it   The sharin't with Montgomerie's Peggy.

THE LASS OF CESSNOCK BANKS

TUNE: *The Butcher Boy*

1

On Cessnock banks a lassie dwells,
  Could I describe her shape and mien;
Our lasses a' she far excels—
eyes   An' she has twa sparkling, rogueish een!

2

She's sweeter than the morning dawn,
  When rising Phœbus first is seen,
And dew-drops twinkle o'er the lawn—
  An' she has twa sparkling, rogueish een!

3

yonder   She's stately like yon youthful ash,
slopes   That grows the cowslip braes between,
And drinks the stream with vigour fresh—
  An' she has twa sparkling, rogueish een!

4

She's spotless like the flow'ring thorn
  With flow'rs so white and leaves so green,
When purest in the dewy morn—
  An' she has twa sparkling, rogueish een!

5

Her looks are like the vernal May,
  When ev'ning Phœbus shines serene,
While birds rejoice on every spray—
  An' she has twa sparkling, rogueish een!

6

Her hair is like the curling mist,
   That climbs the mountain-sides at e'en,
When flow'r-reviving rains are past—
   An' she has twa sparkling, rogueish een!

7

Her forehead's like the show'ry bow,
   When gleaming sunbeams intervene,
And gild the distant mountain's brow—
   An' she has twa sparkling, rogueish een!

8

Her cheeks are like yon crimson gem,
   The pride of all the flowery scene,
Just opening on its thorny stem—
   An' she has twa sparkling, rogueish een!

9

Her teeth are like the nightly snow,
   When pale the morning rises keen,
While hid the murm'ring streamlets flow—
   An' she has twa sparkling, rogueish een!

10

Her lips are like yon cherries ripe,
   That sunny walls from Boreas screen:
They tempt the taste and charm the sight—
   An' she has twa sparkling, rogueish een!

11

Her breath is like the fragrant breeze,
   That gently stirs the blossom'd bean,
When Phœbus sinks behind the seas—
   An' she has twa sparkling, rogueish een!

12

Her voice is like the ev'ning thrush,
   That sings on Cessnock banks unseen,
While his mate sits nestling in the bush—
   An' she has twa sparkling, rogueish een!

13

But it's not her air, her form, her face,
   Tho' matching Beauty's fabled Queen:
'Tis the mind that shines in ev'ry grace—
   An' chiefly in her rogueish een!

THO' FICKLE FORTUNE

TUNE: *I dream'd I lay*

1

Tho' fickle Fortune has deceived me
  (She promis'd fair, and perform'd but ill),
Of mistress, friends, and wealth bereaved me,
  Yet I bear a heart shall support me still.

2

I'll act with prudence as far as I'm able;
  But if success I must never find,
Then come, Misfortune, I bid thee welcome—
  I'll meet thee with an undaunted mind!

RAGING FORTUNE

TUNE: *(Unknown)*

1

O, raging Fortune's withering blast
  Has laid my leaf full low!
O, raging Fortune's withering blast
  Has laid my leaf full low!

2

My stem was fair, my bud was green,
  My blossom sweet did blow;
The dew fell fresh, the sun rose mild,
  And made my branches grow.

3

But luckless Fortune's northern storms
  Laid a' my blossoms low!
But luckless Fortune's northern storms
  Laid a' my blossoms low!

MY FATHER WAS A FARMER

TUNE: *The Weaver and his Shuttle*

1

My father was a farmer upon the Carrick border, O,
And carefully he bred me in decency and order, O.
He bade me act a manly part, though I had ne'er a
    farthing, O,
For without an honest, manly heart no man was
    worth regarding, O.

2

Then out into the world my course I did determine,
    O:
Tho' to be rich was not my wish, yet to be great was
    charming, O.
My talents they were not the worst, nor yet my
    education, O—
Resolv'd was I at least to try to mend my situation,
    O.

3

In many a way and vain essay I courted Fortune's
    favour, O:
Some cause unseen still stept between to frustrate
    each endeavour, O.
Sometimes by foes I was o'erpower'd, sometimes by
    friends forsaken, O,
And when my hope was at the top, I still was worst
    mistaken, O.

4

Then sore harass'd, and tir'd at last with Fortune's
    vain delusion, O,
I dropt my schemes like idle dreams, and came to
    this conclusion, O:—
The past was bad, and the future hid; its good or ill
    untrièd, O,
But the present hour was in my pow'r, and so I
    would enjoy it, O.

5

No help, nor hope, nor view had I, nor person to
    befriend me, O;
So I must toil, and sweat, and broil, and labour to
    sustain me, O!
To plough and sow, to reap and mow, my father bred
    me early, O:
For one, he said, to labour bred was a match for
    Fortune fairly, O.

6

Thus all obscure, unknown, and poor, thro' life I'm
    doom'd to wander, O,
Till down my weary bones I lay in everlasting
    slumber, O.
No view nor care, but shun whate'er might breed me
    pain or sorrow, O,
I live to-day as well's I may, regardless of to-morrow,
    O!

7

But, cheerful still, I am as well as a monarch in a
    palace, O,
Tho' Fortune's frown still hunts me down, with all
    her wonted malice, O:
I make indeed my daily bread, but ne'er can make
    it farther, O,
But, as daily bread is all I need, I do not much
    regard her, O.

8

When sometimes by my labour I earn a little money,
    O,
Some unforeseen misfortune comes gen'rally upon
    me, O:
Mischance, mistake, or by neglect, or my good-
    natur'd folly, O—
But, come what will, I've sworn it still, I'll ne'er be
    melancholy, O.

9

All you who follow wealth and power with unremit-
    ting ardour, O,
The more in this you look for bliss, you leave your
    view the farther, O.

Had you the wealth Potosi boasts, or nations to
  adore you, O,
A cheerful, honest-hearted clown I will prefer before
  you, O!

O, LEAVE NOVÉLS

TUNE: *Donald Blue*

1

O, leave novéls, ye Mauchline belles—
  Ye're safer at your spinning-wheel!
Such witching books are baited hooks
  For rakish rooks like Rob Mossgiel.

2

Your fine *Tom Jones* and *Grandisons*
  They make your youthful fancies reel!
They heat your brains, and fire your veins,
  And then you're prey for Rob Mossgiel.

3

Beware a tongue that's smoothly hung,
  A heart that warmly seems to feel!
That feeling heart but acts a part—
  'Tis rakish art in Rob Mossgiel.

4

The frank address, the soft caress
  Are worse than poisoned darts of steel:
The frank address and politesse
  Are all finesse in Rob Mossgiel.

THE MAUCHLINE LADY

TUNE: *I had a horse, and I had nae mair*

1

When first I came to Stewart Kyle,
  My mind it was na steady:
Where'er I gaed, where'er I rade,   went; rode
  A mistress still I had ay.

2

But when I came roun' by Mauchline toun,
  Not dreadin anybody,
My heart was caught, before I thought,
  And by a Mauchline lady.

ONE NIGHT AS I DID WANDER

TUNE: *John Anderson my jo*

One night as I did wander,
  When corn begins to shoot,
I sat me down to ponder
  Upon an auld tree-root:
Auld Ayr ran by before me,
  And bicker'd to the seas;
A cushat crooded o'er me,
  That echoed through the trees.

past
hastened
cooed

THERE WAS A LAD

TUNE: *Dainty Davie*

CHORUS

Robin was a rovin boy,
  Rantin, rovin, rantin, rovin,
Robin was a rovin boy,
  Rantin, rovin Robin!

roystering

1

There was a lad was born in Kyle,
But whatna day o' whatna style,
I doubt it's hardly worth the while
  To be sae nice wi' Robin.

what

2

Our monarch's hindmost year but ane
Was five-and-twenty days begun,
'Twas then a blast o' Janwar' win'
  Blew hansel in on Robin.

one

January
wind

3

The gossip keekit in his loof,   glanced;
                                                         palm
Quo' scho:—' Wha lives will see the proof,   Quoth she
This waly boy will be nae coof: thumping;
                                                         dolt
    I think we'll ca' him Robin.

4

' He'll hae misfortunes great an' sma',
But ay a heart aboon them a'.   above
He'll be a credit till us a':   to
    We'll a' be proud o' Robin!

5

' But sure as three times three mak nine,
I see by ilka score and line,   every
                                                        kind
This chap will dearly like our kin',   Commend
                                                        me to
    So leeze me on thee, Robin!

6

' Guid faith,' quo' scho, ' I doubt you gar   make
The bonie lasses lie aspar;   aspread
But twenty fauts ye may hae waur—   faults; worse
    So blessins on thee, Robin! '

WILL YE GO TO THE INDIES, MY MARY

TUNE: *Ewe-bughts Marion*

1

Will ye go to the Indies, my Mary,
    And leave auld Scotia's shore?
Will ye go to the Indies, my Mary,
    Across th' Atlantic roar?

2

O, sweet grows the lime and the orange,
    And the apple on the pine;
But a' the charms o' the Indies
    Can never equal thine.

3

I hae sworn by the Heavens to my Mary,
    I hae sworn by the Heavens to be true,
And sae may the Heavens forget me,
    When I forget my vow!

4

O, plight me your faith, my Mary,
  And plight me your lily-white hand!
O, plight me your faith, my Mary,
  Before I leave Scotia's strand!

5

We hae plighted our troth, my Mary,
  In mutual affection to join;
And curst be the cause that shall part us!
  The hour and the moment o' time!

HER FLOWING LOCKS

TUNE: *(Unknown)*

1

Her flowing locks, the raven's wing,
hang   Adown her neck and bosom hing.
How sweet unto that breast to cling,
  And round that neck entwine her!

2

wet   Her lips are roses wat wi' dew—
O, what a feast, her bonie mou!
Her cheeks a mair celestial hue,
  A crimson still diviner!

THE LASS O' BALLOCHMYLE

TUNE: *Ettrick Banks*

1

'Twas even: the dewy fields were green,
hung   On every blade the pearls hang,
The zephyr wanton'd round the bean,
  And bore its fragrant sweets alang,
In ev'ry glen the mavis sang,
All Nature list'ning seem'd the while,
  Except where greenwood echoes rang
heights   Amang the braes o' Ballochmyle.

2

With careless step I onward stray'd,
  My heart rejoic'd in Nature's joy,
When, musing in a lonely glade,
  A maiden fair I chanc'd to spy.
  Her look was like the Morning's eye,
Her air like Nature's vernal smile.
  Perfection whisper'd, passing by:—
' Behold the lass o' Ballochmyle! '

3

Fair is the morn in flowery May,
  And sweet is night in autumn mild,
When roving thro' the garden gay,
  Or wand'ring in the lonely wild;
  But woman, Nature's darling child—
There all her charms she does compile!
  Even there her other works are foil'd
By the bonie lass o' Ballochmyle.

4

O, had she been a country maid,
  And I the happy country swain,
Tho' shelter'd in the lowest shed
  That ever rose on Scotia's plain,
  Thro' weary winter's wind and rain
With joy, with rapture, I would toil,
  And nightly to my bosom strain
The bonie lass o' Ballochmyle!

5

Then Pride might climb the slipp'ry steep,
  Where fame and honours lofty shine,
And thirst of gold might tempt the deep,
  Or downward seek the Indian mine!
  Give me the cot below the pine,
To tend the flocks or till the soil,
  And ev'ry day have joys divine
With the bonie lass o' Ballochmyle.

THE NIGHT WAS STILL

TUNE: (*Unknown*)

1

The night was still, and o'er the hill
    The moon shone on the castle wa',
hung The mavis sang, while dew-drops hang
    Around her on the castle wa';

2

evening; Sae merrily they danc'd the ring
crow Frae eenin' till the cock did craw,
refrain; And ay the o'erword o' the spring
tune Was:—' Irvine's bairns are bonie a'! '

MASONIC SONG

TUNE: *Over the water to Charlie*

1

Ye sons of old Killie, assembled by Willie
    To follow the noble vocation,
Your thrifty old mother has scarce such another
    To sit in that honorèd station!
I've little to say, but only to pray
    (As praying's the *ton* of your fashion).
A prayer from the Muse you well may excuse
    ('Tis seldom her favourite passion):—

2

' Ye Powers who preside o'er the wind and the tide,
    Who markèd each element's border,
Who formèd this frame with beneficent aim,
    Whose sovereign statute is order,
Within this dear mansion may wayward Contention
    Or witherèd Envy ne'er enter!
May Secrecy round be the mystical bound,
    And brotherly Love be the centre! '

THE BONIE MOOR-HEN

TUNE: *The Tailor's March*

CHORUS

I rede you, beware at the hunting, young men!   advise
I rede you, beware at the hunting, young men!
Take some on the wing, and some as they spring,
But cannily steal on a bonie moor-hen.   cautiously

1

The heather was blooming, the meadows were mawn,   mown
Our lads gaed a-hunting ae day at the dawn,   went; one
O'er moors and o'er mosses and monie a glen:
At length they discovered a bonie moor-hen.

2

Sweet-brushing the dew from the brown heather bells,
Her colours betray'd her on yon mossy fells!
Her plumage outlustred the pride o' the spring,
And O, as she wanton'd sae gay on the wing.

3

Auld Phœbus himsel', as he peep'd o'er the hill,
In spite at her plumage he tryèd his skill:
He level'd his rays where she bask'd on the brae—   height
His rays were outshone, and but mark'd where she
   lay!

4

They hunted the valley, they hunted the hill,
The best of our lads wi' the best o' their skill;
But still as the fairest she sat in their sight,
Then, whirr! she was over, a mile at a flight.

5

But by cam a retret ohon and alas!   reaver
A slee cunning loun wi' a firelock o' brass.
The brass sae did glitter, it dazzled her eyes,
And now in his budget he boasts o' the prize.

HERE'S A BOTTLE

There's nane that's blest of human kind
But the cheerful and the gay, man.

TUNE: *(Unknown)*

I

Here's a bottle and an honest friend!
    What wad ye wish for mair, man?

more

Wha kens, before his life may end,
    What his share may be o' care, man?

2

Then catch the moments as they fly,
    And use them as ye ought, man!
Believe me, Happiness is shy,
    And comes not ay when sought, man!

THE BONIE LASS OF ALBANIE

TUNE: *Mary's Dream*

I

My heart is wae, and unco wae,
    To think upon the raging sea,

sad; ex-
tremely

That roars between her gardens green
    An' the bonie lass of Albanie.

2

This noble maid's of royal blood,
    That rulèd Albion's kingdoms three;
But O, alas for her bonie face!
    They hae wranged the lass of Albanie.

3

In the rolling tide of spreading Clyde
    There sits an isle of high degree,
And a town of fame, whose princely name
    Should grace the lass of Albanie.

4

But there is a youth, a witless youth,
    That fills the place where she should be;
We'll send him o'er to his native shore,
    And bring our ain sweet Albanie!

5

Alas the day, and woe the day!
    A false usurper wan the gree,   *gained the prize*
Who now commands the towers and lands,
    The royal right of Albanie.

6

We'll daily pray, we'll nightly pray,
    On bended knees most fervently,
That the time may come, with pipe and drum
    We'll welcome hame fair Albanie.

AMANG THE TREES

TUNE: *The king o' France he rade a race*

1

Amang the trees, where humming bees
    At buds and flowers were hinging, O,   *hanging*
Auld Caledon drew out her drone,
    And to her pipe was singing, O.
'Twas Pibroch, Sang, Strathspeys and Reels—
    She dirl'd them aff fu' clearly, O,   *rang*
When there cam' a yell o' foreign squeels,   *knocked;*
    That dang her tapsalteerie, O!   *head over heels*

2

Their capon craws an' queer ' ha, ha's,'
    They made our lugs grow eerie, O.   *ears; frightened*
The hungry bike did scrape and fyke,   *swarm; make ado*
    Till we were wae and weary, O.   *disgusted*
But a royal ghaist, wha ance was cas'd   *ghost*
    A prisoner aughteen year awa,   *eighteen*
He fir'd a Fiddler in the North,
    That dang them tapsalteerie, O!

THE CHEVALIER'S LAMENT

TUNE: *Captain O'Kane*

I

The small birds rejoice in the green leaves returning,
    The murmuring streamlet winds clear thro' the
        vale,
The primroses blow in the dews of the morning,
    And wild scatter'd cowslips bedeck the green dale:
      But what can give pleasure, or what can seem fair,
      When the lingering moments are number'd by
        care?
        No flow'rs gaily springing,
        Nor birds sweetly singing
    Can soothe the sad bosom of joyless despair!

2

The deed that I dar'd, could it merit their malice,
    A king and a father to place on his throne?
His right are these hills, and his right are those
      valleys,
    Where the wild beasts find shelter, tho' I can find
      none!
      But 'tis not my suff'rings thus wretched, for-
        lorn—
      My brave gallant friends, 'tis your ruin I mourn!
        Your faith prov'd so loyal
        In hot bloody trial,
    Alas! can I make it no better return?

Last night

YESTREEN I HAD A PINT O' WINE

TUNE: *Banks of Banna*

I

    Yestreen I had a pint o' wine,
nobody saw   A place where body saw na;
    Yestreen lay on this breast o' mine
      The gowden locks of Anna.

2

The hungry Jew in wilderness
 Rejoicing o'er his manna
Was naething to my hiney bliss   honey
 Upon the lips of Anna.

3

Ye monarchs take the East and West
 Frae Indus to Savannah:
Gie me within my straining grasp   Give
 The melting form of Anna!

4

There I'll despise Imperial charms,
 An Empress or Sultana,
While dying raptures in her arms
 I give and take wi' Anna!

5

Awa, thou flaunting God of Day!
 Awa, thou pale Diana!
Ilk Star, gae hide thy twinkling ray,   Each; go
 When I'm to meet my Anna!

6

Come, in thy raven plumage, Night
 (Sun, Moon, and Stars, withdrawn a'),
And bring an Angel-pen to write
 My transports with my Anna!

POSTSCRIPT

1

The Kirk an' State may join, and tell
 To do sic things I maunna: such;
The Kirk an' State may gae to Hell,   mustn't
 And I'll gae to my Anna.

2

She is the sunshine o' my e'e,
 To live but her I canna: without
Had I on earth but wishes three,
 The first should be my Anna.

SWEET ARE THE BANKS

TUNE: *Cambdelmore*

1

Sweet are the banks, the banks o' Doon,
  The spreading flowers are fair,
And everything is blythe and glad,
  But I am fu' o' care.
Thou'll break my heart, thou bonie bird,
  That sings upon the bough!
reminds   Thou minds me o' the happy days
  When my fause Luve was true.
Thou'll break my heart, thou bonie bird,
  That sings beside thy mate,
For sae I sat, and sae I sang,
  And wist na o' my fate!

2

Aft hae I rov'd by bonie Doon,
  To see the woodbine twine,
each   And ilka bird sang o' its luve,
  And sae did I o' mine.
plucked   Wi' lightsome heart I pu'd a rose
  Upon its thorny tree,
stole   But my fause luver staw my rose,
  And left the thorn wi' me.
Wi' lightsome heart I pu'd a rose
  Upon a morn in June,
And sae I flourish'd on the morn,
before   And sae was pu'd or noon.

YE FLOWERY BANKS

TUNE: *Cambdelmore*

1

Ye flowery banks o' bonie Doon,
  How can ye blume sae fair?
How can ye chant, ye little birds,
  And I sae fu' o' care?

2

Thou'll break my heart, thou bonie bird,
  That sings upon the bough:
Thou minds me o' the happy days   *reminds*
  When my fause Luve was true!

3

Thou'll break my heart, thou bonie bird,
  That sings beside thy mate:
For sae I sat, and sae I sang,
  And wist na o' my fate!

4

Aft hae I rov'd by bonie Doon
  To see the woodbine twine,
And ilka bird sang o' its luve,   *each*
  And sae did I o' mine.

5

Wi' lightsome heart I pu'd a rose
  Frae aff its thorny tree,   *From off*
And my fause luver staw my rose,   *stole*
  But left the thorn wi' me.

CALEDONIA

TUNE: *Caledonian Hunt's Delight*

I

There was on a time, but old Time was then young,
  That brave Caledonia, the chief of her line,
From some of your northern deities sprung
  (Who knows not that brave Caledonia's divine?).
From Tweed to the Orcades was her domain,
  To hunt, or to pasture, or do what she would.
Her heav'nly relations there fixed her reign,
  And pledged her their godheads to warrant it good.

2

A lambkin in peace but a lion in war,
  The pride of her kindred the heroine grew.
Her grandsire, old Odin, triumphantly swore:—
  'Whoe'er shall provoke thee, th' encounter shall
  rue!'

With tillage or pasture at times she would sport,
    To feed her fair flocks by her green rustling corn;
But chiefly the woods were her fav'rite resort,
    Her darling amusement the hounds and the horn.

3

Long quiet she reign'd, till thitherward steers
    A flight of bold eagles from Adria's strand.
Repeated, successive, for many long years,
    They darken'd the air, and they plunder'd the land.
Their pounces were murder, and horror their cry;
    They'd conquer'd and ravag'd a world beside.
She took to her hills, and her arrows let fly—
    The daring invaders, they fled or they died!

4

The Camelon savage disturb'd her repose,
    With tumult, disquiet, rebellion, and strife.
Provok'd beyond bearing, at last she arose,
    And robbed him at once of his hopes and his life.
The Anglian Lion, the terror of France,
    Oft, prowling, ensanguin'd the Tweed's silver flood,
But, taught by the bright Caledonian lance,
    He learnèd to fear in his own native wood.

5

The fell Harpy-Raven took wing from the north,
    The scourge of the seas, and the dread of the shore;
The wild Scandinavian Boar issued forth
    To wanton in carnage and wallow in gore;
O'er countries and kingdoms their fury prevail'd,
    No arts could appease them, no arms could repel;
But brave Caledonia in vain they assail'd,
    As Largs well can witness, and Loncartie tell.

6

Thus bold, independent, unconquer'd, and free,
    Her bright course of glory for ever shall run,
For brave Caledonia immortal must be,
    I'll prove it from Euclid as clear as the sun:—
Rectangle-triangle, the figure we'll chuse;
    The upright is Chance, and old Time is the base,
But brave Caledonia's the hypothenuse;
    Then, *ergo*, she'll match them, and match them
      always!

YOU'RE WELCOME, WILLIE STEWART

TUNE: *Ye're welcome, Charlie Stewart*

CHORUS

You're welcome, Willie Stewart!
You're welcome, Willie Stewart!
There's ne'er a flower that blooms in May,
That's half sae welcome's thou art!

1

Come, bumpers high! express your joy!
    The bowl we maun renew it—   must
The tappet hen, gae bring her ben,   go
    To welcome Willie Stewart!

2

May foes be strong, and friends be slack!
    Ilk action, may he rue it!   Each
May woman on him turn her back.
    That wrangs thee, Willie Stewart!   wrongs

WHEN FIRST I SAW

TUNE: *Maggy Lauder*

CHORUS

She's aye, aye sae blithe, sae gay,
She's aye sae blithe and cheerie,
She's aye sae bonie, blithe and gay,
O, gin I were her dearie!

1

When first I saw fair Jeanie's face,
    I couldna tell what ail'd me:
My heart went fluttering pit-a-pat,
    My een they almost fail'd me.
She's aye sae neat, sae trim, sae tight,
    All grace does round her hover!
Ae look depriv'd me o' my heart,
    And I became her lover.

2

Had I Dundas's whole estate,
  Or Hopetoun's wealth to shine in;
Did warlike laurels crown my brow,
  Or humbler bays entwining;
I'd lay them a' at Jeanie's feet,
  Could I but hope to move her,
And, prouder than a belted knight,
  I'd be my Jeanie's lover.

3

But sair I fear some happier swain,
  Has gain'd sweet Jeanie's favour.
If so, may every bliss be hers,
must   Though I maun never have her!
go   But gang she east, or gang she west,
  'Twixt Forth and Tweed all over,
While men have eyes, or ears, or taste,
  She'll always find a lover.

BEHOLD THE HOUR

First Set

TUNE: *Oran gaoil*

1

Behold the hour, the boat, arrive!
  My dearest Nancy, O, farewell!
Sever'd frae thee, can I survive,
  Frae thee whom I hae lov'd sae well?

2

Endless and deep shall be my grief,
  Nae ray of comfort shall I see,
But this most precious, dear belief,
  That thou wilt still remember me.

3

Along the solitary shore,
  Where flitting sea-fowl round me cry,
Across the rolling, dashing roar,
  I'll westward turn my wistful eye.

4

'Happy thou Indian grove,' I'll say,
  'Where now my Nancy's path shall be!
While thro' your sweets she holds her way,
  O, tell me, does she muse on me?'

HERE'S A HEALTH TO THEM
THAT'S AWA

TUNE: (*As Title*)

1

Here's a health to them that's awa,
  Here's a health to them that's awa!
And wha winna wish guid luck to our cause,   will not
  May never guid luck be their fa'!   lot
It's guid to be merry and wise,
  It's guid to be honest and true,
It's guid to support Caledonia's cause
  And bide by the buff and the blue.   stand

2

Here's a health to them that's awa,
  Here's a health to them that's awa!
Here's a health to Charlie, the chief o' the clan,
  Altho' that his band be sma'!
May Liberty meet wi' success,
  May Prudence protect her frae evil!
May tyrants and Tyranny tine i' the mist   be lost
  And wander their way to the Devil!

3

Here's a health to them that's awa,
  Here's a health to them that's awa!
Here's a health to Tammie, the Norlan' laddie,
  That lives at the lug o' the Law!
Here's freedom to them that wad read,
  Here's freedom to them that would write!
There's nane ever fear'd that the truth should be
  heard
  But they whom the truth would indite!   indict

4

Here's a health to them that's awa,
  An' here's to them that's awa!

Here's to Maitland and Wycombe! Let wha does na
    like 'em
  Be built in a hole in the wa'!
timber   Here's timmer that's red at the heart,
    Here's fruit that is sound at the core,
And may he that wad turn the buff and blue coat
    Be turn'd to the back o' the door!

5

  Here's a health to them that's awa,
    Here's a health to them that's awa!
gold   Here's Chieftain M'Leod, a chieftain worth gowd,
    Tho' bred amang mountains o' snaw!
  Here's friends on baith sides o' the Firth,
    And friends on baith sides o' the Tweed,
And wha wad betray old Albion's right,
    May they never eat of her bread!

AH, CHLORIS

TUNE: *Major Graham*

1

Ah, Chloris, since it may not be
  That thou of love wilt hear,
must   If from the lover thou maun flee,
  Yet let the friend be dear!

2

Altho' I love my Chloris mair
  Than ever tongue could tell,
My passion I will ne'er declare—
  I'll say, I wish thee well.

3

Tho' a' my daily care thou art,
  And a' my nightly dream,
I'll hide the struggle in my heart,
  And say it is esteem.

PRETTY PEG

TUNE: (*Unknown*)

1

As I gaed up by yon gate-end,   went:
  When day was waxin weary,   yonder road-
Wha did I meet come down the street
  But pretty Peg, my dearie?

2

Her air so sweet, her shape complete,
  Wi' nae proportion wanting—
The Queen of Love could never move
  Wi' motion mair enchanting!

3

With linkèd hands we took the sands
  Down by yon winding river;
And O! that hour, and shady bow'r,
  Can I forget it? Never!

MEG O' THE MILL

Second Set

TUNE: *O bonie lass, will ye lie in a barrack?*

1

O, ken ye what Meg o' the mill has gotten?   got
An' ken ye what Meg o' the mill has gotten?
She's gotten a coof wi' a claute o' siller,   dolt: hoard
And broken the heart o' the barley miller!   of money

2

The miller was strappin, the miller was ruddy,
A heart like a lord, and a hue like a lady.
The laird was a widdifu', bleerit knurl—   gallows-
She's left the guid fellow, and taen the churl!   worthy:
                                                dwarf

3

offered

The miller, he hecht her a heart leal and loving.
The laird did address her wi' matter more moving:

bright

A fine pacing-horse wi' a clear, chainèd bridle,
A whip by her side, and a bonie side saddle!

4

woe: potent

O, wae on the siller—it is sae prevailing!

farm

And wae on the love that is fixed on a mailen!

dowry;
speech

A tocher's nae word in a true lover's parl,

world

But gie me my love and a fig for the warl!

PHILLIS THE FAIR

TUNE: *Aileen a roon*

1

While larks with little wing
    Fann'd the pure air,
Viewing the breathing Spring,
    Forth I did fare.
Gay, the sun's golden eye
Peep'd o'er the mountains high;
' Such thy bloom,' did I cry—
    ' Phillis the fair! '

2

In each bird's careless song,
    Glad, I did share;
While yon wild flowers among,
    Chance led me there.
Sweet to the opening day,
Rosebuds bent the dewy spray;
' Such thy bloom,' did I say—
    ' Phillis the fair! '

3

Down in a shady walk
    Doves cooing were;
I mark'd the cruel hawk
    Caught in a snare.
So kind may Fortune be!
Such make his destiny,
He who would injure thee,
    Phillis the fair!

O SAW YE MY DEAR, MY PHILLY

TUNE: *When she cam ben she bobbit*

1

O, saw ye my Dear, my Philly?
O, saw ye my Dear, my Philly?
She's down i' the grove, she's wi' a new love,
She winna come hame to her Willy.   will not

2

What says she my Dear, my Philly?
What says she my Dear, my Philly?
She lets thee to wit she has thee forgot,   know
And for ever disowns thee, her Willy.

3

O, had I ne'er seen thee, my Philly!
O, had I ne'er seen thee, my Philly!
As light as the air, and fause as thou's fair,
Thou's broken the heart o' thy Willy.

'TWAS NA HER BONIE BLUE E'E

TUNE: *Laddie, lie near me*

1

'Twas na her bonie blue e'e was my ruin:
Fair tho' she be, that was ne'er my undoin.
'Twas the dear smile when naebody did mind us,
'Twas the bewitching, sweet, stoun glance o' kind-   stolen
    ness!

2

Sair do I fear that to hope is denied me,   Sore
Sair do I fear that despair maun abide me;   must
But tho' fell Fortune should fate us to sever,
Queen shall she be in my bosom for ever.

3

Chloris, I'm thine wi' a passion sincerest,
And thou hast plighted me love o' the dearest,
And thou'rt the angel that never can alter—
Sooner the sun in his motion would falter!

WHY, WHY TELL THY LOVER

TUNE: *Caledonian Hunt's Delight*

1

Why, why tell thy lover
Bliss he never must enjoy?
Why why undeceive him.
And give all his hopes the lie?

2

O, why, while Fancy, raptur'd. slumbers,
' Chloris, Chloris,' all the theme,
Why, why wouldst thou, cruel,
Wake thy lover from his dream?

THE PRIMROSE

TUNE: *Todlin Hame*

1

Dost ask me, why I send thee here
The firstling of the infant year:
This lovely native of the vale,
That hangs so pensive and so pale?

2

Look on its bending stalk, so weak.
That, each way yielding, doth not break,
And see how aptly it reveals
The doubts and fears a lover feels.

3

Look on its leaves of yellow hue
Bepearl'd thus with morning dew,
And these will whisper in thine ears:—
' The sweets of loves are wash'd with tears.'

O, WERT THOU IN THE CAULD BLAST

TUNE: *Lenox love to Blantyre*

1

O. wert thou in the cauld blast
  On yonder lea, on yonder lea,
My plaidie to the angry airt,   quarter
  I'd shelter thee, I'd shelter thee.
Or did Misfortune's bitter storms
  Around thee blaw, around thee blaw,
Thy bield should be my bosom,   shelter
  To share it a', to share it a'.

2

Or were I in the wildest waste,
  Sae black and bare, sae black and bare,
The desert were a Paradise,
  If thou wert there, if thou wert there.
Or were I monarch of the globe,
  Wi' thee to reign, wi' thee to reign,
The brightest jewel in my crown
  Wad be my queen, wad be my queen.

YOUR FRIENDSHIP

TUNE: *Banks of Spey*

1

Your friendship much can make me blest—
  O, why that bliss destroy?
Why urge the only, one request
  You know I will deny?

2

Your thought, if Love must harbour there,
  Conceal it in that thought,
Nor cause me from my bosom tear
  The very friend I sought.

FOR THEE IS LAUGHING NATURE

TUNE: *Scots Queen*

For thee is laughing Nature gay,
For thee she pours the vernal day:
For me in vain is Nature drest,
While Joy's a stranger to my breast.

NO COLD APPROACH

TUNE: *Ianthy the lovely*

No cold approach, no alter'd mien,
　Just what would make suspicion start,
No pause the dire extremes between:
　He made me blest—and broke my heart.

LET LOOVE SPARKLE

TUNE: *Jockey fou and Jenny fain*

Ithers seek they kenna what,
Features, carriage and a' that;
Gie me loove in her I court—
Loove to loove maks a' the sport.

Let loove sparkle in her e'e,
Let her lo'e nae man but me:
dower　That's the tocher guid I prize,
There the luver's treasure lies.

brook

AS DOWN THE BURN

TUNE: *Down the burn, Davie*

As down the burn they took their way,
　And thro the flowery dale;
His cheek to hers he aft did lay,
　And love was ay the tale,

With:—' Mary, when shall we return,
   Sic pleasure to renew? '   *such*
Quoth Mary:—' Love, I like the burn,
   And ay shall follow you.'

SKETCH

1

HAIL, Poesie! thou nymph reserv'd!
In chase o' thee, what crowds hae swerv'd
Frae Common Sense, or sunk ennerv'd
        'Mang heaps o' clavers;   *nonsense*
And Och! o'er aft thy joes hae starv'd   *sweethearts*
        'Mid a' thy favors!

2

Say, Lassie, why thy train amang,
While loud the trump's heroic clang,
And Sock and buskin skelp alang   *spank*
        To death or marriage;
Scarce ane has tried the Shepherd-sang   *one*
        But wi' miscarriage?

3

In Homer's craft Jock Milton thrives;
Esch'ylus' pen Will Shakespeare drives;
Wee Pope, the knurlin, 'till him rives   *dwarf; tugs*
        Horatian fame;
In thy sweet sang, Barbauld, survives
        E'en Sappho's flame.

4

But thee, Theocritus, wha matches?
They're no' Herd's ballats, Maro's catches;
Squire Pope but busks his skinklin patches   *small*
        O' Heathen tatters:
I pass by hunders, nameless wretches,   *hundreds*
        That ape their betters.

5

fine;
learning

In this braw age o' wit and lear,
Will nane the Shepherd's whistle mair
Blaw sweetly in its native air
                    And rural grace;
And wi' the far-fam'd Grecian share
                    A rival place?

6

youth
forward
cower; porch
fellow

Yes! there is ane;—a Scottish callan!
There's ane: come forrit, honest Allan!
Thou need na jouk behint the hallan,
                    A chiel sae clever;
The teeth o' Time may gnaw Tantallan,
                    But thou's for ever.

7

perfection

golden

Thou paints auld Nature to the nines,
In thy sweet Caledonian lines;
Nae gowden stream thro' myrtles twines
                    Where Philomel,
While midnight gales rustle clustering vines,
                    Her griefs will tell!

8

floods
smart

Thy rural loves are Nature's sel';
Nae bombast spates o' nonsense swell;
Nae snap conceits, but that sweet spell
                    O' witchin loove,
That charm that can the strongest quell,
                    The sternest move.

9

daisied;
brooklet
clothes
woods;
slopes

In gowany glens thy burnie stray,
Where bonie lasses bleach their claes;
Or trots by hazelly shaws and braes
                    Wi' hawthorns gray,
Where blackbirds join the shepherd's lays
                    At close o' day.

FOR THE AUTHOR'S FATHER

O ye whose cheek the tear of pity stains,
　　Draw near with pious rev'rence, and attend!
Here lie the loving husband's dear remains,
　　The tender father, and the gen'rous friend.

The pitying heart that felt for human woe,
　　The dauntless heart that fear'd no human pride,
The friend of man—to vice alone a foe;
　　For ' ev'n his failings lean'd to virtue's side '.

A BARD'S EPITAPH

I

Is there a whim-inspirèd fool,
Owre fast for thought, owre hot for rule,　　*too*
Owre blate to seek, owre proud to snool?—　　*modest;*
　　　　　　Let him draw near;　　　　　　*cringe*
And owre this grassy heap sing dool,　　　　*woe*
　　　　　　And drap a tear.

2

Is there a Bard of rustic song,
Who, noteless, steals the crowds among,
That weekly this aréa throng?—
　　　　　　O, pass not by!
But with a frater-feeling strong,
　　　　　　Here, heave a sigh.

3

Is there a man, whose judgment clear
Can others teach the course to steer,
Yet runs, himself, life's mad career
　　　　　　Wild as the wave?—
Here pause—and, thro' the starting tear,
　　　　　　Survey this grave.

4

The poor inhabitant below
Was quick to learn and wise to know,
And keenly felt the friendly glow
        And softer flame;
But thoughtless follies laid him low,
        And stain'd his name.

5

Reader, attend! whether thy soul
Soars Fancy's flights beyond the pole,
Or darkling grubs this earthly hole
        In low pursuit;
Know, prudent, cautious, self-control
        Is wisdom's root.

ON THE AUTHOR

He who of Rankine sang, lies stiff and deid,
And a green, grassy hillock hides his heid:
Alas! alas! a devilish change indeed!

GLOSSARY

A, *sometimes used for he, she, or it.*
A', *all; every one, with the sense of each.*
ABEIGH, *at a distance, aloof.*
ABLINS, *v.* AIBLINS.
ABOON, *above, overhead, upstairs.*
ABREAD, *abroad.*
ABREED, *in breadth.*
ADLE, *cow lant, putrid water.*
ADO, *to do.*
ADVISEMENT, *advice, counsel.*
AE, *one.*
AFF, *off.*
AFF-HAND, *at once.*
AFF-LOOF, *off-hand, extempore.*
A-FIEL, *a-field.*
AFORE, *before.*
AFT, *oft.*
AFTEN, *often.*
AGLEY, *askew.*
AHIN, *behind.*
AIBLINS, *perhaps, possibly.*
AIK, AIKEN, *oak, oaken.*
AIL, *to be ill, to complain.*
AILSA CRAIG, *an island rock in the Firth of Clyde.*
AIN, *own.*
AIR, *early.*
AIRLE-PENNY, AIRLES, *earnest-money.*
AIRN, AIRNS, *iron, fetters.*
AIRT, *to direct; a direction, point of the compass.*
AITH, *oath.*
AITS, *oats.*
AIVER, *an old horse.*
AIZLE, *a cinder.*
AJEE, *ajar; twisted; sulky, cross.*
ALAKE, *alas.*
ALANE, *alone.*
ALANG, *along.*
AMAIST, *almost.*
AMANG, *among.*
AN, *if.*
AN', *and.*
ANCE, *once.*
ANDRO, *Andrew.*
ANE, *one, an.*
ANEATH, *beneath.*
ANES, *ones.*

ANEUGH, ANEUCH, *enough.*
ANITHER, *another.*
AQUA-FONTIS, *spring-water.*
AQUA-VITAE, *whisky.*
ARLE *v.* AIRLE-PENNY.
A'S, *all is.*
ASE, *ashes.*
ASKLENT, *awry, off the plumb.*
ASPAR, *spread out.*
A'THEGITHER, *altogether.*
ATHORT, ATHWORT, *athwart, across, over.*
ATTOUR, *moreover, beyond, beside.*
ATWEEL, *truly, indeed, assuredly, of course.*
ATWEEN, *between.*
AUGHT, *to own, to possess; possession; eight.*
AUGHTEEN, *eighteen.*
AUGHTLINS, *at all, in any way.*
AULD, *old.*
AULD REEKIE, *Edinburgh.*
AULD SHOON, *old shoes; a discarded lover.*
AULD-WARLD, *old-world.*
AUMOUS, *alms.*
AUMOUS-DISH, *a beggar's collecting dish, the poor-box.*
AVA, *at all.*
AWA, *away.*
AWALD, *folded or doubled up. A sheep is* AWALD *when it is on its back and cannot rise. Applied to a drunken person having fallen.*
AWAUK, *to awake.*
AWE, *owe.*
A-WEE, *a short time.*
AWKART, *awkward.*
AWNIE, *bearded.*
AY, AYE, *always, assent;* "AY, BUT" *=qualified assent.*
AYONT, *beyond, later than, farther.*

BA', *a ball.*
BABIE-CLOUTS, *baby clothes.*
BACKET, *bucket or box.*
BACKIT, *backed.*
BACKLINS-COMIN, *coming back, returning.*

687

BACK-YETT, *gate at the back.*

BADE, *did bid; endured.*

BAGGIE, *the belly, the stomach.*

BAIG'NETS, *bayonets.*

BAILLIE, *magistrate of a Scots burgh.*

BAINIE. *bony, big-boned.*

BAIRN, *a child.*

BAIRNTIME, *brood, issue.*

BAITH. *both.*

BAKES, *biscuits.*

BALLATS, *ballads.*

BALOO, BALOW. *hush! a lullaby.*

BAMBOOZLE, *to trick by mystifying.*

BAN, *to curse.*

BAN' *a bond; an agreement.*

BANE, *bone.*

BANG, *an effort, a blow, a large number.* UNCO BANG, *great or prolonged effort.*

BANG, *to thump.*

BANIE, *v.* BAINIE.

BANN'D, *cursed, sworn.*

BANNET. *bonnet.*

BANNOCK, BONNOCK, *a thick cake baked on a flat pan of iron.*

BARDIE, *dim. of bard.*

BAREFIT, *barefoot.*

BARKET. *barked.*

BARLEY-BREE, *malt liquor, whisky or ale.*

BARM, *yeast.*

BARMIE, *yeasty.*

BARN-YARD, *stackyard.*

BARTIE, *the Devil.*

BASHING, *abashing.*

BASIN, *a dish for holding oatmeal.*

BATCH. *a number, a company*

BATTS, *the botts (applied to horses), the colic.*

BAUCKIE-BIRD, *a bat.*

BAUDRONS, *a cat.*

BAUK, *a cross-beam.*

BAUK, *v.* BAWK.

BAUK-EN', *beam-end.*

BAULD. *bold.*

BAUMY. *balmy.*

BAWBEE, *a halfpenny.*

BAWDRONS, *v.* BAUDRONS.

BAWK, *a pathway through growing crops.*

BAW NT, *white-faced.*

BAWTIE, *pet name for a dog.*

BE, BY, *as denoting the cause; let be, let alone.*

BEAR, *barley.*

BEAS' *beast, vermin (i.e. lice).*

BEASTIE, *dim. of beast.*

BECK, *a curtsy; to make obeisance.*

BEET, *to kindle, to mend (the fire).*

BEFA'. *befall.*

BEHINT, *behind.*

BEILD, *v.* BIELD.

BELANG, *belong.*

BELD, *bald.*

BELLUM. *assault.*

BELLYS, *bellows.*

BELYVE. *by-and-by.*

BEN. *within; the inner room or parlour.*

BENMOST BORE, *the farthest crevice, chink. or hole.*

BE-NORTH, *to the northward of.*

BENT, *moorland grass; the open field.*

BE-SOUTH, *to the southward of.*

BEUK, *a book.*

BEYONT, *beyond.*

BICKER, *a beaker, an ale-pot; to flow, to dispute.*

BICKER, *a short run.*

BICKER'D, *flowed, rippled, disputed.*

BICKERIN *rippling; disputing, wrangling.*

BID, *to ask, to wish, to offer.*

BIDE, *to wait, to stay, to remain.*

BIELD. *a shelter, refuge.*

BIEN. *thriving. comfortable, cosy, snug.*

BIG. *'o build; large, swollen.*

BIGGIN, *building.*

BIKE, *v.* BYKE.

BILL, *the bull.*

BILLIE, *fellow, comrade, brother.*

BING, *a heap.*

BIRK, *a birch.*

BIRKEN-SHAW, *a birch-wood.*

BIRKIE, *a smart or conceited person.*

BIRLE, *to drink in company, to carouse.* BIRLE THE BAWBEE, *to spend money in social drinking.*

BIRR, *force, vigour.*

BIRRING, *whirring.*

BIRSES, *bristles.*

BIT. *a morsel, a piece; a short time.*

BITCH-FOU, *completely drunk.*

BIZZ, *a flurry.*

BIZZ, *to buzz.*

BIZZARD-GLED, *the buzzard-hawk; a coward.*

BIZZIE, *busy.*

BLACK-BONNET, *the kirk elder.*

BLACK-NEBBIT, *black-beaked.*

BLAE, *blue, the colour of the pollen on the sloe.*

BLASTET, BLASTIT, *blasted.*

BLASTIE, *a blasted (i.e. damned) creature.*

BLATE, *shy, bashful, timid.*

BLATHER, *bladder.*

BLAUD, *a large quantity, a screed.*

BLAUD, *to slap.*

BLAUDIN, *driving, pelting.*

BLAW, *to boast, to exaggerate.*

BLAW, *to blow.*

BLAWING, *blowing.*

BLAWN, *blown.*

BLEER, *to obscure the vision, to deceive.*

BLEERIE, *red about the eyes.*

BLEER'T, BLEERIT, *dimmed, obscured (with weeping).*

BLEEZ'D, *blazed.*

BLEEZE, *a blaze.*

BLEEZIN, *blazing.*

BLELLUM, *a babbler.*

BLETHER, *blethers, nonsense.*

BLETHER, *to talk nonsense.*

BLETHERIN', *talking nonsense.*

BLIN', *blind.*

BLINK, *a glance, an amorous look; a short space of time.*

BLINKERS, *spies, oglers.*

BLINKIN, *blinking, shining.*

BLINKIN, *smirking, leering.*

BLIN'T, *blinded.*

BLITTER, *the common snipe.*

BLUE-BELL, *the harebell, campanula montanis.*

BLUE-GOWN, *the livery of the licensed beggar.*

BLUID, BLUDE, *blood.*

BLUME, *bloom; to bloom.*

BLUNTIE, *having a sheepish look; a stupid or simple person.*

BLYPES, *shreds.*

BLYTH, *cheerful, gay, merry.*

BOBBIT, *to curtsy; up and down motion.*

BOCKED. *vomited.*

BODDLE, *a farthing (properly two pennies Scots, or one-third of an English penny).*

BODE, *a bid, a price offered; to bid.*

BODIE, *a person.*

BODKIN, *tailor's needle.*

BOGGIE, *dim. of bog.*

BOGLE, *a hobgoblin, a spectre.*

BOLE, *a hole or cupboard in the wall.*

BONIE, *beautiful, handsome, pretty, plump; pleasant to see.*

BONNOCK, *v.* BANNOCK.

'BOON, *v.* ABOON.

BOORD, *board, surface.*

BOORD-EN', *board-end.*

BOORTREES, *the shrub—elder.*

BOOST, *behove, must needs.*

BOOT, *payment to the bargain.*

BORE, *a chink, a small hole, an opening.*

BOTCH, *an angry tumour.*

BOUK, BOWK, *bulk; the whole body.*

BOUNTITH, *bounty, reward, bonus.*

BOW-HOUGHED, *bow-thighed.*

BOW-KAIL, *cabbage.*

BOW'T, *bent.*

BRACHENS, *ferns.*

BRACKEN, *the common fern, pteris aquilina.*

BRAE, *a steep bank, the slope of a hill, the broken bank of a river.*

BRAG, *to boast.*

BRAID, *broad.*

BRAID-CLAITH, *broad-cloth.*

BRAIK, *a harrow.*

BRAING'T, *pulled rashly.*

BRAK, *broke, broken.*

BRANKIE, *gaudy, lively, prancing, showy.*

BRANKS, *a (wooden) horse-bridle.*

BRASH, *short illness.*

BRATS, *small pieces, rags.*

BRATS, *small children.*

BRATTLE, *a spurt, a scamper.*

BRATTLE, *noisy onset.*

BRAW, *brave, well-dressed, handsome; very, extremely.*

BRAWLIE, *in good health and cheerful.*

BRAWNIT, *of a mixed red and brown colour, applied to cattle.*

BRAXIES, *sheep that have died.*

BREASTIE, *dim. of breast.*

BREASTIT, *sprang forward.*

BRECHAN, *a horse-collar.*

BRECKAN, *a horse-collar, ferns.*

BREEDIN, *breeding.*

BREEKS, *breeches.*

BREER, *briar.*

BRENT, *smooth, unwrinkled, high.*

BRENT, *brand.*

BRIE, *the brow.*

BRIEF, *writ.*

BRIER, *the briar; to sprout.*

BRIERY, *briary.*

BRIG, *a bridge.*

BRISKET, *breast.*

BRITHER, *brother.*

BROCK, *a badger.*

BROGUE, *a trick.*

BROO, *broth, juice, liquor.*

BROOSES, *wedding races from the church to the home of the bride.*

BROSE, *raw oatmeal mixed with water.*

BROWST, *a brew; the consequence of one's own action.*

BROWSTER WIVES, *ale wives.*

BRUGH, *a burgh, a borough.*

BRULZIE, BRULYIE, *a brawl.*

BRUNSTANE, *brimstone.*

BRUNT, *burned.*

BRUST, *burst.*

BRUYLIE, *a broil, a quarrel.*

BUCKIE, *dim. of buck.*

BUCKLE, *a curl.*

BUCKSKIN, *Virginian.*

BUDGET, *tinker's bag of tools.*

BUFF, *to bang, to thump.*

BUFFET-STOOL, *a low wooden stool set on a frame.*

BUGHT, *a sheepfold.*

BUGHTIN TIME, *the time when cattle are housed for the night.*

BUIRDLY, *stout, stalwart.*

BUM, *the buttocks; to hum.*

BUM-CLOCK, *the beetle.*

BUMMLE, *a drone, a useless fellow.*

BUNKER, *a seat.*

BUNTERS, *harlots.*

BURDIES, *dim. of bird or burd.*

BURE, *bore.*

BURN, *a small stream, a rivulet.*

BURNEWIN, *the blacksmith.*

BURNIE, *dim. of burn.*

BURR-THISTLE, *spear-thistle.*

BUSK, *to dress, to garb.*

BUSKING, *v. BUSK.*

BUSKIT, *v. BUSK.*

BUSKIT, *adorned, dressed.*

BUSS, *a bush.*

BUSSLE, *bustle.*

BUT, *except, unless, as well as.*

BUT, *the kitchen.*

BUT AND BEN, *the kitchen and parlour; backwards and forwards.*

BY, *relating to, towards, beside, past, aside.*

BYE ATTOUR, *besides, into the bargain.*

BYKE, *a beehive, a swarm, a crowd.*

BYRE, *a cow-house.*

CA', *to call, to knock, to drive.*

CA', *a call, a whistle, a summons.*

CA'D, CA'T, *called.*

CA'D, CA'T, *knocked, driven.*

CADDIE, CADIE, *a servant lad, a varlet.*

CADGER, *a hawker.*

CAFF, *chaff.*

CAIRD, *a tinker.*

CAIRN, *a loose heap of stones.*

CALF-WARD, *grazing plot for calves (i.e. churchyard).*

CALLAN, CALLANT, *a stripling.*

CALLER, *fresh, bracing, healthy.*

CALLET, *a drab, a dirty woman, trull.*

CAM, *came, did come.*

CAN, *a tin vessel, a dish of liquor.*

CANKERS, *to be querulous, to grumble.*

CANKERT, *bad-tempered, soured.*

CANKRIE, *crabbed.*

CANNA, *cannot.*

CANNIE, CANNY, *pleasant, cautious, knowing, skilful.*

CANNIEST, *quietest.*

CANNILY, CANNILIE, *softly, gently.*

CANTIE, CANTY, *cheerful, merry.*

CANTRAIP, *magic*

CANTS, *merry stories; canters or sprees or merry doings.*

CAP, CAUP, *a small wooden dish with a handle; a quaich.*

CAPE-STANE, *cope-stone.*

CAPON, *a castrated cock.*

CAPON-CRAWS, *crowing like a capon (the capon was taken for an emblem of stupidity).*

CARDIN, *combing (wool, flax, etc.).*

CARE NA BY, *do not care.*

CARL, CARLE, *a churl, a fellow, an old man, a peasant, a clown.*

CARLIE, *dim. of carl.*

CARLIN, CARLINE, *an old wrinkled woman, a shrew.*

CARMAGNOLE, *a violent Jacobin.*

CAR'T NA BY, *cared not at all.*

CARTES, *playing cards.*

CARTIE, *dim. of cart.*

CASTOCKS, *stem and pith of the cabbage or colewort.*

CATCH-THE-PLACK, *the hunt for coin.*

CAUDRON, *a caldron.*

CAUF, *a calf, a silly and ridiculous person.*

CAUK, *chalk.*

CAULD, *a cold, the cold shivers.*

CAUSEY-CLEANERS, *causeway-cleaners.*

CAVIE, *a hen-coop.*

CESS, *to tax; the land-tax.*

CHAMER, CHAUMER, *chamber.*

CHANGE-HOUSE, *tavern.*

CHANTER, *bagpipes, the part of the bagpipes which produces the melody.*

CHAP, *a person, a lover; to rap.*

CHAPMAN, *a pedlar.*

CHAPPIN, *a quart pot; calling (the landlord).*

CHAUMER, *v. CHAMER.*

CHAUP (*or* CHAP), *a stroke, a blow.*

CHEAP, CHEEP, *to chirp, to peep.*

CHEAR, *cheer, to cheer.*

CHEARFU', *cheerful.*

CHEARLESS, *cheerless.*

CHEARY, *cheery.*

CHEEK-FOR-CHOW, *cheek-by-jowl.*

CHIEL, CHIELD, *a young fellow.*

CHIMLA, *chimney.*

CHITTERING, *shivering.*

CHOW, *v. CHEEK-FOR-CHOW.*

CHOWS, *chews.*

CHUCK, *a hen, a chicken; a dear.*

CHUCKIE, *dim. of chuck, but usually signifies mother-hen, an old dear.*

CHUFFIE, *fat-faced.*

CHUSE, *to choose.*

CIT, *the civet.*

CIT, *a citizen, a merchant.*

CLACHAN, *a small village about a church, a hamlet.*

CLAEDING, *clothing.*

CLAES, *clothes.*

CLAITH, CLAITHING, *cloth, clothing.*

CLAIVERS, *v. CLAVERS.*

CLAMB, *climbed.*

CLANKIE, *a striking noise, a sounding blow.*

CLAP, *the clapper of a mill.*

CLAPPIN, *patting gently.*

CLARK, *clerkly, scholarly.*

CLARK, *a clerk.*

CLARKIT, *clerked, wrote.*

CLARTY, *dirty.*

CLASH, *an idle tale, the story of a day.*

CLASH, *to tattle.*

CLATTER, *noise; disputation.*

CLAUGHT, *clutched.*

CLAUGHTIN, *clutching, grasping.*

CLAUT, *to clutch, to hold, to scrape.*

CLAUTET, *scraped.*

CLAVER, *clover; to talk nonsense.*

CLAVERS, *idle talk.*

CLAW, *to scratch, to thrash.*

CLAY-CAULD, *clay-cold.*

CLAYMORE, *a two-handed sword.*

CLECKIN, *a brood.*

CLEED, *to clothe, to cover.*

CLEG, *gadfly.*

CLEEK, *to seize, to snatch.*

CLEEKIT, *hooked, seized.*

CLEEKS, *cramp in the legs.*

CLINK, *money; to jingle, to rhyme.*

CLINKIN, *a bell-like sound; abrupt motion.*

CLINKUM, CLINKUMBELL, *the beadle, the bellman.*

CLIPS, *shears.*

CLISH-MA-CLAVER, *gossip, tale-telling; nonsense.*

CLOCKIN-TIME, *clucking — (= hatching-) time.*

CLOOT, *a hoof; Auld Clootie, the Devil.*

CLOOTIE, CLOOTS, *hoofie, hoofs (a nickname of the Devil).*

CLOUR, *a bump or swelling after a blow.*

CLOUT, *a patch; to patch, to repair.*

CLOUTIN, *patching, repairing.*

CLOUTS, *ragged clothes.*

CLUDS, *clouds.*

CLUE, *a ball of worsted, cotton, etc.*

CLUNK, *the hollow sound produced by emptying a bottle hastily.*

COATIE, *dim. of coat.*

COBLE, *a broad and flat boat.*

COCK, *the mark (in curling).*

COCKETS, *ornamental head-gear.*

COCKIE, *dim. of cock (applied to an old man).*

COCKS, *fellows, good fellows.*

COD, *a pillow, a cushion.*

COFT, *to buy.*

COG, COGGIE, *a small wooden dish without handles.*

COIL, COILA, *Kyle (one of the ancient districts of Ayrshire).*

COLLIE, *a general, and sometimes a particular, name for country curs; a sheep-dog.*

COLLIESHANGIE, *a squabble.*

COMPLEENIN, *complaining.*

COOD, *cud.*

COOF, CUIF, *a blockhead, a dolt.*

COOKIN, *cooking.*

COOKIT, *hid.*

COOL'D IN HER LINENS, *laid in her shroud.*

COOR, *to cover, to duck down.*

COOSER, *a courser, a stallion.*

COOST, *to cast, to throw.*

COOT, *the water-hen.*

COOTIE, *rough-legged; a small dish.*

COOTS, *hoofs.*

CORBIES, *ravens, crows.*

CORE, *a chorus, a convivial company.*

CORN-MOU', *a stack of corn; where the corn is stacked.*

CORN'T, *fed with corn.*

CORSE, *a corpse.*

CORSS, *cross.*

COU'DNA, COULDNA, *couldn't.*

COUNTRA, *country.*

COUP, *to capsize; head over heels.*

COUR, *to crouch, to duck down.*

COUTHIE, COUTHY, *kind, pleasant, affectionate.*

COWE, *to scare, to daunt.*

COWE, *to crop.*

COWTE, *a colt.*

CRACK, *conversation; to converse.*

CRACKIN, *conversing.*

CRACKS, *stories; conversation.*

CRAFT, *croft.*

CRAFT-RIG, *a croft—ridge; used equiv.*

CRAIBIT, CRABBIT, *crabbed, fretful.*

CRAIG, *a crag, a rock; the neck.*

CRAIG, *the throat.*

CRAIGIE, *the throat, the gullet; craggy.*

CRAIK, *the landrail; to croak.*

CRAMBO-CLINK, *rhyme.*

CRAMBO-JINGLE, *rhyming.*

CRAN, *the support for a pot or kettle.*

CRANKOUS, *fretful.*

CRANKS, *creakings.*

CRANREUCH, *hoar-frost.*

CRAP, *a crop; the top.*

CRAPS, *growing crops.*

CRAW, *crow.*

CREEL, *an osier basket, a hamper; perplexity, confusion of mind*

CREEPIE-CHAIR, *the stool of repentance in the kirk.*

CREESHIE, *greasy.*

CROCKS, *old ewes.*

CRONIE, *an intimate, a companion.*

CROODED, CROODL'D, *cooed, murmured.*

CROODS, *coos.*

CROOKS, *curvature of the neck or spine.*

CROON, *moan, a low.*

CROON, *to toll.*

CROON'D, *hummed.*

CROONING, *humming.*

CROUCHIE, *hunchbacked.*

CROUSE, *elated; courageous, bold.*

CROUSE, *cheerfully.*

CROUSELY, *confidently.*

CROWDIE, *oatmeal gruel made with water; breakfast-time.*

CROWLIN, *crawling.*

CRUMMIE, *a horned cow.*

CRUMMOCK, CUMMOCK, *a cudgel, a crooked staff.*

CRUMP, *crisp.*

CRUNT, *a blow.*

CUDDLE, *to caress, to embrace; to lie close.*

CUDDLE, *to fondle.*

CUDDL'D, *fondled.*

CUIF, COOF, *a dolt, a ninny, a weakling, a dastard.*

CUMMER (*Fr. commere*), *a gossip; a midwife, a godmother, a hag.*

CUMMOCK, *v.* CRUMMOCK.

CURCH, *a kerchief; a woman's head-cover.*

CURCHIE, *a curtsy; a head-dress.*

CURLER, *one who plays at curling (a game on the ice).*

CURMURRING, *commotion.*

CURPIN, *the crupper of a horse.*

CURPLE, *the crupper (i.e. buttocks).*

CUSHAT, *the wild pigeon.*

CUSTOCK, *the pith of the colewort.*

CUTES, *feet (properly of an animal), ankles.*

CUTTY, *short, bob-tailed.*

CUTTY-STOOL, *a low stool, v.* CREEPIE-CHAIR.

DADDY, *father, an old person.*

DAEZ'T, *dazed.*

DAFFIN, *folly, pastime, matrimonial intercourse.*

DAFT, *merry, giddy.*

DAFT, *mad, foolish.*

DAIDLIN, *waddling; inactive or tardy.*

DAILS, *planks.*

DAIMEN ICKER, *an odd ear of corn.*

DAINTIE, *pleasant, good-humoured, agreeable.*

DAM, *pent up water, urine.*

DAMIE, *dim. of dame.*

DANG, *knocked over; pushed about, surpassed.*

DANTON, *v.* DAUNTON.

DARENA, *dare not.*

DARG, *labour, task, a day's labour.*

DARKLINS, *in the dark.*

DAUD, *to pelt.*

DAUNTON, *to intimidate, to terrify, to depress.*

DAUNTON, *to daunt.*

DAUR, *to dare.*

DAURNA, *dare not.*

DAUR'T, *dared.*

DAUT, DAWTE, *to caress, to pet, to fondle.*

DAUTIE, *a pet; term of affection.*

DAUTIT, *fondled, caressed, petted.*

DAW, *dawn.*

DAWDS, *lumps, large portions.*

DAWIN, *the dawning.*

DEAD, *death.*

DEARIE, *dim. of dear.*

DEAVE, *to deafen, to stun with noise.*

DEEVIL, *v.* DEIL.

DEIL, *the devil.*

DEIL-HAET, *nothing; De'il have my soul.*

DEIL MA CARE, *do not care a straw.*

DELEERET, *delirious, mad.*

DELVE, *to dig.*

DERN'D, *hid.*

DESCRIVE, *to describe.*

DESCRIVING, *describing.*

DEUK, *a duck.*

DEVEL, *a stunning blow.*

DIDDLE, *to move quickly (of fiddling).*

DIEIN, *dying.*

DIGHT, DIGHTED, *to wipe, wiped; to clean corn from chaff.*

DIN, *noise; to make a noise.*

DIN, *dun, of complexion.*

DING, *to overcome, to surpass.*

DINK, *neatly, dainty; precise, proper.*

DINMONT, *a two-year-old male sheep.*

DINNA, *do not.*

DIRL'D, *thrilled, vibrated.*

DIRT, *a contemptuous term for money.*

DIZ'N, DIZEN, *dozen.*

DOCHTER, *daughter.*

DOGGIE, *dim. of dog.*

DOITED, *stupid, as in frail old age.*

DONSIE, *self-important, restive.*

DOO, *a dove; term of endearment.*

DOOL, *sorrow; to lament, to mourn.*

DOOLFU', *doleful.*

DORTY, *pettish.*

DOUCE, DOUSE, *steady, grave, gentle, sedate.*

DOUCE, DOUCELY, *dousely, sedately.*

DOUDL'T, *dandled.*

DOUGHT, *pret. of* DOW, *to be able, to possess strength.*

DOUK, DOUKIT, *to duck, ducked.*

DOUN, *down.*

DOUP, *the bottom.*

DOUP-SKELPER, *bottom-smacker.*

DOUR, *obstinate, sullen, mentally strong.*

DOURE, *stubborn, obstinate.*

DOUSE, *v.* DOUCE.

DOUSER, *sedater.*

DOW, *a dove, a pigeon.*

DOW, DOWE, *am able.*

DOWF, DOWFF, *pithless, wanting force, sad, dismal.*

DOWIE, *dull, sorrowful.*

DOWILIE, *drooping.*

DOWN, *low-lying land.*

DOWNA, *cannot; not able.*

DOWNA-DO'S, *listless, fatigued, unable.*

DOXY, *a paramour.*

DOYLT, *stupid, crazed, hebetated.*

DOYEN, *shrivelled, dried up.*

DOYTIN, *doddering.*

DOZEN'D, *torpid.*

DOZIN, *torpid.*

DRAIGL'T, *soaked with mud or water.*

DRAM, *a portion of whisky.*

DRANTS, *tedious talk, long whining prayers.*

DRAP, DRAPPIE, *a drop; a small portion of liquor.*

DRAUNTING, *tedious.*

DREE, *to dread, to suffer, to endure.*

DREIGH, *long and uninteresting, long-winded.*

DRIBBLE, *drizzle.*

DRIDDLE, *to move slowly; more action than motion.*

DRIEGH, *tedious, dull.*

DRODDUM, *the breech.*

DRONE, *the monotonous pipe of the bagpipe; a prosy person.*

DROOP-RUMPL'T, *short-rumped.*

DROUK, *to wet, to soak.*

DROUKIT, *soaked, wet through.*

DROUTH, *drought.*

DROUTHIE, *very thirsty; always thirsty.*

DRUKEN, DRUCKEN, *drunken.*

DRUMLIE. *drumly, muddy, discoloured.*

DRUMMOCK, *raw meal and cold water.*

DRUNT, *the huff.*

DRY, *thirsty.*

DUB, *puddle, slush.*

DUB, *a puddle.*

DUDDIE, *ragged.*

DUDS, DUDDIES, *ragged clothes.*

DUN, *to stun with a great noise; a brown colour.*

DUNE, *done.*

DUNG, *knocked or pushed about.*

DUNTED, *throbbed.*

DUNTS, *blows; wounds caused by a blow.*

DURK, *dirk.*

DUSHT, *touch'd.*

DWALLING, *dwelling.*

DWALT, *dwelt.*

DYKE, *a wall of undressed stones without mortar.*

DYKE-BACK, *the back of a fence.*

DYKE-SIDE, *side of a fence.*

DYVOR, *a bankrupt, a rascal, a ne'er-do-well.*

EAR', *early.*

EASTLIN, *eastern.*

E'EBRIE, *eyebrow.*

E'E, *eye.*

EEN, *eyes.*

E'EN, *even, even so, just so.*

E'EN, E'ENIN, *evening, the eve of a feast.*

E'ER, *ever.*

EERIE, *sad, weird, ghostly; in fear of future misfortune, feeling superstitious fear.*

EILD, *old age.*

EKE, *also.*

ELBUCK, *elbow.*

ELDRITCH, *unearthly.*

ELEKIT, *elected.*

ELL (Scots), *thirty-seven inches.*

ELLER, *an elder of the kirk.*

EN', *end.*

ENEUGH, *enough.*

ENFAULD, *infold, to encompass.*

ENOW. *enough.*

ERSE, *Gaelic.*

ETHER-STANE, *the adder-stone; an amulet.*

ETTLE, *aim.*

EVERMAIR, *evermore.*

EV'NDOWN, *downright, positive.*

EXPECKIT, *expected.*

EYDENT, *diligent.*

FA', *a fall, autumn; to fall.*

FA', *portion, lot.*

FAEN, FAUN, *fell, has fallen.*

FADDOM'D, *fathomed.*

FAEM, *foam.*

FAIKET, *let off, excused.*

FAIN, *fond, desirous.*

FAINNESS, *fondness.*

FALLOW, *fellow.*

FA'N, *fallen.*

FAIR-FA', *good luck, welcome.*

FAND, *found.*

FAR-AFF, *far-off.*

FARLS, *small, thin oat-cakes.*

FASH, *annoyance.*

FASH, *to trouble, worry.*

FASH'D, FASH'T, *bothered.*

FASHIOUS *troublesome.*

FASTEN-E'EN, *Fasten's Even (the evening before Lent).*

FAUGHT, *worry, fight, trouble.*

FAULD, *a fold; to fold.*

FAULDING, *folding; a sheepfold or farm enclosure.*

FAUN, *fallen.*

FAUSE, *false.*

FAUSE-HOUSE, *hole in a cornstack.*

FAUT, *a fault.*

FAUTLESS, *faultless.*

FAUTOR, *a defaulter, a transgressor.*

FAWSONT, *seemly, well-doing, good-looking.*

FEAT, *spruce.*

FECHT, *a fight.*

FECHT, *to fight.*

FECHTIN, *fighting.*

FECK, *the most or greater part.*

FECKET, *a sleeved waistcoat.*

FECKLESS, *feeble, wanting resource.*

FECKLY, *partly, or mostly.*

FEG, *a fig.*

FEGS, *faith.*

FEIDE, *feud.*

FEINT, *v.* FIENT.

FEIRRIE, *lusty.*

FELL, *keen, biting, fierce, cruel, relentless.*

FELL, *a tableland mountain.*

FELLY, *relentless.*

FEN, *a shift; to get along.*

FEN', *fend, to look after, to care for.*

FENCELESS, *defenceless.*

FERLIE, FERLY, *wonder, marvel, surprise.*

FERLIE, *to marvel.*

FETCHES, *catches, gurgles.*

FETCH'T, *stopped suddenly.*

FEY, *fated, doomed, predestined.*

FIDGE, *to be restless, to be uneasy.*

FIDGIN-FAIN, *to be restless with eagerness.*

FIEL, *comfortable, cosy, clean, neat.*

FIENT, *fiend, a petty oath.*

FIENT A, *not a.*

FIENT A HAIR, *not in the least.*

FIENT HAET, *nothing.*

FIENT HAET O', *not one of.*

FIENT-MA-CARE, *no matter.*

FIER, *sound, healthy.*

FIERE, FEIRE, *friend, companion, comrade.*

FIERIE, FEIRIE, *clever, active, nimble, vigorous, mettlesome.*

FILLABEG, *'he short kilt worn by the Highlanders.*

FIN', *to find.*

FISH-CREEL, *v.* CREEL.

FISSLE, *tingle, fidget with delight (it is also used of the agitation caused by frying).*

FIT, *the foot.*

FITTIE-LAN', *the near horse of the hindmost pair in the plough.*

FLAE, *a flea.*

FLAFFIN, *flapping.*

FLAININ, FLANNEN, *flannel.*

FLANG, *flung.*

FLEE, *to fly.*

FLEECH'D, *coaxed, cajoled, wheedled.*

FLEECHIN, *wheedling.*

FLEESH, *fleece.*

FLEG, *either a scare or a blow; action, movement.*

FLETH'RIN, *flattering.*

FLEWIT, *a sharp lash.*

FLEY, FLEY'D, *to frighten; frightened, scared.*

FLICHTERIN, *fluttering.*

FLIE, *a fly; to fly.*

FLINDERS, *shreds, broken pieces.*

FLINGING, *kicking out in dancing, capering.*

FLINGIN-TREE, *a piece of timber hung by way of partition between two horses in a stable; a flail.*

FLISKIT, *fretted, capered.*

FLIT, *to shift.*

FLITTERING, *fluttering.*

FLYTE, *to scold.*

FODGEL, *dumpy.*

FOCK, *folk.*

FOOR, *went, fared.*

FOORSDAY, *Thursday.*

FORBEARS, *forebears.*

FORBY, *besides.*

FORFAIRN, *worn out, forlorn.*

FORFOUGHTEN, } *exhausted (i.e. by labour or conflict).*

FORGATHER, *to meet, to assemble accidentally.*

FORGIE, *to forgive.*

FORJESKET, *jaded with fatigue.*

FORRIT, *forward.*

FOTHER, *fodder.*

FOU, FOW, *full; not sober, drunk.*

FOUGHTEN, *troubled (i.e. by conflict with difficulties).*

FOUMART, *the polecat.*

FOURSOME, *a quartette.*

FOUTH, *abundance, plenty; numerous.*

FOW, *v.* FOU.

FOW, *a bushel.*

FRAE, *from.*

FREATH, *to froth.*

FREMIT, *strange, foreign, unrelated.*

FREWCH, *brittle.*

FRIEN, *a friend.*

FU', *full.*

FU'-HAN'T, *full-handed.*

FUD, *a short tail; the buttocks.*

FUFF'T, *puffed.*

FUR-AHIN, *the hindmost plough-horse in the furrow.*

FURDER, *further.*

FURDER, *to succeed.*

FURM, *a wooden form.*

FUR, FURR, *a furrow.*

FUSHIONLESS, *tasteless, sapless, insipid.*

FYKE, *to fidget, to be restless.*

FYLE, FYLED, *to dirty, to soil; soiled.*

GAB, *the mouth, insolence.*

GABS, *talk.*

GAE (GANG); GAEN, GANE; GAED; GAUN, *to go; gone; went, going.*

GAETS, *ways, manners.*

GAIRS, *ornamental slashes in a lady's dress.*

GAIT, *way, manner, practice, deportment.*

GANE, *gone.*

GANG, *to go.*

GANGREL, *a vagrant.*

GAPIN, *gaping, looking foolish or idiotic.*

GAR, *to make, to cause, to compel.*

GAR'T, *compelled, caused, forced.*

GARTEN, *garter.*

GARTEN'D, *gartered.*

GASH, *wise, sagacious; pert or insolent speech.*

GASHING, *talking, gabbing.*

GAT, *got.*

GATE, *a way, path, road.*

GAUCIE, GAUSIE, *plump, portly, well-conditioned.*

GAUD, *a goad.*

GAU'N, *Gavin.*

GAUN, *going.*

GAUNTED, *gaped, yawned.*

GAWKY, *awkward, ungainly.*

GAWSIE, *buxom, buxom and jolly; big and joyous.*

GAYLIES, *gaily.*

GEAR, *goods, property, wealth, money, harness, tools, tackle, etc.*

GECK, *to toss the head, to sport.*

GED, *a pike.*

GENTLE, *well-born.*

GENTY, *courteous, having good manners.*

GEORDIE, *dim. of George; a guinea.*

GET, *issue, offspring, breed.*

GHAIST, *a ghost.*

GIE, GAE; GIED; GIEN; *to give; gave; given.*

GIF, *if, whether.*

GIFTIE, *dim. of gift.*

GIGLETS, *giggling youngsters or maids.*

GILL, *a half-pint glass; a quarter-pint glass of whisky.* A HAWICK GILL = *two gills.*

GILLIE, *dim. of gill.*

GILPEY, *young girl.*

GIMMER, *a young female sheep, a ewe that has not borne young.*

GIN, *before, until, unless, if, whether, should.*

GIRDLE, *a circular iron plate for baking cakes.*

GIRN, GIRNIN, *to grin, grinning; peevish, complaining.*

GIRR, *a hoop.*

GIZZ, *wig.*

GLAIKIT, *foolish, thoughtless, giddy.*

GLAIKS, TO GET THE, *to be deceived, deluded, cheated, jilted.*

GLAIVE, *a sword, a broadsword.*

GLAIZIE, *glossy, shiny.*

GLAUM'D, *grasped, clutched, snatched.*

GLED, *the common kite, a hawk.*

GLEEDE, *a spark, ember, red-hot coal.*

GLEG, *clear-sighted, sharp, eager.*

GLEIB, *a piece, a portion; the land belonging to the clergy benefice.*

GLENTURIT, *a small lateral valley to the Earn in Perthshire.*

GLIBBER, *smoothly.*

GLIB-GABBET, *smooth-tongued.*

GLINTED, *flashed.*

GLINTIN, *sparkling.*

GLOAMIN, *twilight, dusk, evening.*

GLOAMIN-SHOT, *sunset; a twilight interview.*

GLOOVES, *gloves.*

GLOW'R, *a frown; to stare, to scowl.*

GLOWRIN. *threatening (weather); staring, stormy.*

GLUNCH, *a frown, a growl.*

GLUNCH, *to frown, to growl.*

GOAVIN, *looking dazedly; mooning.*

GOR-COCK, *the moorcock.*

GOTTEN, *got.*

GOWAN, *a generic name for the daisy.*

GOWANY, *covered with wild daisies.*

GOWD, *gold, money.*

GOWDEN, *golden.*

GOWDIE, *the head.*

GOWFF'D, *struck; hit as in the game of golf.*

GOWK, *a blockhead, simpleton, an awkward fellow; the cuckoo.*

GOWLING, *lamenting (as a dog in grief).*

GRAFF, *a grave.*

GRAIN, *a branch; the fork of a tree or the junction of its branches.*

GRAIN'D, *groaned.*

GRAIP, *to grope; a dung-fork.*

GRAITH, *tools, harness, equipment of any kind.*

GRAITHING, *gearing, vestments.*

GRANE, *a groan; to groan.*

GRANNIE, GRAUNIE, *grandmother.*

GRAPE, *a dung-fork.*

GRAPED, GRAPET, *groped.*

GRAT, *wept.*

GRAUNIE, *v.* GRANNIE.

GREE, *to agree; the first place, the highest honours.*

GREET; GRAT; GREETIN, *to cry, to weep; wept; weeping.*

GRIPPIT, *arrested, clasped.*

GRIST, *the corn sent to the mill; used equiv.*

GROANIN-MAUT, *the lying-in drink for the midwife and friends.*

GROZET, *a gooseberry.*

GRUMPHIE, *the pig.*

GRUNTLE, *the face, the phiz.*

GRUNTLE, *dim. of grunt.*

GRUNZIE, *the snout, mouth, face, visage.*

GRUPE, *caught hold, seized.*

GRUSHIE, *growing.*

GRUTTEN, *wept.*

GUDE, GUID, *God, good.*

GUIDE'EN, *good evening, a salutation.*

GUID-FATHER, *father-in-law.*

GUID-WIFE, (also GUDE-WIFE), *the mistress of the house, the landlady.*

GUID-WILLY, *hospitable, kindly, generous good-will.*

GUDEMAN, GUIDMAN, *the master of the house, a husband, a tenant farmer.*

GUDESAKE, *God sake!*

GULLIE, GULLY, *a large knife.*

GUMLIE, *muddy.*

GUMPTION, *wisdom, skill.*

GUSE, *a goose.*

GUSTY, *tasty.*

GUTCHER, *grandfather, grandsire.*

GUT-SCRAPER, *a fiddler.*

HA', *the hall.*

HADDEN, HADDIN, *holding, inheritance.*

HAE, HAEN, *to have; had, been having.*

HAET, *an atom, a very small quantity.*

HAFFETS, *the temples, the side locks.*

HAFFINS, *half, partly.*

HAG, *a moss, a broken bog.*

HAGGIS, *a dish generally consisting of the lungs, heart, and liver of a sheep minced with suet, onions etc., and cooked in a sheep's maw.*

HAIRST, HAR'ST, *harvest.*

HAITH, *" in faith! " an exclamation.*

HAILL, *whole, well, healthful.*

HAIN, HAIN'D, *to spare, to save; saved.*

HAIVERS, *v.* HAVERS.

HAL', HALD, *holding, possession;* '*house an' hal'(d)'* = *house and possession.*

HALE, HAIL, *the whole.*

HALE, HAIL, *whole, healthy.*

HALESOME, *wholesome.*

HALLAN, *a porch, a dwelling, a house.*

HALLAN-EN', *the end of the porch or partition-wall between the door and the fire.*

HALLOWEEN, *All Saints' Eve* (31st October).

HALLOWMAS, *All Saints' Day* (1st November).

HALS, *the neck, the throat.*

HALY, *holy.*

HAME, *home.*

HAMMER, *a clumsy, noisy person.*

HAN', *the hand.*

HAN-DARG (or DAURK), *v.* DARG.

HAND-BREED, *a handbreadth.*

HAND-WAL'D, *hand-picked* (i.e. *choicest*).

HANGIE, *hangman* (nickname of the Devil).

HANKERS, *desires, covets.*

HANSEL, *to use a thing for the first time; the first gift, the first buyer; earnest-money.*

HANSELLING, *the first use or celebration.*

HAP, *to cover for warmth, to wrap, to tuck in; a covering, a wrap.*

HAPPER, *hopper* (of a mill).

HAPPING, *hopping* (as a bird).

HAP-STEP-AN'-LOWP, *hop-step-and-jump.*

HARKIT, *hearkened.*

HARN, *coarse cloth.*

HARRY, HERRY, *to rob, to plunder, to ravage.*

HARST, *v.* HAIRST.

HASH, *an oaf, a dunderhead.*

HASLOCK, *v.* HALS.

HASLOCK-WOO', *the finest wool on the hals or throat of a sheep.*

HAUD, *to hold.*

HAUF, *the half; to halve.*

HAUGHS, *low-lying rich lands, valleys.*

HAUN, *v.* HAN'.

HAURL, HAURL'D, *to drag, dragged.*

HAUSE, *to embrace, to hug, v.* HALS.

HAUVER-MEAL, *oatmeal.*

HAVERIL, HAV'RD, *one who talks nonsense, a half-witted person.*

HAVERS, *nonsense.*

HAVINS, *sense, manners, behaviour.*

HAWKIE, *a white-faced cow, a cow.*

HAWKIT, *a white face, applied to kine.*

HEADIN-MAN, *a headsman, an executioner.*

HEAL, *v.* HALE.

HEALSOME, *v.* HALESOME.

HECHT, *a promise, an offer; to promise, to engage.*

HECKLE, *a flax-comb; to cross-examine.*

HEE, *a call.*

HEELS-O'ER-GOWDIE, *v.* GOWDIE.

HEEZE, *to hoist, to exalt, to raise.*

HEICH, HEIGH, *high.*

HELLIM, *a helm.*

HEM-SHIN'D, *bow-legged, like the shape of the half of a horse-collar.*

HERE AWA, *here about.*

HERN, *the heron.*

HERRYMENT, *spoliation.*

HERSEL, *herself.*

HET, *hot.*

HETTEST, *hottest.*

HEUGH, *a crag, a pit, a hollow.*

HEUK, *a hook, reaping-hook.*

HIE-GATE, *a thoroughfare through a town.*

HILCH, *to hobble, to halt.*

HILLOCK, *dim. of hill, a mound.*

HILTIE-SKILTIE, *helter-skelter.*

HIMSEL, *himself.*

HINEY, HINNY, *honey; a term of endearment.*

HING, *to hang.*

HIRPLE, *to hobble, to limp, to walk lamely.*

HISSELS, *so many cattle as one person can attend.*

HISTIE, *bare.*

HIZZIE, *a huzzy; a wench.*

HOAST, *a cough; to cough.*

HODDEN, HODDIN, *homespun cloth made of natural-coloured wool.*

HODDEN-GREY, *a grey homespun.*

HODDIN, *the motion of a sage countryman riding on a cart horse.*

HOG, HOGGIE, *a first-year-old sheep before shearing, v.* DINMONT *and* GIMMER.

HOG-SCORE. *a term in curling.*

HOG-SHOUTHER, *a kind of horseplay by justling with the shoulder. to justle.*

HOLLAN, HOLLAND, *linen imported from there.*

HOODIE, *the hooded and common crow.*

HOODOCK, *grasping, vulturish.*

HOOKED, *caught.*

HOOL, *the outer case, the sheath.*

HOOLIE, *softly.*

HOORD, *hoard.*

HOORDET, *hoarded.*

HORN, *a horn spoon; a toothed comb of horn.*

HORNIE, *the Devil.*

HOST, *v.* HOAST.

HOTCH'D, *jerked.*

HOUGHMAGANDIE, *fornication.*

HOULET, *v.* HOWLET.

HOUPE, *hope.*

HOWDIE, HOWDY, *a midwife.*

HOWE, *a hollow, a dell.*

HOWE, *hollow.*

HOWKET, *digged, dug, unearthed.*

HOWLET, *the owl.*

HOYSE, *a hoist.*

HOY'T, *urged.*

HOYTE, *to amble crazily.*

HUGHOC, *dim. of Hugh.*

HULLIONS, *slovens.*

HUNDER, *a hundred.*

HUNKERS, *bent knees, pleading, in a squatting position, with the haunches, knees, and ankles acutely bent.*

HURCHEON, *the hedgehog.*

HURCHIN, *an urchin.*

HURDIES, *the loins, the crupper (i.e. the buttocks).*

HURL, *to trundle.*

HUSHION, *a footless stocking.*

HYTE, *furious.*

I', *in.*

ICKER, *an ear of corn.*

IER-OE, *a great-grandchild.*

ILK, ILKA, *the same, each, every.*

ILL O'T, *bad at it.*

ILL-TAEN, *ill-taken.*

ILL-THIEF, *the Devil.*

ILL-WILLIE, *ill-natured, malicious, niggardly.*

INDENTIN, *indenturing.*

INGINE, *genius, ingenuity, wit.*

INGLE, *the fireplace, a chimney-corner.*

INGLE-GLEEDE, *a blazing fireside.*

INGLE-LOWE, INGLE LOW, *the flame or light of the fire.*

IN-KNEE'D, *knock-kneed.*

IS, *often used for the plural are.*

I'SE, *I shall or will.*

ITHER, *other.*

ITSEL', *itself.*

JAD, *an old worn-out horse; a scurvy woman.*

JANWAR, *January.*

JAUK, *to trifle, to dally.*

JAUNER, *to talk at random, to jabber.*

JAUNTIE, *dim. of jaunt.*

JAUP, *to splash.*

JAW, *impudent talk; to pour, to dash, to splash.*

JAWPISH, *frolicsome, mischievous, tricky.*

JEE'D, *stirred, rocked, jogged.*

JEEG, *to jerk.*

JILLET, *a jilt.*

JIMP, JIMPY *or* JIMPLY, *neatly, elegantly.*

JIMPS, *easy stays open in front.*

JINK, *to frisk, to sport, to dodge, move out and in.*

JINKER, *' a jinker noble '=a noble goer, dodger, gamester (i.e. coquette).*

JINKIN, *dodging, moving quickly.*

JINKS, *tricks, dodges.*

JIRKINET, *a woman's outside jacket.*

JIRT, *a jerk.*

JIZ, *a wig.*

JO, *a sweetheart.*

JO, *joy, an expression of good will, friendly address.*

JOCTELEG, *a clasp-knife.*

JORUM, *a large drinking jug or bowl.*

JOUK, *to cower, to bend, to stoop.*

JOW, *to jow, a verb which includes both the swinging motion and pealing sound of a large bell.*

JUMPET, JUMPIT, *jumped.*

JUNDIE, *to justle.*

JURR, *a servant wench.*

KAE, *a jackdaw.*

KAIL, *colewort, cabbage; broth made from greens.*

KAIL-BLADE, *the leaf of the colewort.*

KAIL-GULLIE, *a cabbage-knife; v.* GULLIE.

KAIL-RUNT, *the stem of the corewort.*

KAIL-WHITTLE, *a cabbage-knife.*

KAIL-YARD, *a kitchen-garden.*

KAIN, KANE, *rents in kind.*

KAME, KAIM'D, *to comb, combed.*

KEBARS, *beams, rafters.*

KEBBUCK, *a large cheese uncut.*

KECKLE, *to cackle, to giggle loudly (as a girl).*

KEEK, *a look, a glance.*

KEEK, *to look, to peep, to glance.*

KEEKIN-GLASS, *a looking-glass.*

KEEKIT, *pryed, peered, gazed.*

KEEL, *v.* CAUK.

KEEPIT, *kept.*

KELPIES, *river-demons.*

KEN, KEND, KEN'T, *to know; known.*

KENNA, *know not.*

KENNIN, *a very little.*

KENT, *v.* KEND.

KEP, *to catch.*

KET, *the fleece on a sheep's body.*

KEY, *quay.*

KEY-STANE, *key-stone.*

KIAUGH, *cark.*

KILBAIGIE, *a favourite brand of whisky manufactured at Kilbaigie, Clackmannan, one of the earliest distilleries after the abolition of the Ferintosh monopoly.*

KILLOGIE, *a vacuity before the fire-place in a kiln.*

KILT, *a short dress; to tuck up the skirts.*

KIMMER, *v.* CUMMER.

KIN, *blood relations.*

KIN', *kind.*

KING'S-HOOD, *the second stomach in a ruminant (equivocal for the scrotum).*

KINTRA, *country, neighbours.*

KIRK, *a church.*

KIRN, *a churn.*

KIRN, *harvest-home.*

KIRSEN, *to christen.*

KIRTLE, *a woman's short skirt or outer petticoat.*

KIST, *kissed; a chest.*

KITCHEN, *to relish (to add relish to).*

KITH, *acquaintance, those not related by blood.*

KITTLE, *difficult; to tickle.* TO KITTLE HAIR ON THAIRMS=*to play the fiddle.*

KITTLE, *difficult; ticklish, delicate, fickle.*

KITTLE, *to tickle.*

KITTLIN, *a kitten.*

KIUTLIN, *cuddling.*

KNAGGIE, *knobby.*

KNAGGS, *knobs. protuberances.*

KNAPPIN-HAMMERS, *hammers for breaking stones.*

KNOWE, *a knoll, a hillock.*

KNURL, *a dwarf, a hunchback; stunted.*

KYE, *cattle.*

KYLES, *nine-pins (form of skittles).*

KYTES, *bellies.*

KYTHE, *to show.*

LABOUR LEA, *to plough grass land.*

LADDIE. *dim. of lad.*

LADE, *a load.*

LAG, *backward.*

LAGGEN, *the bottom of a wooden dish.*

LAIGH, *low.*

LAIK, *lack, want.*

LAIRD, *a landowner; an abbey laird=one who took refuge from his creditors in Holyrood Abbey.*

LAIRING, *sticking or sinking in moss or mud.*

LAITH, *loath.*

LAITHFU', *loathful, sheepish.*

LALLAN, LALLAND, *lowland.*

LALLANS, *Scots Lowland vernacular.*

LAMMIE, *dim. of lamb.*

LAN', *land.*

LAN'-AFORE, *the foremost horse on the unploughed land side.*

LAN'-AHIN, *the hindmost horse on the unploughed land side.*

LANE, *alone, solitary, lonely.*

LANG, *long.*

LANG-NECKIT, *long-necked.*

LANG-SYNE, *long since.*

LAP, *leaped.*

LAPWING, *the plover.*

LASS, *a girl, a young woman, a sweet-heart, the complement of lad.*

LAVE, *flowing freely; the rest or remainder.*

LAVEROCK, *the lark.*

LAW, *low; a round-capped mountain which ascends by stages.*

LAWIN, *the expense, the cost, the bill.*

LEA, *grass, untilled land (also used in an equivocal sense).*

LEAL, *loyal, true, trusty.*

LEAR, LAIR, *learning, knowledge, education.*

LEA-RIG, *a ridge in a field left unploughed between ridges bearing grain.*

LEARN, *to teach.*

LEDDY, *lady, the wife of a landlord.*

LEE, *the slope of a hill; warm, sheltered; (in phrase) an intensive meaning of loneliness.*

LEE-LANG, *livelong.*

LEESOME, *lawful, pleasant.*

LEEZE ME, *an expression of pleasure= dear is to me.*

LEISTER, *a fish-spear.*

LEN', *to lend.*

LET BE, *to let alone, to cease from.*

LEUGH, *laughed.*

LEUK, *looked.*

LEY-CRAP, *the first crop after the ploughing of grass or fallow land.*

LIBBET, *castrated.*

LICKIT MY WINNINS=*dissipated my means or money.*

LICKS, *a beating, punishment.*

LIEIN, *lying, equivocating.*

LIEN, *lain.*

LIFT, *the sky, the heavens; to collect, to steal.*

LIFT, *a load.*

LIGHTLY, *to disparage, to scorn.*

LILT, LILTING, *a song; merry singing.*

LIMMER, *a jade, a mistress.*

LIMPET, LIMPIT, *limped.*

LIMPIN, *limping, hobbling.*

LIN, *v.* LINN.

LINENS, *underclothing; death-clothes.*

LINGLES, *shoemaker's thread.*

LINK, *to trip or dance with the utmost possible activity; to hurry.*

LINKIN, *tripping, dancing, hurrying.*

LINN, *a waterfall.*

LINT, *flax.*

LINTWHITE, LINTIE, *the linnet.*

LINT-WHITE, *flaxen-coloured.*

LIPPEN, *to trust, to believe.*

LIPPIE, *dim. of lip.*

LOAN, LOANING, *a lane, a farm road.*

LO'E, LOO, LO'ED, *to love; loved.*

LOGIE, *v.* KILLOGIE.

LON'ON, *London.*

LOOF, *the palm of the hand, the open hand.*

LOON, LOUN, LOWN, *a rascal, a fellow, a servant, a varlet.*

LOOT, *did let.*

LOOVE, *love.*

LOOVES, *v.* LOOF.

LOSH, *a minced oath (a mild form of Lord).*

LOUGH, *a pond, a lake.*

LOUP, LOWP, *to leap.*

LOUR, *lowering, impending.*

LOWE, *a flame; to flame.*

LOWIN, *lowing, flaming, burning.*

LOWN, *v.* LOON.

LOWPIN, *leaping, jumping.*

LOWRY, *Lawrence; a crafty person.*

LOWSE, *to loose, to untie.*

LUCKIE, LUCKY, *an elderly woman, an alewife, a familiar address.*

LUG, *the ear, a handle.*

LUGGET, *having ears.*

LUGGIE, *a small wooden vessel with a handle.*

LUM, *the chimney.*

LUME, *a loom.*

LUNARDI, *a balloon-bonnet (named after Lunardi, a famous balloonist).*

LUNCHES, *full portions.*

LUNT, *a column of smoke or steam.*

LUNTIN, *smoking.*

LUVE, *love.*

LUNZIE-BANES, *the loin bones.*

LYART, *grey, of a mixed colour.*

LYE, *to lie down.*

LYMMAR *or* LIMMER, *a knave, a jade.*

LYNIN, *lining.*

MAE, *more.*

MAILEN, MAILIN, *a farm, holding, rent; the outfit for a bride.*

MAILIE, *Molly.*

MAIR, *more.*

MAIST, *most, almost.*

MAK, *to make.*

MAK O', MAKE O', *to pet, to fondle.*

MALL, MALLY, *Moll, Molly, (Mary).*

MALVOSIE, *Malmsey wine.*

MANTEELE, *a mantle.*

MANTIE, *a mantle, a lady's cloak.*

MARK, or MERK, *an old Scots coin (13⅓d. sterling).*

MASHLUM, *of mixed meal.*

MASKIN-PAT, *a tea-pot, a still.*

MAUKIN, *a hare; a slattern, a term of abuse.*

MAUN, *must.*

MAUNNA, *must not.*

MAUT, *malt, liquor.*

MAVIS, *the thrush.*

MAWIN, *mowing.*

MAWN, *a basket or hamper; mown.*

MAY, *a maid.*

MEAR, MEARE, *a mare.*

MEIKLE, MICKLE, MUCKLE, *much, great, large.*

MELDER, *the quantity of corn sent to be ground.*

MELL, *to mix, to mingle, to have intercourse with.*

MELVIE, *to meal-dust.*

MEN', *to mend.*

MENSE, *tact, discretion.*

MENSELESS, *unmannerly.*

MENZIE, *retainers, followers, men.*

MERLE, *a blackbird.*

MERRAN, *Marian.*

MESS JOHN, *Mass John (the parish priest, the minister).*

MESSIN, *a cur, a mongrel.*

MIDDEN, *a dunghill.*

MIDDEN-CREELS, *manure baskets carried on the back.*

MIDDEN DUB, *midden puddle.*

MIDDEN-HOLE, *a gutter at the bottom of the dunghill.*

MILKIN-SHIEL, *the milking-shed.*

MIM, *prim, affectedly meek.*

MIM-MOU'D, *said of one who speaks affectedly.*

MIN', *mind, remembrance; to recollect.*

MIND, *to remember, to bear in mind.*

MINDNA, *to mind not, to forget.*

MINNIE, MINNY, *mother.*

MIRK, *gloomy, dark; darkness.*

MIRKEST, *gloomiest, darkest.*

MISCA', *to miscall, to abuse.*

MISHANTER, *mishap.*

MISLEAR'D, *mischievous, unmannerly.*

MISS'T, MIST, *missed.*

MISTAK, *mistake.*

MISTEUK, *mistook.*

MITHER, *mother.*

MITTEN'D, *covered, gloved.*

MONIE, MONY, *many.*

MOOLS, *crumbling earth, dust.*

MOOP, *to mump, to nibble as a sheep.*

MORN, *the next day, to-morrow.*

MOTTIE, *dusty.*

MOU', *the mouth.*

MOUDIEWART, MOUDIEWORTS, *the mole; moles.*

MUCK, *manure.*

MUCKIN, *cleansing the stable or cow-house.*

MUCKLE, *v. MEIKLE.*

MUIR, *moorland, a fell.*

MULTURE or MOUTER, *the portion retained by the miller for grinding the corn.*

MUSLIN-KAIL, *beefless broth.*

MYSIE, *Mary.*

MUTCHKIN, *an English pint.*

MYSEL, *myself.*

NA, NAE, *no, not, but, than.*

NAEBODY, *nobody, no one.*

NAETHING, NAITHING, *nothing.*

NAIG, *a nag.*

NAIGIE, *a small riding-horse.*

NANE, *none.*

NAPPY, *ale, liquor.*

NATCH, *a notching implement.*

NAUR, *near to, close to.*

NEB, *the nose, a beak.*

NEBBIT, *shaped like a bird's bill.*

NEEDNA, *needn't.*

NEGLECKIT, *neglected.*

NEIBOR, *a neighbour.*

NEIST, NIEST, *next, nearest.*

NEIVES, NIEVES, *the fists, the closed hands.*

NEUK, NEWK, *a nook, a corner.*

NEW-CA'D, *newly-driven.*

NICHER, *to neigh; the call of a mare to her foal.*

NICK (AULD), NICKIE-BEN, *a name of the Devil.*

NICK, *to sever, to slit, to nail, to seize away.*

NICKIE-BEN, *v.* NICK (AULD).

NICK-NACKETS, *curiosities.*

NICKS. *cuts, the rings on a cow's horns.*

NIEST, *next.*

NIEVE, *the fist.*

NIEVE-FU', *fistful.*

NIFFER, *exchange.*

NIGHT-FA', *nightfall, twilight.*

NIPT, *pinched, shrivelled.*

NIT, *a nut.*

NO, *not.*

NOCHT, *nothing, no more.*

NORLAND, *northland.*

NOWT, NOWTE, *cattle, nolt.*

O', *of.*

OCHILS, *the mountain range dividing Perthshire from Clackmannan.*

O'ERLAY, *a blouse, a smock.*

O'ERWORD, *a refrain, a chorus.*

ONIE, ONY, *any.*

OR, *ere, before.*

ORRA, *extra, superfluous.*

O's, *of his, of us.*

O'T, *of it.*

OUGHT, *aught.*

OUGHTLINS, AUGHTLINS, *aught in the least, at all.*

OURIE, *shivering, drooping.*

OURSEL, OURSELS, *ourselves.*

OUTLER, *unhoused, in the open fields.*

OUTSKIN'D, *shin-bones turned outwards.*

OUTWITTENS, *without the knowledge of.*

OWRE, *over.*

OWSEN, *oxen.*

OXTER, *the armpit.*

OXTER'D, *held up under the arms.*

PACK AN' THICK, *confidential.*

PACTION, *an agreement, an arrangement.*

PAIDLE, *to paddle.*

PAINCH, *the paunch.*

PAITRICK, *a partridge.*

PANG, *to cram.*

PARISHEN, *the parish.*

PARLE, *speech.*

PARLEY, *a truce, a conference.*

PARRITCH, *porridge.*

PARRITCH-PATS, *porridge-pots.*

PAT, *a pot; did put, ejected.*

PATTLE, PETTLE, *a plough-staff.*

PAUGHTY, *haughty.*

PAUKIE, PAWKIE, *sly, artful, knowing.*

PEAT-CREEL, *a basket for carrying dried bog turf for fuel.*

PECHAN, *the stomach.*

PECHIN, *out of breath, panting.*

PENDLES, *earrings.*

PENNY-FEE, *wages, income.*

PEENY-WHEEP, *small beer.*

PETTLE, *v.* PATTLE.

PHEMIE, *Euphemia.*

PHILIBEG, *the kilt, or Highlander's short dress.*

PHRAISIN, *flattering, wheedling.*

PHRASE, *to flatter, to wheedle.*

PICKLE, *a few, a small quantity.*

PIN, *a wooden bar or door-latch.*

PINE, *pain, care.*

PINK, *to glimmer, to contract the eye in looking; a woman who glimmers.*

PINT (Scots), *two English quarts.*

PINT-STOUP, *a pint-vessel containing two English quarts.*

PIT, *to put.*

PLACADS, *shouts.*

PLACK, *four pennies Scots.*

PLACKLESS, *penniless.*

PLAIDEN, *coarse woollen cloth.*

PLAIDEN-WAB, *homespun tweeled woollen.*

PLAIDIE or PLAID, *a broad unformed piece of cloth for wrapping about the shoulders and body.*

PLAISTER, *plaster.*

PLASHY, *applied to a body of water driven violently.*

PLENISH'D, *stocked.*

PLEUGH, *a plough; to plough.*

PLEUGH-PETTLE, *v.* PATTLE.

PLISKIE, *a trick.*

PLIVER, *the plover.*

POCKS, *pockets, bags.*

POIND, *to seize (originally in war, or as prey), to distrain, to impound.*

POIND, *distrained.*

POORTITH, *poverty.*

POU, PU', *to pull.*

POUCH, *a pocket.*

POUK, *to poke.*

POUPIT, *pulpit.*

POUSE, *a push.*

POUSSIE, *a hare (also a cat).*

POUTHERED, *powdered; sanctified.*

POUTS, *chicks.*

POW, *the poll, the head.*

POWNIE, *a pony.*

POW'T, *pulled.*

PREE'D, *tasted.*

PREEN, *a pin; to pin.*

PRENT, *print.*

PRIE, PREE, *to prove, to taste, to try.*

PRIEF, *proof.*

PRIESTIE, *a priest; used derisively.*

PRIGGIN, *haggling.*

PRIMSIE, *dim. of prim, precise.*

PROVESES, *provosts.*

PU', *to pull.*

PUDDOCK-STOOLS, *toad-stools.*

PUIR, *pure, poor.*

PUMPS, *light shoes.*

PUN', PUND, *a pound.*

PURSIE, *a small purse.*

PUSSIE, *a hare.*

PYET, *a magpie.*

PYKE, *to pick.*

PYLES, *grains.*

QUAT, *quit, did quit.*

QUEAN, QUINE, *a young attractive woman.*

QUEY, *a cow that has not calved.*

QUIRE, *choir.*

QUO', QUOD., *quoth.*

RAB, *Rob (dim. of Robert).*

RADE, *rode.*

RAEP, *a rope.*

RAGWEED, *ragwort, benweed.*

RAIBLES, *recites by rote.*

RAIR, *to roar.*

RAIRIN, *roaring.*

RAIR'T, *roared.*

RAISE, *rase, rose.*

RAIZE, *to excite.*

RAMFEEZL'D, *exhausted.*

RAMGUNSHOCH, *surly, cross-grained.*

RAM-STAM, *headlong.*

RANDIE, *randy, a sturdy, abusive or threatening beggar.*

RANT, *to rollick; to roister.*

RANTS, *merry meetings, sprees, rows.*

RANTIN, *boisterous, rollicking.*

RAPE, *v.* RAEP.

RAPLOCH, *homespun.*

RASH, *a rush.*

RASH-BUSS, *a clump of rushes.*

RASHY, *rushy.*

RATTON, RATTAN, *a rat.*

RATTON-KEY, *the Rat-Quay.*

RAUCLE, RAUCKLE, *stout, clever, rash, fearless.*

RAUGHT, *reached.*

RAW, *a row.*

RAX, *to stretch, to extend.*

REAM, *cream, foam.*

REAVE, *to rob.*

REBUTE, *a rebuff; to rebuke.*

RECK, *to take heed.*

RED, *advised, afraid.*

RED, REDE, *to advise, to counsel.*

REDE, *counsel; to counsel, to advise.*

REEK, *smoke.*

REEKIE, REEKY, *smoky.*

REEKIT, *smoked, dingy.*

REEL, *a dance probably indigenous to Britain (but known in Scandinavia), performed by one or two couples. The chief feature is a circular movement, the dancers standing face to face and describing rapidly a series of figures of 8 with a gliding motion.*

REESTIT, *refused to go.*

REESTIT, *scorched.*

REIF, *to reave, to thieve.*

REMEAD, *remedy.*

REW, *to rue.*

RICKLES, *ricklets (small stacks of corn in the fields).*

RIEF, *plunder.*

RIG, *a ridge.*

RIGGIN, *the roof-tree.*

RIGWOODIE, *ancient, lean.*

RIN, *to run.*

RINGLE-EY'D, *with much white in the eye.*

RIPP, *a handful of corn from the sheaf.*

RIPPLES, RIPELLS, *shooting pains in the back and reins.*

RIPPLIN-KAME, *a comb for separating the bolls of flax from the stem; used equiv.*

RISKIT, *cracked.*

RITHER, *a rudder.*

RIVE, *to split, to tear, to tug, to burst.*

ROCK, *a distaff.*

ROOD, *a crucifix, a cross.*

ROON, *round.*

ROOSE, *reputation.*

ROOS'D, *praised, flattered.*

ROOSE, *to praise, to commend.*

ROOSTY, *rusty, disused.*

ROTTAN, ROTTIN, *the rat.*

ROUN', *round.*

ROUPET, *exhausted in voice.*

ROUTH, *plenty, good store.*

ROUTHIE, *well-stocked, of comfortable means.*

ROW'D, *rolled, wrapt.*

ROWE, *to roll, to wrap; to flow.*

ROWIN, *rolling, wrapping.*

ROWTE, *to low, to bellow.*

ROWTH, *plenty, a store.*

ROZET, *rozin.*

RUMPLE-BANE, *the rump-bone.*

RUN-DEILS, *downright devils.*

RUNG, *a stout stick, a cudgel.*

RUNKL'D, *wrinkled.*

RUNT, *a cabbage, or colewort-stalk.*

RYKE, *to reach up.*

SAB, *to sob.*

SAE, *so.*

SAFT, *soft.*

SAIR, SAIR'D, *to serve, served.*

SAIR, SAIRLY, *sore, sorely, severely.*

SAIRIE, *sorrowful.*

SALL, *shall.*

SARK, *a shirt, a smock.*

SASSENACH, SASUNNACH, *the Gaelic for Saxon.*

SAUL, *soul.*

SAUMONT, SAWMONT, *the salmon.*

SAUNT, *saint.*

SAUT, *salt.*

SAUT-BACKETS, *v.* BACKET.

SAW, *to sow.*

SAWNEY, SANDIE, *Alexander.*

SAX, *six.*

SCAITH, SKAITH, *damage, hurt, injury.*

SCANT, *devoid, little or few.*

SCAR, *to scare.*

SCAUD, *to scald.*

SCAUL, *scold.*

SCAULD, *to scold, a scold.*

SCAUR, *afraid, apt to be scared.*

SCAUR, *a jutting cliff or bank of earth.*

SCHO, *she.*

SCONE, *a soft cake.*

SCONNER, *disgust.*

SCONNER, *sicken (with disgust).*

SCRAICHIN, *calling hoarsely.*

SCREED, *a rip, a rent.*

SCREED, *to repeat rapidly, to rattle.*

SCRIECHIN, *screeching.*

SCRIEVIN, *careering.*

SCRIMP, *to save, to deal sparingly.*

SCROGGY, *applied to hill slopes covered with brushwood.*

SCUDS, *brisk beer, foaming ale.*

SCULDUDD'RY, *fornication, bawdry.*

SEE'D, *saw (pret. of see).*

SEISINS, *freehold possessions.*

SEL', *self.*

SELL'D, SELL'T, *sold.*

SEMPLE, *simple, low-born.*

SEN', *send.*

SET, *to set off, to start.*

SET, *sat.*

SETS, *becomes.*

SHACHL'D, *twisted, bent, shapeless.*

SHAIRD, *shred, shard.*

SHANGAN, *a cleft stick.*

SHANKS, *the legs.*

SHANNA, *shall not.*

SHAUL, *shallow.*

SHAVER, *a funny fellow.*

SHAVIE, *a prank.*

SHAW, *a wood; to show.*

SHEARER, *a reaper.*

SHEEP-SHANK, *a sheep's trotter.*

SHEERLY, *wholly.*

SHEERS, *scissors.*

SHELLIN-HILL, *the hill or eminence where grain was dried and husked by the wind.*

SHERRA-MOOR, *Sheriffmuir.*

SHEUGH, *a ditch, a trench; the seed-furrow.*

SHEUK, *shook, did shake.*

SHIEL, *a shelter, a hut.*

SHILL, *shrill.*

SHOG, *a shake.*

SHOOL, *a shovel; to shovel.*

SHOOLING, *shovelling.*

SHOON, *shoes.*

SHORE, SHOR'D, *to offer; to threaten; offered.*

SHORT SYNE, *a little time ago.*

SHOULDNA, *should not.*

SHOUTHER, *the shoulder.*

SHURE, *sheared, did shear.*

SHUTE, *to shoot.*

SIC, *such.*

SICCAN, *such kind of.*

SICKER, *steady.*

SIDELINS, *sideways.*

SILLER, *silver, money, wealth.*

SILLY, *frail, in delicate health; harmless.*

SIMMER, *summer.*

SIN', *since.*

SINDRY, *sundry.*

SINGET, *singed, shrivelled.*

SINN, *the sun.*

SINNY, *sunny.*

SINSYNE, *since then.*

SKAIL, *to spill, to pour.*

SKAITH, *damage.*

SKAITH, *to harm, to injure.*

SKEIGH, *skittish, mettlesome.*

SKELLUM, *a good-for-nothing, a scullion.*

SKELP, SKELPIN, *to slap, to smack, to trounce; a smack, smacking.*

SKELPIE-LIMMER'S-FACE, *a technical term in female scolding.*

SKELPIT, *trounced; hastened, ran quickly.*

SKELVY, *shelvy.*

SKIEGH, *v.* SKEIGH.

SKINKING, *watery.*

SKINKLIN, *small.*

SKIRL, *a piercing sound; to shriek.*

SKLENT, *a slanting devious course.*

SKOUTH, *play (freedom).*

SKRIECH, *a scream.*

SKRIEGH, *to scream, to whinny.*

SKYRIN, *flaring.*

SKYTE, *to squirt, to glide, to skate.*

SLADE, *slid.*

SLAE, *the sloe.*

SLAP, *a field gate; a broken fence.*

SLAW, *slow.*

SLEE, *sly.*

SLEEKIT, *sleek, crafty.*

SLIDD'RY, *slippery.*

SLOKEN, *to slake.*

SLYPET, *slipped.*

SMA', *small.*

SMACK, *a sounding kiss; to slap.*

SMEDDUM, *a powder.*

SMEEK, *smoke.*

SMIDDY, *smithy.*

SMOOR, SMOOR'D, *to smother; smothered.*

SMOUTIE, *smutty.*

SMYTRIE, *a small collection, a litter.*

SNAKIN, *sneering.*

SNAPPER, *to stumble; to fail in moral conduct.*

SNASH, *abuse.*

SNAW, *snow.*

SNAW-BROO, *snow-brew (melted snow).*

SNAWDRAP, *the snowdrop.*

SNED, *to crop, to prune.*

SNEESHIN MILL, *a snuff-box.*

SNELL, *keen, sharp, biting.*

SNICK, *a latch.*

SNIRTLE, *to snigger.*

SNOOD, *a ribbon or fillets round the head, worn by maidens.*

SNOODED, *of hair in ribbons.*

SNOOL, *to snub.*

SNOOVE, *to go slowly.*

SNOWKIT, *pried with the nose.*

SNUFF'T, *snuffed, repressed, extinguished.*

SOJER, SODGER, SOGER, *a soldier.*

SONSIE, SONSY (*from sons, plenty*), *pleasant, comfortable, comely.*

SOOM, *to swim.*

SOOR, *sour.*

SORN, *to take bed and board without payment.*

SOUDIE, SOWDY, *a gross heavy person.*

SOUGH, *south, a sigh; to hum or whistle softly; the sighing noise of wind or water.*

SOUK, *to suck; a draught (of liquor).*

SOUN', *sound.*

SOUPE, *sup, liquid.*

SOUPLE, *supple.*

SOUTER, *cobbler.*

SOUTER or SOWTER, *a shoemaker.*

SOWPS, *sups.*

SOWTH, *to hum or whistle in a low tone.*

SOWTHER, *to solder, to cement.*

SPAE, *to foretell.*

SPAILS, *chips.*

SPAIRGE, *to splash, to spatter.*

SPAK, *spoke, did speak.*

SPATES, *floods.*

SPAVIE, *the spavin.*

SPAVIT, *spavined.*

SPEAN, *to wean.*

SPEAT, *a flood.*

SPEEL, *to climb.*

SPEER v. SPIER.

SPEET, *to spit, to impale.*

SPELL, *to narrate, to discourse.*

SPENCE, *the parlour.*

SPIER, *to ask, to inquire.*

SPLEUCHAN, *tobacco-pouch made of some sort of peltry.*

SPLORE, *to boast; a ramble; a revel, partaking of horse-play.*

SPONTOON, *a half pike or halberd discarded in the British Army in 1787.*

SPRACHL'D, *clambered.*

SPRATTLE, *scramble.*

SPRECKLED, *speckled.*

SPRING, *a quick and cheerful tune, a dance.*

SPRITTIE, *full of roots of sprits (a kind of rush).*

SPRUSH, *spruce, dressed up.*

SPULZIE, *plunder; to despoil or rob.*

SPUNK, *spirit, fire, energy; a splint of wood tipped with sulphur.*

SPUNKIE, *spirited.*

SPUNKIES, *jack-o'-lanthorns.*

SPURTLE-BLADE, *the pot-stick.*

SQUATTLE, *to squat, to settle.*

STACHER, *to totter, to stagger.*

STACK, *stuck; remainder.*

STAGGIE, *dim. of staig (a young horse).*

STAIG, *a young horse under three years.*

STAMMER, *to stutter.*

STAN', *stand.*

STANCED, *stationed.*

STANE, *stone.*

STAN'T, *stood.*

STANG, *stung; a sting.* RIDING THE STANG: *a man who beat his wife or who was an impotent bridegroom was set astride a long pole and carried shoulder-high through the town by his fellows as a mark of infamy.*

STANK, *a pool of standing water.*

STAP, *to stop.*

STAPPLE, *a stopper.*

STARK, *strong.*

STARNIES, *dim. of starn or star.*

STARNS, *stars.*

STARTLE, *to course.*

STAUKIN, *stalking, marching.*

STAUMREL, *half-witted.*

STAW, *a stall; did steal; surfeited.*

STECHIN, *cramming*

STEEK, *a stitch, to stitch; to shut, to close.*

STEER, *to stir, to rouse, to remove.*

STEEVE, *compact.*

STELL, *a still.*

STEN, *a spring, a leap, to rear as a horse.*

STEN'T, *sprang.*

STENTED, *erected, set on high.*

STENTS, *assessments, dues.*

STEYEST, *steepest.*

STIBBLE, *stubble.*

STIBBLE-RIG, *chief harvester.*

STICK-AN-STOWE, *completely.*

STICKIT, *stuck, stopped.*

STILT, *limp.*

STIMPART, *a quarter peck.*

STIRK, *a heifer or bullock between one and two years old.*

STOCK, *a plant of cabbage or colewort.*

STOITED, *stumbled.*

STOITER'D, *staggered, staggering in walk.*

STOOR, STOURE, *flying dust, used fig.*

STOT, *a bull, or ox three years old.*

STOUN, *a sudden pang.*

STOUP, *a vessel for holding liquid.*

STOURIE, *dusty.*

STOWN, *stolen.*

STOWNLINS, *by stealth, clandestinely.*

STOYT, *to stagger.*

STRAE DEATH, *death in bed (i.e. on straw).*

STRAIK, *a stroke; to stroke.*

STRAK, *struck, did strike.*

STRANG, *strong.*

STRAPPIN, *tall and handsome.*

STRATHSPEY, *a reel (which see) deriving its name from the valley of the Spey. The music with the title first appears in a collection, c.1780. It is danced slower than the reel, but the motion is more jerky. The*

music is a series of alternate dotted
quavers and semiquavers, whilst a
REEL usually consists of equal
notes.

STRAUGHT, straight; stretched.

STREEKIT, stretched.

STRIDDLE, to straddle.

STROAN'T, lanted.

STRUNT, strong drink; to swagger.

STUDDIE, an anvil.

STUMPIE, curtailed, mutilated.

STUMPS, legs and feet.

STURT, trouble, strife; to molest.

STURTIN, frighted, staggered.

STYME, the faintest outline.

SUCKER, sugar.

SUD, should.

SUGH, SOUGH, sigh, wail, swish.

SUMPH, a churl.

SUNE, soon.

SUTHRON, Southern.

SWAIRD, the sward.

SWALL'D, swelled.

SWANK, limber.

SWANKIES, strapping fellows.

SWAPPED, exchanged.

SWARF, to swoon.

SWAT, sweated.

SWATCH, a sample.

SWATS, new light foaming ale.

SWEER, lazy, unwilling.

SWIRL, a curl.

SWIRLIE, twisted, knaggy.

SWITH, get away!

SWITHER, doubt, hesitation.

SWOOM, swim.

SWOOR, swore.

SYBOW, a young onion.

SYNE, since, then, ago, afterwards, late
as opposed to soon.

TACK, possession, lease.

TACKET, shoe-nail.

TAE, the toe.

TAE'D, having toes or forks.

TAED, the toad.

TAEN, taken.

TAK, to take.

TAIRGE, to target (with importunities).

TALD, told.

TANE, the one.

TANGS, tongs.

TAP, top.

TAPETLESS, pithless.

TAPMOST, topmost.

TAP-PICKLE, the grain at the top of
the stalk.

TAPPIT-HEN, a large round bottle for
holding whisky.

TAPSALTEERIE, topsy-turvy.

TARROW, to tarry.

TASSIE, a glass, a goblet.

TAUK, talk.

TAULD, told.

TAWIE, tractable.

TAWPIE, a foolish woman.

TAWTED, matted.

TEATS, small quantities.

TEEN, vexation.

TEETHIN, teething.

TELL'D, told.

TEMPER-PIN, the wooden pin for
regulating the motion of a spinning-
wheel.

TENT, to take heed or care for.

TENTIE, careful, attentive.

TENTIER, more watchful.

TENTLESS, careless, heedless.

TESTER, an old Scots silver coin about
sixpence in value.

TEUGH, tough.

TEUK, took.

THACK, thatch.

THAE, those.

THAIRMS, catgut fiddle-strings.

THEEKIT, thatched, covered.

THEGITHER, together.

THEMSEL, THEMSELS, themselves.

THICK, v. PACK AN' THICK.

THIEVELESS, forbidding, spiteful.

THIGGIN, begging.

THIR, these.

THIRL'D, thrilled, vibrated; enslaved.

THOLE, to endure.

THOU'SE, thou shalt.

THOWE, a thaw; to thaw.

THOWLESS, lazy, useless.

THRANG, busy, thronging in crowds,
at work.

THRANG, a throng, a crowd.

THRAPPLE, the windpipe.

THRAVE, twenty-four sheaves of corn.

THRAW, to oppose, to resist.

THRAWIN-BROW, cross-grained, per-
verse.

THRAWS, *death-pangs, last agonies.*

THREAP, *maintain (with asseverations).*

THREESOME, *a trio.*

THRETTEEN, *thirteen.*

THRETTY, *thirty.*

THRIPPLIN-KAME, *v.* RIPPLIN-KAME.

THRISTED, *thirsted.*

THROU'THER (*through other*), *pellmell.*

THRUMS, *the sound of a spinning-wheel in motion; ends of threads.*

THUDS, *blows, sounding knocks.*

THUMMART, *polecat.*

THY LANE, *alone.*

TIBBIE, *Elizabeth.*

TIGHT, *girt, prepared.*

TILL, *until.*

TILL'T, *unto it; tilled.*

TIMMER, *timber; a timmer-tun'd person is one devoid of musical perception, or who sings out of tune.*

TINE, TYNE, *to lose.*

TINKLER, *a tinker.*

TINT, *lost.*

TIPPENCE, *twopence.*

TIPPENNY, *two-penny ale.*

TIRL, TIRL'D, *to knock, to rattle, rattled; tirl'd at the pin, rattled the door-latch.*

TITHER, *the other.*

TITTLIN, *whispering.*

TOCHER, *marriage portion; to endow.*

TOCHER-BAND, *the marriage contract.*

TOD, *a fox.*

TO-FA', *the fall of the year; a lean-to building against a house; a refuge.*

TOOM, TOOM'D, *empty, to empty; emptied.*

TOOP, *tup, a ram.*

TOSS, *a toast, a fashionable beauty.*

TOUN, *a farm enclosure.*

TOURS, *turf.*

TOUSIE, *rough, shaggy.*

TOW, *flax; a rope.*

TOWMOND, *twelve months.*

TOWSING, *teasing, romping, ruffling.*

TOYTE, *to totter.*

TOZIE, *flushed with liquor; crapulous.*

TRAMS, *shafts (of a barrow or cart).*

TRASHTRIE, *small trash.*

TREWS, *trousers, breeches.*

TRIG, *neat, spruce.*

TRINKLIN, TRINKLING, *dropping.*

TRIN'LE, *the wheel of a barrow.*

TROGGIN, *small wares, a pedlar's stock-in-trade.*

TROKE, *to barter.*

TROWSE, *trousers.*

TROW'T, *believed.*

TROWTH, *in truth.*

TRYSTE, *an engagement to meet at a particular place; an appointment; a cattle-market.*

TRYSTED, *trusted, engaged to meet.*

TRYSTING, *meeting.*

TULYIE, TULZIE, *a squabble, a tussle.*

TWA, TWAE, *two.*

'TWAD, *it would.*

TWA-FAULD, *twofold; bent in double.*

TWAL, *twelve.*

TWAL-HUNDRED, *linen of 1200 divisions, not so fine as that of 1700.*

TWALPENNIE WORTH = *a penny worth (sterling).*

TWANG, *a twinge.*

TWA-THREE, *two or three.*

TWAY, *two.*

TWIN, *also* TWINE, *to rob.*

TWISTLE, *a twist, a sprain.*

TYESDAY, *Tuesday.*

TYKE, *a mongrel dog; a rough uncultured person.*

TYNE, *to tine.*

TYSDAY, *Tuesday.*

ULZIE, *oil.*

UNCHANCY, *dangerous.*

UNCO, *strange, not allied, alien.*

UNCOS, *news, strange things, wonders.*

UNFAULD, *to unfold.*

UNKEND, *unknown.*

UNSICKER, *uncertain.*

UNSKAITHED, *unhurt.*

USQUE *or* USGIE, *Celt. for water* = *whisky; usquebah* = *water of life or whisky.*

VAUNTIE, *proud.*

VERA, *very.*

VIRLS, *rings.*

VITTLE, *victuals, food.*

VOGIE, *vain, proud.*

WA', *a wall; at the wa', in desperate circumstances.*

WAB, *a web.*

WABSTER, *a weaver.*

WAD, *to wed.*

WAD, *would, would have.*

WAD'A, *would have.*

WADNA, *would not.*

WADSET, *a pledge, a mortgage.*

WAEFU', *woeful.*

WAESUCKS, *alas!*

WAE WORTH, *woe befall.*

WAIR'D, *worn.*

WALE, *the choice; to choose, to select.*

WALIE, *ample, large.*

WALLOP, *to dangle, to move quickly.*

WALY, *an interjection of distress.*

WAME, *the belly.*

WAMEFOU, *bellyful.*

WAN, *won; pale, dark-coloured.*

WANCHANCIE, *dangerous.*

WANRESTFU', *restless.*

WAP, *to wrap, to envelop, to cover.*

WARE, WAIR, *to spend, bestow.*

WARE, *worn.*

WARK, *work.*

WARK-LUME, *v.* LUME.

WARL', WARLD, *world.*

WARLOCK, *a wizard, one familiar with the Devil.*

WARLOCK-KNOWE, *a knoll reputed to be haunted.*

WARLY, *worldly.*

WARPIN-WHEEL, *a part of the spinning-wheel.*

WARRAN, *warrant.*

WARSE, *worse.*

WARSLE, WARSTLE, *wrestle.*

WAST, *west.*

WASTRIE, *waste.*

WAT, *wet; to wot.*

WATER-FIT, *water-foot (the river's mouth).*

WATER-KELPIES, *v.* KELPIES.

WAUBLE, *to wobble.*

WAUGHT, *a long drink.*

WAUK, *to wake.*

WAUKENS, *wakens.*

WAUKRIFE, *sleepless, in a light sleep.*

WAUR, *worse.*

WAUR'T, *worsted, beat (in running).*

WEAN, *a child.*

WEANIES, *babies.*

WEAPON-SHAW, *an exhibition of arms; (lit.) showing the weapons.*

WEASON, *weasand.*

WECHT, *a measure for corn.*

WEE, *small, little; a short time.*

WEE THINGS, *children.*

WEEL, *well.*

WEEL-FAURED, *well-favoured.*

WEEL-GAUN, *well-going.*

WEEL-HAIN'D, *well-saved.*

WEEL-STOCKIT, *well-stocked.*

WEEPERS, *mournings (on the sleeve, or hat).*

WEET, *wet.*

WERENA, *were not.*

WE'SE, *we shall.*

WESTLIN, *westerly.*

WHA, *who.*

WHA'S, *who is.*

WHAIZLE, *wheeze.*

WHALPET, *whelped.*

WHAM, *whom.*

WHAN, *when.*

WHANG, *a shive, a large slice.*

WHANG, *flog.*

WHAR, WHARE, WHAUR, *where.*

WHASE, *whose.*

WHAT FOR, *whatfore, wherefore: 'what for no?' = why not?*

WHATNA, *what (partly in contempt).*

WHAT RECK, *what matter.*

WHATT, *whittled.*

WHAUP, *a curlew.*

WHEEP, *jerk.*

WHID, *a fib.*

WHIDDIN, *scudding.*

WHIDS, *gambols.*

WHIGMELEERIES, *crotchets.*

WHILES, *sometimes.*

WHINGIN, *whining.*

WHINS, *furze.*

WHIRLYGIGUMS, *flourishes.*

WHIRRIN, *the sound produced by the wings of a flying bird.*

WHISHT, *silence.*

WHISKIN, *sweeping, lashing.*

WHISSLE, *whistle.*

WHITTER, *a draught.*

WHITTLE, *a knife; to cut.*

WI', *with.*

WI'S, *with his.*

WIDDIFU', *peevish, angry; worthy of the gallows.*

WIDDLE, *wriggle.*

WIEL, *eddy.*

WIGHT, *a sturdy person.*

WIGHTER, *stronger.*

WIL'D, WYL'D, *enticed, artfully captured.*

WILLCAT, *wild cat.*

WILLYART, *disordered.*

WIMPLE, *to meander.*

WIMPLE, *a winding or folding.*

WIMPLING, *winding, meandering (of a course).*

WI'M, *with him.*

WIN, *won.*

WINN, *to winnow.*

WINNA, *will not.*

WINNIN, *winding.*

WINNINS, *means, earnings.*

WINNOCK, *window.*

WI'T, *with it.*

WIN'T, *did wind.*

WINTLE, *a somersault.*

WINTLE, *to stagger, to swing, to wriggle.*

WINZE, *a curse.*

WISS, *wish.*

WITHA', *with all.*

WON, *to win, to dwell; dry by exposure to the air.*

WONNER, *a wonder, a marvel.*

WONS, *dwells, lives.*

WOO', *wool.*

WOODIE, *dim. of wud.*

WOODIES, *twigs, withes.*

WOOER-BABS, *love-knots.*

WORDY, *worthy.*

WORSET, *worsted.*

WORTH, *v, WAE WORTH.*

WRACK, *to vex, to trouble, to contradict.*

WRANG, *wrong.*

WUD, *a wood; mad, distracted, outrageous.*

WUMBLE, *wimble.*

WYLIECOAT, *undervest.*

WYLIN, *enticing, wheedling, beguiling.*

WYTE, *the blame; to blame.*

YARD, *a garden, a stackyard.*

YAUD, *an old mare.*

YEALINGS, *coevals.*

YELL, *dry (milkless).*

YERD, *a yard, an enclosure.*

YERKIT, *jerked.*

YERL, *an earl.*

YE'SE, *ye shall.*

YESTREEN, *last evening or night.*

YETT, *a gate.*

YEUKS, *the itch; a kind of eczema.*

YILL, *ale.*

YILL-CAUP, *ale-stoup.*

YIRD, *earth, the soil.*

YOKIN, YOKING, *a spell, a day's work, a set-to.*

YON, YONDER, *over there; used equiv.*

'YONT, *beyond.*

YOWE, *a ewe.*

YOWIE, *dim. of ewe; a pet ewe.*

INDEX OF TITLES AND FIRST LINES

PAGE